BIBLICAL COUNSELING FOUNDATION

Matthew 7:1-5

SELF-CONFRONTATION

A Manual for In-Depth Discipleship

Based on the
Old and New Testaments
as the only authoritative rule of
faith and conduct.

Syllabus for Course I

Biblical Counseling Training Program

Developed by John C. Broger

Biblical Counseling Foundation (BCF)

SELF-CONFRONTATION
A MANUAL FOR IN-DEPTH DISCIPLESHIP
(INTERNATIONAL VERSION)

This discipleship training material is published by the Biblical Counseling Foundation Inc., a non-profit, non-stock corporation founded in 1974 and incorporated in 1977 in the Commonwealth of Virginia, USA.

Copyright: The contents of this material are Copyrighted © 1978, revised 1980, 1987, and 1991 by the Biblical Counseling Foundation, Inc. All rights reserved. Reproduction in any manner in whole or in part, in English and/or other languages, or storage in a retrieval system, or transmission in any form or by any means – electronic, mechanical, photocopy, recording, or any other – except for brief quotations in printed reviews is prohibited without written permission of the Biblical Counseling Foundation (BCF).

Scripture taken from the New American Standard Bible, © 1960, 1962, 1963, 1968, 1971, 1972, 1973, 1975, 1977 by The Lockman Foundation. Used by permission.

ISBN 1-878114-01-8

1991 EDITION
First-Third Printings, 1991-1992, printed in California, USA
Fourth Printing, February, 1993, printed in India
Fifth Printing, October 1993, printed in California, USA
Sixth Printing, January, 1994 by Thomas Nelson Publishers, Inc.
Seventh Printing, June, 1994, printed in India
Eighth-Ninth Printing, 1994 by Thomas Nelson Publishers, Inc.
Tenth-Twelfth Printing, 1995-1997, International Version, printed in Hong Kong
Thirteenth Printing, Fall 1997, printed in India
Fourteenth Printing, Fall 1998, International Version, printed in Hong Kong

BIBLICAL COUNSELING FOUNDATION

42-600 Cook Street, Suite 100
Palm Desert, California 92211-5143
Telephone: (760) 773-2667
Fax: (760) 340-3778

Email address for:
Orders – **orders@bcfministries.org**
Correspondence – **admin@bcfministries.org**
Website address:
http://www.bcfministries.org

Printed by Capstone Enterprises Ltd.

Other materials available through BCF: ***Instructor's Guide for the Self-Confrontation Course*** with 24 audio tapes, the *What God's Word says about ...* series of in-depth discipleship booklets, *Self-Confrontation* video series, and ***Handbook for the Ministry of Biblical Discipleship/Counseling***.

USES OF THE SELF-CONFRONTATION MANUAL

The purpose of this manual is to teach you how to examine yourself biblically so you can live in a manner that pleases the Lord and help others to do the same.

The material in this manual also has been used in Bible studies for youth and adults, classes for Christian students (junior high, high school, college, and seminary level), courses of study designed to prepare missionaries for their ministry, evangelism training, discipleship training in prison ministries, Sunday school classes, home group studies, personal devotional studies, and Scripture memorization programs. In addition, it has proved valuable as a resource for pastors, counselors, health care professionals, personnel managers, educators, social workers and other professionals who are responsible to deal with personal and interpersonal problems. As you progress through this manual, you will discover many other uses for this material in your life and personal ministry.

Please do not be intimidated by the volume of Scripture references contained in this manual. A new believer in Jesus Christ can find great comfort and help from looking up only one verse out of many that are listed on a particular subject. On the other hand, the Bible scholar or seminary student may desire to research many of the Scripture references from the original languages of the Bible. No matter how proficient you are in using Scripture, this manual encourages you to rely on the Word of God to discover God's sufficiency for every aspect of your life.

John C. Broger, president emeritus of the Biblical Counseling Foundation, is known internationally for his missionary and evangelical endeavors spanning five decades.

He served four years in World War II and wrote or edited 38 manuals for naval radar training. Subsequently, he was commissioned electronics officer of Night Torpedo Squadron 91 aboard the aircraft carrier Bon Homme Richard which participated in the Pacific campaigns. The experience gained in electronics gave him the expertise to plan and build the Christian radio stations envisioned in the 1930's to preach the Gospel to the world by means of radio.

At the war's conclusion in 1945, he co-founded and was named the first president of the Far East Broadcasting Company (FEBC), a non-profit, non-commercial, Christian broadcasting corporation. He obtained the first radio franchise granted by the new Philippine Republic and placed the early FEBC transmitters on the air.

During his twelve years with FEBC, he walked the back-trails of Asia to determine better ways of getting the life-changing message of Jesus Christ into the languages of Asia. He was constantly in the midst of the power struggle between the forces of freedom and those who deny the existence of a loving God. (Today, 32 FEBC transmitters carry the Christian message to Asia, Russia, Africa, Latin America, and the Middle East in 141 languages and dialects.)

In 1954, at the height of the cold war between the super-powers, because of his understanding and first-hand experience of the spiritual and ideological conflicts in Asia, Admiral Arthur Radford, Chairman of the Joint Chiefs of Staff requested that he come to Washington D.C. as consultant to the Joint Chiefs of Staff. After much prayer and deliberation with missionary co-workers, he accepted Admiral Radford's request and subsequently resigned his position with the Far East Broadcasting Company. In 1960 he was appointed Director of Information for the Armed Forces of the United States thus becoming the first civilian to hold that position since Thomas Paine in General George Washington's army of American independence.

As Director of Information for the U.S. Armed Forces, his responsibilities included oversight of 1,100 Armed Forces radio and television stations worldwide and 1,900 newspapers, including *Stars and Stripes*. He also supervised the production of all Department of Defense publications and directed its press and motion picture services.

In his governmental capacity, he was responsible to inform the U.S. armed forces world-wide on such subjects as world affairs, democracy, its freedoms and responsibilities based on the Golden Rule and its accompanying values as opposed to humanistic theories advocating repressive totalitarianism. He frequently lectured to civilian and military colleges and universities on subjects necessary to the high calling and privilege of responsible citizenship. Over a period of ten years, he spoke to civic, educational, religious, and private organizations including the Harvard Business School, the U.S. Military Academy at West Point, National War College, Marine Corps Senior Schools, Armed Forces Staff College, Air Command and Staff College, Industrial College of the Armed Forces, and the Military Assistance Institute.

In 1974 he began to develop biblical counseling training material for the Chiefs of Chaplains of the U.S. Armed Forces. In 1977 after 23 years with the Office of the Secretary of Defense and the Joint Chiefs of Staff under six presidents, he retired from federal service.

Knowing the power of God's Word to change lives, he has devoted his retirement years to the further development of biblical counseling material. In addition, he has originated training classes and seminars to help Christian men and women find God's plan for every problem of life through the total sufficiency of Scripture.

Born in Nashville, Tennessee in 1913, he studied at Georgia Institute of Technology, Texas A & M College, and graduated from Southern California Bible College in 1939. He and his wife, Dorothy, were married in 1941 and now reside in Palm Desert, California.

AWARDS AND AFFILIATIONS

Honorary Doctor of Laws (Wheaton College) • Co-founder and President, Biblical Counseling Foundation • Founding Member and first President, National Association of Nouthetic Counselors • Consultant on Biblical Counseling, National Association of Evangelicals • Board Member, Christian Counseling and Educational Foundation • Member of the Academy, National Association of Nouthetic Counselors • Council, International Christian Leadership • Chairman, National Association of Evangelicals' Churchmen Commission • Chairman, National Capital Area Association of Evangelicals • Honorary Faculty Member, U. S. Army Chaplain's School • Vice-Chairman, Armed Services Committee, President Eisenhower's People-to-People Program • Evangelical Layman of the Year, National Association of Evangelicals • AMVETS Annual Americanism Award • Principle Freedoms Foundation Award • Citation Armed Forces Chaplain's Board • Secretary of Defense Meritorious Civilian Service Medal • Department of Defense Distinguished Civilian Service Medal.

ACKNOWLEDGMENTS

I would like to express my deep appreciation to Bracy Ball, Joe Gearo, Robert Schneider, and Shashi Smith, who comprise the team that worked with me in the preparation of this manual.

Bracy Ball
Pastor/Teacher

Robert Schneider
President

Joe Gearo
Vice-President, Business and
Professional Ministries

Shashi Smith
Vice-President,
Policies and Plans

Parenthetically, I am grateful to the members and elders of Family Life Church, Rancho Mirage, California, who so generously approved a leave of absence for Bracy Ball, to oversee the revision and publication of this manual.

Much credit also is due Virginia Baker, Jack Bennett, Becky Elgin, Paul Hoesterey, Cindy Johnson, Maija Jussila, Mike Lane, Patti Lane, Anne Newman, and Carl Smith for their work in various aspects of the development of these materials. Sincere appreciation is extended as well to Beverly Gearo, Elizabeth Wayne, and Christie Welch who have faithfully and patiently typed the numerous revisions along with Ellen Applegate, Kate O'Donnell, and Carol Ruvolo who were responsible for editing and proofreading.

The Lord has used the gifts and talents of this highly skilled team. I do not wish to imply that any individual contribution is more important than another and, thus, have listed each category alphabetically. To all of these and many more, too numerous to record here, I am deeply grateful. This pioneering effort to re-establish the Word of God as the sole authority for life and as the only basis to counsel others has been a labor of love by many of God's people.

We also owe a great debt to Dr. Jay E. Adams and Dr. Henry Brandt for their consultation during our early days. Dr. Brandt's emphasis on Jesus Christ as the only source of true peace and joy greatly helped our focus in training. Dr. Adams was particularly instrumental in providing prudent and discerning guidance. He very generously provided many hours of instruction and critique with no hint of a desire for personal gain. His knowledge of Scriptures and his ability to apply them to the problems of life are unsurpassed in the area of authoritative biblical counseling.[*] We thank God for their dedication and singleness of purpose in this important field of ministry.

John C. Broger

[*] *Lesson 15, Pages 6-9 and Lesson 20, Page 8 are based on corresponding material in* <u>The Christian Counselor's Manual </u> *by Dr. Jay Adams.*

TABLE OF CONTENTS

APPLICATION TO SPECIFIC PROBLEM AREAS

CONCLUSION

SUPPLEMENTS AND PRACTICAL HELPS

PREFACE: WHY SELF-CONFRONTATION?

Self-confrontation? Isn't that just another way of saying "self-condemnation?" Isn't that counter-productive to a fulfilling life? Instead of confronting myself, shouldn't I be building myself up? Shouldn't I avoid doing anything that would lower my self-esteem or self-image? Don't I have to learn to love myself before I can love others? Don't I have to know how to forgive myself before I can have true peace and joy?

Questions like these reflect the fact that many people are following false teaching that has been present since the beginning of time but is gaining unprecedented popularity in the church today. It is the "doctrine" of self-exaltation and self-gratification. This preoccupation with self is based on a misunderstanding of one's relationship with God, is unbiblical, and deters spiritual growth.

Self-exaltation and self-gratification have always had devastating consequences. This self-focus was the basis for Satan's downfall *(Isaiah 14:13-14)* and was also at the heart of the first temptation on earth *(Genesis 3:1-6)*. An unsuccessful appeal to self-exaltation and self-gratification was the focus of the temptation of the Lord Jesus Christ by Satan *(Luke 4:2-12)*. Self-exaltation and self-gratification reaches its pinnacle when in these last days, as Scripture predicts, men are lovers of self *(II Timothy 3:1-2)*.

Instead of pleasing or exalting yourself, Scripture tells you to examine (or confront) and humble yourself *(Matthew 23:12; I Corinthians 11:31)*. You must do this because your heart is deceitful, desperately wicked, and beyond full understanding *(Jeremiah 17:9)*. The first step in self-confrontation is to realize your own sinful, lost condition before God *(Psalm 14:1-3; Romans 3:10-12)* and, second, to turn to God as your only hope of eternal salvation *(Romans 6:23)*. According to His mercy, God provides salvation through faith as a free gift of His grace, not because of any good thing in you and not because of any good work you could do to merit His love and favor *(Ephesians 2:8-9; Titus 3:5-7)*.

Self-confrontation must continue throughout your Christian walk if you are to avoid the hypocrisy of judging the failures of others without first examining your own life in a biblical manner *(Matthew 7:1-5; Luke 6:41-42)*. Most importantly, self-confrontation must be achieved in accordance with the Word of God *(II Timothy 3:16-17; Hebrews 4:12)*.

Confronting yourself in a biblical manner will often be difficult and will sometimes be a grievous experience. However the Holy Spirit, the Helper, will assist you *(John 16:8, 13-14)* to face your own sins, failures, and shortcomings. Then He will comfort you, teach you, and guide you into all truth so that your sorrow may be turned into everlasting joy *(John 14:16, 26; 15:11)*.

If there is a single emphasis that underlies this training, it is for you to determine biblically whether you are seeking to please yourself or seeking to please God in all you think and do *(II Corinthians 5:9; Colossians 1:10; 3:2, 17)*. As you will soon discover, the objective of this course in personal discipleship and biblical counseling training is not to learn how to save your life but instead how to lose it for Jesus' sake *(Matthew 16:24-25; Luke 9:23-24)* through the process of evaluating yourself biblically.

May God bless the truths of His Word to your life as you faithfully begin a lifelong process of biblical self-confrontation.

PURPOSES OF THIS COURSE

In every culture throughout history, mankind has sought solutions to life's problems. Each generation offers new man-made philosophies and models, but personal and interpersonal problems continue to plague us. Even in the Body of Christ, there are unhappy and broken marriages, substance abuse, depression, anxiety, fear, worry, and many other problems resulting in distress, physical illness, and immobility.

The only complete source that identifies causes and provides solutions to all of life's problems is the Bible. Written over a period of 16 centuries, it has endured another 1,900 years. The promises and authority of God in the Old and New Testaments offer the basis for a vital, abundant life. The Bible contains solutions to every problem of attitude, relationships, communication, and behavior.

This course presents essential biblical principles that can change your life. If you earnestly desire to overcome problems and to develop spiritual maturity, you must be willing to confront your failures and shortcomings and make appropriate changes according to biblical standards *(Romans 12:1-2; II Corinthians 5:9; Colossians 3:1-17)*. If you do this, you will be able to grow up in the Lord Jesus Christ and be in a position to help others in an effective and biblical manner *(Matthew 7:1-5; II Corinthians 1:3-4; Galatians 6:1-5; II Timothy 2:2)*. The biblical principles listed in this course form the foundation for lasting change in your life. They are also the basis for the Biblical Counseling Foundation's (BCF) training programs.

PURPOSES OF THIS COURSE

The Self-Confrontation course has two purposes:

I. To teach you how to approach circumstances, relationships, and situations of life from a biblical perspective and to experience victory and contentment in all of life's trials, testings, and problems.

II. To prepare you to help others face and deal with their problems biblically.

The Self-Confrontation course is built upon biblical principles for living. These biblical principles provide patterns for living a victorious and contented life and are applicable to the young and the elderly, to the poor and the wealthy, to the healthy and the ill, and to the skilled and the unskilled. These biblical principles apply to all of life's circumstances, in any culture, and in every part of the world regardless of the age in which one lives.

Each lesson is designed, first, to explain the meaning of specific biblical principles and, then, to build them into your life through very practical homework assignments. The course consists of 24 lessons, usually taught in two-hour classes once a week. The first eight lessons consist of principles describing how change takes place. These eight lessons provide the foundation for the next 14 lessons which deal with some of the most common problems of life. The last two lessons are for review, examination, and preparation for the next course entitled BCT II: Biblical Counseling Basic Course.

OBJECTIVES OF THIS COURSE

You can expect to learn the following in the Self-Confrontation course:

- The biblical principles for understanding problems from God's point of view
- The biblical principles for gaining hope in every situation
- The biblical principles for establishing change
- The characteristics and practical importance of biblical homework

- Biblical principles pertinent to:
    - Dealing with self-belittlement, self-exaltation, and self-pity
    - Personal difficulties such as greed, envy, anger, bitterness, depression, fear, and worry
    - Relationships (interpersonal, marital, parent-child),
    - Life-dominating sins (such as homosexuality or alcohol and drug abuse)

MATERIALS NEEDED FOR THIS COURSE
- Literal translation of the Bible
- *Self-Confrontation* manual
- Comprehensive concordance

CLASS LESSONS IN THE COURSE
A class lesson consists of:
- Review of Scripture memory verses and other homework
- Explanation of biblical principles associated with the lesson
- Teaching on the practical application of God's Word to your life
- Discussion of a biblical counseling case study (introduced in Lesson 9 and continuing throughout the remainder of the course)
- Assignment of homework

You should complete each lesson's homework and then attend class with the manual and a literal translation of the Bible. (While a paraphrased Bible may be useful as an accessory to Bible study, it is important to memorize and understand the Bible in its most literal form). An exhaustive concordance of the Bible will be helpful in completing the homework. Instructions for using a concordance are found in Supplement 5.

YOUR COMMITMENT AND DISCIPLINE FOR THIS COURSE
In order to receive the intended benefit from this course, you should plan to spend a minimum of thirty minutes to an hour each day in doing the homework. The homework is designed to help you establish biblical habit patterns that will change your life. Establishing a daily practice of doing your homework will help you accomplish this; therefore, you should prayerfully establish a realistic daily schedule *(Ephesians 5:15-17)* and commit this time to the Lord *(Proverbs 16:3, 9)*. It may be difficult at first to discipline yourself to maintain your schedule, but remember that establishing any new habit requires time. Plan to rearrange or, if necessary, eliminate activities from your present schedule in order to spend an adequate amount of time doing your homework. Spiritual discipline is a necessary ingredient for godliness *(I Timothy 4:7-8)*.

Since this course focuses on understanding and applying God's Word to your life, consider doing your homework as a part of your daily devotional time. If you choose this pattern of study, a **STUDY GUIDE FOR DAILY DEVOTIONS** is included in every lesson to assist you in completing each lesson's homework. The important factors are faithfulness *(Luke 16:10; I Corinthians 4:2)* and diligence *(II Timothy 2:15)*. A suggestion: If you do not complete your homework for a particular week, go on to the new homework for the current week before you finish your uncompleted homework assignment. Keep all of your completed homework in a separate notebook for practical help and reference as necessary.

YOUR MANUAL FOR THIS COURSE
This manual is divided into two major sections: the **Lessons** and the **Supplements and Practical Helps**. The 24 lessons in the manual are in outline form; they present many major truths of God's Word. You must read the referenced verses in your Bible for a more complete understanding of the biblical principles which are presented. The **Supplements**

and **Practical Helps** section further explains the foundational, biblical principles and provides instruction by which you can apply these truths to your life in a practical manner.

I.   **The Lessons**

A.   Purposes and Contents - The first page of each lesson lists the purposes and contents of the lesson. Reading this first page will help you to gain a quick overview of the teaching points in the lesson.

B.   Biblical Principles - Page two introduces the major biblical principles for each lesson. A brief synopsis of the teaching is given in a box at the top of the page.

C.   Outline - The next pages contain an expanded outline of the lesson. You will learn how to gain biblical perspective, understanding, and hope for the problem discussed. Further, you will see why and how to change.

D.   Homework - Near the end of each lesson are homework assignments, listed in the order in which they should be completed. Scripture memory will always be the first item for homework.

Assignments marked with an asterisk (*) should be completed if you wish to continue to the next course. On the **HOMEWORK** page of each lesson, you may check each homework assignment that you complete. All written homework denoted by an asterisk must be handed in to your instructor for evaluation. Consistent class attendance, participation, and completion of the homework will prepare you to pass the written examination at the end of the course.

E.   The final pages of each lesson contain a **STUDY GUIDE FOR DAILY DEVOTIONS** to help you complete your homework in a regular, consistent manner. If you do the homework using this guide, you will also be establishing a consistent study period during your daily devotions; thus, your devotional life will be significantly enhanced.

(Note: You will probably recognize repetition of Scriptures and biblical principles throughout the course. This purposeful repetition is designed to assist you in learning God's Word and in discovering its multi-faceted applicability to all of life. Repetition also helps those unlearned in the Scripture to grasp the life-changing truths of God's Word more easily. Repetition is an axiom of good training, which is the mission of these courses. The Bible itself is proof of the axiom.)

II.   **Supplements and Practical Helps**

The section titled **Supplements and Practical Helps** contains specific steps by which biblical change can be accomplished in your life. You will find examples of some homework items, particularly forms, to help you in completing your own homework. This section will become a valuable reference tool as well as a means by which practical discipleship can be expressed in your life and in the lives of those entrusted to your care.

DISCIPLESHIP TRAINING

Over the years, the Self-Confrontation Course has proved effective in personal discipleship training. While the Self-Confrontation Course is the first part of a comprehensive training program in biblical counseling, its effectiveness in helping believers in Christ to be "doers of the Word" *(James 1:22-25)* has been proven in various cultures and different countries throughout the world. Consequently, many churches, groups, and ministry leaders have incorporated the Self-Confrontation Course as foundational to the discipleship training offered in their ministries.

After experiencing further spiritual growth in their own lives, many believers completing the Self-Confrontation Course then choose to receive further training in biblical counseling. These students are then able to discover an even greater applicability of Scripture to every problem of life and are more effectively equipped to help others as part of their ministry in the Body of Christ.

OVERVIEW OF BIBLICAL COUNSELING TRAINING

The overall objective of biblical counseling training is to teach members of the local church body to face the challenge of living biblically in a fallen world and to prepare them to counsel others in a strictly biblical manner. Refer to **WHAT MAKES COUNSELING BIBLICAL?** (Supplement 1).

This discipleship training ministry is intended to equip men and women to serve as biblical counselors within the context of the local church. Emphasis is placed on "how" to counsel individuals with personal, interpersonal, or family problems through a proper application of biblical truths and principles. As the Apostle Paul wrote to the church at Rome, *"And concerning you, my brethren, I myself also am convinced that you yourselves are full of goodness, filled with all knowledge, and able also to admonish* (counsel and instruct) *one another" (Romans 15:14).*

COURSES OFFERED IN BIBLICAL COUNSELING TRAINING

There are five levels of training offered in the BCF biblical counseling training program. An explanation of this training is given in **THE BCF BIBLICAL COUNSELING TRAINING PROGRAM** (Supplement 2).

HISTORY OF THESE COURSES

Work on these courses began in 1973 and has involved many thousands of hours of classroom teaching and evaluation as well as application to thousands of biblical counseling cases. Continuing research in the Scriptures has been necessitated by the many difficult problems brought to the counselors of the Biblical Counseling Foundation.

There are many who have made outstanding contributions in preparing these training materials. More than a dozen experienced biblical counselors have spent more than a decade drafting and evaluating the material in this edition. The team consists of pastors and lay persons from a variety of backgrounds, including senior executives, homemakers, retired and active duty military officers, scientists, and managers. Their experience in biblical counseling includes many years of teaching and supervising training programs as well as counseling of individuals.

It is our fervent hope that this training will help pastors, Christian leaders and all others in the Body of Christ to meet the pressing needs of this generation and that, in turn, they will bear the fruit of the victorious and overcoming Gospel of our Lord Jesus Christ.

John C. Broger, President
Biblical Counseling Foundation

A SPECIAL NOTE ON THE SCRIPTURE REFERENCES
FOUND IN THIS MANUAL

As you study this manual, you will find that the biblical principles and precepts presented are substantiated with Scripture references which you are encouraged to look up as you study. The Scripture references are listed in the order they are found in the Bible, not necessarily in the order of importance or clarity.

Whenever you see italicized parentheses with Scripture references listed, the verses/passages directly substantiate the principle or teaching. For example in *Principle 23*, the statement, "Trials and testings will develop and mature you in Christ if you respond to them in God's way" is stated fully in each of the verses that follow (i.e. *Romans 5:3-5; James 1:2-4*).

In addition, every series of Scripture references prefaced with the words *"based on"* must be studied all together as a whole. The truth of these statements cannot be understood from a single verse, but can be understood from a study of all the referenced verses put together. For example the statement in the summary box at the top of Lesson 3, Page 6, "The Holy Spirit is your Guide, your Instructor, and your sensitive Counselor who reveals the wisdom of God to you" is true, but you need to study all the Scriptures that follow (i.e. *John 14:16, 26; 16:7-13; I Corinthians 2:6-13*) to understand the entire sentence.

LESSON 1

YOU CAN CHANGE BIBLICALLY
(PART ONE)

"For by grace you have been saved through faith; and that not of yourselves, it is the gift of God; not as a result of works, that no one should boast."

Ephesians 2:8-9

LESSON 1: YOU CAN CHANGE BIBLICALLY (PART ONE)

> The most significant decision you will ever make concerns
> your willingness to follow God's plan for your life as revealed
> in the Bible. This decision directly impacts your daily life and
> your eternal destiny *(based on Psalm 119:165; Proverbs 1:33;
> Matthew 6:25-34; Mark 8:34-38; John 3:16-21, 36; Acts 2:38-39;
> II Timothy 3:16-17; II Peter 1:2-10; Revelation 20:15).*

I. **The purposes of this lesson are:**

    A. To provide an introduction to the course;

    B. To show the importance and the need for biblical self-confrontation; and

    C. To present the first step of confronting yourself in a biblical way.

II. **The outline of this lesson**

    A. Self-confrontation

        1. **WHY SELF-CONFRONTATION?** (Preface, Page vi)

        2. **PURPOSES OF THIS COURSE** (Pages vii-x)

        3. **BIBLICAL PRINCIPLE: YOU CAN CHANGE BIBLICALLY (PART ONE)** (Lesson 1, Page 2)

        4. **YOU CAN CHANGE BIBLICALLY (PART ONE)** (Lesson 1, Pages 3-7)

    B. Biblical counseling

        1. **WHAT MAKES COUNSELING BIBLICAL?** (Supplement 1)

        2. **THE BCF BIBLICAL COUNSELING TRAINING PROGRAM** (Supplement 2)

    C. Steps for spiritual growth

        1. **LESSON 1: HOMEWORK** (Lesson 1, Page 8)

        2. **STUDY GUIDE FOR DAILY DEVOTIONS** (Lesson 1, Pages 9-10)

BIBLICAL PRINCIPLE: YOU CAN CHANGE BIBLICALLY
(PART ONE)

> God enables you to take the necessary first step towards lasting biblical change. This step is your response to God's demonstrated love for you in Christ Jesus *(based on John 1:12, 3:16-21; Romans 5:8; II Corinthians 5:17; Ephesians 2:8-9; I John 4:10).*

God's plan for you to change in a biblical way centers on His Son, Jesus Christ.

(Principle 1)   Because God's standard is one of perfection *(Leviticus 19:2; Matthew 5:48)*, you cannot meet it by your own efforts *(Psalm 143:2; Ecclesiastes 7:20; Romans 3:23)*. You cannot save yourself *(Proverbs 20:9)* nor depend on any other human being to redeem you *(Psalm 49:7)*. You need to recognize your helplessness to meet God's standard *(Isaiah 64:6; Romans 3:9-12)* and need to repent of your sin *(Luke 15:7; Acts 2:38, 3:19, 17:30-31, 26:19-20; Romans 2:4; II Peter 3:9)*. By God's grace and mercy, you recognize your lost condition and believe wholeheartedly and sincerely on the Lord Jesus Christ to receive the gift of eternal life *(John 3:16, 36; 5:24; 11:25-26; Romans 6:23; Ephesians 2:8-9; Titus 3:5-7; I John 5:11-13)* and forgiveness for your sins *(Mark 16:16; John 3:16-18, 8:24; Acts 2:38, 4:12; Romans 10:9-13; Ephesians 1:7)*.

YOU CAN CHANGE BIBLICALLY (PART ONE)

> Even though eternal life is a gift, many reject it
> (*Matthew 7:13-14; John 1:9-12, 3:16-21; Romans 6:23*).

I. **If you do not already have a sincere (guileless, pure, genuine), personal relationship with the Lord Jesus Christ, you have a spiritual problem that only God can solve. Without this relationship to Jesus, you are:**

   A.   Hopelessly separated from God (*Romans 6:23a; Ephesians 2:1-3, 11-12; Colossians 1:21*),

   B.   Spiritually dead in your own sin (*Romans 3:23, 5:12; Ephesians 2:1, 5; Colossians 2:13*),

   C.   Hostile to God (*Romans 5:10a, 8:7; Colossians 1:21*),

   D.   Blinded by Satan (*II Corinthians 4:3-4*) and held captive by him to do his will (*II Timothy 2:24-26, esp. verse 26*),

   E.   Powerless to overcome sin's hold on your life (*Ecclesiastes 7:20; John 8:34; Romans 1:28-32, 5:6, 6:16; Galatians 5:19-21; II Peter 2:19*),

   F.   Unable to understand the things of God (*Proverbs 14:12, 16:25; Isaiah 55:8-9; I Corinthians 2:14*),

   G.   Unable to please God or to walk in His way (*Psalm 143:2b; Isaiah 64:6; Romans 3:9-12, 23; 8:7-8; Galatians 2:16; Ephesians 2:8-9; II Timothy 1:9; Titus 3:5-7; Hebrews 11:6*), and

   H.   Incapable of living a spiritually fruitful and meaningful life (*John 15:4-6*).

II. **God's answer to your spiritual problem is based on His character.**

   A.   God is just, so you face His wrath and judgment in your sinful state (*Romans 1:18, 6:23a; Ephesians 2:3; Hebrews 9:27; II Peter 3:7*).

   B.   On the other hand, God is loving and doesn't want you to perish in your sin (*John 3:16; Romans 5:8; I Timothy 2:3-4; II Peter 3:9*), so He draws you toward His Son, Jesus (*John 6:44-45, 65*).

III. **The answer to your spiritual problem is found in God's Son, Jesus Christ.**

   A.   By His gracious and merciful love, God gave His one and only begotten Son, Jesus, as the *only* answer for your helpless spiritual condition (*Isaiah 53:2-12; John 3:16, 14:6; Acts 4:12; Romans 5:6; Ephesians 1:3-12; I Timothy 2:5-6; I John 4:10*).

   B.   Since you could not save yourself or do anything to merit God's favor and mercy (*Galatians 2:16; Ephesians 2:8-9; II Timothy 1:9; Titus 3:5-7*), Jesus paid the full price for your redemption by dying on the cross for the penalty for your sin (*Romans 5:8; I Corinthians 15:3-4; II Corinthians 5:21; Ephesians 1:7; I Thessalonians 1:10; I Timothy 2:5-6; Hebrews 10:10-14; I Peter 1:18-19, 3:18*).

C. God accepted and approved His Son's sacrificial death for your sin by raising Jesus from the dead *(Romans 1:4, 4:25)*. Jesus Christ is eternally alive *(Acts 2:32; Romans 6:9; Revelation 1:17-18)*, is with God *(Romans 8:34; Hebrews 8:1)*, and is Lord of all *(Philippians 2:9-11; Revelation 17:14, 19:16)*. Through His death and resurrection, the Lord Jesus Christ is victorious over sin *(Romans 6:10)*, death *(Romans 6:9)*, and the devil *(Hebrews 2:14)*.

D. Through Jesus, you can:

1. Have your sins forgiven *(Acts 5:31, 10:43; Ephesians 1:7, 4:32; Colossians 1:13-14, 2:13-14)* and be reconciled to God *(II Corinthians 5:18-19)*;

2. Experience a spiritual new birth *(John 3:3; I Peter 1:3, 23; I John 5:1)*;

3. Receive the gift of eternal life through God's gracious gift of faith *(John 3:16; 5:24; 6:40, 47; 11:25-26; 17:1-3; Romans 6:23; Ephesians 2:8-9; I Timothy 1:16; I John 5:11-12)*;

4. Have access to God *(John 14:6; Ephesians 2:18, 3:11-12; Hebrews 10:19-22)*;

5. Be a member of God's family *(John 1:12; Romans 8:15-17; Galatians 3:26; Ephesians 1:5, 2:19; I John 3:1-2)*;

6. Understand the things of God *(John 14:26, 16:13-15; I Corinthians 2:9-13)*;

7. Become a new person with the capability for living in a totally new manner *(Romans 6:4-22; II Corinthians 5:17; Philippians 4:13)*; and

8. Be empowered to change, to mature into Christlikeness, and to have an increasingly intimate knowledge of God Himself *(John 17:3; Romans 8:2, 28-29; II Corinthians 5:17; Philippians 1:6, 4:13; Colossians 1:9-11; I Thessalonians 2:13; II Peter 1:3-4)*.

IV. God empowers you to choose His solution to your spiritual problem.

A. When you recognize God's love (John 3:16; I John 4:10) and accept His Truth as revealed in the Lord Jesus Christ *(John 14:6)*, you will be enabled through faith to:

1. Believe in Jesus *(John 5:24; Romans 10:8-13)* who once and for all offered Himself as a sacrifice for your sin *(Hebrews 10:4-22)*;

2. Repent of your sin *(Mark 1:15; Luke 15:7; Acts 2:38, 3:19, 26:20; II Peter 3:9)*;

3. Wholeheartedly believe that the blood of Jesus Christ which was shed on the Cross provides forgiveness for your sin *(Romans 3:23-25; Ephesians 1:7; Colossians 1:19-23; I Peter 1:18-19)* and likewise believe that God raised Jesus from the dead so that you might walk in newness of life *(Romans 4:24-25, 6:4, 8:11, 10:9; I Corinthians 15:12-22)*; and

4. Sincerely receive the Lord Jesus Christ into your life *(John 1:12; I John 5:12)*, and as a new creation *(II Corinthians 5:17)*, live in faithful and loving obedience to God's Word (the Bible) *(I John 2:3-6)*.

B. If you reject God's truth by refusing to repent of your sin and thus fail to receive the gift of eternal life through God's Son, Jesus Christ, you will remain:

1. Under God's judgment *(John 3:18, 36; Romans 1:28-32)*;

2. Ignorant of spiritual matters *(Isaiah 55:8-9; I Corinthians 1:18a, 2:14)*;

3. Powerless to overcome sin in your life *(John 8:34; II Peter 2:19)*;

4. Unable to please God *(Romans 8:8; Hebrews 11:6)*;

5.   Guaranteed increasing heartache, problems, and difficulty for yourself *(Proverbs 13:15, 14:12, 17:20, 26:12; Romans 2:8-9; Colossians 3:25)*;

6.   Doomed to die in your sins *(John 8:21-24);* and

7.   Under condemnation to eternal punishment, forever separated from God's presence *(II Peter 3:7; Revelation 20:15).*

C.   If you decide to alter God's plan of salvation in Christ Jesus to accommodate:

Your own wisdom which is foolish and inadequate to know God *(I Corinthians 1:21, 3:19-20),*

Your own thoughts which are contrary to God's ways *(Isaiah 55:8-9; Romans 8:6-8),* or

Your own desires which are contrary to the Spirit of God *(Galatians 5:17);* then

You thereby place yourself under God's condemnation *(Mark 16:16),* His reproof *(Proverbs 30:6),* His chastisement *(Revelation 22:18-19),* and His curse *(Galatians 1:6-9).*

V.   By faith, you can take the first step of biblical change.

If you have never taken this first step to change biblically, you can do so right now. Simply tell God you know you are a sinner and need His forgiveness of your sin. Acknowledge to God that neither you nor anyone else but Jesus Christ can save you because He alone died to pay the penalty for sin and rose from the dead so that you might have a new life. By faith, receive the Lord Jesus Christ as Savior and thank God for His grace and love to you through Jesus. With a sincere and repentant heart, demonstrate your commitment to Him by being obedient to His Word.

VI.   You must understand that man's way of solving problems falls short of God's solutions.

A.   There are two reasons the plan of salvation has been explained in detail.

1.   To begin with, it is essential that you understand the spiritual principle that all of man's wisdom, philosophy, devices, procedures, manipulations, and sincerity cannot substitute for God's plan of salvation through Jesus Christ (see **IV.**, point C. above). Any person claiming to have taken a different way to salvation except through Jesus Christ is likened in Scripture to a thief and a robber *(John 10:1, 7).*

2.   The next reason is consistent with, and follows, the same basic spiritual principle as the first. The problems brought on by man as a result of his sin of disobedience in the Garden of Eden *(Genesis chapter 3; Romans 5:12)* cannot be solved by man's devices and philosophies *(I Corinthians 3:19-20; Colossians 2:6-8),* regardless of the futile attempts to mix God's Word with unregenerate suppositions and theories *(Deuteronomy 4:2; Proverbs 30:6; Revelation 22:19).*

    a.   This futility is especially realized when you see that God's Word claims total sufficiency to solve all of life's problems *(II Timothy 3:16-17; II Peter 1:2-4).*

    b.   By merely dealing in a superficial way with the basic problems of rebellion and disobedience, man's wisdom seeks to thwart the very will and plan of God to bring him to a saving knowledge of Jesus Christ and to a subsequent reliance on the Word of God for every area of life.

B.   The Word of God has been given to man as the sole source for finding God's solutions to the real problems that plague him *(Psalm 19:7-11; II Timothy 3:16-17; Hebrews 4:12; II Peter 1:2-4).*

VII.   **You need to understand the difference between man's way and God's way in your search for a contented, joyful, and peaceful way of life.**

A.   The primary difference is that man's way is oriented to *self:* to please self, to comfort self, to rely on self, to fulfill self, to forgive self, to exalt self, and to love self. This is described in Scripture as the old self-nature *(Romans 6:6; Ephesians 4:22; Colossians 3:9).*

B.   God's way is

1.   To regenerate and change you by:

a.   Putting off from you the old nature *(Romans 6:6; Ephesians 4:22; Colossians 3:9),*

b.   Putting on you the new nature *(Romans 6:7-8; Ephesians 4:24; Colossians 3:10),* and

c.   Renewing the spirit of your mind as part of your continual process of maturing in Christlikeness *(Romans 12:2; Ephesians 4:23; Colossians 3:10).*

2.   To empower and strengthen you to mature as you:

a.   Deny self and follow Jesus *(Luke 9:23-24);*

b.   Lay aside (put off) the practices of the old self-nature *(Romans 6:11-22; Ephesians 4:25-32; Colossians 3:5-17; Revelation 2:4-5)* and walk in a manner worthy of the Lord *(Ephesians 4:1; Colossians 1:10);* and

c.   Please God in all things *(II Corinthians 5:9; Colossians 1:10).*

C.   God's plan, instead of the ideologies which focus on self, establishes your true position in Christ and gives provision for you to be:

1.   Forgiven of all your sins *(Colossians 2:13-14)* and become a new creation *(II Corinthians 5:17)* by partaking of God's divine nature *(II Peter 1:4);*

2.   A child and heir of God and a joint-heir with Jesus Christ *(Romans 8:14-17);*

3.   A citizen of heaven *(Philippians 3:20),* blessed with every spiritual blessing *(Ephesians 1:3)* and fully complete in Christ Jesus *(Colossians 2:9-10);*

4.   Strong in the Lord *(Ephesians 6:10-17)* as a functioning and maturing member of the body of Christ *(Ephesians 4:11-16);*

5.   More than a conqueror through the Lord Jesus Christ *(Romans 8:37; I John 4:4),* since you have been released from sin's slavery *(Romans 6:5-7)* and have been delivered out of the domain (authority) of darkness and into the kingdom of Christ *(Colossians 1:13);*

6.   An ambassador for Christ *(II Corinthians 5:20),* a member of a chosen race, a royal priesthood, a citizen of a holy nation, a possession of God *(I Peter 2:9),* and a holy temple of the living God *(II Corinthians 6:16; Ephesians 2:21);*

7.   Transformed by the renewing of your mind *(Romans 12:2),* taking every thought captive to the obedience of Christ *(II Corinthians 10:5);*

8.   Full of His peace *(John 16:33)* and joy *(John 15:11, 17:13);*

9.   Changed by the Word of God *(I Thessalonians 2:13; II Timothy 3:16-17);*

10. Led by the Spirit of God *(Romans 8:14)* to understand the things of God *(I Corinthians 2:9-13);*

11. Able to accomplish (or endure) anything in God's will for you through Christ Jesus *(Philippians 4:13),* knowing that God is in total control of your life *(Romans 8:28-29; I Corinthians 10:13; Philippians 1:6);* and

12. Empowered to practice biblical love, thus proving yourself to be a disciple of Christ *(John 13:35).*

D. Throughout this course, the difference between Satan's plan and God's plan for your life will be shown.

1. Satan's plan is to keep you oriented toward gratifying, pleasing, exalting, and esteeming self.

2. God's plan emphasizes that you are to live for Him, since your old self-nature was crucified and buried with Christ in order that you might walk in newness of life *(Romans chapter 6; II Corinthians 5:15-21; Colossians 3:2-17).*

E. Even as man has sought continuously for substitutes to the new birth, he also seeks self-centered solutions to his problems resulting from his original sin.

These man-contrived solutions to problems of the mind, heart, and spirit are as unacceptable to God as are man's futile speculations and substitutes for salvation and the unalterable truths of God's Word *(based on Psalm 119:160; Proverbs 14:12, 30:5-6; Jeremiah 17:9-10; Matthew 15:1-20; John 4:23-24; Acts 4:12; Romans 1:21, 25, 28; 8:5-10; I Corinthians 3:18-20; II Corinthians 7:1; Ephesians 4:22-24; Philippians 2:3-5, 3:18-19; II Timothy 3:1-5).*

LESSON 1: HOMEWORK

> Daily devotions are vital to your spiritual development. To assist you in this practice, the lesson's **HOMEWORK** is correlated to this week's **STUDY GUIDE FOR DAILY DEVOTIONS**, which follows on the next page. Basic steps of spiritual growth are presented along with the basis for true biblical counseling *(based on Psalm 1:1-4; I Thessalonians 5:17; II Timothy 2:15, 3:16-17; I Peter 2:2).*

✔ *homework completed*

☐ A.   * In your own words, write the meaning of *Ephesians 2:8-9*. Memorize *Ephesians 2:8-9*. Begin memorizing *Matthew 7:1 and 7:5*.

☐ B.   * Read **BIBLICAL PRINCIPLE: YOU CAN CHANGE BIBLICALLY (PART ONE)** (Lesson 1, Page 2). Highlight the listed verses in your Bible.

☐ C.   * Describe how you can have eternal life through Jesus Christ (refer to *Principle 1*, on Lesson 1, Page 2, or refer to **IV. God empowers you to choose His solution to your spiritual problem** on Lesson 1, Page 4). Write at least one Scripture reference for each point.

☐ D.   * Explain in writing how you can know for certain that you have eternal life.

☐ E.   Review **YOU CAN CHANGE BIBLICALLY (PART ONE)** (Lesson 1, Pages 3-7). In your Bible, look up the referenced verses, highlighting those that are meaningful to you.

☐ F.   Read **PREFACE: WHY SELF-CONFRONTATION?** (Page vi) and **PURPOSES OF THIS COURSE** (Pages vii-x).

☐ G.   Read **WHAT MAKES COUNSELING BIBLICAL?** (Supplement 1) and **THE BCF BIBLICAL COUNSELING TRAINING PROGRAM** (Supplement 2).

☐ H.   * You can complete the **COURSE EXAM** (Lesson 23) while going through this course. In conjunction with Lesson 1, answer questions 1 and 2 under **Open Book Test** (Lesson 23, Page 1).

*   *The completion of assignments marked with an asterisk (*) is a prerequisite for further biblical counseling training.*

LESSON 1: STUDY GUIDE FOR DAILY DEVOTIONS
(INCLUDING SCRIPTURE MEMORY AND HOMEWORK)

> Daily devotions are vital to your spiritual development. To assist you in this practice, each lesson's **STUDY GUIDE FOR DAILY DEVOTIONS** is correlated to the lesson's **HOMEWORK**. This lesson's **STUDY GUIDE** highlights basic steps of spiritual growth and presents the basis for true biblical counseling *(based on Psalm 1:1-4; I Thessalonians 5:17; II Timothy 2:15, 3:16-17; I Peter 2:2).*

Scripture Memory

1. * Memorize *Ephesians 2:8-9*; begin memorizing *Matthew 7:1 and 7:5.*
2. Write both verses and their appropriate Scripture references on separate cards and carry them with you throughout the day. At every opportunity during the day, read, meditate on, and memorize *Ephesians 2:8-9.* Preview *Matthew 7:1 and 7:5* whenever possible.

Daily Devotional Study Guide

FIRST DAY

1. Open in prayer.
2. * Read **BIBLICAL PRINCIPLE: YOU CAN CHANGE BIBLICALLY (PART ONE)** (Lesson 1, Page 2). Highlight the listed verses in your Bible.
3. * In your own words, write the meaning of *Ephesians 2:8-9.*
4. Close in prayer.
5. Take your Scripture memory card with you today wherever you go and use your spare moments to memorize *Ephesians 2:8-9.*

SECOND DAY

1. Open in prayer.
2. Begin to study **YOU CAN CHANGE BIBLICALLY (PART ONE)** (Lesson 1, Pages 3-7). This is the first day of a three-day study in this important section. Look up any listed verses necessary for you to understand these biblical truths.
3. Close in prayer.

THIRD DAY

1. Open in prayer.
2. Continue your study through **YOU CAN CHANGE BIBLICALLY (PART ONE)** (Lesson 1, Pages 3-7).
3. Close in prayer.

FOURTH DAY

1. Open in prayer.
2. Continue your study through **YOU CAN CHANGE BIBLICALLY (PART ONE)** (Lesson 1, Pages 3-7).
3. Did you fail to take advantage of spare moments to memorize your verse? List these "lost opportunities" and when they occurred; make a plan to improve. If you have already memorized *Ephesians 2:8-9*, begin memorizing *Matthew 7:1 and 7:5*.
4. Close in prayer.

FIFTH DAY

1. Open in prayer.
2. * Write how you can have eternal life through Jesus Christ (refer to *Principle 1*, Lesson 1, Page 2, or refer to **IV. God empowers you to choose His solution to your spiritual problem on Page 4** of Lesson 1). Write at least one Scripture reference for each point.
3. Read **PREFACE: WHY SELF-CONFRONTATION?** (Page vi) and **PURPOSES OF THIS COURSE** (Pages vii-x).
4. Close in prayer.

SIXTH DAY

1. Open in prayer.
2. * In a brief paragraph, write how a person can know for certain that he has eternal life.
3. Read **WHAT MAKES COUNSELING BIBLICAL?** (Supplement 1).
4. Close in prayer.

SEVENTH DAY

1. Open in prayer.
2. Read **THE BCF BIBLICAL COUNSELING TRAINING PROGRAM** (Supplement 2).
3. Review **YOU CAN CHANGE BIBLICALLY (PART ONE)** (Lesson 1, Pages 3-7), looking up any verses that may have been overlooked in your previous study.
4. * You can complete the **COURSE EXAM** (Lesson 23) while going through this course. In conjunction with Lesson 1, answer questions 1 and 2 under **Open Book Test** (Lesson 23, Page 1).
5. Close in prayer.
6. Evaluate your use of spare moments to memorize *Ephesians 2:8-9* and *Matthew 7:1 and 7:5* this week. List improvements that you will make in the next week to use your spare moments better in memorizing God's Word.

---

*   *The completion of assignments marked with an asterisk (*) is a prerequisite for further biblical counseling training.*

LESSON 2

YOU CAN CHANGE BIBLICALLY
(PART TWO)

"Do not judge lest you be judged."

"You hypocrite, first take the log out of your own eye, and then you will see clearly to take the speck out of your brother's eye."

Matthew 7:1, 5

LESSON 2: YOU CAN CHANGE BIBLICALLY (PART TWO)

> Since God has graciously provided everything that is necessary for you to live a life pleasing to Him, you are to depend solely on His power, plan, and resources to accomplish His purpose in your life *(based on Isaiah 55:6-11; Romans 8:28-39; I Corinthians 1:30-31, 2:9-13; Ephesians 1:3-6, 2:8-10; Philippians 1:6, 2:12-13; I Thessalonians 2:13; II Peter 1:2-10; I John 5:4-5).*

I. **The purposes of this lesson are:**

A. To explain the process of biblical change that begins the moment you receive eternal life by God's grace and mercy and then continues until you are in His presence forever, and

B. To show you the importance of self-confrontation to personal discipleship and to help others change biblically.

II. **The outline of this lesson**

A. Self-confrontation

1. **BIBLICAL PRINCIPLES: YOU CAN CHANGE BIBLICALLY (PART TWO)** (Lesson 2, Page 2)

2. **YOU CAN CHANGE BIBLICALLY (PART TWO)** (Lesson 2, Pages 3-5)

3. **BIBLICAL SELF-CONFRONTATION: AN ESSENTIAL FOR DISCIPLESHIP** (Lesson 2, Page 6)

4. **BIBLICAL SELF-CONFRONTATION: A PREREQUISITE FOR HELPING OTHERS BIBLICALLY** (Lesson 2, Pages 7-8)

B. Steps for spiritual growth

1. **BIBLICAL BASIS FOR DAILY DEVOTIONS AND SCRIPTURE MEMORY** (Lesson 2, Pages 9-11)

2. **FOUR PLANS FOR MEMORIZING SCRIPTURE** (Lesson 2, Pages 12-13)

3. **BIBLE STUDY AND APPLICATION FORMAT** (Supplement 3)

4. **LESSON 2: HOMEWORK** (Lesson 2, Page 14)

5. **STUDY GUIDE FOR DAILY DEVOTIONS** (Lesson 2, Pages 15-16)

BIBLICAL PRINCIPLES: YOU CAN CHANGE BIBLICALLY
(PART TWO)

> After you receive salvation by God's grace through our Lord Jesus Christ, your growth in Christ and fitness to help others biblically will be in proportion to your faithfulness in biblically examining yourself and applying God's truths to your life *(based on Matthew 7:1-5; Romans 12:1-2; I Corinthians 11:31; Galatians 6:1-5; Hebrews 5:12-14; I John 1:8-9).*

7/27/44

I. **You are to establish a biblical pattern of life.**

(Principle 2) You are to be rooted, built up, and established in the Lord Jesus Christ and are not to be conformed to the world *(Romans 12:1-2; Colossians 2:6-10).* You must practice God's Word to grow into maturity *(Matthew 7:24-27; II Timothy 3:16-17; Hebrews 5:12-14; James 1:22-25; I Peter 2:2; II Peter 1:4-11; I John 2:5).*

II. **You are to prepare yourself to help others.**

(Principle 3) Practicing God's Word begins with judging yourself and removing sinful obstructions from your own life *(Matthew 7:1-5; I Corinthians 11:28-31; Hebrews 12:1).* Then, you have the privilege and responsibility of restoring others to victorious living *(Matthew 7:5; Romans 15:14; II Corinthians 1:3-4; Galatians 6:1-5).*

YOU CAN CHANGE BIBLICALLY (PART TWO)

> The process of biblical change, explained in God's Word, begins when you repent of your sin and believe in the Lord Jesus Christ. God has given you everything you need to make the changes in your life that will please Him and will lead to His blessings. As you continue to obey God's Word, biblical change toward maturity will occur in your life until you see Jesus face to face *(based on John 1:12; Acts 26:20; Romans 8:28-39; II Corinthians 5:17; Philippians 1:6, 3:12-14; Colossians 2:13-14; James 1:25; II Peter 1:2-10).*

I. **The process of lasting biblical change begins when you are converted to the Lord Jesus Christ.**

A. **God's perspective and your assurance** – After you sincerely and wholeheartedly believe in the Lord Jesus as your Savior, you can change biblically because you have a different relationship with God and can have a different view of yourself, others, and your problems.

1. You are declared righteous through Jesus Christ on the basis of faith *(Romans 3:21-22; I Corinthians 1:30; II Corinthians 5:21; Philippians 3:9)* and are no longer under judgment of God's wrath *(John 3:36; Romans 5:9, 8:1).*

2. You are at peace with God because you have been reconciled to Him through Jesus and stand totally justified before God Almighty *(Romans 3:24-26; 5:1, 11; II Corinthians 5:18).*

3. You are no longer separated from God or a stranger to God's family *(Ephesians 2:12-13, 19-20).* You have been adopted into His family *(Romans 8:14-16; Ephesians 1:4-5),* are a joint-heir with Christ *(Romans 8:16-17; Galatians 4:7),* and are a recipient of His loving care forever *(Psalm 121; John 10:28; Romans 8:31-39; I Peter 5:7).*

4. You have been given the gift of eternal life *(John 10:28)* and have the certainty that God's work in you will continue until you are in His presence *(Philippians 1:6; Jude 1:24).*

5. Because of what God has done for you through Jesus, you may have confidence that He will help you in any and all situations of life *(Romans 8:32; Hebrews 2:18; 4:15-16).*

6. As a child of God, you are a new creation *(II Corinthians 5:17).* You no longer need to be enslaved to sin *(Romans 6:6, 14, 17-18, 22),* but you are to be a slave of righteousness *(Romans 6:16-18).* You have been set free to serve the Lord and others *(Romans 15:1-3; Galatians 5:13; Colossians 3:24).*

7. You have God's promise that He will enable you to handle any problem that comes into your life. Furthermore, you no longer need to be defeated by any problem because God will not permit any difficulty in your life that can overwhelm you *(Romans 8:35-37; I Corinthians 10:13).* In addition to this, He will actively work in every difficulty for good as you continue to walk in His way *(Romans 8:28-29).*

8. You are now enabled to see that God uses trials and problems as opportunities for spiritual growth *(Romans 5:3-5; James 1:2-4)*.

9. You can have confidence because Jesus will never leave you *(Matthew 28:20; Hebrews 13:5)*. He knows about every problem you will ever encounter and is merciful towards you. Moreover, He invites you to come confidently to Him for grace to help in time of need *(Hebrews 4:15-16)*.

B. **God's sufficiency and your resources** – After your conversion to Jesus (a sincere, wholehearted belief in the Lord Jesus Christ), you can change biblically because of God's divine power available to you.

1. God's Spirit is within you *(John 14:16-17; Romans 8:9)*, always available to teach you God's truths *(John 14:26, 16:13; I Corinthians 2:10-13)*, to strengthen you *(Romans 8:11)*, to intercede for you *(Romans 8:26-27)*, to help you discern between truth and error *(based on I John 2:18-27)*, and to develop Christlike character in your life *(Galatians 5:16-17, 22-23)*.

2. God's Word is completely sufficient to change you *(I Thessalonians 2:13; Hebrews 4:12; II Peter 1:2-4)*, to give you hope *(Romans 15:4)*, and to counsel you in any situation *(II Timothy 3:16-17)*.

3. Instead of relying on the wisdom of this world – which is foolishness *(I Corinthians 3:19)*, or your own ideas – which are inadequate *(Isaiah 55:8-9)*, or your own strength – which is ineffectual *(I Corinthians 1:25; I Peter 1:24)*, you can have God's wisdom *(James 1:5)*, empowering, strength *(Ephesians 6:10; II Thessalonians 3:3; I John 4:4)* and sufficiency *(II Corinthians 9:8-10; Philippians 4:19)* in every circumstance *(I Corinthians 10:13; Philippians 4:11-13)*.

4. The Lord Jesus Christ will always remain with you *(Matthew 28:20; Hebrews 13:5)*, sustain you *(John 15:1-11)*, and care for you *(John 10:27-29; Ephesians 5:29)*. Jesus is and will always be your defender *(I John 2:1)*, and He will always intercede to God the Father on your behalf *(Romans 8:34; Hebrews 7:25)*.

C. **God's purpose and your focus** – After your conversion to Jesus, you can change biblically because God gives you a different purpose for living.

1. You are to worship and serve God *(Luke 4:8; John 4:23-24)*, pleasing Him in all respects *(II Corinthians 5:9; Colossians 1:10)* as you are being conformed to the image of Jesus Christ, the firstborn among many brethren *(Romans 8:29; II Corinthians 3:18)*. As a responsible member of God's family, you are to give glory to God in all things *(Psalm 115:1; I Corinthians 10:31; Colossians 3:17)*. You can now be a slave to righteousness *(Romans 6:16-18)*, and you are an ambassador for the Lord Jesus Christ *(II Corinthians 5:20)*.

2. Instead of living for yourself, you can focus on learning to die to self *(Matthew 10:38; Luke 9:23; I Corinthians 15:31)*. In following Christ, you are to lose your life for the Lord's sake *(Matthew 10:39; Luke 9:24)*. This change in allegiance is demonstrated by practical expressions of loving God *(Matthew 22:37-38; John 14:15, 21; I John 5:3)* and loving others *(Matthew 22:39; I Corinthians 13:4-8a; Philippians 2:1-4; I John 4:7-8, 11, 20)*.

D. **God's plan and your obedience** – After your conversion to Jesus, you can change biblically by obeying the biblical directives given to accomplish these changes.

1. Biblical change in you, sovereignly originated, sustained, and to be completed by God *(Philippians 1:6, 2:13)*, is always linked to your obedience to God's Word *(Luke 6:46-49; Philippians 2:12; Hebrews 5:14; James 1:22-25)*. Your obedience to

His Word is a grateful response to God's love that is revealed in Christ Jesus *(John 14:15, 21, 23-24; I John 5:3; II John 1:6)*; it is not to be dependent on circumstances *(Acts 5:28-29; II Timothy 3:1-17)*, your feelings *(Genesis 4:7; Galatians 5:17; I Peter 4:2)*, or other people *(Ezekiel 18:20; I Peter 3:8-17)*.

2.   A commitment to please God *(II Corinthians 5:9; Colossians 1:10)* begins with biblical self-confrontation *(Matthew 7:1-5; I Corinthians 11:31)*. Confronting yourself biblically will enable you to develop and practice plans for change in your thoughts *(Romans 12:2; II Corinthians 10:5; Ephesians 4:23; Philippians 4:8; Colossians 3:2)*, words *(Ephesians 4:29; Colossians 4:6)*, and actions *(the following references indicate the vast number and kinds of changes in actions that are outlined for the people of God: Romans chapters 12-14; Ephesians chapters 4-6; Philippians chapters 2-3; Colossians chapters 2-3; I Thessalonians chapter 4; Titus chapters 2-3; James chapters 1-5; I Peter chapters 2-3)*.

II.   **The process of biblical change ends when you enter into eternal fellowship with Him and with those who, throughout history, have been redeemed by our Heavenly Father.**

A.   A believer in Christ now has an eternal relationship with the Lord, will continue to dwell with Him in heaven, and is promised the following:

1.   You will meet Jesus when He returns with power and great glory *(Matthew 16:27, 26:64; Acts 1:11; Colossians 3:4; I Thessalonians 4:13-18; Hebrews 9:28)*.

2.   You can anticipate the transformation of your earthly body of corruptible flesh into an immortal, incorruptible, and glorified body *(Romans 8:23; I Corinthians 15:36-58; Philippians 3:20-21; I John 3:2)*.

3.   You can be assured of living forever with Jesus Christ in a heavenly, eternal city not made with hands *(II Corinthians 5:1; Hebrews 11:10; Revelation 21:1-2, 10-27; 22:1-7)*.

4.   You will be a part of a great host of righteous brothers and sisters in Christ who will dwell in peace and joy forever *(Matthew 24:31; I Thessalonians 4:13-18; Revelation 7:9, 22:14)*, where there will be no more tears, sorrow, or darkness *(Revelation 21:2-4, 23-25)*.

B.   In the present, you can anticipate this eternal fellowship.

1.   You must keep your heart and mind established, ready, and clear with your activities in proper perspective, anticipating His glorious appearing *(Philippians 3:20; Titus 2:11-13; I Peter 1:13; I John 3:3)*.

2.   Be careful of your walk and make the most of your time *(Ephesians 5:15-16; I Thessalonians 5:6-10)*.

3.   Encourage other believers *(I Thessalonians 5:11; Hebrews 10:23-25)* and comfort them with the hope of His coming *(I Thessalonians 4:13-18, esp. verse 18)*.

BIBLICAL SELF-CONFRONTATION: AN ESSENTIAL FOR DISCIPLESHIP

> Discipleship is a process which enables you to "grow up" in the Lord Jesus Christ and equips you to overcome joyfully the pressures and trials of this present life *(based on Luke 9:23-24; James 1:2-4)*. Discipleship requires constant self-examination that is in accordance with God's Word *(based on Matthew 7:1-5; I Corinthians 11:31; Galatians 6:4)*.

The following will help you evaluate your faithfulness as a disciple of Christ. For each question, rate yourself on a scale of 0 (no faithfulness, complete self-centeredness) to 10 (perfect faithfulness, total Christ-centeredness). Regardless of your present level of faithfulness, remember that God will help you make the necessary changes to be conformed to the image of His Son (Romans 8:29; II Corinthians 3:18; Philippians 1:6). All of the characteristics of discipleship mentioned below are covered during this course. Biblical steps by which these characteristics can be incorporated into your life will also be explained.

1. Are you diligent in learning to handle accurately the Word of God *(II Timothy 2:15)*?

2. Do you consistently examine yourself in light of God's Word instead of comparing yourself with the lives or expectations of others *(I Samuel 16:7; Isaiah 55:8-11; Romans 3:23; II Corinthians 10:12; Hebrews 4:12)*?

3. Are you a doer of the Word? Being a doer of the Word requires continual hearing of God's Word and walking in it to receive the blessings of the Lord *(Deuteronomy 11:26-28; Romans 10:17; Hebrews 5:14; James 1:22-25)*. The Word is completely adequate for every area of life as it teaches, reproves, corrects, trains, and equips you in order that you may mature in Christ *(II Timothy 3:16-17)*.

4. Do you deny yourself by putting off your natural self-centeredness to follow the Lord Jesus Christ *(Matthew 10:38-39; Luke 9:23-24)*?

5. Do you seek to please God in all things *(John 8:29; II Corinthians 5:9; Ephesians 6:6-7; Colossians 1:10; I Thessalonians 2:4, 4:1; Hebrews 13:21; I John 3:22)*?

6. Are you a person of prayer? Continual prayer, with thanksgiving, leads to God's peace guarding your heart and mind in Christ Jesus *(Philippians 4:6-7; I Thessalonians 5:17-18)*.

7. Do you place the welfare of others ahead of your own, thus following the example of the Lord Jesus Christ *(Matthew 20:25-28; Romans 15:1-3; Philippians 2:3-8)*?

8. Do you love others in biblical ways *(I Corinthians 13:4-8a)*? By loving in this manner, you will follow the example of our Lord Jesus Christ and will become known as His disciple *(John 13:34-35, 15:12-13)*.

9. Are you faithfully using your spiritual gift(s) for God's glory and for the benefit of others *(Romans 12:3-8; Ephesians 4:1-16; I Peter 4:10-11)*?

10. Do you regularly worship the Lord, remaining in fellowship and in ministry with other believers *(Psalm 29:1-2, 122:1; John 4:23-24; Hebrews 10:24-25; I Peter 2:5; I John 1:7)*?

11. Are you ready at all times to give testimony for the hope that is within you *(I Peter 3:15)*, giving glory to the Lord with your life *(Matthew 5:16)*, seeking to reconcile others to God, and discipling them to walk in His way *(Matthew 28:19-20; II Corinthians 5:18-20)*?

BIBLICAL SELF-CONFRONTATION:
A PREREQUISITE FOR HELPING OTHERS BIBLICALLY

> You can never truly understand or help others, even in your own family, unless you first look thoroughly into your own life and deal with your own sins without compromise, excuses, or evasion *(based on Matthew 7:1-5; II Corinthians 1:3-5).*

"Test yourselves to see if you are in the faith; examine yourselves!" (II Corinthians 13:5a)

Establishing a personal, genuine, and intimate relationship with the Lord Jesus Christ and thus receiving eternal life (being born again) is a prerequisite to biblical change.

"Therefore bring forth fruit in keeping with repentance." (Matthew 3:8)

Your life must change, and your new biblical conduct (thoughts, words, and actions) should be proof of that change.

"For in the way you judge, you will be judged; and by your standard of measure, it shall be measured to you. And why do you look at the speck that is in your brother's eye, but do not notice the log that is in your own eye?" (Matthew 7:2-3)

The standard you use to judge another's life implies its validity in judging your own life. Be careful to use God's standard and not rely on your own judgments or any other standard that is of the world.

"But if we judge ourselves rightly we should not be judged." (I Corinthians 11:31)

You are not subject to God's judgment resulting in discipline when you rightly judge yourself, confess your sins, and take steps consistent with your repentance.

"You hypocrite, first take the log out of your own eye, and then you will see clearly to take the speck out of your brother's eye." (Matthew 7:5)

You must be correcting your own failures to go God's way before you can attempt to help others with their problems.

"Therefore you are without excuse, every man of you who passes judgment, for in that you judge another, you condemn yourself; for you who judge practice the same things." (Romans 2:1)

When you self-righteously judge others, you reveal areas in your own life in which you are sinning.

"You shall consecrate yourselves therefore and be holy, for I am the Lord your God. And you shall keep my statutes and practice them; I am the Lord who sanctifies you." (Leviticus 20:7-8)

You need and should desire to be set apart from the world. In order to accomplish this, you must be a doer of the Word.

"But solid food is for the mature, who because of practice have their senses trained to discern good and evil." (Hebrews 5:14)

You must continually practice what you have learned from God's Word in order for your senses to be sharpened (i.e., to become sensitive) in discerning right and wrong.

"Watch yourselves, that you might not lose what we have accomplished, but that you may receive a full reward." (II John 1:8)

Your reward from God will correspond to your faithfulness.

"Let not many of you become teachers, my brethren, knowing that as such you shall incur a stricter judgment." (James 3:1)

If you are going to teach or lead someone, you must recognize that God holds you more responsible to keep His standard, not only for your words but for your whole manner of life.

"Brethren, even if a man is caught in any trespass, you who are spiritual, restore such a one in a spirit of gentleness; each one looking to yourself, lest you too be tempted." (Galatians 6:1)

You must gently restore fallen brothers and sisters who are caught in sin. However, you must continue to judge yourself so that you do not also fall short of God's standards.

"Therefore let him who stands take heed lest he fall." (I Corinthians 10:12)

You must continually evaluate yourself in a biblical manner.

BIBLICAL BASIS FOR DAILY DEVOTIONS AND SCRIPTURE MEMORY

> Your daily devotions (time spent each day in prayer, study of God's Word, and biblical self-evaluation) and Scripture memory are vital to your spiritual development (*based on Psalm 1:1-4, 119:9-11; I Corinthians 11:31; I Thessalonians 5:17; II Timothy 2:15; I Peter 2:2*).

DAILY DEVOTIONS

I. **Developing a habit of daily devotions (prayer, study of God's Word, and biblical self-evaluation) will help you to:**

    A. Follow the example of many people in Scripture who had a heart for God *(Psalm 5:3, 63:6, 119:62, 147-148; Daniel 6:10; Acts 10:1-2, 17:11)*;

    B. Be equipped for spiritual warfare *(Ephesians 6:10-18)* and to remain alert to your adversary, the devil *(I Peter 5:8)*;

    C. Be obedient to the scriptural command of habitual and continual prayer *(Luke 18:1; Ephesians 6:18; Philippians 4:6-7; Colossians 4:2; I Thessalonians 5:17)*;

    D. Be sustained and nourished continually by the Word of God *(Psalm 1:2-3; Jeremiah 15:16; Matthew 4:4; I Thessalonians 2:13)*;

    E. Be directed in all of life by the Word of God *(Psalm 19:7-11; Psalm 119; II Timothy 2:15, 3:16-17; Hebrews 4:12; II Peter 1:3-4)*;

    F. Focus your life on the worship and praise of God *(Psalm 16:11, 34:1, 48:1, 63:1-4, 92:1-2, 95:6, 119:164; John 4:23-24; Hebrews 13:15)*;

    G. Examine yourself daily in the light of God's Word *(Psalm 119:105; Hebrews 4:12)*, confess your sins *(I John 1:9)*, and practice self-discipline *(Galatians 5:23-24; I Timothy 4:7-8; II Peter 1:6)*, thus avoiding the necessity of the discipline of the Lord *(I Corinthians 11:31-32; Hebrews 12:5-11)*; and

    H. Keep yourself in a biblical position to help others *(Matthew 7:1-5; Galatians 6:1-5)*.

II. **Your daily devotions will enhance your own spiritual development as you:**

    A. List your prayer requests and God's answers to those requests. This will help you to:

        1. Become persistent in prayer *(Daniel 10:12-13; Luke 18:1-8)*,

        2. Learn patience in waiting for God's answers *(Psalm 40:1; Galatians 6:9b)*,

        3. Avoid anxiety *(Philippians 4:6-7)*, and

        4. Be thankful to God for His greatness *(Psalm 92:1-5, 105:1-2, 106:1; Hebrews 13:15; James 1:17)*.

B.   Develop a pattern of prayer that embraces:

    1.   Worshipping God (P*salm 95:6; John 4:23-24),*

    2.   Confessing your own sins *(Psalm 139:23-24; Proverbs 28:13; I John 1:9),*

    3.   Thanking God for what He has accomplished *(Psalm 119:164; Ephesians 5:20; I Thessalonians 5:18),*

    4.   Interceding on behalf of others (I *Samuel 12:23; Luke 10:2; Ephesians 6:18; I Timothy 2:1-2),* and

    5.   Acknowledging your dependence on the Lord to supply your needs *(Matthew 6:9-13).*

C.   Meditate on specific passages or principles of God's Word (Psalm 1:2-3, 119:48) as well as on God's majesty and His wonderful works *(Psalm 145:5).*

D.   Develop a plan of scriptural study that includes application of biblical principles to everyday life *(Matthew 7:24-27; II Timothy 2:15; James 1:22-25)*

See: **BIBLE STUDY AND APPLICATION FORMAT** *(Supplement 3).*

E.   Examine your life according to Scripture on a continual basis *(Matthew 7:1-5; I Corinthians 11:31; II Timothy 3:16-17)* and make appropriate, biblical changes *(Romans 6:1-14; 12:1, 2; Colossians 3:1-17).*

SCRIPTURE MEMORY

I.   **Memorizing Scripture is beneficial because it:**

A.   Helps to renew your mind and change your thought life, establishing permanent change in your entire manner of life and conduct *(Joshua 1:8; Psalm 1:2-3);*

B.   Follows the example of the Lord Jesus Christ *(Matthew 4:1-10);*

C.   Equips you to use Scripture in everyday situations *(for example: Acts 2:16-21, 25-28; 3:22-23; 13:40-41, 47);*

D.   Allows God's Word to be the foundation of your life *(Deuteronomy 6:6-8);*

E.   Provides guidance *(Psalm 119:24, 105);*

F.   Develops confidence in witnessing *(Isaiah 55:11);*

G.   Establishes a foundation to conquer temptation *(for example: Matthew 4:1-10)* and to gain victory over sin *(Psalm 119:9-11);*

H.   Becomes an integral part of your prayer life *(for example: Acts 4:24-31);*

I.   Enables you to teach, counsel, encourage, and build up others in the Body of Christ *(Colossians 3:16);*

J.   Provides a basis for meditation on God's Word *(Psalm 119:15-16, 97);*

K.   Makes the Word of God readily available for comfort *(Psalm 119:52);*

L.   Keeps God's Word ready to refresh or revive *(Psalm 119:93);*

M.   Provides stability in your spiritual life *(Psalm 37:31, 40:8);* and

N.   Gives you the truth so that, at times of need, you are ready to answer others concerning your source of hope *(Proverbs 22:17-21; I Peter 3:15)*.

II.   **Memorizing Scripture can extend your devotional time throughout the day as you:**

A.   Read the verse in your Bible and meditate on it *(Psalm 1:2; II Timothy 2:15)*,

B.   Take advantage of free moments throughout each day to learn your verses *(Ephesians 5:16)*, and

C.   Review the verses you have learned *(Psalm 19:14, 119:15-16; Philippians 4:8)*.

FOUR PLANS FOR MEMORIZING SCRIPTURE

> You are commanded to put aside the sinful practices of
> your old self, to be changed by a renewing of the mind,
> and to put on Christlike practices of your new self.
> Memorizing God's Word is foundational to that process
> *(based on Psalm 40:8; Psalm 119:9-11, 15-16, 24, 97;*
> *Romans 12:2; Ephesians 4:22-24; Colossians 3:8-10).*

The following are four suggested plans for memorizing Scripture. Although they are not the only ways by which you can memorize, these plans have proven helpful in the lives of many Christians. The important thing to remember, regardless of the memory plan you choose, is that God's Word is to be treasured in your heart (Psalm 119:11). Ask God to give you understanding and wisdom for your life through the Scripture passages that you memorize.

I. Scripture memory – plan 1

A. Read the context of the verse in your Bible (literal translation) and meditate on it. This helps you understand the verse in its setting.

B. Thoughtfully read the verse through several times aloud or in a whisper. This will help you grasp the verse as a whole.

C. Include the reference as part of the verse by saying it before and after the verse every time you repeat it.

D. Print your memory verses neatly on individual index cards. Using a paper punch, you may also make a hole in the top of your card and use a ring clasp to keep your cards together. Carry them with you at all times by placing them in a packet or putting an elastic band around them.

E. Break the passage into natural phrases. Learn the reference and first phrase. Then repeat the reference, first phrase, and second phrase. Continue adding phrases until the verse is memorized.

F. Take advantage of your spare time during the day to pull out your packet and memorize your verses. Use the time spent waiting in line, on the bus, doing dishes, mowing the lawn – any time your mind is not required for attention to detail. This habit will help to renew your thought life.

G. Review the verse frequently during the first few weeks after learning it. This is crucial to getting the verse fixed firmly in mind. Many find it beneficial to review the previously memorized verses every day for at least six weeks before placing them in a box for periodic review.

II. Scripture memory – plan 2

A. Print verse and Scripture reference on an index card. Ask God for His help in understanding and applying this portion of His Word to your life.

B. Recite the week's memory verse and reference five to ten times when you awaken in the morning and five to ten times before you go to sleep at night.

C. Carry your Scripture memory card pack with you throughout the day to review past memory verses. Insert your new verse into your Scripture memory card pack at the end of the week.

D. Review each verse in your Scripture memory card pack at least once per day for six weeks before placing it in a weekly review box.

III. Scripture memory – plan 3

A. Choose a number of places in your daily routine that you regularly visit (for example: a mirror, a briefcase, a purse, the bathroom, the kitchen, a favorite book).

B. Print your memory verse and its Scripture reference on as many index cards as you have places listed in your daily routine and post your Scripture memory cards in these places.

C. Whenever you visit your regular places each day, quote the verse and the reference listed on the card.

D. At the end of a week, remove your current memory verse cards from their posted spots and replace each one with a new verse (multiple verses can be posted while others are reviewed daily, weekly, or monthly).

IV. Scripture memory – plan 4

A. Read the verse and its reference into a tape recorder, reciting it as many times as you want to repeat it.

B. Play back what you have recorded and, with the tape, recite the reference and the verse at various times each day.

C. Recite your past memory verses and their references into your tape recorder. On a weekly basis, evaluate your retention of these verses by reciting them when you play back the verses.

For all four plans, ask someone to listen to your memorized verses on a weekly basis. When you recite your verses to this person, also explain what the verse(s) mean and how they are to be applied to your life.

LESSON 2: HOMEWORK

> Central to God's plan for you is your redemption through the Lord Jesus Christ's sacrifice on the Cross and His resurrection from the dead. Understanding the meaning of your redemption and responding biblically will give you hope in any situation of life *(based on Romans chapter 6; I Corinthians 1:18-24; 2:2; 15:3-4; Ephesians 1:18-23; Philippians 3:8-14; Hebrews 5:12-14; James 1:22-25).*

✔ *homework completed*

☐ A. * In your own words, write the meaning of *Matthew 7:1 and 7:5*. Memorize *Matthew 7:1 and 7:5* and begin memorizing *II Timothy 3:16-17*.

☐ B. * Complete a **BIBLE STUDY AND APPLICATION FORMAT** (Supplement 3, Page 1) for *Psalm 1:1-2*.

*You may make copies of the **BIBLE STUDY AND APPLICATION FORMAT** (Supplement 3, Page 1) for your study of Scripture. To help you use this form effectively, examples are provided in Supplement 3, Pages 2-3.*

*Use this plan of study as an opportunity to establish a daily devotional time with the Lord. If you have already developed the habit of daily devotions, use this study as part of your regular devotional time. A **STUDY GUIDE FOR DAILY DEVOTIONS** for this week is provided in Lesson 2, Pages 15-16.*

☐ C. * Read **BIBLICAL PRINCIPLES: YOU CAN CHANGE BIBLICALLY (PART TWO)** (Lesson 2, Page 2). Highlight the listed verses in your Bible.

☐ D. Read **YOU CAN CHANGE BIBLICALLY (PART TWO)** (Lesson 2, Pages 3-5). Look up the listed verses to help you better understand this study.

☐ E. Read **BIBLICAL SELF-CONFRONTATION: AN ESSENTIAL FOR DISCIPLESHIP** (Lesson 2, Page 6), answering each question in order to gain a biblical perspective of your current walk with the Lord. As the first step in correcting any failures or deficiencies, confess your shortcomings, as sin, to the Lord *(I John 1:9)*.

☐ F. Read **BIBLICAL SELF-CONFRONTATION: A PREREQUISITE FOR HELPING OTHERS BIBLICALLY** (Lesson 2, Pages 7-8) to continue your process of biblical self-evaluation.

☐ G. Read **BIBLICAL BASIS FOR DAILY DEVOTIONS AND SCRIPTURE MEMORY** (Lesson 2, Pages 9-11), which illustrates the need for you to incorporate these areas of spiritual discipline into your life.

☐ H. Read **FOUR PLANS FOR MEMORIZING SCRIPTURE** (Lesson 2, Pages 12-13). Prayerfully choose a plan for Scripture memory and begin using that plan.

☐ I. * To complete the **COURSE EXAM** (Lesson 23) while going through this course, answer question 3 under **Open Book Test** (Lesson 23, Page 1).

* *The completion of assignments marked with an asterisk (*) is a prerequisite for further biblical counseling training.*

LESSON 2: STUDY GUIDE FOR DAILY DEVOTIONS
(INCLUDING SCRIPTURE MEMORY AND HOMEWORK)

> Central to God's plan for you is your redemption through the Cross of Jesus Christ. Understanding the meaning of your redemption and responding biblically will give you hope in any situation of life. This week's **STUDY GUIDE** will assist you in this process (*based on Romans chapter 6; I Corinthians 1:18-24, 2:2; Ephesians 1:18-23; Philippians 3:8-14; Hebrews 5:12-14; James 1:22-25*).

Scripture Memory

1. * Memorize *Matthew 7:1 and 7:5* and begin memorizing *II Timothy 3:16-17*.
2. With your memory verse from last week (*Ephesians 2:8-9*), you should now have three memory verse cards that can be carried with you throughout the day. At every opportunity, review *Ephesians 2:8-9* and read, meditate on, and memorize *Matthew 7:1 and 7:5*. Preview *II Timothy 3:16-17* whenever possible.

Daily Devotional Study Guide

FIRST DAY

1. Open in prayer.
2. * Read **BIBLICAL PRINCIPLES: YOU CAN CHANGE BIBLICALLY (PART TWO)** (Lesson 2, Page 2). In your Bible, highlight the verses listed under *Principle 2* and *Principle 3*.
3. Read **DAILY DEVOTIONS** under **BIBLICAL BASIS FOR DAILY DEVOTIONS AND SCRIPTURE MEMORY** (Lesson 2, Pages 9-11).
4. * In your own words, write the meaning of *Matthew 7:1 and 7:5*.
5. Close in prayer.

SECOND DAY

1. Open in prayer.
2. Study Section I. A., points 1-4, under **YOU CAN CHANGE BIBLICALLY (PART TWO)** (Lesson 2, Page 3). This is the first day of a six day study that highlights the process of biblical change. Look up the listed verses to help you understand the different relationship you have with God through Jesus Christ.
3. * Start a **BIBLE STUDY AND APPLICATION FORMAT** (Supplement 3, Page 1) for *Psalm 1:1-2*. Examples in the use of this study form are provided in Supplement 3, Pages 2-3.
4. Read **SCRIPTURE MEMORY** under **BIBLICAL BASIS FOR DAILY DEVOTIONS AND SCRIPTURE MEMORY** (Lesson 2, Page 9-11).
5. Read **FOUR PLANS FOR MEMORIZING SCRIPTURE** (Lesson 2, Pages 12-13).
6. Close in prayer.

THIRD DAY

1. Open in prayer.
2. Study Section I. A., points 5-9, in **YOU CAN CHANGE BIBLICALLY (PART TWO)** (Lesson 2, Pages 3-4). Refer to listed verses as necessary.
3. * From the previous day, continue to work on your **BIBLE STUDY AND APPLICATION FORMAT** (Supplement 3, Page 1) for *Psalm 1:1-2*.
4. Close in prayer.

FOURTH DAY

    1.   Open in prayer.

    2.   Study Section I. B. in **YOU CAN CHANGE BIBLICALLY (PART TWO)** (Lesson 2, Page 4). Refer to the listed Scriptures to help you understand the supernatural power granted for your biblical change.

    3.   * Continue work on your **BIBLE STUDY AND APPLICATION FORMAT** (Supplement 3, Page 1) for *Psalm 1:1-2.*

    4.   Close in prayer.

    5.   How is your progress in Scripture memorization? Are you taking your cards with you and using your spare moments for Scripture memory? Have you contacted someone to whom you could recite your memory verses this week?

FIFTH DAY

    1.   Open in prayer.

    2.   Study Section I. C. in **YOU CAN CHANGE BIBLICALLY (PART TWO)** (Lesson 2, Page 4). Look up verses as needed.

    3.   * Complete your **BIBLE STUDY AND APPLICATION FORMAT** (Supplement 3, Page 1) for *Psalm 1:1-2.*

    4.   Read **BIBLICAL SELF-CONFRONTATION: AN ESSENTIAL FOR DISCIPLESHIP** (Lesson 2, Page 6) and answer the questions to give you a biblical perspective of your present walk in Jesus Christ *(Ephesians 4:1).* If you have failed, confess these sins to the Lord *(I John 1:9).*

    5.   Close in prayer.

SIXTH DAY

    1.   Open in prayer.

    2.   Study Section I. D. in **YOU CAN CHANGE BIBLICALLY (PART TWO)** (Lesson 2, Pages 4-5), referring to passages as necessary.

    3.   Read through **BIBLICAL SELF-CONFRONTATION: A PREREQUISITE FOR HELPING OTHERS BIBLICALLY** (Lesson 2, Pages 7-8) to realize the importance of confronting yourself biblically before attempting to help others.

    4.   Close in prayer.

    5.   Evaluate your use of spare moments in memorizing Scripture. List improvements you will make to use your time more effectively in memorizing God's Word.

SEVENTH DAY

    1.   Open in prayer.

    2.   Study Section II. in **YOU CAN CHANGE BIBLICALLY (PART TWO)** (Lesson 2, Page 5), looking up the listed verses to help you understand the promised eternal fellowship with our Lord Jesus Christ.

    3.   * To complete the **COURSE EXAM** (Lesson 23) while going through this course, answer question 3 under **Open Book Test** (Lesson 23, Page 1).

    4.   Close in prayer.

    5.   Ask someone to hear you recite your memory verses. Remember to explain the meaning of the verses and their application to your life.

    *   *The completion of assignments marked with an asterisk (*) is a prerequisite for further biblical counseling training.*

LESSON 3

MAN'S WAY AND GOD'S WAY
(PART ONE)

"All Scripture is inspired by God and profitable for teaching, for reproof, for correction, for training in righteousness; that the man of God may be adequate, equipped for every good work."

II Timothy 3:16-17

LESSON 3: MAN'S WAY AND GOD'S WAY (PART ONE)

> Learning to live God's way requires you to respond to God's salvation through His Son, Jesus Christ. Then, you are to begin a new way of living based on the Lord's truth, resources, and wisdom rather than your own or anyone else's wisdom, philosophy, or experience *(based on Proverbs 3:5-6; John 14:6; Romans 10:9-10, 13, 17; 12:1-2; II Corinthians 5:21; Colossians 2:6-10; James 3:13-15).*

I.   **The purposes of this lesson are:**

A.   To show you God's resources which enable you to live God's way; and

B.   To provide an opportunity for you to develop your own personal testimony of God's grace and mercy given to you through Jesus Christ.

II. **The outline of this lesson**

A.   Self-confrontation

1.   **BIBLICAL PRINCIPLES: MAN'S WAY AND GOD'S WAY (PART ONE)** (Lesson 3, Page 2)

2.   **SCRIPTURE IS YOUR AUTHORITY** (Lesson 3, Pages 3-5)

3.   **THE HOLY SPIRIT EMPOWERS YOU TO SOLVE YOUR PROBLEMS** (Lesson 3, Pages 6-8)

4.   **PRAYER PROVIDES COMMUNICATION WITH GOD** (Lesson 3, Pages 9-12)

B.   Steps for spiritual growth

1.   **LESSON 3: HOMEWORK** (Lesson 3, Page 13)

2.   **STUDY GUIDE FOR DAILY DEVOTIONS** (Lesson 3, Pages 14-15)

3.   **PREPARING A PERSONAL TESTIMONY** (Supplement 4)

4.   **HOW TO USE A CONCORDANCE** (Supplement 5)

BIBLICAL PRINCIPLES: MAN'S WAY AND GOD'S WAY
(PART ONE)

> You can live God's way because of the abundant resources and provisions He has graciously and mercifully given to you *(based on John 14:26; Romans 8:11; II Corinthians 1:20-24; Ephesians 1:13-14; Philippians 4:13; Colossians 4:2; I Thessalonians 5:16-18; II Timothy 3:16-17; James 1:5; I John 5:14-15).*

I. **The Bible is adequate**

(Principle 4)   Since God's Word is the only authority for faith and conduct and is the sole, legitimate standard by which all aspects of living are evaluated, you are to rely on no other source. God's Word provides hope and gives direction for change in deeds (thoughts, speech, and actions) and is adequate to equip you for every good work *(Psalm 19:7-11; Proverbs 30:5-6; Colossians 2:8; II Timothy 3:16-17; Hebrews 4:12; II Peter 1:2-4)* and to develop a Christlike attitude of servanthood within you *(II Corinthians 3:5-6; Philippians 2:5-8).*

II. **The Holy Spirit is necessary**

(Principle 5)   Only through the power of the Holy Spirit are you able to live an abundant life *(John 14:26, 16:7-14; Romans 8:5-11; I Corinthians 2:9-14; Ephesians 1:13-14, 5:18).*

III. **Prayer is vital**

(Principle 6)   Prayer is essential to a Spirit-controlled life *(Psalm 145:18-19; Matthew 7:7-8; Ephesians 5:18-20; 6:18; I Thessalonians 5:17; I John 3:22).* You are to be devoted to prayer, according to God's will, and to bring everything and everyone unceasingly before the Lord in prayer *(Luke 18:1; Ephesians 6:18; Philippians 4:6; Colossians 4:2; I Thessalonians 5:17; I Timothy 2:1; I John 5:14-15).*

SCRIPTURE IS YOUR AUTHORITY

> God's Word is changeless and is as powerful and
> applicable to you and your circumstances today as it was to
> those living thousands of years ago *(based on Joshua 1:8;
> Psalm 19:7-11, 119:160; Isaiah 55:11; Matthew 24:35;
> Romans 15:4; Hebrews 4:12; I Peter 1:24-25).*

God's Word Is:

A.	**Permanent and eternal**	*Isaiah 40:8*
	1. It will all be fulfilled	*Matthew 5:18*
	2. Heaven and earth shall pass away but God's Word will not pass away	*Matthew 24:35*
	3. It will abide forever	*I Peter 1:25*
	4. It is everlasting and forever	*Psalm 119:89, 160*
B.	**Inspired by God for our training and equipping**	*II Timothy 3:16-17*
	1. Holy men of God spoke as they were moved by the Holy Spirit	*II Peter 1:21*
	2. God's Word provides a new pattern of living	*II Timothy 3:16-17*
	a. It teaches you *(commands and guidelines)*	*Psalm 25:4-5; 94:12*
	b. It reproves you *(identification of error)*	*Hebrews 4:12*
	c. It corrects you *(change/repentance)*	*Psalm 25:8-9; 119:9*
	d. It trains you in righteousness *(growth and stability through practice)*	*Hebrews 5:13-14*
	e. It will make you adequate *(ready and able to do God's work)*, and	*I Peter 1:22-23; II Peter 1:3-4*
	f. It will equip you for every good work *(used by God in this world)*	*I Thessalonians 2:13*
C.	**Truth**	*John 17:17*
	1. All of God's Word is truth	*Psalm 119:151, 160*
	2. The gospel of salvation is truth	*Ephesians 1:13*
	3. You are brought forth by the Word of truth	*James 1:18*
	4. You are to handle accurately the Word of truth	*II Timothy 2:15*
D.	**A powerful, spiritual force**	*Jeremiah 23:29*
	1. It is living, active, and sharper than any two-edged sword	*Hebrews 4:12*
	2. It is a weapon against spiritual forces of wickedness	*Ephesians 6:11-17*
	3. It is to be used to resist Satan's wiles	*Matthew 4:4-10; Ephesians 6:11, 17*
	4. It makes you wiser than your enemies	*Psalm 119:98*

5. It can make you tremble — *Ezra 10:3; Isaiah 66:2, 5*

E. Cleansing to your ways — *Psalm 119:9*

1. You are cleansed through God's Word — *John 15:3;*
   Ephesians 5:26

2. You are sanctified by the truth of God's Word — *John 17:17*

3. You are purified by obeying the truth — *I Peter 1:22*

F. A source of grace that builds you up — *Acts 20:32*

1. It strengthens in grief — *Psalm 119:28*

2. It sustains you — *Psalm 119:116*

3. It comforts in affliction — *Psalm 119:50, 92*

4. It is a comfort and consolation — *Psalm 119:52*

5. It gives hope — *Psalm 119:49;*
   Romans 15:4

6. It provides peace — *Psalm 119:165*

7. It produces a reverence for God — *Psalm 119:38*

8. It gives freedom — *Psalm 119:45; John 8:32*

G. A testimony to its own sufficiency — *II Peter 1:3-4*

1. It is a reproach to those who do not listen — *Jeremiah 6:10*

2. You must not add to it or subtract from it — *Deuteronomy 4:2*

3. You are in peril if you take anything away from or add anything to God's Word — *Proverbs 30:6;*
   Revelation 22:19

4. You are accursed if you preach a different gospel — *Galatians 1:8, 9*

5. Distortion of Scripture brings about destruction — *II Peter 3:16*

6. It contains examples for our instruction — *Romans 15:4;*
   I Corinthians 10:6, 11

7. It is foolishness to those who are perishing — *I Corinthians 1:18*

8. It is not to be used deceitfully nor taken lightly — *II Corinthians 2:17, 4:2*

9. It is pure and refined — *Psalm 12:6, 19:8*

10. It has been tested — *II Samuel 22:31;*
    Psalm 18:30;
    Proverbs 30:5

11. It is perfect — *Psalm 19:7*

12. It is fully confirmed — *Psalm 93:5*

H. Always effective in accomplishing God's purpose — *Isaiah 55:11*

1. The Scriptures bear witness of Jesus Christ — *John 5:39*

2. It is used to bring a person to faith in Jesus Christ — *Romans 10:17*

3. It performs its work in you who believe — *I Thessalonians 2:13*

I.	**The standard for judgment**	*John 12:48*
	1. Your acceptance of God's Word determines your eternal destiny	*John 5:24, 38; 8:47, 51*
	2. It judges the thoughts and intentions of the heart	*Hebrews 4:12*
J.	**To dwell within you**	*Colossians 3:16*
	1. It helps to keep you from sinning	*Psalm 37:31, 119:11*
	2. It helps you meditate biblically	*Joshua 1:8; Psalm 1:2; 119:15, 23, 48, 97*
K.	**To be obeyed, not just heard**	*Matthew 7:24-27*
	1. You should be a doer, not just a hearer	*James 1:22-24*
	2. You are blessed when you observe God's Word	*Luke 11:28; John 13:17; James 1:25*
	3. You have greater spiritual discernment through obedience to God's Word	*Hebrews 5:14*
L.	**Food – man lives not only by bread but by God's Word**	*Deuteronomy 8:3; Matthew 4:4*
	1. God's Word is more treasured than necessary food	*Job 23:12*
	2. God's Word is sweeter than honey	*Psalm 19:10*
	3. You grow on the milk of God's Word	*I Peter 2:2*
	4. God's children are delighted when they partake of His words	*Jeremiah 15:16*
	5. His servants are nourished by words of faith	*I Timothy 4:6*
M.	**A light to guide your way**	*Psalm 119:105*
	1. It gives light and understanding	*Psalm 19:7; 119:99, 104, 130*
	2. It is able to keep you from stumbling	*Psalm 119:9, 165*
	3. It is a light shining in a dark place	*II Peter 1:19*
	4. It provides the light of instruction	*Proverbs 6:23*

THE HOLY SPIRIT EMPOWERS YOU
TO SOLVE YOUR PROBLEMS

> The Holy Spirit is your Guide, your Instructor, and your
> sensitive Counselor who reveals the wisdom of God to you
> *(based on John 14:16, 26; 16:7-13; I Corinthians 2:6-13).*

I. **The Holy Spirit is fully divine and is identified as being equal with God the Father and Jesus Christ the Son** *(based on Matthew 28:19; John 14:16-18; Acts 5:3-4, 16:6-7; II Corinthians 13:14).*

    A. Divine characteristics (a partial list to illustrate the deity of the Holy Spirit)

        1. The Holy Spirit is eternal *(Hebrews 9:14)* as is God the Father *(Deuteronomy 33:27a; Psalm 90:1-2)* and Jesus Christ the Son *(Hebrews 1:8-12, 7:24-25).*

        2. The Holy Spirit is truth *(John 14:16-17, 15:26, 16:13)* as is God the Father *(Psalm 31:5; Isaiah 65:16)* and Jesus Christ the Son *(John 14:6).*

        3. The Holy Spirit is present everywhere *(Psalm 139:7-10)* as is God the Father *(Psalm 139:7-10; Jeremiah 23:23-24)* and Jesus Christ the Son *(Matthew 18:20, 28:20; Romans 8:34; Hebrews 13:5b).*

    B. Divine works (a partial list to illustrate the cooperation of God the Father, God the Son, and God the Holy Spirit)

        1. The creation of the world was accomplished through God the Father *(Genesis 1:1; Isaiah 44:24; 45:12, 18; 51:13a; Ephesians 3:9)*, Jesus Christ *(Colossians 1:16; Hebrews 1:2, 10)*, and the Holy Spirit *(Genesis 1:2).*

        2. The Holy Spirit and God the Father were present and active in the virgin birth of Jesus Christ *(Luke 1:35)*, the baptism of Jesus Christ at the hands of John the Baptist *(Matthew 3:16-17; Luke 3:21-22)*, the earthly life and ministry of Jesus Christ *(Luke 4:1, 14; 9:28-36, esp. verse 35; Acts 10:38)*, and the resurrection of Jesus Christ *(Acts 5:30; Romans 8:11).*

        3. The Holy Spirit, God the Father, and Jesus Christ are all involved in the eternal plan of redemption *(Hebrews 9:11-15, esp. verse 14; I Peter 1:1-2).*

        4. Eternal life is granted to a believer through the work of God the Father *(Ephesians 2:4-7, esp. verse 5; I John 5:11)*, Jesus Christ *(John 6:40; I John 4:9, 5:11-12)*, and the Holy Spirit *(Romans 8:9-11).*

        5. The wisdom of God the Father is revealed through the ministry of the Holy Spirit *(I Corinthians 2:10-11)* and Jesus Christ the Son *(I Corinthians 1:24, 30).*

        6. Believers are justified through the work of God the Father *(Romans 8:33)*, Jesus Christ *(Galatians 2:16)*, and the Holy Spirit *(I Corinthians 6:11).*

        7. A believer is sealed in Jesus Christ by God the Father through the pledge (guarantee, promise) of the Holy Spirit *(II Corinthians 1:21-22; Ephesians 1:13-14).*

        8. The Holy Spirit is sent to believers by God the Father *(John 14:26)* and Jesus Christ *(John 15:26, 16:7).*

---

9. A believer is supernaturally indwelt by God the Father *(II Corinthians 6:16)*, Jesus Christ *(John 14:18-20; Romans 8:10; Colossians 1:27)*, and the Holy Spirit *(Romans 8:9; II Timothy 1:14)*.

10. Comfort is provided for the children of God by God the Father *(Isaiah 51:12a; II Corinthians 1:3; II Thessalonians 2:16-17)*, Jesus Christ *(II Corinthians 1:5; II Thessalonians 2:16-17)*, and the Holy Spirit *(Acts 9:31)*.

11. Love is imparted to a believer through God the Father *(John 3:16; Romans 5:8; I John 4:7-8, 19)*, Jesus Christ *(John 14:21, 15:9; Ephesians 5:25; II Timothy 1:13)*, and the Holy Spirit *(Romans 15:30; Galatians 5:22-23; Colossians 1:8)*.

12. Joy for a believer is found in God the Father *(Psalm 16:11, 43:4)*, Jesus Christ *(John 15:11, 16:24, 17:13)*, and the Holy Spirit *(Romans 14:17; Galatians 5:22-23; I Thessalonians 1:6)*.

II. **The Holy Spirit provides an overcoming and abundant life for you in Christ**

A. In the world, the Holy Spirit:

1. Is present everywhere and at all times *(Psalm 139:7-10)*;

2. Is the author of Scripture *(II Peter 1:20-21)* and is the empowerment for effective preaching *(Romans 15:18-19; I Corinthians 2:1-5, esp. verse 4; I Peter 1:12)*; and

3. Convicts the world concerning sin, righteousness, and judgment *(John 16:8-11)*.

B. In the life of a believer, the Holy Spirit:

1. Is the regenerating power for his spiritual new birth *(John 3:5-8; Titus 3:5)*;

2. Baptizes him into the body of Christ *(I Corinthians 12:13)*;

3. Gives him life *(John 6:63; Romans 8:11)*;

4. Seals him in Jesus Christ (gives evidence of belonging) *(II Corinthians 1:21-22; Ephesians 4:30)*;

5. Is given as a pledge (deposit, downpayment) of our inheritance *(II Corinthians 1:22, 5:5; Ephesians 1:14)*, which will reach completion when we see the Lord face to face *(I Corinthians 13:12; I John 3:2)*;

6. Indwells him *(John 14:16-17; I Corinthians 3:16, 6:19; Galatians 4:6-7; II Timothy 1:14)* and is proof that he belongs to Christ *(Romans 8:9)*;

7. Bears witness to the truth of God as revealed in His Son, Jesus Christ *(I John 5:6-8)* and bears witness to a believer that he is a child of God *(Romans 8:16)*;

8. Testifies of the Lord Jesus Christ *(John 15:26; Acts 5:30-32)* and glorifies Him *(John 16:14)*;

9. Sanctifies a believer (sets him apart for God's use and conforms him to the image of Jesus Christ) *(II Thessalonians 2:13; I Peter 1:2)*;

10. Washes (cleanses him from sin) and justifies him (declares him righteous) *(I Corinthians 6:11)*;

11. Anoints him to discern between truth and error *(I John 2:18-27, esp. verses 20 and 27)*;

12. Provides guidance by:

   a. Revealing the mind of God to him *(I Corinthians 2:9-16)*,

   b. Teaching him *(Luke 12:11-12; I Corinthians 2:9-16; I John 2:27)* and bringing the words of Christ to remembrance *(John 14:26)*,

      c.   Leading him to all truth *(John 16:13-14)*,

      d.   Giving direction for ministry decisions *(for example: Acts 13:2-4, 16:6-7)*, and

      e.   Helping him in times of prayer *(Romans 8:26-27; Ephesians 6:18; Jude 1:20)*;

13. Encourages him by:

      a.   Giving hope *(Romans 5:3-5, 15:13)*,

      b.   Interceding for him *(Romans 8:26)*,

      c.   Providing help (coming alongside) *(John 14:16, 15:26; Romans 8:26)*, and

      d.   Giving comfort *(Acts 9:31)*;

14. Empowers him to:

      a.   Know Jesus Christ and God the Father in their fulness *(Ephesians 3:14-19)*,

      b.   Proclaim the Lordship of Jesus Christ *(I Corinthians 12:3)* and to be a witness for Him throughout the world *(John 15:26-27; Acts 1:8)*,

      c.   Speak effectively in time of trial and persecution *(Mark 13:11)*, and

      d.   Not carry out the desire of the flesh *(Romans 8:13; Galatians 5:16)*;

15. Fills him (controls him) for:

      a.   A new and higher dimension of living *(Ephesians 5:18-21)* and

      b.   Effective ministry *(for example, Acts 6:3, 13:9-12)*;

16. Gives spiritual gift(s) to equip him for ministry *(I Corinthians 12:7-11)*;

17. Develops Christlike character (spiritual fruitfulness) in him *(Galatians 5:22-23)* through His transforming power *(II Corinthians 3:18)*;

18. Helps a believer in worship *(Philippians 3:3)*; and

19. Must not be grieved *(Ephesians 4:30)* nor quenched *(I Thessalonians 5:19)*.

PRAYER PROVIDES COMMUNICATION WITH GOD

> Prayer gives you opportunity to praise God and to request His divine intervention in your life and/or the lives of others. Prayer allows you to glorify His Name and also provides an avenue for you to be filled with joy *(based on Psalm 65:2, 145:1; Matthew 7:7; John 14:13, 16:23-24; Hebrews 13:15; James 1:5; I John 5:14-15).*

I. **Biblical truths about God's work as it relates to prayer**

   A. His listening

      1. He hears prayer *(Psalm 65:2)* and responds to the cry of those who reverence Him *(Psalm 34:15, 145:19);*

      2. He knows what you need before you ask *(Matthew 6:8, 32);*

      3. He delights to hear the prayer of the upright *(Proverbs 15:8),* which accomplishes much *(James 5:16);*

      4. He is near to those who call upon Him in truth *(Psalm 145:18);* and

      5. He does not listen when you hold on to (harbor, regard) sin in your heart *(Psalm 66:18).*

   B. His answering

      1. He answers in response to your asking *(Matthew 7:7);*

      2. He answers as you continue to obey Him *(I John 3:22);*

      3. He answers YES when you ask according to His will *(I John 5:14-15);*

      4. He answers in greater measure than you can ask *(Ephesians 3:20);*

      5. He will not give bad gifts as answers to your prayer *(Matthew 7:7-11; Luke 11:9-13);*

      6. He does not answer when you ask in doubt *(James 1:6-7);*

      7. He answers NO when your prayer is not according to His will *(II Corinthians 12:7-10);* and

      8. He answers NO when His glory and grace is better revealed by your going through a trial instead of your being rescued from it *(Matthew 26:39; II Corinthians 12:7-9).*

II. **Observations from the Gospels about the prayer life of Jesus Christ**

   A. How Jesus prayed

      1. He made prayer a priority and a frequent practice *(Matthew 14:23; Mark 1:35; Luke 5:16);*

      2. He prayed knowing the Father heard Him always *(John 11:41-42);*

      3. He prayed alone *(Matthew 14:23);* and

      4. He prayed specifically and persistently but always in submission to God and in accordance with the will of the Father *(Matthew 26:36-44).*

B.   When Jesus prayed

1.   He consistently prayed in the beginning, during, and at the close of His ministry *(Luke 3:21, 5:16, 23:46)*;

2.   He prayed after ministering all day *(Matthew 14:23; Mark 1:35)*;

3.   He prayed after ministering through the evening *(Mark 1:32-35)*;

4.   He prayed all night *(Luke 6:12)*;

5.   He prayed in the midst of His own suffering *(Luke 23:34)*;

6.   He prayed before making major decisions *(Luke 6:12-13)*; and

7.   He prayed while in the midst of a trial *(Matthew 26:36-44)*.

C.   What Jesus prayed and what He taught about prayer

1.   He taught His disciples the basics of prayer *(Matthew 6:9-13; Luke 11:1-4)*;

2.   He demonstrated how to pray *(John chapter 17)*;

3.   He prayed for the strengthening of others *(Luke 22:32)*;

4.   He prayed for His disciples and for the disciples who were to follow *(John 17:20)*; and

5.   He prayed for God's forgiveness of those who were His enemies *(Luke 23:34)*.

III.   **Scriptural teaching to believers about prayer**

A.   Truths about your prayer life

1.   You sometimes do not know how to pray as you should *(Romans 8:26)*, and

2.   You sin before the Lord when you fail to pray *(I Samuel 12:23; I Thessalonians 5:17; James 4:17)*.

B.   Truths about answers to your prayers

1.   You should not expect answers from God when you meaninglessly repeat requests *(Matthew 6:7)*;

2.   You receive answers to prayer when you ask according to God's will *(I John 5:14-15)*, when you ask in faith *(Matthew 17:20, 21:21-22)*, and when you ask in the Name of Christ (asking just as Jesus would ask) *(John 14:13-14)*;

3.   You receive answers to prayer by abiding in Christ and having His words abide in you *(John 15:7)*;

4.   You receive answers and fullness of joy by asking *(John 16:24)*;

5.   You receive answers to prayer when you are obedient to God's will *(I John 3:22)*;

6.   Even though you are obedient to the Lord, you will sometimes not receive what you ask for so you may learn more of God's grace and power *(Matthew 26:39; II Corinthians 12:7-10)*;

7.   You will not receive if you do not ask *(James 4:2)*;

8.   You will not receive if you ask in doubt *(James 1:6-7)* or if you ask with selfish motives *(James 4:3)*;

9.   You should not expect answers to prayer when there is any unconfessed and unforsaken sin in your life *(Psalm 66:18; Isaiah 59:1-2; I Peter 3:12)*; and

10. You are hindered in receiving answers to prayer when you are not obedient to God's Word in your relationships *(I Peter 3:7; I John 3:22)*.

C. How you are to pray

1. You are to follow the example of Jesus by praying always in submission to God and in accordance with His will *(Matthew 26:36-44; Mark 14:36)*;

2. You are to pray specifically *(Matthew 7:7-8; John 14:13-14, 16:24)*;

3. You are to pray so God may be glorified *(John 14:13)*;

4. You are to pray with thanksgiving *(Philippians 4:6)*;

5. You are to ask in faith *(Hebrews 11:6; James 1:6)*;

6. You are to be alert and devoted to prayer *(Colossians 4:2)*;

7. You are to persist in meaningful prayer *(Matthew 7:7-8; Luke 11:5-10)*;

8. You are urged to pray in a variety of ways *(I Timothy 2:1)*;

9. You should sometimes fast and pray in times of specific need *(Joel 2:12-13; Matthew 4:1-2, 6:17-18; Acts 9:9-11, 13:1-3, 14:23)*;

10. You are to pray through (in, by means of) the Holy Spirit *(Ephesians 6:18; Jude 1:20)*;

11. You are to be clear-minded and self-controlled for the purpose of prayer *(I Peter 4:7)*; and

12. You are not to pray hypocritically for the approval or notice of man. Rather, you are to pray to the Lord for His hearing and favor *(Matthew 6:5-6)*.

D. When you are to pray

1. You should pray diligently and not lose heart *(Luke 18:1)*;

2. You are to pray if you are suffering, if you are sick, if you have sinned *(James 5:13-16)*, or if you face any kind of trial, temptation, or trouble *(Psalm 86:6-7; II Thessalonians 3:1-2)*; and

3. You are to pray without ceasing *(I Thessalonians 5:17)*.

E. What you are to pray

1. You are to praise God *(Psalm 111:1, 112:1, 113:1; Psalm 150)* for:

   a. His character *(Psalm 148:13-14; 150:2b; Matthew 6:9)*,

   b. His works *(Psalm 150:2a)*,

   c. His lovingkindness *(Psalm 106:1, 108:3-4)*, and

   d. His mercy through Jesus Christ *(Romans 15:8-12)*.

2. You are to thank God for:

   a. His goodness *(Psalm 106:1, 107:1)*,

   b. His lovingkindness *(Psalm 106:1; 107:1, 8; 108:3-4)*,

   c. His grace that has been provided through Jesus Christ *(I Corinthians 1:4; II Corinthians 9:15)*,

   d. His effectual working in your life and in the lives of others *(Romans 1:8; II Corinthians 2:14; I Thessalonians 2:13; II Thessalonians 1:3)*,

   e. Victory over death and the grave through Jesus Christ *(I Corinthians 15:50-57, esp. verse 57)*,

   f. The fearful and wonderful way He made you *(Psalm 139:14)*, and

g.   All that is in your life *(Ephesians 5:20; Philippians 4:6; I Thessalonians 5:18)*.

3.   You are to ask God's forgiveness (based on Matthew 6:12), confessing your sins to Him, in order to receive His forgiveness and cleansing *(I John 1:9)*.

4.   You are to pray for everything and everyone *(Ephesians 6:18-19; Philippians 4:6; I Timothy 2:1-2)*.

5.   You are to pray for necessities of life *(Matthew 6:11; Luke 11:3)*.

6.   You are to pray for more laborers to enter the harvest *(Matthew 9:37-38; Luke 10:2)* and are to pray for the Word of the Lord to spread rapidly and be glorified *(II Thessalonians 3:1)*.

7.   You are to lay your anxious concerns before God when you pray *(Philippians 4:6-7)*.

8.   You are to pray that you may resist or avoid entering into temptation *(Matthew 6:13, 26:41; Mark 14:38; Luke 11:4, 22:40)*.

9.   You are to pray for others in specific situations *(Luke 22:32; Romans 10:1; Ephesians 6:18-19; Philippians 1:19, 4:6)*.

10.   You are to pray for grace to help in time of need *(Hebrews 4:16)*.

11.   You are to pray for wisdom *(James 1:5)*.

IV.   Unprofitable practices in your prayer life

You are not to pray thoughtlessly *(based on I Peter 4:7)*. Instead you are carefully to consider what you are to pray. For example:

1.   You do not need to plead hopelessly for the Lord to be with you or with any other believer, because He is with you already and has promised never to leave nor forsake you *(Matthew 28:20b; Hebrews 13:5)*. Instead, thank the Lord for His continual presence with you *(Hebrews 13:6)*.

2.   You do not need to pray that God will grant you love for another person, because He has already poured out His love within you *(Romans 5:5)* and has commanded and enabled you to love *(I John 4:7-12)*. Pray instead for His wisdom *(James 1:5)* and leading *(Romans 8:4; Galatians 5:16)* to show you how to increase and abound in your love to others *(I Thessalonians 3:12)*.

3.   As a true believer, you do not need to pray to be freed from the power of sin because you already have been freed *(Romans 6:1-14)*. However, you are to pray to be delivered from evil (or the evil one) *(Matthew 6:13)* and are to thank the Lord that He has provided you freedom from the power of sin as you keep on presenting yourself as a living sacrifice to Him *(Romans 6:6-7, 12:1-2)*.

4.   You do not need to pray for help in either putting off your old self-nature or in putting on the new righteous self, because that was already accomplished at salvation *(Romans 6:6-11; Galatians 2:20; Ephesians 4:22-24)*. Pray instead for His wisdom, grace, and help in putting off the practices of the old self and in putting on the new righteous practices *(Hebrews 4:15-16; James 1:5)*.

LESSON 3: HOMEWORK

> This week's lesson will become a valuable reference tool for you to use in the future. Ask the Lord to give you wisdom in determining what is especially beneficial for you and what will help you help others *(based on II Corinthians 1:3-5; Ephesians 5:15-16; James 1:5).*

✔ *homework completed*

☐ A. * In your own words, write the meaning of *II Timothy 3:16-17.* Memorize *II Timothy 3:16-17* and begin memorizing *II Corinthians 3:5-6.* Review previous memory verses.

☐ B. Read *Psalm 19* and *Psalm 119.* Note especially what these Psalms tell you about the importance of God's Word in your life.

☐ C. * Read **BIBLICAL PRINCIPLES: MAN'S WAY AND GOD'S WAY (PART ONE)** (Lesson 3, Page 2). In your Bible, highlight the verses listed under *Principles 4, 5, and 6.*

☐ D. * Complete a **BIBLE STUDY AND APPLICATION FORMAT** (Supplement 3, Page 1) for *Ephesians 5:15-16.*

☐ E. Read **SCRIPTURE IS YOUR AUTHORITY** (Lesson 3, Pages 3-5). Look up as many verses as are necessary for you to realize that Scripture is totally sufficient for every facet of your life and the lives of others.

☐ F. Read **THE HOLY SPIRIT EMPOWERS YOU TO SOLVE YOUR PROBLEMS** (Lesson 3, Pages 6-8), looking up listed verses as necessary to understand the purposes of the Holy Spirit.

☐ G. Read **PRAYER PROVIDES COMMUNICATION WITH GOD** (Lesson 3, Pages 9-12). Study any verses which point out the changes you need to make in your own prayer life and make adjustments accordingly.

☐ H. * Review **PREPARING A PERSONAL TESTIMONY** (Supplement 4). Write a brief sentence or two for each portion of your testimony (Before Conversion, Conversion, After Conversion). Develop and write a ten-second testimony and a thirty-second testimony following the suggested format of Supplement 4. If you turn in your testimonies to your instructor, keep another copy for your own reference.

☐ I. If you do not already use a Concordance, read **HOW TO USE A CONCORDANCE** (Supplement 5).

☐ J. * To complete the **COURSE EXAM** (Lesson 23) while going through this course, answer questions 4, 5, 6, 7, and 8 under **Open Book Test** (Lesson 23, Page 2).

* *The completion of assignments marked with an asterisk (*) is a prerequisite for further biblical counseling training.*

LESSON 3: STUDY GUIDE FOR DAILY DEVOTIONS (INCLUDING SCRIPTURE MEMORY AND HOMEWORK)

> This week's lesson should become a valuable reference tool for you to use in the future. Ask the Lord to give you wisdom in determining what is especially beneficial for you and what will help you help others (based on II Corinthians 1:3-5; Ephesians 5:15-16; James 1:5).

Scripture Memory

1. * Memorize *II Timothy 3:16-17* and begin memorizing *II Corinthians 3:5-6*.
2. Remember to carry your Scripture memory cards with you throughout the day. At every opportunity, review past memory verses and read, meditate on, and memorize this week's verse.

Daily Devotional Study Guide

FIRST DAY

1. Open in prayer.
2. Read *Psalm 19* and *Psalm 119:1-16*. Note especially what these Psalms tell you about the importance of God's Word in your life.
3. * Under **BIBLICAL PRINCIPLES: MAN'S WAY AND GOD'S WAY (PART ONE)** (Lesson 3, Page 2), read *Principle 4*, highlighting the listed verses in your Bible.
4. * Begin a **BIBLE STUDY AND APPLICATION FORMAT** (Supplement 3, Page 1) for *Ephesians 5:15-16*.
5. * In your own words, write the meaning of *II Timothy 3:16-17*.
6. Close in prayer.
7. Take your Scripture memory cards with you throughout the day. Use your spare moments to review past verses while memorizing the current verse.

SECOND DAY

1. Open in prayer.
2. Read *Psalm 119:17-48*.
3. Read **SCRIPTURE IS YOUR AUTHORITY** (Lesson 3, Pages 3-5), highlighting appropriate verses in your Bible that give greater understanding to these descriptive statements of God's Word. This is the first day of a two-day study.
4. * Complete the **BIBLE STUDY AND APPLICATION FORMAT** (Supplement 3, Page 1) on *Ephesians 5:15-16*.
5. Close in prayer.

THIRD DAY

1. Open in prayer.
2. Read *Psalm 119:49-80*.
3. * Read *Principle 5* under **BIBLICAL PRINCIPLES: MAN'S WAY AND GOD'S WAY (PART ONE)** (Lesson 3, Page 2). Highlight the verses in your Bible.
4. Finish your study of **SCRIPTURE IS YOUR AUTHORITY** (Lesson 3, Pages 3-5).
5. * Write a brief sentence or two for each portion of your testimony using the "Before Conversion, Conversion, After Conversion" format. Write your ten second testimony. Refer to **PREPARING A PERSONAL TESTIMONY** (Supplement 4).
6. Close in prayer.

FOURTH DAY

1. Open in prayer.
2. Read *Psalm 119:81-104.*
3. Read **THE HOLY SPIRIT EMPOWERS YOU TO SOLVE YOUR PROBLEMS** (Lesson 3, Pages 6-8), looking up verses to help you realize the many purposes of the Holy Spirit. This is the first day of a two-day study.
4. Review your ten-second testimony and say it aloud a few times.
5. Close with prayer.
6. Are you staying current with your Scripture memorization? Are you taking your memory cards with you throughout each day? Evaluate your present plan of Scripture memory, make necessary changes, and commit yourself to continued faithfulness to the Lord *(I Corinthians 4:2).*

FIFTH DAY

1. Open with prayer.
2. Read *Psalm 119:105-136.*
3. * Read *Principle 6* under **BIBLICAL PRINCIPLES: GOD'S WAY AND MAN'S WAY (PART ONE)** (Lesson 3, Page 2) and highlight the listed verses in your Bible.
4. Complete your study of **THE HOLY SPIRIT EMPOWERS YOU TO SOLVE YOUR PROBLEMS** (Lesson 3, Pages 6-8).
5. * Write a thirty-second testimony that builds on and expands your ten-second testimony. If needed, refer to Supplement 4, Page 2.
6. Close in prayer.

SIXTH DAY

1. Open in prayer.
2. Read *Psalm 119:137-160.*
3. Read **PRAYER PROVIDES COMMUNICATION WITH GOD** (Lesson 3, Pages 9-12), highlighting statements that point out changes you need to make in your prayer life. Look up the verses for statements that you highlight and make the necessary adjustments in your prayer life. This is the first day of a two-day study.
4. Review your thirty-second testimony.
5. Close in prayer.

SEVENTH DAY

1. Open in prayer.
2. Read *Psalm 119:161-176.*
3. Complete your study of **PRAYER PROVIDES COMMUNICATION WITH GOD** (Lesson 3, Pages 9-12).
4. Review your ten-second and thirty-second testimonies.
5. Read **HOW TO USE A CONCORDANCE** (Supplement 5).
6. * To complete the **COURSE EXAM** (Lesson 23) while going through this course, answer questions 4, 5, 6, 7, and 8 under **Open Book Test** (Lesson 23, Page 2).
7. Close in prayer.
8. Recite your memory verses to someone, explaining the meaning of the verses and their application to your life.

* *The completion of assignments marked with an asterisk (*) is a prerequisite for further biblical counseling training.*

LESSON 4

MAN'S WAY AND GOD'S WAY
(PART TWO)

"Not that we are adequate in ourselves to consider anything as coming from ourselves, but our adequacy is from God, who also made us adequate as servants of a new covenant, not of the letter, but of the Spirit; for the letter kills, but the Spirit gives life."

II Corinthians 3:5-6

LESSON 4: MAN'S WAY AND GOD'S WAY (PART TWO)

> Man, in his own wisdom, has developed a vast number of philosophies and theories seeking to explain one's thoughts, words, and actions. In doing so, man has pridefully sought to deny his own sinfulness and has confused any clear definition of God's standards of right and wrong (*based on Proverbs 14:9a, 12, 16; 21:2, 24; 26:12; Isaiah 5:20-21; I Corinthians 3:19-20; I Timothy 1:5-7; II Timothy 3:1-5*).

I.   **The purposes of this lesson are:**

   A.   To contrast man's philosophies of life with God's truths for living;

   B.   To illustrate the folly and confusion of this world's wisdom in solving problems as compared to the certainty of God's plan for overcoming any difficulty of life;

   C.   To evaluate biblically the differences between man's way and God's way; and

   D.   To give you further opportunity to prepare your own testimony of God's grace and mercy and to demonstrate your own commitment to follow God's way.

II.   **The outline of this lesson**

   A.   Self-confrontation

   1.   **BIBLICAL PRINCIPLES: MAN'S WAY AND GOD'S WAY (PART TWO)** (Lesson 4, Page 2)

   2.   **THE BIBLICAL MODEL OF MAN'S FAILURE** (Lesson 4, Pages 3-4)

   3.   **THE BIBLICAL VIEW OF SELF** (Lesson 4, Pages 5-10)

   4.   **BASIC APPROACHES TO SOLVING PERSONAL PROBLEMS** (Lesson 4, Page 11)

   5.   **EXAMPLES OF MAN'S WAY COMPARED TO GOD'S WAY** (Lesson 4, Pages 12-13)

   6.   **KNOWING THE DIFFERENCE BETWEEN MAN'S WAY AND GOD'S WAY** (Lesson 4, Page 14)

   B.   Steps for spiritual growth

   1.   **LESSON 4: HOMEWORK** (Lesson 4, Page 15)

   2.   **STUDY GUIDE FOR DAILY DEVOTIONS** (Lesson 4, Pages 16-17)

BIBLICAL PRINCIPLES: MAN'S WAY AND GOD'S WAY
(PART TWO)

> God's Word clearly shows that man's way of living is futile. Man has very serious shortcomings that he cannot change by himself *(based on Proverbs 14:12; Isaiah 55:8-9; Romans 1:28-32, 3:10-12; I Corinthians 2:14).*

I. Man's way

A. The natural man is inadequate

(Principle 7)   You cannot live according to God's design in your own way or by your own wisdom *(Proverbs 14:12; Isaiah 55:8-9; I Corinthians 2:14).*

B. The natural man is rebellious

(Principle 8)   The natural man is self-centered and rebels against God's way *(Genesis 3:1-6; Romans 1:20-32; 3:9-18, 23; 10:1-3).* Furthermore, partial obedience to God is just as unacceptable to Him as even your deliberate rebellion *(based on I Samuel 15:1-23, esp. verses 22-23; Isaiah 1:10-20; Hosea 6:6; Micah 6:6-8; Mark 12:28-33, esp. verse 33).*

II. God's way

Man needs to be changed

(Principle 9)   It is necessary to be born again (to be born from above; to have a spiritual birth) in order to recognize, admit, and solve your problems in a biblical manner. Only God's solutions, grace, empowering, and wisdom are completely adequate for abundant living *(Ecclesiastes 12:13-14; John 3:3-8; 10:10; 14:16-17, 26; Romans 8:5-14; I Corinthians 2:10-14; Ephesians 2:8-10).*

THE BIBLICAL MODEL OF MAN'S FAILURE

> God's Word is the only true source and authority for living *(based on Psalm 19:7-11; II Timothy 3:16-17)*. It reveals man's failure, the subsequent consequences, and the effect that man's original sin has on today's world *(based on Genesis 1:26-27; 3:1 - 4:12; 5:1-3; Romans 5:12)*.

I. **Mankind was created in God's image.** *Genesis 1:26-27*
(Unique, created in righteousness, recipient of blessings and responsibilities)

II. **Mankind sinned and has borne the many consequences** *Romans 5:12*
of that sin unto the present day.

A.	Spiritually *(warning of separation from God)*	"In the day that you eat … you shall surely die."	*Genesis 2:17*
B.	Physically *(focus on self)*	Gave in to the desires of self-gratification and self-exaltation, knew they were naked, sewed fig leaves together and covered themselves.	*Genesis 3:6-7*
C.	Mentally *(fear, worry, anxiety, deceptiveness)*	Hid themselves – were afraid.	*Genesis 3:8-10*
D.	Socially – the man *(blameshifting, discontent with marriage)*	"The woman you gave me, she gave me and I ate."	*Genesis 3:12*
	– the woman *(blameshifting; seeking to justify sin)*	"The serpent deceived me and I ate."	*Genesis 3:13*
E.	Environmentally *(the natural realm suffers)*	"Cursed is the ground because of you."	*Genesis 3:17-19*
F.	Interpersonally *(anger)*	Abel's offering accepted. Cain's offering rejected; Cain became angry and his countenance fell	*Genesis 4:4; Genesis 4:5*
	(God's exhortation and solution to depression)	"If you do well, will not your countenance be lifted up? If you do not do well, sin is crouching at the door … you must master it."	*Genesis 4:7*

(God's way refused)	Cain refused God's solution and murdered Abel.	*Genesis 4:8*	
G. Personally *(fugitive)*	Cain did not repent and was cursed as a vagrant and a wanderer.	*Genesis 4:9, 12*	
(self-pity)	"My punishment is too great to bear."	*Genesis 4:13*	
H. Perpetually	Adam became the father of a son, according to his own image ...	*Genesis 5:3*	
I. Universally *(born in sin)*	"Through one man, sin entered into the world and death through sin, and so death spread to all men, because all sinned."	*Romans 5:12*	

III. **Man's primary need is to be justified (declared righteous) by God and reconciled through faith in the Lord Jesus Christ** *(Romans chapter 5).*

    A. In **YOU CAN CHANGE BIBLICALLY (PART ONE)** (Lesson 1, Pages 3-7), note section **IV. God empowers you to choose His solution to your spiritual problem.**

    B. In **YOU CAN CHANGE BIBLICALLY (PART TWO)** (Lesson 2, Pages 3-5), note the different relationship God the Father has with you through His Son, Jesus Christ.

IV. **A regenerated person is called to holiness (purity, without blame) and sanctification (set apart for God)** *(I Corinthians 6:9-20; I Thessalonians 4:7, 5:23; Titus 2:11-14; I Peter 1:16, 2:9).*

In Lesson 2, Pages 4-5, biblical change is shown to be possible because of the divine sources of power, a different purpose for living, and your obedience to God's Word. This is outlined in section I. The process of lasting biblical change begins when you receive the Lord Jesus Christ, explained under points B., C., and D.

For further illustrations of the contrast between man's way and God's way, refer to:
    THE BIBLICAL VIEW OF SELF *(Lesson 4, Pages 5-10),*
    BASIC APPROACHES TO SOLVING PERSONAL PROBLEMS *(Lesson 4, Page 11), and*
    EXAMPLES OF MAN'S WAY COMPARED TO GOD'S WAY *(Lesson 4, Pages 12-13).*

THE BIBLICAL VIEW OF SELF

> The wisdom of this world deceptively teaches that believing in the inherent goodness of one's "self" is foundational to a fulfilled life. However, this erroneous viewpoint overlooks the devastating results of Adam and Eve's failure to obey God. Scripture teaches that a fulfilled life is not dependent on having a "good self-image" or "higher self-esteem." Instead, fulfillment in living depends on your relationship to God and a biblical response to the problem of "self" *(based on Proverbs 14:12; Matthew 10:38-39; Luke 9:23-24; Romans 5:6-21, 7:15-25, 14:7-8; I Corinthians 1:26-31; II Corinthians 10:17-18; Ephesians 2:1-9; Titus 3:3-7; James 4:14-17).*

I. **Sinless self to the sinful self (the fall of mankind)**

   A. Adam and Eve were:

   1. Created in the image of God *(Genesis 1:27, 5:1),*

   2. In a sinless world *(Romans 5:12),*

   3. Blessed by God *(Genesis 1:28),*

   4. Together as one flesh *(Genesis 2:22-25),*

   5. To rule over the earth *(Genesis 1:28),* and

   6. In personal communication with their Creator God *(Genesis 1:28-30, 2:16-17).*

   B. God placed only one restraint on Adam and Eve, which required simple obedience to His command regardless of their desires or feelings *(Genesis 3:3).* Adam and Eve lost their privileged status with God when they fell to temptation by focusing on self (coveting, prideful wisdom, and gratifying their fleshly desires, which is all that the world offers – *I John 2:16).* They then disobeyed God's clear command by choosing to eat the forbidden fruit *(Genesis 3:1-7).* When they chose to focus on self, Adam and Eve sinned, bringing the consequences of sin upon themselves *(Genesis 3:16-24)* and upon every generation that has followed *(Romans 5:12-21).*

   Refer to: **THE BIBLICAL MODEL OF MAN'S FAILURE** *under points I. and II., Lesson 4, Pages 3-4.*

II. **Scripture speaks of the natural man's self-importance**

   A. Since nothing and no one in the world can compare with God *(Exodus 15:11; II Chronicles 6:14; Psalm 40:5, 89:6-8; Jeremiah 10:6-7),* He only is to be exalted *(Psalm 57:11, 97:9).* You are not in any manner to exalt yourself *(Proverbs 30:32).* In comparison to the Creator God, the natural man is:

   1. Like dust *(Psalm 90:3, 103:14);*

   2. Like a mere breath and a passing shadow, with a lifetime that is nothing in the Lord's sight *(Psalm 39:4-5, 62:9, 144:4);*

   3. Like grass *(Isaiah 40:6-8, 51:12; I Peter 1:24);*

4.   Like a flower of the field that flourishes and then is no more *(Psalm 103:15-16; Isaiah 40:6-8; I Peter 1:24);*

5.   Like a vapor that appears for a little while and then vanishes away *(James 4:14);*

6.   Stupid and devoid of knowledge *(Jeremiah 51:17a);*

7.   Accounted as nothing and meaningless *(Isaiah 40:17; Daniel 4:35);* and

8.   Like a worm and not a man *(Job 25:6; Psalm 22:6).*

B.   If you refuse to respond biblically to God's plan of salvation revealed only through the Lord Jesus Christ, in God's sight you are:

1.   Worthless (depraved, unapproved), detestable *(Jeremiah 13:10; Titus 1:16),* rejected in regards to faith *(II Timothy 3:1-8)* and worthy of death *(Romans 1:28-32, 6:23);*

2.   Corrupt, unrighteous, and useless *(Psalm 14:1-3, 53:1-3, 143:2; Ecclesiastes 7:20; Romans 3:10-18);* and

3.   Dead in your sins *(Ephesians 2:1, 5; Colossians 2:13).*

Refer to: **YOU CAN CHANGE BIBLICALLY (PART ONE)** *(Lesson 1, Pages 4-5) under* **IV. B.,** *to see further consequences of rejecting God's truth in Jesus.*

C.   Trusting in yourself is futile since:

1.   Nothing inherently good dwells within your heart or flesh *(Jeremiah 17:9; Romans 7:18);*

2.   You can do nothing fruitful apart from Jesus *(John 15:5);*

3.   Apart from Jesus Christ, you are a slave to sin *(Romans 6:16-18; Hebrews 2:14-15);* and

4.   Your natural wisdom is inadequate to direct your steps *(Psalm 94:11; Proverbs 14:12; Jeremiah 10:23)*

Refer to: **EXAMPLES OF MAN'S WAY COMPARED TO GOD'S WAY** *(Lesson 4, Pages 12-13).*

III.   The image of God in each person has been marred by sin (effects of the fall of mankind)

A.   Every person's natural bent is to sin *(Ecclesiastes 7:20, 29; Romans 3:10-18),* even though mankind is:

1.   Able to know the difference between good and evil *(Genesis 3:22),*

2.   Divinely enabled to have dominion on the earth *(Psalm 8:6-8),*

3.   Made a little lower than heavenly beings *(Psalm 8:4-5),* and

4.   Fashioned in the likeness of God *(James 3:9).*

B.   God's image in you cannot be seen in its sinless perfection as it was seen in Adam, since you also bear Adam's image after he sinned *(Genesis 5:3; I Corinthians 15:47-50).*

C.   You were fearfully and wonderfully fashioned by the Lord in your mother's womb *(Psalm 139:13-15; Isaiah 44:24).* Prior to your birth, God ordained the number of days for your life *(Psalm 139:16)* with a view to your responding to the truth as revealed in the Lord Jesus Christ *(I Timothy 2:3-6; II Peter 3:9).*

IV. **Only God can and does enable a person to re-acquire the perfect image of God (restoration after the fall of mankind)**

   A. The Lord Jesus Christ is fully divine *(John 1:1, 18; Titus 2:13)* and came to earth in the image of the invisible God *(II Corinthians 4:4; Colossians 1:15)*. Crowned with God's glory and honor because of His death and resurrection *(Hebrews 2:9; I Peter 1:20-21)*, He is the radiance of God's glory and the exact representation of God's nature *(John 12:45, 14:9; Hebrews 1:3)*.

   B. Through your spiritual new birth *(John 3:3; I Peter 1:3-5)*, you partake of God's divine nature *(II Peter 1:4)* and are a new creation in Christ *(II Corinthians 5:17)*. Your body becomes a temple of the Holy Spirit *(I Corinthians 3:16, 6:19)*, who dwells within you *(John 14:16-17; Romans 8:9; Galatians 4:6; II Timothy 1:14)*.

       1. As a new creation in Christ, the corrupt old self has been crucified with Christ *(Romans 6:6)* and the old self has been put off *(Ephesians 4:22)*. The new self, which has been created in righteousness and holiness of the truth, has been put on *(Ephesians 4:24)*. You now are able to be transformed into the image of Jesus Christ *(Romans 8:29; II Corinthians 3:18; Colossians 3:10)*.

       2. As a new creation in Christ *(II Corinthians 5:17; Galatians 2:20)*, you are to put off the sinful practices of your old self *(Romans 6:12-13; Colossians 3:3-9)* and put on the Christlike characteristics of the new self *(Romans 6:17-18; Colossians 3:10-24; II Peter 1:5-10)*, as you are being renewed in the spirit of your mind *(Romans 12:2; Ephesians 4:23; Colossians 3:10)*.

       3. To follow Jesus, you must deny yourself *(Luke 9:23-24)*. You are to:

           a. Become a servant like the Lord Jesus Christ *(Matthew 20:26-28, 23:11-12; John 13:12-17; Romans 15:1-3; Philippians 2:3-8)*,

           b. Please God in all things by walking in a manner worthy of Him *(II Corinthians 5:9; Colossians 1:10)*, and

           c. Give God glory in everything you do *(Matthew 5:16; John 15:8; I Corinthians 6:20, 10:31; I Peter 2:12, 4:10-11)* as Jesus did *(John 17:4)*.

   Refer to:
   YOU CAN CHANGE BIBLICALLY (PART ONE) (Lesson 1, Pages 3-7);
   YOU CAN CHANGE BIBLICALLY (PART TWO) (Lesson 2, Pages 3-5);
   BIBLICAL PRINCIPLES: BIBLICAL STRUCTURE FOR CHANGE (Lesson 7, Page 2);
   BIBLICAL CHANGE IS A PROCESS (Lesson 7, Pages 3-4);
   THE EFFECTS OF UNBIBLICAL THOUGHTS, SPEECH, AND ACTIONS (Lesson 7, Page 5); and
   RENEWING YOUR MIND (Lesson 7, Pages 6-7).

V. **You can be more than a conqueror in Christ by dying to self (living victoriously after the fall of mankind)**

   A. God has graciously provided for you so that you may give glory and exaltation to Him and not to yourself *(Psalm 115:1; Romans 1:19-21; 5:1-2, 6-11; Ephesians 2:8-9)*. Your example in giving glory to God and disregarding yourself is Jesus, who did not seek His own glory *(John 7:17-18; 8:50, 54; Hebrews 5:5)*. Instead Jesus lived to do the will of the Father *(John 4:34, 5:30, 6:38)* as a servant who learned obedience from the things which He suffered *(Hebrews 5:8)* and remained obedient even to death *(Matthew 20:26-28; Philippians 2:5-8)*.

       1. **The error of man's way concerning "self-worth"** – While you are more valuable than the lower forms of God's creation *(Matthew 6:26, 10:29-31, 12:12; Luke 12:7, 24)* and are intimately known by God *(I Samuel 16:7; Psalm 139:13-16; Matthew*

10:30; Luke 16:15), you still deserve death because of your inherent sinfulness *(Romans 1:18-32, 5:12, 6:23)*.

Being adopted into God's family should cause you to praise and thank Him for the glory of His grace *(Ephesians 1:5-6)*. It is wrong for you to think that you are worthy in any way to receive His unmerited favor *(Romans 5:8; I Corinthians 1:26-31)*.

2. **The error of man's way regarding "self-assurance"** – Even God's people can mistakenly think that they are the source of material blessings which are, in reality, provided solely by God *(Deuteronomy 8:11-18)*. Pride (a dependence on yourself or your "possessions" instead of a dependence on God) will lead to a fall *(Proverbs 11:28, 16:18; I Corinthians 10:12)*. Since you can do nothing fruitful apart from Jesus *(John 15:5)*, you are to live in total dependence upon Him, who is the power and wisdom of God *(Proverbs 3:5-6; I Corinthians 1:24; Galatians 2:20; Philippians 4:13)*.

3. **The error of man's way in "self-love"** – You are to love God *(Deuteronomy 6:5; Matthew 22:37-38)*, but nowhere in Scripture are you told to love yourself. A command to love yourself is unnecessary since you already do that; in fact, you are commanded to love others in the same way in which you already love yourself *(Matthew 22:39; Galatians 5:14; Ephesians 5:28-29)*. Note that one of the self-centered characteristics of those who reject the faith in the last days is "loving self" *(II Timothy 3:1-2)*.

4. **The error of man's way related to "self-assertiveness"** – Through Jesus Christ, you are more than a conqueror in any situation of life *(Romans 8:35-39)*, and the Lord has not given you a spirit of timidity (fear) but of power and love and discipline *(II Timothy 1:7)*. However, Scripture never tells you to assert yourself; you are commanded, instead, to trust wholly in God's plan for your life *(Matthew 6:33-34; Romans 8:28-29; Philippians 4:19)* while you minister to others as a servant *(Matthew 20:26-28)*, esteeming them as more important than yourself *(Philippians 2:3-4)*.

5. **The error of man's way pertaining to "self-confidence"** – You are not to trust in yourself but instead are to trust only in the Lord *(Psalm 60:11-12, 73:26; Proverbs 3:5-7; Jeremiah 9:23-24, 17:5-8; I Corinthians 1:26-31)*. The Lord is your confidence *(Proverbs 3:26)*, and you are to place no confidence in your flesh *(Philippians 3:3)*. You are not adequate in yourself to consider anything as from yourself, but your adequacy is from God *(II Corinthians 3:5)*. As a servant of the new covenant *(II Corinthians 3:6)*, you can be an overcomer only through your faith in Christ Jesus *(Philippians 4:13; I John 5:4-5)* and not because of your own strength *(John 15:5; Romans 7:14 – 8:8)*.

6. **The error of man's way regarding "self-esteem"** – Apart from Jesus Christ, you have no inherent value in yourself (refer above to **II. Scripture speaks of the natural man's self-importance**); yet, God in His merciful love cares for you *(Psalm 8:4)*. After receiving Jesus Christ into your life, your value is found in being in Him *(Ephesians 2:4-7, 19-22)* and knowing Him *(Philippians 3:7-11)*.

7. **The error of man's way regarding "self-righteousness"** – You are not righteous in yourself *(Psalm 14:2-3; Ecclesiastes 7:20; Romans 3:10-12, 7:18)*, and it is impossible for you to earn a righteous standing before God *(Luke 18:9-14; Titus 3:5)*. The best you could do in your own strength or merit is considered as a filthy garment in God's sight *(Isaiah 64:6)* and is worthless when compared to the value of faith in Christ Jesus *(Philippians 3:7-11, esp. verse 9)*. Your true righteousness is based *solely* on the Lord Jesus Christ *(Romans 10:8-10; II Corinthians 5:21)* and is a free gift of God's grace *(Romans 5:17)*.

8. **The error of man's way concerning "self-exaltation"** – Commending yourself has no value *(II Corinthians 10:18)* and shows your lack of biblical understanding *(II Corinthians 10:12)*. Exalting one's self is characteristic of a person who is rebellious *(Psalm 66:7)* or of one who doesn't truly know the Lord *(Psalm 10:4, 83:2, 94:4)*. Those who exalt themselves will be humbled *(Matthew 23:12; Luke 18:9-14, esp. verse 14)*. Self-exaltation is descriptive of a self-centered person who is rejected in regard to faith in the difficult times of these last days *(II Timothy 3:1-9, esp. verses 2 and 8)*.

Exalting self in any dimension is to forget or deny that your praise should be to the glory of God's grace *(Ephesians 1:5-6)*. The Lord alone is to be exalted *(Psalm 148:13)*. You are to boast:

a. In the Lord *(Psalm 20:7, 34:1-3, 44:8; Jeremiah 9:24; I Corinthians 1:31; II Corinthians 10:17)*,

b. In the cross of Jesus Christ *(Galatians 6:14)*, and

c. In your weaknesses *(II Corinthians 11:30, 12:9)*.

If you exalt yourself, you will be humbled; yet, if you humble yourself under the mighty hand of God, He will exalt you at the proper time *(Matthew 23:12; I Peter 5:6)*.

B. Remember your identity in Christ

Refer to:
YOU CAN CHANGE BIBLICALLY (PART ONE) *(Lesson 1, Pages 3-7)* **III. D.** and **VII. C.** and
YOU CAN CHANGE BIBLICALLY (PART TWO) *(Lesson 2, Pages 3-5)*.

VI. Conclusion

A. From Adam and Eve to the present, mankind has sinfully exalted self. Death to self can only occur through Jesus Christ *(Romans 5:12-21)*. Disregarding God's way, man habitually turns to his own inadequate wisdom to deal with problems *(Proverbs 14:12; Isaiah 55:8-9)* and develops unbiblical solutions that focus on self instead of focusing on God

Refer to: **BASIC APPROACHES TO SOLVING PERSONAL PROBLEMS** *(Lesson 4, Page 11)*.

B. Man's philosophies, having rejected God's redemptive solutions, place man on the throne and substitute a self-oriented focus as the substance and solution to life's failures and successes. Since this is the essence of materialistic humanism, the integration of man's way and God's way is an impossibility

Refer to: **YOU CAN CHANGE BIBLICALLY (PART ONE)** *(Lesson 1, Pages 3-7, under points VI. and VII.)*.

C. God's solution to the problem of "self" is a transformation *(Romans 6:3-6, 12:2; II Corinthians 5:17; Ephesians 4:22-24)*, which allows you to die to self and live for Jesus Christ *(Matthew 10:38-39; Luke 9:23-24; Galatians 2:20)*.

D. Even the so-called "difficult" problems of life (for example: chronic depression, child abuse, battered spouse, alcohol or drug abuse, homosexuality) are only solved effectively from a biblical perspective of pleasing God *(Colossians 1:10)* and relying on God's Word *(Psalm 19:7-11; II Timothy 3:16-17; II Peter 1:3-4)* instead of pleasing self *(Luke 9:23-24; II Corinthians 5:15; Galatians 5:16-17)* and relying on human wisdom

(Proverbs 16:9, 25; I Corinthians 3:18-20).   Remember that God has given complete provision for you to face and deal with problems His way

Refer to: **MAN'S WAY AND GOD'S WAY (PART ONE)** *(Lesson 3, Pages 3-7).*

E.   The philosophies of self-exaltation or self-reliance are given the death blow by Jesus in the Beatitudes of the Sermon on the Mount *(Matthew 5:3-12).*

For further illustrations of the contrast between man's way and God's way, refer to:
BASIC APPROACHES TO SOLVING PERSONAL PROBLEMS *(Lesson 4, Page 11) and*
EXAMPLES OF MAN'S WAY COMPARED TO GOD'S WAY *(Lesson 4, Pages 12-13).*

Overcoming the problem of "self" in order to live for the Lord is the subject of **DEALING WITH SELF (PART ONE)** *(Lesson 9) and* **DEALING WITH SELF (PART TWO)** *(Lesson 10). First, however, it is essential to study the principles of biblical change outlined in Lessons 5 – 8.*

BASIC APPROACHES TO SOLVING PERSONAL PROBLEMS (Isaiah 55:7-9)

	MAN'S WAY (Proverbs 14:12; I Corinthians 3:19-20; Colossians 2:8)				GOD'S WAY (John 10:9-10; Romans 11:33-36) Heart Transformation (Psalm 51:10; Ezekiel 36:26; Acts 15:6-9)
	Instinctual	Behavioral	Positive Potential	Spiritist	
BASIC VIEW OF MAN	Driven by instincts (i.e., instinctively does things: fight, flight, seek food and gratification)	Behavior is conditioned or "programmed"	Intrinsically good – has everything necessary within self to solve own problems	Helpless before all spirits	Sinner – Saint (Romans 5:12, 19; II Corinthians 5:17-18, 21)
CAUSE OF PROBLEMS	Instincts are thwarted by society, family, and upbringing	Wrongly influenced by environment and circumstances	Mind blocked by negative thinking or influences	Committed to or under control of spirits, demons, ancestors	Rebellion (Romans 1:20-21), Unbelief (John 3:16-18, 5:38-40), Disobedience (Ephesians 2:1-2, 5:6; Titus 3:3), Denial of God's power (Hebrews 2:14-15; I John 3:8)
CURE	Follow instincts	Recondition or "reprogram"	Release potential within self	Appease ancestors; Appease or cast out demons, spirits; Discover your spirit guide	Be saved by grace through faith (Ephesians 2:8-9), and in loving obedience to God (Romans 6:16-19) be matured in Christ (Ephesians 4:13) through the power of the Holy Spirit (Galatians 5:16; Ephesians 5:18)
COUNSELING TECHNIQUE	Psychoanalysis (Interpretation of irrational thoughts, analysis of dreams); Hypnosis therapy; Psychodrama; Resocialization; Personality testing and analysis	Manipulation of behavior by use of positive and negative stimuli; Train to respond to reward and punishment	Reflection of thoughts and feelings; No presentation of answers - draw answer out of counselee's own inner resources; Positive thinking	Potions, charms, amulets, fetishes; Curses on enemy; Curse nullification; Ritual offerings; Communion with spirits; Mantras, chants; Horoscopes; "Visualization"	Listen (Proverbs 18:2, 13, 17); Reprove, rebuke, exhort (II Timothy 4:2); Encourage (Hebrews 3:13); Admonish (Romans 15:14; Colossians 1:28); Stimulate (Hebrews 10:24); Strengthen (Hebrews 12:12); Restore (Galatians 6:1-2, 5); Teach (Romans 6:17-18; Colossians 3:16); Train (II Timothy 2:2)
COUNSELOR'S TERMINOLOGY	Ego, Id, Drives, Libido, Conscious and Subconscious, Neurosis/ Psychosis, Phobia, Mania, Catharsis, Self-actualization, Free Association	Stimulus, Conditioning, Automatic response, Positive/negative reinforcement, Self-fulfillment, Self-improvement	Inner potential, Inherent goodness, Self-assertion, Self-esteem, Self-worth	Curses; god within; Higher power; Appeasal of spirits; Binding of demons; Generational sins; Demons or spirits of anger, fear, lust, etc.	Sin (Romans 3:23); Put off practices of the old self and put on practices of the new self (Ephesians 4:22-24; Colossians 3:5-17); Self-denial (Luke 9:23-25); Judge self (Matthew 7:1-5); Godliness (I Timothy 4:7-8); Do the Word (James 1:22-25)
COUNSELING FOCUS	Liberate Self (contrary to Ezekiel 18:20-21; Philippians 2:3-4)	Improve Self (contrary to John 15:4-5; Romans 1:18-32; James 4:10)	Elevate Self (contrary to Psalm 62:9; Romans 3:10-18, 23, 7:18)	Release self from bondage (contrary to John 15:4-5; II Thessalonians 3:3; I John 5:4-5)	Deny Self (Luke 9:23-24); Please God (II Corinthians 5:9; Colossians 1:10) and bless others (I Peter 3:8-9) through ministry (I Peter 4:10) and service (Matthew 20:25-28)

EXAMPLES OF MAN'S WAY COMPARED TO GOD'S WAY

GOD SAYS: *"For my thoughts are not your thoughts, neither are your ways My ways," declares the Lord. "For as the heavens are higher than the earth, so are My ways higher than your ways, and My thoughts higher than your thoughts." (Isaiah 55:8-9)*

EXAMPLES	MAN'S WAY *(Proverbs 14:12; I Corinthians 2:14)*	GOD'S WAY *(Proverbs 30:5-6; Colossians 2:8; Hebrews 4:12)*
The human heart	People say "Mankind is basically good." We hear, "I'm OK, you're OK."	The heart is desperately wicked, who can know it *(Jeremiah 17:9)*? All have sinned *(Romans 3:23)*. Trust the Lord completely; do not ever trust yourself *(Proverbs 3:5, 28:26)*.
Trust/ dependence	Some say, "If I don't take care of myself no one else will." Self-reliance is supposed to be a goal for life.	God says if you will seek first His kingdom and His righteousness, He will meet your needs *(Matthew 6:33)*. Do not depend on your own understanding; instead, seek God's way *(Proverbs 3:5-6)*.
Freedom	We're told everyone must protect and guard his own rights and that each person is born to live free (i.e., freedom of expression, free speech). It is said we only live under authority because of our common social contract.	Apart from God, you are a slave to sin *(Romans 6:16)*. The one who focuses on saving his life will lose it; but if you are willing to lose your life for His sake, God promises your life will be saved *(Luke 9:23-24)*. Be subject to those in authority over you *(Romans 13:1; Hebrews 13:17)*.
My problems	We sometimes think "No one can really understand my problems;" and we may believe that each problem and set of circumstances are unique.	Your problems are common to mankind. God promises to help you through them so that you do not have to sin or lose your peace and joy if you will choose to live life His way *(I Corinthians 10:13)*.
Love	Marriage is often viewed as a social convenience. People seek to find a spouse who can meet their own needs. Loving another depends on a reciprocal love from that person.	Your focus in marriage is to put the interests of your spouse above your own and to reflect Christ in your marriage relationship *(Ephesians 5:22-33; Philippians 2:3-4)*. Biblical love is giving not getting *(John 3:16; I Corinthians 13:4-8a)*.
My enemy is successful	Enemies are to be hated and their success is to be envied. We try to discredit our adversaries and to win over them.	Rejoice in any situation *(Romans 12:14-15; I Thessalonians 5:16)*. Love and pray for those who view themselves as your enemies *(Matthew 5:44)*.
I hurt someone	We seek to justify our actions and give excuses for our behavior. Some even enjoy hurting others.	Go to that one, ask forgiveness, and be reconciled *(Matthew 5:23-24; Romans 12:18; James 5:16)*.

EXAMPLES	MAN'S WAY (*Proverbs 14:12; I Corinthians 2:14*)	GOD'S WAY (*Proverbs 30:5-6; Colossians 2:8; Hebrews 4:12*)
Problems/ conflicts	We avoid problems and do everything we can to get out of them. We look for excuses or shift blame to others. We fail to admit we even have problems or say they are someone else's fault.	Conflicts and problems are for your good and for your spiritual growth. They help you to see what is within yourself (*Matthew 15:18-20*). Rejoice that God uses them to bring you to maturity (*Romans 5:3-5; James 1:2-4*).
Leadership	We are told to assert ourselves. Learn to take charge and give orders; these are keys to success.	Be willing to be a servant. The best leader is the one who serves. God gives more grace to the humble (*Matthew 20:26-28*).
Sex	We seek lovers to satisfy us. We say it is our spouse's duty to meet our desires; "After all, my spouse belongs to me."	You and your spouse belong to the Lord; you must seek to meet your spouse's best interests and to bless your spouse. Sex is to be reserved for marriage only (*I Corinthians 7:4; I Thessalonians 4:3; Hebrews 13:4*).
Anger: rights	We retaliate in order to get even. We protect our rights and don't let them be violated.	Your response to difficulties is to put off anger, forgive, and return a blessing (*Romans 12:14; Ephesians 4:31-32*). Be willing to give up your freedoms or "rights" for the sake of others (*Matthew 5:43-48; Romans 14:15-21*).
I've been offended/ hurt	"The best defense is a good offense." We all must defend ourselves. We're told we should not let our "self-esteem" be destroyed by letting others discredit us.	Examine yourself (*Matthew 7:5*). Die to self (*Luke 9:23-24*). Do not judge others by your standards but be a blessing instead (*Luke 6:27-28, 36-38; John 7:24; Romans 14:1-13; James 4:11-12; I Peter 3:8-9*). Consider others as more important than yourself (*Philippians 2:3-4*).
My enemy needs help	We say our enemy deserves it when they get in trouble. We show little patience for incompetence and want to say, "Get rid of those people."	Love your enemies and meet their needs (*Matthew 5:43-48; Luke 6:35*). In fact, go beyond what is expected (*Matthew 5:38-42*).
Riches	We learn we can't have too much money. "Always get it while the getting's good."	Fix your hope on God, not on riches (*I Timothy 6:17*). All riches are God's; give to Him and those in need (*Psalm 24:1; Proverbs 3:9-10; Luke 12:33; II Corinthians 9:6-12*).
Duties	People say "If you feel like it, do it." "Don't worry about those things; they'll get done eventually." We find good excuses for not fulfilling our responsibilities.	Be obedient to God's Word and do your responsibilities heartily as to the Lord, regardless of your feelings; God blesses obedience (*Genesis 4:6-7; I Samuel 15:22; John 14:15; James 1:22, 4:17*).

© Biblical Counseling Foundation

KNOWING THE DIFFERENCE BETWEEN MAN'S WAY AND GOD'S WAY

> You must be firmly rooted, built up, and established in the Lord. Only in this way can you avoid the empty deception, philosophy, and elementary principles of the world *(based on Colossians 2:6-10)*.

I. **The basics of knowing God's way**

   A. Test the spirits to determine if they are from God and if they sincerely and wholeheartedly believe in the Lord Jesus Christ *(I John 4:1-3)*.

   B. Check the foundation/basic premises *(I Corinthians 3:10-11; Colossians 2:8)*.

   C. Identify the source of authority, which must be the Word of God *(II Timothy 3:16-17; Hebrews 4:12)*.

II. **The importance of following God's way**

   A. There will be a judgment of what you have done *(Matthew 16:27; Romans 14:10; I Corinthians 3:10-15; II Corinthians 5:10)*.

   B. Only God's standard is eternal *(Psalm 119:89, 160; I Peter 1:24-25)*, acceptable, and valid *(Deuteronomy 11:26-28; Psalm 119:118; Isaiah 55:8-11; Hebrews 4:12)*.

III. **The hope in going God's way**

   A. You have freedom over sin *(Romans 6:6-7, 14, 18; Galatians 2:20)*.

   B. God promises you victory to overcome sin in any temptation or trial *(Romans 8:31-39; I Corinthians 10:13)*.

   C. The Lord Jesus Christ is your advocate for every failure and in every need *(Hebrews 4:15-16; I John 2:1)*.

   D. God controls circumstances for your good as He conforms you to the image of the Lord Jesus Christ *(Romans 8:28-29; James 1:2-4)*.

   E. God's peace and joy for you do not depend on circumstances, people, or things *(John, chapters 14-17; Romans 14:17)*.

   F. God is solely responsible (not you or any other) for causing change in others *(Ezekiel 18:20; II Corinthians 3:18; Philippians 1:6)*.

   G. God forgives your sins *(Psalm 103:12; Colossians 1:13-14; Hebrews 10:17; I John 1:9)*.

   H. God provides abundant life for you which begins now *(John 5:24, 10:10)*.

LESSON 4: HOMEWORK

> God's Word can be relied upon for every situation of life. You can know the basic principles of Scripture to face and deal with every problem and be able to distinguish between the folly of man's wisdom and the promises of God *(based on Psalm 19:7-14; II Corinthians 1:19-20; II Timothy 3:16-17; Hebrews 5:14; James 1:5; II Peter 1:2-4).*

✔ *homework completed*

☐ A. * In your own words, write the meaning of *II Corinthians 3:5-6*. Memorize *II Corinthians 3:5-6*. Begin memorizing *I Corinthians 10:13*. Review past verses.

☐ B. * Read **BIBLICAL PRINCIPLES: MAN'S WAY AND GOD'S WAY (PART TWO)** (Lesson 4, Page 2). Highlight verses not marked in previous lessons.

☐ C. * Choose one verse from each principle listed on Lesson 4, Page 2, that is applicable to your life and complete a **BIBLE STUDY AND APPLICATION FORMAT** (Supplement 3, Page 1) for each one.

   *You may make copies of the **BIBLE STUDY AND APPLICATION FORMAT** (Supplement 3, Page 1) for your study of Scripture throughout this course.*

☐ D. * You are to examine yourself to test the validity of your faith *(II Corinthians 13:5)*. One New Testament book *(I John)* was written specifically to help you know that you have received eternal life *(I John 5:13)*. This week, read through *I John* for your personal study and highlight the verses that present the measurable proofs that God's gift of eternal life is yours. Write how each of these proofs of salvation has been incorporated into your life.

☐ E. Review **THE BIBLICAL MODEL OF MAN'S FAILURE** (Lesson 4, Pages 3-4).

☐ F. Study **THE BIBLICAL VIEW OF SELF** (Lesson 4, Pages 5-10).

☐ G. Study **BASIC APPROACHES TO SOLVING PERSONAL PROBLEMS** (Lesson 4, Page 11), and mark any terminology in the **"Man's Way"** columns that you have been using. Look up the Scripture passages that are listed on this chart.

☐ H. Read **EXAMPLES OF MAN'S WAY COMPARED TO GOD'S WAY** (Lesson 4, Pages 12-13). Place a check mark beside statements applicable to you.

☐ I. Study **KNOWING THE DIFFERENCE BETWEEN MAN'S WAY AND GOD'S WAY** (Lesson 4, Page 14).

☐ J. * Refer to **PREPARING A PERSONAL TESTIMONY** (Supplement 4). Review your ten-second and thirty-second testimonies from the last lesson's homework. Write your sixty-second testimony and be prepared to give your testimony in class.

☐ K. * Respond to statement 9 under **Open Book Test**, Lesson 23, Page 2.

*   *The completion of assignments marked with an asterisk (*) is a prerequisite for further biblical counseling training.*

LESSON 4: STUDY GUIDE FOR DAILY DEVOTIONS
(INCLUDING SCRIPTURE MEMORY AND HOMEWORK)

> God's Word can be relied upon for every situation of life. You can know the basic principles of Scripture to face and deal with every problem and be able to distinguish between the folly of man's wisdom and the promises of God *(based on Psalm 19:7-14; II Corinthians 1:19-20; II Timothy 3:16-17; Hebrews 5:14; James 1:5; II Peter 1:2-4).*

Scripture Memory

1. * Memorize *II Corinthians 3:5-6.* Begin memorizing *I Corinthians 10:13.*
2. With previous memory verses, four memory verse cards can be carried with you throughout the day *(Matthew 7:1, 5; Ephesians 2:8-9; II Corinthians 3:5-6; II Timothy 3:16-17).* At every opportunity, review the previous three weeks' memory verses and read, meditate on, and memorize *II Corinthians 3:5-6.* Whenever possible, preview *I Corinthians 10:13.*

Daily Devotional Study Guide

FIRST DAY

1. Open in prayer.
2. * Read **BIBLICAL PRINCIPLES: MAN'S WAY AND GOD'S WAY (PART TWO)** (Lesson 4, Page 2). Highlight the verses that you have not marked in previous lessons.
3. Study through **THE BIBLICAL MODEL OF MAN'S FAILURE** (Lesson 4, Pages 3-4). Look up the passages that accompany each point.
4. * In your own words, write the meaning of *II Corinthians 3:5-6.*
5. Close with prayer.
6. Take your Scripture memory cards with you and use your spare moments each day to review *Ephesians 2:8-9, Matthew 7:1, 5, and II Timothy 3:16-17.* Memorize *II Corinthians 3:5-6.* Preview *I Corinthians 10:13* whenever possible.

SECOND DAY

1. Open in prayer.
2. * Begin a **BIBLE STUDY AND APPLICATION FORMAT** (Supplement 3, Page 1) on any verse listed under *Principle 7* (Lesson 4, Page 2).
3. Read **THE BIBLICAL VIEW OF SELF** (Lesson 4, Pages 5-10). Look up verses as necessary.
4. Close in prayer.

THIRD DAY

1. Open in prayer.
2. * Complete the **BIBLE STUDY AND APPLICATION FORMAT** (Supplement 3, Page 1) that you began yesterday.
3. Review **BASIC APPROACHES TO SOLVING PERSONAL PROBLEMS** (Lesson 4, Page 11). Be sure to look up the listed Scripture passages. Mark the terminology in the **"Man's Way"** columns that you have been using.

4.   * Review your ten-second and thirty-second testimonies from your last lesson and write your sixty-second testimony. Follow the format in **PREPARING A PERSONAL TESTIMONY** (Supplement 4).

5.   Close in prayer.

6.   How is your progress in Scripture memorization? Are you taking your cards with you each day and using spare moments to review and memorize? Be faithful (*Psalm 119:11; I Corinthians 4:2*).

FOURTH DAY

1.   Open with prayer.

2.   * Begin a **BIBLE STUDY AND APPLICATION FORMAT** (Supplement 3, Page 1) on any verse listed under *Principle 8* (Lesson 4, Page 2).

3.   * Begin to read through *I John*, highlighting verses that give you proof that God's gift of eternal life is yours. Write how these proofs of salvation have been incorporated into your life. This is the first day of a three-day study.

4.   Read **EXAMPLES OF MAN'S WAY COMPARED TO GOD'S WAY** (Lesson 4, Pages 12-13). Place a check mark beside any areas that need to be corrected in your own life.

5.   Close in prayer.

FIFTH DAY

1.   Open with prayer.

2.   * Complete the **BIBLE STUDY AND APPLICATION FORMAT** (Supplement 3, Page 1) that you began yesterday.

3.   * Continue your study through *I John*.

4.   Review your sixty-second testimony, making any changes as necessary.

5.   Close with prayer.

SIXTH DAY

1.   Open in prayer.

2.   * Begin a **BIBLE STUDY AND APPLICATION FORMAT** (Supplement 3, Page 1) on any verse listed under *Principle 9* (Lesson 4, Page 2).

3.   * Complete your study through *I John* and write how these proofs of salvation have been incorporated into your life.

4.   Close in prayer.

SEVENTH DAY

1.   Open with prayer.

2.   * Complete the **BIBLE STUDY AND APPLICATION FORMAT** (Supplement 3, Page 1) that you began yesterday.

3.   Read through **KNOWING THE DIFFERENCE BETWEEN MAN'S WAY AND GOD'S WAY** (Lesson 4, Page 14), looking up the listed verses to reinforce these truths in your life.

4.   * Refer to **PREPARING A PERSONAL TESTIMONY** (Supplement 4). Make any changes in your sixty-second testimony and write a final copy. Prepare to give your testimony in class.

5.   Recite your memory verses to someone, explaining the meaning of the verses and their application to your life.

6.   * To complete the **COURSE EXAM** (Lesson 23) while going through this course, respond to statement 9 under **Open Book Test** (Lesson 23, Page 2).

7.   Close in prayer.

*   The completion of assignments marked with an asterisk (*) is a prerequisite for further biblical counseling training.

LESSON 5

BIBLICAL DYNAMICS OF CHANGE

"No temptation has overtaken you but such as is common to man; and God is faithful, who will not allow you to be tempted beyond what you are able, but with the temptation will provide the way of escape also, that you may be able to endure it."

I Corinthians 10:13

LESSON 5: BIBLICAL DYNAMICS OF CHANGE

> Neglecting or refusing God's ways brings multiplied problems. To deal effectively with your problems, you must realize your inadequacy and turn to the power of God for salvation. Then, you will be able to make the necessary biblical changes that characterize a child of God as you reverently depend on God and His Word *(based on Proverbs 1:22-33; Romans 1:16-32; 6:4-7, 11-14; Philippians 2:12-13; James 1:25; II Peter 1:5-10).*

I. **The purposes of this lesson are:**

   A. To illustrate the consequences of following your own natural desires instead of God's pattern for change as outlined in His Word;

   B. To help you identify a specific problem or difficulty in your life on which God wants you to work during this course;

   C. To point out the importance of being a doer of the Word; and

   D. To encourage you to be prepared always to give your testimony of biblical change regarding your salvation and focus of life.

II. **The outline of this lesson**

   A. Self-confrontation

      1. **BIBLICAL PRINCIPLES: BIBLICAL DYNAMICS OF CHANGE** (Lesson 5, Page 2)

      2. **THE DOWNWARD SPIRAL: NEGLECTING OR REFUSING GOD'S WAY** (Lesson 5, Page 3)

      3. **BEGINNINGS OF BIBLICAL CHANGE** (Lesson 5, Page 4)

      4. **THE UPWARD PATH: WALKING GOD'S WAY** (Lesson 5, Page 5)

      5. **THE IMPORTANCE OF DOING THE WORD** (Lesson 5, Pages 6-9)

   B. Steps for spiritual growth

      1. **LESSON 5: HOMEWORK** (Lesson 5, Page 10)

      2. **STUDY GUIDE FOR DAILY DEVOTIONS** (Lesson 5, Pages 11-12)

   C. Biblical Counseling

      1. **PERSONAL HISTORY/PROBLEM EVALUATION** (Supplement 6)

BIBLICAL PRINCIPLES: BIBLICAL DYNAMICS OF CHANGE

> Biblical change begins with your spiritual birth and continues throughout your life. Your purpose for living changes from a focus of living for self to one of dying to self as you learn to love God and love others in a biblical manner *(based on Matthew 22:37-39; Luke 9:23; John 3:3; Romans 12:1-2; Titus 2:11-14).*

I. The downward spiral

(Principle 10)   God's thoughts and ways are far higher (superior) than yours *(Isaiah 55:8-9),* and His Word is truth *(Psalm 119:160; John 17:17).* If you neglect or refuse God's ways or His truth, you will experience ever-increasing problems; and the problems you have will grow worse *(Proverbs 1:25-32, 13:15, 28:13-14; Romans 1:20-32; Galatians 5:16-21; Hebrews 3:7-19; James 1:14-15).*

II. Beginnings of biblical change

(Principle 11)   A transforming new birth is necessary for you to live victoriously and to be empowered to overcome the world and problems of life *(John 3:3-7; Romans 12:1-2; II Corinthians 5:17-21; Titus 3:3-7; I John 5:4-5).*

(Principle 12)   The whole duty of man is to fear (reverence) God and keep His commandments *(Ecclesiastes 12:13-14; I Peter 1:17).* You are to love God and others in response to God's love for you *(Matthew 22:37-39; John 15:9-14; I John 4:11, 19).* You are to walk in a manner worthy of God and to please Him in every area of your life *(II Corinthians 5:9; Colossians 1:10)* by being a doer of the Word *(John 14:15; James 1:22; I John 2:3-4).* As you obediently respond to God's love, you become mature in the Lord and are blessed with peace and joy *(John 15:10-11, 16:33).* Numerous other blessings from the Lord follow *(Matthew 6:33; James 1:25; I John 3:22).* If you do not obey God's Word, He will judge and discipline you *(I Corinthians 11:31-32; Hebrews 12:5-10).*

(Principle 13)   To appropriate God's gracious wisdom in facing and dealing with your problems, you must ask in faith *(Hebrews 4:16; James 1:5-8),* live according to God's Word *(James 1:22-25),* and depend on His power *(II Corinthians 3:4-5; Philippians 4:13).*

III. The upward path

(Principle 14)   You must obey God's Word consistently *(I John 2:3-6)* to grow increasingly into godliness *(I Timothy 4:7-8; II Peter 1:3-11)* and to realize true peace *(Psalm 119:165; John 16:33)* and joy *(John 15:10-11).*

THE DOWNWARD SPIRAL:
NEGLECTING OR REFUSING GOD'S WAY

> If you neglect or refuse God's direction for your life and choose to follow the path of least resistance (your feelings and desires or what seems good at the moment), you will be headed toward defeat and ultimate ruin (*based on Psalm 1:4-6; Proverbs 1:22-32, 16:25; Matthew 7:13; Galatians 5:17; James 1:14-15*).

Problems start in the **heart** (*Jeremiah 17:9-10; Matthew 15:18-19; Mark 7:20-23*). Heart problems lead to:

Unbiblical **deeds** (thoughts, words, actions) (*for example: Romans 1:18-32*). Unbiblical deeds may be accompanied by and often lead to:

Bad **feelings** (*for example: Genesis 4:6-7; Psalm 38:1-10, 17-18*).

AN EXAMPLE OF A STUDENT CAUGHT IN THE
DOWNWARD SPIRAL:

A. **Heart level**

Focus on self (*Luke 9:23-24*)

B. **Doing level (unbiblical deeds)**

Tempted to follow fleshly desires instead of a commitment to God **(thought life)** (*Galatians 5:16-17; Ephesians 2:3; Titus 2:11-12*)

Lazy – doesn't want to study **(thought life)** (*Proverbs 6:9-11, 10:4; Ecclesiastes 11:4; Matthew 25:26-29; Ephesians 5:15-16*)

Doesn't study **(actions)** (*II Thessalonians 3:11*)

Keeps bad company **(actions)** (*Proverbs 1:10-19, 24:1; I Corinthians 15:33*)

Worries about failing course **(thought life)** (*Proverbs 12:25a; Philippians 4:6*)

Lies to parents about readiness for exams **(words)** (*Ephesians 4:25; Colossians 3:9*)

Cheats on exams **(actions)** (*Exodus 20:15; Ephesians 4:28*)

Fails course (consequence) (*Proverbs 28:13; Colossians 3:25*)

C. **Feeling level**

Depression, despair, guilt feelings (*Psalm 38:4-8*)

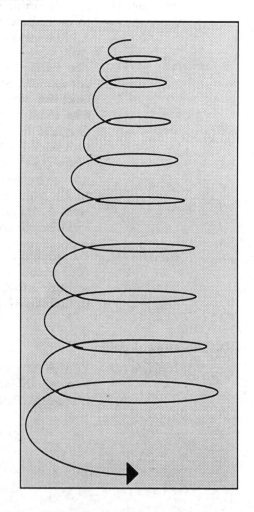

BEGINNINGS OF BIBLICAL CHANGE

> Man's "solutions" to your difficulties will ultimately fail because they do not deal with the source of your problems: your heart. God's solutions, as revealed in Scripture, go to the heart of the matter where permanent change is accomplished *(based on Jeremiah 17:9-10; Matthew 15:18-19; John 15:5; I Corinthians 3:19, 6:9-11; II Timothy 3:16-17; Hebrews 4:12).*

I. **Commit yourself to God's sovereignty and rule in your life.**

    A.   Receive the Lord Jesus Christ as Savior *(John 1:12; Romans 10:9-13; I Corinthians 15:1-4; Ephesians 2:8-10).*

    B.   Determine to live each day in a manner that pleases God *(II Corinthians 5:9; Ephesians 4:1; Colossians 3:17).*

II. **Determine specific ways you have sinned against God and confess these sins to Him (I John 1:9). Repent of your sinful ways, since they are contrary to Scripture and displeasing to God** *(Proverbs 28:13; Acts 26:20; Revelation 2:5, 3:19).*

III. **Ask God for wisdom to know what changes to make and how to make them** *(James 1:5).* **Ask with faith that He will answer** *(Hebrews 11:6; James 1:5-8).*

IV. **Confess your specific sins to those against whom you have sinned by your words or actions** *(James 5:16).* **Forgive those who have sinned against you** *(Mark 11:25-26; Ephesians 4:31-32)* **and reconcile with them if at all possible** *(Matthew 5:23-24; Romans 12:18).*

V. **Diligently study God's Word on a regular basis** *(Joshua 1:8; Psalm 1:2; II Timothy 2:15, 3:16-17)* **and memorize Scripture to store His truth in your heart** *(Psalm 119:11, 16).*

VI. **Pray unceasingly, at all times, and in everything** *(Luke 18:1; Philippians 4:6-7; I Thessalonians 5:17).*

VII. **Do what God says to do in His Word** *(Matthew 7:24-26; James 1:22-25)* **regardless of your feelings** *(Genesis 4:6-7; Romans 13:14; Galatians 5:16-17; I Peter 4:2)* **in order to glorify Him** *(Matthew 5:16; I Corinthians 10:31),* **staying under the control and guidance of the Holy Spirit** *(John 14:26, 16:13; Romans 8:14; Ephesians 5:18-20).*

Problems That Need God's Solutions (A Sample List)

Adultery, outbursts of anger, anorexia, arrogance, bitterness, bulimia, ineffective or evil communications, depression, lack of discipline in specific areas, drunkenness, fear, financial problems, fornication, frustration, gluttony, greed, guilt, homosexuality, impatience, interpersonal disputes, jealousy, laziness, loneliness, lust, lying, marriage problems and failures, parent and child difficulties, pride, procrastination, rebellion, self-pity, stealing, substance abuse, suffering, unforgiving spirit, and worry.

THE UPWARD PATH : WALKING GOD'S WAY

> **NOTE: This page should be read from the bottom to the top.** Living God's way means putting away your self-centeredness and committing yourself to follow God's Word in spite of any feelings to the contrary *(based on Psalm 1:1-3; Matthew 7:13-14; Luke 9:23; Galatians 5:17).* If you do this, God will bless you *(based on John 14:27, 15:11; Galatians 5:22-23; James 1:25).*

- Realize abundant life, filled with God's peace and joy *(John 10:10, 14:27, 15:11, 16:33)*
- Experience Christlike character development through God's Spirit working within you *(II Corinthians 3:18; Galatians 5:22-23)*
- Rejoice always *(Philippians 4:4; I Thessalonians 5:16),* giving thanks in all things *(I Thessalonians 5:18)* and for all things *(Ephesians 5:20)*
- Pray unceasingly about everything *(Philippians 4:6-7; I Thessalonians 5:17)*
- Speak the truth in love *(Ephesians 4:15; Colossians 3:9)*
- Work heartily as unto the Lord *(Ephesians 6:7; Colossians 3:23-24)*
- Do everything without grumbling or disputing *(Philippians 2:14)*
- Continually live in a manner consistent with your calling in Christ *(Ephesians 4:1)*
- Count all trials as joy since God uses your trials to develop Christlike character in you *(Romans 5:3-5, 8:28-29; James 1:2-4)*
- Practice forgiveness and reconciliation *(Matthew 5:23-24, 6:14; Mark 11:25-26; Ephesians 4:32; Colossians 3:12-13)* and return a blessing for any evil you might receive from others *(Romans 12:17-21; I Peter 3:8-9)*
- Continually show deeds appropriate to repentance *(Luke 3:8; Acts 26:20; Revelation 2:5; 3:3, 19)*
- Be compassionate, kind, humble, gentle, and patient *(Colossians 3:12)*
- Learn to love God's way *(John 3:16, 15:17; Romans 5:8; I Corinthians 13:4-8a; I John 4:11, 19)*
- Dwell in your thoughts on what is true, honorable, right, pure, lovely, of good repute, excellent, and praiseworthy *(Philippians 4:8-9)* and set your mind on things above instead of on things that are on earth *(Colossians 3:2)*
- Regard others as more important than yourself, as did Jesus *(Philippians 2:3-8)*
- Continually judge yourself biblically *(Matthew 7:5; I Corinthians 11:31)*
- Be controlled by the Holy Spirit *(Ephesians 5:18-20)* and the Word of God *(Psalm 119:11; Colossians 3:16)*
- Be obedient to the Word out of your love for the Lord *(John 14:15, 21)*
- Commit your ways to God unreservedly *(Proverbs 3:5-8; Matthew 22:37; II Corinthians 5:9; Colossians 3:17)* and deny self to follow Jesus *(Matthew 10:24-26; Luke 9:23-24)*
- In faith, pray for wisdom in all matters *(James 1:5-8)*
- Repent *(Proverbs 9:6, 28:13; Acts 26:20; II Corinthians 7:9-11; Revelation 2:5)*
- Confess specific, recognized sins *(Psalm 51:1-4, 6-10, 17; James 5:16; I John 1:9)*

BIBLICAL CHANGE AFFECTS YOUR THOUGHTS, WORDS AND ACTIONS

(While a commitment of discipleship to Jesus Christ will be evidenced by specific and measurable steps of obedience to God's Word, the description of biblical living highlighted on this page is not intended to be exhaustive nor in a rigid sequence).

The UPWARD PATH (Comprised of Biblical Understanding, Hope, Change, and Practice)

THE IMPORTANCE OF DOING THE WORD

> Your love for Jesus Christ is evidenced by your obedience to God's Word *(based on Luke 6:46; John 14:23-24; I John 2:3-4, 5:3; II John 1:6)*. Your rewards in heaven will also be based on your obedience to Him *(based on II Corinthians 5:10; Colossians 3:23-25; I Peter 1:17)*.

I. You are SAVED by God's grace and not by your works, but you are created in Christ for good works *(Ephesians 2:8-10; Titus 2:11-14; James 2:17-18)*.

II. You are JUSTIFIED (declared righteous) by faith *(Romans 3:23-28, 5:1; Galatians 2:16)*.

III. You are JUDGED as a child of God by your obedience to God's Word and REWARDED accordingly.

    A. Your first step of obedience is to respond to the Lord Jesus Christ for salvation. Your response has eternal significance.

John 3:16	"For God so loved the world, that He gave His only begotten Son, that whoever believes in Him should not perish, but have eternal life."
John 3:36	"He who believes in the Son has eternal life; but he who does not obey the Son shall not see life, but the wrath of God abides on Him."
John 5:28-29	"Do not marvel at this; for an hour is coming, in which all who are in the tombs shall hear His voice, and shall come forth; those who did the good deeds, to a resurrection of life, those who committed the evil deeds to a resurrection of judgment."
Acts 17:30-31	"Therefore having overlooked the times of ignorance, God is now declaring to men that all everywhere should repent, because He has fixed a day in which He will judge the world in righteousness through a Man whom He has appointed, having furnished proof to all men by raising Him from the dead."
Romans 2:5-10	"But because of your stubbornness and unrepentant heart you are storing up wrath for yourself in the day of wrath and revelation of the righteous judgment of God, who will render to every man according to his deeds: to those who by perseverance in doing good seek for glory and honor and immortality, eternal life; but to those who are selfishly ambitious and do not obey the truth, but obey unrighteousness, wrath and indignation, there will be tribulation and distress for every soul of man who does evil, of the Jew first and also of the Greek, but glory and honor and peace to every man who does good, to the Jew first and also to the Greek."
Romans 6:23	"For the wages of sin is death, but the free gift of God is eternal life in Christ Jesus our Lord."

II Thessalonians 1:7b-8	*"...when the Lord Jesus shall be revealed from heaven with His mighty angels in flaming fire, dealing out retribution to those who do not know God and to those who do not obey the gospel of our Lord Jesus."*
II Peter 3:9	*"The Lord is not slow about His promise, as some count slowness, but is patient toward you, not wishing for any to perish but for all to come to repentance."*

B.   Blessings for obedience and judgment leading to discipline for disobedience have always been part of God's eternal plan.

Deuteronomy 11:26-28	*"See, I am setting before you today a blessing and a curse: the blessing, if you listen to the commandments of the Lord your God, which I am commanding you today; and the curse, if you do not listen to the commandments of the Lord your God, but turn aside from the way which I am commanding you today, by following other gods which you have not known."*
Psalm 62:12	*"And lovingkindness is Thine, O Lord, For Thou dost recompense a man according to his work."*
Jeremiah 17:10	*"I, the Lord, search the heart, I test the mind, Even to give to each man according to his ways, According to the results of his deeds."*
Ecclesiastes 12:13-14	*"The conclusion, when all has been heard, is: fear God and keep His commandments, because this applies to every person. Because God will bring every act to judgment, everything which is hidden, whether it is good or evil."*
Matthew 12:35-37	*"The good man out of his good treasure brings forth what is good; and the evil man out of his evil treasure brings forth what is evil. And I say to you, that every careless word that men shall speak, they shall render account for it in the day of judgment. For by your words you shall be justified, and by your words you shall be condemned."*
Matthew 16:27	*"For the Son of Man is going to come in the glory of His Father with His angels; and will then recompense every man according to his deeds."*
I Corinthians 3:8	*"Now he who plants and he who waters are one; but each will receive his own reward according to his own labor."*
II Corinthians 5:10	*"For we must all appear before the judgment seat of Christ, that each one may be recompensed for his deeds in the body, according to what he has done, whether good or bad."*
II Corinthians 11:14-15	*"And no wonder, for even Satan disguises himself as an angel of light. Therefore it is not surprising if his servants also disguise themselves as servants of righteousness; whose end shall be according to their deeds."*
Colossians 3:23-25	*"Whatever you do, do your work heartily, as for the Lord rather than for men; knowing that from the Lord you will receive the reward of the inheritance. It is the Lord Christ whom you serve. For he who does wrong will receive the consequences of the wrong which he has done, and that without partiality."*

I Peter 1:17	*"And if you address as Father the One who impartially judges according to each man's work, conduct yourselves in fear during the time of your stay upon earth."*
Revelation 2:23, 26	*"And I will kill her children with pestilence; and all the churches will know that I am He who searches the minds and hearts; and I will give to each one of you according to your deeds...And he who overcomes, and he who keeps My deeds until the end, to him I will give authority over the nations."*
Revelation 3:15-16	*"I know your deeds, that you are neither cold nor hot; I would that you were cold or hot. So because you are lukewarm, and neither hot nor cold, I will spit you out of My mouth."*
Revelation 14:13	*"And I heard a voice from heaven, saying, 'Write, "Blessed are the dead who die in the Lord from now on!" ' 'Yes' says the Spirit, 'that they may rest from their labors, for their deeds follow with them.'"*
Revelation 20:12-13	*"And I saw the dead, the great and the small, standing before the throne, and books were opened; and another book was opened, which is the book of life; and the dead were judged from the things which were written in the books, according to their deeds."*
Revelation 22:12	*"Behold, I am coming quickly, and My reward is with Me, to render to every one of them according to what he has done."*

C.   God consistently blesses those who, as a pattern of life, obediently respond to His Word.

Deuteronomy 28:1-2	*"Now it shall be, if you will diligently obey the Lord your God, being careful to do all His commandments which I command you today, the Lord your God will set you high above all the nations of the earth. And all these blessings shall come upon you and overtake you, if you will obey the Lord your God."*
Psalm 119:165	*"Those who love Thy law have great peace, and nothing causes them to stumble."*
Isaiah 1:19	*"If you consent and obey, You will eat the best of the land."*
John 1:12	*"But as many as received Him, to them He gave the right to become children of God, even to those who believe in His name."*
John 14:13	*"And whatever you ask in My name, that will I do, that the Father may be glorified in the Son."*
John 15:7	*"If you abide in Me, and My words abide in you, ask whatever you wish, and it shall be done for you."*
John 15:10-11	*"If you keep My commandments, you will abide in My love; just as I have kept my Father's commandments, and abide in His love. These things I have spoken to you, that My joy may be in you, and that your joy may be made full."*
I Corinthians 10:13	*"No temptation has overtaken you but such as is common to man; and God is faithful, who will not allow you to be tempted beyond what you are able, but with the temptation will provide the way of escape also, that you may be able to endure it."*

Galatians 6:9	*"And let us not lose heart in doing good, for in due time we shall reap if we do not grow weary."*
James 1:25	*"But one who looks intently at the perfect law, the law of liberty, and abides by it, not having become a forgetful hearer but an effectual doer, this man shall be blessed in what he does."*
I John 3:22	*"and whatever we ask we receive from Him, because we keep His commandments and do the things that are pleasing in His sight."*

D. Out of love for His children, God warns and disciplines those who are disobedient to His Word so that they may be restored to His righteous path in everyday life.

Deuteronomy 28:15	*"But it shall come about, if you will not obey the Lord your God, to observe to do all His commandments and His statutes which I charge you today, that all these curses shall come upon you and overtake you."*
Psalm 32:3-4	*"When I kept silent about my sin, my body wasted away through groaning all day long. For day and night Thy hand was heavy upon me; my vitality was drained away as with the fever-heat of summer."*
I Corinthians 11:31-32	*"But if we judged ourselves rightly, we should not be judged. But when we are judged, we are disciplined by the Lord in order that we may not be condemned along with the world."*
Hebrews 12:5-10	*"and you have forgotten the exhortation which is addressed to you as sons, 'My son, do not regard lightly the discipline of the Lord, nor faint when you are reproved by Him; for those whom the Lord loves He disciplines, and He scourges every son whom He receives.' It is for discipline that you endure; God deals with you as with sons; for what son is there whom his father does not discipline? But if you are without discipline, of which all have become partakers, then you are illegitimate children and not sons. Furthermore, we had earthly fathers to discipline us, and we respected them; shall we not much rather be subject to the Father of spirits, and live? For they disciplined us for a short time as seemed best to them, but He disciplines us for our good, that we may share His holiness."*

LESSON 5: HOMEWORK

> In this Self-Confrontation course, you have now covered enough scriptural basics for the life-long process of biblical self-confrontation *(based on Matthew 7:1-5; Romans 2:21; Hebrews 5:12-14; James 3:1)*. This lesson's **HOMEWORK** will present opportunities for you to judge yourself scripturally and, in the process, gain hope as you discover the biblical changes that can occur in your own life *(based on Acts 26:20; Romans 5:3-5, 6:6, 8:26-31; I Corinthians 11:31; II Corinthians 5:17; Philippians 2:12-13, 4:13)*.

✔ *homework completed*

☐ A.   * Review previous memory verses. In your own words, write the meaning of *I Corinthians 10:13*. Memorize *I Corinthians 10:13* and begin memorizing *Romans 8:28-29*.

☐ B.   * Complete a **BIBLE STUDY AND APPLICATION FORMAT** (Supplement 3, Page 1) for both of the following passages: *Romans 12:1-2* and *Galatians 5:16-17*.

☐ C.   * Describe a problem you are experiencing on which God wants you to work during this course. Complete the **PERSONAL HISTORY/PROBLEM EVALUATION** form (Supplement 6). See Lesson 5, Page 4, for a sample list of problems. Do not write anything on this form that you do not want your instructor to see.

☐ D.   * Read **BIBLICAL PRINCIPLES: BIBLICAL DYNAMICS OF CHANGE** (Lesson 5, Page 2). Look up the verses supporting these principles. Highlight the verses in your Bible if you have not already done so.

☐ E.   * Read *John, chapters 14-17*, highlighting the verses that mention the Source of true peace and joy. In your own words, write how God has provided for His Source of peace and joy to be in your life.

☐ F.   Review **THE DOWNWARD SPIRAL: NEGLECTING OR REFUSING GOD'S WAY** (Lesson 5, Page 3), observing the relationship between the heart, unbiblical deeds, and distressingly bad feelings.

☐ G.   Read **BEGINNINGS OF BIBLICAL CHANGE** (Lesson 5, Page 4). Determine if some of your present problems are listed at the bottom of the page and circle them.

☐ H.   Study **THE UPWARD PATH: WALKING GOD'S WAY** (Lesson 5, Page 5). Mark the statements that identify the biblical changes you need to make to overcome problems in your own life. Look up any verses as necessary.

☐ I   Read **THE IMPORTANCE OF DOING THE WORD** (Lesson 5, Pages 6-9).

☐ J.   * Review your ten-second, thirty-second, and sixty-second testimonies this week. (Refer to Supplement 4). State your testimonies to a friend for your own personal review.

☐ K.   * To complete the **COURSE EXAM** (Lesson 23) while going through this course, respond to statement 10 under **Open Book Test** (Lesson 23, Page 2).

   *   *The completion of assignments marked with an asterisk (*) is a prerequisite for further biblical counseling training.*

© Biblical Counseling Foundation   **Lesson 5, Page 10**

LESSON 5: STUDY GUIDE FOR DAILY DEVOTIONS
(INCLUDING SCRIPTURE MEMORY AND HOMEWORK)

> This week's **STUDY GUIDE FOR DAILY DEVOTIONS** will present opportunities for you to judge yourself scripturally and, in the process, gain hope as you discover the biblical changes that can occur in your own life *(based on Acts 26:20; Romans 5:3-5, 6:6, 8:26-31; I Corinthians 11:31; II Corinthians 5:17; Philippians 2:12-13, 4:13).*

Scripture Memory

1. * Memorize *I Corinthians 10:13* and begin memorizing *Romans 8:28-29.*
2. You now have six memory verse cards to carry with you throughout the day (listed in lesson order: *Ephesians 2:8-9; Matthew 7:1, 5; II Timothy 3:16-17; II Corinthians 3:5-6; I Corinthians 10:13; Romans 8:28-29).*

Daily Devotional Study Guide

FIRST DAY

1. Open with prayer.
2. * Read **BIBLICAL PRINCIPLES: BIBLICAL DYNAMICS OF CHANGE** (Lesson 5, Page 2). Look up the listed verses and highlight them in your Bible.
3. * In your own words, write the meaning of *I Corinthians 10:13.*
4. Close with prayer.
5. Take your six Scripture memory cards with you throughout the day, begin memorizing *I Corinthians 10:13* and preview *Romans 8:28-29.*

SECOND DAY

1. Open with prayer.
2. * Begin a **BIBLE STUDY AND APPLICATION FORMAT** (Supplement 3, Page 1) for *Romans 12:1-2.*
3. * Review your ten-second, thirty-second, and sixty-second testimonies. If necessary, refer to **PREPARING A PERSONAL TESTIMONY** (Supplement 4).
4. Read **THE IMPORTANCE OF DOING THE WORD** (Lesson 5, Pages 6-9).
5. * Describe a problem on which God wants you to work during this course. Complete a **PERSONAL HISTORY/PROBLEM EVALUATION** form (Supplement 6), on this problem. Do not put anything on this form that you do not want your instructor to see.
6. Close with prayer.

THIRD DAY

1. Open with prayer.
2. * Complete the **BIBLE STUDY AND APPLICATION FORMAT** (Supplement 3, Page 1) on *Romans 12:1-2* that you began yesterday.
3. Practice giving your spoken testimonies. Evaluate and change words that a non-believer would not understand.

4. Review **THE DOWNWARD SPIRAL: NEGLECTING OR REFUSING GOD'S WAY** (Lesson 5, Page 3). Notice the relationship between the heart level of problems and subsequent unbiblical thoughts, words, actions, and bad feelings.

5. Close with prayer.

FOURTH DAY

1. Open with prayer.

2. * Read *John chapter 14,* highlighting verses that indicate the Source of God's peace and joy in your life.

3. Read **BEGINNINGS OF BIBLICAL CHANGE** (Lesson 5, Page 4). Look up verses as needed.

4. Continue to review your ten-second, thirty-second, and sixty-second testimonies, getting their presentations firmly in mind.

5. Close with prayer.

6. Determine the effectiveness of your plan of memorizing verses this week. Today, recite all of your memory verses with their proper references.

FIFTH DAY

1. Open with prayer.

2. * Read *John chapter 15,* and highlight the verses that speak of peace and joy.

3. * Begin a **BIBLE STUDY AND APPLICATION FORMAT** (Supplement 3, Page 1) for *Galatians 5:16-17.*

4. Repeat your sixty-second testimony for your own assessment.

5. Close with prayer.

SIXTH DAY

1. Open with prayer.

2. * Read *John chapter 16,* highlighting the verses that speak of the Origin of peace and joy.

3. * Complete the **BIBLE STUDY AND APPLICATION FORMAT** (Supplement 3, Page 1) for *Galatians 5:16-17.*

4. For review, say your ten-second, thirty-second, and sixty-second testimonies.

5. Close with prayer.

SEVENTH DAY

1. Open with prayer.

2. * Read *John chapter 17* (the High Priestly prayer of the Lord Jesus Christ) and highlight verses that speak of a believer's peace and joy. As a summary of the highlighted verses marked in this study of *John chapters 14-17,* write how God has provided for His source of peace and joy to be in your life.

3. Study **THE UPWARD PATH: WALKING GOD'S WAY** (Lesson 5, Page 5). Place a check by the statements which identify the biblical changes you need to make in order to please the Lord and overcome problems in your life. Look up the verses associated with these steps of biblical change and meditate on them.

4. * To complete the **COURSE EXAM** (Lesson 23) while going through this course, respond to statement 10 under **Open Book Test** (Lesson 23, Page 2).

5. Close with prayer.

6. Ask someone to hear you recite your memory verses. Remember to explain the meaning of the verses and their application to your life. Also ask your friend to hear your ten-second, thirty-second, and sixty-second testimonies.

*   *The completion of assignments marked by an asterisk (*) is a prerequisite for further biblical counseling training.*

94

LESSON 6

BIBLICAL BASIS FOR CHANGE

"And we know that God causes all things to work together for good to those who love God, to those who are called according to His purpose. For whom He foreknew, He also predestined to become conformed to the image of His Son, that He might be the first born among many brethren."

Romans 8:28-29

LESSON 6: BIBLICAL BASIS FOR CHANGE

> As you obey God's Word and rely on His strengthening power, you can count on biblical change to occur in every area of your life *(based on Isaiah 40:29; Romans 8:29; II Corinthians 10:3-5; Philippians 2:12-15, 4:13; II Timothy 3:16-17; James 1:22-25; II Peter 1:3-10).*

I. **The purposes of this lesson are:**

   A. To describe the three levels of any problem in your life;

   B. To identify, from God's Word, the hope you can have in any difficulty; and

   C. To disclose how God's peace and joy can be yours in any circumstance and relationship.

II. **The outline of this lesson**

   A. Self-confrontation

      1. **BIBLICAL PRINCIPLES: BIBLICAL BASIS FOR CHANGE** (Lesson 6, Pages 2-3)

      2. **THREE LEVELS OF PROBLEMS** (Lesson 6, Pages 4-5)

      3. **BIBLICAL HOPE** (Lesson 6, Pages 6-7)

      4. **BIBLICAL BASIS FOR PEACE AND JOY** (Lesson 6, Pages 8-10)

   B. Steps for spiritual growth

      1. **LESSON 6: HOMEWORK** (Lesson 6, Page 11)

      2. **STUDY GUIDE FOR DAILY DEVOTIONS** (Lesson 6, Pages 12-13)

BIBLICAL PRINCIPLES: BIBLICAL BASIS FOR CHANGE

> Your hope as a believer is in the Lord. He causes all things in your life (including problems and trials) to work together for good as you continually respond in love (demonstrated through obedience) to Him. Out of the hope that God provides, your faith and love can be biblically expressed in any situation. Understanding and responding biblically to problems glorifies God while He further conforms you to the image of Jesus Christ (based on *Proverbs 3:5-6; Romans 8:28-29, 15:13; II Corinthians 3:16-18; 4:7-10, 16-18; Galatians 5:22-25; James 1:2-4, 22-25; I John 3:2-3*).

I. **Understanding your problems at the:**

A. Feeling level (often reflects your focus in life and may also reveal upon whom or what you are depending for your peace and joy)

(Principle 15)   Feelings of being mistreated indicate a focus on self and not on Jesus Christ *(Philippians 2:14-15; II Timothy 2:24-25; Hebrews 12:3)*.

(Principle 16)   The way you feel and the way you view yourself, your relationships, and your circumstances are often indications of whether you are living to please yourself or living to please God *(Genesis 4:6-7; Psalm 119:165; John 14:27, 15:10-11; Romans 14:17-18; II Corinthians 7:10; Philippians 4:6-7; I John 4:18-21)*.

B. Doing level (reveals the extent of your faithfulness to the Lord)

(Principle 17)   If you hear God's Word and do it, you will be blessed *(Joshua 1:8; Psalm 19:11; Proverbs 29:18; Matthew 7:20-27; James 1:25; I John 3:22)*, and your ability to discern good and evil will be increased *(Hebrews 5:14)*.

(Principle 18)   If you do not become a doer of the Word, you deceive yourself *(James 1:22-24)*, show your lack of love for the Lord *(John 14:23-24)*, place yourself under the corrective discipline of the Lord *(I Corinthians 11:32; Hebrews 12:5-11)*, and deny the reality of His life within you *(Romans 6:11-13, 17-18; I John 2:3-4; 3:7, 10)*.

C. Heart level (partially revealed by your thoughts, words, and actions)

(Principle 19)   Since even you cannot fully understand your heart *(Jeremiah 17:9)*, God's own Word is the measure and the instrument by which the heart level of your problems is discerned *(Hebrews 4:12)*. Your responses to problems need not be dependent on people, circumstances, or things. Your deeds (thoughts, words, and actions) in any situation are used by God to reveal the condition of your heart *(Matthew 15:18-20; Mark 7:20-23; Luke 6:45)*.

II. Your hope in the midst of trials

(Principle 20)   Those in Christ are freed from the power and penalty of sin *(Romans 6:6-7, 14, 18, 23)*.

(Principle 21)   God will not allow believers to be tested or tempted beyond what they can bear. He gives you His grace and strength to endure every test and resist every temptation so that you never have to sin *(Romans 8:35-39; I Corinthians 10:13; II Corinthians 4:7-10, 12:9-10; Philippians 4:13; Hebrews 4:15-16; II Peter 2:4-9)*.

(Principle 22)   Our Lord Jesus Christ will grant mercy and provide grace to help in every need. He constantly intercedes as an advocate for you to God the Father and fully understands your weaknesses *(Hebrews 2:18, 4:15-16, 7:25; I John 2:1)*.

(Principle 23)   Trials and testings will develop and mature you in Christ if you respond to them in God's way *(Romans 5:3-5; James 1:2-4)*. He never devises evil or harm for you; rather His plans for you are for good *(Genesis 50:20; Deuteronomy 8:2, 5, 16; Psalm 145:17; Ecclesiastes 7:13-14; Jeremiah 29:11-13; Romans 8:28-29; James 1:13-17)*.

(Principle 24)   God's peace and joy are available to believers regardless of others, possessions, or circumstances *(Psalm 119:165; Matthew 5:3-12; John 14:27, 15:11, 16:33, 17:13; Romans 14:17; Philippians 4:4-7; I Peter 1:6-9)*.

(Principle 25)   Only God can change people *(Ezekiel 36:26-27; Philippians 1:6, 2:13)*, so you are not and cannot be responsible for changing them. You are accountable to God solely for your own deeds *(Jeremiah 17:10; Ezekiel 18:1-20, especially verse 20; Matthew 16:27; Romans 2:5-10; Colossians 3:23-25; I Peter 1:17)* and are to do your part in living at peace with others *(Matthew 5:23-24; Mark 11:25; Romans 12:9-21, 14:19; I Peter 3:8-9, 4:8)*.

(Principle 26)   When you confess your sins, God forgives and cleanses you *(I John 1:9)*.

THREE LEVELS OF PROBLEMS

> While you may only be alert to your problems at one or two levels, all problems have three levels: feeling, doing, and heart. Generally, you perceive problems only at the feeling and doing levels. Since you often do not understand the full scope of your problems, it is important to examine your perceptions in light of God's Word *(based on Genesis 4:7; Psalm 38; Jeremiah 17:9; Matthew 7:1-5; I Corinthians 11:31; Galatians 5:17).*

I. **Feeling level**

   A. Your feelings cover a wide range of emotions and do not always accurately reflect the condition of your heart. Some distressing feelings may be the result of sin committed at the "doing" and "heart" level, as experienced by David *(Psalm 38:3-10).*

   B. You may sometimes be happy or elated as a result of unrighteous deeds that are displeasing to God and harmful to others, as the people of Israel were *(Exodus 32:2-6, 17-19).* Thus, feelings may or may not indicate whether you are living to please self or living to please God.

   C. However, feelings must not be overlooked in dealing with problems. Powerful feelings may be one of the first indications that a problem exists in your life, as the following examples in Scripture attest *(Genesis 4:5; Judges 7:3; I Samuel 18:8-9; I Kings 19:1-3; Psalm 38:3-10, 49:5; Ecclesiastes 7:9; Matthew 6:34; Mark 10:22; Luke 10:41).*

II. **Doing level**

   Your problems also involve your thoughts, words, and actions – the "doing level" *(Matthew 5:21-22, 27-28; Galatians 5:19-21; Colossians 3:5-9);* for example:

SELF - CENTERED LIFE		SELF - CENTERED DEEDS
Arrogance	Demonstrated by:	Saying unkind words, being critical
Deceitfulness	Demonstrated by:	Lying, using manipulative words
Immorality	Demonstrated by:	Committing adultery or fornication, viewing pornographic films, participating in homosexual activity
Anger	Demonstrated by:	Striking others, slamming doors, throwing things, attacking others verbally, shouting at others
Lack of fellowship	Demonstrated by:	Sporadic church attendance, unwillingness to meet others' needs
Lack of discipline	Demonstrated by:	Overeating, irregular devotions, failing to complete assignments or tasks

SELF - CENTERED LIFE		SELF - CENTERED DEEDS
Bitterness	Demonstrated by:	Brooding, not speaking, gossiping, planning for and carrying out revenge
Anxiety	Demonstrated by:	Blaming people or circumstances for lack of peace; talking constantly about your problems to others
Jealousy	Demonstrated by:	Belittling or criticizing others or their accomplishments

III. Heart level

A. The heart is described in Scripture in many varied but related ways. For example:

1. The "heart" refers to one's character or inner life with its desires and purpose for living *(Genesis 6:5, 8:21; Deuteronomy 11:13; I Samuel 12:24; Psalm 57:7, 84:2, 95:10; Jeremiah 32:38-41; Ezekiel 11:21; Matthew 5:8, 11:29, 22:37; Mark 3:5; Acts 2:46-47, 4:32; Romans 2:5; Colossians 3:22);*

2. The heart is impossible for man to understand fully *(Jeremiah 17:9)* and is impossible for man to cleanse *(Proverbs 20:9)*; and

3. The heart is the basis for all issues of life *(Proverbs 4:23; Matthew 12:34-35; Mark 7:20-23; Luke 6:43-45)* and, as such, focuses on living to please self or living to please God *(Luke 9:23-24; Galatians 5:16-17)*.

B. Your heart is revealed by your deeds, which include your:

1. Thoughts *(Matthew 15:19; Mark 7:20-23)*,

2. Speech *(Matthew 12:34; Luke 6:45)*, and

3. Actions *(Matthew 15:18-20; Mark 7:20-23)*.

C. When your heart is not focused on loving God, problems inevitably occur *(Matthew 15:18-20)*. A partial list of these problems includes:

Pride, greed (coveting), fleshly lusts *(I John 2:16)*, selfishness *(Philippians 2:21)*, bitterness *(Hebrews 12:15)*, envy/jealousy *(James 3:14-16)*, laziness or slothfulness *(Matthew 25:26)*, self-righteousness *(Luke 18:9-14)*, immorality, idolatry, enmities, strife, jealousy, outbursts of anger, dissensions, drunkenness, and envy *(Galatians 5:19-21)*.

D. In many instances the heart is equated with the mind *(Mark 7:18-23; Luke 5:22; Acts 5:4; Romans 10:8-10; II Corinthians 9:7; Hebrews 4:12)*.

E. The heart is also equated with the location of belief and faith *(Acts 16:14; Romans 10:10; Hebrews 3:12)*.

F. Only God can accurately judge the entire spiritual condition of the heart *(I Samuel 16:7; I Chronicles 28:9; Proverbs 17:3; Jeremiah 17:10; I Corinthians 4:5; I Thessalonians 2:4)*, and only He can change it *(Psalm 51:10; Ezekiel 36:26)*.

G. When God cleanses your heart through faith in the Lord Jesus Christ *(Acts 15:8-9; II Corinthians 4:6; Galatians 4:4-7)*, He seals you and gives you His Spirit as a pledge *(II Corinthians 1:21-22)*. Your response is to love and serve Him with your "whole heart" (the totality of your life and being) *(Matthew 22:37; Romans 6:17-18; Ephesians 6:5-8)*.

BIBLICAL HOPE

> The hope that God has provided for you is not merely a wish. Neither is it dependent on other people, possessions, or circumstances for its validity. Instead, biblical hope is an application of your faith that supplies a confident expectation in God's fulfillment of His promises. Coupled with faith and love, hope is part of the abiding characteristics in a believer's life *(based on Psalm 39:7, 119:49-50; Lamentations 3:21-24; Romans 5:1-5, 8:24-25; I Corinthians 13:13; II Corinthians 1:3-11; Colossians 1:3-6; I Thessalonians 1:2-3; I Timothy 1:1; Hebrews 6:17-20, 11:1, 13-16; I Peter 1:3).*

I. **The basis for biblical hope**

    A. According to God's Word, to have biblical hope means to remain steadfast while you eagerly wait for and have the sure expectation of divine, saving actions that are grounded in:

        1. The character of God the Father *(Psalm 33:18, 62:5-6, 71:5; Jeremiah 29:11; Lamentations 3:21-24; Romans 15:13; II Corinthians 1:8-10; I Peter 1:21);*

        2. God's Word *(Psalm 119:49, 130:5; Romans 15:4);*

        3. God's Son, the Lord Jesus Christ *(Matthew 12:21; Ephesians 1:9-12; Colossians 1:27; I Thessalonians 1:3; I Timothy 1:1; Titus 2:13; I John 3:3);* and

        4. The power of the Holy Spirit *(Romans 15:13).*

    B. "Hope" that depends on any other foundation will fail *(Job 8:13, 27:8; Psalm 33:16-17; Proverbs 11:7)* or will be no hope at all *(Ephesians 2:12; I Thessalonians 4:13).*

II. **The accompaniments of biblical hope**

    A. Hope is closely linked with faith and love *(I Corinthians 13:13; Galatians 5:5-6; Ephesians 4:1-6).*

    B. Faith, hope, and love are foundational characteristics of a godly person *(Ephesians 1:15-18; Colossians 1:3-5; I Thessalonians 1:2-3).*

III. **The realization of biblical hope**

    A. Biblical hope is a gift of God's grace *(II Thessalonians 2:16-17)* and is linked to the Good News of Jesus Christ *(Romans 5:1-2, 8:23-25; Ephesians 1:18-23, 4:4; Colossians 1:21-23; I Thessalonians 5:8; I Peter 1:3).*

    B. Since your hope is an unquestioned certainty through the Lord Jesus Christ *(Colossians 1:27)*, you are dramatically transformed by your biblical response to Him *(II Corinthians 5:17; Galatians 2:20; I John 3:1-3).*

    C. As a believer, you are to exult in hope at the glory of God revealed in Jesus Christ. Responding to this hope, you can joyfully cooperate with God's development of your Christlike character by persevering in any and all tribulations. By doing this, you will acquire hope for everyday living that can never disappoint *(based on Romans 5:1-5)*.

D. Because of God's sovereign and loving care for you in every situation *(Romans 8:28-29)*, remember:

1. You have freedom from the power and penalty of sin (see *Principle 20, Lesson 6, Page 3)*;

2. In any difficulty, you have the promise of victory that Jesus Christ has already attained through His death and resurrection (see *Principle 21, Lesson 6, Page 3)*;

3. You have personal support from the Lord Jesus Christ (see *Principle 22, Lesson 6, Page 3)*;

4. You have the promise that God will work out trials for your benefit as you live according to His Word (see *Principle 23, Lesson 6, Page 3)*;

5. You can have God's peace and joy in any situation (see *Principle 24, Lesson 6, Page 3)*;

6. You have no biblical responsibility to change others – only yourself (see *Principle 25, Lesson 6, Page 3)*; and

7. You can have hope renewed even if you fail (see *Principle 26, Lesson 6, Page 3)*.

Refer to: **KNOWING THE DIFFERENCE BETWEEN MAN'S WAY AND GOD'S WAY** *(Lesson 4, Page 14)* under III. *The hope in going God's way.*

IV. **Characteristics of those who exhibit biblical hope in their daily walk**

A. They have received salvation through the Lord Jesus Christ *(Romans 8:24-25; I Thessalonians 5:8; I Peter 1:3)*,

B. They are joyful *(Romans 5:2, 12:12, 15:13)*,

C. They are peaceful *(Romans 15:13)*,

D. They are encouraged by Scripture *(Romans 15:4)*,

E. They persevere in any situation *(Romans 8:24-25; Hebrews 6:9-12)*,

F. They have an expectancy to see the Lord Jesus Christ *(Galatians 5:5; Titus 2:11-13)*,

G. They are confidently steadfast in Christ Jesus *(Colossians 1:21-23; I Thessalonians 1:2-3; Hebrews 3:5-6)*,

H. They are dependent on God *(II Corinthians 1:8-10)*,

I. They are disciplined and faithful *(I Timothy 4:7-10)*,

J. They trust in God's promises *(Hebrews 6:17-20)*, and

K. They purify themselves *(I John 3:3)*.

BIBLICAL BASIS FOR PEACE AND JOY

> Experiencing and maintaining God's peace and joy are directly related to a believer's continued intimate relationship with the Lord Jesus Christ *(based on John 14:27, 15:11, 16:33; Romans 14:17; Galatians 5:22).*

God's peace and joy characterize a Spirit-filled life *(Galatians 5:22)*. His peace and joy are not dependent on any of the following:

1.   All others (i.e., spouse, parents, children, relatives, friends, enemies, supervisor/boss, roommates, classmates, neighbors, etc.);

2.   Circumstances (i.e., heritage, upbringing, job, school, vacation, neighborhood, holidays, authorities over us, "inconveniences," health problems, financial difficulties, weather, popularity, etc.); or

3.   Things (i.e., money, car, educational degree, house, apartment, clothes, furniture, pets, etc.).

However, many of God's children are not experiencing the peace and joy found in Jesus Christ *(John 14:27, 15:11, 16:33)*, even though these traits are to be characteristic of the abundant life that is promised in God's Word *(John 10:10; Romans 14:17, 15:13)*.

I.   **Peace**

A.   The world's peace

The "peace" offered by the world is neither steadfast nor secure. The world's peace is temporal and lasts only as long as everything is going smoothly *(John 14:27, 16:33; Romans 3:16-17).*

B.   The scriptural dimensions of peace

1.   Peace is used in the obvious sense of a lack of hostility between groups of people *(Joshua 9:15; I Samuel 16:4-5; Matthew 10:34-36; Luke 14:31-32; Acts 7:26, 12:20, 24:2-3)*. Peace also describes harmonious relationships between individuals *(I Chronicles 12:16-18; Romans 14:19; Ephesians 4:1-3; Hebrews 12:14)*.

2.   Peace is the opposite of confusion *(I Corinthians 14:33)* and is descriptive of godly wisdom *(James 3:17)*. Since self-serving peace is linked to people or circumstances, it is temporary and deceptive *(Deuteronomy 29:19-21; Jeremiah 6:10-15, 8:8-11; Ezekiel 13:8-16; Micah 3:5)*. Biblical peace is dependent solely on living God's way *(Psalm 85:8-10; Isaiah 32:17, 48:22, 57:21; James 3:14-18)*.

3.   The highest dimension of peace in Scripture describes a person who has a right relationship with God, resulting in a clear conscience, sense of well-being, and state of rest *(Psalm 4:8, 29:11; Isaiah 26:12, 32:17; Malachi 2:3-6; Luke 2:14; II Timothy 1:2-3)*. This right relationship with God can be yours, and it is found only through Jesus Christ *(Luke 1:67-79; Acts 10:34-36; Romans 5:1; Ephesians 2:13-18)*.

C. Your realization of true peace

1. Peace is characteristic of the kingdom of God *(Romans 14:17)* and may be experienced even when difficulties surround you and circumstances change. Since the peace of God is in His Son, Jesus Christ *(Isaiah 9:6; Ephesians 2:13-18; Colossians 3:15; II Thessalonians 3:16)*, it surpasses comprehension *(Philippians 4:7)* and is not like the world's peace which is based on people, circumstances, or possessions *(John 14:27)*.

2. Jesus said that in the world you will have tribulation; but since He has overcome the world, you can still have peace in Him *(John 16:33)*.

3. When you stop worrying but instead pray with thanksgiving in every situation, then you will realize God's peace as the guardian of your heart and mind *(Philippians 4:6-7)*. God's peace is experienced through your sustained trust in Him *(Isaiah 26:3; Romans 8:6)* and a continual love for the Word of God that is demonstrated by loving and wholehearted obedience *(Psalm 119:165-168)*.

II. **Joy**

A. The world's joy

Anything offered by the world, including its "joy," is temporal and short-lived *(I John 2:15-17)*. An individual who is seeking joy in either a person, a circumstance, or another "thing" soon finds that this type of joy is shallow. When people fail, circumstances change, or things disappoint, the "joy" that seemed to beam brightly soon disappears. The typical reaction then is to find a different individual, a change in circumstances, or more "things" in a vain attempt to attain joy anew.

B. The scriptural dimensions of joy

1. Joy (to glory, to exult, to be satisfied, to take delight in) is a multi-faceted term that is used in a variety of circumstances. In every instance, joy results from a definite cause. The basis for joy in each situation determines whether it is steadfast joy that pleases God or temporal joy that pleases self. For example, while it is possible to be joyful at others' distress *(Psalm 35:26)*, at calamity *(Proverbs 17:5)*, in unrighteousness *(I Corinthians 13:6)*, or in the midst of sin *(James 4:1-9)*, that kind of rejoicing focuses on self-gratification and is displeasing to God.

Lasting joy that comes from God must be rooted and grounded in God, His character, and His works *(Deuteronomy 16:13-15; II Chronicles 30:20-22; Psalm 9:2, 31:7, 33:21, 35:9, 40:16, 43:4, 92:1-4, 118:24; Isaiah 61:10; Luke 1:46-55)*.

2. Since Jesus is fully God *(Colossians 1:15-20; Hebrews 1:1-6)* and never changing *(Hebrews 13:8)*, lasting joy is found in Him *(Luke 1:14, 2:10; John 15:11, 17:13; Philippians 4:4)* and in the salvation He has provided *(Luke 10:20; 15:7, 10; Romans 15:8-13; Philippians 1:15-18; I Peter 1:3-8)*.

3. True joy can even be consistently experienced in the midst of sorrows and distress *(II Corinthians 6:1-10, especially verse 10; I Thessalonians 5:16)*.

C. Your realization of true joy

1. Like peace, the joy that God gives is a distinctive characteristic of the kingdom of God *(Romans 14:17)*. Fullness of joy is found in God's presence *(Psalm 16:11)* and in His strength *(Nehemiah 8:10)*. This joy, found in the Lord Jesus Christ *(Romans 5:11)*, cannot be taken away from you *(John 16:22, 17:13)*. It does not

depend on people, circumstances, or possessions; but it is dependent only upon your relationship with Jesus *(John 15:1-11; Galatians 5:22; I Peter 1:3-8)*.

2. The joy that Jesus provides can fill you *(John 17:13)* and can be consistently experienced through a prayer life centered on the Lord Jesus Christ *(John 16:24)*.

3. Since lasting joy is yours through a right relationship with Jesus, you can endure trials joyfully *(Matthew 5:11-12; James 1:2-4; I Peter 1:6-7, 4:12-13)*. Our example in this regard is Jesus Himself, who endured the ultimate trial, death on a cross, for the lasting joy that was set before Him *(Hebrews 12:1-2)*.

4. When you rejoice in the Lord always *(Philippians 3:1, 4:4; I Thessalonians 5:16)*, you respond in the way that is characteristic of a faithful believer in Christ. For example:

   a. After being flogged and threatened by the authorities, the apostles rejoiced that they had been considered worthy to suffer shame for the Name of Jesus Christ *(Acts 5:40-41)*.

   b. Paul and Silas prayed and sang hymns to God in spite of being beaten and imprisoned *(Acts 16:22-25)*. Later, even though imprisoned again, the Apostle Paul continued to rejoice in spite of his sufferings *(Colossians 1:24)*. No matter what trials and sorrows were experienced, Paul continually rejoiced as a servant of God *(II Corinthians 6:4-10)*.

   c. Not only were individuals filled with God's joy in spite of adversity, but groups of believers are likewise described. For example:

      1) The churches in Macedonia were abundantly filled with joy in spite of being afflicted and in great poverty *(II Corinthians 8:2)*;

      2) The recipients of Peter's letter were to be joyful in their fiery trial, since their difficulties meant they were sharing the sufferings of Christ *(I Peter 4:13)*; and

      3) The recipients of the letter to the Hebrews had their property seized yet continued to be joyful, since their hope centered on heavenly values and not earthly circumstances *(Hebrews 10:34)*.

LESSON 6: HOMEWORK

> This week's **HOMEWORK** provides an opportunity for you
> to deal biblically with a specific problem in your life. Also
> presented are scriptural insights concerning difficulties,
> your reactions to them, and their subsequent influence in
> your life (based on *Romans 5:1-5, 8:28-29; I Corinthians 11:31;*
> *II Corinthians 1:3-5; II Timothy 2:15; Titus 2:11-12; James 1:2-4*).

✔ *homework completed*

☐ A. * In your own words, write the meaning of *Romans 8:28-29.* Memorize *Romans 8:28-29* and begin memorizing *Ephesians 4:22-24.* Review past memory verses.

☐ B. * In your devotions this week, use a concordance to find at least two scriptural references that are applicable to the problem on which God wants you to work and complete a **BIBLE STUDY AND APPLICATION FORMAT** (Supplement 3, Page 1) for each reference.

☐ C. * Study **BIBLICAL PRINCIPLES: BIBLICAL BASIS FOR CHANGE** (Lesson 6, Pages 2-3). This lesson has a number of scriptural passages that are foundational for the remainder of this course. You are encouraged to highlight the verses in your Bible that are listed with each biblical principle.

☐ D. * Read **THREE LEVELS OF PROBLEMS** (Lesson 6, Pages 4-5). Write a description of the three levels of a problem as they apply to the problem on which God wants you to work during this course.

☐ E. * Study **BIBLICAL HOPE** (Lesson 6, Pages 6-7). Highlight the referenced verses in your Bible. These explain God's plan for establishing true and lasting hope in your life.

☐ F. Read **BIBLICAL BASIS FOR PEACE AND JOY** (Lesson 6, Pages 8-10). Mark any statements that are presently applicable to you. Following the statements you have marked, look up the verses that are referenced and highlight these verses in your Bible.

☐ G. * To complete the **COURSE EXAM** (Lesson 23) while going through this course, answer questions 11, 12, and 13 under **Open Book Test** (Lesson 23, Page 2).

* *The completion of assignments marked with an asterisk (*) is a prerequisite for further biblical counseling training.*

LESSON 6: STUDY GUIDE FOR DAILY DEVOTIONS
(INCLUDING SCRIPTURE MEMORY AND HOMEWORK)

> This week's **STUDY GUIDE** provides an opportunity for
> you to deal biblically with a specific problem in your life.
> Also presented are scriptural insights concerning
> difficulties, your reactions to them, and their subsequent
> influence in your life *(based on Romans 5:1-5, 8:28-29;*
> *I Corinthians 11:31; II Corinthians 1:3-5; II Timothy 2:15;*
> *Titus 2:11-12; James 1:2-4).*

Scripture Memory

1.   * Memorize *Romans 8:28-29* and begin memorizing *Ephesians 4:22-24.*

2.   With your previous lesson's verses, you now have seven memory verse cards that you can carry throughout the day *(listed in lesson order: Ephesians 2:8-9; Matthew 7:1, 5; II Timothy 3:16-17; II Corinthians 3:5-6; I Corinthians 10:13; Romans 8:28-29; Ephesians 4:22-24).* This week, be faithful in reviewing past memory verses and learning your new verses during your spare moments each day.

Daily Devotional Study Guide

FIRST DAY

1.   Open with prayer.
2.   * Read *Principles 15 and 16* under **BIBLICAL PRINCIPLES: BIBLICAL BASIS FOR CHANGE** (Lesson 6, Pages 2-3). Highlight the verses in your Bible.
3.   * In your own words, write the meaning of *Romans 8:28-29.*
4.   Close with prayer.
5.   Take your seven Scripture memory cards with you throughout the day and review memory verses from previous lessons. Memorize *Romans 8:28-29* and preview *Ephesians 4:22-24.*

SECOND DAY

1.   Open with prayer.
2.   * Read *Principles 17 and 18* under **BIBLICAL PRINCIPLES: BIBLICAL BASIS FOR CHANGE** (Lesson 6, Pages 2-3). Highlight verses not marked previously.
3.   * Read **THREE LEVELS OF PROBLEMS** (Lesson 6, Pages 4-5). Write a description of the three levels of a problem as they apply to the problem on which God wants you to work during this course.
4.   Close with prayer.

THIRD DAY

1.   Open with prayer.
2.   * Read *Principle 19* under **BIBLICAL PRINCIPLES: BIBLICAL BASIS FOR CHANGE** (Lesson 6, Pages 2-3). Highlight the listed verses in your Bible.
3.   * Using a concordance, choose two scriptural references that are applicable to the problem on which God wants you to work. Over the next three days, complete a **BIBLE STUDY AND APPLICATION FORMAT** (Supplement 3, Page 1) for both references that you have chosen.
4.   Close with prayer.

FOURTH DAY

1.   Open with prayer.
2.   * Study **BIBLICAL HOPE** (Lesson 6, Pages 6-7). Look up and highlight the referenced verses. These explain God's plan for establishing true and lasting hope in your life.
3.   * Using one Scripture reference that you chose yesterday, complete a **BIBLE STUDY AND APPLICATION FORMAT** (Supplement 3, Page 1) for the problem on which God wants you to work.
4.   Close with prayer.
5.   How is your progress in Scripture memorization? Be faithful in using spare moments to review and memorize.

FIFTH DAY

1.   Open with prayer.
2.   * Read *Principles 20 and 21* under **BIBLICAL PRINCIPLES: BIBLICAL BASIS FOR CHANGE** (Lesson 6, Pages 2-3) and highlight the listed passages in your Bible.
3.   * With your other chosen reference that is applicable to your problem complete a second **BIBLE STUDY AND APPLICATION FORMAT** (Supplement 3, Page 1).
4.   Close with prayer.

SIXTH DAY

1.   Open with prayer.
2.   * Read *Principles 22 and 23* under **BIBLICAL PRINCIPLES: BIBLICAL BASIS FOR CHANGE** (Lesson 6, Pages 2-3). Highlight your verses accordingly.
3.   Read **BIBLICAL BASIS FOR PEACE AND JOY** (Lesson 6, Pages 8-10). Mark any statements that are presently applicable to you. Following your marked statements, look up the verses that are referenced and highlight these verses in your Bible. This is the first day of a two-day study.
4.   Close with prayer.

SEVENTH DAY

1.   Open with prayer.
2.   * Read *Principles 24, 25, and 26* under **BIBLICAL PRINCIPLES: BIBLICAL BASIS FOR CHANGE** (Lesson 6, Pages 2-3) and highlight verses accordingly.
3.   Complete your study of **BIBLICAL BASIS FOR PEACE AND JOY** (Lesson 6, Pages 8-10) that you began yesterday.
4.   * To complete the **COURSE EXAM** (Lesson 23) while going through this course, answer questions 11, 12, and 13 under **Open Book Test** (Lesson 23, Page 2).
5.   Close with prayer.
6.   Determine the effectiveness of your Scripture memory this week. Ask someone to listen to you recite all of your memory verses with their proper references. Explain how this lesson's Scripture memory *(Romans 8:28-29)* has application to your life.

*   *The completion of assignments marked with an asterisk (*) is a prerequisite for further biblical counseling training.*

LESSON 7

BIBLICAL STRUCTURE FOR CHANGE

"...that, in reference to your former manner of life, you lay aside the old self, which is being corrupted in accordance with the lusts of deceit, and that you be renewed in the spirit of your mind, and put on the new self, which in the likeness of God has been created in righteousness and holiness of the truth."

Ephesians 4:22-24

LESSON 7: BIBLICAL STRUCTURE FOR CHANGE

> You need to become a doer of the Word (be obedient to Scripture) in order to mature in Christ *(based on II Timothy 3:16-17; Hebrews 5:13-14; James 1:22-25; II Peter 1:2-10, esp. verse 10).*

I.   **The purposes of this lesson are:**

   A.   To present the methodology of biblical change that will accomplish spiritual maturity;

   B.   To illustrate how unbiblical thoughts lead to unbiblical deeds; and

   C.   To show how you must cooperate with God's plan in order for your mind to be renewed.

II. **The outline of this lesson**

   A.   Self-Confrontation

      1.   **BIBLICAL PRINCIPLES: BIBLICAL STRUCTURE FOR CHANGE** (Lesson 7, Page 2)

      2.   **BIBLICAL CHANGE IS A PROCESS** (Lesson 7, Pages 3-4)

      3.   **THE EFFECTS OF UNBIBLICAL THOUGHTS, SPEECH, AND ACTIONS** (Lesson 7, Page 5)

      4.   **RENEWING YOUR MIND** (Lesson 7, Pages 6-7)

   B.   Steps for spiritual growth

      1.   **LESSON 7: HOMEWORK** (Lesson 7, Page 8)

      2.   **STUDY GUIDE FOR DAILY DEVOTIONS** (Lesson 7, Pages 9-10)

BIBLICAL PRINCIPLES: BIBLICAL STRUCTURE FOR CHANGE

> Biblical change is initiated in your life through the regenerating power of the Holy Spirit. As a new creation in Christ, you are empowered to make biblical changes in your thoughts, words, and actions as you die to self and lovingly serve God and others *(based on Matthew 22:37-39; Luke 9:23; John 3:5-6; Romans 12:1-2; I Corinthians 10:31; II Corinthians 5:15, 17; Ephesians 4:22-24; Philippians 2:3-8, 3:12-14; Titus 3:5).*

Your steps for biblical change

A. The process

(Principle 27)   Effective and lasting biblical change is a continuing process. You are to obey the commands and guidelines in God's Word for every area of your life (your thoughts, words, and actions) *(Romans 15:4; II Timothy 3:16-17; James 1:21-25; II Peter 1:2-4).* As you stop (put off) the old continuing pattern of sin and begin (put on) the new practice of righteousness and holiness, you are renewed in the spirit of your mind *(Romans 6:11-14, 16-23; 12:1-2; Ephesians 4:22-24; Philippians 2:12-13; Colossians 3:5-17; II Timothy 2:19).*

B. The "put-offs"

(Principle 28)   In order to put off the old sinful habits, you must first identify them by examining (judging) your life in light of God's Word *(Matthew 7:1-5; I Corinthians 11:28-31; II Timothy 3:16-17; Hebrews 4:12).* Once you have specifically identified sins in your life, you must repent of them *(Proverbs 28:13; II Corinthians 7:9-10; Revelation 2:5),* confess them *(I John 1:9),* and immediately put them aside *(Romans 6:12-13a; II Corinthians 10:5; Ephesians 4:25, 29, 31; 5:4; Colossians 3:2, 5-9; II Timothy 2:22a).*

C. The "put-ons"

(Principle 29)   As you put on righteous deeds *(II Timothy 2:22b; Titus 2:11-12)* in the power of the Holy Spirit *(Galatians 5:16; Ephesians 3:16-21, 5:18),* you will glorify God *(I Corinthians 10:31; I Peter 4:11),* demonstrate your love for Him *(Deuteronomy 10:12; Matthew 22:37; I John 5:3; II John 1:6),* and please Him in all things *(II Corinthians 5:9; Colossians 1:10).*

BIBLICAL CHANGE IS A PROCESS

> You may experience conflict within you as you constantly make choices between good and evil, between doing what you want and doing what God wants. You must set your mind to please God instead of yourself *(based on Romans 7:19-25, 8:5-9; II Corinthians 5:15; Galatians 5:17; Philippians 3:12-14; Colossians 3:1-2).*

I. Put-offs and put-ons

A. In order to change your thoughts, words, and actions while following Christ, you must learn and obey God's Word. His Word lists many trangressions (a transgression is a deliberate crossing over of God's boundary between right and wrong). These are to be put off and Christlike deeds are to be put on *(for example: Ephesians 4:22-32; Colossians 3:5-17).* When a "put-off" is listed in Scripture, there is an appropriate "put-on" given, often in the same passage. For example:

Put-off		Put-on
Falsehood	*Ephesians 4:25*	Speaking the truth
Stealing	*Ephesians 4:28*	Working and giving to those in need
Unwholesome speech	*Ephesians 4:29*	Edifying speech, according to the need of the moment
Bitterness, wrath, anger clamor, slander, malice	*Ephesians 4:31-32*	Kindness, tenderheartedness, forgiveness

B. Sometimes, a "put-on" is given in Scripture without an associated "put-off." This instruction is provided by God so you can know His will for your life in those areas where you may be ignorant or neglectful of His way. Putting on biblical deeds that you have previously omitted to practice brings glory to God's name *(Matthew 5:16; I Corinthians 10:31-33).* For example:

1. Make disciples, baptizing and teaching them *(Matthew 28:19-20);*

2. Do all in the name of the Lord Jesus, giving thanks to God through Christ *(Colossians 3:17);*

3. Put on the full armor of God and stand firm *(Ephesians 6:13-20);*

4. Walk in a manner worthy of the Lord, to please Him *(Colossians 1:10);* and

5. Rejoice always, pray without ceasing, in everything give thanks *(I Thessalonians 5:16-18).*

II. Prayer and action

A. Prayer is necessary to the obedient Christian life *(Philippians 4:6-7; Colossians 4:2; I Thessalonians 5:17).* It is the first action you should take and is essential to experience God's peace *(Philippians 4:6-7)* and forgiveness in your life *(I John 1:9).*

B. However, prayer alone will not bring about the fulness of God's plan for your life. You also need to act specifically and obediently *(Matthew 7:24-27; Philippians 2:12-13, 4:9; James 1:22-25; I John 3:22)* by putting off thoughts, words, and actions that dishonor the name of Christ and, in their place, putting on new ways of thinking, speaking, and acting that reflect the character and image of Christ *(Romans 6:6-7, 12-13, 17-19; 8:29; Ephesians 4:29; Colossians 3:1-15, 4:5-6).*

Refer to: **PRAYER PROVIDES COMMUNICATION WITH GOD** *(Lesson 3, Pages 9-12).*

III. Failure and confession

A. If you fail, it is possible to please God again by responding biblically. You do this by acknowledging and repenting of your sins to God, which is part of confession *(I John 1:9).* At the time that is biblically appropriate, confess your sin to those against whom you have sinned *(James 5:16)* with a view to reconciliation *(Matthew 5:23-24; Romans 12:18).*

Refer to: **RECONCILIATION (REMOVING ALL HINDRANCES TO UNITY AND PEACE)** *(Lesson 12, Pages 6-8).*

B. When you confess your sins to God and develop a pattern of recognizing sin and dealing with it God's way, you acknowledge His Lordship *(Psalm 51:1-4; Luke 6:46).* This enables you to have unhindered communication with your Heavenly Father *(Psalm 66:18)* and to have a fruitful prayer life *(I John 3:22).*

C. When you consistently confess your sins to others, you encourage harmonious relationships *(Romans 12:18)* and demonstrate the difference that Jesus makes in your life *(Matthew 5:16; Ephesians 4:32-5:1).*

THE EFFECTS OF UNBIBLICAL THOUGHTS, SPEECH, AND ACTIONS

Living for Jesus Christ requires that you direct your thoughts away from self and toward pleasing the Lord *(based on Romans 12:2; II Corinthians 10:5; Ephesians 4:22-24; Colossians 3:1-2, 5-10).*

Results of focusing on self in your thought life

Hatred *(I John 3:15)*
Rebellion *(I Samuel 15:23)*
Resentment/Bitterness
  (Ephesians 4:31-32)
Selfishness
  (Philippians 2:3-4)

Jealousy/Envy *(Galatians 5:20-21)*
Pride *(Proverbs 16:18, 29:23)*
Anger *(Proverbs 16:32, 29:11;*
  James 1:19-20)
Anxiety *(Philippians 4:6-7)*

Fear *(I John 4:18)*
Lust *(Matthew 5:28)*
Doubt *(James 1:6-8)*

Deceitfulness
  (Proverbs 12:20a, 26:24)

Lead to and increase:

(Matthew 15:18-20;
Romans 1:24-32;
I Corinthians 6:9-10, 12;
James 1:14-15)

May result in:

(Psalm 32:3-4;
I Corinthians 11:28-30;
Galatians 6:7-8;
Colossians 3:25;
I John 5:16)

Unbiblical speech and actions

Lying
Hostility, Disputes
Worrying
Impatience
Treachery, Slander
Unkindness
Intolerance
Grumbling
Bragging
Fornication
Adultery
Murder
Homosexuality

May result in:

(based on Psalm 32:3-4,
38:1-10; Acts 5:1-11,
esp. verses 5 and 10;
I Corinthians 5:1-6,
esp. verse 5; 11:28-30)

Bodily damage

Heart Malfunction
Colitis
Migraine Headaches
High Blood Pressure
Cramps
Spasms
Ulcers
Insomnia
Stomach Disorders
Arthritis
Kidney Disease
Hypertension
Venereal Diseases
Death

RENEWING YOUR MIND

> Your enemy, Satan, will tempt you repeatedly and continually by appealing to your self-oriented feelings and desires. You can resist his onslaughts by cooperating with God's plan to renew your mind. Salvation is the first step in this process, and a committed life of obedience to God's Word will insure that your mind will be continually renewed to increasing Christlikeness *(based on Genesis 3:1-7; Romans 12:2; II Corinthians 2:11, 11:3; Galatians 5:17; Philippians 2:5-8, 13; Hebrews 5:14; James 1:14-15; I Peter 5:8; I John 4:4).*

I. **The renewal of your mind with regard to your growth in Christ**

   A. Renewing your mind is the process by which your thoughts and your will become more and more Christlike. The renewal of your mind is recognized by an increasingly faithful and obedient response to God's Word *(based on Romans 12:1-2; Ephesians 4:22-32; Colossians 3:10-17).*

   B. The consistent renewing of your mind is an integral part of your spiritual development *(Romans 12:2; Ephesians 4:23; Colossians 3:10).*

II. **The renewal of your mind with regard to your personal responsibilities**

   A. Graciously enabled by divine power *(John 15:4-5; Philippians 2:13)*, you are to practice biblical thinking *(II Corinthians 10:5; Philippians 4:8-9; Colossians 3:1-2).*

   B. Your obedience to Scripture furthers the development of a Christlike mind *(Hebrews 5:14; James 1:22-25).* Scripture tells us to:

   1. Hear the Word *(Romans 10:17)* (e.g., by listening to preaching or teaching from God's Word);

   2. Read the Word *(I Timothy 4:13; Revelation 1:3)* (e.g., by having daily devotions);

   3. Study the Word *(II Timothy 2:15)* (e.g., by investigating and learning scripturally based principles of living, accurate doctrine, and godly examples to follow);

   4. Memorize the Word *(Psalm 119:11)* (e.g., by reviewing your memory verse cards throughout the day); and

   5. Meditate on the Word *(Joshua 1:8; Psalm 1:2)* (e.g., by thinking of the personal application of God's promises and commands to you).

   By doing the above, you provide opportunities for the Word of Christ to dwell richly within you *(Colossians 3:16).* Of equal importance, you are to practice the Word especially in known areas of needed biblical change. As you continually do this, the spirit of your mind is being renewed to Christlikeness *(based on Colossians 3:8-10; Hebrews 5:14).*

III. The renewal of your mind within the process of your biblical change

	Your old self	Your new self	Renewing your mind
Hope	Through the Cross of Jesus Christ, your debt of sin has been paid *(Romans 5:6-9; Ephesians 1:7; Colossians 2:13-14),* and your old self has been crucified with Christ *(Romans 6:3-7; Galatians 2:20; Colossians 3:3).*	Since the old self has been put off and the new self has been put on, you are a totally new person and are empowered by the resurrected life of Jesus Christ to be conformed to His image *(Romans 6:4; 8:11, 29; II Corinthians 5:17; Galatians 2:20; Ephesians 4:22-24).*	As a result, you are directed by God's Spirit *(John 14:26, 16:13; Romans 8:14)* and are able to understand the things of God *(I Corinthians 2:10-14),* which are revealed in His Word *(II Timothy 3:16-17; Hebrews 4:12).*
Change	The sinful and destructive practices of your old self are to be put off *(Romans 6:12-13; Ephesians 4:17-22; Colossians 3:5-9; Titus 2:11-12).*	Putting on Christlike characteristics *(Colossians 3:10-17)* leads you to please God and edify others instead of simply living to please yourself *(Luke 9:23-24; Romans 12:16, 15:2; II Corinthians 5:14-15; Galatians 5:13-17; Philippians 2:3-4).*	As a result, your mind is being continually renewed *(Colossians 3:8-10).*
Practice	You are continually to consider yourself dead to sin and free from slavery to sin *(Romans 6:6-7, 11-12)* and self-gratification *(I Peter 1:14).*	Faithful and diligent obedience to the Lord enables you to overcome trials *(James 1:2-4)* and failures *(Philippians 3:13-14; I John 1:9)* and produces Christlike maturity and fruitfulness in your life *(II Peter 1:4-11).*	As a result, continual obedience to the Word of God protects you from delusion and increases your spiritual discernment and sensitivity to sin *(Hebrews 5:14; James 1:22).*

For a more detailed review of God's plan and provisions for you to change biblically, refer to:
YOU CAN CHANGE BIBLICALLY (PART TWO) (Lesson 2, Pages 3-5) and
MAN'S WAY AND GOD'S WAY (PART TWO) (Lesson 4, Pages 2-11)

LESSON 7: HOMEWORK

> "Putting off" unbiblical thoughts, words, and actions and "putting on" new practices of righteousness are vital to having your mind renewed in Christlikeness. This lesson's **HOMEWORK** highlights this principle of biblical change while giving you an opportunity to focus on a particular problem of your life *(based on Romans 12:2; Philippians 4:13; Colossians 3:1-17; Hebrews 5:14; I John 5:1-5).*

✔ *homework completed*

☐ A. * In your own words, write the meaning of *Ephesians 4:22-24.* Memorize *Ephesians 4:22-24* and begin memorizing *Hebrews 5:14* and *James 4:17.* Review past memory verses.

☐ B. * Read **BIBLICAL PRINCIPLES: BIBLICAL STRUCTURE FOR CHANGE** (Lesson 7, Page 2). Look up the referenced verses in your Bible and highlight the verses that you have not marked in previous studies.

☐ C. * As you progress through this week, identify and list at least five (5) incidents in which you recognize the problem that God wants you to work on during this course. Remember, it is through your deeds (thoughts, words, and actions) that you show what is in your heart.

☐ D. Read **BIBLICAL CHANGE IS A PROCESS** (Lesson 7, Pages 3-4). Notice how prayer is to be coupled with "putting off" unbiblical patterns of life while appropriate biblical thoughts, words, and actions are being "put on." Especially note the first step of biblical restoration if you fail by choosing to please yourself instead of the Lord (under **III. Failure and Confession**).

☐ E. Study **THE EFFECTS OF UNBIBLICAL THOUGHTS, SPEECH, AND ACTIONS** (Lesson 7, Page 5). Observe the relationship among unbiblical thoughts, unbiblical deeds, and the possible harm that can occur to your body when you focus on self.

☐ F. Read **RENEWING YOUR MIND** (Lesson 7, Pages 6-7), noting the relationship between obedience to God's Word and the renewal of your mind. If you consistently fail by continuing to please yourself instead of the Lord, check the steps under **II. The renewal of your mind with regard to your personal responsibilities**, under point B., to see if your failure can be traced to a breakdown in one of these areas. Take corrective action immediately.

☐ G. * In conjunction with this lesson, answer question 14 under **Open Book Test** (Lesson 23, Page 2).

　*　 *The completion of assignments marked with an asterisk (*) is a prerequisite for further biblical counseling training.*

LESSON 7: STUDY GUIDE FOR DAILY DEVOTIONS
(INCLUDING SCRIPTURE MEMORY AND HOMEWORK)

> "Putting off" unbiblical thoughts, words, and actions and "putting on" new practices of righteousness are vital to having your mind renewed in Christlikeness. This lesson's **STUDY GUIDE** highlights this principle of biblical change while giving you an opportunity to focus on a particular problem of your life *(based on Romans 12:2; Philippians 4:13; Colossians 3:1-17; Hebrews 5:14; I John 5:1-5).*

Scripture Memory

1. * Memorize *Ephesians 4:22-24* and begin memorizing *Hebrews 5:14* and *James 4:17.*
2. Carry your memory verse cards from previous weeks along with this week's memory verses. Review your Scriptures in your spare moments throughout the day.

Daily Devotional Study Guide

FIRST DAY

1. Open in prayer.
2. * Read *Principle 27* under **BIBLICAL PRINCIPLES: BIBLICAL STRUCTURE FOR CHANGE** (Lesson 7, Page 2). Highlight the referenced verses in your Bible.
3. * Begin to identify and list at least five (5) incidents in which you recognize the problem that God wants you to work on during this course. This is the first day in a seven-day exercise of learning to judge yourself in an accurate, biblical manner. You should carry your list with you throughout the day and note incidents as they occur. Keep in mind that you are to identify the logs that you need to remove from your own life.
4. * In your own words, write the meaning of *Ephesians 4:22-24.*
5. Close in prayer.

SECOND DAY

1. Open in prayer.
2. * Read *Principle 28* under **BIBLICAL PRINCIPLES: BIBLICAL STRUCTURE FOR CHANGE** (Lesson 7, Page 2). Highlight the listed verses in your Bible.
3. * Stay current in making your list of incidents that happened today.
4. Close in prayer.

THIRD DAY

1. Open in prayer.
2. * Read *Principle 29* under **BIBLICAL PRINCIPLES: BIBLICAL STRUCTURE FOR CHANGE** (Lesson 7, Page 2). Highlight the referenced verses in your Bible.
3. * Complete your list of deeds that show your problem for today. (Are you carrying this form with you to gather accurate information on your problem?)
4. Close in prayer.
5. Are you faithful in memorization of Scripture? Take time to review all of your verses with their proper Scripture references.

FOURTH DAY

1. Open in prayer.
2. * Fill out your list of sinful deeds for today.
3. Read **BIBLICAL CHANGE IS A PROCESS** (Lesson 7, Pages 3-4). Notice how prayer, biblical "put-offs" and "put-ons," plus confession after failure are vital to a biblical pattern of living.
4. Close in prayer.

FIFTH DAY

1. Open in prayer.
2. * Complete your list of sinful deeds for today.
3. Study **THE EFFECTS OF UNBIBLICAL THOUGHTS, SPEECH, AND ACTIONS** (Lesson 7, Page 5).
4. Close in prayer.

SIXTH DAY

1. Open in prayer.
2. * Stay current in completing your list of sinful deeds.
3. Study **RENEWING YOUR MIND** (Lesson 7, Pages 6-7), noting the relationship between obedience to God's Word and the renewal of your mind. This is the first day of a two-day study.
4. Close in prayer.

SEVENTH DAY

1. Open in prayer.
2. * Complete your final day of identifying deeds that show your problem. Circle those activities, situations, locations, or people which have been listed at least twice on the list.
3. Complete your study of **RENEWING YOUR MIND** (Lesson 7, Pages 6-7). If you consistently fail by continuing to please yourself instead of the Lord, check the steps under **II. The renewal of your mind with regard to your personal responsibilities**, under point B., to see if your failure can be traced to a breakdown in one of these areas. Take corrective action immediately.
4. * In conjunction with this lesson, answer question 14 under **Open Book Test** (Lesson 23, Page 2).
5. Close in prayer.
6. Review your memory verses for the week. Are you continuing to review your verses at spare moments throughout the day? Ask a friend to listen to the verses you have memorized this week; remember to tell how this portion of God's Word applies to your life.

---

*   *The completion of assignments marked with an asterisk (*) is a prerequisite for further biblical counseling training.*

LESSON 8

BIBLICAL PRACTICE ACHIEVES LASTING CHANGE

"But solid food is for the mature, who because of practice have their senses trained to discern good and evil."

Hebrews 5:14

"Therefore, to one who knows the right thing to do, and does not do it, to him it is sin."

James 4:17

LESSON 8: BIBLICAL PRACTICE ACHIEVES LASTING CHANGE

> Specific, biblical steps of obedience demonstrate and deepen your love for the Lord and lead to Christlike changes that God intends and plans for your life *(based on John 14:15; Romans 8:29, 12:1-2; Philippians 2:12-13; Hebrews 5:14).* Lasting biblical change is a result of faithful, disciplined living that is in accordance with God's Word *(based on Luke 16:10; I Timothy 4:7-8; II Peter 1:2-10).*

I.   **The purposes of this lesson are:**

A.   To show that biblical practice is necessary for spiritual growth leading to maturity;

B.   To present a specific plan to help you change biblically;

C.   To illustrate how trials (tests and temptations) can affect your life; and

D.   To give you an opportunity to develop a biblical plan to overcome a specific problem in your life.

II. **The outline of this lesson**

A.   Self-Confrontation

1.   **BIBLICAL PRINCIPLES: BIBLICAL PRACTICE ACHIEVES LASTING CHANGE** (Lesson 8, Page 2)

2.   **BIBLICAL PERSPECTIVE ON TESTS AND TEMPTATIONS** (Lesson 8, Pages 3-7)

3.   **PRACTICAL STEPS FOR ACHIEVING BIBLICAL CHANGE** (Lesson 8, Pages 8-10)

B.   Steps for spiritual growth

1.   **LESSON 8: HOMEWORK** (Lesson 8, Page 11)

2.   **STUDY GUIDE FOR DAILY DEVOTIONS** (Lesson 8, Pages 12-13)

3.   **GUIDELINES: VICTORY OVER FAILURES WORKSHEET** (Supplement 7) and **VICTORY OVER FAILURES WORKSHEET** (Supplement 8)

4.   **GUIDELINES: THE "THINK AND DO" LIST** (Supplement 9) and **"THINK AND DO" LIST** (Supplement 10)

BIBLICAL PRINCIPLES: BIBLICAL PRACTICE ACHIEVES LASTING CHANGE

> Biblical change that pleases and glorifies the Lord requires more than merely understanding correct doctrines. Only as you practice God's Word in every area of your life will you see lasting change *(based on Matthew 7:24-27; Luke 6:39-49; I Corinthians 10:31; II Corinthians 5:9; James 1:21-25, 4:17).*

Your practice of biblical change

A. Starting

(Principle 30)   Change results when you remember from where you have fallen, repent, and do the deeds you did when you first received the Lord Jesus into your life *(Revelation 2:4-5).* Acknowledge the Lordship of Jesus Christ and make a commitment to be a doer of the Word *(Luke 6:46-49).* If you are merely a hearer and not a doer of the Word, then you remain foolish *(Matthew 7:24-27),* spiritually deluded *(James 1:22),* and spiritually immature *(I Corinthians 3:1-3; Hebrews 5:11-13; James 1:22-24).*

B. Continuing

(Principle 31)   To continue the process of biblical change, you must faithfully practice your daily responsibilities *(Ephesians 5:15-16; Colossians 3:23-24; James 4:17)* and discipline yourself toward godliness *(I Timothy 4:7-11; II Peter 1:5-11; I John 3:7).* As you continue to be a doer of the Word, your senses will be trained to discern good and evil *(Hebrews 5:14).* Your spiritual growth is a sovereign work of God *(Galatians 5:22-23; Philippians 1:6, 2:13; Hebrews 12:2a, 13:20-21)* that is divinely linked to your living in a biblical manner *(Ephesians 2:10, 4:14-16; I Timothy 4:7-8; Hebrews 13:20-21; I Peter 2:2; II Peter 1:5-11).*

C. Maturing

(Principle 32)   In order to mature (grow up) in Christ, you must persevere in doing what is good in the Lord's sight by being obedient to Scripture *(Luke 17:10; John 14:15; Romans 2:7; I Corinthians 15:58; Galatians 6:9; James 1:22-25).* Instead of living according to your self-centered feelings and desires *(II Corinthians 5:15; Galatians 5:16-17; I Peter 2:19-20, 4:1-6),* continue to press forward to your high calling in Christ Jesus *(Ephesians 4:1; Philippians 3:12-14; Hebrews 6:1-3).* Discipline your thought life *(II Corinthians 10:5; Colossians 3:1-2; Philippians 4:8),* speak in a manner that is helpful to others *(Ephesians 4:29; Colossians 4:6),* and faithfully love others in a biblical manner *(Matthew 22:39; I Corinthians 13:4-8a; I John 4:7-8, 10-11, 20).* Do not focus on physical or immediate results; instead, focus on eternal values in order to mature in Christ *(II Corinthians 4:17-18; Colossians 3:1-2; I Timothy 4:7-8; II Peter 1:4-10),* to glorify God *(I Corinthians 10:31),* and to please the Lord in all things *(II Corinthians 5:9; Colossians 1:10).*

BIBLICAL PERSPECTIVE ON TESTS AND TEMPTATIONS

> Every person in the world, including yourself, will encounter various trials throughout life. Satan seeks to defeat you by tempting you to trust your own wisdom, to live according to your self-centered feelings, and to gratify the desires of your flesh. In contrast, God's will is for you to be an overwhelming conqueror in all of these tests for His honor and glory *(based on Genesis 3:1-6; Proverbs 14:12; Matthew 5:45; Romans 8:31-39; Galatians 2:20, 5:16-17; I Peter 5:8; I John 2:16-17).*

I. **The difference between tests and temptations**

   A. A test is an opportunity for you to practice Christlikeness by obeying God's Word, thus giving honor to Jesus Christ *(based on Job 23:10; Romans 5:3-5; II Corinthians 2:9; James 1:2-4, 12; I Peter 1:6-7).*

   B. A temptation, which cannot originate from God, is a solicitation for you to disobey God's Word and to gratify your fleshly desires. When you yield to temptation, you inevitably experience consequences *(based on I Thessalonians 3:5; I Timothy 6:9; James 1:13-15).*

   C. In any circumstance, the appeal to your self-centered feelings and fleshly desires is used by Satan as a temptation to entice you to sin *(Genesis 3:1-7; II Samuel chapter 11; James 1:14-15).* In stark contrast, the same circumstance is used by God as a test to help strengthen you as you obey His Word. Your response in this circumstance determines whether you will stand firm in your faith and please God or fall to temptation and please yourself *(based on Galatians 5:16-17; Colossians 1:10; Hebrews 4:15; James 4:7-10; I Peter 5:8-9).*

II. **God and tests**

   A. God tests individuals *(Genesis 22:1-19; Job 1:8-12, 2:3-6; Daniel 3:17-18, 28; Jonah chapters 1-4; Luke 22:31-34).* He also tests groups of people *(Exodus 16:4, 20:20; Deuteronomy 8:2, 16; 13:1-4; Judges 2:22, 3:1; Hebrews 10:32-39; I Peter 1:6-9, 4:12-19).* God tests both the righteous and the wicked *(Psalm 11:4-7),* and He uses tests to refine His people *(Job 23:10; Psalm 66:10; Romans 5:3-5; James 1:2-4; I Peter 1:6-7).*

   B. God's tests are designed to strengthen your commitment to follow Him and obey His Word, no matter what the cost. For your benefit and instruction *(Romans 15:4),* the Old Testament records examples of God testing His people regarding their obedience *(Genesis 22:1-19; Exodus 15:22-26, 20:20; Deuteronomy 8:2; Judges 2:21-23; Malachi 3:10).* This same emphasis on obedience to God is recorded in the life of Jesus *(Philippians 2:5-8; Hebrews 5:8)* as well as in the lives of His followers *(John 6:52-69; Acts 6:8 - 7:60; 9:10-17; 11:1-18).*

   C. God forbids people to test (tempt) Him and His character *(Deuteronomy 6:16; Matthew 4:7; I Corinthians 10:9; Hebrews 3:7-11),* unless He specifically asks them to do so *(Malachi 3:10).* People test (tempt) God when they forget His past blessings and power exercised on their behalf, when they harden their hearts, and when they fail to live by His Word *(Numbers 14:22-23; Psalm 78:40-42, 56-64; 95:8-9; 106:13-15)*. It is important to remember that God will discipline people when they test Him, because testing the Lord is in itself an act of disobedience and disbelief *(Psalm 95:8-11; Acts 5:1-10; I Corinthians 10:9)*.

D. God promises to rescue His people in any difficulty *(Psalm 34:19; II Peter 2:9)*. Scripture states that God will never allow any temptation to be more than His children can bear but will always provide a way of escape from sin *(I Corinthians 10:13)*.

III. Satan and temptations to self-gratification

A. Satan's very nature is to tempt (solicit to do evil) *(Matthew 4:3; I Thessalonians 3:5)*, and he lives to devour people *(I Peter 5:8)*.

B. As the ruler of this world *(John 12:31; Ephesians 2:2)*, Satan uses the three attractions of the world – the lust of the flesh (gratification of desires and living by one's feelings), the lust of the eyes (coveting, greed, desire for more), and the boastful pride of life (self-centered living) *(I John 2:16)* – as an enticement for you to do evil. His diabolical efforts *(II Corinthians 2:11; Ephesians 6:11)* are designed to seduce you away from your devotion to Jesus Christ *(II Corinthians 11:3)* so you will gratify your lusts and selfish desires *(James 1:13-15)*.

1. In Satan's initial temptation of mankind *(Genesis 3:1-6)*, he used all three worldly avenues of attraction *(I John 2:16)*. In viewing the forbidden tree, Eve noticed that it was "good for food" (lust of the flesh), "a delight to the eyes" (lust of the eyes), and "desirable to make one wise" (pride of life). Eve became deceived, yielded to temptation, and chose to disobey God. Adam also yielded to temptation and willfully chose to sin *(Genesis 3:6)*.

2. In Satan's temptation of Job *(Job 1:8-2:7)*, Satan appealed to Job's self-centered feelings and desire for self-gratification by taking away Job's possessions, his children and servants, his health, and his notable position of prestige among his contemporaries. All of these trials were aimed at the lust of the flesh, the lust of the eyes, and the pride of life; but Job was not overcome in these specific trials because he trusted God and did not yield to his own self-centered feelings and desires *(Job 23:10-12, 42:1-6)*.

3. In Satan's initial temptation of Jesus, he tempted our Lord through the three attractions of the world. Satan tempted Jesus through hunger and challenged Him to turn stones into bread (lust of the flesh), asked Jesus to throw Himself off the temple (pride of life), and promised Jesus the kingdoms of the world (lust of the eyes). However, Jesus overcame this temptation by obeying God and His Word *(Matthew 4:1-11)*.

IV. Three Levels of Temptation

A. For your instruction, Scripture records examples of those who yielded to the appeal of temptation *(Romans 15:4)*. (Refer above to **III. Satan and temptations to self-gratification**, B. 1.). For example:

1. Eve was tempted by the lust of the flesh *("saw that the tree was good for food" – Genesis 3:6)*, the lust of the eyes *("saw that it was a delight to the eyes" – Genesis 3:6)*, and the pride of life *("was desirable to make one wise" – Genesis 3:6)*.

Notice the failure to resist temptation at the "feeling," "doing," and "heart" levels of life.

a. Failure at the "feeling" level began when gratifying the flesh became more important than remaining obedient to God. Not surprisingly, after giving in to temptation, the "feeling level" was dominated by fear *(Genesis 3:10)*.

b. Adam and Eve's failure at the "doing" level was evidenced when they listened to Satan instead of God, ate the fruit, tried to hide their sin by hiding themselves, and tried to shift the blame for their sinful behavior to others *(Genesis 3:2-13)*.

c. Their failure at the "feeling" and "doing" levels revealed the orientation of their "heart," which was directed at pleasing themselves instead of pleasing God. Their unrepentant, self-centered hearts were also evidenced in their failure to confess their sin and ask for forgiveness from the Lord and from one another *(Genesis 3:8-24)*.

2. David was tempted by the lust of the eyes *("he saw a woman bathing and the woman was very beautiful"* – II Samuel 11:2), the lust of the flesh, and the pride of life *("Is this not Bathsheba, the daughter of Eliam, the wife of Uriah the Hittite? And David sent messengers and took her ..."* – II Samuel 11:3-4).

Notice how the "feeling," "doing," and "heart" levels were affected in David's response to temptation.

a. David failed at the "feeling" level when he responded to his purely physical attraction to Bathsheba.

b. David failed at the "doing" level when he deliberately watched Bathsheba's nakedness, made inquiry about the woman, committed adultery with her, and subsequently planned her husband's death.

c. David exhibited his heart's self-centeredness by taking another man's wife when he already had many wives and by trying to hide his sin *(II Samuel 12:7-9)*. Even though David later repented at the "heart" level *(II Samuel 12:13; Psalm 32:3-5; Psalm 51)*, he still suffered the consequences of his sin *(II Samuel 12:10-12, 14; Colossians 3:25)*.

B. Jesus' resistance to temptation and His defeat of Satan are recorded in Scripture to give you hope *(Matthew 4:1-11)* and to give you confidence that you have a High Priest who did not sin *(Hebrews 4:15-16)* (Refer back to **III. Satan and temptations to self-gratification**, B. 3. on Page 4).

1. Jesus was tempted by the lust of the flesh *("... If you are the Son of God, command that these stones become bread."* – Matthew 4:3), the pride of life *("... If you are the Son of God throw yourself down for it is written, 'He will give His angels charge concerning you; and on their hands they will bear you up, lest you strike your foot against a stone.' "* – Matthew 4:6), and the lust of the eyes *("... All these things will I give You, if You fall down and worship me."* – Matthew 4:9).

Jesus was an overwhelming conqueror at the "feeling" level, "doing" level, and "heart" level in this temptation, leaving an example for you to follow *(Matthew 4:1-11; Hebrews 2:18, 4:15-16)*.

a. Jesus, with an unwavering focus away from Himself and toward pleasing the Father, had no place for self-centered feelings as He chose to live according to God's Word.

b. Our Lord was victorious at the "doing" level when He responded to each temptation with an answer from God's Word and refused to do what

Satan asked. Notice that Jesus Christ's answers from the Scriptures were not given to become a point of discussion regarding the temptation. Rather, Jesus stated these to end any further talk of the temptation. He stood firmly and confidently on the Word of God.

    c.   At the heart level, Jesus revealed His purity (holiness) by His unwavering commitment to please and obey God the Father by resisting Satan and not giving temptation any foothold in His mind.

  2. Jesus, tempted in all points as you are *(Matthew 4:1-11; I John 2:16-17)*, never sinned. Thus, He understands the power of temptation and your weakness and will assist you in your time of need *(Hebrews 2:18, 4:15-16)*.

V. Your tests and temptations (a review to give you hope)

A.   God cannot be tempted by evil and does not tempt you *(James 1:13)*.

B.   The intent of temptation is to entice you to please yourself instead of being obedient to God and His Word *(examples of giving in to temptation: Genesis 3:1-7; II Samuel chapter 11; example of not giving in to temptation: Matthew 4:3-11)*. Temptation is directed by Satan *(II Corinthians 11:3; I Thessalonians 3:5)* to appeal to your flesh (gratification of your desires and/or living by your self-centered feelings) *(James 1:14)*. However, the decision to sin or to obey God's Word and resist temptation victoriously is yours *(Joshua 24:15; Psalm 119:101; Romans 6:12-22; I Corinthians 6:18-20; Galatians 5:16-17)*.

C.   Being led by feelings and yielding to the gratification of your flesh characterizes one's pattern of living prior to salvation in the Lord Jesus Christ. Thus, apart from Jesus, giving in to temptation cannot be avoided and is a way of life for the natural man *(Ephesians 2:3; Titus 3:3)*. When Jesus comes into your life, obedience to God conflicts with the gratification of fleshly desires. However, God's Spirit within you gives you the power to overcome temptation and live for Him *(Romans 6:16, 8:12-14; Galatians 5:16-17; I Peter 1:14-15, 4:1-2)*.

D.   Tests and related sufferings are common to every follower of Jesus. These trials enable you to share the sufferings of Christ and allow you to follow His example of obedient, sacrificial living *(Romans 8:17; II Corinthians 6:4-11; Philippians 1:29; Hebrews 5:8; I Peter 2:19-21, 4:12)*. While you may be distressed in various tests, any suffering you experience is not to be compared with the value of knowing Jesus Christ *(Philippians 3:8-10)* and cannot compare with the glory that is to be revealed *(Romans 8:18; II Corinthians 4:16-18)*. Any suffering that you have is just for a little while; and God promises to perfect (mature), confirm, strengthen, and establish you after you experience this suffering *(I Peter 5:10)*.

E.   Those who remain faithful in trials (tests or temptations) prove the reality of their faith *(James 1:12; I Peter 1:6-7)* and will be rewarded by the Lord *(James 1:12; Revelation 2:10)*.

F.   You will never face any temptation that is not common to man. In any situation, God has promised that you will never have more than you can bear and that He will be faithful to give you a way of escape from sin *(I Corinthians 10:13; II Peter 2:9)*. No matter what tests may come your way, God has promised to deliver you *(Psalm 34:19)*; therefore, you can be an overwhelming conqueror through Jesus Christ *(Romans 8:35-39)*.

G. Your trials are used by God to develop Christlike character in your life and are to be received with joy *(Romans 5:3-5; James 1:2-4)*. These trials are designed to show forth the power of God and the life of Jesus Christ within you *(II Corinthians 4:7-11)*.

H. Jesus, as your High Priest, was tempted in all things as you are, yet without sin. Therefore, He is able to provide mercy and grace to help in any difficulty, no matter how prolonged the trial may be *(Hebrews 2:18, 4:15-16)*.

PRACTICAL STEPS FOR ACHIEVING BIBLICAL CHANGE

> Making biblical changes in your life requires prayerful and purposeful action *(based on Matthew 7:24-25; Romans 6:12-13; Colossians 3:5-14; I Thessalonians 5:17; Titus 2:11-12; James 1:22-25).*

I. **Respond immediately to your need for biblical change** *(Psalm 37:27; Proverbs 3:5-8; Romans 6:1-4; Ephesians 4:22-24; Colossians 3:5-14; Titus 2:11-12; James 1:22-25).*

   A. Ask God for wisdom *(James 1:5).*

   B. Be subject to (place yourself under the control of) the Holy Spirit, who dwells within you *(John 14:15-18, 26; Romans 8:9-11; Galatians 5:16; Ephesians 5:18).*

   C. Conduct a thorough self-evaluation and make a list of all the ways you have failed to think, speak, and act in a biblical manner. These are your "put-offs" as identified by God in His Word *(for example: Romans 6:12-14; Ephesians 4:25-31; Colossians 3:8-9).*

   D. Confess these unbiblical deeds (thoughts, words, and actions) to the Lord *(based on Matthew 7:1-5; I Corinthians 11:31; I John 1:9).*

   E. Make a list of the biblical "put-ons" that are to replace your unbiblical thoughts, words, and actions *(based on Romans 6:19; Ephesians 4:25, 28-29, 32; Colossians 3:10, 12-17; II Peter 1:5-8).*

   F. Develop a **basic plan** for living a changed life on a daily basis. Your basic plan should list specific steps by which your sinful "put-offs" are replaced by biblical "put-ons" *(based on Ephesians 2:10; 4:1, 25-32; Colossians 2:6, 3:1-17)* and should include:

      1. Prayer *(Philippians 4:6-7; Colossians 4:2; I Thessalonians 5:17);*

      2. Study of Scripture, especially to find out how God's Word relates to changes necessary in your life *(II Timothy 2:15);*

      3. Scripture memory, which should be focused on God's answers to the temptation(s) in which you are prone to sin *(Psalm 119:11);*

      4. Avoidance of all forms (i.e., the appearance) of evil *(I Thessalonians 5:22);*

      5. Obedience to God in all things *(Matthew 7:24; John 14:15; I John 5:3)* instead of pleasing "self" by gratifying fleshly desires *(Galatians 5:16-17; II Timothy 2:22a; Titus 2:12);*

      6. Consistent and faithful fellowship, worship, and ministry in the Body of Christ *(Hebrews 10:24-25; I Peter 4:10);* and

      7. Continual biblical self-evaluation *(Matthew 7:1-5; I Corinthians 11:31)* dealing with thoughts *(II Corinthians 10:5; Philippians 4:8-9; Colossians 3:1-2),* words *(Ephesians 4:29; Colossians 4:6),* and actions *(Matthew 5:16; Ephesians 2:10; Colossians 1:10).* In biblically evaluating your thoughts, words, or actions in any situation, answer the following questions. You should memorize both the questions and the referenced verses.

a.   Is this profitable (in other words, does this contribute toward the development of godly traits or help to accomplish biblical responsibilities in my life or in the lives of others) *(I Corinthians 6:12, 10:23a)*?

b.   Does this bring me under its power or am I controlled by it in any way *(I Corinthians 6:12)*?

c.   Is this an area of spiritual weakness (a stumbling block) in my life *(Matthew 5:29-30, 18:8-9)*?

d.   Could this lead another believer in Christ to stumble *(Romans 14:13; I Corinthians 8:9-13)*?

e.   Does this edify (build up) others or, stated in another way, is this the biblically loving thing to do *(Romans 14:19; I Corinthians 10:23-24)*?

f.   Does this glorify God *(Matthew 5:16; I Corinthians 10:31)*?

G.   Develop a **contingency plan** to deal immediately with temptation when it occurs *(I Peter 5:8-9)*. Remember that sin's power over you has been broken *(Romans 6:4-14)* so that you can overcome temptation and live righteously *(I Corinthians 10:13; I John 5:4-5, 18)*. Your **contingency plan** should include:

1.   Prayer for wisdom, direction, and grace to withstand the temptation *(Philippians 4:6-7; I Thessalonians 5:17; Hebrews 4:16; James 1:5)*;

2.   Biblical thoughts *(II Corinthians 10:5; Philippians 4:8-9; Colossians 3:2)*, utilizing Scripture memory *(Psalm 119:11)* and remembering to stay dependent on God *(James 4:7)*;

The questions and verses to be memorized (listed above under F., point 7.) will help you gain God's perspective in your thoughts when faced with any temptation.

3.   Biblical speech *(Ephesians 4:29; Colossians 4:6)*, especially quoting Scripture *(Psalm 119:11; Matthew 4:3-10)* and giving a reason for the hope within you to others *(I Peter 3:15)*; and

4.   Biblical action: flee temptation *(Genesis 39:7-12; I Corinthians 6:18; II Timothy 2:22a)*. If prohibited from fleeing temptation immediately, remain obedient to Scripture as Jesus did in His temptation *(Matthew 4:1-11)*, in order for God to provide you with strength and a way of escape in which you will not sin *(I Corinthians 10:13)*.

H.   Whenever possible or necessary, obtain help from others *(Proverbs 11:14, 15:22; Ecclesiastes 4:9-10, 12; I Corinthians 12:25-27; Galatians 6:1-2; II Timothy 2:22)*.

To develop both your basic plan for biblical living and your contingency plan for overcoming temptation, refer to:
GUIDELINES: VICTORY OVER FAILURES WORKSHEET *(Supplement 7) and*
GUIDELINES: THE "THINK AND DO" LIST *(Supplement 9)*

Note: Both your basic plan and contingency plan are coordinated with the five steps for renewing your mind, listed in RENEWING YOUR MIND (Lesson 7, Page 6) under II. The renewal of your mind with regard to your personal responsibilities, point B.

II.   **Consistently and faithfully practice your new biblical pattern for daily living *(Galatians 6:9; Philippians 4:9; Hebrews 5:14; James 1:25)*.**

III. **If you sin and respond biblically to your failure, you can rely on God's sustaining care *(Psalm 37:24, 145:14)* as you return quickly to your obedient walk in Christ *(Proverbs 24:16; I John 5:4-5).***

   A.   Whenever you fail, you should:

   1.   Identify your failure *(Matthew 7:1-5; I Corinthians 11:31)* and confess your sin to God *(Psalm 51:1-4; I John 1:9);*

   2.   Confess your sins to those against whom you have sinned *(James 5:16);*

   3.   Show the deeds of repentance corresponding to this change in direction *(based on James 4:7-10; Revelation 2:4-5);* and

   4.   Reconstruct or revise your **basic** and/or **contingency plans** *(Philippians 2:12-13; 3:12-14),* remembering that God has promised you victory over failures *(Proverbs 24:16; II Corinthians 2:14; I John 5:4-5, 18).*

   B.   Begin again to live God's way *(Romans 12:2; Philippians 3:13-14; Revelation 2:5),* not dwelling on past failures *(Philippians 3:13-14);* since God has completely forgiven you *(I John 1:9)* and is continuing to perfect His work in you *(Philippians 1:6, 2:13).*

LESSON 8: HOMEWORK

> This lesson is specifically designed to help you take measurable steps of practical obedience to God's Word in order to accomplish biblical changes in your life. You must be diligent to carry out faithfully the changes that God's Word directs you to make *(based on Luke 6:46; John 14:23-24; I Corinthians 4:2-5; Ephesians 5:15-16; I Timothy 4:7; II Peter 1:2-10).*

✔ *homework completed*

☐ A.   * In your own words, write the meaning of *Hebrews 5:14* and *James 4:17.* Memorize *Hebrews 5:14* and *James 4:17* and begin memorizing *Luke 9:23-24.*

☐ B.   * Read **BIBLICAL PRINCIPLES: BIBLICAL PRACTICE ACHIEVES LASTING CHANGE** (Lesson 8, Page 2). Look up the referenced verses and highlight the verses in your Bible that you have not marked in previous studies.

☐ C.   Study **BIBLICAL PERSPECTIVE ON TESTS AND TEMPTATIONS** (Lesson 8, Pages 3-7). Notice how "tests" are directed at your commitment to obey God's Word, while "temptations" appeal to your self-centered feelings and fleshly desires. Especially note how falling to temptation affects all three levels of problems (feeling, doing, and heart). Look up the referenced verses to help you understand this vital area of spiritual development.

☐ D.   Study the overview of biblical change presented in **PRACTICAL STEPS FOR ACHIEVING BIBLICAL CHANGE** (Lesson 8, Pages 8-10). Place a check by the steps that you need to take to make biblical changes in your life or to recover biblically from failure.

☐ E.   * During your daily devotional time, begin to apply biblical solutions to the problem that God wants you to work on during this course by completing a **VICTORY OVER FAILURES WORKSHEET** (Supplement 8, Pages 1-2). Before starting on this worksheet, carefully read the **GUIDELINES: VICTORY OVER FAILURES WORKSHEET** (Supplement 7). *You may make copies of the VICTORY OVER FAILURES WORKSHEET (Supplement 8, Pages 1-2) for your personal use.*

☐ F.   * To further your understanding of how to make biblical changes in your life, read **GUIDELINES: THE "THINK AND DO" LIST** (Supplement 9). Study the **"THINK AND DO" LIST - EXPLANATION** (Supplement 10, Page 2). Note the completed **"THINK AND DO" LIST - EXAMPLE** (Supplement 10, Page 3). A blank **"THINK AND DO" LIST** is also provided for your use (Supplement 10, Page 1). *You may make copies of the "THINK AND DO" LIST (Supplement 10, Page 1) for your personal use.*

☐ G.   * In conjunction with this lesson, respond to statement 15 under **Open Book Test** (Lesson 23, Page 2).

   *   *The completion of assignments marked with an asterisk (*) is a prerequisite for further biblical counseling training.*

LESSON 8: STUDY GUIDE FOR DAILY DEVOTIONS
(INCLUDING SCRIPTURE MEMORY AND HOMEWORK)

> This lesson is specifically designed to help you to take measurable steps of practical obedience to God's Word in order to accomplish biblical changes in your life. You must be diligent to carry out faithfully the changes that God's Word directs you to make *(based on Luke 6:46; John 14:23-24; I Corinthians 4:2-5; Ephesians 5:15-16; I Timothy 4:7; II Peter 1:2-10).*

Scripture Memory

1. * Memorize *Hebrews 5:14* and *James 4:17*; begin memorizing *Luke 9:23-24*.
2. Carry your memory verse cards from previous weeks along with this week's memory verses. Review your Scriptures in your spare moments throughout the day.

Daily Devotional Study Guide

FIRST DAY

1. Open in prayer.
2. * Read *Principle 30* under **BIBLICAL PRINCIPLES: BIBLICAL PRACTICE ACHIEVES LASTING CHANGE** (Lesson 8, Page 2). Highlight the indicated verses in your Bible.
3. * In preparing to work on the problem that God wants you to overcome, read through **GUIDELINES: VICTORY OVER FAILURES WORKSHEET** (Supplement 7).
4. * In your own words, write the meaning of *Hebrews 5:14* and *James 4:17*.
5. Close in prayer.

SECOND DAY

1. Open in prayer.
2. * Read *Principle 31* under **BIBLICAL PRINCIPLES: BIBLICAL PRACTICE ACHIEVES LASTING CHANGE** (Lesson 8, Page 2). Highlight the indicated verses in your Bible.
3. * Review **GUIDELINES: VICTORY OVER FAILURES WORKSHEET** (Supplement 7). Complete columns 1 and 2 of your **VICTORY OVER FAILURES WORKSHEET** (Supplement 8, Pages 1-2) for the problem that God wants you to overcome.
4. * Read **GUIDELINES: THE "THINK AND DO" LIST** (Supplement 9). Study the **"THINK AND DO" LIST - EXPLANATION** (Supplement 10, Page 2). Note the completed **"THINK AND DO" LIST - EXAMPLE** (Supplement 10, Page 3).
5. Close in prayer.

THIRD DAY

1. Open in prayer.
2. * Read *Principle 32* under **BIBLICAL PRINCIPLES: BIBLICAL PRACTICE ACHIEVES LASTING CHANGE** (Lesson 8, Page 2). Highlight the referenced verses in your Bible.
3. * Continue to work on your **VICTORY OVER FAILURES WORKSHEET** (Supplement 8, Pages 1-2) by completing column 3.
4. Close in prayer.

FOURTH DAY

    1.   Open in prayer.

    2.   Read **BIBLICAL PERSPECTIVE ON TESTS AND TEMPTATIONS** (Lesson 8, Pages 3-7), noting how "tests" are directed at your commitment to obey God and His Word while "temptations" appeal to your self-centered feelings and fleshly desires. Especially note how falling to temptation affects all three levels of problems (feeling, doing, and heart). Look up the referenced verses to help you understand this vital area of spiritual development. This is the first day of a three-day study.

    3.   * Complete column 4 of your **VICTORY OVER FAILURES WORKSHEET** (Supplement 8, Pages 1-2) by formulating a biblical plan to overcome your problem.

    4.   Close in prayer.

    5.   Have you been faithful to memorize Scripture and review past memory verses?

FIFTH DAY

    1.   Open in prayer.

    2.   Read **PRACTICAL STEPS FOR ACHIEVING BIBLICAL CHANGE** (Lesson 8, Pages 8-10). Place a check by the steps that you need to take to stabilize biblical changes in your life or to recover biblically from failure. Many of these specific steps in making biblical changes will be used in column 4 of your **VICTORY OVER FAILURES WORKSHEET** (Supplement 8, Pages 1-2).

    3.   * Review your biblical plan recorded in column 4 of your **VICTORY OVER FAILURES WORKSHEET** (Supplement 8, Pages 1-2) to overcome your problem. Is each step biblical? Is each step measurable? Are you listing specific steps to keep you from repeating your sinful behavior? *Refer to:* *GUIDELINES: THE "THINK AND DO" LIST (Supplement 9) for further assistance.*

    4.   Continue your study of **BIBLICAL PERSPECTIVE ON TESTS AND TEMPTATIONS** (Lesson 8, Pages 3-7).

    5.   Close in prayer.

SIXTH DAY

    1.   Open in prayer.

    2.   * Make any necessary adjustments in your biblical plan of action as recorded in column 4 of your **VICTORY OVER FAILURES WORKSHEET** (Supplement 8, Pages 1-2). If you have not already done so, take the first steps of biblical action that are necessary to overcome your problem.

    3.   Complete your study of **BIBLICAL PERSPECTIVE ON TESTS AND TEMPTATIONS** (Lesson 8, Pages 3-7).

    4.   Close in prayer.

SEVENTH DAY

    1.   Open in prayer.

    2.   * Continue to take steps of biblical action that are recorded in column 4 of your **VICTORY OVER FAILURES WORKSHEET** (Supplement 8, Pages 1-2). Have you included specific biblical responses to deal with unexpected temptation?

    3.   * In conjunction with this lesson, respond to statement 15 under **Open Book Test** (Lesson 23, Page 2).

    4.   Close in prayer.

    5.   Review your memory verses for the week. Are you continuing to review your verses at spare moments throughout the day? Ask someone to hear you recite your memory verses. Be sure to explain their application to your life.

    *   *The completion of assignments marked with an asterisk (*) is a prerequisite for further biblical counseling training.*

LESSON 9

DEALING WITH SELF (PART ONE)

"And He was saying to them all, 'If anyone wishes to come after Me, let him deny himself, and take up his cross daily, and follow Me. For whoever wishes to save his life shall lose it, but whoever loses his life for My sake, he is the one who will save it.'"

Luke 9:23-24

LESSON 9: DEALING WITH SELF (PART ONE)

> The supreme challenge you will face in making Christ-honoring, biblical changes is dying to self. The biblical perspective concerning "self" is exactly opposite to what the wisdom of this world proclaims (*based on Proverbs 14:12; Isaiah 55:8-9; Jeremiah 10:23; Luke 9:23-24; I Corinthians 3:19-20; I John 2:15-17*).

I. **The purposes of this lesson are:**

A. To contrast the truth of God's Word regarding self with the erroneous view of the natural man regarding self-belittlement, self-exaltation, and self-pity;

B. To contrast God's Word and man's philosophy regarding envy, jealousy, covetousness, and greed;

C. To illustrate how your responses to problems indicate either a focus on pleasing God or pleasing self;

D. To introduce a continuing case study that focuses on the use of biblical principles to face and deal with problems; and

E. To give you further opportunity to design and implement a biblical plan to overcome a specific problem in your life.

II. **The outline of this lesson**

A. Self-confrontation

1. **BIBLICAL PRINCIPLES: DEALING WITH SELF (PART ONE)** (Lesson 9, Pages 2-3)

2. **SELF-BELITTLEMENT, SELF-EXALTATION, AND SELF-PITY** (Lesson 9, Pages 4-5)

3. **ENVY, JEALOUSY, COVETOUSNESS, AND GREED** (Lesson 9, Pages 6-9)

4. **PLEASING SELF OR PLEASING GOD** (Lesson 9, Pages 10-11)

B. Steps for spiritual growth

1. **LESSON 9: HOMEWORK** (Lesson 9, Page 14)

2. **STUDY GUIDE FOR DAILY DEVOTIONS** (Lesson 9, Pages 15-16)

C. Biblical counseling

1. **A CASE STUDY: MARY'S HUSBAND HAS LEFT HER** (Lesson 9, Pages 12-13)

2. **FACTS ABOUT BIBLICAL COUNSELING** (Supplement 11)

BIBLICAL PRINCIPLES: DEALING WITH SELF (PART ONE)

> You will face constant temptations to self-centeredness that lead to thoughts, words, and actions that are devastating to the Body of Christ and your own walk with the Lord. Because they characterize your life apart from Christ, these sins must be confessed and overcome if you are to mature as a child of God *(based on Proverbs 28:13; Jeremiah 17:9; Mark 7:20-23; Romans 6:12-13; I Corinthians 3:1-3; Galatians 5:16-26; Ephesians 4:1, 5:3-5; I Peter 1:14-17, 2:11-12).*

I. God's view

(Principle 33) No one hates himself; rather, he loves, cherishes, and nourishes himself *(Matthew 22:39; Ephesians 5:29).* Man's problem is that he pays too much attention to self, not too little *(Luke 9:24; Philippians 2:19-21; II Timothy 3:1-5).*

(Principle 34) A proper view of self comes from an understanding of who you are in Christ *(Romans 8:14-17; Ephesians 1:3-14; Colossians 2:9-12; I Peter 2:9-10).* As a child of God, you have the assurance that your Heavenly Father, out of His grace and mercy, is involved actively in your life *(Philippians 1:6, 2:13; I Peter 2:9-10; II Peter 1:3-4)* in spite of your natural inadequacies *(Psalm 62:9; Isaiah 64:6; John 15:4-5; II Corinthians 3:5).* While you are totally inadequate to live God's way in your own strength, God has chosen you to be a testimony of His power to the world *(I Corinthians 1:26-31).* He gives you a purpose for living by conforming you to the image of Christ *(Matthew 5:16; Romans 8:28-29; I Corinthians 1:26-31; II Corinthians 5:17-20; Ephesians 2:10).*

(Principle 35) Your contentment in all circumstances is dependent on your obedient response to God in your deeds (thoughts, words, actions) *(Genesis 4:7; Psalm 119:165; Isaiah 26:3; Luke 11:28; John 15:10-11; II Corinthians 4:7-10, 16-18; Philippians 4:6-11).* By obeying the Lord in your daily walk, you show your love for the Lord Jesus Christ *(John 14:15, 21, 23-24; I John 2:4-5)* and demonstrate His Lordship in your life *(Matthew 7:21).* God has delight and pleasure in your obedience of faith *(I Samuel 15:22; Hebrews 11:6),* not merely in your protestations of loyalty *(Proverbs 20:6; Matthew 7:21; I John 2:4),* your expressions of remorse *(for example, I Samuel 15:24-26),* or your good but meaningless activities *(Psalm 40:6; 51:16-17; Jeremiah 6:20; Hebrews 10:1-4).*

II. Your Hope

(Principle 36)   You should be thankful to God because you are fearfully and wonderfully made *(Psalm 119:73, 139:13-14)*. Even though you might have physical deformities or a chronic affliction, God's plan is to use them for your good and His glory *(Romans 5:3-5, 8:28; I Corinthians 10:13; II Corinthians 12:9-10)*. God loves you with perfect love regardless of any weaknesses and "limitations" you may have, even though you do not merit, do not deserve, and cannot earn His love *(Isaiah 53:6; Luke 15:4-7; John 3:16; Romans 5:8; I John 4:10)*.

(Principle 37)   You can quickly overcome self-belittlement, self-exaltation, or self-pity. This is possible when you realize that a preoccupation with self is sin *(Matthew 23:12; Luke 9:23; Romans 14:7-8; II Corinthians 5:15; Galatians 2:20; Philippians 2:3-4; James 4:16-17)*. You are to confess this unbiblical focus and begin immediately to live in accordance with His Word *(Psalm 51:10; Philippians 3:12-14; I John 1:9)*.

(Principle 38)   You have been freed from the power of all sins *(Romans 6:6, 12-13; 12:21; Colossians 3:2-17)*, including those of envy, jealousy, covetousness, and greed, which have a pronounced self-focus. You can be content in any circumstance *(Philippians 4:11-13)* and can have the attitude of Christ developed within you *(Philippians 2:5)*.

NOTE - Remember that your Heavenly Father is the Sovereign God of the universe, has your best interests at heart *(Jeremiah 29:11; Matthew 6:7-8; Romans 8:28)*, and will accomplish His purposes in your life *(Isaiah 46:9-11; Romans 8:29; Philippians 1:6, 2:13)*. He promises to meet every need that you will ever have *(Psalm 34:10, 15-18; 37:23-25; Matthew 6:33-34; Philippians 4:19)*, to equip you fully for every good work *(I Corinthians 12:7; II Timothy 3:16-17; I Peter 4:10-11)*, and to be with you through every circumstance of your life *(Psalm 23:1-6, 121:1-8; II Timothy 4:18; I John 5:18)*.

This outline continues in **BIBLICAL PRINCIPLES: DEALING WITH SELF (PART TWO)** *(Lesson 10, Pages 2-3) under* **III. Your change** *and* **IV. Your practice.**

SELF-BELITTLEMENT, SELF-EXALTATION, AND SELF-PITY

> Self-belittlement, self-exaltation, and self-pity all indicate a preoccupation with self. Inordinate attention to self is the exact opposite of God's commandments to love Him and others. A self-focus also prohibits the development of a Christlike servant attitude in you. If you try to save your life by focusing on self, you will reap a certain consequence; instead of saving your life, you will lose it *(based on Matthew 10:34-39, 22:37-40; Luke 9:23-25).*

I. **Man's view**

The wisdom of this world teaches that many of your problems stem from a "bad self-image" or "low self-esteem." The natural man's wisdom also states that you must learn to love yourself before you can love others, that you must raise your self-esteem, that your "perceived" needs must be met so you can help others, that you must forgive yourself before you can find peace, that you are of infinite worth because of "the god within" you, or that you must "get in touch" with yourself and your feelings before finding fulfillment in living. All of these views are in error, since they conflict with the truth of God's Word.

II. **Some of man's mistaken explanations for a low view of self ("poor self-esteem")**

Poor surroundings	Lack of money	Slow to learn
Unfulfilling work	Minimal education	No job opportunities
Physical handicaps	No respect from others	Nagging spouse
Belittlement by others	Inability to communicate	Abused as a child
Rejection by parents	Misunderstood by people	Poor relationships

III. **Some of man's futile ways of building up self ("high self-esteem")**

Accept yourself	Learn to love yourself	Assert yourself
Do not get mad – get even	Discover the "god" within	Tell of accomplishments
If you feel like it, do it	Forgive yourself	Be your own person
Be sure your perceived needs are met	Get in touch with yourself	Blameshift
	Pursue self-actualization	Practice visualization

IV. **Some unbiblical viewpoints about "self" being taught in some churches today**

- You have to love yourself before loving others *(ignores John 15:12-13; I John 4:7-8).*

- You are created in God's image, which makes you inherently worthy of God's grace and of infinite value in His sight *(ignores Romans 5:8, 10; I Corinthians 1:26-31).*

- Without good self-esteem, you cannot solve problems, relate to others effectively, and grow spiritually *(ignores II Corinthians 3:5-6; Philippians 4:13; James 4:6).*

- The most serious sin in the world is the one in which a person says he is unworthy. The need for self-worth is the greatest of all human needs in the world today *(ignores Jeremiah 9:23-24; Luke 17:10).*

- In order to accomplish anything of significance, positive thinking about one's self is a necessity *(ignores John 15:4-5; Philippians 3:7-14).*

- We should not talk of sin, hell, or eternal separation from God; we should only build up people *(ignores Ezekiel 33:8-9; Luke 3:7, 12:5)*.

- You must learn to forgive yourself in order to find peace and fulfillment in life. If you do not forgive yourself, you cannot understand Jesus' death on the cross *(ignores John 16:33; I Corinthians 1:18-21, 2:14; Colossians 2:8-14)*.

- God wants us all to feel good about ourselves; after all, Jesus possessed the greatest self-esteem in the history of mankind *(ignores Philippians 2:3-8)*.

- To be born again actually means to be transformed from a negative self-image to a positive self-image *(ignores John 3:3-8; I Peter 1:23)*.

Refer to: **THE BIBLICAL VIEW OF SELF** *(Lesson 4, Pages 5-10) to note the numerous scriptural distortions and errors which are evidenced in the above information.*

V.   God's view

"When pride comes, then comes dishonor ..." (Proverbs 11:2)

"There is a way which seems right to a man, but its end is the way of death." (Proverbs 14:12)

"If you have been foolish in exalting yourself ... put your hand on your mouth." (Proverbs 30:32)

"Woe to those who call evil good, and good evil; who substitute darkness for light and light for darkness; who substitute bitter for sweet, and sweet for bitter! Woe to those who are wise in their own eyes, and clever in their own sight." (Isaiah 5:20-21)

"And whoever exalts himself shall be humbled ..." (Matthew 23:12)

"For whoever wishes to save his life shall lose it ..." (Luke 9:24)

"Where is the wise man? Where is the scribe? Where is the debater of this age? Has not God made foolish the wisdom of the world? ... Because the foolishness of God is wiser than men, and the weakness of God is stronger than men ... but God has chosen the foolish things of the world to shame the wise, and God has chosen the weak things of the world to shame the things which are strong." (I Corinthians 1:20, 25, 27)

"Therefore let him who thinks he stands take heed lest he fall." (I Corinthians 10:12)

"For men will be lovers of self ... led on by various impulses, always learning and never able to come to the knowledge of the truth." (II Timothy 3:2, 6-7)

"But He gives a greater grace. Therefore it says, 'God is opposed to the proud ...'" (James 4:6)

"... there will also be false teachers among you, who will secretly introduce destructive heresies, even denying the Master who bought them, bringing swift destruction upon themselves. And many will follow their sensuality, and because of them the way of the truth will be maligned; and in their greed they will exploit you with false words; their judgment from long ago is not idle, and their destruction is not asleep." (II Peter 2:1-3)

"For all that is in the world ... the boastful pride of life, is not from the Father but is from the world." (I John 2:16)

ENVY, JEALOUSY, COVETOUSNESS, AND GREED

> Envy, jealousy, covetousness, and greed are sins that reveal a self-focus that questions God's work and provision in your life. These sins must be "put off" out of your commitment to live for Jesus Christ *(based on Romans 6:3-4; 13:14; Galatians 5:19-21; Colossians 3:5-11; Titus 3:3; I Peter 2:11-12).*

I. **Characteristics of envy, jealousy, covetousness, and greed**

A. When you belittle others in thought or speech, you disobey specific commands of Scripture *(based on Ephesians 4:29; Philippians 4:8; James 3:5-18, 4:11).* God's Word teaches that:

1. You are not to think or speak about others' accomplishments or abilities in a demeaning manner;

2. You are not to think or speak of others' lives or actions in a way which questions their motives or character; and

3. You are not to think, speak, or act in ways which imply that another person is selfish because he has material goods.

B. If you compare yourself or your circumstances with those whose material goods, benefits, abilities, talents, spiritual gifts, or honors you desire, you question God's sovereignty in your life *(based on Psalm 75:6-7; Matthew 20:1-16; I Corinthians 13:5; II Corinthians 10:12; I Timothy 6:6-8).* You sin in this manner by:

1. Desiring or demanding an equal measure of others' benefits whether or not you did anything to deserve or earn them;

2. Complaining in your thoughts or in your conversation about your present situation in life; or

3. Striving to accumulate or acquire more wealth, honor, power, fame, or popularity than others.

II. **Some common thoughts, words, and actions that reveal envy, jealousy, covetousness, or greed**

A. Complaining about your circumstances or making unwholesome, unedifying statements about other people while comparing yourself with them reveals a problem of envy, jealousy, covetousness, or greed within your own heart *(based on Matthew 12:34-37; Luke 6:45; Romans 14:10-13; Ephesians 4:29; James 3:3-6, 4:11).* In reviewing the following statements, it is important to examine yourself in a biblical manner and not judge others. Some examples that indicate envy, jealousy, covetousness, or greed are:

1. "Well, that's another feather he can add to his cap. I'll bet he stepped on quite a few people to get that position." *(belittling accomplishments)*

2. "Oh, anybody with half a brain could have figured that out! She just happened to do it first." *(belittling ability)*

3. "Sure, they're rich. But did you ever wonder how they managed to get that much money? And I'm sure they don't give sacrificially or help others in need like we do." *(belittling deeds; comparing self with others)*

4. "You think she's beautiful? Do you know how long it must take her to get that way every morning?" *(belittling physical appearance)*

5. "I don't know why he is in charge of that ministry. You'd think the whole church revolved around him, since everyone thinks he can do everything. Well, pride goes before a fall, I always say." *(belittling accomplishments and responsibilities)*

B. When your thoughts, words, or actions indicate envy, jealousy, covetousness, or greed, you displease the Lord through your lack of love for others and your exaltation of yourself. In addition, you reveal the spiritual condition of your heart, which is focused on self *(based on Matthew 15:19-20, 22:39; Romans 12:9, 13:8-10; I Corinthians 13:1-8a; II Corinthians 10:17-18; Galatians 5:14; Philippians 2:3-8).* Examine yourself in light of Scripture, using the following examples:

1. You pretend outwardly that you are happy for another's recognition or accomplishment but brood in private about the unfairness of life and how deprived you are *(in violation of Romans 12:3-9; I Corinthians 13:1; Philippians 2:14, 4:13);*

2. You practice "one-upmanship" and seek to have more honor, or goods, or praise for yourself to show that you can do at least as well as the other person *(in violation of Proverbs 25:27, 27:2; Mark 10:43-45; Luke 14:8-11);*

3. You plan or try to take away the very thing that the other person has (such as a friendship, popularity, honors, spouse, reputation, etc.) *(in violation of Exodus 20:17; Deuteronomy 5:21; Ephesians 4:28);*

4. You ignore or avoid those who are honored *(in violation of Romans 12:10, 15; I Peter 2:17);*

5. You protest that a particular item or honor really belongs to you; you complain that the other person "stole" what was rightly yours; or you angrily demand a recount, a re-evaluation, or an equal measure for yourself *(in violation of James 4:11-12, 5:9; I Peter 2:19-23);*

6. You pretend that the other person's position, honor, or goods do not matter to you and put on a jovial "it is no big thing" attitude *(in violation of Psalm 34:13; Proverbs 26:24-28; I Peter 3:10);*

7. You try and make another feel guilty by expressing your opinion that he is shallow to take pleasure in any particular benefit that has come his way *(in violation of Matthew 7:1-5; Romans 2:1-2; James 3:13-18);* or

8. You boast about your own accomplishments, especially in an effort to advance your own cause with those around you *(in violation of Proverbs 25:27, 27:2; I Corinthians 1:30-31; II Corinthians 11:30).*

III. Recognizing the difference between godly jealousy and sinful jealousy

A. God is completely holy *(Leviticus 19:2; Psalm 99:3, 5, 9; Isaiah 6:3; I Peter 1:16),* totally loving *(I John 4:8),* unchanging in His character *(Malachi 3:6; James 1:17),* and is never described as envious, covetous, or greedy.

B. God, in His holiness, is jealous *(Exodus 34:14)* but in a distinctly different way from the kind of earthly jealousy that prohibits your spiritual development *(James 3:13-16)*. The difference between godly jealousy and sinful jealousy is in its focus.

    1. While God's jealousy focuses on His honor, His holiness, the worship due His Name, and the purity of His people *(Exodus 20:4-5; Deuteronomy 4:23-24, 5:8-9, 6:14-15; Joshua 24:16-21; Ezekiel 39:25; Zechariah 1:14, 8:1-3)*, sinful jealousy focuses on pleasing self and being harmful to others *(Romans 13:12-14; I Corinthians 3:1-3; James 3:13-18)*.

    2. When servants of God exhibited godly jealousy, the incidents show that the focus was to please God and bless others instead of gratifying self or harming others *(Numbers 25:11; II Corinthians 11:2)*.

IV. God's view of envy, jealousy, covetousness, and greed

A. **Envy** (resentment or displeasure at another's attainments, material goods, or endowments, often resulting in efforts to deprive others of what they have) and **jealousy** (a selfish desire accompanied by resentment, suspicion, or fear that another person is seeking to take away what you perceive to be yours) both reveal a self-centeredness that is unloving and destructive *(based on Proverbs 27:4; Matthew 27:15-18; Acts 5:12-18, 13:45; I Corinthians 13:4-8a; Titus 3:3)*.

    1. Envy is:

        a. Not compatible with good will in the Body of Christ *(Philippians 1:15; I Timothy 6:3-5)*,

        b. One of the deeds of the flesh *(Galatians 5:19-21)*,

        c. Characteristic of a life separated from God *(Titus 3:3)*,

        d. Not compatible with a Spirit-controlled life *(Galatians 5:25-26)*, and

        e. Indicative of a depraved mind *(Romans 1:28-32, esp. verse 29)*.

    2. Jealousy is:

        a. One of the deeds of darkness *(Romans 13:12-14)*,

        b. Considered fleshly and leads to foolish comparisons and competitiveness *(I Corinthians 3:1-4, 19)*,

        c. In opposition to godly wisdom *(James 3:13-18)*,

        d. A denial of biblical love *(I Corinthians 13:4)*,

        e. A prelude to disorder and evil *(James 3:16)*,

        f. Associated with strife *(Romans 13:13; II Corinthians 12:20)*, and

        g. One of the deeds of the flesh *(Galatians 5:19-21)*.

B. **Covetousness** (a wrongful desire to possess what God has not ordained you to have; this desire is usually directed at what belongs to another) and **greed** (giving free rein to an overwhelming desire for more than is God's will for your life) are both sins that reveal a focus on self-gratification *(based on Exodus 20:17; Ecclesiastes 5:10-11; Micah 2:1-2; Luke 12:15-21; Ephesians 4:17-19, esp. verse 19)*. Both covetousness and greed are linked with idolatry *(Ephesians 5:5; Colossians 3:5)*.

    1. Covetousness:

        a. Has always been forbidden by God *(Exodus 20:17; Deuteronomy 5:21; Romans 13:9)*,

        b. Is characteristic of those who have no part in the kingdom of God *(I Corinthians 6:9-10)*, and

    c.   Is so detrimental to the Body of Christ that believers are forbidden to associate with any so-called brother who is covetous *(I Corinthians 5:11-13)*.

2.   Greed is:

    a.   To be guarded against *(Luke 12:15)*,

    b.   Characteristic of false teachers *(II Peter 2:1-3)* and those who reject the Lord *(Psalm 10:3; II Peter 2:9-16, esp. verse 14)*,

    c.   Indicative of a depraved mind *(Romans 1:28-32, esp. verse 29)*,

    d.   Descriptive of a life separate from the Lord *(Psalm 10:3-4; Colossians 3:5-7)*, and

    e.   Improper among believers *(Ephesians 5:3)*.

PLEASING SELF OR PLEASING GOD

> Your focus for living – either to please self or to please God – is revealed by your responses to life's situations *(based on Mark 7:20-23, 8:34-35; II Corinthians 5:14-15; Galatians 5:17-25; Colossians 1:9-12; James 1:14-15, 22-25; 4:17).* This focus is dramatically illustrated by the translation of various New Testament words describing some of these responses. The same words in the original language of the New Testament are translated differently according to their emphasis on pleasing self or pleasing God, as illustrated below.

I. **Worry versus Concern**

    A.   You sin when you **worry** or are **anxious**, because both are self-centered responses that reveal a lack of trust in God's care and sovereignty in your life *(Matthew 6:25-34, 10:16-20; Luke 12:22-31; Philippians 4:6-7).*

    B.   However, you walk in God's way when you have **concern** or **care for** the welfare of others and the glory of God *(I Corinthians 12:25; II Corinthians 11:28; Philippians 2:20).* (The New Testament word translated **"concern"** or **"care for"** is translated **"worry"** or **"anxiety"** when self-focus is involved.)

II. **Fear versus Reverence**

    A.   You sin by focusing on self when you live in **fear** of men (what they think of you or what they can do to you) *(Matthew 10:28; Luke 12:4; I Peter 3:13-14).*

    B.   However, you please God when you are living a holy life, **reverencing** (the same New Testament word translated as **"fearing"**) the Lord *(II Corinthians 7:1; I Peter 1:14-17),* with the promise of His blessings to follow *(Psalm 103:17; 112:1; 128:1, 4; Acts 10:34-35).*

III. **Covetousness/Lust versus Desire**

    A.   You sin when you **covet**. It is forbidden by God since it selfishly focuses on possessing what does not belong to you *(Romans 13:9).* The same New Testament word translated as **"covet"** is also used for **"lust"** (a desire for self-gratification) *(Romans 13:14; James 1:14-15).*

    B.   However, you demonstrate godliness when you **desire** or **have great desire** to please God and edify others *(Philippians 1:23; I Thessalonians 2:17; Hebrews 6:11).* (The New Testament word translated **"desire"** or **"have great desire"** is translated as **"covet"** or **"lust"** when there is a self-focus in view.)

IV. **Jealousy versus Zeal**

   A. You sin when you are **jealous**. **Jealousy** is full of evil *(James 3:13-18)*, is part of the deeds of darkness *(Romans 13:12-14)*, and is a detriment to spiritual maturity *(I Corinthians 3:1-3)*.

   B. However, you please the Lord when you have **zeal**, an earnest desire to please God and edify others (the same New Testament word is translated **"jealousy"** when focused on self) *(John 2:17; I Corinthians 12:31, 14:39; II Corinthians 7:6-7, 11; 9:2)*.

A CASE STUDY: MARY'S HUSBAND HAS LEFT HER

> Broken and fractured lives are all around us. Scripture tells us to prepare ourselves to meet the needs of others. This preparation must be done in accordance with God's Word to achieve God's purposes *(based on Matthew 7:1-5; Romans 15:14; II Corinthians 1:3-5, 5:18-19; Galatians 6:1-2; II Timothy 2:15, 3:16-17; James 1:25)*. The following case study illustrates the practical sufficiency of God's Word and His resources in any difficulty, no matter how severe or prolonged. The case study will be expanded in later lessons.

Mary and her husband (Tom) have lived in your neighborhood for six years. Mary is a professing believer in Christ. Tom seems to have no interest in spiritual matters. They have three children: two teenagers (a boy, 14, and a girl, 13) and a small daughter (3 years old). Mary began participating with your local body of believers about four months ago, but she had always attended by herself. On two occasions, you had talked briefly to Mary after the worship service, but you did not have an opportunity to discuss spiritual matters. Even though you had looked for her, you had not seen Mary in your assembly for three weeks.

A few days ago, you unexpectedly saw Mary at the market and briefly talked to her. At that meeting, Mary introduced you to her husband, Tom. When Mary mentioned your church, Tom said that people would probably faint if he ever came. In the course of conversation, you discovered that Tom and Mary live half a mile from your home.

Later that week, Mary came to your home in the early evening. She asked to speak privately with you and announced that her husband had left her quite unexpectedly.

She was in a highly emotional state (weeping, frantic in her tone of voice, disheveled) and told you that she and her husband argued last night and had continued their argument throughout that day. She went on to say that their children had overheard much of their conversation, and their smallest daughter had cried during much of this time.

She continued by saying that Tom had gathered up his clothes about an hour ago and said he was leaving her and wasn't coming back. She tearfully exclaimed that this was quite a surprise.

She told you she has been a good wife and could not understand how this could have happened to her. She stated that she could not understand how her husband could be so insensitive.

She said that she is now bitter toward her husband and also threatened to get even with him for walking out on her. She went on to say that she was miserable and wanted you to help her.

In light of the above description, answer the following questions.

1. At this point, what is Mary's understanding of the basic problem?

2.   What is Mary's primary problem from God's view?

3.   What additional problems could result if Mary continues responding in the same way (for example: depression, anxiety, suicide, murder, living as a recluse, physical or emotional breakdown, alcohol and drug use)? What else?

4.   Will studying this case only help married people or do the principles apply to everyone regardless of age and marital status? Explain.

5.   How would you give hope to Mary using **FACTS ABOUT BIBLICAL COUNSELING** (Supplement 11)?

LESSON 9: HOMEWORK

> In order to please God instead of seeking to please yourself, you must have a biblical plan that affects your thoughts, words, and actions. This plan must apply to your daily routine as well as provide biblical guidelines for any emergency situations that arise *(based on Matthew 10:38-39, 22:37-39; II Corinthians 10:5; Colossians 3:2; Hebrews 4:12; James 1:22; I Peter 5:8).*

✔ *homework completed*

☐ A.   * In your own words, write the meaning of *Luke 9:23-24.* This week, memorize *Luke 9:23-24* and begin memorizing *Romans 6:12-13.* Review previous verses.

☐ B.   * Read through **BIBLICAL PRINCIPLES: DEALING WITH SELF (PART ONE)** (Lesson 9, Pages 2-3). Highlight the listed verses in your Bible.

☐ C.   Read **SELF-BELITTLEMENT, SELF-EXALTATION, AND SELF-PITY** (Lesson 9, Pages 4-5). Contrast man's way of dealing with self and God's view of solving this problem. Mark the statements that you have erroneously accepted as "truth" before realizing God's perspective.

☐ D.   Read **ENVY, JEALOUSY, COVETOUSNESS, AND GREED** (Lesson 9, Pages 6-9). Mark any statements that describe these sins in your life.

☐ E.   * Continue work on the problem you are beginning to overcome biblically during this course by completing a **VICTORY OVER FAILURES WORKSHEET** (Supplement 8, Pages 1-2). Give special attention to those aspects that focus on self (for example: self-belittlement, self-gratification, self-pity, self-love, self-exaltation, envy, jealousy, covetousness, or greed). Refer to your marked statements in C. or D. above in order to confront yourself biblically. Af necessary, refer to the list you have already begun.

☐ F.   Study **PLEASING SELF OR PLEASING GOD** (Lesson 9, Pages 10-11). Does this study reveal your focus of pleasing self or pleasing God? If your response indicates a self-focus, refer to **RENEWING YOUR MIND** (Lesson 7, Pages 6-7).

☐ G.   * Read **FACTS ABOUT BIBLICAL COUNSELING** (Supplement 11).

☐ H.   * Read **A CASE STUDY: MARY'S HUSBAND HAS LEFT HER** (Lesson 9, Pages 12-13) and answer the questions after the case study introduction. Using the **FACTS ABOUT BIBLICAL COUNSELING** (Supplement 11), list at least three scriptural truths with their verse references that would give Mary hope and help her begin to see God's view of her problem.

☐ I.   * In conjunction with this lesson, answer question 16 under **Open Book Test** (Lesson 23, Page 2).

*   *The completion of assignments marked with an asterisk (*) is a prerequisite for further biblical counseling training.*

LESSON 9: STUDY GUIDE FOR DAILY DEVOTIONS
(INCLUDING SCRIPTURE MEMORY AND HOMEWORK)

> In order to please God instead of seeking to please yourself, you must have a biblical plan that affects your thoughts, words, and actions. This plan must apply to your daily routine as well as provide biblical guidelines for any emergency situations that arise *(based on Matthew 10:38-39, 22:37-39; II Corinthians 10:5; Colossians 3:2; Hebrews 4:12; James 1:22; I Peter 5:8).*

Scripture Memory

1. * Memorize *Luke 9:23-24* and begin memorizing *Romans 6:12-13.*
2. Carry your memory verse cards from previous weeks along with this week's memory verses. Review your Scriptures during your spare moments throughout the day.

Daily Devotional Study Guide

FIRST DAY

1. Open in prayer.
2. * Read *Principle 33* under **BIBLICAL PRINCIPLES: DEALING WITH SELF (PART ONE)** (Lesson 9, Pages 2-3). Look up the verses and highlight them in your Bible.
3. Read **SELF-BELITTLEMENT, SELF-EXALTATION, AND SELF-PITY** (Lesson 9, Pages 4-5). Note the contrast between man's way and God's way of dealing with "self". Mark any statements that you have erroneously accepted as "truth" before you realized and accepted God's plan for overcoming the problem of self.
4. * In your own words, write the meaning of *Luke 9:23-24.*
5. Close in prayer.

SECOND DAY

1. Open in prayer.
2. * Read *Principle 34* under **BIBLICAL PRINCIPLES: DEALING WITH SELF (PART ONE)** (Lesson 9, Pages 2-3). Highlight the listed verses in your Bible.
3. Read **ENVY, JEALOUSY, COVETOUSNESS, AND GREED** (Lesson 9, Pages 6-9). Mark any statements that describe these sins in your life. This is the first day of a two-day study.
4. Close in prayer.

THIRD DAY

1. Open in prayer.
2. * Read *Principle 35* under **BIBLICAL PRINCIPLES: DEALING WITH SELF (PART ONE)** (Lesson 9, Pages 2-3). Highlight the listed verses in your Bible.
3. Continue work on the problem that God wants you to overcome by completing the first three columns of a **VICTORY OVER FAILURES WORKSHEET** (Supplement 8, Page 1). Give special attention to those aspects of your problem which exhibit self-belittlement, self-exaltation, self-pity, envy, jealousy, covetousness, or greed. Af necessary, refer to the list you have already begun.

4. Complete your study of **ENVY, JEALOUSY, COVETOUSNESS, AND GREED** (Lesson 9, Pages 6-9).

5. Close in prayer.

FOURTH DAY

1. Open in prayer.

2. * Read *Principle 36* under **BIBLICAL PRINCIPLES: DEALING WITH SELF (PART ONE)** (Lesson 9, Pages 2-3). Highlight the verses in your Bible.

3. * Continue work that you began yesterday on the first three columns of your **VICTORY OVER FAILURES WORKSHEET** (Supplement 8, Page 1). If necessary, use a blank **"THINK AND DO" LIST** (Supplement 10, Page 1).

4. Close in prayer.

FIFTH DAY

1. Open in prayer.

2. * Read *Principle 37* under **BIBLICAL PRINCIPLES: DEALING WITH SELF (PART ONE)** (Lesson 9, Pages 2-3). Highlight the listed verses in your Bible.

3. * Continue work on your first three columns of your **VICTORY OVER FAILURES WORKSHEET** (Supplement 8, Page 1). In evaluating failures in your first column, highlight unbiblical thoughts, words, or actions that you tend to repeat as a pattern of life.

4. Read **PLEASING SELF OR PLEASING GOD** (Lesson 9, Pages 10-11). Does this study indicate you are living to please God or living to please self? If you are focused on pleasing self, refer to **RENEWING YOUR MIND** (Lesson 7, Pages 6-7).

5. Close in prayer.

SIXTH DAY

1. Open in prayer.

2. * Read *Principle 38* under **BIBLICAL PRINCIPLES: DEALING WITH SELF (PART ONE)** (Lesson 9, Pages 2-3). Highlight the verses in your Bible.

3. * Continue work on your **VICTORY OVER FAILURES WORKSHEET** (Supplement 8, Pages 1-2). Add to any columns as necessary.

4. Read **FACTS ABOUT BIBLICAL COUNSELING** (Supplement 11).

5. Read **A CASE STUDY: MARY'S HUSBAND HAS LEFT HER** (Lesson 9, Pages 12-13) and answer the questions after the case study introduction. Using the **FACTS ABOUT BIBLICAL COUNSELING** (Supplement 11), list at least three scriptural truths and their verse references that would give Mary hope and help her discover God's view of her problem.

6. Close in prayer.

SEVENTH DAY

1. Open in prayer.

2. * Review your work this past week on your **VICTORY OVER FAILURES WORKSHEET** (Supplement 8, Pages 1-2). If any additions need to be made, complete the list today.

3. * Answer question 16 under **Open Book Test** (Lesson 23, Page 2).

4. Close in prayer.

5. Review your memory verses. Ask someone to hear you recite your memory verses and their Scripture references. Explain their application to your life.

* *The completion of assignments marked with an asterisk (*) is a prerequisite for further biblical counseling training.*

LESSON 10

DEALING WITH SELF (PART TWO)

"Therefore do not let sin reign in your mortal body that you should obey its lusts, and do not go on presenting the members of your body to sin as instruments of unrighteousness; but present yourselves to God as those alive from the dead, and your members as instruments of righteousness to God."

Romans 6:12-13

LESSON 10: DEALING WITH SELF (PART TWO)

> You must decisively "put off" a preoccupation with self,
> which is sin, and "put on" a life committed to Christ,
> pleasing to the Lord *(based on Romans 6:12-14; 12:9, 21;*
> *Galatians 5:19-21, 25-26; Ephesians 4:1-3, 22-24; 5:5;*
> *Colossians 3:5-10; Titus 2:11-14, 3:3; James 4:17).*

I. **The purposes of this lesson are:**

   A. To provide a scriptural foundation for developing a pattern of stewardship in your life;

   B. To present the use of spiritual gifts for Christ-honoring ministry;

   C. To provide a biblical plan for overcoming a preoccupation with self; and

   D. To present the essential elements of biblical counseling through a continuation of a case study.

II. **The outline of this lesson**

   A. Self-confrontation

   1. **BIBLICAL PRINCIPLES: DEALING WITH SELF (PART TWO)** (Lesson 10, Pages 2-3)

   2. **BIBLICAL PRINCIPLES OF STEWARDSHIP** (Lesson 10, Pages 4-6)

   3. **DYING TO SELF BY SERVING OTHERS** (Lesson 10, Pages 7-8)

   B. Steps for spiritual growth

   1. **OVERCOMING A PREOCCUPATION WITH SELF** (Lesson 10, Pages 9-12)

   2. **LESSON 10: HOMEWORK** (Lesson 10, Page 15)

   3. **STUDY GUIDE FOR DAILY DEVOTIONS** (Lesson 10, Pages 16-17)

   C. Biblical counseling

   A CASE STUDY: MARY'S HUSBAND HAS LEFT HER (Lesson 10, Pages 13-14)

BIBLICAL PRINCIPLES: DEALING WITH SELF (PART TWO)

> God's view concerning self emphasizes the need for biblical change. Instead of a preoccupation with "self" in its varied forms, God's plan focuses on a denial of self in order to please Him and be a blessing to others *(based on Ecclesiastes 7:20; Luke 9:23-24; Romans 1:20-21, 3:9-18, 12:1-12; I Corinthians 2:14, 3:19-20; II Corinthians 5:17; Galatians 2:20; Ephesians 5:8-10; Philippians 3:8-9, 12-14; Hebrews 13:20-21).*

III. **Your change** (outline continues from Lesson 9, Pages 2-3)

(Principle 39)   You must take the focus off yourself in daily situations and relationships *(Luke 9:23-24; John 3:30, 12:24-26; Romans 12:3, 14:7-8; II Corinthians 5:15)* by following God's commandments *(Matthew 22:37-39)*. Instead of sinning through self-belittlement, self-exaltation, or self-pity, you are to regard others as more important than yourself and be a servant to God and others *(Matthew 20:26-28; Luke 4:8; John 13:3-17, esp. verses 14-15; Romans 15:1-3; I Corinthians 9:19; 10:24, 32-33; Philippians 2:3-8; Colossians 3:23-24; I Peter 4:10).*

(Principle 40)   You are to put off the sins of envy, jealousy, covetousness, and greed, which characterized your life apart from Jesus Christ. Rather, you are to delight yourself in the Lord, commit your ways to Him, and wait patiently for Him *(Psalm 37:1-9)*. Instead of being jealous and having selfish ambition, you are to be pure, peaceable, gentle, reasonable, full of mercy and good fruits, and unwavering without hypocrisy *(James 3:13-17).*

(Principle 41)   Since you have been bought with the precious sacrifice of Jesus Christ and are not your own *(I Corinthians 6:19-20; I Peter 1:17-19)*, you are God's possession and a steward (managing servant) of all that the Lord has provided for you. As the Lord's servant, you have the privilege and responsibility to be faithful with all that He has placed in your care *(Matthew 25:14-30; Luke 16:10-13; I Corinthians 4:1-2; I Peter 4:10)*. As a servant of the Lord, you should not seek to be served *(Mark 10:42-45)* or to receive credit from men *(Colossians 3:23; I Thessalonians 2:4-6)* but instead should seek only to please the Lord *(I Corinthians 10:31; II Corinthians 5:9; Hebrews 13:20-21).*

IV. **Your practice**

(Principle 42)   Examine (judge) yourself continually in a biblical manner *(Matthew 7:5; I Corinthians 11:26-32)* and do not compare yourself with others *(II Corinthians 10:12; Galatians 6:3-4)* to determine whose approval you ultimately seek *(II Corinthians 5:9; Galatians 1:10; Colossians 3:23-24; I Thessalonians 2:4).*

(Principle 43)   Thank God for "apparent deficiencies" that you cannot correct *(II Corinthians 12:7-10; Ephesians 5:20; I Thessalonians 5:18)* and correct all actual deficiencies in your life that hinder you from serving God and edifying others *(Matthew 22:37-39; Romans 6:19, 14:12-13; I Corinthians 10:31-33; Philippians 2:12-16; Colossians 3:2-15; Hebrews 12:1-2; James 4:8).*

(Principle 44)   You are to practice love without hypocrisy (play-acting) *(Romans 12:9),* demonstrating the fruit of Christ's life in your thoughts, speech, and actions *(Matthew 5:16; Galatians 5:22-23; Ephesians 5:1-2).*

BIBLICAL PRINCIPLES OF STEWARDSHIP

> Sins such as envy, jealousy, covetousness, and greed very markedly reveal a focus on self. Instead you are to please God and bless others by practicing biblical stewardship which is to care for and give of the physical and spiritual resources that God has provided for you *(based on Mark 12:41-44; Luke 8:16-18; 12:15-21, 35-48; 16:10-13; Acts 20:35; Romans 12:1-2, 6-8; I Corinthians 4:2, 6:12-20; II Corinthians 8:5, 8-9, 13-15; 9:6-15; Ephesians 4:28; I Timothy 6:6-19; I Peter 4:10-11)*. The following guidelines will help you develop a biblical plan of stewardship that characterizes a servant of the Lord Jesus Christ.

I. **God is sovereign over every facet of His creation, yet He graciously allows you to be a steward (managing servant) over what He places in your care.**

   A. You should recognize that everything you have – your body, material goods, time, abilities, and spiritual gifts – has been graciously given to you by God *(based on Deuteronomy 8:18; I Chronicles 29:12; Psalm 24:1, 50:12b, 139:16; I Corinthians 6:19-20; 12:4-6, 11)*.

   B. As a steward of all that the Lord has entrusted to you, you are to be faithful in the care and use of God's provisions *(based on Matthew 25:14-30; Luke 12:13-48, 16:10-13; I Corinthians 4:1-2; Ephesians 5:15-17; I Peter 4:10)*.

II. **Your motivation to be a faithful steward is to be centered on God and His objectives instead of a preoccupation with self.**

   A. As a trustworthy steward of God's grace, you must demonstrate Christlikeness in your own walk *(I Corinthians 4:1-4)* as you remain faithful to present God's message of reconciliation through Jesus Christ to others *(II Corinthians 5:17-20, esp. verse 19)*.

   B. The goal of your service must be to give glory to God instead of receiving honor from others or gratifying your own self-centered desires *(based on Matthew 6:1; I Corinthians 6:19-20, 10:31; II Corinthians 9:12-13; Colossians 3:17; I Thessalonians 2:1-6, esp. verses 4 and 6; I Peter 4:10-11, esp. verse 11b)*. The exercise of spiritual gifts should not bring glory to yourself but should build up the body of Christ and cooperate with God in fulfilling His purposes in the world *(based on Romans 12:3-8; I Corinthians 12:4-27; Ephesians 4:11-16)*.

      *Refer to: **DYING TO SELF BY SERVING OTHERS** (Lesson 10, Pages 7-8) for a more complete study on this subject.*

   C. The stewardship of your time is not to be focused on fulfilling your self-centered desires but instead must:

      1. Acknowledge and demonstrate God's sovereignty in your life *(Proverbs 16:1, 3, 9; Matthew 6:25-33; James 4:13-16)*;

      2. Include study *(II Timothy 2:15)*, memorization *(Psalm 119:11)*, and meditation on God's Word *(Psalm 1:1-3, 119:97)*;

---

3.   Give ample opportunity for you to examine yourself in a biblical manner on a continual basis *(Matthew 7:1-5; Ephesians 5:15-16);*

4.   Provide opportunity for ministering to others *(Galatians 6:10);*

5.   Allow for assembling with other believers to encourage one another *(Hebrews 10:23-25);*

6.   Take into account the trials and spiritual warfare that are a part of everyday life *(Matthew 6:34; Ephesians 5:15-17);* and

7.   Reflect your anticipation and preparation for the soon return of the Lord Jesus Christ *(Luke 12:35-40; John 9:1-4, esp. verse 4; II Corinthians 5:1-11; Hebrews 10:23-25, esp. verse 25; I Peter 1:14-19, esp. verse 17; II Peter 3:8-18, esp. verses 11-13; I John 3:1-3, esp. verse 3).*

D.   The care and discipline of your body is to:

1.   Enable your body to be used for the Lord instead of being used to gratify fleshly desires *(Romans 6:12-13; I Corinthians 6:13-20; I Thessalonians 4:3-7);*

2.   Give evidence that you are not your own but have been bought with a price *(I Corinthians 6:19-20);*

3.   Demonstrate that you give glory to God as a temple of the Holy Spirit *(I Corinthians 6:19-20);*

4.   Give the Lord your spiritual service of worship by presenting your body as a living sacrifice to Him *(Romans 12:1);* and

5.   Demonstrate self-control so that you may receive a heavenly reward *(I Corinthians 9:24-27).*

E.   Your stewardship of material goods indicates your level of spiritual maturity *(Luke 16:10-13, esp. verse 10; I Timothy 6:6-10).*

1.   One of the greatest spiritual battles you will fight is in choosing whether to serve the God of the universe or the god of money. There is no middle ground in your allegiance *(Matthew 6:24; Luke 16:13).*

   a.   Your real interests and "treasures" are revealed by your perspective on and use of material goods *(based on Matthew 6:19-21).*

   b.   Not giving to the Lord or giving of your "leftovers" robs God and insures spiritual leanness for yourself *(based on Proverbs 3:9-10, 11:24-25; Malachi 1:7-8, 10b; 3:8-9; Luke 16:11-12).*

2.   Your primary motive in giving is to be your love and commitment to the Lord *(based on II Corinthians 8:5, 7b-8; Colossians 3:17).*

   a.   When you give to the Lord, you are returning what is already His *(based on I Chronicles 29:14).*

   b.   You should have a readiness to give *(based on II Corinthians 8:11-12).*

   c.   Giving is to be marked by generosity, good spirit, and personal determination *(based on Exodus 35:5, 36:6b; Luke 19:8; II Corinthians 8:2b, 9:7).*

3.   Be content with what you have. Whether God gives you abundant riches or meager poverty, pleasant circumstances or suffering, you are to trust Him as He continues to work in your life *(based on Ecclesiastes 7:14; Romans 8:28-29; Philippians 1:6, 4:11-13; I Timothy 6:6-8; Hebrews 13:5-6).*

   a.   Having riches, not having riches, or desiring riches are all potentially dangerous *(based on Deuteronomy 6:10b-12; Proverbs 30:8b-9; Ecclesiastes 5:10-11; I Timothy 6:9-10).*

b.   God promises to take care of your needs as you honor Him with your material substance *(based on Proverbs 3:9-10; Matthew 6:33-34; II Corinthians 9:6, 8-11; Philippians 4:19)*.

4.   Giving is not a matter of how much you give; it is a matter of what you have after you give *(based on Mark 12:43b-44)*.

a.   Giving is to be done sacrificially, even in times of great financial difficulty *(based on II Corinthians 8:2-4)*.

b.   Believers with a greater abundance of wealth are expected to give more to advance the Lord's work and bless others instead of selfishly spending excess funds merely on their own pleasures *(based on Luke 12:15, 18-21; Acts 4:34-35; II Corinthians 8:13-15, 9:8; I Timothy 6:17-19)*.

c.   You should plan to give on a regular basis in addition to responding to immediate needs *(based on I Chronicles 29:9; Acts 4:34-35; I Corinthians 16:2; II Corinthians 8:4)*.

d.   Giving has greater value than receiving *(Acts 20:35b)*.

5.   Using material goods to provide for others is one way to show a thankful response for God's love to you in Christ Jesus *(based on II Corinthians 8:1-5, esp. verse 4; 8:7-9, esp. verse 7; I John 3:14-17)*.

a.   You should freely provide for your spiritual teachers and leaders *(Galatians 6:6; I Timothy 5:17-18)*.

b.   You should be especially sensitive to help those who find it difficult to help themselves, for example: prisoners *(Matthew 25:36, 39-40; Hebrews 13:3)*, strangers, the poor, the sick, *(Matthew 25:31-46, esp. verses 35-36; Hebrews 13:2)*, widows and orphans *(I Timothy 5:3, 5, 9-10; James 1:27)*, and other believers in need *(Romans 12:13; II Corinthians 8:3-5, esp. verse 4; 8:13-15; I John 3:16-18; III John 1:5-6)*.

c.   Whenever biblically necessary, you should provide for every member of your family *(I Timothy 5:4, 8, 16)*.

d.   You should even meet the needs of those who consider themselves your enemy *(Luke 6:27-38; Romans 12:20-21)*.

e.   You should not give with a self-focus to earn the praise of others, but instead you should give so that God will receive all the glory *(based on Psalm 115:1; Matthew 6:1-3; I Corinthians 10:31)*.

DYING TO SELF BY SERVING OTHERS

> As a child of God, you have a privileged responsibility to be in ministry alongside others in the Body of Christ. To accomplish His purposes in your area(s) of service, God has provided you with everything needed to fulfill this ministry so that you may do your part to build up the Body of Christ and to bring glory to His Name *(based on Psalm 119:105; Matthew 28:18-20; John 16:13; Acts 1:8; Romans 12:4-8; I Corinthians 12:7; Ephesians 4:11-12, 16; II Timothy 3:16-17; James 1:5; I Peter 4:10-11; I John 5:14-15).*

I. **As a believer in Jesus Christ, you have been given all the provisions you need for ministry.**

   A. God has given you His Son, who alone can provide you with abundant life and access to God, the Father *(John 10:10; Ephesians 2:14-18).*

   Refer to:
   YOU CAN CHANGE BIBLICALLY (PART ONE) (Lesson 1, Pages 3-7) and
   YOU CAN CHANGE BIBLICALLY (PART TWO) (Lesson 2, Pages 3-5).

   B. God has given you His Word which alone will provide specific direction for every area of life *(II Timothy 3:16-17; II Peter 1:3-4; Hebrews 4:12).*

   Refer to: **SCRIPTURE IS YOUR AUTHORITY** (Lesson 3, Pages 3-5).

   C. God has sent His Spirit to indwell you, to empower you, to help you in times of prayer, and to help you understand the things of God *(Romans 8:9-11, 26-27; I Corinthians 2:10, 12; Ephesians 3:16).*

   Refer to: **THE HOLY SPIRIT EMPOWERS YOU TO SOLVE YOUR PROBLEMS** (Lesson 3, Pages 6-8)

II. **God has a unique plan of ministry for you and for every other believer to fulfill.**

   A. God gives at least one spiritual gift, in addition to talents and abilities, to every believer. These gracious provisions are not for your own use but are to be used for service and edification in the Body of Christ *(I Corinthians 12:7; Ephesians 4:16; I Peter 4:10).* Each spiritual gift is sovereignly distributed by the will of the Holy Spirit *(I Corinthians 12:8-11).*

   B. God has given a variety of spiritual gifts to His children to accomplish a number of ministries in an effective and harmonious manner, consistent with the unity in the Body of Christ *(Romans 12:6-8; I Corinthians 12:4-6).*

   C. In the history of the Church, God has sovereignly chosen and spiritually gifted leaders (apostles, prophets, evangelists, pastors, and teachers) to fulfill specific functions in the Body of Christ *(I Corinthians 12:28; Ephesians 4:11-12).*

   D. In the life and history of the Church, spiritual gifts have been granted to individuals for the benefit of the Body of Christ and the glory of God. There are three main Scripture passages listing these spiritual gifts. The three passages and their lists are:

© Biblical Counseling Foundation

1. Prophecy, service, teaching, exhortation, giving, leadership, mercy *(Romans 12:6-8)*;

2. Word of wisdom, word of knowledge, faith, gifts of healing, effecting of miracles, prophecy, distinguishing of spirits, kinds of tongues, interpretation of tongues, teaching, helps, administrations *(I Corinthians 12:8-10, 28)*; and

3. Speaking the utterances of God, service *(I Peter 4:11)*.

III. **As a believer in Jesus Christ, you need to minister and are needed in ministry by the rest of the Body of Christ.**

A. As a believer, you are to exercise spiritual gift(s) in love *(I Corinthians 12:31 - 13:13)*. When each child of God faithfully serves in ministry, the entire body is built up in love *(Ephesians 4:16)*.

B. Using spiritual gifts in a biblical manner fosters care for one another, eliminates division in the Body of Christ *(I Corinthians 12:18-27; Ephesians 4:16)*, and glorifies God *(I Peter 4:11)*.

C. You become a good steward of God's grace as you use spiritual gift(s) to serve others *(I Peter 4:10)*. Faithfulness in ministry is expected *(Luke 17:7-10; I Corinthians 4:2, 12:7; Ephesians 4:16; I Peter 4:10)*, and you are to desire spiritual gifts *(I Corinthians 14:1)*. To use your spiritual gift in an effective manner, the following guidelines for ministry are suggested:

1. Continually place the highest priority on your relationship and walk with God *(Psalm 37:3-5; Matthew 22:37-38; Ephesians 4:1)*.

2. Prayerfully evaluate your motives for ministry, which should be to cooperate with God in fulfilling His purposes in the world, to edify the Body of Christ, and to glorify God *(I Corinthians 12:4-6; Ephesians 4:11-12, 16; I Peter 4:11)*. Ask God for wisdom as you seek your area of ministry *(Philippians 4:6; James 1:5)*.

3. Be aware of the spiritual gifts that God has provided in the Body of Christ *(I Corinthians 12:1)*. Beware of false teaching contrary to God's Word that may be presented in this area of spiritual life *(II Peter 2:1-3; I John 4:1)*.

4. Seek and take advantage of opportunities to minister, especially in areas that keep you in a Christlike servant attitude before others *(Matthew 20:25-28; I Corinthians 4:2, 12:22; Philippians 2:3-8)*.

5. Seek counsel from spiritually mature believers about ministry needs before you begin to serve. Continue to listen to this counsel concerning the effectiveness of your service during your time of ministry *(Proverbs 11:14, 12:15, 27:17; Ephesians 5:21; Hebrews 13:17)*.

6. Continue to judge yourself and your motivation to serve in the light of God's Word. Don't compare yourself with others or evaluate your service merely by your feelings *(based on John 5:41, 44; II Corinthians 4:5; 5:15; 10:12, 18; I Thessalonians 2:5-8; Hebrews 4:12)*. You must not think too little or too highly of your part in the Body of Christ. Each member is a vital part of the unity and care of the Body *(Romans 12:3-6a; I Corinthians 12:12, 14, 18, 24b-25)*.

OVERCOMING A PREOCCUPATION WITH SELF

> A focus on self is crippling to your spiritual development and must be put off if you are to mature in Christ. As with all sinful deeds, your preoccupation with self must be consistently replaced by a commitment to please God and be a blessing to others. Regardless of your feelings or desires, you must obey God's Word in every situation by being content with what God has given you and by disciplining yourself for the purpose of godliness (*based on Matthew 10:38-39, 22:37-39; Romans 6:12-13, 13:9-13; II Corinthians 10:5; Galatians 5:16-26; I Timothy 4:7, 6:6-8; Hebrews 13:5; I Peter 1:13-16*).

I. Cross-references

Sins such as self-belittlement, self-exaltation, self-pity, envy, jealousy, covetousness, and greed indicate a severe preoccupation with self. To overcome this unbiblical condition, review carefully:

A. The foundational, biblical requirements for change (Lessons 1 and 2), recognizing the differences between living man's way and living God's way (Lessons 3 and 4);

B. The essential elements of biblical change (Lessons 5 - 8) as you die to self and live for the Lord (Lesson 9);

C. The necessity of dealing with anger in a biblical manner (Lesson 11);

D. The applicability of this situation to loving your neighbor (Lessons 12 and 13) and family relationships (Lessons 14 - 17);

E. The possible links between fear, worry, or depression (Lessons 18 and 19) and a self-focus;

F. The seriousness of life-dominating sins and their relationship to a preoccupation with self (Lessons 20 and 21); and

G. The need to establish specific godly standards for life which are to be faithfully maintained (Lesson 22).

NOTE: The cross-references cited above are important in dealing with specific problem areas (Lessons 9-21), since no problem can be dealt with biblically without regard to the other aspects of your life. For example, the problem of envy cannot be overcome by dealing with it as an end in itself. Rather, any specific problem must be dealt with in light of scriptural principles for all of life. As you will note, previous lessons are listed in addition to those not yet covered. This is done to emphasize that you are to focus the full range of essential scriptural principles upon particular problems in your own life.

If you proceed in biblical counseling training, you will be able to find God's solutions to problems of life other than the ones covered in this manual through the full range of scriptural principles presented in this course.

II. To become aware of the patterns of sin or temptations regarding a preoccupation on self, list people, places, times, or circumstances where ongoing problems are evident in your life.

III. Use the VICTORY OVER FAILURES WORKSHEET (Supplement 8). To complete columns 1-3, follow the instructions in GUIDELINES: VICTORY OVER FAILURES WORKSHEET (Supplement 7).

IV. When completing column four of the VICTORY OVER FAILURES WORKSHEET (Supplement 8):

A. Develop a **basic plan** to overcome the sins you have recognized. In your plan, include deeds (thoughts, speech, and actions) that will help you develop a Christlike manner by taking into account the following guidelines:

1. Think biblically

a. Confess all sinful thoughts to God *(I John 1:9)* and ask for His help in changing this sinful pattern *(I Thessalonians 5:17; Hebrews 4:15-16; James 1:5)*.

b. Develop a thought life that focuses on glorifying and pleasing God and being a blessing to others in all situations *(based on Matthew 22:37-39; Luke 9:23-24; II Corinthians 5:9, 15; 10:5; Galatians 5:16-17; Philippians 2:3-4, 4:8; Colossians 3:2)*.

c. Stop comparing yourself with others *(II Corinthians 10:12)*.

d. Instead, rejoice *(Philippians 4:4; I Thessalonians 5:16)* and give thanks in and for every situation *(Ephesians 5:20; I Thessalonians 5:18)*. Remain content in God's provision for all areas of your life *(Matthew 6:25-34; Philippians 4:11-13, 19; I Timothy 6:6-8)* knowing that endurance in trials helps conform you to the image of Christ *(based on Romans 5:3-5; James 1:2-4)*.

e. Find or remind yourself of ways to bless others, beginning with those against whom you have sinned through envy, jealousy, covetousness, or greed *(Matthew 5:38-48; Romans 12:9-21)*.

f. Commit to please the Lord in all things instead of living to gratify your fleshly desires *(based on Luke 9:23-24; Romans 13:13-14; II Corinthians 5:15; Galatians 5:16-17; Colossians 1:10; I Peter 1:14-16)*.

g. No matter what the situation, discipline your mind to dwell on those things that give honor to the Lord and that edify others within that very circumstance *(based on II Corinthians 10:5; Philippians 4:8; Colossians 3:2)*.

h. Recognize that God has given you, as a believer, at least one spiritual gift by which you are to serve others *(Romans 12:3-8; I Corinthians 12:12-13; Ephesians 4:15-16; I Thessalonians 5:11; I Peter 4:10-11)*.

2. Speak biblically

a. Let your speech be truthful, edifying, and gracious to others *(Ephesians 4:15, 25, 29; Colossians 4:6)* instead of being abusive or unedifying to those around you *(Ephesians 5:4; Colossians 3:8)*. You are not to grumble or complain (dispute) in any situation *(Philippians 2:14)*.

b. Do not talk about your past accomplishments *(Proverbs 27:2, 30:32; II Corinthians 10:18)*, sorrows or defeats *(Philippians 3:13-14)*, worries about the future *(Matthew 6:34)*, comparisons between yourself and others *(II Corinthians 10:12)*, or supposed personal accomplishments in the future *(Proverbs 27:1; James 4:13-16)*. Instead, thankfully speak of the goodness of the Lord and the difference He has made, and continues to make, in your life *(Luke 10:20; Hebrews 13:15; I Peter 3:15).*

c.   Confess your sin of envy, jealousy, covetousness, or greed to those against whom you have sinned *(James 5:16).*

3.   Act biblically

a.   Correct deficiencies in your life that exist because of a lack of discipline or neglect *(I Corinthians 10:32-33; Colossians 3:1-17; James 4:17).*

b.   Take advantage of opportunities to minister, especially in areas that keep you in a Christlike servant attitude toward others *(Matthew 20:25-28; I Corinthians 4:2; Philippians 2:3-8).*

c.   Prayerfully construct a scriptural plan whereby you can bless others through tangible expressions of biblical love and set up a schedule to fulfill your plan consistently. This plan should include fulfilling your daily responsibilities as a husband, wife, parent, student, roommate, employer, employee, etc. *(Matthew 7:12; Romans 12:9-21, 13:8-13; I Corinthians 13:4-8a; Ephesians 4:28; Philippians 2:3-8; I Timothy 6:17-19; I Peter 3:8-9).*

Refer to: **MY PROPOSED BIBLICAL SCHEDULE** *(Supplement 15).*

d.   Memorize Scripture verses and study Scripture passages specifically related to overcoming a preoccupation with self *(based on Psalm 119:9, 11, 16; II Corinthians 10:5; Philippians 4:8; II Timothy 2:15).*   Also memorize psalms, hymns, and spiritual songs to help set your mind on the Lord and on being a blessing to others *(based on Ephesians 5:19-20; Colossians 3:16).*

e.   Show God's wisdom in your actions by being pure, peaceable, gentle, reasonable (willing to yield), full of mercy and good fruits, unwavering, and without hypocrisy *(James 3:13-18).*

f.   Practice biblical stewardship to honor the Lord and to be a blessing to others

Refer to:
BIBLICAL PRINCIPLES OF STEWARDSHIP *(Lesson 10, Pages 4-6) and*
DYING TO SELF BY SERVING OTHERS *(Lesson 10, Pages 7-8).*

B.   Develop a **"THINK AND DO" LIST** (Supplement 10) using **GUIDELINES: THE "THINK AND DO" LIST** (Supplement 9).

C.   Implement your **basic plan** *(James 1:22)* and do it heartily for the Lord *(Colossians 3:23-24).*

D.   Develop a **contingency plan** to deal with unexpected situations that provide temptation for you to be preoccupied with or focused on self. Take into account the following guidelines:

1.   Immediately ask God for help *(I Thessalonians 5:17; Hebrews 4:15-16; James 1:5).*

2.   Immediately seek God's perspective.

a.   See this situation as an opportunity for further spiritual maturity *(James 1:2-4).*

b.   Remember that God looks on your heart, not on your outward appearance *(I Samuel 16:7).* You must stand blameless before Him in your thoughts, whether others know about it or not *(based on Acts 23:1, 24:16; Romans 14:12; Ephesians 4:1; Philippians 1:9-11; Colossians 1:21-22).*

        c.   Continue to trust God because He will work all things together for good in your life, regardless of your feelings or circumstances *(Psalm 37; Proverbs 3:5-12; Romans 8:28-29; Ephesians 1:3-14; Philippians 1:6)*.

        d.   Remind yourself that you can do all things through Christ who gives you strength *(Philippians 4:11-13)*, since your adequacy is from God *(II Corinthians 3:5)*. Remember that you can do nothing fruitful apart from Jesus Christ *(John 15:5)*.

3.   If you even begin to think sinful thoughts in this unforeseen circumstance, confess them to the Lord *(I John 1:9)*. Remember that it is not the amount of time spent sinning or the immensity of the sin (by human standards) by which you are to judge yourself. Rather, the fact that you stopped going God's way even momentarily is what matters *(James 2:10, 4:17)*.

4.   Praise and glorify God that He is sufficient even in your areas of weakness *(II Corinthians 12:9-10)* and that He will keep you from stumbling and make you stand blameless and with great joy in the presence of His glory *(Jude 1:24-25)*.

5.   Thank God that you are His servant in your present circumstance *(Ephesians 5:20; I Thessalonians 5:18)*. Determine how you will give glory to God *(I Corinthians 10:31; I Peter 4:11)*, and seek ways to edify others by serving them *(Ephesians 4:29; Philippians 2:3-4)*.

6.   Review Scripture verses *(such as Luke 9:23-24)* that point out the error of being preoccupied with self *(based on Psalm 119:9, 11, 16)*.

E.   Implement your **contingency plan** vigorously, as soon as you detect temptation to be focused on self *(based on I Thessalonians 5:22; II Timothy 2:19-22)*. Then, begin again to do those things written in your **basic plan** *(Proverbs 24:16; James 1:22-25)*.

A CASE STUDY: MARY'S HUSBAND HAS LEFT HER

> No matter how severe a problem may seem, there are basic scriptural principles to follow that will enable you to fulfill God's plan for your life and give biblical counsel to others *(based on Matthew 7:1-5; Romans 8:28, 15:14; I Corinthians 10:13; II Corinthians 1:3-5; II Timothy 3:16-17; Hebrews 4:15-16).*

Mary and her husband (Tom) have been your neighbors for six years. They have three children: two teenagers (a boy, 14, and a girl, 13) and a small daughter (3 years old). Mary came to your local church regularly until three weeks ago; her husband, Tom, has never attended. You are casually acquainted with Tom and Mary but have not discussed spiritual matters with them.

After Mary's abrupt entrance into your house, telling you with great emotion that her husband has left her (refer to Lesson 9, Page 12), she asks you not to tell the pastor about this present situation. You explain that she may not get all the help available to her if her pastor is not informed of this difficulty *(Proverbs 11:14)*. She agrees that you may call him, but she refuses to talk to him herself.

You call the pastor. He tells you to keep him informed and encourages you to rely only on God's Word. He gives you a few starting helps, knowing that you are attending the Self-Confrontation class. Your pastor's directions to you are:

1. Pray with Mary now.

2. Set a specific time and place for Mary to come tomorrow and discuss her problem with you and other biblical counselors *(Proverbs 11:14; 15:22)*. Designate how long the session will last (for example, "We will spend an hour together and see what we ought to do"). Don't make it a social call. Tell Mary that because you intend to take her problem seriously and to work with her toward overcoming it *(Proverbs 17:17; 18:2, 13, 24)*, she must come prepared for a working session by bringing her Bible, a notebook, and pen or pencil.

3. In your first session, start with prayer *(Luke 18:1; Philippians 4:6-7)*.

4. Using the **FACTS ABOUT BIBLICAL COUNSELING** (Supplement 11), point out to Mary the following:

    a. The Bible is the only guide that never fails *(Psalm 19:7-8; Proverbs 30:5-6; II Timothy 3:16-17; Hebrews 4:12; II Peter 1:3-4)*.

    b. The Holy Spirit is the One who does the work in her life *(Romans 8:5-11; Galatians 5:22-23)*.

    c. There are four elements to be emphasized in every counseling session: **Understanding the problem, Hope, Change, and Practice**

        Refer to: WHAT MAKES COUNSELING BIBLICAL (Supplement 1) under the section titled, ESSENTIAL ELEMENTS OF BIBLICAL COUNSELING (Page 3 of that supplement).

        First: **Understand the problem.** Make biblical inquiry by asking "what, who, when, where, and how" questions, but avoid "why" questions; get all the facts *(Proverbs 18:13, 17; James 1:19)*. It is important that you help Mary gain God's

---

perspective on her problem *(Proverbs 3:5-6; Isaiah 55:8-9; Romans 5:3-5, 8:28-29; James 1:2-4).*

Second: There is **hope**. In the Scriptures, God has promised that He will not let His children be tried or tempted, suffer pressure or anxiety, or face any problem that is beyond their endurance; but He will always provide a way to endure in every situation without sinning *(based on I Corinthians 10:13; Hebrews 4:15-16).*

Third: You must learn how to **change**. In other words, you must learn how to lay aside the old selfish ways, the destructive anxieties, the old habits, and learn to implement the new biblical ways of thinking and living *(Ephesians 4:22-24; Philippians 4:6-9; Colossians 3:2-17).*

Fourth: You must **practice** being a doer of the Word. If you hear His Word and do not change in accordance with its principles and precepts, you delude and deceive yourself; and your problems get worse. However, if you learn to obey His Word, He has promised that you will be blessed and enjoy days filled with peace and joy in spite of any circumstance *(Matthew 7:24-27; John 15:10-12, 16:33; James 1:22-25; I Peter 3:8-17).*

After receiving these guidelines from your pastor, you ask Mary to read and memorize *I Corinthians 10:13* before your meeting tomorrow. Using this verse, show her the hope that God has promised in this situation. You ask Mary to read *I Corinthians 13:4-8a, Philippians 4:6-9,* and *James 1:22-25* in order to be prepared to discuss these passages at tomorrow's session. Because of Mary's distraught state, you ask her to write down these Scripture references so she will not forget them. After prayer, you arrange a meeting time with Mary the following day at your home. You also encourage her to call a friend or one of the women at church to provide care for her daughter during the time of the counseling session tomorrow.

Especially note the four essential elements of biblical counseling (understanding the problem, hope, change, and practice). If you have not already done so, mark the verses in your Bible which provide the scriptural foundation for these four elements.

At this stage in the case study, observe especially how scriptural hope can be given to Mary in spite of her present difficulty.

LESSON 10: HOMEWORK

> God desires that you honor Him in every area of your life. This week's **HOMEWORK** is designed to help you overcome a preoccupation with self in order for you to mature in Christ Jesus *(based on Mark 7:20-23; Romans 13:9; I Corinthians 13:4; Galatians 5:26; Ephesians 5:3; I Peter 2:1-2).*

✔ *homework completed*

☐ A. * In your own words, write the meaning of *Romans 6:12-13.* Memorize *Romans 6:12-13* and begin memorizing *Ephesians 4:31-32* and *James 1:19-20.* Review previous memory verses.

☐ B. * Read **BIBLICAL PRINCIPLES: DEALING WITH SELF (PART TWO)** (Lesson 10, Pages 2-3). Highlight any verses that you have not marked in previous lessons.

☐ C. * Complete the fourth column of your **VICTORY OVER FAILURES WORKSHEET** (Supplement 8, Page 2) that you began last week. Read **OVERCOMING A PREOCCUPATION WITH SELF** (Lesson 10, Pages 9-12). When working on the fourth column, develop specific plans for blessing the very individuals against whom you have sinned (base your plans on *Romans 12:9-21* and *James 3:5-18*).

☐ D. * Using your list of blessings in the fourth column of the **VICTORY OVER FAILURES WORKSHEET** (Supplement 8, Page 2), bless at least one person daily. Make a note of the day and time you practiced your plan. Place a check mark by the ones you did and record the names of the people you blessed. Give thanks to God for empowering you to bless others.

☐ E. Read **BIBLICAL PRINCIPLES OF STEWARDSHIP** (Lesson 10, Pages 4-6). Place a check mark by the statements that describe areas of your life that need to change. Formulate a plan to practice biblical stewardship in those areas that need to change and begin to implement your plan.

☐ F. Read **DYING TO SELF BY SERVING OTHERS** (Lesson 10, Pages 7-8). Notice how God has equipped you for service. Do your actions show a life committed to pleasing God by ministering to others? If not, make plans whereby you will be faithful in this ministry. Include your ministry plans this week as part of the completion of the fourth column in your **VICTORY OVER FAILURES WORKSHEET** (Supplement 8, Page 2).

☐ G. Read **A CASE STUDY: MARY'S HUSBAND HAS LEFT HER** (Lesson 10, Pages 13-14). Especially note the four key elements of biblical counseling and mark the verses in your Bible which support each element. Observe how scriptural hope can be given to Mary in spite of her present difficulty.

☐ H. * In conjunction with this lesson, answer statement 17 under **Open Book Test** (Lesson 23, Page 2).

 * *The completion of assignments marked with an asterisk (*) is a prerequisite for further biblical counseling training.*

LESSON 10: STUDY GUIDE FOR DAILY DEVOTIONS
(INCLUDING SCRIPTURE MEMORY AND HOMEWORK)

> God desires that you honor Him in every area of your life. This week's **STUDY GUIDE** is designed to help you overcome a preoccupation with self in order for you to mature in Christ Jesus *(based on Mark 7:20-23; Romans 13:9; I Corinthians 13:4; Galatians 5:26; Ephesians 5:3; I Peter 2:1-2).*

Scripture Memory

1.   * Memorize *Romans 6:12-13* and begin memorizing *Ephesians 4:31-32* and *James 1:19-20.*
2.   Carry your memory verse cards from previous weeks along with this week's memory verses. Review your memory verses during your spare moments throughout the day.

Daily Devotional Study Guide

FIRST DAY

1.   Open with prayer.
2.   * Read *Principle 39* under **BIBLICAL PRINCIPLES: DEALING WITH SELF (PART TWO)** (Lesson 10, Pages 2-3). Highlight referenced verses in your Bible.
3.   Read **OVERCOMING A PREOCCUPATION WITH SELF** (Lesson 10, Pages 9-12).
4.   * In your own words, write the meaning of *Romans 6:12-13.*
5.   Close with prayer.

SECOND DAY

1.   Open with prayer.
2.   * Read *Principle 40* under **BIBLICAL PRINCIPLES: DEALING WITH SELF (PART TWO)** (Lesson 10, Pages 2-3). Highlight verses not previously marked.
3.   * Continue to work on the **VICTORY OVER FAILURES WORKSHEET** (Supplement 8, Page 2) that you began last week. Complete the fourth column by developing specific plans for blessing the very individuals against whom you have sinned.
4.   Close with prayer.

THIRD DAY

1.   Open with prayer.
2.   * Read *Principle 41* under **BIBLICAL PRINCIPLES: DEALING WITH SELF (PART TWO)** (Lesson 10, Pages 2-3). Highlight referenced verses in your Bible.
3.   * Continue to work on your **VICTORY OVER FAILURES WORKSHEET** (Supplement 8, Page 2). Do at least one blessing today from your list in the fourth column of this worksheet, recording the name of the person receiving the blessing. Give thanks to God for empowering you to bless others.
4.   Read **BIBLICAL PRINCIPLES OF STEWARDSHIP** (Lesson 10, Pages 4-6). Place a check mark by the statements that describe areas of your life that need to change. This is the first day of a two-day study.
5.   Close with prayer.
6.   Make necessary adjustments in your use of spare moments throughout the day to review and memorize Scripture.

FOURTH DAY

1. Open with prayer.
2. * Read *Principle 42* under **BIBLICAL PRINCIPLES: DEALING WITH SELF (PART TWO)** (Lesson 10, Pages 2-3). Highlight verses in your Bible that have not been marked in previous studies.
3. * Take specific steps of action that you have listed in column 4 of your **VICTORY OVER FAILURES WORKSHEET** (Supplement 8, Page 2), keeping a record of the blessings you give. Continue working on the fourth column by adding blessings for others.
4. Complete your study of **BIBLICAL PRINCIPLES OF STEWARDSHIP** (Lesson 10, Pages 4-6). Formulate a plan to practice biblical stewardship in those areas of your life that need to change. Begin to implement your plan.
5. Close with prayer.

FIFTH DAY

1. Open with prayer.
2. * *Read Principle 43* under **BIBLICAL PRINCIPLES: DEALING WITH SELF (PART TWO)** (Lesson 10, Pages 2-3). Highlight the referenced verses.
3. * Work on your **VICTORY OVER FAILURES WORKSHEET** (Supplement 8, Pages 1-2). Complete your plan to overcome self-belittlement, self-exaltation, self-pity, envy, jealousy, covetousness, or greed; and continue to give blessings to those listed in column 4 of the worksheet.
4. Read **DYING TO SELF BY SERVING OTHERS** (Lesson 10, Pages 7-8). If you are not already ministering to others, make plans to do so. Include these plans as part of the fourth column in your **VICTORY OVER FAILURES WORKSHEET**.
5. Close with prayer.

SIXTH DAY

1. Open with prayer.
2. * Read *Principle 44* under **BIBLICAL PRINCIPLES: DEALING WITH SELF (PART TWO)** (Lesson 10, Pages 2-3). Highlight verses in your Bible not marked previously.
3. * Read **A CASE STUDY: MARY'S HUSBAND HAS LEFT HER** (Lesson 10, Pages 13-14). Note the basic premises of biblical counseling and observe how scriptural hope can be given to Mary in spite of the crisis in which she finds herself.
4. * Follow through on your plan to overcome self-belittlement, self-exaltation, self-pity, envy, covetousness, jealousy, or greed as recorded in column 4 of your **VICTORY OVER FAILURES WORKSHEET** (Supplement 8, Page 2).
5. Close with prayer.

SEVENTH DAY

1. Open with prayer.
2. * In conjunction with this lesson, answer statement 17 under **Open Book Test** (Lesson 23, Page 2).
3. Close in prayer.
4. Ask someone to hear you recite your most recent memory verses with their proper references. Explain how these Scriptures have application to your life.

* *The completion of assignments marked with an asterisk (*) is a prerequisite for further biblical counseling training.*

LESSON 11

ANGER AND BITTERNESS

"Let all bitterness and wrath and anger and clamor and slander be put away from you, along with all malice. And be kind to one another, tender-hearted, forgiving each other, just as God in Christ also has forgiven you."

Ephesians 4:31-32

"This you know, my beloved brethren. But let everyone be quick to hear, slow to speak and slow to anger; for the anger of man does not achieve the righteousness of God."

James 1:19-20

LESSON 11: ANGER AND BITTERNESS

> Anger and bitterness are two noticeable signs of being focused on self and not trusting God's sovereignty in your life. When you believe that God causes all things to work together for good to those who belong to Him and love Him, you can respond to trials with joy instead of anger or bitterness *(based on John 14:15; Romans 5:3-5, 8:28-29; Ephesians 4:31; James 1:2-4; I Peter 1:13-16; I John 5:3).*

I. **The purposes of this lesson are:**

A. To present the biblical view of anger and bitterness;

B. To help you recognize unbiblical responses to anger and bitterness;

C. To develop a plan for overcoming anger and bitterness;

D. To continue the development of a case study in biblical counseling; and

E. To introduce procedures for biblical counseling sessions.

II. **The outline of this lesson**

A. Self-confrontation

1. **BIBLICAL PRINCIPLES: ANGER AND BITTERNESS** (Lesson 11, Pages 2-3)

2. **UNBIBLICAL RESPONSES TO ANGER AND BITTERNESS** (Lesson 11, Pages 4-5)

3. **A BIBLICAL VIEW OF ANGER** (Lesson 11, Pages 6-9)

4. **A BIBLICAL VIEW OF BITTERNESS** (Lesson 11, Pages 10-11)

B. Steps for spiritual growth

1. **OVERCOMING ANGER AND BITTERNESS** (Lesson 11, Pages 12-16)

2. **LESSON 11: HOMEWORK** (Lesson 11, Page 18)

3. **STUDY GUIDE FOR DAILY DEVOTIONS** (Lesson 11, Pages 19-21)

C. Biblical counseling

1. **A CASE STUDY: MARY'S HUSBAND HAS LEFT HER** (Lesson 11, Page 17)

2. **BIBLICAL COUNSELING RECORD** (Supplement 12)

3. **BIBLICAL COUNSELING SUMMARY AND PLANNING** (Supplement 13)

BIBLICAL PRINCIPLES: ANGER AND BITTERNESS

> Anger and bitterness are formidable detriments to biblical love, harmonious relationships, and maturity in Christ. Failing to put off anger and bitterness grieves the Holy Spirit, gives Satan an opportunity in your life, obscures your witness to others, and disrupts the unity in the Body of Christ. Dealing biblically with anger and bitterness requires wholehearted obedience to God's Word in every circumstance and with every person, even if your feelings dictate otherwise *(based on Matthew 5:16; Romans 14:19; I Corinthians 13:4-5; II Corinthians 2:10-11, 5:14-15; Galatians 5:17-26; Ephesians 4:1-3, 26-27, 31-32; 6:11; Colossians 3:8-15; Hebrews 12:15).*

I. God's View

(Principle 45)   Anger (great displeasure, animosity) that is quickly aroused or quickly expressed is characteristic of your old self apart from Jesus Christ and is contrary to Scripture *(Galatians 5:19-20; Colossians 3:8; James 1:19-20).* Bitterness is related to anger and demonstrates a great dissatisfaction with God's sovereignty in your life. Bitterness arises out of living to please self instead of living to please the Lord *(Acts 8:18-23; Romans 3:10-18, esp. vs. 14)* and causes much trouble *(Hebrews 12:15).*

II. Your Hope

(Principle 46)   Since God's Word commands you to put away anger and bitterness *(Psalm 37:8; Ephesians 4:31; Colossians 3:8),* it is possible to do so *(I Corinthians 10:13; Hebrews 2:17-18, 4:15-16).*

(Principle 47)   You do not need to defend or preserve what you perceive to be your "rights" *(based on Psalm 37:23, 84:11-12; I Peter 2:19-25),* because God causes all things to work together for good to those who belong to Him and love Him *(Romans 8:28-29).*

III. Your Change

(Principle 48)   You are to control your spirit *(Proverbs 25:28),* be slow to anger *(James 1:19),* and deal with anger quickly *(Ephesians 4:26-27).* You are to put off anger, wrath, bitterness, quick-temperedness, dissension, abusive speech, and strife; and you are not to take into account a wrong suffered *(Matthew 5:21-22; I Corinthians 13:5; Ephesians 4:31; Colossians 3:8; I Timothy 2:8; Titus 1:7).* Instead, you are to put on patience, kindness, humility, bearing with one another, tenderheartedness, forgiveness, love, and self-control *(Ephesians 4:31-32; Colossians 3:12-14).*

IV. Your Practice

(Principle 49)   List the circumstances or relationships in which you are (or have been) tempted to become angry or bitter *(based on Proverbs 9:6, 14:16; Matthew 7:1-5; Galatians 5:16-21)*. Develop a biblical plan for overcoming anger or bitterness in those situations and formulate a contingency plan for dealing with anger or bitterness that may arise quickly or unexpectedly *(based on Proverbs 28:13; Ephesians 4:26-27; I Thessalonians 5:22; II Timothy 2:15, 22; James 1:19; I Peter 1:13-16)*. As you rely on God's power and provisions *(John 15:5; Galatians 5:24-25; II Timothy 3:16-17)*, diligently do what you have planned to avoid further sin with regard to anger or bitterness *(James 1:22-25, 4:17)*.

*Refer to: **OVERCOMING ANGER AND BITTERNESS** (Lesson 11, Pages 12-16) to help you determine specific, biblical steps to take in overcoming anger or bitterness.*

(Principle 50)   Practice biblical love *(Proverbs 10:12; I Corinthians 13:4-8a; I Peter 1:22, 4:8; I John 4:11)* by forgiving others just as God has forgiven you *(Mark 11:25; Ephesians 4:32; Colossians 3:13)* and by doing kind and tenderhearted deeds to the very individuals with whom you become irritated *(Ephesians 4:32; I Peter 3:8-9)*.

To help you gain a biblical perspective on biblical forgiveness and biblical love, refer to:
FORGIVENESS (FORGIVING OTHERS AS GOD HAS FORGIVEN YOU) (Lesson 12, Pages 3-5); and
THE MEANING OF BIBLICAL LOVE (Lesson 13, Pages 4-6).

UNBIBLICAL RESPONSES TO ANGER AND BITTERNESS

> At times, you may try to justify your anger by saying, "God was angry *(Numbers 25:4)* and Jesus was angry *(Mark 3:5),* so I can be angry too." However, God is perfectly holy, and you are not. His holiness, justice, love, and perfection remain constant even though He is jealous *(Exodus 20:5),* has wrath *(II Chronicles 28:11),* exercises vengeance *(Romans 12:19),* and is indignant every day *(Psalm 7:11).* Unlike God, your flesh is in continual conflict between good and evil *(Romans 7:14-25; Galatians 5:17).* As a result, you will have difficulty responding to emotionally-charged situations without sinning.

I. **Some examples from Scripture of unbiblical deeds resulting from anger and bitterness**

   A. Cain, in his anger, killed his brother. As a result, he became a vagrant and a wanderer *(Genesis 4:5-8, 11-12).*

   B. Simeon and Levi were self-willed men, murdering others in their cruel anger. As a result, their families were scattered *(Genesis 49:5-7).*

   C. Saul became angry and tried to kill his oldest son *(I Samuel 20:30-33).*

   D. Naaman became furious and refused to follow a simple command in order to be healed of leprosy. However, when he finally obeyed, he was healed *(II Kings 5:10-14).*

   E. Uzziah, confronted by the priests for his unfaithfulness to the Lord, became enraged and was struck with leprosy until the day of his death *(II Chronicles 26:16-23).*

   F. Jonah was greatly displeased and angry when the Lord showed compassion on Nineveh, and God subsequently rebuked and humbled him *(Jonah 4:1-11).*

   G. Simon, in his bitterness, tried to buy the authority of God and was openly rebuked by Peter *(Acts 8:14-24).*

II. **Some unbiblical ways of dealing with anger and bitterness**

   A. You explode in a rage or temper, striking out physically or verbally at people or things *(this disregards Proverbs 16:32; Matthew 7:12; Romans 14:19; I Corinthians 13:4-5; Galatians 5:19-20, 22-23; Colossians 3:17).*

   B. You express anger outwardly ("ventilate your anger") by beating a pillow (or another inanimate object) while thinking (or speaking) about the person with whom you are angry or bitter *(this disregards Psalm 19:14; II Corinthians 10:5; Philippians 2:3-4, 4:8-9; Colossians 3:2).*

   C. You control your temper at work (in front of your boss) and at church (in front of Christian brothers and sisters), but you exercise little or no control at home with your loved ones *(this disregards Proverbs 25:28; Matthew 5:13-16, 7:12; Romans 12:9, 14:13; I Corinthians 13:4-5; Galatians 5:19-20, 22-23; Ephesians 4:1-3).*

D.   You exercise strenuously to release feelings of anger yet fail to deal with the sinful basis of your anger *(this disregards I Samuel 16:7; Mark 7:20-23; I Timothy 4:8)*.

E.   You "lose your temper" by honking your horn in traffic, throwing objects, yelling at others, or thinking and speaking obscenities *(this disregards Proverbs 16:32; Matthew 5:16, 7:12; I Corinthians 13:4-5; Galatians 5:19-20, 22-23; Philippians 4:8-9; Colossians 3:17)*.

F.   You seethe inwardly and become bitter *(this disregards Psalm 19:14; Proverbs 25:28; Philippians 4:8-9; Hebrews 12:15)*.

G.   You verbally attack or slander individuals who persecute you or take advantage of you *(this disregards Matthew 5:10-12, 38-48; Romans 12:17-21, 13:10, 14:19, 15:2; Ephesians 4:29, 31-32; I Peter 2:20-25, 3:8-9)*.

H.   You discuss everything about your anger or bitterness "to get in touch with your feelings" and to release repressed emotions ("catharsis") *(this disregards Matthew 15:18; II Corinthians 5:17; Galatians 5:17-25; Philippians 2:3-4, 3:13-14, 4:8-9)*.

I.   You deny ("internalize") that you are angry or bitter *(this disregards Ephesians 4:15, 25; James 3:14, 5:16; I John 1:8-10)*.

J.   You write vengeful letters to express your anger or bitterness but don't mail them (to combine "ventilation of anger" and "catharsis") *(this disregards Matthew 5:22-24, 44; Mark 11:25-26; Romans 12:9-21, 14:10-12; Ephesians 4:29; Philippians 2:3-4, 4:8-9)*.

K.   You characterize your anger as "righteous indignation" and your bitterness as "justifiable" instead of biblically examining your anger and bitterness and responding accordingly *(this disregards Isaiah 5:20-21, 55:7-9; Matthew 7:1-5; Ephesians 4:31; Hebrews 12:15; James 1:19-25, 3:13 - 4:2)*.

III.   Some unbiblical justifications for anger or bitterness

A.   You claim that others and/or their actions are responsible for your anger or bitterness *(this disregards Ezekiel 18:20; Mark 7:20-23; I Corinthians 10:13; Ephesians 4:31-32; Colossians 3:12-14)*.

B.   You claim that past, present, and possible future circumstances have led to your anger or bitterness *(this disregards Matthew 15:18-19; Romans 5:3-5, 8:28-29; James 1:2-4)*.

*Note: You are living to please yourself when you respond unbiblically to the sins of anger and bitterness. Review **THE BIBLICAL VIEW OF SELF** (Lesson 4, Pages 5-10). As you focus on self, you may attempt to "solve" your problem of anger or bitterness; but this "solution" will be based on the wisdom of man. Trusting in man's wisdom leads to a further emphasis on self. Review **BASIC APPROACHES TO SOLVING PERSONAL PROBLEMS** (Lesson 4, Page 11). Without relying solely on the Lord and His Word, you cannot overcome anger or bitterness in a manner that gives glory to God.*

A BIBLICAL VIEW OF ANGER

> If you fail to deal biblically with anger, increasing disobedience to Scripture is inevitable *(based on Genesis 4:5-8; I Samuel 18:7-9; Psalm 37:8; Proverbs 19:19, 29:22; Ephesians 4:26-27).* However, God's abundant resources and promises enable you to be an overwhelming conqueror as you deal biblically with the problem of anger in your life *(based on John 16:13, 23-24; Romans 8:31-39, esp. vs. 37; I Corinthians 10:13; Ephesians 4:31-32; Philippians 1:6, 4:13; II Timothy 3:16-17; James 1:5; I John 3:22).*

I. Anger of God

A. While Scripture describes God as angry *(Exodus 4:14, 22:24; Numbers 11:33, 25:4, 32:10-15; Deuteronomy 29:27-28; 32:16, 19-22; Joshua 23:16; I Kings 11:9; II Kings 22:13; Psalm 78:49-50, 90:7; Isaiah 30:27; Daniel 9:16),* He remains holy *(Leviticus 11:45; I Peter 1:16)* and without sin *(Job 34:10; Matthew 5:48; James 1:13).*

B. God is slow to anger and simultaneously merciful, gracious, compassionate, forgiving, and abundant in lovingkindness and truth *(Nehemiah 9:17; Psalm 86:15, 103:8, 145:8; Nahum 1:3).*

C. God's favor is for a lifetime, but His anger is for a moment *(Psalm 30:5).* He often restrains His anger *(Psalm 78:38).*

D. God's anger is always directed at rebellion or disobedience to His commands, which are always holy and just *(Deuteronomy 29:14-21, 24-28; Psalm 78:21-22; Lamentations 3:42-43; Zephaniah 2:2-3; Romans 2:5; Hebrews 3:7-11).*

II. Anger of Jesus

A. Jesus was angry at the hypocrisy and legalism of the religious leaders while simultaneously grieving over their hardness of heart. In spite of being angry, He healed a man *(Mark 3:5).*

B. In the first cleansing of the Temple *(John 2:13-16),* Scripture does not teach that Jesus was angry but instead teaches that He was motivated by a divine jealousy (zeal) for His Father's house *(John 2:17).* Afterwards, He answered questions from the religious leaders *(John 2:18-21).* Nor is it recorded in Scripture that Jesus was angry at the second cleansing of the temple *(Matthew 21:12-13; Mark 11:15-17; Luke 19:45-46).* After His actions on this occasion, He healed the sick and responded to questions of the religious leaders *(Matthew 21:14-16; Mark 11:17-18).*

III. Anger that is not sinful

A. On extremely rare and exceptional occasions in Scripture, a person devoted to God was recorded as being angry with no accompanying sin *(for example: Exodus 16:20; Leviticus 10:16-20; I Samuel 11:6, 20:34; II Kings 13:19; Nehemiah 5:6).*

B. Since Scripture states that it is possible for a child of God to be angry and not sin *(Ephesians 4:26-27)*, it is possible to do so *(Romans 6:12-13; I Corinthians 10:13; I Peter 1:13-16)*.

C. In order to "be angry and sin not," you must obey God's Word with **no** exceptions *(II Timothy 3:16-17)* and must completely follow the example of God *(Matthew 5:48; Ephesians 5:1)* and our Lord Jesus Christ *(I Peter 1:14-16, 2:21-22)*.

IV. Sinful anger

A. Scripture teaches that the anger of man cannot achieve the righteousness of God *(James 1:20)*. Your anger, whether explosive in expression or settled as a disposition, is to be decisively put off if you are to be conformed to the image of Jesus Christ *(Ephesians 4:31; Colossians 3:8, 10)*.

B. Outbursts of anger are part of the deeds of the flesh *(Galatians 5:19-21)* and are characteristic of a fool *(Proverbs 29:11)*. Besides showing a lack of the fruit of the Spirit *(Galatians 5:22-23)*, a person with a quick temper abounds in transgressions *(Proverbs 29:22)* and is not fit to assume church leadership responsibilities *(Titus 1:7)*.

C. Anger is a prelude to and is often compounded by further sins *(Genesis 4:5-8, 49:6; I Samuel 20:30-33; Psalm 37:8; Matthew 2:16)*, is devastating *(Proverbs 27:4)*, and is associated with both strife *(Proverbs 15:18, 29:22, 30:33)* and foolishness *(Proverbs 14:29, 29:11; Ecclesiastes 7:9)*.

D. Anger against another is condemned by our Lord *(Matthew 5:22)* and shows a lack of biblical love *(I Corinthians 13:4-8a)*.

E. Anger demonstrates a lack of trust in God's sovereignty *(Psalm 37:1-11, esp. vss. 7-9)* and may also indicate a failure to follow the Lord Jesus Christ *(based on I Peter 2:19-24)*.

F. A person with great anger will continually be in difficulty *(Proverbs 19:19, 29:22)*, will wrongly influence others, and should be avoided *(Proverbs 22:24-25)*.

G. Your anger is sinful when you:

1. Are quick-tempered or have angry outbursts *(Galatians 5:20; Ephesians 4:31; James 1:19)*;

2. Become angry and are not merciful, compassionate, and forgiving *(Nehemiah 9:17; Psalm 86:15; Ephesians 4:32)*;

3. Seek vengeance or retaliation against another *(Romans 12:17-19; Hebrews 10:30)*;

4. Violate biblical love in your anger *(I Corinthians 13:4-8; I Peter 4:8)*;

5. Fail to demonstrate the fruit of the Spirit in your thoughts, words, or actions: love, joy, peace, patience, kindness, goodness, faithfulness, gentleness, and self-control *(Galatians 5:22-23)*;

6. Use words that are not edifying *(Matthew 12:36-37; Ephesians 4:29; I Peter 3:10)*;

7. Respond angrily in order to "protect your rights" or "get your own way" *(Luke 9:23; II Corinthians 5:15; I Peter 2:21-23)*;

8. Have an abiding (continuing) anger against another *(Matthew 5:21-22)* or let the sun go down on your anger *(i.e., fail to deal with your anger in a biblical manner but harbor it instead) (Ephesians 4:26)*;

9. Respond to anger in a manner that does not please the Lord *(II Corinthians 5:9; Colossians 1:10)* or bring honor to His Name *(I Corinthians 10:31; Colossians 3:17; I Peter 1:6-7);* and

10. Become angry and neglect to rejoice, to pray, or to give thanks in the very situation in which you find yourself *(I Thessalonians 5:16-18).*

H. You also sin if you respond angrily in areas where Scripture has already told you how to act. For example, with regard to:

1. An enemy, you must look for and meet his needs *(Romans 12:20)* and show love to him *(Luke 6:35);*

2. The civic authorities, you are to obey them and give to them what is due *(Romans 13:1-8; I Peter 2:13-15),* unless their demands contradict God's Word and would force you to sin *(Acts 4:19-20, 5:29);*

3. An unreasonable supervisor, you are to submit *(I Peter 2:18),* except when doing so would cause you to disobey Scripture *(Genesis 39:7-9);*

4. Your circumstances, you are to trust God and be content *(Ecclesiastes 7:14; Romans 8:28-29; Philippians 4:11-13; I Timothy 6:6-8);*

5. Your trials, you are to cooperate with God and respond joyfully as He develops Christlike character in your life *(Romans 5:3-5; James 1:2-4);*

6. Unjust treatment, you are patiently to endure and thus find favor with God *(I Peter 2:19-20);*

7. Fellow-believers who are caught in sin, you are to restore them in gentleness *(Galatians 6:1)* and not regard them as enemies *(II Thessalonians 3:15);*

8. Your parents (while they are in biblical authority over you), you are to obey them in a manner that pleases the Lord *(Ephesians 6:1; Colossians 3:20);*

9. Your children, you are not to provoke them to wrath but are to teach them with the discipline and instruction of the Lord *(Ephesians 6:4);*

10. Husbands and wives, each is to submit to one another *(Ephesians 5:21)* and to love each other in a consistently biblical manner *(I Corinthians 13:4-8; Ephesians 5:25; Titus 2:4);* and

11. Scripturally qualified church leaders, you are to obey them *(Hebrews 13:17)* and to esteem them highly in love *(I Thessalonians 5:12-13).*

V. Anger and the inner man

A. Since your heart is revealed by your thoughts, words, and actions *(Matthew 12:34-35, 15:18-20; Mark 7:20-23; Luke 6:45),* sinful anger reveals that you are living to please yourself *(based on II Corinthians 5:15; Galatians 5:16-21; Colossians 1:10).*

B. One who is slow to anger has great understanding *(Proverbs 14:29),* is better than the mighty *(Proverbs 16:32),* is able to pacify contention *(Proverbs 15:18),* and is obedient to God's Word *(James 1:19-20).*

C. One who is wise turns away anger *(Proverbs 29:8)* and holds back his anger *(Proverbs 29:11).*

D. One often reveals his failure to deal biblically with his own anger by judging others for this same sin *(Romans 2:1).*

E. One who becomes angry quickly shows himself to be a fool *(Proverbs 14:17, 29:11; Ecclesiastes 7:9).*

VI. Conclusions about anger

A. It is possible for you to be angry and not sin *(I Corinthians 10:13; Ephesians 4:26)*. However, sinful anger violates Scripture *(James 4:17)*, doesn't conform to the character of Christ *(part of which is described in I Corinthians 13:4-8a, Galatians 5:22-23, and I Peter 2:20-25)*, is characterized by outbursts *(Galatians 5:20; James 1:19-20)*, and often is allowed to remain into the future *(Ephesians 4:26-27)*.

B. Following the example of God the Father and His Son, Jesus Christ, anger is righteous only if it is aroused by specific violations of God's Word and remains righteous only if it is acted upon with a spirit of compassion *(Nehemiah 9:17; Psalm 86:15, 103:8-14; Mark 3:5)*.

C. Because of the ever-present temptation to live for self rather than to live for God *(Luke 9:23; Romans 7:14-25; Galatians 5:16-17)*, you must obey God's Word *(Psalm 119:165; II Timothy 2:15, 3:16-17; Hebrews 4:12)*, pray habitually *(Luke 18:1; I Thessalonians 5:17; James 1:5)*, constantly depend on God's Spirit *(John 14:16, 16:13)*, and consistently do the Word *(James 1:22-25)* in order to deal biblically with anger *(based on Romans 12:2; Hebrews 5:14)*.

D. You are not to allow anger to get the upper hand and gain control of your mind or conduct, since Satan uses this as an opportunity to affect your life *(Ephesians 4:27)*. You must live in a manner that pleases the Lord no matter how you feel *(based on II Corinthians 5:15; Galatians 5:17; Ephesians 4:31-32; Colossians 1:10)*.

E. Your deeds (thoughts, words, actions) reveal whether you are living to please yourself or living to please God *(Mark 7:20-23; Luke 9:23; Romans 6:12-13, 17-18)*. If you are focused on self and become angry, you run the risk of:

1. Carrying out fleshly desires instead of being led by the Holy Spirit *(Galatians 5:16-17)*;

2. Having your prayer life hindered *(Psalm 66:18; I John 3:22)*;

3. Damaging your relationships with others *(Romans 12:18)* by becoming judgmental and placing a stumbling block in their paths *(Romans 14:13)*;

4. Being unwilling to overlook others' transgressions *(Proverbs 19:11)* or to forgive them *(Ephesians 4:31-32)*;

5. Thinking unbiblically *(II Corinthians 10:5; Philippians 4:8; Colossians 3:2)* and using words that do not edify *(Ephesians 4:29)*;

6. Returning evil instead of giving blessings *(Romans 12:17-21; I Peter 3:8-9)* and stirring up more anger and strife *(Proverbs 15:1, 29:22)*;

7. Impairing your own judgment *(Hebrews 5:14; James 1:22)*;

8. Falling into foolish mistakes *(Proverbs 14:29, 19:19; Ecclesiastes 7:9)* and becoming unfit for spiritual leadership *(Titus 1:7)*;

9. Judging others in the area of your own sin *(Romans 2:1)*; and

10. Failing to love others biblically *(I Corinthians 13:4-5)*.

A BIBLICAL VIEW OF BITTERNESS

> The sin of bitterness hinders your spiritual growth and harms your relationships with others. It causes much trouble and must be put away quickly from your life and be replaced by compassionate kindness and forgiveness *(based on Ephesians 4:31-32; Hebrews 12:14-15; James 3:8-18, esp. verses 11, 14).*

I. **The root words for "bitter" or "bitterness" in the original languages of the Old and New Testaments are the basis for words meaning:**

   A. "Sharp," "pointed" (as arrows are sharp, or as a sharp smell or taste), "brackish" (the opposite of "sweet" or "fresh"), or "inedible" *(for example: Exodus 15:23-25; Proverbs 27:7; Isaiah 5:20; James 3:11; Revelation 8:11);*

   B. "Rebellious" *(Deuteronomy 21:18, 20; Isaiah 30:9; Jeremiah 5:23; Ezekiel 2:5-8, 44:6);*

   C. "Rebellion" *(Deuteronomy 31:27a; I Samuel 15:23; Proverbs 17:11);*

   D. "Discontented" *(I Samuel 22:2);*

   E. "Disobedient" *(I Kings 13:20-26, esp. verses 21 and 26; Nehemiah 9:26);* and

   F. "Gall of bitterness" (bitterness of spirit) or "bitterness" *(Acts 8:23; Romans 3:14; Hebrews 12:15; James 3:14).*

II. **Bitterness is compounded by a lack of repentance and is connected with:**

   A. Holding an angry grudge against someone who has wronged you *(for example: Genesis 27:30-41, esp. verses 34 and 41)* or against someone whom you think has wronged you *(for example: I Samuel 30:1-6, esp. verse 6);*

   B. The speech of evildoers *(Psalm 64:1-4; Romans 3:10-18, esp. verse 14);* and

   C. The sins of wrath (a settled disposition to sinful passion), anger (being provoked, irritation), clamor (shouting, uproarious crying out), slander (defamation, blasphemy), and malice (wickedness, a special kind of moral deficiency) *(Ephesians 4:31).*

III. **The sin of bitterness results from living to please yourself. It is often directed at harming other people and, if not dealt with biblically, results in even more sin. For example:**

   A. It comes short of (literally, "is backwards with respect to") the grace of God *(Hebrews 12:15a);*

   B. It causes trouble for others (crowds in, annoys) *(Hebrews 12:15b);*

   C. It defiles (stains, leaves a mark on) many *(Hebrews 12:15b);* and

   D. It ultimately connects you to godless (irreligious) and immoral people *(Hebrews 12:15-17).*

IV. Bitterness is not to characterize your life in Christ (your new self), and it is to be put off. You can overcome the sin of bitterness by remembering the following and responding in a biblical manner.

   A. Bitterness is sin and defiles many *(Hebrews 12:15)*. You must confess your bitterness as sin to obtain God's forgiveness and cleansing *(I John 1:9)*.

   B. Instead of being bitter toward others, you are to be tender-hearted and kind to one another, forgiving each other just as God in Christ has forgiven you *(Ephesians 4:31-32)*.

   C. To avoid any bitterness toward God and His dealings in your life or the lives of others, be diligent to rejoice always, pray without ceasing, and give thanks in everything and for all things in the Name of Jesus Christ *(Ephesians 5:20; I Thessalonians 5:16-18)*. Remember that God is graciously working in your life *(Psalm 121; Romans 8:28-29; Philippians 1:6, 2:13)* and is merciful and righteous in all His ways *(Psalm 145:8-9, 17)*.

   For specific help in overcoming the sin of bitterness, refer to: **OVERCOMING ANGER AND BITTERNESS** *(Lesson 11, Pages 12 - 16)*

OVERCOMING ANGER AND BITTERNESS

> Anger and bitterness often accompany life apart from Jesus Christ (your old self). These sinful habits are not to be part of your new life in Christ (your new self). By following God's way, you can overcome these sinful deeds of the natural man, even if anger or bitterness has dominated your life for years *(based on John 15:3-5; Romans 6:12-14; II Corinthians 5:17; Ephesians 4:22-24, 31-32; I Peter 1:13-16).*

I. **Carefully review the following cross-references:**

A. The foundational, biblical requirements for change (Lessons 1 and 2), recognizing the differences between living man's way and living God's way (Lessons 3 and 4);

B. The essential elements of biblical change (Lessons 5 - 8) as you die to self and live for the Lord (Lessons 9 and 10);

C. The applicability of this situation to loving your neighbor (Lessons 12 and 13) and family relationships (Lessons 14 - 17);

D. The possible links between fear, worry, or depression (Lessons 18 and 19) and this problem;

E. The seriousness of life-dominating sins and their relationship to this particular problem (Lessons 20 and 21); and

F. The need to establish and faithfully maintain specific standards from God's Word for every area of your life (Lesson 22).

NOTE: The cross-references cited above are important in dealing with this specific problem area. In dealing with problems biblically, you must examine all aspects of your life. For example, the problem of anger cannot be overcome by dealing with it as an end in itself. Rather, any specific problem must be dealt with as it relates to scriptural principles for all of life. As you can see, references to previous lessons are listed in addition to those lessons not yet covered.

II. **To become aware of patterns of sin or temptations with regard to anger or bitterness, make a list of people, places, times, or circumstances where ongoing problems are evident in your life.**

III. **Use the VICTORY OVER FAILURES WORKSHEET (Supplement 8). To complete columns 1-3, follow the instructions given in GUIDELINES: VICTORY OVER FAILURES WORKSHEET (Supplement 7).**

IV. **When completing column four of the VICTORY OVER FAILURES WORKSHEET (Supplement 8):**

A. Develop a **basic plan** to overcome the sins you have recognized. In your plan, include deeds (thoughts, speech, and actions) that will help you develop a Christlike manner by taking into account the following guidelines:

---

1.   Think biblically

   a.   Remember that God has promised to care for you in any situation, no matter how unsettling it may seem (*Psalm 23:1-6, 37:5; Proverbs 3:25-26; Matthew 10:28-31; Romans 8:28-29, 36-39; I Corinthians 10:13*).

   b.   Confess all sinful thoughts to God (*I John 1:9*) and ask for His help in changing this sinful pattern (*based on I Thessalonians 5:17; Hebrews 4:15-16; James 1:5*).

   c.   Rejoice (*I Thessalonians 5:16*) and give thanks in and for every situation (*Ephesians 5:20; I Thessalonians 5:18*), knowing that endurance in trials helps conform you to the image of Christ (*based on Romans 5:3-5; James 1:2-4*).

   d.   Remember that God's forgiveness of you is the basis for you to forgive others (*Matthew 18:21-35; Ephesians 4:32; Colossians 3:13*).

   e.   Remember that your love for others demonstrates the love that you have for God (*I John 2:9-11; 3:14-16; 4:7-11, 20-21*).

   f.   Focus your thoughts on glorifying and pleasing God and on being a blessing to others in all situations (*based on Matthew 22:37-39; Luke 9:23-24; II Corinthians 5:9, 15; 10:5; Galatians 5:16-17; Philippians 2:3-4, 4:8; Colossians 3:2*).

   g.   Within the very situation in which you find yourself, do not dwell on things that contribute to further sin. Instead discipline your mind to think on things that please the Lord (*Philippians 4:8; Colossians 3:2*). Remember to pray for those who persecute you (*Matthew 5:44*).

   h.   "Think" kind and tender thoughts toward the very individuals with whom you are or have been irritated (*based on I Corinthians 13:4-8a; Ephesians 4:32*). Focus your thoughts on facing and dealing with the current problem (*based on Philippians 4:6-8; James 1:5, 3:13-18*).

   i.   Review psalms, hymns, and spiritual songs that you have memorized (*based on Ephesians 5:19-20; Colossians 3:16*).

2.   Speak biblically

   a.   Confess your current sins to the Lord and to those whom you have failed to love in a biblical manner, including the sins of failing to complete your responsibilities. Confess any other remembered sins that you have failed to confess earlier (*based on Psalm 51:1-4; James 5:16; I John 1:9*).

   To review how to confess your sins to those you have sinned against, refer to:
   GUIDELINES: VICTORY OVER FAILURES WORKSHEET (Supplement 7) *under* **VI. Application of biblical change**, *point D. and*
   RECONCILIATION (REMOVING ALL HINDRANCES TO UNITY AND PEACE) (Lesson 12, Pages 6-8) *under* II. Confession.

   b.   Do not talk about your past accomplishments (*Proverbs 27:2, 30:32; II Corinthians 10:18*), sorrows or defeats (*Philippians 3:13-14*), worries about the future (*Matthew 6:34*), comparing yourself to yourself and/or others (*II Corinthians 10:12*), or boastfully promising what you will do in the future (*Proverbs 27:1; James 4:13-16*). Instead, edify others by thankfully speaking of the goodness of the Lord and the recent difference He has made in your life, especially in this situation (*based on Luke 10:20; Ephesians 4:29; Colossians 4:6; Hebrews 13:15; I Peter 3:15*).

   c.   Do not slander, gossip, quarrel, or use words that do not edify others (*Proverbs 10:18; Ephesians 4:29, 31; 5:4; Colossians 3:8; II Timothy 2:24; I Peter 2:1*). Instead, let your speech be truthful and gracious, according to the need of the moment, that you may know how to answer each person *(Ephesians 4:15, 25, 29; Colossians 4:6).*

d.   Do not bring up another's sin in an accusing or vengeful manner, either to others, yourself, or to the person who has sinned *(Proverbs 10:18, 17:9, 20:19; Ephesians 4:29, 31; Colossians 3:8; I Peter 2:1).*

e.   Encourage reconciliation with God and others, being careful to follow biblical guidelines *(Matthew 5:9, 23-24; Romans 12:18; II Corinthians 2:6-8, 5:18).*

Refer to: **RECONCILIATION (REMOVING ALL HINDRANCES TO UNITY AND PEACE)** *(Lesson 12, Pages 6-8).*

3.   Act biblically

a.   Forgive others just as God has forgiven you *(Ephesians 4:32; Colossians 3:13).*

Refer to: **FORGIVENESS (FORGIVING OTHERS AS GOD HAS FORGIVEN YOU)** *(Lesson 12, Pages 3-5) and determine if you are practicing biblical forgiveness. Make changes as necessary.*

b.   Memorize Scripture verses and study Scripture passages specifically related to overcoming anger or bitterness *(based on Psalm 119:9, 11, 16; II Corinthians 10:5; Philippians 4:8; II Timothy 2:15).* Also, memorize psalms, hymns, and spiritual songs to help set your mind on the Lord and to be a blessing to others *(based on Ephesians 5:19-20; Colossians 3:16).*

c.   Pray always with thanksgiving *(Philippians 4:6; I Thessalonians 5:17-18)* and according to God's will *(I John 5:14-15).* Cast all your cares on the Lord *(I Peter 5:7)* and pray for those who persecute you *(Matthew 5:44).*

d.   Identify all danger signals – such as situations, places, and personal contacts that bring temptation – and take immediate steps to eliminate, flee, or resist the temptation *(based on Psalm 1:1; Proverbs 27:12; I Corinthians 10:13, 15:33; II Timothy 2:22; James 4:7; I Peter 5:8-9).*

e.   Make amends for wrongdoing and seek reconciliation with those you have offended *(based on Matthew 5:23-24).* Remember that although you have already confessed your sins *(see 2. a. above),* you need to demonstrate actively your serious intent to change.

See: **RECONCILIATION (REMOVING ALL HINDRANCES TO UNITY AND PEACE)** *(Lesson 12, Pages 6-8) under* **III.   Restitution** *and* **IV.   The importance of reconciliation.**

f.   Bless others through tangible and genuine expressions of biblical love and service (this includes your daily responsibilities as a husband, wife, parent, roommate, student, employer, employee, etc.) *(based on Matthew 7:12; Romans 12:9-13, 15-16; 13:8-10; I Corinthians 13:4-8a; Philippians 2:3-8; I Timothy 6:17-19; I Peter 3:8-9; I John 3:18).* You are to do this:

1)   Regardless of how you feel *(based on Genesis 4:7; II Corinthians 5:14-15; Galatians 5:16-17; Philippians 4:13; James 4:17);*

2)   Especially to those who seem to be your enemies or to those against whom you have sinned *(based on Matthew 5:23-24, 43-48; Mark 11:25-26; Romans 12:14, 17-21);*

3)   With kindness and tenderheartedness for the very individuals with whom you are or have been irritated *(Ephesians 4:31-32);*

4)   By taking advantage of opportunities to minister, especially in ways that keep you in a Christlike servant attitude toward others *(based on Matthew 20:25-28; Philippians 2:3-8; I Peter 4:10);* and

5) By practicing biblical stewardship to honor the Lord and to be of practical help to others *(based on Psalm 24:1; Matthew 25:14-29; I Corinthians 4:1-2; Ephesians 5:15-17; I Timothy 6:17-19; I Peter 4:10).*

Refer to:
BIBLICAL PRINCIPLES OF STEWARDSHIP *(Lesson 10, Pages 4-6); and* **DYING TO SELF BY SERVING OTHERS** *(Lesson 10, Pages 7-8).*

For specific examples of how and when to express biblical love, even in difficult situations, refer to: **THE MEANING OF BIBLICAL LOVE** *(Lesson 13, Pages 4-6).*

g. Whenever necessary, conduct a "conference table" using the guidelines outlined in **OVERCOMING PROBLEMS THROUGH BIBLICAL COMMUNICATION (USING A CONFERENCE TABLE FOR RECONCILIATION)** (Lesson 15, Pages 6-9).

h. Correct deficiencies in your life that exist because of a lack of discipline or neglect *(based on Colossians 3:1-17; I Timothy 4:7b; James 4:17).*

i. If you need help, ask a Christian friend to hold you accountable to carry out your **basic** and **contingency plans** until you have established a new pattern of godly living *(Proverbs 27:17; Ecclesiastes 4:9-10; Hebrews 10:23-25).* If necessary, seek biblical counsel from others *(Proverbs 11:14, 15:22).*

j. Do not associate (do not have close fellowship or friendship) with others given to anger *(Proverbs 22:24-25).*

B. As necessary, develop a **"THINK AND DO" LIST** (Supplement 10) using **GUIDELINES: THE "THINK AND DO" LIST** (Supplement 9).

C. Implement your **basic plan** *(James 1:22)* and do it heartily for the Lord *(Colossians 3:23-24).*

D. Develop a **contingency plan** to deal with typical situations that provide temptation for you to sin in anger or bitterness. Take into account the following guidelines:

1. Immediately ask God for help *(I Thessalonians 5:17; Hebrews 4:15-16; James 1:5).*

2. Review your memorized Scripture verses that deal specifically with the sins of anger or bitterness *(based on Psalm 119:9, 11, 16).*

3. Immediately seek God's perspective.

a. Regardless of your feelings or circumstances, view this situation as an opportunity for further spiritual maturity *(James 1:2-4)* because God will work all things together for good in your life *(based on Psalm 37; Proverbs 3:5-12; Romans 8:28-29; Ephesians 1:3-14; Philippians 1:6).*

1) Remind yourself that you can do all things through Christ who gives you strength *(Philippians 4:11-13),* since your adequacy is from God and not from any natural "inner strength" *(II Corinthians 3:5).* Remember that you can do nothing fruitful apart from Jesus Christ *(John 15:5).*

2) Praise and glorify God that He is sufficient even in your areas of weakness *(II Corinthians 12:9-10)* and that He will keep you from stumbling and make you stand blameless and with great joy in the presence of His glory *(Jude 1:24-25).*

b. Remember that God looks on your heart, not on your outward appearance *(I Samuel 16:7).* You must stand blameless before Him in your thoughts, whether others know about it or not *(based on Acts 23:1, 24:16; Romans 14:12; Ephesians 4:1; Philippians 1:9-11; Colossians 1:21-22).*

    1) If you even begin to think sinful thoughts in this unforeseen circumstance, confess them to the Lord *(I John 1:9)*.

    2) Remember that it is not the amount of time spent sinning or the immensity of the sin (by human standards) by which you should judge yourself. Rather, the fact that you stopped going God's way even momentarily is what matters *(based on James 2:10, 4:17)*.

4. Thank God that you are His servant in your present circumstance *(Ephesians 5:20; I Thessalonians 5:18)*. Determine how you will give glory to God *(I Corinthians 10:31; I Peter 4:11)* and seek ways to edify others by serving them in this situation *(Ephesians 4:29; Philippians 2:3-4)*.

5. Especially when dealing with anger, determine to overcome the immediate temptation to sin by being:

    a. Quick to hear *(James 1:19)* – listen carefully, ask questions, get the facts, and make no pre-judgments or hasty decisions *(Proverbs 18:13, 15)*.

    b. Slow to speak *(James 1:19)* – discuss biblical solutions to the problem, speak only words that edify instead of tearing down the other person *(based on Proverbs 15:1; Ephesians 4:29)* – speak the truth with a gentle and quiet spirit *(Ephesians 4:15; I Peter 3:8-17)*. Gather factual information related to the circumstances in which anger or bitterness rose within you *(based on Proverbs 18:13; Matthew 7:1-5)*.

    c. Slow to anger *(Proverbs 16:32; James 1:19)* – deal with the problem and do not attack the person.

        1) In someone else, deal with the deeds (speech, actions), not the motive *(based on I Samuel 16:7b; Jeremiah 17:9; Matthew 12:36-37)*.

        2) In yourself, deal with your own motive *(based on Matthew 7:1-5, 12:34-37, 15:19; I Corinthians 11:31)* and change your deeds *(based on Job 42:5-6; Colossians 3:8-10)*.

Continue to refine your plan to put off the practices of the old self as you put on the righteous deeds of the new self (Ephesians 4:22, 24; Colossians 3:2-17). When you are quick to hear, slow to speak, and slow to anger and when you practice your biblical plan for overcoming anger or bitterness, you are being renewed in the spirit of your mind (based on Romans 12:1-2; Ephesians 4:23; Colossians 3:10; Hebrews 5:14).

6. Act according to your **contingency plan** as soon as you detect temptation to sin in anger or bitterness *(based on I Thessalonians 5:22; II Timothy 2:19-22)*. Then, begin again to do those things written in your **basic plan** *(based on Proverbs 24:16; James 1:22-25)*.

A CASE STUDY: MARY'S HUSBAND HAS LEFT HER

> You can help others through any difficult situation by following a specific, scriptural plan of action *(based on Proverbs 3:5-6, 11:14; Ezekiel 18:20; Matthew 7:1, 5; Romans 15:14; II Corinthians 1:3-5, 3:5-6; Galatians 6:1-5; I Thessalonians 5:16-18; II Timothy 3:16-17; James 1:2-7).*

Immediately after Mary's departure, you pray for God's wisdom *(James 1:5)*. Realizing the spiritual challenges that are in Mary's life *(Ephesians 6:12; I Peter 5:8)*, you begin to make specific preparations for your meeting with Mary. You call the pastor at your church to ask if there are biblical counselors who can assist you in tomorrow's session *(Proverbs 11:14, 15:22)*. He encourages you to take notes during the sessions. He reminds you to review the session carefully and make biblical plans for future meetings following each counseling session for the information of the pastor, who is responsible for Mary's spiritual oversight *(Hebrews 13:17)*. He reports that all the biblical counselors of your church are involved in counseling or are in discipleship meetings with those who have previously completed counseling sessions. However, he recommends two women (Jane and Teresa) and a man (Jim) to be your assistants. None have had any biblical counseling experience, but all have completed the Self-Confrontation Course and have indicated a desire to be trained to counsel others. Realizing that these are the assistant counselors whom God has sovereignly chosen for this situation *(Proverbs 16:9; Romans 8:28)*, you prayerfully thank the Lord *(I Thessalonians 5:16-18)* and call your assistants to review guidelines for the first session.

When you contact the proposed assistant counselors, all mention their lack of experience to help in an actual counseling case. You remind them that, as maturing believers, they have a responsibility and privilege to help others in their difficulties *(Romans 15:14; Galatians 6:1)*. You also say that no one, regardless of his level of training, is adequate within himself to accomplish anything spiritually fruitful and that a believer's adequacy is totally from the Lord *(John 15:5; II Corinthians 3:5-6)*. You encourage them with the biblical truth that we are able to comfort others with the same comfort that we have been comforted by Almighty God *(II Corinthians 1:3-5)*. You remind them that God's Word is your guide *(II Timothy 3:16-17)*, His Spirit is your empowerment *(I Corinthians 2:9-16)*, and this situation has provided an opportunity for all involved to grow in Christ *(John 15:5-7; Romans 8:28-29)*. All of the recommended assistant counselors agree with these biblical truths, and all pray with you for God's will to be accomplished for each person in this situation.

The persons involved in this situation include every member of Mary's family, Jane, Teresa, Jim, you, and other members of the biblical counseling team. Besides you and your assistants, other members of the biblical counseling team who may or may not be present in all sessions are the pastor, and any other male biblical counselors (disciplers) who may counsel with Mary's husband. Most importantly, the key personage of the biblical counseling team on whom all are to depend is the Holy Spirit.

After prayer, you review with your assistants the biblical plan for the coming session and the importance of taking notes. Everyone agrees on proposed topics to be covered in the session, which are comprised of the four essential elements of biblical counseling *(understanding the problem, hope, change, practice)*. You ask your assistants to arrive thirty minutes ahead of tomorrow's scheduled counseling time so that you may pray together and go over a final review of the proposed biblical plan for Mary's first session. *(From a biblical perspective, identify the important elements in the above description, most of which are followed by italicized verse references.)*

LESSON 11: HOMEWORK

> You must deal scripturally with anger and bitterness in order to continue your growth in Christ. This week's **HOMEWORK** will help you understand God's view of anger and bitterness as well as provide an opportunity for you to develop and implement a biblical plan for overcoming these problem areas *(based on Psalm 119:105, 165; Matthew 7:5; I Corinthians 10:13; II Corinthians 5:17; Galatians 5:16-25; Ephesians 4:31-32; Colossians 3:8-17; I Peter 1:13-16; II Peter 1:2-11).* Specific and practical steps for learning to counsel biblically are also presented.

✔ *homework completed*

☐ A. * Write the meaning of *Ephesians 4:31-32* and *James 1:19-20.* Memorize *Ephesians 4:31-32* and *James 1:19-20* and begin memorizing *Matthew 5:23-24.*

☐ B. * Read **BIBLICAL PRINCIPLES: ANGER AND BITTERNESS** (Lesson 11, Pages 2-3). Highlight the listed verses in your Bible.

☐ C. * Continue working on the problem you chose earlier in the course by completing a **VICTORY OVER FAILURES WORKSHEET** (Supplement 8, Pages 1-2) on those aspects of your problem in which you have exhibited anger or bitterness. Include specific plans for change in column 4 of your worksheet.

Study **OVERCOMING ANGER AND BITTERNESS** (Lesson 11, Pages 12-16) and make a list of ways that anger or bitterness may be evident in your life.

☐ D. Read **UNBIBLICAL RESPONSES TO ANGER AND BITTERNESS** (Lesson 11, Pages 4-5). Confess your own unbiblical responses to the Lord.

☐ E. Study **A BIBLICAL VIEW OF ANGER** (Lesson 11, Pages 6-9). This study describes the sinless anger of God, Jesus, and notable men of Scripture. It also gives you a biblical basis for determining if your anger is sinful.

☐ F. Study **A BIBLICAL VIEW OF BITTERNESS** (Lesson 11, Pages 10-11) and note God's plan for you to avoid this sin.

☐ G. Read **A CASE STUDY: MARY'S HUSBAND HAS LEFT HER** (Lesson 11, Page 17). List the important truths that a biblical counselor should learn in this situation (these are accompanied by verse references in the case study).

☐ H. Review the form entitled **BIBLICAL COUNSELING RECORD** (Supplement 12). Note the explanation (Supplement 12, Page 2) and the use (Supplement 12, Page 3) of this helpful tool in biblical counseling. Read the **BIBLICAL COUNSELING SUMMARY AND PLANNING** sheet (Supplement 13). Take note of the summary points of each biblical counseling session and review the specific planning that prepares the counseling team for future sessions.

☐ I. * In conjunction with this lesson, respond to statement 18 under **Open Book Test** (Lesson 23, Page 2).

* *The completion of assignments marked with an asterisk (*) is a prerequisite for further biblical counseling training.*

LESSON 11: STUDY GUIDE FOR DAILY DEVOTIONS
(INCLUDING SCRIPTURE MEMORY AND HOMEWORK)

> You must deal scripturally with anger and bitterness in order to continue your growth in Christ. This week's **STUDY GUIDE** will help you understand God's view of anger and bitterness as well as provide an opportunity for you to develop and implement a biblical plan for overcoming these problem areas (*based on Psalm 119:105, 165; Matthew 7:5; I Corinthians 10:13; II Corinthians 5:17; Galatians 5:16-25; Ephesians 4:31-32; Colossians 3:8-17; I Peter 1:13-16; II Peter 1:2-11*). Additionally, specific and practical steps for learning to counsel biblically are presented.

Scripture Memory

1. * Memorize *Ephesians 4:31-32* and *James 1:19-20*. Begin memorizing *Matthew 5:23-24*.
2. Carry your memory verse cards from previous weeks along with this week's memory verses. Review your Scriptures during your spare moments throughout the day.

Daily Devotional Study Guide

FIRST DAY

1. Open with prayer.
2. * Read *Principle 45* under **BIBLICAL PRINCIPLES: ANGER AND BITTERNESS** (Lesson 11, Pages 2-3). Highlight the referenced verses in your Bible.
3. * Continuing to work on the problem you have chosen, read through **OVERCOMING ANGER AND BITTERNESS** (Lesson 11, Pages 12-16). Begin a **VICTORY OVER FAILURES WORKSHEET** (Supplement 8, Pages 1-2) on those aspects of your problem in which you have exhibited anger or bitterness.
4. * In your own words, write the meaning of *Ephesians 4:31-32* and *James 1:19-20*.
5. Begin listing any angry or bitter deeds (thoughts, words, or actions) that you became alert to in your life this week.
6. Close with prayer.

SECOND DAY

1. Open with prayer.
2. * Read *Principle 46* under **BIBLICAL PRINCIPLES: ANGER AND BITTERNESS** (Lesson 11, Pages 2-3). Highlight verses in your Bible not marked previously.
3. * Continue to work on your **VICTORY OVER FAILURES WORKSHEET** (Supplement 8, Pages 1-2). Include specific plans for change in column 4.
4. Read **UNBIBLICAL RESPONSES TO ANGER AND BITTERNESS** (Lesson 11, Pages 4-5). If you recognize your own unbiblical viewpoints, confess them as sin to the Lord. Update your list from the first day.
5. Close with prayer.

THIRD DAY

1. Open with prayer.
2. * Read *Principle 47* under **BIBLICAL PRINCIPLES: ANGER AND BITTERNESS** (Lesson 11, Pages 2-3). Highlight verses in your Bible not marked previously.
3. * Implement the first steps toward biblical change listed in column 4 of your **VICTORY OVER FAILURES WORKSHEET** (Supplement 8, Pages 1-2).
4. Read **A BIBLICAL VIEW OF ANGER** (Lesson 11, Pages 6-9). This three-day study will help you determine if your anger is sinful.
5. Update your list of angry or bitter deeds.
6. Close with prayer.

FOURTH DAY

1. Open with prayer.
2. * Read *Principle 48* under **BIBLICAL PRINCIPLES: ANGER AND BITTERNESS** (Lesson 11, Pages 2-3). Highlight verses in your Bible not marked previously.
3. * Further implement the specific steps of action that you have listed in column 4 of your **VICTORY OVER FAILURES WORKSHEET** (Supplement 8, Pages 1-2).
4. Continue studying **A BIBLICAL VIEW OF ANGER** (Lesson 11, Pages 6-9) and update your list of angry or bitter responses.
5. Read **A CASE STUDY: MARY'S HUSBAND HAS LEFT HER** (Lesson 11, Page 17). From a biblical perspective, list the important truths that a biblical counselor should learn in this situation (these are accompanied by verse references in the case study).
6. Close with prayer.

FIFTH DAY

1. Open with prayer.
2. * Read *Principle 49* under **BIBLICAL PRINCIPLES: ANGER AND BITTERNESS** (Lesson 11, Pages 2-3). Highlight appropriate verses in your Bible.
3. * If necessary, adjust your plan of action listed in column 4 of your **VICTORY OVER FAILURES WORKSHEET** (Supplement 8, Pages 1-2) and take biblical steps of obedience.
4. Complete your study of **A BIBLICAL VIEW OF ANGER** (Lesson 11, Pages 6-9) and update your list of angry or bitter responses.
5. Review the **BIBLICAL COUNSELING RECORD** (Supplement 12), noting its explanation (Supplement 12, Page 2) and its use (Supplement 12, Page 3). Also review the **BIBLICAL COUNSELING SUMMARY AND PLANNING** sheet (Supplement 13) which gives guidelines for recording results of a counseling session. Notice the basic steps of preparation a counseling team should prayerfully take for upcoming biblical counseling sessions.
6. Close with prayer.

SIXTH DAY

1. Open with prayer.
2. * Read *Principle 50* under **BIBLICAL PRINCIPLES: ANGER AND BITTERNESS** (Lesson 11, Pages 2-3). Highlight verses in your Bible not marked previously.
3. * Be faithful to your plan for change recorded in column 4 of your **VICTORY OVER FAILURES WORKSHEET** (Supplement 8, Pages 1-2).
4. Study **A BIBLICAL VIEW OF BITTERNESS** (Lesson 11, Pages 10-11) and note God's plan for you to avoid this sin. This is the first day of a two-day study.
5. Update your list of angry or bitter deeds.
6. Close with prayer.

SEVENTH DAY

1. Open with prayer.
2. Complete your study of **A BIBLICAL VIEW OF BITTERNESS** (Lesson 11, Pages 10-11).
3. Complete your list of angry or bitter deeds.
4. Evaluate the steps of biblical action you have taken to overcome anger and bitterness in your life. Have you pleased yourself or have you pleased God?
5. * In conjunction with this lesson, respond to statement 18 under **Open Book Test** (Lesson 23, Page 2).
6. Close with prayer.
7. Review your memory verses for the week and contact someone to hear you recite them. Remember to explain the meaning of the verses and their application to your life.

---

*   *The completion of assignments marked with an asterisk (*) is a prerequisite for further biblical counseling training.*

LESSON 12

INTERPERSONAL PROBLEMS (PART ONE)

(LEARNING HOW TO LOVE YOUR NEIGHBOR)

"If therefore you are presenting your offering at the altar, and there remember that your brother has something against you, leave your offering there before the altar, and go your way; first be reconciled to your brother, and then come and present your offering."

Matthew 5:23-24

LESSON 12: INTERPERSONAL PROBLEMS (PART ONE)
(LEARNING HOW TO LOVE YOUR NEIGHBOR)

> The practice of Christlike love is the distinctive characteristic of a disciple of the Lord Jesus Christ. As part of loving others biblically, faithful and consistent forgiveness of them indicates your thankfulness and understanding of God's forgiveness which is available to you through the death and resurrection of His Son, Jesus *(based on Matthew 18:21-35; John 13:35; Ephesians 4:32).*

I. **The purposes of this lesson are:**

A. To present God's forgiveness of you as an example of how you are to forgive others biblically;

B. To present the necessary components and steps of biblical reconciliation;

C. To examine common misconceptions about biblical forgiveness;

D. To help you begin practicing biblical forgiveness; and

E. To continue the development of a case study in biblical counseling.

II. **The outline of this lesson**

A. Self-Confrontation

1. **BIBLICAL PRINCIPLES: INTERPERSONAL PROBLEMS (PART ONE) (LEARNING HOW TO LOVE YOUR NEIGHBOR)** (Lesson 12, Page 2)

2. **FORGIVENESS (FORGIVING OTHERS AS GOD HAS FORGIVEN YOU)** (Lesson 12, Pages 3-5)

3. **RECONCILIATION (REMOVING ALL HINDRANCES TO UNITY AND PEACE)** (Lesson 12, Pages 6-8)

4. **QUESTIONS AND ANSWERS ABOUT BIBLICAL FORGIVENESS** (Lesson 12, Pages 9-13)

B. Steps for spiritual growth

1. **LESSON 12: HOMEWORK** (Lesson 12, Page 16)

2. **STUDY GUIDE FOR DAILY DEVOTIONS** (Lesson 12, Pages 17-18)

C. Biblical counseling

A CASE STUDY: MARY'S HUSBAND HAS LEFT HER (Lesson 12, Pages 14-15)

BIBLICAL PRINCIPLES: INTERPERSONAL PROBLEMS
(PART ONE)
(LEARNING HOW TO LOVE YOUR NEIGHBOR)

> The great and foremost commandment is to love the Lord your God with all your heart, with all your soul, with all your mind, and with all your strength. The second great commandment is to love your neighbor as you already love yourself. The first statement may sound simple to do, but the reality of loving God with such intensity is directly linked to your loving others in a biblical manner *(based on Matthew 22:36-40; Mark 12:30-31; I John 2:10-11; 4:7-11, 20-21).*

I. God's View

(Principle 51) If you do not love others, you do not love God *(I John 4:20-21)*. If you do not biblically forgive others, you will not be forgiven by God *(Matthew 6:14-15, 18:21-35; Mark 11:25-26)*. Your forgiveness of others demonstrates your obedience to God's Word *(Ephesians 4:32; Colossians 3:13)* and, thus, your love for the Lord *(John 14:15; I John 5:3; II John 1:6)*. When you forgive others, you indicate your gratefulness to God for His gracious forgiveness of you through the Lord Jesus Christ *(based on Matthew 18:21-35, esp. verses 32-33).*

(Principle 52) Do not judge others by your own standards, perspectives, or experiences *(John 7:24; Romans 14:1-13; James 4:11-12)*. You will be judged in the very same way you judge others *(Matthew 7:1-2; Luke 6:36-38).*

(Principle 53) Even when you are worshipping the Lord and remember that someone (spouse, brother, neighbor, co-worker, etc.) has something against you, you are to cease your worship, go and seek reconciliation, and then return to your worship *(Matthew 5:23-24)*. You are commanded in the Name of the Lord Jesus Christ to eliminate divisions among believers, since the unity of the body of Christ is from and in the Holy Spirit. Unity of mind and purpose should characterize believers *(John 17:20-23; I Corinthians 1:10, 12:22-27; Philippians 2:1-2).*

II. Your Hope

(Principle 54) God has enabled you to forgive others *(based on Ephesians 4:32)*. You can love even your enemies *(Matthew 5:43-48; Luke 6:27-35)*. Both forgiveness and biblical love are not dependent upon your feelings *(based on I Corinthians 13:4-8a; Colossians 3:13)* but upon an act of your will *(John 14:15; II Corinthians 5:14-15; I John 3:18-24; 4:10-11, 21)* as you respond to God's love to you *(I John 4:19).*

FORGIVENESS
(FORGIVING OTHERS AS GOD HAS FORGIVEN YOU)

> God's forgiveness is an outpouring of abundant grace and mercy that provides pardon to the guilty. Although God's forgiveness does not necessarily release the offender from the physical or material consequences of his sin, it provides full release from the guilt of the wrongdoing. For you to practice biblical forgiveness, you must understand and accept God's gracious forgiveness of you and must follow His example in providing forgiveness to others *(based on II Samuel 12:13-14; Psalm 103:10-14; Luke 23:39-43; Romans 5:8, 8:1; Ephesians 4:32; Colossians 3:12-14, 25).*

I. **Understanding God's forgiveness**

    A.   The nature of God is to forgive sins *(Nehemiah 9:16-17; Psalm 86:5; Isaiah 43:22-25).*

        1.   Every type of wrongdoing can be forgiven by God *(Exodus 34:6-7, esp. verse 7; Psalm 103:3, 10-12),* except that of blasphemy against the Holy Spirit, which is to attribute the works of God to Satan *(Matthew 12:22-32, esp. verses 31-32; Mark 3:20-30, esp. verses 28-29).*

            a.   He forgives "iniquity" (a lack of integrity, honesty, or justice).

            b.   He forgives "transgression" (crossing over the boundary from right to wrong).

            c.   He forgives "sin" (missing the mark of God's perfection; self-centered lawlessness).

        2.   He was ready to forgive you while you were still His enemy *(Romans 5:10)* and before you were ready to ask for or receive forgiveness *(Psalm 86:5; Romans 5:8).*

        3.   He forgives you out of His mercy and grace and not because you merit (deserve or have earned) His forgiveness *(Romans 5:6-8; Ephesians 2:4-7; Colossians 2:13-14).*

    B.   When God forgives you, He forgives completely *(Psalm 103:10-12; Jeremiah 50:20; Romans 5:16-21; 8:1, 33-34; I John 1:9).* The completeness of His forgiveness is revealed by the following statements.

        1.   When God forgives you, you are changed.

            a.   At your spiritual birth, God establishes a new relationship with you as your Father and removes the judgment of condemnation from you. *Review:* **YOU CAN CHANGE BIBLICALLY (PART ONE)** *(Lesson 1, Pages 3-7).*

            b.   As your Father, He cleanses you from all unrighteousness as you confess your sins to Him *(I John 1:9).*

        2.   When God forgives you, He no longer deals with you according to your sin *(Psalm 103:10).* Instead, He covers your sin *(Psalm 32:1)* and blots it out *(Psalm 51:9; Isaiah 43:25, 44:22).*

---

3.   When God forgives you, He no longer will charge the guilt (condemnation) of your sin to your account *(Psalm 32:2; Romans 3:24-25, 4:8, 8:1; II Corinthians 5:19)*.

4.   When God forgives you, He removes your sin from you and from His presence *(Psalm 103:12; Isaiah 38:17; Micah 7:19)* and promises not to remember it against you any longer *(Hebrews 10:14-18)*.

C.   God's forgiveness cost you nothing *(Ephesians 2:8-9)*, but it was very costly to God *(Isaiah 53:4-12; John 3:16; Acts 20:28; Romans 5:8; II Corinthians 5:21; I Peter 1:17-19, esp. verse 19)*.

D.   God never withholds forgiveness when sins (any wrongdoings) are confessed in a sincere, biblical manner *(I John 1:9)*.

II.   Responding to God's forgiveness

A.   You are to forgive others just as God in Christ has forgiven you *(Ephesians 4:32; Colossians 3:13)*.   (Refer to **I.   Understanding God's forgiveness**).   You are to:

1.   Willingly *grant* forgiveness whenever another confesses sin to you;

Refer to: **RECONCILIATION (REMOVING ALL HINDRANCES TO UNITY AND PEACE)** *(Lesson 12, Pages 6-8) under* **V.   Hindrances to reconciliation**, *point C.*

2.   Forgive any type of sin, no matter how severe or devastating it might seem to be;

3.   Forgive on the basis of grace, not on the merit of the person to be forgiven;

4.   Expect a renewed relationship with the one who is forgiven;

5.   Recognize that it may be costly to you when you grant forgiveness; and

6.   Forgive completely and do not remind the forgiven person of his sin in an accusing manner, even though it may not be appropriate to release the offender from all the consequences of his sin. (The only reason to remind anyone of his sins is for restoration or teaching purposes, and even then it must be done in a spirit of gentleness).

B.   Forgive others *in your heart (mind)* even before they ask to be forgiven *(Mark 11:25)*.

III.   Reviewing principles of forgiveness

A.   Forgiveness is an act of obedience to the Lord *(Luke 17:3-10; Ephesians 4:32; Colossians 3:13)* and must be granted from the heart *(Matthew 18:35)*.

B.   Forgiveness gives the offender what he needs rather than what he deserves *(Psalm 103:10; Luke 23:39-43; Romans 5:8)*.

C.   Forgiveness is the love of Jesus Christ in action and is a promise to:

1.   Not keep a record of wrongs suffered *(I Corinthians 13:5)*;

2.   Not gossip about a person's sins to others *(Ephesians 4:29)*;

3.   Not dwell on the offense yourself *(Philippians 4:8)*; and

4.   Restore fellowship with the forgiven person or the offender, as far as is biblically possible *(Romans 12:18; II Corinthians 2:6-8)*.

To understand your responsibility to forgive and deal biblically with non-repentant believers, refer to:
RESTORATION/DISCIPLINE (YOUR BIBLICAL RESPONSE TO THE SIN OF ANOTHER BELIEVER) *(Lesson 13, Pages 7-8); and*
GUIDELINES: THE RESTORATION/DISCIPLINE PROCESS *(Lesson 13, Pages 9-11).*

In certain situations, Scripture prohibits you from having fellowship with them, thus making biblical reconciliation an impossibility.

D. Loving God without loving people is an impossibility *(I John 4:20-21)*. Forgiveness should include comforting those who have sinned and have repented, as well as reaffirming your love to them *(II Corinthians 2:6-8)*.

E. Forgiveness is to be granted when requested without limitation *(Matthew 18:21-22; Luke 17:3-4)*.

F. When you forgive another who has sinned against you, you are not to *demand* restitution; but, instead, you are to demonstrate mercy and love toward him with a goal of reconciling with him *(based on Matthew 18:21-35, esp. verses 32-33; Luke 6:27-38; I Corinthians 6:5-7, esp. verse 7; II Corinthians 2:5-7)*.

It is important to remember that even though you are not to demand restitution, restitution is part of the reconciliation process for the one who has sinned. This should be lovingly brought to his attention.

Refer to: **RECONCILIATION (REMOVING ALL HINDRANCES TO UNITY AND PEACE)** *(Lesson 12, Pages 6-8) under* **III. Restitution.** *Also take special note of the illustration on Page 8 of Lesson 12 under* **V. Hindrances to reconciliation,** *point D.*

G. Especially when you pray, if you have something against someone, you must forgive him from your heart *(based on Matthew 18:35; Mark 11:25)*.

IV. Refusing to forgive

A. Because you are commanded to forgive others *(Ephesians 4:32)*, you sin when you refuse to forgive *(James 4:17)*.

B. You show your base ingratitude for God's merciful forgiveness toward you when you do not forgive others *(Matthew 18:21-35)*.

C. God as your Father withholds His forgiveness of your everyday transgressions when you do not forgive others *(Matthew 6:14-15; Mark 11:25-26)*.

To discover the relationship between your forgiveness of others and God's forgiveness of your shortcomings, study: **QUESTIONS AND ANSWERS ABOUT BIBLICAL FORGIVENESS** *(Lesson 12, Pages 9-13) under point* **III.**

RECONCILIATION
(REMOVING ALL HINDRANCES TO UNITY AND PEACE)

> Asking for forgiveness from others in a scriptural manner involves acknowledging that you have sinned against them and that you desire mercy and pardon (not to be given what you deserve). Asking for forgiveness is vital for reconciliation and may lead to a difference in the relationship. For complete restoration to occur, specific steps of biblical action must be taken *(based on Matthew 5:23-24, 18:21-35; Romans 12:18, 14:19; II Corinthians 5:17-19; Ephesians 4:32; Colossians 3:12-14; James 5:16; I John 1:9).*

I. **Repentance (changing your mind from pleasing self to pleasing God, which is followed by a corresponding biblical change in your life)**

   A. Biblical repentance results in a change from disobedience to biblically obedient behavior *(Psalm 51:12-13; Matthew 3:8; Luke 3:8; Acts 26:20).*

   B. Biblical repentance acknowledges sin and takes personal responsibility for it *(Psalm 51:1-6; I John 1:8-10).*

   C. Biblical repentance results from a sorrow for sins committed against God and others *(Psalm 38:1-18, esp. verse 17; II Corinthians 7:9-10).*

   D. Biblical repentance results in a broken (sorrowful for the sin) and contrite heart (completely putting away or crushing any previous reliance on self) *(Psalm 51:16-17; James 4:8-10).*

   E. Biblical repentance removes reminders of past sins, since these reminders themselves often provide temptations to sin *(based on I Kings 15:12; Jeremiah 4:1; Acts 19:8-19, esp verses 18-19).*

II. **Confession (agreeing with God about sins that you have committed against Him and against others, with a commitment to forsake those sins)**

   A. You are to confess sins to God in all aspects of thought, word, and action *(based on Psalm 51:1-4; I John 1:9).*

   B. Confess your sins to those against whom you have sinned *(based on James 5:16).* When confessing sin(s) you have committed against another:

   1. Do not accuse him, judge him, or bring up his failures *(Matthew 7:1-5; Romans 2:1; I Corinthians 13:5).* For example, you should say, "Please forgive me for slamming the door in your face." Don't say, "Please forgive me for slamming the door in your face when you called me stupid" *(based on I Peter 3:8-9).*

   2. Do not give excuses. For example, say, "Please forgive me for using bad language and unwholesome words." Don't say, "Please forgive me for my use of bad language, but today is just not a good day for me." Remember that

there is no justification or excuse for sinning against someone or causing anyone to stumble *(based on Matthew 18:7; Romans 14:13; I Corinthians 10:13)*.

3. Do not stop at merely expressing your feelings by saying, "I'm sorry." "I'm sorry" simply means "I feel sorrow" and is not a statement of a desire to be reconciled. When seeking forgiveness, also identify your wrong as sin *(Ephesians 4:15)*. For example, you might say, "I'm sorry; please forgive me for sinning against you when I yelled at you and called you names."

Refer to: **GUIDELINES: VICTORY OVER FAILURES WORKSHEET** *(Supplement 7)*, under **VI. Application of biblical change, D.**

III. Restitution (restoring or compensating for damages your sin has caused)

A. Biblical restitution should be made whenever possible *(based on Leviticus 6:2-5; Numbers 5:5-8; Proverbs 6:30-31)*. In the case of adultery, forgiveness is available from the Lord *(I John 1:9)* and may be granted by those sinned against *(Luke 17:3; Ephesians 4:32)*. However, restitution is not possible *(Proverbs 6:32-35)*.

B. Biblical restitution is to be made to those against whom you have sinned *(based on Exodus 22:1-17; Luke 19:8-9)*.

C. Since the goal of biblical restitution is to be at peace with another, you are not to attempt to "buy back" the relationship or "manipulate" the other person to respond in a way that you desire *(based on Romans 12:9a, 18)*.

IV. The importance of reconciliation (putting away enmity with a view to establishing or restoring a relationship of unity and peace)

A. Biblical reconciliation can only begin with being reconciled to God through Jesus Christ *(Romans 5:10-11; II Corinthians 5:17-20; Colossians 1:21-22)*.

B. The ministry and message of reconciliation between God and mankind is a responsibility and privilege that has been entrusted to you *(II Corinthians 5:17-20, esp. verses 18-19)*.

C. Biblical reconciliation with others is so important that it must be done before your worship and service to the Lord. You are not able (fit) to worship or serve the Lord unless you have sought reconciliation with others who are estranged from you *(Matthew 5:23-24)*.

V. Hindrances to reconciliation

A. Inadequate understanding or a lack of biblical forgiveness on the part of another may impede reconciliation.

1. The one you have offended may minimize the matter by saying, "Oh, that's all right. It's no problem." You must let him see that it was serious to God and you because it was sin in your life *(James 2:10, 4:17)*. You must assure him that you want to reconcile with him completely. You are to emphasize that you do not wish to ignore or minimize your failure and that you intend to change in this area and live God's way *(Matthew 5:23-24; Romans 12:18)*.

2. The one offended may not forgive you. In this case, remember you are only responsible for what God instructs you to do; the other person's response is between him and God *(Proverbs 16:7; Ezekiel 18:20; Romans 12:18)*. However, in seeking to be reconciled and at peace with another, assure him that you really

do desire his forgiveness and that you intend to change. Tell him the specific steps you will take to make this change. This is especially important in a close relationship (i.e., spouse, family, boss, roommate, co-worker, etc.) so that you can be held accountable to change that will demonstrate Christlikeness in your future deeds.

Refer also to: **GUIDELINES: VICTORY OVER FAILURES WORKSHEET** *(Supplement 7) under* **VI. Application of biblical change.**

B. Waiting for another to initiate and demonstrate forgiveness delays reconciliation. Regardless of who is at fault, it is the responsibility of an obedient believer to begin the process of reconciliation *(based on Matthew 5:23-24, 18:15; Mark 11:25-26).*

C. Unscriptural demands for "sinlessness" or perfection restrict reconciliation. Remember that you are to forgive on the strength of another's verbal statement of repentance, not his "sinless," perfect walk of repentance *(Luke 17:4).*

If forgiveness by a professing believer is sought and granted yet the one seeking forgiveness persists in sinful behavior, it will be necessary to apply biblical discipline prayerfully and in a spirit of gentleness (Galatians 6:1-5).

Refer to:
THE MEANING OF BIBLICAL LOVE *(Lesson 13, Pages 4-6), especially noting* **IV.** *point* E.;
RESTORATION/DISCIPLINE (YOUR BIBLICAL RESPONSE TO THE SIN OF ANOTHER BELIEVER) *(Lesson 13, Pages 7-8);*
GUIDELINES: THE RESTORATION/DISCIPLINE PROCESS *(Lesson 13, Pages 9-11); and*
BIBLICAL COMMUNICATION *(Lesson 13, Pages 12-14).*

D. Reconciliation with a person who has sinned is not possible when that person will not respond with true repentance, confession, and restitution. *See below:*

1. An employee steals from his company. Other co-workers witness this theft and report it to their manager, a true believer in Christ. When the manager confronts the person about the allegation of theft, the person admits the crime, says he will not do it again, and asks for forgiveness for violating the manager's trust. The manager forgives him and counsels him not to do it again. *(If the employee is a believer, the manager counsels him regarding put-offs and put-ons, renews fellowship, and admonishes him not to steal again).* The manager knows that he must file a report about this situation with his supervisors and does so.

2. Those in authority review the situation and decide to place the employee on probation. The manager discusses his options concerning the employee with his supervisors. After this consultation, two things are decided for the job: (1) the employee is transferred to another department with job restrictions that are appropriate to the confessed theft, and (2) a payment schedule is worked out so that the employee can make restitution for his theft.

3. A short time later, the employee again steals from his company but is caught once more. As earlier, the employee admits his theft to his manager, says he will not do it again, and asks his manager to forgive him once again for violating the manager's trust. The manager again forgives him and counsels him about the consequences of his actions *(If the employee is a believer, the manager warns him of the consequences of continued wrongdoing).* The manager again reports the situation to his supervisors and requests guidance concerning job termination, the filing of criminal charges, and possible restitution.

QUESTIONS AND ANSWERS ABOUT BIBLICAL FORGIVENESS

> While God's plan of forgiveness is stated clearly in Scripture, man's humanistic wisdom has introduced confusion. To protect yourself from accepting and believing erroneous teaching about forgiveness, follow this simple truth: If a particular viewpoint is not supported by Scripture, it is not from God and must be discarded *(based on Proverbs 21:30; Isaiah 55:8-9; Jeremiah 10:23; II Timothy 3:16-17; Hebrews 4:12; II Peter 1:3-4).*

I. **Is it possible or necessary for you to forgive yourself?**

   A. Man's wisdom often teaches that "forgiving self" is a prerequisite for experiencing peace and joy. Forgiving self is usually heard in statements such as, "I just can't forgive myself for what I have done," or "You must learn to forgive yourself to get rid of your guilt." Even a believer might erroneously say, "Now that God has forgiven me, I need to forgive myself."

   B. Any teaching that emphasizes a need "to forgive yourself" is trusting and exalting "self" instead of relying solely on God's promises and provision for total and complete forgiveness. If you believe that it is necessary to "forgive yourself" in addition to receiving God's forgiveness for your sins, you indicate that God's plan of forgiveness for salvation – *Refer to:* **YOU CAN CHANGE BIBLICALLY (PART ONE)** *(Lesson 1, Pages 3-7)* – and His plan of forgiveness for your continued daily cleansing *(I John 1:9)* are not adequate. Remember the following:

   1. Receiving God's forgiveness is not a matter of "feeling forgiven;" rather, it is a matter of trusting God *(Hebrews 11:6)* and His promises *(such as Romans 5:1-2; Colossians 1:21-23; I John 1:9).*

   2. Since God says there is no condemnation (no guilt, complete forgiveness) for you in Christ Jesus, then it is true, regardless of your feelings *(Romans 8:1).*

   3. When God says that He forgives you and cleanses you from *all* unrighteousness *(I John 1:9),* there is absolutely nothing you can or need to do to complete His work.

   4. The "need" to "forgive yourself" presupposes that you have a sense of guilt concerning past sin(s). Since guilt is the result of sin, you are to repent and confess your sin(s) to the Lord *(I John 1:9)* and confess to others at the appropriate time *(based on Proverbs 15:23, 25:11; James 5:16).* Subsequent steps of repentance should include cooperation with God in renewing your mind.

      Refer to: **RENEWING YOUR MIND** *(Lesson 7, Pages 6-7).*

   5. Instead of thinking you need to "forgive yourself" in addition to receiving God's forgiveness, you should forget what lies behind, reach forward to what lies ahead, and press on toward the goal for the prize of the upward call of God in Christ Jesus *(Philippians 3:13-14).*

C.   "Forgiving self" has no biblical support. Scripture has only two perspectives on forgiveness:

   1.   You can and need to be forgiven by God *(Colossians 1:13-14; I John 1:9)*; and

   2.   You are wholeheartedly to forgive others, following the example of God's forgiveness to you *(Matthew 18:32-33; Ephesians 4:32; Colossians 3:13)*.

II.   Will all the consequences of your sins be removed when you receive forgiveness?

A.   When you receive God's forgiveness for salvation, you pass from death to life *(John 5:24)*, thus having the ultimate judgment and consequence of your sin removed *(Romans 6:23)*.   In your daily life as a child of God, you do not need to be judged by the Lord (and subsequently disciplined) when you judge yourself rightly and deal with sin immediately *(based on I Corinthians 11:31-32)*.

B.   However, receiving God's forgiveness does not guarantee that all the consequences of your wrongdoing will be removed *(Colossians 3:25)*. For example:

   1.   Even though the Lord forgave David for his adultery with Bathsheba *(II Samuel 12:13)*, the child that was born out of this adulterous relationship died *(II Samuel 12:14-23)*.

   2.   The repentant thief on the cross responded in faith to Jesus Christ but still died for the crimes he had committed *(Luke 23:39-43)*.

   3.   You can receive God's forgiveness for sins committed against another *(I John 1:9)*, but you still are responsible to reconcile with the person against whom you have sinned *(Matthew 5:23-24)*.

III.   What is the relationship between your granting forgiveness to others and God's granting forgiveness to you?

A.   Before your spiritual new birth *(John 3:3)*, your primary need was to be forgiven by God *(Romans 5:8-9; Colossians 2:13-14)*, which is a sovereign work of grace and is not dependent on anything that you can do *(Ephesians 2:8-9; Titus 3:5)*.

B.   Prior to your spiritual new birth, it was impossible for you to forgive sincerely because apart from Christ:

   1.   You could not understand the things of God *(I Corinthians 2:14)*;

   2.   You were powerless to obey Him *(Romans 8:7)*; and

   3.   You could not conform to something you knew nothing about and had not experienced yourself *(Ephesians 4:32)*.

C.   Since your spiritual new birth, your eternal inheritance in Christ is protected by God *(I Peter 1:3-5)*. Your heavenly inheritance depends only on God's purpose, mercy, and grace; and you are sealed in Him with the Holy Spirit of promise *(Ephesians 1:3-14; II Timothy 1:9)*.

D.   A *consistent* refusal to forgive others biblically reveals a spirit of vindictiveness and indicates that a spiritual new birth has not occurred *(I John 2:3-4; 3:6, 9-10)*. However, a true child of God might sin by placing his focus on himself and fail to grant forgiveness to another person in a particular situation.

1. If you as a child of God sin by failing to forgive another, you show that:

    a. You are empty of gratitude for God's forgiveness granted to you in Christ Jesus *(Matthew 18:21-33)*,

    b. You are not following the example of sacrificial love given by God through Jesus Christ *(Ephesians 4:32; I John 4:10-11)*, and

    c. You are choosing to disobey God's Word by keeping count of a wrong suffered (harboring a grudge) *(I Corinthians 13:5)* and by refusing to grant forgiveness *(Ephesians 4:32)*.

2. If you as a child of God sin by failing to forgive another:

    a. God the Father's forgiveness of your current sins will be withheld *(Matthew 6:14-15; Mark 11:25-26)*; and

    b. God will discipline you in a corrective, appropriate, and loving manner *(I Corinthians 11:32; Hebrews 12:5-11)*.

3. If you object by asking, "What about *I John 1:9* which says I receive forgiveness and cleansing from God when I confess my sins," remember the true meaning of confession. To confess rightly before the Lord means that you "agree with God about your sin with a corresponding commitment to forsake that sin."

    a. You are spiritually deluded *(James 1:22)* if you "confess" some of your sins and expect God's forgiveness and cleansing from all unrighteousness, yet choose to continue in sin by failing to forgive others *(Mark 11:25)*.

    b. You receive answers to your prayers (including those of "confession" of sins) when you are obedient to God's Word *(I John 3:22)* and ask according to God's will *(I John 5:14-15)*. If you will not forgive another, you are not obedient to God's Word and will not be asking in accordance with His will. By withholding forgiveness from another, you choose to continue sinning *(James 4:17)*. As a result, you will not receive cleansing from the Lord for this transgression. In addition, many times the memory of the hurt you received will often continue to drain your spiritual vitality. You are to forgive that person and be free from that bondage.

IV. Does God require you to "forgive and forget?"

A. Scripture says that God's forgiveness involves remembering sins against you no more *(Isaiah 43:25; Jeremiah 31:34; Hebrews 10:17)*. This means that He will not hold your sins against you since He has cleansed you with the precious blood of Jesus Christ *(Romans 3:23-25; Ephesians 1:7; Hebrews 10:19-22; I John 1:7)*.

1. While God forgives, He cannot forget (erase His memory) since He is the Almighty God and final Judge who will bring every act and every careless word to judgment whether good or evil *(Ecclesiastes 12:14; Matthew 12:36-37; II Corinthians 5:10; I Peter 1:17)*. Therefore, since God's character and His Word give assurance that He does forgive completely, forgetting is not required in order to forgive

    Refer to:
    FORGIVENESS (FORGIVING OTHERS AS GOD HAS FORGIVEN YOU)
    (Lesson 12, Pages 3-5), under **I. Understanding God's forgiveness,** *and*
    THE IMPORTANCE OF DOING THE WORD *(Lesson 5, Pages 6-9).*

2. Your responsibility is to forgive another as God has forgiven you *(Ephesians 4:32)*, which involves not holding another's sin against him (i.e., "not remembering"). Then, you are to commit the fault and the person to the Lord since He is the final and righteous Judge *(Matthew 16:27; II Timothy 4:8; James 5:9)*.

B. Scripture uses the term "not to remember" as meaning "not to mention or bring to mind" or "not to keep an account." For example, David requested of the Lord "not to remember" (literally, "not to mention") the previous sins of his youth *(Psalm 25:7)*.

C. Scripture uses "forget" in the sense of "escaping notice." For example, the Apostle Paul could remember (bring to mind) his earlier sins *(I Timothy 1:12-15)* yet confidently proclaimed "to forget" ("not take notice") of those things that were behind in order to press on toward the goal for the prize of the upward call of God in Christ Jesus *(Philippians 3:13-14)*.

D. Nowhere does Scripture require you to have a blank memory about your own sins or sins committed against you. In fact, the memory of certain sins (even though these sins have been forgiven by God) is important for your training in righteousness, to help you not repeat them *(for example, notice David's remembrance of his sins in II Samuel 12:13-23 and Psalm 38)*. The only requirement is for you to forgive others as God in Christ has forgiven you *(Ephesians 4:32)*, even when you clearly remember sins committed against you, which now have no power over you.

Review: **FORGIVENESS (FORGIVING OTHERS AS GOD HAS FORGIVEN YOU)** *(Lesson 12, Pages 3-5)*.

V. **Is it necessary, as some teach, for you to "forgive God" for what has happened in your life?**

A. God, in His majestic holiness *(Exodus 15:11; Isaiah 6:3; Revelation 4:8)* and righteous judgment *(Psalm 7:11, 50:6)*, is kind in all His deeds and is righteous in all His ways *(Psalm 145:17)*, is abundant in lovingkindness *(Psalm 118:1-4; Lamentations 3:22-23)*, and is blameless *(Psalm 18:30)*.

B. Needing to "forgive God" implies that:

1. You can usurp God's authority as the sole Judge when you are forbidden even to judge your neighbor *(James 4:12)*; and

2. God has sinned, which is an impossibility *(Deuteronomy 32:3-4; Psalm 145:17; James 1:17; I John 1:5)*.

C. Forgiveness requires the shedding of blood *(Hebrews 9:22)*.

1. God the Father sent His sinless Son, Jesus Christ, to shed His blood *(Hebrews 9:14)* in order that you could be forgiven of sin for all eternity and thus have a basis to forgive others *(Ephesians 1:7; Colossians 3:13)*.

2. Neither you nor any other person (besides Jesus Christ) can ever shed sinless blood *(Romans 3:23)* in order to have a basis to forgive others eternally.

D. The unbiblical concept of "forgiving God" is not only an affront to God's holiness, the sanctity of His plan of sacrificial forgiveness, and His sovereign rule in this life; but it further illustrates the steps that man will take to exalt self instead of dying to self.

Note: Often, the mistaken emphasis on "forgiving God" results from dealing unbiblically with anger or bitterness in one's life. Refer to: **ANGER AND BITTERNESS** *(Lesson 11, Pages 2-16)*.

VI. **What about not feeling like forgiving another or not feeling like you have been forgiven?**

A.   Even if you do not "feel like" forgiving another, you can and must obey Scripture and forgive others as God has forgiven you *(Ephesians 4:32; Colossians 3:13)*. Biblical forgiveness is costly and often difficult, but it is possible *(based on II Corinthians 3:5-6; Philippians 2:12-13)*. It is not necessary for you to think your forgiveness of another is "fair" or equitable. Forgiving others is not to be based on your "feelings" or perceived equity but instead is based on God's merciful forgiveness of you *(for example: Romans 5:8)*.

Refer to: **FORGIVENESS (FORGIVING OTHERS AS GOD HAS FORGIVEN YOU)** *(Lesson 12, Pages 3-5)*.

B.   As a child of God, even if you do not "feel forgiven" after sincerely confessing your sin(s), God's Word promises that you are completely forgiven and cleansed by God, who is completely faithful and just *(I John 1:9)*. God's promise of forgiveness seals the fact of your forgiveness, regardless of your feelings.

1.   As a child of God, your sins which have been forgiven by God do not hinder your present standing before the Lord *(Romans 8:31-34; I Corinthians 6:9-11; Ephesians 2:1-7)*.

2.   In spite of how you "feel" about your forgiven sins, you are to press forward to your high calling in Christ Jesus and forget (don't take notice of, disregard) what is in your past *(Philippians 3:12-14)*.

A CASE STUDY: MARY'S HUSBAND HAS LEFT HER

> Helping another to solve his problems biblically requires that you deal with that person's relationship with the Lord and his subsequent obedience in practicing biblical love in all of his relationships *(based on Matthew 22:37-39; John 13:35, 14:23-24; I Corinthians 13:4-8a; II Corinthians 2:14; I John 4:8, 10-11, 19; 5:3).*

At a pre-session meeting with your assistant counselors, you review the importance of taking notes during the counseling session with Mary. As a team, you also review the four essential elements of biblical counseling (i.e., understanding the problem, hope, change, practice). Realizing that Mary needs to gain God's perspective on her problem, you establish a session plan (along with corresponding scriptural references) which: (a) explores Mary's relationship with the Lord and (b) asks questions that leads each of you to an understanding of God's perspective in this difficulty. You commit this planning to the Lord in prayer.

When Mary arrives, you introduce her to the other members of the counseling team. After praying together, you encourage everyone to take notes and remind everyone present that the Bible is the sole authority in solving this difficulty. Mary reports that she has partially memorized *I Corinthians 10:13* since your time with her last night. She also says that the other verses given to her in preparation for today's session were helpful. After she explains how these verses ministered to her, you (as the counselor) ask Mary about her salvation experience.

(As you read through this role play, make a list of Mary's unbiblical words and actions).

Counselor: "MARY, TELL ME HOW YOU CAME TO KNOW JESUS CHRIST."

Mary: "I ACCEPTED THE LORD AT A CHRISTIAN SUMMER CAMP WHEN I WAS 16. I HAD REAL JOY IN THE LORD. I REGULARLY ATTENDED CHURCH AND SUNDAY SCHOOL FOR A COUPLE OF YEARS AFTER THAT. I ALSO HAD PLENTY OF CHRISTIAN FRIENDS. (PAUSE) IN COLLEGE I STARTED DOWN A SPIRAL. I MET TOM WHO WAS NOT INTERESTED IN THE CHRISTIAN LIFE. I MARRIED HIM EVEN THOUGH I KNEW I SHOULDN'T BE MARRYING AN UNBELIEVER. I THOUGHT HE WOULD CHANGE, BUT HE DIDN'T. THERE HAS BEEN NO COMMUNICATION OR COMPANIONSHIP OR ROMANCE FOR YEARS NOW. I AM TOTALLY MISERABLE. THERE IS NO PEACE OR JOY IN MY LIFE. EVERYTHING HAS GONE WRONG IN OUR MARRIAGE, AND I HAVE NO HOPE LEFT."

Counselor: "WHEN DID THE PROBLEMS FIRST START BETWEEN YOU AND YOUR HUSBAND TOM?"

Mary: "HE STOPPED WRITING ME LOVE NOTES AND BRINGING ME GIFTS. I FELT SO LET DOWN. I DIDN'T THINK HE LOVED ME ANYMORE. BESIDES THAT, HE EXPECTED ME TO GET UP EVERY MORNING AND FIX BREAKFAST."

Counselor: "WHAT WAS YOUR RESPONSE TO THAT?"

Mary:	"I TOLD HIM TO FIX HIS OWN. I'M NOT HIS COOK OR SERVANT. I REALLY FELT HE WAS STEPPING ON MY RIGHTS. (PAUSE) ON TOP OF THAT, HE'S SO IRRESPONSIBLE; HE LEAVES HIS DIRTY CLOTHES JUST LAYING AROUND. IT REALLY IRRITATES ME. HE KNOWS IT IRRITATES ME; I'M CONVINCED THAT'S WHY HE DOES IT."
Counselor:	"WHAT DO YOU TELL HIM WHEN HE LEAVES HIS CLOTHES ON THE FLOOR?"
Mary:	"WELL, I TELL HIM AT LEAST TEN TIMES A DAY TO PICK THEM UP. WHEN HE DOESN'T DO IT, I START YELLING. THAT IS THE ONLY WAY I CAN GET HIS ATTENTION."
Counselor:	"WHAT OTHER SPECIFIC PROBLEMS CAN YOU THINK OF?"
Mary:	"WE NEVER HAVE MONEY FOR ALL OF OUR FAMILY'S NEEDS BECAUSE HE SPENDS IT ON HIMSELF. I EVEN HAVE TO BEG FOR MONEY FOR FOOD."
Counselor:	"WHAT IS YOUR RESPONSE TO THIS?"
Mary:	"I'M REALLY FRUSTRATED. IT'S SOMETHING HE WILL NEVER DO ANYTHING ABOUT. I REMEMBER SEVERAL TIMES HE FORGOT TO PAY SOME BILLS, AND I HAD TO GO STRAIGHTEN IT OUT. I'LL NEVER FORGET IT; I WAS SO EMBARRASSED! I REMIND HIM OF IT EVERY CHANCE I GET, TOO. MAYBE THAT'LL KEEP HIM FROM DOING IT AGAIN. I DOUBT IT THOUGH."
Counselor:	"IS THERE ANYTHING ELSE?"
Mary:	"YES, AS A MATTER OF FACT. HE NEVER TAKES AN INTEREST IN DISCIPLINING THE CHILDREN. I ALWAYS FEEL LIKE I HAVE TO DO IT. WE FIGHT ABOUT THAT THE MOST. I KEEP TELLING HIM HOW HE'S SUPPOSED TO DO THINGS AS A FATHER; BUT, AS USUAL, HE NEVER LISTENS. I TELL THE CHILDREN THAT IT WILL BE ALL THEIR FATHER'S FAULT IF THEY TURN OUT ROTTEN...JUST LIKE HE IS. I'VE TRIED TO MAKE THIS MARRIAGE WORK BUT IT TAKES TWO, AND HE'S JUST NOT WILLING. I HAVE DONE SO MUCH FOR THAT MAN!"

Review your list of Mary's unbiblical words and actions. Using the Bible as the standard, what has Mary indicated about herself? Where should you help Mary focus her attention in this difficulty? What should Mary do initially in her own life in order to face and deal with these problems God's way?

Refer to:
YOU CAN CHANGE BIBLICALLY (PART TWO) *(Lesson 2, Pages 3-5);*
BIBLICAL SELF-CONFRONTATION: AN ESSENTIAL FOR DISCIPLESHIP *(Lesson 2, Page 6);*
BIBLICAL SELF-CONFRONTATION: A PREREQUISITE FOR HELPING OTHERS BIBLICALLY *(Lesson 2, Pages 7-8);*
BIBLICAL BASIS FOR DAILY DEVOTIONS AND SCRIPTURE MEMORY *(Lesson 2, Pages 9-11); and*
THE UPWARD PATH: WALKING GOD'S WAY *(Lesson 5, Page 5).*

LESSON 12: HOMEWORK

> This lesson's **HOMEWORK** presents God's perspective on forgiveness. As you practice biblical forgiveness, you demonstrate the difference Jesus has made in your life *(based on Matthew 5:16; John 13:35; Ephesians 4:32; Colossians 3:13).*

✔ *homework completed*

☐ A. * In your own words, write the meaning of *Matthew 5:23-24*. This week, memorize *Matthew 5:23-24* and begin memorizing *Ephesians 4:29* and *Philippians 2:3-4.*

☐ B. * Read **BIBLICAL PRINCIPLES: INTERPERSONAL PROBLEMS (PART ONE) (LEARNING HOW TO LOVE YOUR NEIGHBOR)** (Lesson 12, Page 2). Highlight verses in your Bible that are not marked from previous studies.

☐ C. * Study **FORGIVENESS (FORGIVING OTHERS AS GOD HAS FORGIVEN YOU)** (Lesson 12, Pages 3-5). Mark any statements that point out changes you will make to forgive others biblically. Using a **VICTORY OVER FAILURES WORKSHEET** (Supplement 8, Pages 1-2), list those whom you will forgive and begin to work on a specific plan by which you will demonstrate this forgiveness. Use a separate sheet for each person.

☐ D. * Study **RECONCILIATION (REMOVING ALL HINDRANCES TO UNITY AND PEACE)** (Lesson 12, Pages 6-8). Mark any statements that indicate changes you will make in your own life to please the Lord. Using a **VICTORY OVER FAILURES WORKSHEET** (Supplement 8, Pages 1-2), list those with whom you will seek reconciliation. Begin to determine the specific steps of reconciliation you will take with those on your list.

☐ E. * As part of your plan to practice biblical forgiveness, write exactly what you need to say in order to ask someone for forgiveness of a wrong you have committed against him. If there is someone of whom you should ask forgiveness, do so (refer to C. above). Remember, you are only responsible for your obedience to the Lord; you are not responsible for another's response.

☐ F. Read **QUESTIONS AND ANSWERS ABOUT BIBLICAL FORGIVENESS** (Lesson 12, Pages 9-13) to discover answers for common questions concerning biblical forgiveness.

☐ G. * Read **A CASE STUDY: MARY'S HUSBAND HAS LEFT HER** (Lesson 12, Pages 14-15). In addition to listing Mary's unbiblical words and actions that are recorded in this case study, answer the questions at the end of the role-play.

☐ H. * In conjunction with this lesson, answer questions 19 and 20 under **Open Book Test** (Lesson 23, Page 2).

  * *The completion of assignments marked with an asterisk (*) is a prerequisite for further biblical counseling training.*

LESSON 12: STUDY GUIDE FOR DAILY DEVOTIONS
(INCLUDING SCRIPTURE MEMORY AND HOMEWORK)

> This lesson's **STUDY GUIDE** presents God's perspective on forgiveness. As you practice biblical forgiveness, you demonstrate the difference Jesus has made in your life *(based on Matthew 5:16; John 13:35; Ephesians 4:32; Colossians 3:13).*

Scripture Memory

1.   * Memorize *Matthew 5:23-24* and begin memorizing *Ephesians 4:29* and *Philippians 2:3-4.*
2.   Carry your memory verse cards from previous weeks along with this week's memory verses. Review your Scriptures during spare moments throughout the day.

Daily Devotional Study Guide

FIRST DAY

1.   Open with prayer.
2.   * Read *Principle 51,* **BIBLICAL PRINCIPLES: INTERPERSONAL PROBLEMS (PART ONE) (LEARNING HOW TO LOVE YOUR NEIGHBOR)** (Lesson 12, Page 2). Highlight the referenced verses in your Bible.
3.   * In your own words, write the meaning of *Matthew 5:23-24.*
4.   Close with prayer.

SECOND DAY

1.   Open with prayer.
2.   * Read *Principle 52,* **BIBLICAL PRINCIPLES: INTERPERSONAL PROBLEMS (PART ONE) (LEARNING HOW TO LOVE YOUR NEIGHBOR)** (Lesson 12, Page 2). Highlight the listed verses in your Bible.
3.   * Study **FORGIVENESS (FORGIVING OTHERS AS GOD HAS FORGIVEN YOU)** (Lesson 12, Pages 3-5). Look up the listed verses to fix these truths in your heart. This is the first in a two-day study.
4.   Close with prayer.

THIRD DAY

1.   Open with prayer.
2.   * Read *Principle 53,* **BIBLICAL PRINCIPLES: INTERPERSONAL PROBLEMS (PART ONE) (LEARNING HOW TO LOVE YOUR NEIGHBOR)** (Lesson 12, Page 2). Highlight the referenced verses in your Bible.
3.   * Complete your study of **FORGIVENESS (FORGIVING OTHERS AS GOD HAS FORGIVEN YOU)** (Lesson 12, Pages 3-5). Besides looking up listed verses, mark any statements that point out changes you will make to forgive others biblically. Using a **VICTORY OVER FAILURES WORKSHEET** (Supplement 8, Pages 1-2), list those whom you will forgive and begin to work on a specific plan by which you will demonstrate this forgiveness. Use a separate sheet for each person.
4.   Close with prayer.
5.   Are you faithful to review your memory verses in your spare moments throughout the day *(Psalm 119:11; Ephesians 5:15-16)*?

FOURTH DAY

1.   Open with prayer.
2.   * Read *Principle 54,* **BIBLICAL PRINCIPLES: INTERPERSONAL PROBLEMS (PART ONE) (LEARNING HOW TO LOVE YOUR NEIGHBOR)** (Lesson 12, Page 2). Highlight the referenced verses in your Bible.
3.   * Study **RECONCILIATION (REMOVING ALL HINDRANCES TO UNITY AND PEACE)** (Lesson 12, Pages 6-8). Mark any statements that indicate changes you will make in your own life to please the Lord. This is the first day of a two-day study.
4.   Close with prayer.

FIFTH DAY

1.   Open with prayer.
2.   * Complete your study of **RECONCILIATION (REMOVING ALL HINDRANCES TO UNITY AND PEACE)** (Lesson 12, Pages 6-8). Remember to mark statements that indicate changes you intend to make. Using a **VICTORY OVER FAILURES WORKSHEET** (Supplement 8, Pages 1-2), list those with whom you will seek reconciliation. Begin to determine the specific steps of reconciliation you will take with those on your list.
3.   * Write exactly what you need to say in order to ask someone for forgiveness of a wrong you have committed against him.
4.   Close with prayer.

SIXTH DAY

1.   Open with prayer.
2.   Begin your study of **QUESTIONS AND ANSWERS ABOUT BIBLICAL FORGIVENESS** (Lesson 12, Pages 9-13). This is the first day of a two-day study.
3.   Using your written statement that outlines what you will say in asking someone for forgiveness (refer to **FIFTH DAY** above), ask that person to forgive you. Remember, you are only responsible for your actions, not another's response.
4.   Close with prayer.

SEVENTH DAY

1.   Open with prayer.
2.   * Read **A CASE STUDY: MARY'S HUSBAND HAS LEFT HER** (Lesson 12, Pages 14-15). In addition to listing Mary's unbiblical words and actions that are recorded in this role-play, answer the questions at the end of the role-play.
3.   Complete your study of **QUESTIONS AND ANSWERS ABOUT BIBLICAL FORGIVENESS** (Lesson 12, Pages 9-13).
4.   * In conjunction with this lesson, answer questions 19 and 20 under **Open Book Test** (Lesson 23, Page 2).
5.   Close with prayer.
6.   Evaluate your Scripture memory this week. Review your memory verses and ask someone to listen to you recite those you have learned this week. Remember to explain the meaning of the verses and their application to your life.

*   *The completion of assignments marked with an asterisk (*) is a prerequisite for further biblical counseling training.*

LESSON 13

INTERPERSONAL PROBLEMS
(PART TWO)
(LEARNING HOW TO LOVE YOUR NEIGHBOR)

"Let no unwholesome word proceed from your mouth, but only such a word as is good for edification according to the need of the moment, that it may give grace to those who hear."

Ephesians 4:29

"Do nothing from selfishness or empty conceit, but with humility of mind let each of you regard one another as more important than himself; do not merely look out for your own personal interests, but also for the interests of others."

Philippians 2:3-4

LESSON 13: INTERPERSONAL PROBLEMS (PART TWO)
(LEARNING HOW TO LOVE YOUR NEIGHBOR)

> Learning how to love your neighbor requires a willingness to draw on the strength of Jesus Christ as you die to self and live for Him. Living in this manner allows you to practice biblical love for others in spite of adverse circumstances or your feelings to the contrary (*based on Matthew 5:38-48, 22:37-39; Luke 23:34; John 13:35, 15:5; I Corinthians 13:4-8a; II Corinthians 4:7-10, 5:14-15; I John 4:7-11*).

I. **The purposes of this lesson are:**

A. To explain the meaning of biblical love and to teach you how to practice it,

B. To present the guidelines for biblical communication,

C. To show the restoration/discipline process that God's Word outlines for an unrepentant believer,

D. To show how biblical love is to be practiced in the Body of Christ,

E. To present a biblical plan to help you overcome interpersonal problems, and

F. To continue the development of a case study in biblical counseling.

II. **The outline of this lesson**

A. Self-Confrontation

B. Steps for spiritual growth

C. Biblical counseling

BIBLICAL PRINCIPLES: INTERPERSONAL PROBLEMS
(PART TWO)

> Every believer in Christ is responsible to do his part in establishing and maintaining harmonious relationships. Your example is the Lord Jesus Christ who, while here on earth, demonstrated how biblical love is expressed toward others *(based on Matthew 5:23-24; Mark 11:25-26; Luke 23:34; Romans 12:18; II Corinthians 5:17-21; I Peter 2:21-25, 3:8-9; I John 3:14, 18; 4:7-8).*

III. Your Change (outline continues from Lesson 12, Page 2)

(Principle 55)   Do unto others as you would want them to do for you *(Matthew 7:12).* In your relationships, you must be careful to remove anything from your life that could become a stumbling block to others *(Matthew 18:7; Romans 14:13; I Corinthians 8:9, 13).*

(Principle 56)   Put off arguing, quarreling, and returning evil for evil; put on kind speech and gentle behavior by giving a blessing instead *(Philippians 2:14-16; Colossians 4:6; I Thessalonians 5:15; II Timothy 2:23-25; I Peter 3:8-9).*

Also applicable:

(Principle 3, Lesson 2, Page 2) Practicing God's Word begins with judging yourself and removing sinful obstructions from your own life *(Matthew 7:1-5; I Corinthians 11:28-31).* Then, you have the privilege and responsibility of restoring others to victorious living *(Matthew 7:5; II Corinthians 1:3-4; Galatians 6:1-5).*

(Principle 4, Lesson 3, Page 2) God's Word is the only authority for faith and conduct and is the sole, legitimate standard by which all aspects of living are evaluated. Since God's Word provides hope and gives direction for change in your deeds (thoughts, speech, and actions), you are to rely on no other source. It is adequate to equip you for every good work *(Psalm 19:7-11; Proverbs 30:5-6; Colossians 2:8; II Timothy 3:16-17; Hebrews 4:12; II Peter 1:4)* and to help you develop a Christlike attitude of servanthood *(based on Matthew 20:25-28; Philippians 2:5-8; I Thessalonians 2:13).*

(Principle 39, Lesson 10, Page 2) You must take the focus off yourself in daily situations and relationships *(Luke 9:23-24; John 3:30, 12:24-26; Romans 12:3, 14:7-8; II Corinthians 5:15)* by following God's commandments *(Matthew 22:37-39).* Instead of sinning through self-belittlement, self-exaltation, or self-pity, you are to regard others as more important than yourself and be a servant to God and others *(Matthew 20:25-28; Luke 4:8; John 13:3-17, esp. verses 14-15; Romans 15:1-3; I Corinthians 9:19; 10:24, 32-33; Philippians 2:3-8; Colossians 3:23-24; I Peter 4:10).*

(*Principle 52*, Lesson 12, Page 2) Do not judge others by your own standards, perspectives, or experiences *(John 7:24; Romans 14:1-13; James 4:11-12).* You will be judged in the very same way you judge others *(Matthew 7:1-2; Luke 6:36-38).*

IV. Your Practice

(*Principle 57*)   Confess your sins to the Lord *(I John 1:9)* and, in a completely biblical manner, confess sins to others against whom you have sinned *(James 5:16).* Express sorrow and repentance *(Matthew 3:8; Acts 26:20; II Corinthians 7:9; James 4:8-10),* formulate a specific biblical plan to change, and begin to implement the plan *(II Corinthians 7:9-11; Ephesians 4:31-32; Colossians 3:12-17; James 1:25; I Peter 4:8-11).*

(*Principle 58*)   When communicating with someone, first establish the habit of listening carefully *(Proverbs 18:2, 13; James 1:19-20).* Then, speaking the truth in love, bless those with whom you speak *(Ephesians 4:15, 25, 29; Colossians 4:6).* Follow God's directives for biblical communication: be honest, be kind and tender-hearted, keep current, speak no unwholesome words, and use only words that build up and make for peace *(Proverbs 12:18, 15:1; Romans 14:19; Ephesians 4:25, 29, 32; Colossians 4:6).*

(*Principle 59*)   Actively seek reconciliation with others *(Matthew 5:9, 23-24; 18:15-18; Romans 12:18; Colossians 3:14-15).*

Also applicable:

(*Principle 44*, Lesson 10, Page 3) You are to practice love without hypocrisy *(Romans 12:9),* demonstrating the fruit of Christ's life in your thoughts, speech, and actions *(Matthew 5:16; Galatians 5:22-23; Ephesians 5:1-2).*

THE MEANING OF BIBLICAL LOVE

> The primary meaning of the word "love" in Scripture is a purposeful commitment to sacrificial action for another. In fact, loving God is demonstrated by obeying His Word *(John 14:15, 21, 23-24; I John 5:3; II John 1:6)*. Powerful emotions may accompany biblical love, but it is the commitment of the will that holds love steadfast and unchanging. Emotions may change, but a commitment to love in a biblical manner endures and is the hallmark of a disciple of Jesus Christ *(based on John 3:16, 13:34-35; Romans 5:8-11; I Corinthians 13:4-8a, 13)*.

I. **All of God's directives for living are based on loving God and loving others in a biblical manner *(Matthew 22:36-40; Mark 12:28-34)*.**

   A. You are to love God with all your heart, soul, might, and mind *(Deuteronomy 6:5; Matthew 22:37; Mark 12:30)*.

   B. You are to love your neighbor as you already love yourself *(Matthew 7:12, 22:39; Mark 12:31; Ephesians 5:29)*.

II. **Love is giving, not getting *(John 3:16)*, with God's love being the basis and the example for the expression of your love *(I John 4:7-10)*.**

   A. God gave His only begotten Son *(John 3:16)*.

   B. The Lord Jesus Christ loves you and gave Himself for you *(Galatians 1:4, 2:20)*.

   C. The Lord Jesus Christ gave Himself as a ransom on your behalf *(Isaiah 53:4-12; I Timothy 2:6)*.

   D. The Lord Jesus Christ, in demonstrating His love, served others even though He is the Master *(John 13:3-17)*.

III. **Love has specific characteristics demonstrated by godly deeds (thoughts, words, and actions) *(I Corinthians 13:4-8a)*.** The test of biblical love is to do the following, especially when you don't feel like it *(Matthew 5:46-48)*:

   A. *LOVE IS PATIENT, even when you feel like forcefully expressing yourself.* Love bears pain or trials without complaint, shows forbearance under provocation or strain, and is steadfast despite opposition, difficulty, or adversity.

   B. *LOVE IS KIND, even when you want to retaliate physically or tear down another with your words.* Love is sympathetic, considerate, gentle and agreeable.

   C. *LOVE IS NOT JEALOUS, especially when you are aware that others are being noticed more than you.* Love does not participate in rivalry, is not hostile toward one believed to enjoy an advantage, and is not suspicious. Love works for the welfare and good of the other.

D. *LOVE DOES NOT BRAG, even when you want to tell the world about your accomplishments.* Love does not flaunt itself boastfully and does not engage in self-glorification. Instead, love lifts (builds up) others.

E. *LOVE IS NOT ARROGANT, even when you think you are right and others are wrong.* Love does not assert itself or become overbearing in dealing with others.

F. *LOVE DOES NOT ACT UNBECOMINGLY, even when being boastful, rude, or overbearing will get you attention and allow you to get your own way.* Love conforms to what is right, fitting, and appropriate to the situation in order to honor the Lord.

G. *LOVE DOES NOT SEEK ITS OWN, even when you feel like grabbing it all or have an opportunity to do so.* Love does not try to fulfill its own desires, does not ask for its own way, and does not try to acquire gain for itself. Love, as an act of the will, seeks to serve and not be served.

H. *LOVE IS NOT PROVOKED, even when others attempt to provoke you or you are tempted to strike out at something or someone.* Love is not aroused or incited to outbursts of anger. Love continues faithfully and gently to train others in righteousness, even when they fail.

I. *LOVE DOES NOT TAKE INTO ACCOUNT A WRONG SUFFERED, even when everyone seems to be against you or when people openly attack you.* Love does not hold a grudge against someone. Love forgives, chooses not to bring up past wrongs in accusation or retaliation, does not return evil for evil, and does not indulge in self-pity. Love covers a multitude of sins.

J. *LOVE DOES NOT REJOICE IN UNRIGHTEOUSNESS, even when it seems like a misfortune was exactly what another person deserved.* Love mourns over sin, its effects, and the pain which results from living in a fallen world. Love seeks to reconcile others with the Lord.

K. *LOVE REJOICES WITH THE TRUTH, even when it is easier and more profitable materially to lie.* Love is joyful when truth is known, even when it may lead to adverse circumstances, reviling, or persecution.

L. *LOVE BEARS ALL THINGS, even when disappointments seem overwhelming.* Love is tolerant, endures with others who are difficult to understand or deal with, and has an eternal perspective in difficulties. Love remembers that God develops spiritual maturity through difficult circumstances.

M. *LOVE BELIEVES ALL THINGS, even when others' actions are ambiguous and you feel like not trusting anyone.* Love accepts trustfully, does not judge people's motives, and believes others until facts prove otherwise. Even when facts prove that the other person is untrustworthy, love seeks to help restore the other to trustworthiness.

N. *LOVE HOPES ALL THINGS, even when nothing appears to be going right.* Love expects fulfillment of God's plan and anticipates the best for the other person. Love confidently entrusts others to the Lord to do His sovereign and perfect will in their lives.

O. *LOVE ENDURES ALL THINGS, especially when you think you just can't endure the people or circumstances in your life.* Love remains steadfast under suffering or hardship without yielding and returns a blessing while undergoing trials.

P. *LOVE NEVER FAILS, even when you feel overwhelmed and the situation seems hopeless.* Love will not crumble under pressure or difficulties. Love remains selflessly faithful even to the point of death.

IV. **Love characterizes the life of a disciple of Christ** *(John 13:34-35; Ephesians 4:1-3; Colossians 3:14; I John 4:7-8).*

A. You must devote yourself to loving one another *(Romans 12:10)* and remain fervent in this love *(I Peter 4:8)*, because God has already given you His love freely *(I John 4:7, 11, 19)*. You do not need to ask God for more love for another, since His love has already been poured out within your heart *(Romans 5:5)*.

B. You must and can practice biblical love even when you do not feel like it *(Luke 6:27-38; I John 3:16-18, 4:18-21)*.

C. You are to practice biblical love even when you must take a stand on biblical principles that might lead to misunderstanding or retaliation *(I Corinthians 13:8a; Ephesians 4:15, 25; I John 4:18)*.

D. Since godly love is to be the dominant trait of a believer's life *(I Corinthians 13:13)* and is the perfect bond of unity *(Colossians 3:14)*, the characteristics of Christlike love are to be demonstrated even in the midst of difficult situations at home, at work, or with friends *(I Corinthians 13:8a)*.

E. Biblical love must be practiced even when difficult situations arise that cannot be ignored. You are to practice biblical love even when you must:

1. Seriously admonish someone *(I Thessalonians 5:14-15)* or take action to reprove a fellow-believer who is sinning *(Matthew 18:15-17)*,

2. Establish firm rules of behavior in dealing with a so-called believer who persists in practicing sin *(I Corinthians 5:11-13)*,

3. Avoid fellowship with an unruly child of God *(II Thessalonians 3:6)*,

4. Reject (avoid) a factious (divisive) person in the Body of Christ *(Titus 3:10-11)*,

5. Discipline your child *(Ephesians 6:4)*, or

6. Resort to police involvement or become involved in a legal process *(Romans 13:1-5)*.

Even though you personally are to deal with any situation in biblical love, other believers should also become involved whenever it is necessary and biblically appropriate.

Review:
RESTORATION/DISCIPLINE (YOUR BIBLICAL RESPONSE TO THE SIN OF ANOTHER BELIEVER) *(Lesson 13, Pages 7-8), and*
GUIDELINES: THE RESTORATION/DISCIPLINE PROCESS *(Lesson 13, Pages 9-11).*

RESTORATION/DISCIPLINE
(YOUR BIBLICAL RESPONSE TO THE SIN OF ANOTHER BELIEVER)

> Biblical principles must be followed by individuals and by
> the church as a body when restoration /discipline is required
> for a fellow-believer who sins. This restoration/discipline
> process is to be exercised with great love and with diligent,
> fervent prayer *(based on Matthew 18:15-17; John 13:35;
> Romans 15:14; Galatians 6:1-5; I Thessalonians 5:17; James 1:5).*

Responding to a fellow-believer's sin requires you continually to: (1) judge yourself biblically, (2) forgive from your heart the one who has sinned, and (3) reprove (admonish) the sinning fellow-believer in a spirit of gentleness so that he may have an opportunity to be reconciled with God and others *(based on Proverbs 17:17, 20:30, 27:5-6; Matthew 7:1-5; 18:15, 21-35; Mark 11:25-26; Luke 17:3-4; Romans 12:16-19, 15:14; Galatians 6:1-2; Ephesians 4:29, 32; Colossians 4:6; I Thessalonians 5:14-15; James 5:19-20; I Peter 4:8).*

If a fellow-believer sins, go to him in private, and reprove him (expose his sin to him).

If he repents, you are to: (1) grant full forgiveness from your heart, (2) provide biblical counsel for him to be reconciled with God and others, and (3) help him return to full fellowship and useful service in the body of Christ, as far as is biblically possible *(based on Proverbs 11:14, 15:22, 17:9; Matthew 7:1-5; 18:15, 35; Luke 17:3-4; Romans 12:18; I Corinthians 12:25-27; Galatians 6:1-2; Colossians 4:6).*

If he chooses not to repent, you are to: (1) continue judging yourself in a biblical manner, (2) forgive him from your heart, (3) remain in a spirit of gentleness, and (4) return to him with one or two witnesses as you urge him to repent *(based on Matthew 7:1-5; 18:16, 35; Galatians 6:1-2).*

If he repents, you are to: (1) grant full forgiveness from your heart, (2) provide biblical counsel for him to be reconciled with God and others, and (3) help him return to full fellowship and useful service in the body of Christ, as far as is biblically possible *(based on Proverbs 11:14, 15:22, 17:9; Matthew 7:1-5, 18:35; Luke 17:3-4; Romans 12:18; I Corinthians 12:25-27; Galatians 6:1-2; Colossians 4:6).*

If a fellow-believer remains unrepentant, you are to: (1) continue judging yourself in a biblical manner, (2) forgive him from your heart, (3) remain in a spirit of gentleness, and (4) report his decision to remain unrepentant to the church leaders who are responsible for the final steps in the discipline/restoration process *(based on Matthew 7:1-5; 18:17, 35; Galatians 6:1-2).*

(continued on next page)

(continued from previous page)

If he repents, you and all others who are now involved in the discipline and restoration process are to: (1) grant full forgiveness from the heart, (2) provide biblical counsel for him to be reconciled with God and others, (3) comfort him and reaffirm your love to him, and (4) help him return to full fellowship and useful service, as far as is biblically possible *(based on Proverbs 11:14, 15:22, 17:9; Matthew 7:1-5; 18:35; Luke 17:3-4; I Corinthians 12:25-27; II Corinthians 2:6-8; Galatians 6:1-2; Colossians 4:6).*

On the other hand:

- You are not to associate or eat with an unrepentant person who persists in open sin (you are not to fellowship with him) *(based on I Corinthians 5:11-13).*

- You are to withdraw from (fellowship is to cease with) an unrepentant person who continues to live an unruly life marked by willful disobedience to God's Word. You are to take special note of him and admonish him as a brother and not as an enemy *(based on II Thessalonians 3:6, 14-15).*

- For the unrepentant one who is factious (creates division in the body), you are to reject him (avoid him, cease to communicate with him) after a first and second warning since he is self-condemned *(based on Titus 3:10-11).*

- If the unrepentant brother is an elder who remains unrepentant and continues in sin, he is to be rebuked in the presence of all other believers in the church, so that the rest may be fearful of sinning *(I Timothy 5:19-21).*

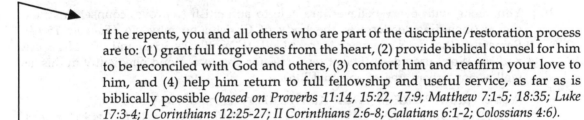

If he repents, you and all others who are part of the discipline/restoration process are to: (1) grant full forgiveness from the heart, (2) provide biblical counsel for him to be reconciled with God and others, (3) comfort him and reaffirm your love to him, and (4) help him return to full fellowship and useful service, as far as is biblically possible *(based on Proverbs 11:14, 15:22, 17:9; Matthew 7:1-5; 18:35; Luke 17:3-4; I Corinthians 12:25-27; II Corinthians 2:6-8; Galatians 6:1-2; Colossians 4:6).*

If he chooses to remain unrepentant after the discipline/restoration process has been prayerfully and faithfully applied to him, then he is to be viewed as someone who does not belong to the family of God *(based on Matthew 18:17; I Corinthians 5:13).*

If he repents, you and all others who are part of the discipline/restoration process are to: (1) grant full forgiveness from the heart, (2) provide biblical counsel for him to be reconciled with God and others, (3) comfort him and reaffirm your love to him, and (4) help him return to full fellowship and useful service, as far as is biblically possible *(based on Proverbs 11:14, 15:22, 17:9; Matthew 7:1-5; 18:35; Luke 17:3-4; I Corinthians 12:25-27; II Corinthians 2:6-8; Galatians 6:1-2; Colossians 4:6).*

If the unrepentant person comes to where believers are gathered (worship services, Bible studies, etc.) after being officially removed from the fellowship of the church, others in the church are to communicate to him consistently his need for repentance. That is the only message that is appropriate for him to hear, since he is outside the fellowship of believers *(based on Matthew 18:17).*

GUIDELINES: THE RESTORATION/DISCIPLINE PROCESS

> You demonstrate biblical love when you take steps to restore a fellow-believer overtaken in sin. This not only encourages a fallen believer to return to his first love of Jesus Christ, but it also gives others involved in the restoration process on-going opportunities to examine the depth of their love to the Lord *(based on Matthew 7:1-5; John 14:15; I Corinthians 13:4-8a; Galatians 6:1-2; Colossians 3:12-13; I Thessalonians 5:14-15; Hebrews 10:23-25; Revelation 2:4-5).*

I. **Initial steps to take in restoring a brother who has sinned**

    A.   Remember that the biblical restoration process is for fellow-believers who sin in direct violation of God's Word. The restoration/discipline process is not to be used for you to "reprove" others who have different preferences or opinions than yourself. In matters of preference or opinions, God's Word directs you to regard others as more important than yourself *(based on Philippians 2:3-4)* and not to judge another *(based on Romans 14:1-19, 15:1-2).*

    B.   You, along with every believer, are able to admonish (reprove, counsel, instruct) others (including leaders) in the body of Christ who may sin *(Romans 15:14)*. Remember that your adequacy is from God *(II Corinthians 3:5-6)* and that His Spirit and His Word provide sufficient resources for you to respond obediently in this, as well as any other, area of spiritual life.

        Review: **SCRIPTURE IS YOUR AUTHORITY** *(Lesson 3, Pages 3-5), and* **THE HOLY SPIRIT EMPOWERS YOU TO SOLVE YOUR PROBLEMS** *(Lesson 3, Pages 6-8).*

    C.   In order to admonish a sinning believer, you are to use only God's Word and not your own "common sense" or the "wisdom" of any other *(based on Psalm 19:7-11; 119:49-50, 92, 104; Proverbs 6:23; Isaiah 55:8-11; II Timothy 3:16-17; Hebrews 4:12)*. In your obedient attempt to restore a fallen brother *(Galatians 6:1-2)*, you are to:

        1.   Privately point out to him the sins that he needs to forsake (the "put-offs") and direct him to the portions of God's Word that show him his deeds are sin *(based on Romans 6:1-2; Colossians 3:1-9)*; and

        2.   Be ready to teach him God's plan for restoration, which involves repentance, confession, reconciliation, and beginning again to live in a manner which pleases the Lord (the "put-ons") *(based on Romans 12:18; Colossians 1:9-12, 3:10-24; James 5:16; I John 1:9; Revelation 2:4-5)*. Biblical counseling from mature believers is often needed at this point to help in the complete restoration of a fallen fellow-believer *(based on Proverbs 11:14, 15:22; Galatians 6:1)*. *Review Lessons 5 - 8, which deal with biblical change.*

    D.   Regardless of a fellow-believer's response to you or to his sin, you are to do the following:

        1.   Examine (judge) yourself in a biblical manner before approaching another believer about his sin(s) and take appropriate biblical steps to overcome any and all sin(s) in your own life to please God and avoid being a hypocrite *(based on Matthew 7:1-5; I Corinthians 11:31; Galatians 6:3-5).*

2. Before God, forgive the sin(s) of your brother in your heart *(Matthew 18:35; Mark 11:26)* and be ready, at all times, to grant forgiveness when your brother repents *(Luke 17:3-4)*.

3. Seek faithfully to win your brother back to a right relationship with the Lord and with the rest of the body of Christ *(Matthew 18:15; Galatians 6:1-2)* as you continually examine yourself by God's Word *(Matthew 7:1-5)*.

4. Remain in a spirit of gentleness in your dealings with your brother who has sinned. Look to yourself to be alert to any temptation while you are trying to restore your brother *(based on Galatians 6:1-2; James 4:7; I Peter 5:8)*, remembering at all times that discipline is sorrowful *(Hebrews 12:11)*.

5. Speak words that edify, according to the need of the moment, in order for your words to provide grace to those who hear *(Ephesians 4:29; Colossians 4:6)*. Do not gossip about another's sins (relating information to anyone not biblically involved in the restoration process) *(based on Leviticus 19:16; Psalm 15:1-3; Proverbs 16:28, 17:9, 20:19; I Peter 4:8)*.

E. When your brother repents at any time in the restoration process, you (and all others who may be involved) are to:

1. Openly grant full (complete, total) forgiveness from your heart *(Matthew 18:35; Luke 17:3-4)* and continue to speak graciously *(Colossians 4:6)*.

    Review: **FORGIVENESS (FORGIVING OTHERS AS GOD HAS FORGIVEN YOU)** *(Lesson 12, Pages 3-5)*.

2. Provide biblical instruction (which usually involves the help, support, and counsel of other believers) to help him overcome the immediate sin(s) in his life and help him develop a biblical pattern of living *(based on Proverbs 11:14, 15:22; II Timothy 3:16-17)*.

    Review: **PRACTICAL STEPS FOR ACHIEVING BIBLICAL CHANGE** *(Lesson 8, Pages 8-10)*; **GUIDELINES: VICTORY OVER FAILURES WORKSHEET** *(Supplement 7)*; **RECONCILIATION (REMOVING ALL HINDRANCES TO UNITY AND PEACE)** *(Lesson 12, Pages 6-8)*; *and* **QUESTIONS AND ANSWERS ABOUT BIBLICAL FORGIVENESS** *(Lesson 12, Pages 9-13)*.

3. Help him to be restored to full fellowship and useful service in the body of Christ, as far as is biblically possible *(based on I Corinthians 12:25-27; Ephesians 4:16; Hebrews 10:23-25; I Peter 4:10)*.

4. Continue to judge yourself in a biblical manner *(Matthew 7:1-5)*.

II. Continuing steps to take when a fellow-believer refuses to repent

A. If a fellow-believer refuses to repent after you have urged him to do so *(Matthew 18:15)*, you are to bring one or two others with you to witness his persistent refusal to repent *(Matthew 18:16)*.

1. It is essential that the witnesses be mature believers who understand the biblical principles associated with the restoration process *(see I. C. above)*. The witnesses are to have a reputation for impartiality so that none of the witnesses are perceived as "taking up one side of the argument" *(based on Leviticus 19:15; Proverbs 24:23; I Timothy 5:21)*.

2. To prepare for possible further steps of restoration/discipline that may involve many others in the church, it is advisable that one witness be a church leader who could institute the next step in the restoration/discipline process *(based on Hebrews 13:17; I Peter 5:1-7)*.

3. Each witness should review and follow the above guidelines under: **I. Initial steps to take in restoring a brother who has sinned**.

B. If a professing believer's persistent unrepentance must be brought before the church (i.e., the known believers, not simply those attending a public meeting where both believers and non-believers might be present), all steps in the biblical restoration process should be reviewed *(based on Matthew 7:1-5; II Timothy 3:16-17; James 4:17)*. Then, these believers, under the supervision of church leaders, are to encourage the one in sin to repent *(based on Matthew 18:17; Galatians 6:1; Hebrews 13:17; James 5:19-20)*.

C. To withdraw fellowship from an unrepentant professing believer *(I Corinthians 5:11; II Thessalonians 3:6, 14-15; Titus 3:10)*, remember the following:

1. To withdraw yourself from fellowship (keeping aloof) does not mean to self-righteously avoid or ignore the unrepentant person. Conversations with an unrepentant believer may occur in the course of everyday living. However, communication should only consist of admonishing him to put off the old sinful pattern and to return to the Lord and be obedient to God's Word (based on *Romans 6:1-2; Colossians 3:3-14; Revelation 2:4-5)*.

2. To "take special note" of an unrepentant person means to note that those involved in the restoration process (which could include an entire church family) must make a prayerful effort to restore that individual. It does not mean to gossip about the person who is choosing to remain unrepentant *(based on Proverbs 17:9)*.

D. If an unrepentant professing believer must be treated as one who does not belong to the family of God *(Matthew 18:17)*, remember the following:

1. You and the others involved in the restoration/discipline process are not to unlovingly ignore the unrepentant person, but you are to avoid speaking with him freely in unhindered fellowship as you would with other fellow-believers.

2. An unrepentant person may choose to attend church functions (as unbelievers do); but, like an unbeliever, he may not minister, should not take communion, or otherwise pretend that he has no problem with which he must deal.

3. Believers in the church must continue to admonish him. However, the reality of his salvation must now be brought up for him to consider, since he is persistently choosing (just like an unbeliever) not to be obedient to the Word of God *(I John 2:3-6, 3:6-9)* and is living like one who has no supernatural power to overcome sin *(Romans 8:7)*.

E. At all times, remember that discipline is sorrowful *(Hebrews 12:11a)*, not only for the one being disciplined; but God the Father and the Holy Spirit are also grieved by the sin of the individual *(based on Ezekiel 18:23, 30-32; Ephesians 4:30)*.

F. Believers who choose not to be diligent and faithful in the complete process of restoration/discipline toward sin in another believer's life face the corrective discipline of the Lord because:

1. They are sinning in their own lives by failing to obey God's Word, which states that believers are to restore a brother caught in sin *(based on Galatians 6:1-2; James 4:17)*; and

2. They are sinning as a group by minimizing sin in the body of Christ and choosing not to deal with it *(based on I Corinthians 5:1-13; James 4:17)*.

BIBLICAL COMMUNICATION

> Your words and the manner in which you speak are critical to harmonious relationships. As you learn to speak the truth in love, you must also determine when to speak, how to speak in an edifying manner, and to whom you should speak. The power of your words is enormous, and they also show the condition of your heart. Even your idle words will be accounted for in the day of judgment *(based on Proverbs 12:18, 18:21, 21:23; Matthew 12:34-37; Ephesians 4:15, 25, 29; Colossians 4:6)*.

I. **What do your words reveal?**

    A. Your words are a mirror of your heart *(Luke 6:45)*.

    B. Your words reflect your intent to heal or to hurt *(Proverbs 11:9, 11; 12:18; 14:25; 15:4; 16:24, 28; 18:21)*.

    C. Your words are indicators of your spiritual maturity *(based on Ecclesiastes 10:12-14; II Timothy 2:16; James 1:26; 3:1-6, esp. vs. 2)*.

    D. Your words reveal a self-focus (by cursing) or a focus on God and others (by blessing) *(based on James 3:9-12; I Peter 3:8-10)*.

II. **To whom should you speak?**

    A. Speak with the Lord first in order to gain His perspective *(James 1:5)*.

    B. Speak to yourself next, to determine changes you may need to make *(based on Matthew 7:1-5; Romans 2:21)*.

    C. Speak to the wise, not to the foolish scoffer *(Proverbs 9:7-9, 19:25, 23:9)*.

    D. Speak to the receptive, not to the quarrelsome *(Proverbs 17:14, 20:3)*.

    E. Speak only to those who need to know *(based on Proverbs 11:13-14)*.

    F. Speak to those who need hope, comfort, restoration, or regeneration (spiritual new birth) *(based on Matthew 28:19-20; II Corinthians 1:3-4, 5:18-20; I Peter 3:15)*.

III. **When should you speak?**

    A. Speak after gathering the facts *(Proverbs 18:13, 29:20)*.

        1. Listen attentively, rather than concentrating on what you are going to say *(Proverbs 10:19, 15:28, 18:2)*.

        2. Listen to all sides; don't jump to conclusions *(based on Proverbs 18:13, 17)*.

        3. Focus on facts, not on opinions. Ask who, what, where, when, and how (not why) questions *(based on Proverbs 13:10, 18:15; II Timothy 2:23)*.

4. Ask questions to gain insight, not those that merely solicit a "yes" or "no" response *(based on Proverbs 20:5)*.

B. Speak after thinking *(based on Proverbs 13:3, 15:28, 18:13, 21:23; James 1:19)*.

C. Speak at the appropriate time *(Proverbs 15:23, 25:11)*.

1. Make the most of any opportunity to provide grace in building up others *(Ephesians 4:29; Colossians 4:5-6)*.

2. Speak with a blessing even when insulted or persecuted *(based on Proverbs 20:22; Romans 12:14; I Peter 3:8-9)*.

3. When appropriate, help another by admonishing, correcting, and restoring him *(Romans 15:14; Galatians 6:1; Colossians 1:28; II Timothy 2:24-25)*.

IV. How should you speak ?

A. Speak in love *(Ephesians 4:15)*.

1. Love is patient, is kind, is not jealous, does not brag, is not arrogant, is not provoked, does not take into account a wrong suffered *(I Corinthians 13:4-5)*.

2. Love covers transgressions whenever possible and biblically appropriate *(Proverbs 10:12; I Peter 4:8)*.

Cross-reference with: **THE MEANING OF BIBLICAL LOVE** *(Lesson 13, Pages 4-6), especially noting the definition of biblical love illustrated under* **III. Love has specific characteristics demonstrated by godly deeds.**

B. Speak with control over emotions *(Proverbs 15:1, 16:32, 17:27; Ephesians 4:25-27)*.

C. Speak without quarrelling *(Proverbs 17:14, 20:3; II Timothy 2:24-25)*.

D. Speak with sweetness, gentleness, graciousness, and reverence *(Proverbs 15:1; 16:21, 24; 25:15; Colossians 4:6; I Peter 3:15)*, and yet with confidence and authority *(Titus 2:15, 3:8)*.

E. Speak with a blessing in response to insults *(Proverbs 20:22; Romans 12:14; I Peter 3:9)*.

F. Speak in a manner that is acceptable and pleasing to God *(Psalm 19:14; I Thessalonians 2:4)*.

V. What should you not say?

A. You should not lie *(based on Exodus 20:16; 23:1; Deuteronomy 5:20; Psalm 31:18; Proverbs 4:24; 6:12, 16-19; 8:13; 12:22; 19:5; Ephesians 4:25; Colossians 3:9; Revelation 22:15)*.

B. You should not use words that are unwholesome, slanderous, malicious, or abusive, since these are practices of the old self *(Ephesians 4:29, 31; Colossians 3:8)*.

C. You should not curse or speak with bitterness since these are signs of wickedness and unrighteousness *(Psalm 10:2-11, esp. verse 7; Romans 3:10-18, esp. verse 14)*.

D. You should not speak in a silly, joking, or coarse manner since this is not fitting behavior for a child of God *(Proverbs 26:18-19; Ephesians 5:4)*.

E. You should avoid worldly and empty chatter since this leads to further ungodliness *(I Timothy 6:20; II Timothy 2:16)*.

F.   You should not talk too much or be quick to speak since this leads to unavoidable transgression and is characteristic of an undisciplined life *(based on Psalm 39:1, 141:3; Proverbs 10:19; James 1:19)*.

G.   It is deceptive to use flattering words for the purpose of gaining an advantage, since this is ruinous to loving relationships *(based on Proverbs 26:28, 29:5; I Thessalonians 2:3-7, esp. verse 5; Jude 1:16)*.

H.   You should not gossip, since this reveals a contentious spirit within you and fosters contention between others *(Proverbs 18:8, 20:19, 26:20)*.

1.   Gossip is to be put away from your life, and you are not to associate with gossips. As *Proverbs 20:19* pointedly states, "He who goes about as a slanderer (talebearer, scandal-monger) reveals secrets, therefore do not associate with a gossip (one who flatters with his lips)."

2.   You can quiet contention by putting off gossip, as *Proverbs 26:20* states, "For lack of wood the fire goes out, and where there is no whisperer (gossip, talebearer), contention quiets down."

I.   You should not boast about what you have accomplished or what you plan to do since all you have accomplished in the past or all you may accomplish in the future is a gift of God's grace. Furthermore, boasting about yourself is a sign of arrogance and a failure to recognize God's sovereignty and enablement in your life *(Psalm 75:1-8; Proverbs 27:1; Jeremiah 9:23-24; James 4:13-16)*.

VI.   What should you speak?

A.   Always speak the truth *(Ephesians 4:15, 25)*.

B.   You should speak God's words rather than your own opinions or man's philosophies *(based on Proverbs 30:5-6; Isaiah 55:8-11; I Peter 1:24-25)*. Don't appeal to your own authority by saying "I think," "I believe," "I don't agree," etc.

1.   Speak only words fitting for (appropriate to) sound doctrine *(Titus 2:1)*.

2.   Speak in psalms, hymns, and spiritual songs *(Ephesians 5:19; Colossians 3:16)*.

C.   Use only wholesome words that give grace to those who hear *(Proverbs 15:1; Ephesians 4:29; Colossians 4:6)*.

1.   Do not tear down or belittle others with words like "that's stupid" or "you are always wrong," but instead concentrate on building up another.

2.   Focus on meeting the need of the moment.

D.   Speak with a view to reconcile others to the Lord *(based on II Corinthians 5:20)*.

E.   Speak to give witness for the Lord *(I Peter 3:15)*.

F.   Your speech should give thanks *(Psalm 9:1; Ephesians 5:4, 20; Colossians 3:17)* and praise to the Lord *(Psalm 145:1-7, 150:1-6)*.

G.   Boast of God's righteousness, mercy, justice and His work of grace provided through Christ Jesus for you *(Psalm 20:7, 44:8; Jeremiah 9:23-24; I Corinthians 1:26-31)*.

BIBLICAL RELATIONSHIPS
(LOVING EACH OTHER IN THE BODY OF CHRIST)

> After your spiritual new birth, you became a member of
> the Body of Christ. Believers in Christ are supernaturally
> related as brothers and sisters in Christ and should
> consistently support one another through the practice of
> biblical love *(based on John 13:35; Romans 12:4-5;*
> *I Corinthians 10:17; Ephesians 1:22-23, 2:11-22, 4:11-16;*
> *Colossians 2:18-19).*

I. Expressions of biblical love in the Gospels

A.   Be gentle with one another, that you may inherit the earth *(Matthew 5:5)*.

B.   Make peace with one another, that you may be called the sons of God *(Matthew 5:9)*.

C.   Reconcile with one another, that you may be fit to worship and serve the Lord *(Matthew 5:23-24)*.

D.   Give to him who asks of you *(Matthew 5:42a)*.

E.   Love your enemies and pray for those who persecute you *(Matthew 5:44)*.

F.   Forgive others that God may forgive you *(Matthew 6:14-15)*.

G.   Do not judge others that you may not be judged *(Matthew 7:1-2)*.

H.   Treat others the same way that you want them to treat you *(Matthew 7:12)*.

I.   Reprove your brother so that he may be reconciled with you and with the Lord *(Matthew 18:15-17)*.

J.   Serve one another, following the example of Christ *(Matthew 20:26-28; John 13:13-17)*.

K.   Love others as you do yourself so they may know that you are one of Christ's disciples *(Matthew 22:39; John 13:34)*.

II. Expressions of biblical love in Acts and Romans

A.   Meet one another's needs by sharing God's provisions that He has placed under your care *(Acts 4:32-37)*.

B.   Minister to others, according to your spiritual giftedness, as a functioning and mutually edifying member of the Body of Christ *(Romans 12:3-8)*.

C.   Be devoted to one another in brotherly love since you are a member of God's family through Christ *(Romans 12:10)*.

D.   Give preference to one another and thus demonstrate honor to a fellow-believer *(Romans 12:10)*.

E. Be of the same mind with one another that you may not be wise in your own estimation but instead that you may glorify the Lord through your unity *(Romans 12:16, 15:5-6)*.

F. Love one another that you may fulfill the law of God in its sum: "You shall love your neighbor as yourself." *(Romans 13:8-10)*.

G. Do not judge one another and thus acknowledge God's sovereignty in the lives of one another *(Romans 14:1-13)*.

H. Pursue things that make for peace and the building up of one another that you may not lead others to stumble *(Romans 14:14-19)*.

I. Accept one another and thus follow Christ's example of acceptance to the glory of God *(Romans 15:7)*.

J. Admonish one another because you are enabled by the Lord to do so *(Romans 15:14)*.

III. Expressions of biblical love in I Corinthians and II Corinthians

A. Be of the same mind with one another to preserve the unity in the Body of Christ *(I Corinthians 1:10)*.

B. Do not be greedy but instead wait for one another when you come to eat and thus express the unity of the Body of Christ *(I Corinthians 11:17-22, 33)*.

C. There should be no divisions in the body but the members should have the same care for one another *(I Corinthians 12:25)*.

D. Give yourself first to the Lord and then to one another that you may demonstrate participation in the support of other believers *(II Corinthians 8:4-5)*.

IV. Expressions of biblical love in Galatians and Ephesians

A. Through love, serve one another *(Galatians 5:13)*.

B. In living by the Spirit, do not become boastful, challenging one another, or envying one another *(Galatians 5:24-26)*.

C. Gently restore those who are caught in any sin *(Galatians 6:1)*.

D. Bear one another's burdens and thus fulfill the law of Christ *(Galatians 6:2)*.

E. Bear with one another in love and thus preserve the unity of the Spirit in the bond of peace *(Ephesians 4:2-3)*.

F. Be truthful because you are a member with others in the Body of Christ *(Ephesians 4:25)*.

G. Forgive one another just as Christ forgave you *(Ephesians 4:32)*.

H. Be kind and tenderhearted toward one another, putting off bitterness, wrath, anger, clamor, and malice *(Ephesians 4:31-32)*.

I. In thankfulness, speak to one another in psalms and hymns and spiritual songs, singing and making melody with your heart to the Lord *(Ephesians 5:18-20)*.

J.   In living a life controlled by the Spirit, be subject to one another in the fear (reverence) of Christ *(Ephesians 5:18-21)*.

V.   Expressions of biblical love in Philippians and Colossians

A.   Be of the same mind with one another to maintain the fellowship of the Spirit in affection and compassion *(Philippians 2:1-2)*.

B.   Regard one another as more important than yourself, not dealing with anyone out of selfishness or empty conceit *(Philippians 2:3)*.

C.   Bear with one another in love since you have been chosen by God *(Colossians 3:12-13)*.

D.   Forgive one another just as the Lord forgave you *(Colossians 3:13)*.

E.   With all wisdom teach and admonish one another with psalms and hymns and spiritual songs, singing with thankfulness in your hearts to God *(Colossians 3:16)*.

VI.   Expressions of biblical love in I Thessalonians

A.   Love one another since the Lord causes you to increase and abound in His love *(I Thessalonians 3:12, 4:9)*.

B.   Comfort one another with the promise of our Lord's return that you may not sorrow without hope *(I Thessalonians 4:13-18)*.

C.   Encourage one another while you await the coming of the Lord Jesus Christ *(I Thessalonians 5:11)*.

D.   Greatly appreciate and highly esteem those who have charge over you and live in peace with one another *(I Thessalonians 5:12-13)*.

E.   Seek after that which is good for one another and do not repay evil for evil *(I Thessalonians 5:15)*.

VII.   Expressions of biblical love in Hebrews and James

A.   Encourage one another lest you become hardened by the deceitfulness of sin *(Hebrews 3:13, 10:25)*.

B.   Stimulate one another to love and good deeds and hold fast the confession of your hope without wavering *(Hebrews 10:23-24)*.

C.   Assemble with one another so that you may encourage one another as the coming of the Lord Jesus Christ draws near *(Hebrews 10:25)*.

D.   Confess your sins to one another and pray for one another so you may be made whole *(James 5:16)*.

VIII.   Expressions of biblical love in I Peter

A.   Love one another out of your obedience to the truth and thus cover many sins *(I Peter 1:22, 4:8)*.

B.   Be a blessing to one another out of your calling in Christ to inherit a blessing *(I Peter 3:9)*.

C.   Be hospitable to one another without complaint *(I Peter 4:9)*.

D.   Through love, serve one another since you have been gifted to do so *(I Peter 4:10)*.

E.   Clothe yourself with humility toward one another because God opposes the proud but gives grace to the humble *(I Peter 5:5)*.

IX.   **Expressions of biblical love in I John and II John**

A.   Fellowship with one another through Christ because you are walking in His light *(I John 1:7)*.

B.   Love one another and be obedient to God in response to His love for you *(I John 3:11, 23; 4:7, 11; II John 1:5)*.

C.   Meet the needs of your brother because of God's abiding love in you *(I John 3:17)*.

OVERCOMING INTERPERSONAL PROBLEMS

> Even though you may have had a spiritual new birth, you have the responsibility of continually dying to self in order to live for the Lord and to minister effectively to others *(based on Matthew 7:12; Mark 10:43-45; Luke 9:23-24; John 3:30, 12:24-26; Romans 12:3; Philippians 2:3-4, 3:7-8; Hebrews 12:1-3).*

I. **Carefully review the following cross-references:**

   A. The foundational, biblical requirements for change (Lessons 1 and 2), recognizing the differences between living man's way and living God's way (Lessons 3 and 4);

   B. The essential elements of biblical change (Lessons 5 - 8) as you die to self and live for the Lord (Lessons 9 and 10);

   C. The necessity of biblically dealing with any anger and bitterness in your life (Lesson 11);

   D. The applicability of this situation to family relationships (Lessons 14 - 17);

   E. The possible links between fear, worry, or depression in your life (Lessons 18 and 19) and interpersonal difficulties;

   F. The seriousness of life-dominating sins and their relationship to any problem (Lessons 20 and 21); and

   G. The need for you to establish and faithfully maintain specific standards from God's Word for every area of your life (Lesson 22).

   NOTE: The cross-references cited above are important in dealing with this specific problem area. In dealing with problems biblically, you must examine all aspects of your life. For example, the problem of envy cannot be overcome by dealing with it as an end in itself. Rather, any specific problem must be dealt with in light of scriptural principles for all of life. As you can see, references to previous lessons are listed in addition to those lessons not yet covered.

   If you proceed in biblical counseling training, you will find that God's solutions as presented in this course apply to all problems, including those not covered in this manual.

II. **To become aware of the patterns of sin or temptations in regard to this particular problem, make a list of people, places, times, or circumstances where ongoing problems are evident in your life.**

III. **Use the VICTORY OVER FAILURES WORKSHEET (Supplement 8). To complete columns 1-3, follow the instructions given in GUIDELINES: VICTORY OVER FAILURES WORKSHEET (Supplement 7).**

IV. **When completing column four of the VICTORY OVER FAILURES WORKSHEET (Supplement 8):**

   A. Develop a **basic plan** to overcome the sins you have recognized in your own life in your interpersonal relationships. In your plan, include deeds (thoughts, speech, and

---

actions) that will help you develop a Christlike manner by taking into account the following guidelines:

1. Think biblically

    a. Remember that God has promised to care for you in any situation, no matter how unsettling it may seem *(Psalm 23:1-6, 37:5; Proverbs 3:25-26; Matthew 10:28-31; Romans 8:28-29, 36-39; I Corinthians 10:13).*

    b. Confess all sinful thoughts to God *(I John 1:9)* and ask for His help in changing this sinful pattern *(based on I Thessalonians 5:17; Hebrews 4:15-16; James 1:5).*

    c. Rejoice *(I Thessalonians 5:16)* and give thanks in and for every situation *(Ephesians 5:20; I Thessalonians 5:18),* knowing that endurance in trials helps to conform you to the image of Christ *(based on Romans 5:3-5; James 1:2-4).*

    d. Remember that God's forgiveness of you is the basis for you to forgive others *(Matthew 18:21-35; Ephesians 4:32; Colossians 3:13).*

    e. Remember that your love for others illustrates the love that you have for God *(I John 2:9-11; 3:14-16; 4:7-11, 20-21).*

    f. Focus your thoughts on glorifying and pleasing God and on being a blessing to others in all situations *(based on Matthew 22:37-39; Luke 9:23-24; II Corinthians 5:9, 15; 10:5; Galatians 5:16-17; Philippians 2:3-4, 4:8; Colossians 3:2).*

    g. Within the very situation in which you find yourself, do not dwell on things that contribute to further sin. Instead discipline your mind to think on things that please the Lord *(Philippians 4:8; Colossians 3:2).* Remember to pray for those who persecute you *(Matthew 5:44).*

    h. Review psalms, hymns, and spiritual songs that you have memorized *(based on Ephesians 5:19-20; Colossians 3:16).*

    i. Think of ways you can encourage other believers, stimulating them to love and good deeds *(Hebrews 10:23-25).*

2. Speak biblically

    a. Confess your current sins to the Lord and to those whom you have failed to love in a biblical manner, including the sins of failing to complete your responsibilities. Confess any other remembered sins that you have failed to confess earlier *(based on Psalm 51:1-4; James 5:16; I John 1:9).*

        To review how to confess your sins to those you have sinned against, refer to:
        GUIDELINES: VICTORY OVER FAILURES WORKSHEET *(Supplement 7)*
             under **VI. Application of biblical change,** *point D. and*
        RECONCILIATION (REMOVING ALL HINDRANCES TO UNITY AND PEACE) *(Lesson 12, Pages 6-8) under* **II. Confession.**

    b. Do not speak about your past accomplishments *(Proverbs 27:2, 30:32; II Corinthians 10:18),* sorrows, or defeats *(Philippians 3:13-14),* worries about the future *(Matthew 6:34),* comparing yourself to yourself and/or others *(II Corinthians 10:12),* or boastfully promising what you will do in the future *(Proverbs 27:1; James 4:13-16).* Instead, edify others by thankfully speaking of the goodness of the Lord and the recent difference He has made in your life in this situation *(Luke 10:20; Ephesians 4:29; Colossians 4:6; Hebrews 13:15; I Peter 3:15).*

    c. Do not slander, gossip, quarrel, or use words that do not edify others *(Proverbs 10:18; Ephesians 4:29, 31; 5:4; Colossians 3:8; II Timothy 2:24; I Peter 2:1).* Instead, let your speech be truthful and gracious, according to the need of the moment, that you may know how to answer each person *(Ephesians 4:15, 25, 29; Colossians 4:6).*

d.   Do not bring up another's sin in an accusing or vengeful manner, either to others, yourself, or to the person who has sinned *(Proverbs 10:18, 17:9, 20:19; Ephesians 4:29, 31; Colossians 3:8; I Peter 2:1).*

e.   Encourage reconciliation with God and others, following biblical guidelines *(Matthew 5:9, 23-24; Romans 12:18; II Corinthians 2:6-8, 5:18).*

Refer to: **RECONCILIATION (REMOVING ALL HINDRANCES TO UNITY AND PEACE)** *(Lesson 12, Pages 6-8).*

3.   Act biblically

a.   Forgive others just as God has forgiven you *(Ephesians 4:32; Colossians 3:13).*

Refer to: **FORGIVENESS (FORGIVING OTHERS AS GOD HAS FORGIVEN YOU)** *(Lesson 12, Pages 3-5) and determine if you are practicing biblical forgiveness. Make changes as necessary.*

b.   Memorize Scripture verses and study Scripture passages specifically related to overcoming your own sins in your interpersonal relationships. Memorize verses that tell you how to love others biblically *(based on Psalm 119:9, 11, 16; II Corinthians 10:5; Philippians 4:8; II Timothy 2:15).* Memorize psalms, hymns, and spiritual songs to be used at appropriate times *(based on Ephesians 5:19-20; Colossians 3:16).*

c.   Pray always with thanksgiving *(Philippians 4:6; I Thessalonians 5:17-18)* and according to God's will *(I John 5:14-15).* Cast all your cares on the Lord *(I Peter 5:7)* and pray for those who persecute you *(Matthew 5:44).*

d.   Identify all danger signals – such as situations, places, and personal contacts that bring temptation – and take immediate steps to eliminate, flee, or resist the temptation *(based on Psalm 1:1; Proverbs 27:12; I Corinthians 10:13, 15:33; II Timothy 2:22; James 4:7; I Peter 5:8-9).*

e.   Make amends for wrongdoing and seek reconciliation with those you have offended *(based on Matthew 5:23-24).* Remember that although you have already confessed your sins *(see 2. a. above),* you need to demonstrate actively your serious intent to change.

See: **RECONCILIATION (REMOVING ALL HINDRANCES TO UNITY AND PEACE)** *(Lesson 12, Pages 6-8) under* **III. Restitution** *and* **IV. The importance of reconciliation.**

f.   Bless others through tangible and genuine expressions of biblical love and service (this includes your daily responsibilities as a family member, student, employer, employee, roommate, etc.) *(based on Matthew 7:12; Romans 12:9-13, 15-16; 13:8-10; I Corinthians 13:4-8a; Philippians 2:3-8; I Timothy 6:17-19; I Peter 3:8-9; I John 3:18).* You are to do this:

1)   Regardless of how you feel *(based on Genesis 4:7; II Corinthians 5:14-15; Galatians 5:16-17; Philippians 4:13; James 4:17);*

2)   Especially to those who seem to be your enemies or to those against whom you have sinned *(based on Matthew 5:23-24, 43-48; Mark 11:25-26; Romans 12:14, 17-21);*

3)   With kindness and tenderheartedness for the very individuals with whom you are or have been irritated *(Ephesians 4:31-32);*

4)   By taking advantage of opportunities to minister, especially in ways that keep you in a Christlike servant attitude towards others *(based on Matthew 20:25-28; Philippians 2:3-8; I Peter 4:10);* and

5) By practicing biblical stewardship to honor the Lord and to be of practical help to others *(based on Psalm 24:1; Matthew 25:14-29; I Corinthians 4:1-2; Ephesians 5:15-17; I Timothy 6:17-19; I Peter 4:10).*

Refer to:
BIBLICAL PRINCIPLES OF STEWARDSHIP *(Lesson 10, Pages 4-6) and* **DYING TO SELF BY SERVING OTHERS** *(Lesson 10, Pages 7-8).*

For specific examples of how and when to express biblical love, even in difficult situations, refer to: **THE MEANING OF BIBLICAL LOVE** *(Lesson 13, Pages 4-6).*

g. Whenever necessary, conduct a "conference table" using the guidelines outlined in **OVERCOMING PROBLEMS THROUGH BIBLICAL COMMUNICATION (USING A CONFERENCE TABLE FOR RECONCILIATION)** (Lesson 15, Pages 6-9).

h. Correct deficiencies in your life that exist because of a lack of discipline or neglect *(based on Colossians 3:1-17; I Timothy 4:7b; James 4:17).*

i. If you need help, ask a Christian friend to help you and hold you accountable to carry out your **basic and contingency plans** until you have established a new pattern of godly living *(Proverbs 27:17; Ecclesiastes 4:9-10; Hebrews 10:23-25).* If necessary, seek biblical counsel from others *(Proverbs 11:14, 15:22).*

j. If an interpersonal problem persists because a fellow-believer will not repent of sin in his own life, take the necessary steps to restore that person to the Lord and to others *(based on Romans 12:18; Matthew 18:15; Galatians 6:1-2).*

To review the necessary steps that must be taken in restoring unrepentant believers, study:
RESTORATION/DISCIPLINE (YOUR BIBLICAL RESPONSE TO THE SIN OF ANOTHER BELIEVER) *(Lesson 13, Pages 7-8) and*
GUIDELINES: THE RESTORATION/DISCIPLINE PROCESS *(Lesson 13, Pages 9-11).*

B. As necessary, develop a **"THINK AND DO" LIST** (Supplement 10) using **GUIDELINES: THE "THINK AND DO" LIST** (Supplement 9).

C. Implement your **basic plan** *(James 1:22)* and do it heartily for the Lord *(Colossians 3:23-24).*

D. Develop a **contingency plan** to deal with typical situations that provide temptation for you to sin in your interpersonal relationships. Take into account the following guidelines:

1. Immediately ask God for help *(I Thessalonians 5:17; Hebrews 4:15-16; James 1:5).*

2. Review your memorized verses that deal specifically with your own sins in your relationships in addition to reviewing your verses that tell you how to love others biblically *(based on Psalm 119:9, 11, 16).*

3. Immediately seek God's perspective.

a. Regardless of your feelings or circumstances, view this situation as an opportunity for further spiritual maturity *(James 1:2-4)* because God will work all things together for good in your life *(based on Psalm 37; Proverbs 3:5-12; Romans 8:28-29; Ephesians 1:3-14; Philippians 1:6).*

1) Remind yourself that you can do all things through Christ who gives you strength *(Philippians 4:11-13),* since your adequacy is from God and not

from any natural "inner strength" *(II Corinthians 3:5)*. Remember that you can do nothing fruitful apart from Jesus Christ *(John 15:5)*.

2) Praise and glorify God that He is sufficient even in your areas of weakness *(II Corinthians 12:9-10)* and that He will keep you from stumbling and make you stand blameless and with great joy in the presence of His glory *(Jude 1:24-25)*.

b. Remember that God looks on your heart, not on your outward appearance *(I Samuel 16:7)*. You must stand blameless before Him in your thoughts, whether others know about it or not *(based on Acts 23:1, 24:16; Romans 14:12; Ephesians 4:1; Philippians 1:9-11; Colossians 1:21-22)*.

1) If you even begin to think sinful thoughts in this unforeseen circumstance, confess them to the Lord *(I John 1:9)*.

2) Remember that it is not the amount of time spent sinning or the immensity of the sin (by human standards) by which you should judge yourself. Rather, the fact that you stopped going God's way even momentarily is what matters *(James 2:10, 4:17)*.

4. Thank God that you are His servant in your present circumstance *(Ephesians 5:20; I Thessalonians 5:18)*. Determine how you will give glory to God *(I Corinthians 10:31; I Peter 4:11)* and seek ways to edify others by serving them in this situation *(Ephesians 4:29; Philippians 2:3-4)*.

5. Act according to your **contingency plan** as soon as you detect temptation to sin in your interpersonal relationships *(based on I Thessalonians 5:22; II Timothy 2:19-22)*. Then, begin again to do those things written in your **basic plan** *(based on Proverbs 24:16; James 1:22-25)*.

A CASE STUDY: MARY'S HUSBAND HAS LEFT HER

> No matter how severe the situation, the biblical steps in dealing with any difficulty begin with judging yourself first and then responding in a manner that pleases the Lord *(based on Matthew 7:1-5; I Corinthians 11:31; II Corinthians 5:9, 15; Galatians 5:17; Colossians 3:17).*

After the counselor shows Mary what she needs to do in order to obey Scripture and honor God, the counseling session continues:

Counselor: "WELL, MARY, AS I SAID LAST TIME, THE LORD HAS SOME WONDERFUL ANSWERS FOR YOUR LIFE. LET'S SEE WHAT HE HAS TO SAY. TO BEGIN WITH, WOULD YOU OPEN YOUR BIBLE TO MATTHEW 22:37-39 AND READ THESE VERSES ALOUD?"

After Mary reads these verses, the counselor explains how a Christlike life is demonstrated by loving God and loving others. The counselor points out that Mary's most serious problem is that she is not loving God, which is evidenced by a lack of obedience to Scripture.

Mary: "BUT I DO LOVE GOD."

Counselor: "HOW DO YOU DEFINE LOVE, MARY?"

Mary: "WELL, GOD IS LOVE."

Counselor: "ANYTHING ELSE?"

Mary stumbles around in her explanation but can't find words to respond adequately.

Counselor: "MARY, LET'S SEE WHAT GOD SAYS LOVE IS. TURN IN YOUR BIBLE TO FIRST CORINTHIANS 13:4-8. PLEASE READ THESE VERSES OUT LOUD, AND STOP AFTER THE FIRST PHRASE IN VERSE 8."

Mary reads the verses describing God's definition of love. The counselor reminds Mary about how she has responded to her husband and children thus far, using her description and words from their earlier sessions. The counselor points out that Mary has violated numerous elements of biblical love. Mary protests but the protests weaken as the evidence piles up, and the Word does its work through the Holy Spirit (Hebrews 4:12).

Mary: "I SEE WHAT YOU MEAN. MY LIFE HAS REALLY COME APART SINCE I WANDERED FROM THE LORD, AND I CAN'T BLAME ANYONE ELSE FOR THAT."

The counselor then gently deals with Mary's sins in violating the elements of love as described in I Corinthians 13:4-8a. This is absolutely essential, since these sins are not only affecting her but also every member of her family.

Counselor: "DO YOU SEE HOW YOU HAVE MADE THE CHOICE TO SIN IN EACH AREA? EACH TIME YOU COULD HAVE GONE GOD'S WAY, BUT YOU CHOSE TO GO YOUR OWN WAY. YOU HAVE BASED YOUR PEACE AND JOY ON YOUR RELATIONSHIP TO TOM, INSTEAD OF ON YOUR RELATIONSHIP TO JESUS. TOM MAY FAIL, BUT JESUS NEVER DOES."

The counselor then reinforces the fact that Mary's commitment must be to do things God's way **whether she feels like it or not** (II Corinthians 5:9, 15; Galatians 5:17; Colossians 3:17).

SPECIAL NOTE: It is important not to get between Mary and God. A counselor may be tempted to feel badly for Mary and wrongfully seek to remove her from her situation, or he may try to help her feel better or find justification for her deeds. Don't do it. Let the Word do its work. Jesus was crucified for Mary. He sent the Holy Spirit to work in her, even in difficult situations. Don't get in the way.

Tom's behavior is **his** problem and can't be dealt with until he wants to change. You will soon be introduced to a way that the Lord may use to help Tom face his own problems biblically.

Counselor: "MARY, LET'S TAKE A LOOK AT WHERE THE LORD WANTS YOU TO START. WOULD YOU TURN TO MATTHEW 7:1-5 AND READ THESE VERSES?"

After Mary reads these verses, the counselor helps Mary understand that she needs to work on her own life before the Lord. The counselor asks Mary if she would like to pray and confess her waywardness to the Lord as well as to pray for the Lord's help in solving this problem His way. Mary agrees to this and prays a prayer of confession along with asking the Lord for His wisdom and strength in solving this problem in a biblical manner.

The counselor then assigns Mary her homework to do in preparation for their next session together. Besides Scripture memory, daily devotions, and church attendance, Mary is to begin work on a **VICTORY OVER FAILURES WORKSHEET** (Supplement 8).

What are at least five scriptural "put-offs" and "put-ons" that Mary could list on her **VICTORY OVER FAILURES WORKSHEET** (Supplement 8) in beginning to restructure her life before the Lord? List the appropriate Scripture references for each item.

LESSON 13: HOMEWORK

> Loving others in a biblical manner involves your thoughts, words, and actions and is a sign of your being a disciple of Christ. Loving others biblically is dependent on your commitment to the Lord Jesus Christ and is not dependent on people, circumstances, or your feelings *(based on Luke 6:45; John 13:35; I Corinthians 13:4-8a; II Corinthians 5:14-15; Philippians 4:8; I John 4:7-11).*

✔ *homework completed*

☐ A.   * In your own words, write the meaning of *Ephesians 4:29* and *Philippians 2:3-4.* Memorize *Ephesians 4:29* and *Philippians 2:3-4.* Begin memorizing *Ephesians 5:21-22 and 25.* Review previous memory verses.

☐ B.   * Read **BIBLICAL PRINCIPLES: INTERPERSONAL PROBLEMS (PART TWO)** (Lesson 13, Pages 2-3). Highlight verses in your Bible not marked previously.

☐ C.   * Study **THE MEANING OF BIBLICAL LOVE** (Lesson 13, Pages 4-6). Place a check by the statements which point out changes you need to make.

☐ D.   Read **BIBLICAL RELATIONSHIPS (LOVING EACH OTHER IN THE BODY OF CHRIST)** (Lesson 13, Pages 15-18). Place a check by statements which point out the changes you need to make in your relationships with other believers.

☐ E.   * Complete a **VICTORY OVER FAILURES WORKSHEET** (Supplement 8) for each person that you have failed to love biblically and develop a plan by which you will begin to practice biblical love with each of them. *(Refer to the changes you need to make that have been pointed out in "C." and "D." above).* Study **OVERCOMING INTERPERSONAL PROBLEMS** (Lesson 13, Pages 19-23) to implement your plans.

☐ F.   * Study **RESTORATION/DISCIPLINE (YOUR BIBLICAL RESPONSE TO THE SIN OF ANOTHER BELIEVER)** (Lesson 13, Pages 7-8) and **GUIDELINES: THE RESTORATION/DISCIPLINE PROCESS** (Lesson 13, Pages 9-11).

☐ G.   * Study **BIBLICAL COMMUNICATION** (Lesson 13, Pages 12-14). Highlight the referenced verses in your Bible and place a check by any statements which point out changes you need to make in your communication.

☐ H.   * Read **A CASE STUDY: MARY'S HUSBAND HAS LEFT HER** (Lesson 13, Pages 24-25). Notice that the scriptural emphasis in dealing with any problem is on learning to examine yourself and to love God and others. List five "put-offs" and "put-ons" on Mary's **VICTORY OVER FAILURES WORKSHEET** (Supplement 8) with associated Scripture references.

☐ I.   * In conjunction with this lesson, respond to statement 21 and 22 under **Open Book Test** (Lesson 23, Page 3).

*   *The completion of assignments marked with an asterisk (*) is a prerequisite for further biblical counseling training.*

LESSON 13: STUDY GUIDE FOR DAILY DEVOTIONS
(INCLUDING SCRIPTURE MEMORY AND HOMEWORK)

> Loving others in a biblical manner involves your thoughts, words, and actions and is a sign of your being a disciple of Christ. Loving others biblically is dependent on your commitment to the Lord Jesus Christ and is not dependent on people, circumstances, or your feelings *(based on Luke 6:45; John 13:35; I Corinthians 13:4-8a; II Corinthians 5:14-15; Philippians 4:8; I John 4:7-11).*

Scripture Memory

1.   * Memorize *Ephesians 4:29* and *Philippians 2:3-4*. Begin memorizing *Ephesians 5:21-22 and 25*.
2.   Review your current and past memory verses in your spare moments throughout the day by carrying Scripture memory cards with you.

Daily Devotional Study Guide

FIRST DAY

1.   Open with prayer.
2.   * Read *Principle 55*, **BIBLICAL PRINCIPLES: INTERPERSONAL PROBLEMS (PART TWO)** (Lesson 13, Pages 2-3). Highlight verses in your Bible.
3.   * Study **THE MEANING OF BIBLICAL LOVE** (Lesson 13, Pages 4-6) and place a check by the statements which point out the changes you need to make.
4.   Read **BIBLICAL RELATIONSHIPS (LOVING EACH OTHER IN THE BODY OF CHRIST)** (Lesson 13, Pages 15-18). Place a check by the statements which point out changes you should make in your relationships with other believers.
5.   * In your own words, write the meanings of *Ephesians 4:29* and *Philippians 2:3-4*.
6.   Close with prayer.

SECOND DAY

1.   Open with prayer.
2.   * Read *Principle 56*, **BIBLICAL PRINCIPLES: INTERPERSONAL PROBLEMS (PART TWO)** (Lesson 13, Pages 2-3). Highlight verses not previously marked.
3.   * Begin work on a **VICTORY OVER FAILURES WORKSHEET** (Supplement 8) for each person that you have failed to love biblically. For each person that you have listed, develop a plan by which you will begin to practice biblical love with each of them *(refer to FIRST DAY studies above, under "3." and "4." for specific changes you have already recognized you need to make)*. This is the first day of a six-day assignment.
4.   * Study **OVERCOMING INTERPERSONAL PROBLEMS** (Lesson 13, Pages 19-23) to discover the steps necessary to love others biblically.
5.   Close with prayer.

THIRD DAY

1.   Open with prayer.
2.   * Read *Principle 57*, **BIBLICAL PRINCIPLES: INTERPERSONAL PROBLEMS (PART TWO)** (Lesson 13, Pages 2-3). Highlight referenced verses in your Bible.

3.   * Continue work on your **VICTORY OVER FAILURES WORKSHEET** (Supplement 8) for each person that you have failed to love biblically.

4.   * Study **RESTORATION/DISCIPLINE (YOUR BIBLICAL RESPONSE TO THE SIN OF ANOTHER BELIEVER)** (Lesson 13, Pages 7-8).

5.   Close with prayer.

FOURTH DAY

1.   Open with prayer.

2.   * Read *Principle 58,* **BIBLICAL PRINCIPLES: INTERPERSONAL PROBLEMS (PART TWO)** (Lesson 13, Pages 2-3). Highlight verses in your Bible.

3.   * Continue to work on your **VICTORY OVER FAILURES WORKSHEET** (Supplement 8), being very specific with your plans to love others biblically.

4.   * Study **GUIDELINES: THE RESTORATION/DISCIPLINE PROCESS** (Lesson 13, Pages 9-11).

5.   Close with prayer.

FIFTH DAY

1.   Open with prayer.

2.   * *Read Principle 59,* **BIBLICAL PRINCIPLES: INTERPERSONAL PROBLEMS (PART TWO)** (Lesson 13, Pages 2-3). Highlight the listed verses in your Bible.

3.   * Continue work on your **VICTORY OVER FAILURES WORKSHEET** (Supplement 8). Have you begun to implement your plan to love in a biblical manner those whom you have failed to love previously?

4.   * Study **BIBLICAL COMMUNICATION** (Lesson 13, Pages 12-14). Place a check by any statements which point out changes you need to make in your communication and highlight these referenced verses. This is the first day of a two-day study.

5.   Close with prayer.

SIXTH DAY

1.   Open with prayer.

2.   * Complete your study of **BIBLICAL COMMUNICATION** (Lesson 13, Pages 12-14).

3.   * Continue work on your **VICTORY OVER FAILURES WORKSHEET** (Supplement 8) for each person that you have chosen to love biblically.

4.   * Read **A CASE STUDY: MARY'S HUSBAND HAS LEFT HER** (Lesson 13, Pages 24-25). Notice the first steps to take in biblically dealing with any problem involves judging one's self in regard to loving God and loving others. List five "put-offs" and corresponding "put-ons" that Mary could list to begin living God's way. List the verse references with each item.

5.   Close with prayer.

SEVENTH DAY

1.   Open with prayer.

2.   * Implement your plans to love others biblically that you have developed through your **VICTORY OVER FAILURES WORKSHEET** (Supplement 8).

3.   * In conjunction with this lesson, respond to statement 21 and 22 under **Open Book Test** (Lesson 23, Page 3).

4.   Close in prayer.

5.   Review your memory verses and ask someone to listen to you recite them. Explain the meaning of the verses and their application to your life.

*   *The completion of assignments marked with an asterisk (*) is a prerequisite for further biblical counseling training.*

LESSON 14

THE MARRIAGE RELATIONSHIP (PART ONE)

"...Be subject to one another in the fear of Christ. Wives, be subject to your own husbands, as to the Lord."

"Husbands, love your wives, just as Christ also loved the church and gave Himself up for her."

Ephesians 5:21-22, 25

LESSON 14: THE MARRIAGE RELATIONSHIP (PART ONE)

> The marriage relationship is to reflect the relationship
> between Jesus Christ and His Church
> *(based on Ephesians 5:21-33).*

I. **The purposes of this lesson are:**

   A. To present God's plan for the marriage relationship,

   B. To teach how to deal with marriage problems in a manner that pleases the Lord, and

   C. To apply principles of biblical hope through the continuation of a case study.

II. **The outline of this lesson**

   A. Self-confrontation

   1. **BIBLICAL PRINCIPLES: THE MARRIAGE RELATIONSHIP (PART ONE)** (Lesson 14, Page 2)

   2. **THE BIBLICAL MODEL FOR MARRIAGE** (Lesson 14, Pages 3-4)

   3. **MARITAL CONFLICTS (MAN'S WAY VERSUS GOD'S WAY)** (Lesson 14, Pages 5-6)

   B. Steps for spiritual growth

   1. **LESSON 14: HOMEWORK** (Lesson 14, Page 8)

   2. **STUDY GUIDE FOR DAILY DEVOTIONS** (Lesson 14, Pages 9-10)

   C. Biblical counseling

   A CASE STUDY: MARY'S HUSBAND HAS LEFT HER (Lesson 14, Page 7)

BIBLICAL PRINCIPLES: THE MARRIAGE RELATIONSHIP
(PART ONE)

> God intends and expects marriage to be a lifetime commitment between a man and a woman, based on the principles of biblical love. The relationship between Jesus Christ and His Church is the supreme example of the committed love that a husband and wife are to follow in their relationship with each other *(based on Ecclesiastes 9:9; Malachi 2:14; Matthew 19:3-6; Mark 10:6-9; I Corinthians 13:4-8a; Ephesians 5:21-33).*

I.   God's View

(Principle 60)   Marriage is not a social convenience nor simply an invention for living together. It is ordained by God to be a covenant of companionship and mutual complement *(based on Genesis 2:18, 22-25; Malachi 2:14; Matthew 19:3-6; I Corinthians 7:10-11)*, and it is meant to keep you set apart in your physical relationship for one another *(I Corinthians 7:2-5).*

(Principle 61)   The marriage relationship is designed to be one of unity and one-flesh permanency *(Genesis 2:24; Mark 10:6-9; Ephesians 5:31)* that reflects the loving relationship between Christ and His Church *(Ephesians 5:21-33).*

II.   Your Hope

(Principle 62)   If you are married, God's Word instructs you to love your spouse *(Ephesians 5:25; Titus 2:4)*; and, if you are a believer in Jesus Christ, you have already been enabled to do so *(Romans 5:5)*. Even if your spouse never practices biblical love, you can still be at peace *(Psalm 119:165; John 14:27, 16:33; Romans 12:18; Galatians 5:22-23)* and can do your part to foster harmony in your home *(I Peter 3:8-9)*. Remember that you are not responsible to change others *(based on Ezekiel 18:20; Philippians 1:6, 2:13)*, but you are responsible to examine yourself continually in a biblical manner *(Matthew 7:1-5; I Corinthians 11:31).*

(Principle 63)   As you continue to be a biblical servant and be a blessing to your spouse *(based on Romans 12:9-21; Ephesians 5:21-33; Philippians 2:3-4)*, you can be assured that God will work all things for good in your relationship with your spouse. No one, not even an unbelieving or unloving or rebellious spouse, can prevent it *(based on Romans 8:28-29).*

Also refer to principles listed in:
INTERPERSONAL PROBLEMS (PART ONE) (LEARNING HOW TO LOVE YOUR NEIGHBOR) *(Lesson 12, Page 2) and*
INTERPERSONAL PROBLEMS (PART TWO) (LEARNING HOW TO LOVE YOUR NEIGHBOR) *(Lesson 13, Pages 2-3).*

THE BIBLICAL MODEL FOR MARRIAGE

> While there are only a few passages in God's Word that specifically address the marriage relationship, they provide all that is necessary to understand God's exalted view of marriage (based on Genesis 1:27-28, 2:18-25; Malachi 2:14; Matthew 19:3-6; Mark 10:6-9; I Corinthians 7:2-5, 10-16, 27-40; Ephesians 5:21-33; Colossians 3:18-19; Titus 2:4-5; Hebrews 13:4; I Peter 3:1-9).

I. **God has ordained marriage.**

A. When you marry, you commit yourself in a covenant before God to a lifetime of companionship with your spouse (Malachi 2:14; Proverbs 2:11-19, esp. verses 17-18; Mark 10:6-9).

   1. Your commitment to companionship is designed to provide for mutual help (Genesis 2:18) and to unify you and your marriage partner in every aspect of life (Genesis 2:24; Mark 10:8; Ephesians 5:31).

   2. Your marriage commitment is sovereignly ordained and established by God and should never be dissolved (Genesis 2:18, 23-24; Proverbs 18:22; Mark 10:9). Only the sinfulness and corresponding hardness of heart in a marriage partner can lead to breaking the covenant relationship of marriage (Matthew 19:8-9; Mark 10:2-11, esp. verses 4-5).

B. Your marriage relationship with your spouse is to be patterned after the relationship of the Lord Jesus Christ and His Church (Ephesians 5:21-33, esp. verses 24-27).

II. **God has established the character of marriage.**

A. Biblical love for your spouse is to be based on God's love for you (based on I John 4:7-11) and must be practiced out of a desire to please the Lord (based on II Corinthians 5:9; Colossians 1:9-12, 3:17).

B. Marriage is to be a one-flesh relationship, not only physically but also in mind and purpose (Genesis 2:24; Matthew 19:5-6; Mark 10:7-8; Ephesians 5:31).

C. In God's sight, marriage partners are equal in value (I Corinthians 11:11-12; Galatians 3:28) but have different responsibilities (Ephesians 5:23-25; Titus 2:3-5; I Peter 3:1-7).

D. As in all biblically based relationships, marriage partners are to seek to have the same mind and same judgment (based on I Corinthians 1:10; Philippians 2:1-7).

   1. All decisions are to be based on the principles of God's Word (Psalm 19:7-11; Isaiah 55:8-11; II Timothy 3:16-17; Hebrews 4:12; II Peter 1:3-4).

      a. If your spouse is an unbeliever, do not lose hope when your spouse does not base decisions solely on the Word of God, since the natural (unbelieving) person cannot understand or accept the things of God (I Corinthians 2:14). This is not an impossible situation (Matthew 19:26; Romans 8:28-29; I Corinthians 10:13; Philippians 4:13) if you seek God's wisdom (James 1:5) and continue to practice Christlike servanthood in your home (Philippians 2:3-4).

b.   A believing spouse has the responsibility to present God's truth to an unbelieving spouse in speech and actions that are Christ-honoring and biblically submissive *(based on Acts 1:8; Ephesians 4:15, 25, 29; 5:21; I Peter 3:1-9, 15)*.

2.   While clear directives of Scripture are to be obeyed without compromise *(based on I Samuel 15:22-23a; Acts 5:29)*, preferring your spouse in matters of preference or opinion is the loving thing to do *(Romans 12:10; Ephesians 5:21; Philippians 2:3-4; I Peter 3:1, 7)*.

E.   Marriage partners are to leave the parent-child relationship with their own respective parents in order to cleave (permanently bond) with one another *(Genesis 2:24; Matthew 19:5; Ephesians 5:31)*.

F.   Marriage is to be undefiled and is to be held in honor by all *(Hebrews 13:4)*.

G.   Marriage is to be marked by the loving servanthood of marriage partners to one another *(Ephesians 5:21-33)*.

1.   You are to serve your spouse lovingly *(I Corinthians 7:3-4; I Peter 3:1-9)*, as a believer is to do in all relationships *(John 13:14-17; I Corinthians 13:4-8a; Ephesians 5:21; Philippians 2:3-4; I John 3:18, 4:10-11)*.

2.   You are to seek to be a fit help to your spouse *(based on Genesis 2:18; Ephesians 5:24-25)*.

3.   Jesus is the example of servanthood for you to follow in ministering to your spouse *(Mark 10:43-45; Ephesians 5:24-25)*.

III.   God has made the marriage relationship basic to society.

A.   Marriage is designed to give society stability in relationships and responsibilities *(based on Genesis 1:28; 2:18, 23-24; Ephesians 5:21-33)*.

B.   Marriage is designed to give the necessary stability for bearing and bringing up children *(based on Genesis 1:28a; Psalm 127:3)*.

C.   A biblical marriage relationship is designed to be a criterion for the evaluation of the maturity and development of potential elders in a church *(based on I Timothy 3:2a, 4-5; Titus 1:5-6)*.

D.   Marriage is integral to the life of a local church *(based on Ephesians 5:21-33; I Timothy 3:2, 4-5; Titus 1:5-6, 2:3-5)*.

IV.   God has designed some to receive the blessing of remaining single.

A.   If you are single, you have a great opportunity for ministry in the life of a church family, since you do not have the responsibilities or potential distractions of married people *(based on I Corinthians 7:32-35)*.

B.   God has given singleness as a gift to some. He desires those who are presently single to be content and to bless others with their time, material goods, and energy, making the most of every opportunity to serve *(based on Romans 12:1-2, 9-21; I Corinthians 7:32-35; Ephesians 5:16; Philippians 4:11-13, 19)*.

MARITAL CONFLICTS
(MAN'S WAY VERSUS GOD'S WAY)

> Many conflicts in a marriage result from living to please self instead of living to please the Lord. These conflicts can be resolved and are actually opportunities for spiritual growth when dealt with in a biblical manner *(based on Matthew 5:3-16; Romans 5:3-5, 8:28-29; II Corinthians 4:7-10; Philippians 2:14-15, 3:12-14; James 1:2-4, 25; 3:16; 4:1-3; 5:16).*

I. When living to please self, each spouse will blame the other for problems and difficulties even though both are sinning *(Genesis 3:12-13; James 4:1).*

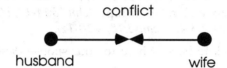

II. When a husband and wife live to please themselves, they often try to solve marital conflicts man's way by:

A. Compromising biblical principles to solve conflicts;

B. Seeking to find trade-offs and bargains in order to get their own way;

C. Basing decisions and actions on the world's erroneous concept of having a good self-esteem or self-image;

D. Trying to find someone "more compatible;"

E. Building a separate life with separate interests, even though continuing to live together;

F. Learning how to argue forcefully;

G. Seeking reasons to leave or threatening to do so;

H. Hoping for and seeking to find satisfaction with someone else or in another location;

I. Allowing their "feelings" or emotions to determine the course of their actions; or

J. Immersing themselves in work, children, travel, sports, alcohol, drugs, friends, etc.

III. God desires that problems in marriages be solved for the good of each spouse, as each seeks to please the Lord within the marriage relationship *(based on Psalm 19:7-11, 127:1; Proverbs 2:6, 3:5-6; Isaiah 55:8-11; II Timothy 3:16-17; Hebrews 4:12; James 1:25).*

A. God commands a believing spouse to love Him *(Matthew 22:37-38)* and to obey His Word *(Luke 6:46-49; John 14:15; I John 5:3; II John 1:6).*

B. Out of a thankful response to God's love through the Lord Jesus Christ, a believer *can* demonstrate love for his spouse in a biblical manner *(Matthew 22:37-39; I John 4:7-11, 18-21).*

C. As a believer esteems his spouse as more important than himself *(based on Ephesians 5:24-25; Philippians 2:3-4),* he will face and deal with all difficulties in a manner that pleases the Lord *(Luke 9:23-24; Romans 14:7-8; II Corinthians 5:9, 14-15; I Peter 4:1-2).* This leads to an increasing oneness of mind and purpose as both spouses receive encouragement from Jesus Christ *(based on Philippians 2:1-2).*

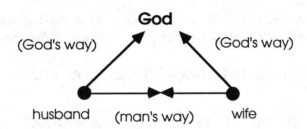

IV. Spouses are to be drawing closer to God, especially during times of conflict.

A. As both believing spouses individually draw closer to God the Father through the Lord Jesus Christ *(John 14:6; Hebrews 4:14-16),* they draw closer to each other *(based on Ephesians 4:1-3; 5:1-2, 21-33).*

B. Even when only one spouse draws closer to God, it is the best hope of drawing the other spouse to the Lord *(based on Matthew 5:16; I Corinthians 7:16; I Peter 3:1).*

A CASE STUDY: MARY'S HUSBAND HAS LEFT HER

> If you begin again to live for yourself after making a
> commitment to live for the Lord, you will be defeated in
> your problems. *(Compare the following passages: Exodus 19:3-8
> and Exodus 32:1-6; I Kings 18:17-40 and I Kings 19:1-10;
> Mark 14:27-29 and Mark 14:66-72; I Corinthians 10:12).*

Even though Mary had confessed her sin to the Lord at the last session and had made a commitment to examine herself biblically in her present difficulty, her focus has changed by the time she returns.

Counselor: "MARY, IT IS GOOD TO SEE YOU AGAIN. WE HAVE BEEN PRAYING FOR YOU. I UNDERSTAND THAT YOU HAVE FACED SOME CHALLENGES THIS WEEK, BUT WE WANT TO HEAR HOW YOU DID IN RESPONDING IN A MANNER THAT PLEASED THE LORD."

The counselors are aware of some of the challenges that Mary has faced during the week because of the personal conversations between the assistant counselor and Mary. In addition, the counseling team noticed on Sunday that Mary had attended the worship service, but she came late and left early without speaking to anyone.

Counselor: "MARY, AFTER WE PRAY, WE WOULD LIKE TO HEAR OF THE PROGRESS YOU HAVE MADE IN DOING YOUR HOMEWORK THIS WEEK."

After one of the assistant counselors prays, Mary begins to speak.

Mary: (blurting out) "EVEN THOUGH MY HUSBAND HAS REMAINED AT HOME, HE ONLY TAKES CARE OF HIMSELF. HE DOESN'T CARE ABOUT ANYONE ELSE! HE GOES TO WORK IN THE MORNINGS AND LEAVES ME TO DEAL WITH MY TWO TEENAGERS AND THEIR FRIENDS WHO MESS UP THE HOUSE AND EAT UP ALL THE FOOD. AND I NEVER KNOW WHERE THEY WILL BE NEXT. I FEEL LIKE A POLICEMAN AND MAID WITH NO PAY. THEN, MY THREE-YEAR-OLD DAUGHTER GETS INTO EVERYTHING. I THOUGHT I WAS JUST GETTING THROUGH WITH THE TOUGH PART OF RAISING KIDS, AND THEN SHE CAME ALONG!"

Mary: (continuing) "TOM IS NEVER AROUND TO HELP! HE DOESN'T APPRECIATE ME AND ALL THAT I DO! MY CHILDREN DON'T APPRECIATE ME EITHER. I GET TIRED; I DO ALL THE WORK AND NOBODY CARES. THEY TREAT ME LIKE A DOORMAT. I'M SICK OF BEING EVERYONE'S VICTIM."

Mary: (continuing) "I JUST DON'T NEED THIS! WHAT I REALLY NEED IS TO GET AWAY FROM ALL THESE FRUSTRATIONS. WHAT'S THE USE? I FEEL LIKE I'M A NOTHING!"

What Scriptures would you use to help Mary see her sin of self-centeredness?

What Scriptures would you use to give hope to Mary?

What must Mary do concerning forgiveness and reconciliation?

What homework should she be assigned?

© Biblical Counseling Foundation

LESSON 14: HOMEWORK

> This week's **HOMEWORK** helps you understand God's
> plan for marriage and the necessity for a married believer
> to please the Lord by biblically serving his spouse *(based on
> Genesis 1:27-28, 2:18-25; Ephesians 5:21-33; Philippians 2:3-4;
> Colossians 3:17-19; I Peter 3:1-12).*

✔ *homework completed*

☐ A. * In your own words, write the meaning of *Ephesians 5:21-22 and 25.* Memorize *Ephesians 5:21-22 and 25,* and begin memorizing *I Peter 3:1 and 7.* Review previous memory verses.

☐ B. * Read **BIBLICAL PRINCIPLES: THE MARRIAGE RELATIONSHIP (PART ONE)** (Lesson 14, Page 2). Highlight any verses that you have not marked in previous lessons.

☐ C. * Study **THE BIBLICAL MODEL FOR MARRIAGE** (Lesson 14, Pages 3-4). Look up the listed verses in the summary box at the beginning of this study and highlight them in your Bible.

☐ D. * Read **MARITAL CONFLICTS (MAN'S WAY VERSUS GOD'S WAY)** (Lesson 14, Pages 5-6). Notice that the way to overcome marital difficulties is for each spouse to live biblically before the Lord and not try to change the other person. Numerous biblical principles and verses introduced in earlier studies are to be applied to the marriage relationship. List ways that you need to change and make plans to complete these biblical changes. (If necessary, use a **VICTORY OVER FAILURES WORKSHEET**, Supplement 8.)

☐ E. * Read **A CASE STUDY: MARY'S HUSBAND HAS LEFT HER** (Lesson 14, Page 7). Answer the questions which follow.

☐ F. * In conjunction with this lesson, answer question 23 under **Open Book Test** (Lesson 23, Page 3).

* *The completion of assignments marked with an asterisk (*) is a prerequisite for further biblical counseling training.*

LESSON 14: STUDY GUIDE FOR DAILY DEVOTIONS
(INCLUDING SCRIPTURE MEMORY AND HOMEWORK)

> This week's **STUDY GUIDE** helps you understand God's plan for marriage and the necessity for a married believer to please the Lord by biblically serving his spouse *(based on Genesis 1:27-28, 2:18-25; Ephesians 5:21-33; Philippians 2:3-4; Colossians 3:17-19; I Peter 3:1-12).*

Scripture Memory

1.   * Memorize *Ephesians 5:21-22 and 25.* Begin memorizing *I Peter 3:1 and 7.*
2.   Carry your memory verse cards from previous weeks along with this week's memory verse cards. Review your Scriptures in spare moments throughout the day.

Daily Devotional Study Guide

FIRST DAY

1.   Open with prayer.
2.   * Read *Principle 60* under **BIBLICAL PRINCIPLES: THE MARRIAGE RELATIONSHIP (PART ONE)** (Lesson 14, Page 2). Highlight the listed verses in your Bible.
3.   * Write the meaning of *Ephesians 5:21-22 and 25* in your own words.
4.   Close with prayer.

SECOND DAY

1.   Open with prayer.
2.   * Read *Principle 61* under **BIBLICAL PRINCIPLES: THE MARRIAGE RELATIONSHIP (PART ONE)** (Lesson 14, Page 2). Highlight the listed verses in your Bible.
3.   * Study **THE BIBLICAL MODEL FOR MARRIAGE** (Lesson 14, Pages 3-4). This is the first day of a three-day study. Look up the listed verses in the summary box on page 3 and highlight them in your Bible.
4.   Close with prayer.

THIRD DAY

1.   Open with prayer.
2.   * Read *Principle 62* under **BIBLICAL PRINCIPLES: THE MARRIAGE RELATIONSHIP (PART ONE)** (Lesson 14, Page 2). Highlight the listed verses in your Bible.
3.   * Continue your study of **THE BIBLICAL MODEL FOR MARRIAGE** (Lesson 14, Pages 3-4). You may be familiar with many of these verses and perhaps have highlighted them in your Bible. Highlight any new verses.
4.   Close with prayer.
5.   Have you carried your memory verse cards with you throughout the day? Have you memorized or reviewed Scriptures in your spare time? Make necessary changes in order to grow spiritually in this area of your life.

FOURTH DAY

1. Open with prayer.
2. * Read *Principle 63* under **BIBLICAL PRINCIPLES: THE MARRIAGE RELATIONSHIP (PART ONE)** (Lesson 14, Page 2). Highlight listed verses.
3. * Complete your study of **THE BIBLICAL MODEL FOR MARRIAGE** (Lesson 14, Pages 3-4).
4. * Begin studying **MARITAL CONFLICTS (MAN'S WAY VERSUS GOD'S WAY)** (Lesson 14, Pages 5-6). This is the first day of a three-day study. Numerous verses introduced in earlier studies will now be applied to the marriage relationship. Notice that the way to overcome marital difficulties biblically is for each believing spouse to live for the Lord and not try to change the other person. Begin to list the changes that you need to make.
5. Close with prayer.

FIFTH DAY

1. Open with prayer.
2. * Continue your study of **MARITAL CONFLICTS (MAN'S WAY VERSUS GOD'S WAY)** (Lesson 14, Pages 5-6). As you list the changes you need to make, use a **VICTORY OVER FAILURES WORKSHEET** (Supplement 8), if necessary, to implement these changes in your life.
3. Close with prayer.

SIXTH DAY

1. Open with prayer.
2. * Complete your study of **MARITAL CONFLICTS (MAN'S WAY VERSUS GOD'S WAY)** (Lesson 14, Pages 5-6). As you discover areas in which you need to change in your marriage, take steps to institute those changes in your life.
3. * Read **A CASE STUDY: MARY'S HUSBAND HAS LEFT HER** (Lesson 14, Page 7). Begin to answer the questions at the end of the case study.
4. Close with prayer.

SEVENTH DAY

1. Open with prayer.
2. * Refer to **A CASE STUDY: MARY'S HUSBAND HAS LEFT HER** (Lesson 14, Page 7) and complete a plan to help Mary by answering the rest of the questions following the case study.
3. * In conjunction with this lesson, answer question 23 under **Open Book Test** (Lesson 23, Page 3).
4. Close in prayer.
5. Evaluate your faithfulness in memorizing Scripture this week *(Psalm 119:11, 16; I Corinthians 4:2; Ephesians 5:15-16)*. Take time to review past memory verses. Ask someone to listen to you recite this week's memory verses. Remember to explain the meaning of these verses and their application to your life.

*   *The completion of assignments marked with an asterisk (*) is a prerequisite for further biblical counseling training.*

LESSON 15

THE MARRIAGE RELATIONSHIP
(PART TWO)

"In the same way, you wives, be submissive to your own husbands so that even if any of them are disobedient to the word, they may be won without a word by the behavior of their wives."

"You husbands likewise, live with your wives in an understanding way, as with a weaker vessel, since she is a woman; and grant her honor as a fellow-heir of the grace of life, so that your prayers may not be hindered."

I Peter 3:1, 7

LESSON 15: THE MARRIAGE RELATIONSHIP (PART TWO)

> Since the marriage relationship is to reflect the relationship between Jesus Christ and His Church, it is imperative that biblical submission and love be practiced in all of its aspects between husband and wife *(based on John 13:12-17; I Corinthians 13:4-8a; Ephesians 5:21-33; Colossians 3:19; Titus 2:4; I Peter 4:8; I John 4:7-8, 20).*

I. **The purposes of this lesson are:**

A. To present God's plan for a husband and wife to make biblical changes in their marriage relationship;

B. To define biblical submission;

C. To help you learn how to show love toward your spouse biblically in every situation;

D. To help you overcome problems in marriage through biblical communication; and

E. To introduce a plan of biblical communication through the continuation of a case study.

II. **The outline of this lesson**

A. Self-confrontation

1. **BIBLICAL PRINCIPLES: THE MARRIAGE RELATIONSHIP (PART TWO)** (Lesson 15, Page 2)

2. **BIBLICAL SUBMISSION** (Lesson 15, Page 3)

3. **YOU CAN LEARN HOW TO SHOW LOVE TOWARD YOUR SPOUSE** (Lesson 15, Pages 4-5)

B. Steps for spiritual growth

1. **OVERCOMING PROBLEMS THROUGH BIBLICAL COMMUNICATION (USING A CONFERENCE TABLE FOR RECONCILIATION)** (Lesson 15, Pages 6-9)

2. **LESSON 15: HOMEWORK** (Lesson 15, Page 13)

3. **STUDY GUIDE FOR DAILY DEVOTIONS** (Lesson 15, Pages 14-15)

C. Biblical counseling

A CASE STUDY: MARY'S HUSBAND HAS LEFT HER (Lesson 15, Pages 10-12)

BIBLICAL PRINCIPLES: THE MARRIAGE RELATIONSHIP
(PART TWO)

> Since a marriage relationship is to be patterned after the relationship between the Lord Jesus Christ and His Church, the commandment to love one another is of paramount importance. Loving in this manner requires a constant dependence on the Lord and a commitment to follow the pattern of servanthood displayed by the Lord Jesus Christ *(based on Matthew 20:25-28; John 13:12-17, 15:5; Ephesians 5:21-33; Philippians 2:3-8; I John 4:7-8).*

III. Your Change (outline continues from Lesson 14, Page 2)

(Principle 64) Husbands, put off being harsh or embittered towards your wives. Put on love and understanding just as Christ also loved the church and gave Himself up for her *(Ephesians 5:25; Colossians 3:19; I Peter 3:7).* Being a true leader requires being a true servant in attitude and action *(Matthew 20:25-28; John 15:11-13; Ephesians 5:21, 25-33; Philippians 2:3-8).*

(Principle 65) Wives, put off being quarrelsome and contentious with your husbands. Put on love, submission, and respect for them *(Proverbs 21:9; John 15:11-13; Ephesians 5:21-24, 33; Colossians 3:18; Titus 2:3-5; I Peter 3:1-6).*

(Principle 66) To love one's spouse as God commands *(I John 3:23)* requires that you die daily to your own selfish desires *(Luke 9:23-24)* and live to please God and serve your spouse *(Matthew 22:37-39; Ephesians 5:21; Philippians 2:3-8).*

IV. Your Practice

(Principle 67) In order to fulfill your marriage responsibilities faithfully, you must rely on the Lord's strength and the wisdom of His Word. Do not depend on your natural strength or wisdom *(based on Proverbs 3:5-6; Isaiah 55:8-11; John 15:1-5; II Timothy 3:16-17; I John 2:4-6, 3:23-24).* As you lovingly and faithfully carry out these responsibilities, you demonstrate your love for God *(Matthew 22:37-38; I John 5:3)* and your spouse *(I Corinthians 13:4-8a; I John 3:18, 4:7-8).*

(Principle 68) When you fail to love your spouse as you should, you can be restored to fellowship with both the Lord and your spouse *(based on Psalm 145:14; Proverbs 24:16; Matthew 5:23-24).* To be restored to the Lord, you must confess your sin to Him *(Psalm 51:1-4; I John 1:9)* and return to your initial commitment to live for Him by: (a) remembering from where you have fallen, (b) repenting, and (c) doing again the deeds you did at first which show your love for the Lord *(John 14:15; I John 5:3; Revelation 2:4-5).*

Refer to Lessons 12 and 13 to review the steps that must be taken to be fully restored to your spouse.

BIBLICAL SUBMISSION

> Biblical submission is an act of the will demonstrated by serving others out of an attitude that regards them as more important than yourself. This does not mean that you place yourself under the control of another. You stand directly accountable to God and not to anyone else's ultimate authority *(based on Matthew 20:26-28; Acts 5:29; Romans 14:12; Philippians 2:3-4).*

I. **You are to be like the Lord Jesus Christ** *(Matthew 20:26-28; I Peter 2:21)*, **who is the supreme example of biblical submission.**

   A. He submitted to the will of His Father *(John 5:30; Philippians 2:5-8).*

   B. He willingly served others by doing for them what was needed, giving you an example to follow *(John 13:12-17).*

   C. He suffered unjustly, not threatening or retaliating but instead entrusting Himself to His Heavenly Father who judges righteously *(I Peter 2:21-25).*

II. **God's Word requires you to submit without a contentious spirit** *(Proverbs 10:12, 28:25; Ephesians 4:31; Philippians 2:14):*

   A. To God by:

   1. Placing yourself continuously under His sole control *(Ephesians 5:18-20; James 4:7; I John 5:3);*

   2. Living with His Word as your only hope, standard, and ultimate authority *(based on Psalm 19:7-11, 119:49; II Timothy 3:16-17; Hebrews 4:12; II Peter 1:3-4);*

   3. Being empowered, strengthened, and led by the Holy Spirit *(John 14:26; Romans 8:2-4, 14; I John 4:4);*

   B. To other believers *(Ephesians 5:21; I Peter 5:5b);*

   C. To your spouse (a husband submits as a loving servant to his wife: *Ephesians 5:21, 25-27;* a wife submits to her husband: *Ephesians 5:21-24; I Peter 3:1-6);*

   D. To your parents, specifically while they are responsible for your training and discipline *(Ephesians 6:1-2);*

   E. To your children by not provoking them to anger, and by bringing them up in the instruction and discipline of the Lord *(Ephesians 6:4);*

   F. To your employers, rendering service to them with good will *(Ephesians 6:5-7; I Peter 2:18);*

   G. To your employees, by not threatening them *(Ephesians 6:5-9, especially verse 9);*

   H. To appointed authority in the church *(Hebrews 13:17; I Peter 5:5a);* and

   I. To authority in civil government *(Romans 13:1-7; I Peter 2:13-17).*

YOU CAN LEARN HOW TO SHOW LOVE
TOWARD YOUR SPOUSE

> Many marriages are disintegrating or have already been destroyed because husbands and wives have failed to love according to God's principles. Even if you have never known or practiced biblical love, God graciously directs you to His perfect picture of love *(John 3:16; I Corinthians 13:4-8a; I John 4:8-11)*, since loving in this manner is possible for any believer *(John 13:34; I John 3:23)*. If you have failed to practice biblical love, you can be restored to the Lord by remembering from where you have fallen, by repenting of your failures, and by beginning to do those things that you did at first out of a loving heart *(based on Revelation 2:4-5)*.

I. **Your marriage is to be a covenant before the Lord to a lifetime of companionship and mutual help with your spouse** *(based on Proverbs 2:17; Malachi 2:14; Mark 10:7-9).*

A. Your love for your spouse is not to be based on your emotions, circumstances, or your spouse's responses *(based on Matthew 5:43-44; John 13:34-35; Galatians 5:16-17)*. Instead, you are to love your spouse in obedience to the Lord *(based on John 14:15)* and in response to His love for you *(based on I John 4:10-11)*. Remember that God does not command you to feel like loving. Instead, He directs you to think, speak, and act in a loving manner *(I John 3:23)* even when your spouse:

1. Chooses to have only casual contact with you, much like your neighbor *(Matthew 22:39)*;

2. Currently acts like your enemy *(Matthew 5:44; Luke 6:27, 35)*; or

3. Is a believer *(based on John 13:34; Hebrews 13:1; I Peter 4:8; I John 4:7-8)* or an unbeliever *(based on I Corinthians 7:12-16; Ephesians 5:25, 28; Titus 2:3-5)*.

B. You can show love toward your spouse in spite of any fears that you may have *(based on Philippians 4:13; I John 5:4)*, since God's abiding and perfect love casts out all fear *(based on I John 4:12, 18)*. You are not being a hypocrite by loving your spouse even if you do not feel like it *(Romans 12:9)*. To love when you do not feel like it is simply a matter of faithful obedience *(John 14:15)* and is a response to God's love for you *(I John 4:10-11, 19)*.

(NOTE: It is not hypocritical to do things that you don't feel like doing. You may not feel like cooking a meal or going to work, but you do it anyway because you know that it is your responsibility. You are a hypocrite only when you do things that you don't feel like doing and say that you enjoy doing them.)

II. **God's solution to problems in your marriage is for you to:**

A. Make a full commitment to please the Lord in all things *(based on II Corinthians 5:9; Ephesians 4:1; Colossians 1:10, 3:17)*;

B. Examine and judge your own failures in a biblical manner *(Psalm 139:23-24; Matthew 7:1-5; I Corinthians 11:31)*;

C.   Confess your sins to the Lord *(Psalm 51:1-4; I John 1:9)* and confess your marital shortcomings as sins to your spouse *(Matthew 5:23-24; James 5:16)*;

D.   Seek to edify your spouse biblically and do it heartily as unto the Lord *(Proverbs 27:17; Romans 14:19, 15:1-2; Ephesians 4:29; Colossians 3:23-25)*; and

E.   Seek to resolve conflicts and live at peace with your spouse *(Romans 12:18, 14:19; Galatians 6:1-5)*. If your spouse refuses to solve problems biblically, continue to trust in Christ Jesus for your peace and joy *(based on John 14:27; 15:11; 16:22, 33)*.

III.   **Diligently practice biblical love *(based on John 13:12-17; I Corinthians 13:4-8a; I John 3:18, 23; 4:7-8, 10-11, 18-21)*.**

A.   Repent of sins committed against God and your spouse *(James 5:16; I John 1:9)*. Return to your initial commitment to live for Him by: (a) remembering from where you have fallen, (b) repenting, and (c) doing again the deeds you did at first which show your love for the Lord *(based on John 14:15; I John 5:3; Revelation 2:4-5)*. In being reconciled with your spouse, you must confess your failure directly to your spouse in order to begin the process of reconciliation *(Romans 12:18; James 5:16)* and begin again to live in a biblically loving manner *(I Corinthians 13:4-8a)*.

Refer to: *RECONCILIATION (REMOVING ALL HINDRANCES TO UNITY AND PEACE) (Lesson 12, Pages 6-8).*

B.   Refrain from being judgmental or critical of your spouse *(based on Romans 14:10, 13; Ephesians 4:29; Philippians 2:14-15)* but instead edify your spouse with words of grace and helpfulness *(based on Romans 15:7; Ephesians 4:29-31; Colossians 4:6)*.

C.   Do not quarrel with your spouse; instead, gently and diligently encourage harmony in your home as you consider your spouse as more important than yourself *(based on Philippians 2:3-4; II Timothy 2:23-26; I Peter 3:8-9)*.

D.   Do not attempt to manipulate your spouse (i.e., practice love with hypocrisy) but instead overcome evil with respectful and understanding devotion *(Romans 12:9-21; I Peter 3:1-9)*.

E.   Be harmonious, sympathetic, kind-hearted, understanding, and humble in spirit toward your spouse, regardless of his or her actions. Do not return an insult if you are insulted but return a blessing instead *(I Peter 3:1-9)*. Initiate reconciliation, no matter who may be at fault *(based on Matthew 5:23-24; Romans 12:18, 14:19)*.

IV.   **You can respond biblically to an "irritating" spouse *(Romans 12:10-18; I Corinthians 10:13; II Corinthians 3:4-5; Galatians 5:16-17, 25-26; I Peter 3:8-9)*.**

A.   Irritation in you is a signal that **you** need to change *(II Timothy 2:23-26)*. Your heart is revealed by how you respond *(Matthew 12:34-37, 15:18-19; Mark 7:20-23)*.

B.   Your peace and joy in the Lord is not dependent on your spouse's actions or attitudes *(Psalm 119:165; Isaiah 26:3; John 14:27, 15:11, 16:33)*.

C.   Difficult situations and difficult people give you an opportunity to grow in Christ *(Romans 5:3-5; James 1:2-4)* and to manifest God's glory to those around you *(Matthew 5:13-16; I Peter 2:12)*.

OVERCOMING PROBLEMS
THROUGH BIBLICAL COMMUNICATION
(USING A CONFERENCE TABLE FOR RECONCILIATION)

> Individuals and families must have a plan, based on biblical principles, to resolve problems and failures in communication. If you will obey God's Word in biblical communication and problem solving, you will be lifted up. However, if you do not obey God's Word, whether through ignorance or willful disobedience, you invite disaster *(based on Genesis 4:7; Proverbs 12:15, 14:12, 16:20; Colossians 3:25; Hebrews 12:5-6; James 1:25, 4:17).*

I. **Overall purposes of conference tables**

   A. To provide people (individuals, couples, families, roommates, co-workers, etc.) a structured environment to communicate biblically *(based on Ephesians 4:15-32);*

   B. To help restore poor relationships and to initiate a pattern of forgiveness and reconciliation between individuals *(based on Matthew 5:23-24; Mark 11:25-26; Romans 12:14, 18; 14:13, 19; Ephesians 4:32);*

   C. To provide a method for finding biblical solutions to disagreements and to maintain unity in relationships *(based on Psalm 133:1; I Corinthians 1:10; Ephesians 4:1-3; Philippians 2:1-4; James 1:5);* and

   D. To develop the habit of making daily decisions in a biblical fashion (for example: scheduling time, making financial decisions, determining personal or family responsibilities, developing biblical goals, etc.) *(based on Proverbs 16:1, 9; Luke 14:28-30; Romans 12:9-13; Ephesians 5:15-17).*

II. **Prerequisites to conducting a first conference table**

   A. Judge yourself first *(Psalm 139:23-24; Matthew 7:1-5; I Corinthians 11:31).* Use **OVERCOMING INTERPERSONAL PROBLEMS** (Lesson 13, Pages 19-23) in this self-evaluation project. Remember to complete all four columns of the **VICTORY OVER FAILURES WORKSHEET** (Supplement 8) for each person against whom you have sinned.

   B. Ask the other individual(s) who are part of your family (or group) to work with you in developing a method for communicating lovingly with one another. Explain your commitment to build up all the others and to learn to speak with them in such a way that focuses on overcoming problems instead of attacking them *(based on Ephesians 4:15, 29, 31-32; Colossians 4:6; II Timothy 2:24-25).*

   As necessary, review: **BIBLICAL COMMUNICATION** (Lesson 13, Pages 12-14).

   C. Forgive other conference table participants in your heart even if they have not asked for forgiveness *(Mark 11:25).*

   Refer to: **FORGIVENESS (FORGIVING OTHERS AS GOD HAS FORGIVEN YOU)** (Lesson 12, Pages 3-5).

D. Thoroughly explain to each individual how to conduct a conference table before beginning:

1. Review the purposes for having a conference table (see above, **I. Purposes of the conference table**).

2. Review the following biblical principles for conducting a conference table:

   a. Base everything on God's Word, since Scripture is the authority for all faith and conduct *(Romans 15:4; II Timothy 3:16-17; Hebrews 4:12)*;

   b. Be truthful *(Ephesians 4:15, 25)*;

   c. Be loving and kind in your speech, avoiding talk that produces quarrels *(Proverbs 15:1; Ephesians 4:15, 5:4; Colossians 4:6; II Timothy 2:23-24)*;

   d. Do not use unwholesome words but use only those words that edify (build up) others *(Romans 14:19; Ephesians 4:29)*;

   e. Do not argue or be contentious *(II Timothy 2:23-24; Titus 3:9; James 4:1-2)*;

   f. Work on changing yourself, not on changing others *(Ezekiel 18:20; Matthew 7:1-5)*;

   g. Be forgiving *(Matthew 6:14-15; Ephesians 4:32; Colossians 3:12-13)*; and

   h. Treat others at the conference table just as you desire to be treated *(Matthew 7:12)*.

III. Procedures for the first conference table

A. The husband (or in the absence of a husband, one chosen to be the leader) is to conduct the time together *(Ephesians 5:21-6:9; I Timothy 3:4-5)* and the wife (or another delegated person) is to act as the recorder.

1. The conference table opens and closes with prayer *(Colossians 4:2; I Thessalonians 5:17; James 1:5)*.

2. The Bible is studied during the conference time in order to discover God's will concerning questions and decisions. All are encouraged to bring their Bibles. For those who do not bring one, have extras on the table for their use *(based on Joshua 1:8; Psalm 19:7-11; Proverbs 13:13; II Timothy 2:15, 3:16-17; Hebrews 4:12; II Peter 1:3-4)*.

B. Select and agree on the time of day, length of each session, and number of times during the week to conduct the conference table *(Ephesians 5:15-16)*. The recommended meeting time is one hour or less to avoid fatigue and to encourage everyone to remain focused on the important matters *(based on Proverbs 10:19a, 15:23, 25:11-12)*.

C. Select a place conducive to serious and effective communication, without interruption.

1. Choose a room with as few distractions as possible.

2. If available, select a table that provides adequate seating and is large enough for open Bibles and note taking. A table serves as a means for joining people together to meet purposefully.

3. Walking to the conference table allows cooling of tempers *(based on Proverbs 14:17, 29; 15:28)*. When one is seated, it is also harder to walk away.

4. The conference table will soon become a symbol of hope, as problems are faced and dealt with there on a regular basis and in a biblical manner.

D. Formulate a plan to deal with unbiblical behavior.

1. Select a silent or quiet signal (such as raising a hand or standing up) to indicate that the behavior of another is unbiblical in the opinion of one or more persons. A silent signal is best because it is less likely to incite anger *(based on Proverbs 15:1; Ecclesiastes 3:7b, 8:17; James 1:19)*.

2. If the one whose behavior is in question repents, confesses, and begins again to speak and act biblically, the conference table resumes. If not, biblical communication has ended and so has the conference table.

3. The conference may resume at another time, either:

   a. That day, as soon as the person who has acted unbiblically recognizes and confesses his sin to the Lord *(I John 1:9)* and to others *(James 5:16)*; or

   b. At the next designated time for the conference table.

E. If, during the conference table, a person does not control his spirit *(Proverbs 25:28)*, he should:

1. Use the preselected signal (raising a hand or standing up) to indicate his need to stop conferring until he has gained control over his spirit; or

2. Excuse himself from the conference table until ready to act in a biblical manner.

F. If anyone continues to argue, refuses to speak, or does anything other than communicate biblically at the conference table, others should rise and stand quietly until everyone is ready to behave biblically.

G. The initial session involves specific activities.

1. At the first conference, read *Ephesians 4:17-32* and *I Corinthians 13:4-8a*.

2. If each person has not done so, take time to make as complete a list as possible of sinful words and actions committed against others, especially those who are at the conference table *(Matthew 7:1, 5)*.

3. The wife (or the designated recorder) keeps a written record of the major points discussed at the conference table (suggestion: keep a separate column for each person's responses, which could be confession of one's own sins, an offer of help to another, quoting of a memory verse, etc.). At the conclusion of the meeting, the recorder reads aloud the decisions and commitments made by the group or individuals in the group. After the meeting record is read, each person is invited to suggest any changes that would help clarify any part of the written record. Appropriate written adjustments are then entered into the record *(based on Proverbs 11:14, 15:22, 16:3; Ecclesiastes 4:9-10; Philippians 2:3-4)*.

   In later meetings, the conference table record helps each person recall the results of earlier meetings. The record also serves as a reminder to pray about specific matters and to give thanks to the Lord for the changes He is making in the lives of conference table participants.

H. Be specific when confessing sins to one another *(Matthew 5:23-24; James 5:16)*.

1. The husband (or the designated leader) should be the first to confess his sins committed against others present, with the wife confessing next, then the children. (If the conference table participants are non-family members, the order of confessing sins should be decided by mutual agreement).

NOTE: Confessing sins at the conference table needs to be voluntary. No one should force another to confess his sins since convicting and prompting is the Holy Spirit's responsibility

(John 14:26, 16:8). The willingness to deal with his own sins is each person's responsibility (Ezekiel 18:20). Since each person is individually responsible for his own sinful behavior (Deuteronomy 24:16), no blameshifting is to be allowed during the conference table (based on Genesis 3:12-13, 19; Romans 14:12).

2. After three or four productive meetings, any member may invite other members to remind him of sins that he may have overlooked *(based on Proverbs 27:6; Matthew 7:1-5, 18:15; Galatians 6:1-2; Ephesians 4:15, 25).*

    a. It is especially important that all aspects of biblical love and Christ-honoring communication be maintained by those who are bringing up overlooked sins in another's life *(based on I Corinthians 13:4-8a; Ephesians 4:29; Colossians 4:6).*

    b. After being reminded of his overlooked sins, each person is provided an opportunity to confess only his own sinful deeds that he has committed against others *(based on Matthew 5:9, 23-24; 7:12; Mark 11:25-26; Romans 12:18, 13:8-10, 14:19).*

    To review how to confess your sins to those you have sinned against, refer to:
    GUIDELINES: VICTORY OVER FAILURES WORKSHEET *(Supplement 7) under*
    VI. D. *and*
    RECONCILIATION (REMOVING ALL HINDRANCES TO UNITY AND PEACE) *(Lesson 12, Pages 6-8),* **II. Confession.**

I. Soon after the first meeting, each person individually should begin to work on his own **VICTORY OVER FAILURES WORKSHEET** (Supplement 8) one failure at a time, moving across all four columns.

    Refer to: **OVERCOMING INTERPERSONAL PROBLEMS** *(Lesson 13, Pages 19-23).*

    1. Remain faithful in this endeavor to develop Christ-honoring maturity *(based on Galatians 6:9; Ephesians 4:1).*

    2. When asked, the entire family (or group) participating in the conference can help each person locate the biblical "put-offs" and "put-ons" listed in the Scriptures along with the biblical basis for a specific plan to change *(Galatians 6:1-2).* This will encourage thorough study of the Scriptures and will challenge growth among those participating in the conference table *(based on Proverbs 27:17; II Timothy 2:15; Hebrews 10:24).*

J. Be steadfast *(I Corinthians 15:58).*

    1. Recognize that not all problems can be solved in just a few conference tables. For multiple problems, develop an agenda and schedule your work together over a period of time *(Ephesians 5:15-16).*

    2. Work to defeat the problem *(based on II Corinthians 7:11-12),* not the other person(s) *(Romans 12:18-19, 14:19).*

K. After the pattern for reconciliation has begun among those at the conference table, the resolution of conflicts, the establishment of goals, and the process of making biblical decisions may continue. The ultimate objective is for the conference table to be used to develop biblical communication with one another as a pattern of life.

A CASE STUDY: MARY'S HUSBAND HAS LEFT HER

> No matter how difficult a situation may seem, you are to follow God's Word in every respect in order for His will to be accomplished *(Isaiah 55:8-11; II Timothy 3:16-17).*

In taking biblical steps to overcome her self-centeredness, Mary had fulfilled her responsibilities in a loving manner to her husband and children for a number of weeks. As a result, her husband had asked her about the counseling she was receiving and later accompanied her to a counseling session.

When Tom came to his first counseling session with Mary, the counseling team had warmly welcomed him and thanked him for coming to assist in Mary's counseling. The lead counselor had explained to Tom that all counseling was based on God's Word and that Tom could ask questions about the counseling at any time during the session. The lead counselor then addressed several subjects in a manner that reinforced the biblical changes in Mary's life. In answering the counselor's questions, Mary was also able to give testimony to Tom about the biblical basis for the changes he had been observing. The counselor had asked questions concerning the following:

Mary's commitment to Jesus Christ and the peace and joy that had resulted;
Her commitment to do things God's way instead of her own self-centered way;
Her "failures list" and her determination to put off the practices of the old nature and to put on biblical practices that demonstrated her new nature in Jesus Christ;
The meaning of biblical forgiveness and reconciliation; and
The personal benefits of Scripture memory and daily personal devotions.

*Tom did not ask any questions in his first session, but he continued to accompany Mary to the following sessions. The counseling team used these sessions to work on various aspects of Mary's **VICTORY OVER FAILURES WORKSHEET** (Supplement 8). At each session, Tom listened intently without participating.*

In the fourth session he attended, Tom admitted that he never believed anything could ever change Mary but that he recognized she was making changes in spite of all the unresolved problems in their home. He also indicated that he wanted God to help him make some changes in his own life.

The lead counselor explained to Tom that the changes in Mary's life were happening because of her commitment to please the Lord and be obedient to God's Word, which began with her spiritual new birth. The counselor then made a clear presentation of God's plan of salvation through the Lord Jesus Christ. Tom listened attentively and indicated that he would like to make a commitment to Jesus Christ. Tom admitted his sin, asked God to forgive him through the sacrificial death of His Son, and invited the Lord Jesus Christ into his life. While praying, Tom also asked God to help him make changes as a husband and father.

*At the conclusion of the session, Tom was assigned homework that helped him understand who he was in Jesus Christ. He also began work on his own **VICTORY OVER FAILURES WORKSHEET** (Supplement 8). In the following weeks, he faithfully completed his homework assignments, which included memorizing verses, having daily devotions, and bringing his family to church for worship services. During this time, Mary also remained faithful in completing her homework assignments.*

While both Tom and Mary are noticeably growing in Christ, there are a number of concerns that have not yet been resolved in their home. As a result, their next counseling session concentrates on developing a plan to overcome these problems. After reviewing Tom and Mary's homework, the lead counselor reviews the purpose and procedures for conducting a "conference table."

Counselor: "TOM AND MARY, REMEMBER THAT THE PURPOSE OF THE CONFERENCE TABLE IS TO PROVIDE A STRUCTURED ENVIRONMENT FOR DEVELOPING THE HABIT OF FACING AND DEALING WITH PROBLEMS IN A BIBLICAL FASHION. IT WILL HELP YOU COMMUNICATE IN A WAY THAT IS MUCH MORE BIBLICAL AND PLEASING TO THE LORD. NOW, TOM, AS THE LEADER IN THE HOME, IT IS YOUR RESPONSIBILITY TO LEAD EACH SESSION."

Mary: "IF HE'S THE LEADER, WHAT DO I DO?"

Counselor: "YOU WILL BE THE RECORDER. THIS WILL HELP BOTH OF YOU REMEMBER WHAT WAS SAID. NOW, LET'S FOLLOW THE OUTLINE **'OVERCOMING PROBLEMS THROUGH BIBLICAL COMMUNICATION'**, WHICH CAN BE FOUND IN LESSON 15, PAGES 6-9, IN THE SELF-CONFRONTATION MANUAL. SINCE BOTH OF YOU HAVE BEEN EXAMINING YOURSELF IN A BIBLICAL MANNER, LET'S REVIEW THE PRINCIPLES FOR CONDUCTING A CONFERENCE TABLE AND THEN FOLLOW THE PROCEDURES LISTED IN PART **III. PROCEDURES FOR THE CONFERENCE TABLE**."

Tom: *(pause)* "SINCE THE CONFERENCE TABLE IS TO BEGIN IN PRAYER, LET'S PRAY AND ASK FOR THE LORD'S HELP EVEN AS WE PRACTICE THESE PROCEDURES."

At the request of the lead counselor, one of the assistant counselors prays. When the "amen" is said, Tom begins to speak.

Tom: "MARY, WHEN DO YOU THINK WE SHOULD HAVE THE CONFERENCE TABLE AT OUR HOME?"

Mary: *(In a sarcastic manner)* "YOU DECIDE; *YOU'RE* SUPPOSED TO BE THE LEADER!!!"

Counselor: *(Breaks in)* "EXCUSE ME, MARY; REMEMBER, LOVE IS KIND. TOM HAS ASKED FOR YOUR OPINION AND AS A LOVING HELPER, YOU SHOULD CONTRIBUTE WITH GENTLENESS."

Mary: *(Looking somewhat embarrassed, Mary quietly replies)* "I THINK MONDAY AND WEDNESDAY EVENINGS AFTER THE CHILDREN GO TO BED WOULD BE OKAY."

Tom: "HOW ABOUT 9:30 TO 10:30 ON THOSE NIGHTS IN THE EATING AREA?"

Mary: "FINE."

The counselor continues to explain further procedures. When reviewing what to do if unbiblical behavior occurs, Tom looks at Mary and speaks.

Tom: "WHAT SIGNAL SHOULD WE USE WHEN WE RECOGNIZE ONE OF US IS GETTING ANGRY?"

Mary: "HOW ABOUT RAISING A HAND?"

Tom: "OK, LET'S TRY THIS. MAKE TWO COLUMNS ON A PIECE OF NOTEBOOK PAPER AND PUT MY NAME AT THE HEAD OF ONE COLUMN AND YOURS AT THE HEAD OF THE OTHER." *(Pause)* "NOW, WE'RE SUPPOSED TO START READING EPHESIANS 4:17-32."

Counselor:	*(Breaks in)* "THE PURPOSE OF READING THESE SCRIPTURES IS TO HELP REMIND EACH OF YOU OF THE SINS YOU'VE COMMITTED AGAINST THE OTHER AND TO REVIEW THE BIBLICAL GROUND RULES FOR CONDUCTING THE CONFERENCE TABLE. I KNOW BOTH OF YOU HAVE WORKED ON YOUR **VICTORY OVER FAILURES WORKSHEETS,** SO HOW ABOUT STARTING WITH YOU, MARY?"
Mary:	*(Hesitatingly)* "WELL, ALL RIGHT; I HOPE I DO THIS RIGHT. *(Looking at her husband, Mary continues)* TOM, I'VE BEEN INCONSIDERATE."
Counselor:	*(Breaks in)* "EXCUSE ME, MARY, BUT AS YOU KNOW FROM YOUR PREVIOUS HOMEWORK, THAT IS TOO GENERAL. CHANGE TAKES PLACE IN SPECIFICS. HOW HAVE YOU DEMONSTRATED BEING INCONSIDERATE?"
Mary:	*(Hesitatingly)* "I DON'T FIX YOU BREAKFAST BECAUSE YOU NEVER APPRECIATE ANYTHING I DO FOR YOU."
Counselor:	"MARY, THAT WAS SPECIFIC BUT YOU ALSO MOVED INTO TOM'S COLUMN. YOU ONLY LIST *YOUR* SINS, NOT TOM'S."
Tom:	*(Very sharply)* "THAT'S RIGHT! SHE ALWAYS BLAMES ME ... SHE SAYS I DON'T APPRECIATE HER ... I'M NOT A GOOD HUSBAND ... I DON'T TAKE CARE OF THE KIDS ... EVEN THOUGH SHE HAS BEEN MAKING CHANGES RECENTLY, SHE'S NO ANGEL."

While Tom continues with a louder voice, the counselor quietly raises his hand and motions for Mary to do the same.

Counselor:	*(After Tom notices the raised hands)* "NOW, TOM AND MARY, WE'VE JUST DEMONSTRATED HOW TO STOP A FIGHT RATHER QUICKLY. *(Pause)* MARY, LET'S START AGAIN EXCEPT THIS TIME STATE *ONLY* YOUR SINS THAT YOU HAVE COMMITTED AGAINST TOM."

Mary states her specific sins that she has committed against Tom since the last time she had asked for his forgiveness. Tom needs some assistance in being specific about the sins he has committed against Mary. After stating a number of these specific sins, he also asks her to forgive him. They both say a prayer of commitment to live in a more biblical manner in their home. The counselor assigns further homework for them to complete during the coming week.

What homework assignments would you give to them if you were the counselor?

LESSON 15: HOMEWORK

> This week's **HOMEWORK** helps husbands and wives love one another biblically. If a spouse violates Scripture and fails to practice biblical love, then God's plan must be followed to restore that one to the Lord and his marriage companion *(based on Isaiah 55:8-11; John 13:35; I Peter 3:1-9; I John 1:9, 4:18-21; Revelation 2:4-5).*

✔ *homework completed*

☐ A. * In your own words, write the meaning of *I Peter 3:1 and 7.* Memorize *I Peter 3:1 and 7* and begin memorizing *Ezekiel 18:20* and *Ephesians 6:4.* Review previous memory verses.

☐ B. * Read **BIBLICAL PRINCIPLES: THE MARRIAGE RELATIONSHIP (PART TWO)** (Lesson 15, Page 2). Highlight the listed verses in your Bible.

☐ C. Study **BIBLICAL SUBMISSION** (Lesson 15, Page 3). Note the definition of biblical submission and the relationships in which it is to be practiced.

☐ D. Read **YOU CAN LEARN HOW TO SHOW LOVE TOWARD YOUR SPOUSE** (Lesson 15, Pages 4-5). Note that biblical love between a husband and wife is based on each one's commitment to God and the covenant relationship they have with one another. Failure to love your spouse biblically cannot be blamed on emotions, circumstances, or people. Instead, a failure to love biblically is a denial of God's love for you through Christ Jesus *(based on Matthew 18:21-35, esp. verses 32-33; I John 4:7-8).* Place a check by those statements that describe changes you need to make in your marriage relationship.

☐ E. * Read **OVERCOMING PROBLEMS THROUGH BIBLICAL COMMUNICATION (USING A CONFERENCE TABLE FOR RECONCILIATION)** (Lesson 15, Pages 6-9). Complete a **VICTORY OVER FAILURES WORKSHEET** (Supplement 8) for each person sinned against in preparation for conducting your first conference table.

☐ F. * Conduct at least one "Conference Table" this week with your family (or others with whom you have a close relationship) using these guidelines. On your **VICTORY OVER FAILURES WORKSHEET** (Supplement 8), place a check mark by each sin confessed.

☐ G. * Read **A CASE STUDY: MARY'S HUSBAND HAS LEFT HER** (Lesson 15, Page 10-12). Answer the question at the end of the case study.

☐ H. * In conjunction with this lesson, begin work on the outline described in statement 24 of the **Open Book Test** (Lesson 23, Page 3).

* *The completion of assignments marked with an asterisk (*) is a prerequisite for further biblical counseling training.*

LESSON 15: STUDY GUIDE FOR DAILY DEVOTIONS
(INCLUDING SCRIPTURE MEMORY AND HOMEWORK)

> This week's **STUDY GUIDE** helps husbands and wives love one another biblically. If a spouse violates Scripture and fails to practice biblical love, then God's plan must be followed to restore that one to the Lord and his marriage companion *(based on Isaiah 55:8-11; John 13:35; I Peter 3:1-9; I John 1:9, 4:18-21; Revelation 2:4-5).*

Scripture Memory

1. * Memorize *I Peter 3:1 and 7.* Begin memorizing *Ezekiel 18:20* and *Ephesians 6:4.*
2. Carry your memory verse cards from previous weeks along with this week's memory verses. Review your Scriptures in spare moments throughout the day.

Daily Devotional Study Guide

FIRST DAY

1. Open with prayer.
2. * Read *Principle 64* under **BIBLICAL PRINCIPLES: THE MARRIAGE RELATIONSHIP (PART TWO)** (Lesson 15, Page 2). Highlight the listed verses in your Bible.
3. * Write the meaning of *I Peter 3:1 and 7* in your own words.
4. Study **BIBLICAL SUBMISSION** (Lesson 15, Page 3). Note the definition of biblical submission and the relationships in which it is to be practiced.
5. Close with prayer.

SECOND DAY

1. Open with prayer.
2. * Read *Principle 65* under **BIBLICAL PRINCIPLES: THE MARRIAGE RELATIONSHIP (PART TWO)** (Lesson 15, Page 2). Highlight the listed verses in your Bible.
3. Study **YOU CAN LEARN HOW TO SHOW LOVE TOWARD YOUR SPOUSE** (Lesson 15, Pages 4-5). Note that biblical love between a husband and wife is based on each one's commitment to God and the covenant relationship with one another. Failure to love your spouse biblically cannot be blamed on emotions, circumstances, or people. Instead, a failure to love biblically is a denial of God's love for you through Christ Jesus *(based on Matthew 18:21-35, esp. verses 32-33; I John 4:7-8).* Place a check by those statements that indicate changes you need to make.
4. Close with prayer.

THIRD DAY

1. Open with prayer.
2. * Read *Principle 66* under **BIBLICAL PRINCIPLES: THE MARRIAGE RELATIONSHIP (PART TWO)** (Lesson 15, Page 2). Highlight the listed verses in your Bible.
3. * Start a **VICTORY OVER FAILURES WORKSHEET** (Supplement 8) for each person sinned against in preparation for conducting your first conference table.

4.   Close with prayer.

FOURTH DAY

1.   Open with prayer.
2.   * Read *Principle 67* under **BIBLICAL PRINCIPLES: THE MARRIAGE RELATIONSHIP (PART TWO)** (Lesson 15, Page 2). Highlight listed verses in your Bible.
3.   * Complete your **VICTORY OVER FAILURES WORKSHEET** (Supplement 8) for each person sinned against who will be at your first conference table.
4.   Close with prayer.

FIFTH DAY

1.   Open with prayer.
2.   Read *Principle 68* under **BIBLICAL PRINCIPLES: THE MARRIAGE RELATIONSHIP (PART TWO)** (Lesson 15, Page 2). Highlight listed verses in your Bible.
3.   * To prepare for your own conference table, study **OVERCOMING PROBLEMS THROUGH BIBLICAL COMMUNICATION (USING A CONFERENCE TABLE FOR RECONCILIATION)** (Lesson 15, Pages 6-9). This is the first day of a two-day study. Set a time to have at least one conference table this week with your family or others with whom you have a close relationship.
4.   Close with prayer.
5.   Are you remaining faithful in memorizing Scripture during the week? Take time to review past memory verses, especially in your spare moments.

SIXTH DAY

1.   Open with prayer.
2.   * Complete your study of **OVERCOMING PROBLEMS THROUGH BIBLICAL COMMUNICATION (USING A CONFERENCE TABLE FOR RECONCILIATION)** (Lesson 15, Pages 6-9). Set the time for your first conference table and conduct it. On your **VICTORY OVER FAILURES WORKSHEET** that you have prepared for the conference table, remember to place a check mark by each sin as you confess them.
3.   Close with prayer.

SEVENTH DAY

1.   Open with prayer.
2.   * Prayerfully evaluate the results of your first conference table. Schedule at least one more conference table for the coming week in which you and other participants can face and deal with problems in a manner that pleases the Lord.
3.   * Read **A CASE STUDY: MARY'S HUSBAND HAS LEFT HER** (Lesson 15, Pages 10-12). Answer the question at the end of the case study.
4.   * In conjunction with this lesson, begin work on the outline described in statement 24 of the **Open Book Test** (Lesson 23, Page 3).
5.   Close in prayer.
6.   Evaluate your faithfulness in memorizing Scripture this week *(Psalm 119:11, 16; I Corinthians 4:2; Ephesians 5:15-16)*. Take time to review past memory verses. Ask someone to listen to you recite this week's memory verses and explain their application to your life.

*   *The completion of assignments marked with an asterisk (*) is a prerequisite for further biblical counseling training.*

LESSON 16

PARENT-CHILD RELATIONSHIPS
(PART ONE)

"The person who sins will die. The son will not bear the punishment for the father's iniquity, nor will the father bear the punishment for the son's iniquity; the righteousness of the righteous will be upon himself, and the wickedness of the wicked will be upon himself."

Ezekiel 18:20

"And, fathers, do not provoke your children to anger; but bring them up in the discipline and instruction of the Lord."

Ephesians 6:4

LESSON 16: PARENT-CHILD RELATIONSHIPS (PART ONE)

> Parents have a blessed privilege and solemn responsibility before the Lord to bring up their children in a manner that pleases Him and to train them to understand the principles of Scripture. Accomplishing this task in a biblical manner will result in the blessings of the Lord. Failing to bring up children according to God's Word will bring heartache and grief *(based on Deuteronomy 6:6-7; Proverbs 10:1, 13:18, 17:25, 22:6, 29:17; Colossians 1:10; James 1:25).*

I. **The purposes of this lesson are:**

A. To introduce God's plan for the parent-child relationship,

B. To contrast man's philosophies with God's directives for bringing up children,

C. To present biblical guidelines for rearing children in the instruction and discipline of the Lord,

D. To review the basic ways that parents provoke their children to anger, and

E. To show the importance of parents providing biblical instruction for their children.

II. **The outline of this lesson**

A. Self-confrontation

1. **BIBLICAL PRINCIPLES: PARENT-CHILD RELATIONSHIPS (PART ONE)** (Lesson 16, Page 2)

2. **MAN'S THEORIES AND PRACTICES FOR REARING CHILDREN** (Lesson 16, Pages 3-6)

3. **GUIDELINES FOR TRAINING CHILDREN** (Lesson 16, Pages 7-9)

4. **WAYS THAT PARENTS PROVOKE THEIR CHILDREN TO ANGER** (Lesson 16, Pages 10-12)

5. **UNDERSTANDING BIBLICAL INSTRUCTION OF CHILDREN** (Lesson 16, Pages 13-16)

B. Steps for spiritual growth

1. **LESSON 16: HOMEWORK** (Lesson 16, Page 17)

2. **STUDY GUIDE FOR DAILY DEVOTIONS** (Lesson 16, Pages 18-19)

C. Biblical counseling

(Case study resumes in Lesson 18)

BIBLICAL PRINCIPLES: PARENT-CHILD RELATIONSHIPS (PART ONE)

> God's principles and precepts are applicable to parents and children alike. Parents are to be of one mind as they teach the Scriptures to their children in a manner that is pleasing to the Lord, and children are to respond faithfully to this teaching as unto the Lord *(based on Deuteronomy 6:6-7; Psalm 19:7-11; Proverbs 22:6; I Corinthians 1:10; Ephesians 6:1-4; Colossians 3:20; II Timothy 3:16-17; II Peter 1:3-4).*

I. God's View

(Principle 69) Children are a gift (heritage) of the Lord *(Psalm 127:3).* They are to be brought up according to the directives of God's Word *(based on Psalm 19:7-11; II Timothy 3:14-17)* and not according to the arbitrary decisions of parents or the philosophies of man *(Proverbs 3:5, 16:2; Isaiah 55:8-11; I Corinthians 3:18-20).* Parents are to train up their children in the discipline and instruction of the Lord *(Deuteronomy 4:9; 6:6-7, 20-25; Proverbs 22:6; Ephesians 6:4).*

(Principle 70) Children are to honor and obey their parents in the Lord, because this is right and is pleasing to the Lord *(Deuteronomy 5:16; Mark 7:8-10; Ephesians 6:1-2; Colossians 3:20).*

II. Your Hope

(Principle 47, revised; from Lesson 11, Page 2) God can and does cause all things to work together for good to those who belong to Him and love Him. No one else, not even your children or your parents, can prevent His work in your life *(based on Romans 8:28-29; Philippians 1:6).*

(Principle 71) As you study and follow God's Word for your life and the training of your children *(based on Ecclesiastes 12:13-14; Isaiah 55:8-11; II Timothy 2:15, 3:16-17)* and decisively put off any reliance on yourself, your background, or your upbringing *(Proverbs 3:5, 14:12, 28:26a; I Corinthians 3:20),* you will gain the wisdom and direction that you need to be a godly parent *(based on Proverbs 3:5-6, 15:33; James 1:25).*

(Principle 72) Children, when you put off disobedience, stubbornness, and rebellion *(based on Deuteronomy 21:18-21; Romans 1:28-32, esp. verse 30; 2:5-11; II Timothy 3:1-5, esp. verse 2; Titus 1:6)* and put on honor and obedience to the Lord and your parents *(Ephesians 6:1-2; Colossians 3:20),* God will bless you *(Ephesians 6:2-3).* Heed (take seriously) your parents' instruction and discipline, that you may be wise *(based on Proverbs 13:1, 19:20, 23:19).*

MAN'S THEORIES AND PRACTICES
FOR REARING CHILDREN

> Many of man's philosophies for the rearing of children typically arise from individual experiences. Moreover, in the area of bringing up children, even Christians often look to ungodly counsel, or to "common sense," rather than to the sole authority and totally sufficient standard of the Scriptures *(based on Deuteronomy 4:9; 6:6-9, 13-14, 17, 20-25; Ephesians 4:11-20; II Timothy 3:16-17; Titus 1:10-11; II Peter 1:3-10).*

I. **Characteristics of man's theories and practices for rearing children**

The modern focus of man's theories about the training of children is the exaltation of self and the importance of emotions in regard to both parents and children. The wisdom of the world teaches that you must bring up your children to have a "good self-image" and that you and your children must "get in touch" with your feelings (which often means to live by your emotions).

II. **Some of man's mistaken explanations for problems between parents and children**

A. The "wisdom of man" has many "reasons" for parental failure in rearing children, such as:

1. Parents are deficient in "parenting" skills;

2. Parents lack "conflict-resolution" skills;

3. Parents did not receive love and "proper role models" from their own mother and father and so are unable to love and bring up their own children;

4. Parents who verbally and physically abuse their children try to trace and blame their actions back to their own parents, who verbally and physically abused them as children;

5. A parent doesn't receive "support" from the other parent for decisions that affect their children;

6. A single parent who is divorced doesn't have enough help to bring up children properly;

7. A parent's lack of money hinders children from having material advantages;

8. Parents may have a child who will not respect them, no matter what;

9. Parents today just don't have the "quality" time necessary to rear children effectively;

10. Parents don't understand all the "pressures" placed on children and youth today; and

11. Parents fail because they have a "poor self-image" themselves.

B. Man's earthly wisdom also gives "reasons" for children's failures, such as:

1. Their parents are inadequate;

2. Their "home atmosphere" isn't "free enough" for self-expression;

3. They have inherited "personality problems;"

4. They lack financial, educational, or social advantages;

5. They are overwhelmed by "peer pressure";

6. They can't be expected to understand the reasons for obedience and are often too young to be responsible for their behavior;

7. Their "family tree" has a history of drug or alcohol abuse ("chemical dependency"); and

8. They have a poor "self-image."

III. **Some of man's futile attempts to solve parent-child problems**

A. Solutions given to parents:

1. Read books and attend parenting seminars;

2. Do not place restrictive guidelines on your children but, instead, allow your children to learn from their own mistakes and experiences;

3. Receive therapy or psychological counseling to deal with the lack of love shown by your own parents;

4. Find someone to listen to the problems associated with your spouse and children;

5. Get a divorce from an uncooperative spouse; then, if possible, marry someone else who will help bring up the children;

6. Find someone to give you "moral support;"

7. Get away from the children and take time for yourself;

8. No matter what, do not harm your children's "self-concept;"

9. Never moralize; be careful how soon you bring up God's standards so that you don't "beat your children over the head" with the Bible;

10. Let children do what they want, since they will do what they feel like doing anyway; and

11. Join a support or therapy group for parents who have similar problems.

B. Solutions given to children:

1. Find an adult to be your "parent-substitute;"

2. Outwardly be nice, but do what you want anyway, since only you can decide what is best for you;

3. Ignore your parents;

4. Leave home if your parents are too restrictive;

5. Accept the "fact" that you will probably have the same problems as your parents;

6. Be more aggressive in expressing to your parents exactly how you feel and give them only the respect they have earned;

7. Write how you feel in a journal and develop your own fantasy life to escape your parents' lack of understanding;

8. Remind parents of their own failures to prove to them that they cannot "moralize" to you;

9.   Improve your "self-image" by excelling in some area or achieving a goal;

10.   Focus on your own development and learn "to be your own person;" and

11.   Join a support or therapy group for young people just like yourself.

To review why these approaches to parent-child problems are unbiblical, refer to:
THE BIBLICAL VIEW OF SELF (Lesson 4, Pages 5-10);
BASIC APPROACHES TO SOLVING PERSONAL PROBLEMS (Lesson 4, Page 11);
BIBLICAL PRINCIPLES: DEALING WITH SELF (PART ONE) (Lesson 9, Pages 2-3);
SELF-BELITTLEMENT, SELF-EXALTATION, AND SELF-PITY (Lesson 9, Pages 4-5);
BIBLICAL PRINCIPLES: DEALING WITH SELF (PART TWO) (Lesson 10, Pages 2-3); and
OVERCOMING A PREOCCUPATION WITH SELF (Lesson 10, Pages 9-12).

IV.   **Some unbiblical views within the church regarding the bringing up of children**

A.   Unbiblical "advice" or "counsel" given to parents:

1.   You have to learn parenting from people who have had the same experiences as you, since they are the only ones who can truly understand your struggles *(disregards Proverbs 14:12; Romans 15:14).*

2.   Teach your children to trust you and rely on you first; then teach them to rely on the Lord. It is essential to gain their trust before they can trust God *(disregards Proverbs 3:5-6).*

3.   Don't constantly use the Bible when you talk to your children about their lives. Using Scripture too much might cause them to resent the Bible *(disregards Deuteronomy 6:5-9; Psalm 19:7-11; II Timothy 3:16-17).*

4.   When it comes to rearing children, you really only need good common sense *(disregards Proverbs 14:12; Jeremiah 17:9).*

5.   If your children are disobedient to your rules, punish them severely. Let them know they cannot get away with breaking your rules *(disregards Ephesians 6:4).*

6.   You are the role model of the Lord for your children. The way your children view you as parents will be the way they view God *(disregards Matthew 11:27; John 14:9; II Corinthians 4:3-6; Colossians 1:15; Hebrews 1:1-3, esp. verse 3a).*

7.   All children will "sow some wild oats." It is a phase they must go through; but don't worry, they'll grow out of it *(disregards Proverbs 19:18, 20:11).*

B.   Unbiblical "advice" or "counsel" given to children:

1.   You are the master of your own destiny because of the potential within you. No one, not even your parents, has any right to dictate to you *(disregards Proverbs 16:18; Isaiah 64:6; I Corinthians 10:12).*

2.   God wants you to feel good about yourself. Find something that you do well and excel at it *(disregards Proverbs 21:2-4).*

3.   Look at the mess your parents have made of their own lives. How could they possibly give you any legitimate guidance *(disregards Proverbs 20:9-10; Matthew 7:1-5; Romans 15:14; II Corinthians 3:5)?*

4.   Certainly there are going to be times you and your parents are at odds with one another. When you disagree, learn to write stories about how you feel and how you would like to deal with your parents. Put all your anger down on paper. You will feel much better because this will help you get rid of your angry feelings *(disregards Proverbs 18:17, 25:28; Ephesians 4:15; Philippians 4:6-9).*

5. Explain to your parents how much you are being deprived by their not allowing you to have or to do what you want. Tell them how you think you have been mistreated *(disregards Philippians 2:3-4, 14; 4:11)*.

6. Release your anger by participating in some kind of strenuous activity *(disregards Proverbs 16:32, 25:28; Ephesians 4:31-32)*.

7. There are other adults who are more understanding and kind than your parents. Find a sympathetic adult in the church or in your school and tell them your problems. If necessary, go to a professional counselor. If your parents do not understand, it is not necessary to try and communicate with them *(disregards Ephesians 4:25, 6:2; Colossians 4:6)*.

8. If all else fails in dealing with problems at home, leave. You do not need this frustration and pain *(disregards Romans 8:28-29; James 1:2-4)*.

9. No one is responsible to obey their parents all the time. There will be times when you need to "clarify your values" and judge "truth" for yourself *(disregards Ephesians 6:1; Colossians 3:20; II Timothy 3:16-17)*.

GUIDELINES FOR TRAINING CHILDREN

> Parents, be diligent in continuously examining your own walk in Jesus Christ as you guide your children in the ways of the Lord. Start discussing and planning the training of your children even before they are born. Pray consistently as you learn and practice scriptural directives for raising your children. After your children are born, firmly hold to your commitment to follow God's Word in training each child according to his age and training needs *(based on Psalm 37:4-5; Proverbs 16:3, 22:6; Matthew 7:1-5; I Corinthians 1:10; Ephesians 4:1-3, 6:4; I Thessalonians 5:17).*

I. **A parent's commitment to the Lord**

   A. A spiritual new birth is required to understand biblical principles for bringing up children *(I Corinthians 2:14).*

   B. Parents are to demonstrate their commitment of love to the Lord by rearing their children in a manner that pleases Him *(based on Colossians 1:10, 3:17).*

II. **A parent's commitment to the Word of God**

   A. Scripture is the sole authority for life and is the only basis by which children can be brought up in order to please the Lord *(II Timothy 3:14-17).* Man's way is totally inadequate *(Proverbs 14:12; Isaiah 55:8-11).*

   B. Continual biblical self-evaluation and faithful obedience to Scripture are required for parents to avoid spiritual delusion concerning the things of God *(James 1:22)* and to avoid hypocrisy in correcting their children *(Matthew 7:1-5).*

III. **The commitment of parents to each other**

   A. Believing parents are to be one in mind and judgment *(based on I Corinthians 1:10; Philippians 2:2).* Even if your spouse is not a believer, your faithful, loving commitment to the one-flesh relationship of marriage is designed by God to help unify you and your spouse, resulting in a godly influence in the lives of your children *(based on Genesis 2:18, 24; Matthew 19:5-6; Mark 10:6-8; I Corinthians 7:10-14, esp. verse 14; Ephesians 5:31).*

   B. Each parent, as a committed believer in Christ, is to submit to the other *(Ephesians 5:21),* to love one another *(Ephesians 5:25, 28; Titus 2:4),* and to regard the other as more important than himself *(Philippians 2:3-4).* However, in loving servanthood *(John 13:14-16; Philippians 2:3-8)* the father, as the head of the family, is to take the responsibility for leadership in the rearing of children *(Ephesians 5:23, 6:4; Colossians 3:21).*

IV. The commitment of believing parents to their children

A. Parents are to carry out their responsibilities to their children as godly servants, following the example of the Lord Jesus Christ *(Matthew 20:25-28; John 13:12-17; Philippians 2:3-8)*.

    1. Because a believing family is a smaller unit of the body of Christ, all involved (both parents and children) are to fulfill all the directives of God's Word. Parents are to be godly examples for their children *(based on Deuteronomy 4:9, 6:8-9; Matthew 18:5-7; I Corinthians 4:14-16, 11:1; I Timothy 4:12; Titus 2:7)*, and are to point to Jesus Christ as the ultimate example for them to follow *(John 13:12-17; Philippians 2:5-8; Hebrews 12:1-3; I Peter 2:21)*.

    2. Parents are to regard their children as more important than themselves and are to lay aside their own self-centered interests. Parents are to respond lovingly to their children and provide for them in a manner that pleases the Lord *(I Corinthians 13:4-8a; II Corinthians 12:14; Philippians 2:3-4)*.

    3. Parents must not be quarrelsome, either with each other or with their children, but instead must be kind, gentle, and patient in all things. Parents must teach God's Word and the practice of it and, as necessary, provide correction when their children violate scriptural standards *(Proverbs 15:10; II Timothy 2:24-26)*.

B. When parents sin against their children, they are to confess these transgressions to the Lord as well as to their children *(based on James 5:16; I John 1:9)*.

    Refer to: **RECONCILIATION (REMOVING ALL HINDRANCES TO UNITY AND PEACE)** *(Lesson 12, Pages 6-8)*, under **II. Confession.**

C. Parents are to put off provoking their children to anger but instead are to rear them in the discipline and instruction of the Lord *(Ephesians 6:4; Colossians 3:21)*. Relying on God's Word, you are to be faithful in helping your children become equipped and adequate for every good work by training them in righteousness through teaching, reproof, and correction *(based on II Timothy 3:16-17)*.

    1. You are to bring up your children in the instruction of the Lord, teaching them how to obey God's Word, the necessity of doing so, and the consequences of disobedience as follows:

        a. Show your children faithful obedience to the Lord by the example of your walk *(based on Deuteronomy 6:5-7; I Corinthians 11:1; I Timothy 4:12; II Timothy 1:5)*;

        b. Teach (instruct) your children God's Word and His way whenever you are with them during the daily routine of life *(Deuteronomy 6:6-7; II Timothy 3:16)*; and

        c. Increase the responsibilities of your children based on their demonstrated and increasing faithfulness and capabilities *(based on Matthew 25:14-29; Luke 16:10)*.

    2. You are to bring up your children in the discipline of the Lord, graciously instructing them by reproof and correction as follows:

        a. Establish simple, clear-cut guidelines and consequences as God did in directing His people *(based on Genesis 2:16-17; Exodus 20:3-17; Deuteronomy 11:26-28)*. Clearly explain these biblically-based standards of conduct to avoid confusion or misunderstandings *(based on Exodus 31:18, 34:1; Deuteronomy 4:13-14; Matthew 22:37-39; John 14:15)*.

    b.   Carry out discipline in a loving manner *(based on Proverbs 6:23, 15:10, 19:18, 22:15, 23:13; I Corinthians 13:4-8a; Hebrews 12:5-11; Revelation 3:19)* and apply it quickly *(Ecclesiastes 8:11)* in order to restore your child while there is hope *(based on Proverbs 19:18, 23:14; Hebrews 12:11).*

    c.   Tailor the sternness of the discipline to the child's willingness to return and follow God's way *(based on Proverbs 15:10).*

        1)   If a child remains foolish (as shown by continued disobedience and disrespect), use the rod as a tool for restoration, not as a punishment *(Proverbs 22:15, 29:15).*

            Refer to: **UNDERSTANDING BIBLICAL DISCIPLINE** *(Lesson 17, Pages 8-10) under* **III. How and when is discipline carried out?**

        2)   If a child repents of his wrongdoings, exercise gracious compassion as God does for those who sin and repent *(based on Psalm 103:10-14).*

V. The commitment of children to the Lord

A.   The necessity of the spiritual new birth applies to all, beginning at the earliest age of comprehension. In fact, children are considered as especially tender to the Lord *(Matthew 18:2-6; Mark 9:35-37; Luke 17:2).*

B.   Children are to demonstrate their commitment to the Lord by their demeanor, speech, and actions *(based on Exodus 20:12; Proverbs 20:11; Ephesians 6:1-2; Colossians 3:20; I Timothy 4:12; II Timothy 3:15).*

VI. The commitment of children to their parents

A.   Out of a commitment to please the Lord in all things *(II Corinthians 5:9; Colossians 1:10),* children are to put off disrespect for their parents and are to honor their father and mother *(Exodus 20:12; Proverbs 23:22; Mark 7:10; Ephesians 6:2).*

B.   Out of a commitment to please the Lord in all things, children are to obey their parents *(Proverbs 6:20; Ephesians 6:1; Colossians 3:20).*

WAYS THAT PARENTS PROVOKE THEIR CHILDREN TO ANGER

> Parents provoke their children to anger by not practicing biblical love, not considering their children as more important than themselves, and not dying to self to become a servant of the Lord Jesus Christ (based on Matthew 5:43-48; Mark 10:42-45; Luke 9:23-24; I Corinthians 13:4-8a; Galatians 5:14; Ephesians 6:4; Philippians 2:3-4; Colossians 3:21; I Peter 4:8; I John 4:7-8).

I. **You can provoke your child to anger when you fail to demonstrate biblical love (I Corinthians 13:4-8a) to your child through:**

A. Impatience (e.g., not waiting for your child to finish a task or hurrying your child to do something that is beyond his capabilities) (violating I Corinthians 13:4; Galatians 5:22; Ephesians 4:1-2; Colossians 1:9-12, 3:12);

B. Unkindness (e.g., not providing for your child's physical needs because you are too busy with your own interests) (violating I Corinthians 13:4; Galatians 5:22; Ephesians 4:32; Philippians 2:3-4; II Timothy 2:24; Titus 2:4-5);

C. Jealousy (e.g., trying to prove to your child that you can do something better than he can) (violating I Corinthians 13:4; Galatians 5:19-20; James 3:13-18);

D. Bragging (e.g., saying things such as "I had it a lot harder when I was your age") (violating Proverbs 27:2; Romans 1:30; I Corinthians 13:4; II Corinthians 10:18);

E. Arrogance (e.g., saying such things as "We'll do it my way because I'm a lot smarter and a lot bigger than you") (violating Romans 1:30; I Corinthians 13:4);

F. Unbecoming actions (e.g., purposefully embarrassing and demeaning your child by discussing his failures and shortcomings in front of others) (violating I Corinthians 13:5; Ephesians 4:29);

G. Seeking to have your own way (e.g., insisting that your child or family do only what you want to do) (violating I Corinthians 13:5; Philippians 2:3-4);

H. Taking into account wrongs suffered (e.g., reminding your child in an accusing manner of his past failures by saying things such as "I've told you this a thousand times...") (violating I Corinthians 13:5; Ephesians 4:32; Colossians 3:12-13);

I. Rejoicing in unrighteousness (e.g., encouraging your child to retaliate for wrongs he has suffered from others) (violating I Corinthians 13:6; II Thessalonians 2:12);

J. Not rejoicing in the truth (e.g., failing to commend your child for being truthful in a difficult situation) (violating I Corinthians 13:6; I Thessalonians 5:16; I Peter 4:13; II John 1:4; III John 1:3);

K. Not bearing all things (e.g., avoiding, criticizing, or neglecting your child because he wasn't perfect in meeting your expectations) (violating I Corinthians 13:7; Galatians 6:2);

L.   Not believing or hoping all things (e.g., consistently doubting what your child says before you know all the facts) *(violating I Corinthians 13:7)*; or

M.   Not enduring all things (e.g., responding in anger to your child because you are focused on your own difficulties) *(violating I Corinthians 13:7; James 1:2-4)*.

II.   **You can provoke your child to anger when you fail to live as an example of the believer *(I Timothy 4:12)* by:**

A.   Acting hypocritically (e.g., judging your child's behavior when you do not continually examine your own life by God's Word) *(violating Matthew 7:1-5)*;

B.   Lying to your child or requesting your child to lie for you *(violating Romans 14:13; Ephesians 4:15, 25)*;

C.   Arguing with your child or arguing with your spouse in the presence of your child *(violating Proverbs 20:3; Philippians 2:14-16; Colossians 4:6; II Timothy 2:24-25)*;

D.   Teasing your child (e.g., tickling him to the point of tears or making fun of him when he has been embarrassed or has failed in an endeavor) *(violating Ephesians 6:4; Colossians 3:12)*;

E.   Speaking to your child in an unwholesome manner (e.g., calling him names or yelling at him in anger) *(violating Ephesians 4:29; Colossians 4:6)*; or

F.   Showing partiality to one child over another *(violating Proverbs 24:23; also see Genesis 25:24-34, esp. verse 28, and Genesis 27:1 - 28:9 for illustrations of the evils precipitated by parents favoring one child over another)*.

III.   **You can provoke your child to anger when you seek to become the ultimate authority in the life of your child instead of showing him the importance of following the Lord *(based on Ezekiel 18:4-20, esp. verses 4 and 20; II Corinthians 3:5-6; II Timothy 3:16-17; James 1:22-25)* by:**

A.   Practicing a double standard and demanding that your child serve you continually, while you fail to serve your child and others *(violating Matthew 20:25-28; Mark 9:35, 10:42-45)*;

B.   Treating your child as a possession or imposing your own aspirations on him (e.g., insisting that he meet the goals that you have arbitrarily set for his life) *(violating Deuteronomy 6:6-7; Psalm 24:1, 127:3; Ephesians 6:4)*;

C.   Swearing at your child or using harsh, contentious language when he does not meet certain standards *(violating Proverbs 12:18, 20:3; Ephesians 4:15, 29, 31; Colossians 4:6; James 3:2-12)*; or

D.   Comparing your child to yourself or others to show him the ways in which he does not measure up to your standards *(violating II Corinthians 10:12, 17-18)*.

IV.   **You can provoke your child to anger when you act in an inconsistent manner in front of, or toward, your child by:**

A.   Failing to keep your word and becoming untrustworthy (e.g., promising to take him someplace and then arbitrarily changing your plans in order to please yourself) *(violating Matthew 5:37; Ephesians 4:15; 25; Colossians 3:9)*;

B.   Failing to discipline biblically when necessary *(violating Proverbs 13:24, 23:13; Hebrews 12:7-8)* or disciplining when provoked and angry *(violating I Corinthians 13:5; Ephesians 4:31)*;

C.   Being erratic and inconsistent in your speech or actions (e.g., showing little or no response to your child's disobedience on one day but at another time becoming visibly upset, using unkind words, and punishing rather than restoring) *(violating Proverbs 15:1; Galatians 6:1; Ephesians 4:15, 29; Colossians 4:6)*;

D.   Failing to confess sins that you have committed against your child or seeking to give excuses for your sinful behavior in an effort to justify yourself *(violating Matthew 5:23-24; Romans 12:18; James 5:16)*; or

E.   Refusing to forgive your child (e.g., making statements such as "I'll never be able to forgive you for what you have done to me") while demanding that your child forgive others for wrongs done against him *(violating Matthew 5:23-24, 18:21-22; Mark 11:25-26; Ephesians 4:32; Colossians 3:12-13)*.

V.   **You can provoke your child to anger when you neglect your child by:**

A.   Failing to spend time with your child in order to show the application of God's Word to everyday life *(violating Deuteronomy 6:6-7)*;

B.   Failing to listen patiently when your child speaks to you because you are "too busy" with your own interests *(violating I Corinthians 13:4-5; Philippians 2:3-4; James 1:19)*; or

C.   Failing to discipline your child biblically or in a timely manner by delaying discipline because "you don't feel like it" or waiting to discipline your child until a number of wrongs have accumulated *(violating Proverbs 13:24, 19:18; Ecclesiastes 8:11)*.

UNDERSTANDING BIBLICAL INSTRUCTION OF CHILDREN

> To instruct children in God's way requires that you live each moment to please the Lord in a deliberate and thoughtful manner. When you teach children, you must take into account each child's level of spiritual understanding and abilities *(based on Deuteronomy 6:6-9; Proverbs 22:6; Romans 12:1-2; I Thessalonians 2:5-8, esp. verses 7-8; I Timothy 1:5; III John 1:4).*

I. **What does biblical instruction mean?**

A. In the Old Testament, the primary word for "instruction" also means "teach," "discipline," and "admonish."

B. In the New Testament, different words convey the concepts of "instruction" and "discipline." For parental instruction of children, the word for "instruction" in *Ephesians 6:4* can also be translated "train" or "admonish" and has within it the idea of biblical counsel. It encompasses:

1. A biblical foundation for the instruction *(based on I Corinthians 10:11; Colossians 3:16);*

2. A loving relationship *(based on Acts 20:31; I Corinthians 4:14; II Thessalonians 3:15);*

3. Wisdom *(Colossians 1:28, 3:16)* and the exercise of patience *(based on Acts 20:31; I Thessalonians 5:14);*

4. A goal of seeing the other complete in Christ *(Colossians 1:28);*

5. Individual attention *(based on Acts 20:31; I Thessalonians 5:14; II Thessalonians 3:15);* and

6. The understood responsibility of a spiritual leader *(I Thessalonians 5:12).*

C. The concept of "instruction" is also part of the broader meaning of "teaching" *(Colossians 1:28, 3:16),* which also serves as a basis for this study.

II. **Why is biblical instruction necessary for both parents and children?**

A. It helps give discernment for true understanding *(Proverbs 1:2, 4:1),* which begins with the knowledge and reverence of God *(Proverbs 9:10).*

B. It gives life to the one who guards it *(Proverbs 4:13).*

C. It teaches wise behavior, righteousness, justice, and equity *(Proverbs 1:3).*

D. It gives sound judgment to the simple and gives knowledge and discretion to youth *(Proverbs 1:4).*

E. It allows one to acquire wise counsel and to increase in learning *(Proverbs 1:5).*

F. It prevents foolishness *(Proverbs 1:7).*

G. It keeps one on the path of life *(Psalm 27:11; Proverbs 10:17)* and helps one to find life *(Proverbs 8:32-36, esp. verse 35).*

H.   It equips and enables one to teach others *(based on Matthew 28:19-20; Romans 15:14; II Timothy 2:2, 3:16-17).*

I.   It gives good judgment (discretion) *(Psalm 119:66; Proverbs 5:1-2).*

J.   It gives hope *(Romans 15:4).*

III. **Who is to instruct biblically and who is to be instructed?**

A.   All believers are to:

1.   Teach one another *(Matthew 28:19-20; Romans 15:14).*

2.   Teach those who are disobedient to the Word *(II Timothy 2:24-26).*

3.   Be ready to teach unbelievers the reason for the hope within them *(Psalm 51:12-13; I Peter 3:15).*

B.   Pastors, teachers *(Romans 12:6-8, esp. verse 7; Ephesians 4:11-12),* and elders *(I Timothy 3:2; Titus 2:1)* are to lead and teach the flock.

C.   Older women are to teach younger women *(Titus 2:3-5).*

D.   Parents (with the father responsible for leadership) are to teach their children *(Deuteronomy 4:9, 6:6-9; Proverbs 1:8; Ephesians 6:4).*

IV. **What are you to teach your children?**

A.   You are to proclaim the gospel (the Good News of salvation through the Lord Jesus Christ) to your children, just as you are to do with all others who have not received a spiritual new birth *(Matthew 28:18-20).*

For help in presenting God's plan for a spiritual new birth, refer to: **YOU CAN CHANGE BIBLICALLY (PART ONE)** *(Lesson 1, Pages 3-7).*

B.   You are to teach them the Scriptures *(Deuteronomy 6:6-9).*

1.   Set aside specific times to teach your children how to study the Word *(based on II Timothy 2:15).*

2.   Also, teach your children God's Word at all opportunities that arise throughout the day *(Deuteronomy 6:7; Proverbs 25:11-12).*

3.   You are to teach them the importance of trusting the Lord *(Proverbs 3:1-12)* and of being doers of the Word of God *(Matthew 7:24-27).*

Refer to: **THE IMPORTANCE OF DOING THE WORD** *(Lesson 5, Pages 6-9).*

C.   You are to help them learn the importance of restoration to obedience through the discipline of the Lord. When your children disobey God's directives for them, you are to teach them about biblical discipline and faithfully discipline them in a loving manner *(Proverbs 3:11-12, 22:15; Hebrews 12:11).* In doing this, remember:

1.   Discipline is sorrowful not only for the one being disciplined, but the individual's sin also grieves the Holy Spirit *(based on Ezekiel 18:23, 30-32; Ephesians 4:30; Hebrews 12:11);* and

2.   You are, at all times, to be judging yourself in a biblical manner *(Matthew 7:1-5; Galatians 6:4)* and, from your heart, are to have a continuing spirit of forgiveness for all your children's sins *(based on Matthew 18:21-22, 35).* You are to grant forgiveness immediately when your children profess repentance *(Luke 17:3-4).*

Refer to:
UNDERSTANDING BIBLICAL DISCIPLINE *(Lesson 17, Pages 8-10),*
RECONCILIATION (REMOVING ALL HINDRANCES TO UNITY AND PEACE)
 (Lesson 12, Pages 6-8),
RESTORATION/DISCIPLINE (YOUR BIBLICAL RESPONSE TO THE SIN OF
 ANOTHER BELIEVER) *(Lesson 13, Pages 7-8), and*
GUIDELINES: THE RESTORATION/DISCIPLINE PROCESS *(Lesson 13, Pages 9-11).*

D.   You are to teach them to love the Lord and others *(based on Matthew 22:37-39; I Corinthians 13:4-8a)* and teach them how to demonstrate that love *(based on John 14:15; I Corinthians 13:4-8a; I John 4:7-8, 5:3).*

Refer to:
DYING TO SELF BY SERVING OTHERS *(Lesson 10, Pages 7-8) and*
THE MEANING OF BIBLICAL LOVE *(Lesson 13, Pages 4-6).*

V.   **How are you as a believer to receive instruction and what are you to do as a result?**

A.   Receive the Word with humility *(James 1:21);*

B.   Hold fast to the word of life *(Philippians 2:12-16, esp. verse 16);*

C.   Share all good things with those who teach you *(Galatians 6:6);*

D.   Esteem very highly those who have charge over you and give you instruction *(I Thessalonians 5:12-13);*

E.   Keep instruction in your heart, and do not let it depart from you *(Proverbs 4:20-21);*

F.   Pay serious attention to (heed) instruction, not neglecting it, that you may be wise and blessed *(Proverbs 8:32-35);*

G.   Leave the presence of fools, because they do not speak words of knowledge *(Proverbs 14:7);*

H.   As a wise man, consider your steps, not naively believing everything or everyone, as do the simple (those who have no reverence for God) *(Psalm 19:7; Proverbs 14:15; I John 4:1);* and

I.   Be a doer of the Word in order to receive the blessings of the Lord *(Matthew 7:24-27; James 1:22-25).*

VI.   **How are you to instruct your children?**

A.   You must live as an example of a believer *(based on I Corinthians 11:1; Ephesians 4:1-3; Colossians 2:6-7; I Timothy 4:12),* demonstrating biblical love at all times *(based on I Corinthians 13:4-8a; John 13:34-35; I John 4:7-8).*

B.   You are to be diligent to instruct your children at all times and in every situation *(based on Deuteronomy 6:7, 11:19).*

C.   Your attitude toward your children is to be one of servanthood (i.e., considering them as more important than yourself) *(Philippians 2:3-8)* without arrogantly imposing your authority over them *(as exemplified through Jesus' washing of the disciples' feet in John 13:12-17 and demonstrated by Paul in his care and teaching of others in I Thessalonians 2:6-8).*

D. You are to teach them without hypocrisy, not using flattering speech to manipulate them or to gain your own selfish ends *(based on Romans 12:9; I Thessalonians 2:1-8, esp. verse 5)*.

E. You are not to seek glory for yourself as you instruct your children, but you are to give glory to the Lord through your life and your instruction *(Psalm 115:1; I Corinthians 10:31)*.

F. You are to refrain from quarreling but instead are to be kind, patient even when wronged, and gentle when you correct your children *(based on II Timothy 2:24-25, 4:2)*. As tenderly as a nursing mother and with fond affection, you are to impart your very life as well as the Word of God to your children *(I Thessalonians 2:7-8)*.

G. You are to train your children to be fruitful disciples of Christ *(based on Matthew 28:19-20; Ephesians 6:4b)*. Remember that all of the scriptural principles that apply to your ministry to others also apply for the instruction of your children.

1. To bring up your children in God's way, your sole authority is God's Word *(II Timothy 3:16-17; Hebrews 4:12; II Peter 1:3-4)*; and you are to follow the example set forth by the Lord Jesus Christ *(based on John 13:12-17, esp. verse 15; Ephesians 5:1-2; Hebrews 5:8-9, 12:1-3; I Peter 2:21-24, esp. verse 21)*.

2. For each activity or responsibility that your child is to do, instruct them as follows:

    a. From God's Word, give your children clear teaching about God's view of life, what people are to do in response to the Lord, and what He can accomplish in the lives of individuals (i.e., show them why they should obey) *(as exemplified by Jesus' call of His disciples in Matthew 4:18-22, 9:9-13; Mark 1:16-17; Luke 5:1-10; John 1:35-51)*.

    b. Show your children how to obey God's Word through your example; help them in every new situation *(based on the example of Jesus' training of His disciples in Matthew 8:18-27; Mark 3:20-6:6; John 13:3-12)*.

    c. For each activity, train your children to make plans for obedience to God's Word and then to be faithful in putting these plans into practice *(based on the example of Jesus having His disciples minister with Him and then commissioning them to leave and minister in other locations without Him, as seen in Matthew 10:1-11:1; Mark 6:7-13; Luke 9:1-6)*.

    d. After your children begin to carry out their responsibilities, oversee their work and give them help as necessary to encourage them in God's way *(based on Jesus' example of giving His disciples help with their questions and difficulties in Matthew 14:13-21; Mark 6:45-52, 7:17-23, 9:14-29)*.

    e. After your children have begun to be established in a biblical pattern of life, challenge, encourage, teach and help them seek opportunities to disciple others *(based on Jesus' commands and training of His disciples in Matthew 28:19-20; Mark 16:15-18; John 20:21, 21:14-22; Acts 1:8)*.

LESSON 16: HOMEWORK

> This week's **HOMEWORK** presents God's plan for parents and children to live together in a manner that pleases the Lord. In addition, common errors that parents make in bringing up their children are highlighted *(based on Deuteronomy 6:6-7; Proverbs 6:23, 22:6; Matthew 7:1-5; I Corinthians 13:4-8a; Ephesians 6:1-4; Colossians 3:12-21).*

✔ *homework completed*

☐ A. * In your own words, write the meaning of *Ezekiel 18:20* and *Ephesians 6:4.* Memorize *Ezekiel 18:20* and *Ephesians 6:4* and begin memorizing *Ephesians 6:1-3.* Review previous memory verses.

☐ B. * Read **BIBLICAL PRINCIPLES: PARENT-CHILD RELATIONSHIPS (PART ONE)** (Lesson 16, Page 2). Note the applicability of principles and verses presented in earlier studies. As you study the new principles, highlight the listed verses in your Bible.

☐ C. * Study **MAN'S THEORIES AND PRACTICES FOR REARING CHILDREN** (Lesson 16, Pages 3-6), and evaluate your own beliefs and practices in rearing your own children. Place a check mark by any unbiblical theories or practices you need to put off.

☐ D. * Study **GUIDELINES FOR TRAINING CHILDREN** (Lesson 16, Pages 7-9). Observe how biblical parent-child relationships are dependent on commitments to the Lord and to one another. In areas of needed biblical change, use the **VICTORY OVER FAILURES WORKSHEET** (Supplement 8). Refer to **GUIDELINES: VICTORY OVER FAILURES WORKSHEET** (Supplement 7) if necessary.

☐ E. * Read **WAYS THAT PARENTS PROVOKE THEIR CHILDREN TO ANGER** (Lesson 16, Pages 10-12). If you are a parent, place a check beside the statements that deal with areas in which you have failed. Confess these sins to the Lord. Then, as applicable, confess them to your child by following the guidelines in **OVERCOMING INTERPERSONAL PROBLEMS** (Lesson 13, Pages 19-23).

☐ F. * Read **UNDERSTANDING BIBLICAL INSTRUCTION OF CHILDREN** (Lesson 16, Pages 13-16). Note that biblical instruction is designed to teach us to follow God's way instead of man's way. Especially study Jesus' methods of training His disciples.

Select a task that your child should carry out on a continuing basis (for example, memorizing Scripture, household chores, helping others in your church or neighborhood). Then, establish a plan for training your child following the steps of training that Jesus used in training His disciples.

☐ G. * In conjunction with this lesson, begin to answer question 25 under **Open Book Test** (Lesson 23, Page 3).

*   *The completion of assignments marked with an asterisk (*) is a prerequisite for further biblical counseling training.*

LESSON 16: STUDY GUIDE FOR DAILY DEVOTIONS
(INCLUDING SCRIPTURE MEMORY AND HOMEWORK)

> This week's **STUDY GUIDE** presents God's plan for parents and children to live together in a manner that pleases the Lord. In addition, common errors that parents make in bringing up their children are highlighted *(based on Deuteronomy 6:6-7; Proverbs 6:23, 22:6; Matthew 7:1-5; I Corinthians 13:4-8a; Ephesians 6:1-4; Colossians 3:12-21).*

Scripture Memory

1. * Memorize *Ezekiel 18:20* and *Ephesians 6:4*. Begin memorizing *Ephesians 6:1-3*.
2. Carry your memory verse cards from previous weeks along with this week's memory verses. Review your memory verses in spare moments throughout the day.

Daily Devotional Study Guide

FIRST DAY

1. Open with prayer.
2. * Read *Principle 69* under **BIBLICAL PRINCIPLES: PARENT-CHILD RELATIONSHIPS (PART ONE)** (Lesson 16, Page 2). Highlight the listed verses in your Bible.
3. Read **MAN'S THEORIES AND PRACTICES FOR REARING CHILDREN** (Lesson 16, Pages 3-6) and evaluate your own beliefs and practices in rearing your children. Place a check mark by any unbiblical theories or practices you need to put off.
4. * Write the meaning of *Ezekiel 18:20* and *Ephesians 6:4* in your own words.
5. Close with prayer.

SECOND DAY

1. Open with prayer.
2. * Read *Principle 70* under **BIBLICAL PRINCIPLES: PARENT-CHILD RELATIONSHIPS (PART ONE)** (Lesson 16, Page 2). Highlight the listed verses in your Bible if you have not already done so.
3. * Study **GUIDELINES FOR TRAINING CHILDREN** (Lesson 16, Pages 7-9). Note how biblical parent-child relationships are dependent on commitments to the Lord and to one another. This is the first day of a two-day study.
4. Close with prayer.

THIRD DAY

1. Open with prayer.
2. * Read *Principle 47, revised,* under **BIBLICAL PRINCIPLES: PARENT-CHILD RELATIONSHIPS (PART ONE)** (Lesson 16, Page 2). Highlight the listed verses in your Bible.
3. * Complete your study of **GUIDELINES FOR TRAINING YOUR CHILDREN** (Lesson 16, Pages 7-9). In areas of needed biblical change, use the **VICTORY OVER FAILURES WORKSHEET** (Supplement 8). Refer to **GUIDELINES: VICTORY OVER FAILURES WORKSHEET** (Supplement 7) if necessary.
4. Close with prayer.

FOURTH DAY

1. Open with prayer.
2. * Read *Principle 71* under **BIBLICAL PRINCIPLES: PARENT-CHILD RELATIONSHIPS (PART ONE)** (Lesson 16, Page 2) Highlight the listed verses in your Bible.
3. * Read **WAYS THAT PARENTS PROVOKE THEIR CHILDREN TO ANGER** (Lesson 16, Pages 10-12). If you are a parent, place a check beside the statements that deal with areas in which you have failed. Confess these sins to the Lord. Then, set aside a specific time to confess these wrongs to your child by following the guidelines in **OVERCOMING INTERPERSONAL PROBLEMS** (Lesson 13, Pages 19-23).
4. Close with prayer.

FIFTH DAY

1. Open with prayer.
2. * Read *Principle 72* under **BIBLICAL PRINCIPLES: PARENT-CHILD RELATIONSHIPS (PART ONE)** (Lesson 16, Page 2). Highlight the listed verses in your Bible.
3. * Study **UNDERSTANDING BIBLICAL INSTRUCTION OF CHILDREN** (Lesson 16, Pages 13-16). This is the first day of a two-day study. Observe that biblical instruction is designed to teach you to follow God's way instead of man's way. If you are a parent, place a check beside each statement which describes a way that you are failing to instruct your child in a biblical manner.
4. Close with prayer.

SIXTH DAY

1. Open with prayer.
2. * Complete your study of **UNDERSTANDING BIBLICAL INSTRUCTION OF CHILDREN** (Lesson 16, Pages 13-16). Refer to the statements that you checked yesterday and develop a biblical plan to overcome your failures in giving biblical instruction. Then, set aside a specific time with your children to explain your new plan for providing them with biblical instruction.
3. Close with prayer.

SEVENTH DAY

1. Open with prayer.
2. Study *Hebrews 12:4-11*, which outlines God's purpose for discipline.
3. Select a task that your child should carry out on a continuing basis (for example, memorizing Scripture, household chores, helping others in your church or neighborhood). Then, establish a plan for training your child following the steps of training that Jesus used in training His disciples.
4. * In conjunction with this lesson, begin to answer question 25 under **Open Book Test** (Lesson 23, Page 3).
5. Close in prayer.
6. Ask a friend to listen to you recite this week's memory verses. Explain how these verses have application to your life.

*   *The completion of assignments marked with an asterisk (*) is a prerequisite for further biblical counseling training.*

LESSON 17

PARENT-CHILD RELATIONSHIPS
(PART TWO)

"Children, obey your parents in the Lord, for this is right. Honor your father and mother (which is the first commandment with a promise), that it may be well with you, and that you may live long on the earth."

Ephesians 6:1-3

LESSON 17: PARENT-CHILD RELATIONSHIPS (PART TWO)

> God has set forth His standards clearly and specifically throughout Scripture. If you and every member of your family will live according to them, you will all receive the blessings of the Lord. On the other hand, those neglecting or disobeying God's standards will receive His judgment resulting in corrective discipline *(based on Ecclesiastes 12:13-14; Matthew 5:2-12; Luke 11:28; John 13:12-17; I Corinthians 11:31-32; Hebrews 12:5-11; James 1:22-25).*

I. **The purposes of this lesson are:**

A. To present principles of biblical discipleship in the home;

B. To review the necessity for parents to discipline their children in a biblical manner;

C. To introduce guidelines and suggestions for family devotions; and

D. To provide a comprehensive, biblical plan for raising children in the instruction and discipline of the Lord.

II. **The outline of this lesson**

A. Self-confrontation

1. **BIBLICAL PRINCIPLES: PARENT-CHILD RELATIONSHIPS (PART TWO)** (Lesson 17, Pages 2-3)

2. **TRAINING CHILDREN TO BE FAITHFUL (BIBLICAL DISCIPLESHIP IN THE HOME)** (Lesson 17, Pages 4-7)

3. **UNDERSTANDING BIBLICAL DISCIPLINE** (Lesson 17, Pages 8-10)

4. **AN OVERALL PLAN FOR REARING CHILDREN** (Lesson 17, Pages 16-21)

B. Steps for spiritual growth

1. **FAMILY DEVOTIONS AND WORSHIP (GUIDELINES & SUGGESTIONS)** (Lesson 17, Pages 11-15)

2. **LESSON 17: HOMEWORK** (Lesson 17, Page 22)

3. **STUDY GUIDE FOR DAILY DEVOTIONS** (Lesson 17, Pages 23-24)

C. Biblical counseling

(Case study resumes in Lesson 18)

BIBLICAL PRINCIPLES: PARENT-CHILD RELATIONSHIPS
(PART TWO)

> God's standards and goals are the same for you and your children. They are revealed in God's Word and are designed to develop Christlike character in you and in every member of your family *(based on Isaiah 55:8-11; Luke 6:40; Romans 8:29; II Timothy 3:16-17; I Peter 1:14-16; II Peter 1:3-10).*

III. Your Change (continued from Lesson 16, Page 2)

(Principle 73)   Parents, stop provoking your children *(Ephesians 6:4; Colossians 3:21)* but instead provide them with discipline and instruction in the Lord *(Deuteronomy 6:6-7; Ephesians 6:4)*. While continuing to judge yourself in all areas of life *(Matthew 7:1-5)*, you are to train your children *(Proverbs 22:6; Ephesians 6:4)* to delight in the Lord and to walk faithfully in His ways *(based on Psalm 1:1-6; Ephesians 4:1-3; II Timothy 3:14-17).*

(Principle 74)   As parents, you are to serve your children lovingly *(based on Philippians 2:3-4)* through your faithful biblical teaching and discipline *(based on Deuteronomy 4:9, 6:4-9; I Corinthians 4:14-16, 11:1; Philippians 3:15-17; II Thessalonians 3:7)* in order to train up your children in the ways of the Lord *(based on Proverbs 4:1-4, 22:6; Ephesians 6:4)*. You are not to insist on your children's obedience merely on the basis of your parental authority, nor are you to rely upon any adequacy as coming from yourself. Rather, you are to minister to your children faithfully as a servant of the Lord Jesus Christ *(based on John 13:12-17; II Corinthians 3:5-6).*

(Principle 75)   Children, you are to learn from your parents willingly as they teach you the precepts, the principles, and the ways of the Lord *(Proverbs 1:2-5, 2:1-9, 6:20-23)*. You are to heed as from the Lord the teaching, reproof, and discipline from your parents and other spiritually mature individuals. In doing this, you will gain wisdom and will not be ensnared by the deceit or wickedness of others and their false ways *(based on Proverbs 2:10-15, 3:13-26, 4:10-27, 5:1-23, 13:1, 20:11; Colossians 1:9-12)*. Put off being wise in your own eyes *(Proverbs 12:15, 21:2)* and put on the fear (reverence) and love of the Lord that results from being obedient to His Word *(Psalm 111:10; Proverbs 3:5-7; John 14:15, 21; I John 5:3)*. In addition, put off abandoning or neglecting the teaching of your parents and put on heeding their teaching and reproof *(based on Proverbs 4:1-6, 15:32-33, 19:26; Ephesians 6:1; Colossians 3:20).*

(Principle 4, revised from Lesson 3, Page 2)   Whether you are a parent or a child, God's Word is to be your only authority for faith and conduct and is to be the only legitimate standard by which you are evaluated. You are to rely on no other source, since God's Word provides hope and gives direction for change in all areas of your life (thoughts, speech, and actions). Scripture is adequate to equip you to be the kind of parent, or the kind of child, you ought to be *(based on Psalm 19:7-11; Proverbs 30:5-6; Colossians 2:8; II Timothy 3:16-17; Hebrews 4:12; II Peter 1:3-4)*. As you are obedient to God's Word, a Christlike attitude of servanthood will develop within you toward your family members and others *(based on Matthew 20:25-28; John 13:12-17; Philippians 2:3-8; I Thessalonians 2:13)*.

IV. Your practice

(Principle 76)   Based on God's standards for life as revealed in His Word *(Psalm 19:7-11; 119:105, 160; II Timothy 3:16-17; II Peter 1:3-4)*, you, as a parent, are to determine biblical responsibilities and tasks that will lead you and your children to discipline yourselves toward godliness *(based on I Timothy 4:7-8; II Peter 1:3-10)*, resulting in glory to God *(based on Psalm 29:1-2, 145:10-13; Matthew 5:16; I Peter 1:7)*.

(Principle 77)   Even though you may not yet be an adult, you are to live in a manner that is pleasing to the Lord as you seek to be an example of a godly believer *(based on Proverbs 20:11; Colossians 1:10; I Timothy 4:12)*. Stubbornness and rebellion are not to be part of your life as you continuously honor and obey your parents *(based on Ephesians 6:1-2; Philippians 2:14-16; Colossians 3:20)*. Be a good steward, even in your youth, of all the Lord has provided you in order to demonstrate your faithfulness to Him *(based on I Corinthians 4:2; Colossians 3:23-24)*.

TRAINING CHILDREN TO BE FAITHFUL
(BIBLICAL DISCIPLESHIP IN THE HOME)

> As parents, you may confidently rear your children according to God's Word. While bringing up your children, you are to remember that your children are not your "possessions" but instead are the Lord's gift to you. You are to exercise faithful stewardship in their lives *(based on Psalm 19:7-11, 24:1, 127:3-5a; Proverbs 22:6; Ezekiel 18:4, 20; I Corinthians 4:2; Ephesians 6:4; I Thessalonians 2:3-13).*

I. **Principles for training children to be faithful to the Lord**

As you rear your children, remember that you are bringing them up to live as individuals who will walk in a manner worthy of the Lord and to please Him in all respects *(Proverbs 20:11, 22:6; Ephesians 6:4; Colossians 1:10).* In order to train your children to be faithful to the Lord:

A. You must teach and lead them in the way they should live, which is not in the way they are "naturally" inclined *(Psalm 14:2-3; Proverbs 22:15a; Jeremiah 17:9; Romans 3:10-12).* Because every individual is born with a sin nature *(based on Psalm 51:5; Proverbs 20:9; Romans 3:23, 5:12-14),* your children must first be regenerated (have a spiritual new birth) *(John 1:12, 3:16-18; Acts 4:12; Romans 6:23; I John 5:11-13);* and then, in the power of the Holy Spirit, they are to walk in the way of the Lord *(Romans 8:1-10; Colossians 1:10, 2:6-7; I John 2:3-6).* This means that:

   1. You are not to look to any worldly source for guidance in training up your children. Your commitment to the Word of God must remain unwavering, since Scripture gives true wisdom for the training of your children *(based on Isaiah 55:8-11; Jeremiah 29:11-14a; II Timothy 3:14-17; James 1:5, 22-25; I John 5:14).*

   2. You must recognize that you are not the ultimate authority in the lives of your children. They are the Lord's gift to you, for your temporary stewardship *(based on Psalm 24:1, 127:3; Ezekiel 18:4).* You are to help your children recognize their need for becoming children of God through salvation *(based on Romans 6:23; II Corinthians 5:14-21)* which will lead them to live in obedience to God's Word *(based on Luke 11:28; John 14:23-24; I Corinthians 2:9-12; II Peter 1:3-10).*

   3. Regardless of how much you love your children, you must recognize that God the Father loves them far more *(based on John 3:16; Romans 5:8).* For your believing children:

      a. He works together all circumstances, relationships, and things in their lives for their good *(based on Jeremiah 29:11-14a; Romans 8:28-29).*

      b. No matter how much you may desire to keep adversity from them, your responsibility is to teach your children to expect trials *(I Peter 4:12-13),* to rejoice in the midst of them *(James 1:2-4),* and to grow into Christlikeness through these tests as they learn obedience through faithfulness *(Romans 5:3-5; James 1:2-4).*

      c. Remind your children that the Lord is continually strengthening each one of them to keep them from sinning *(based on Psalm 121; I Corinthians 10:13; II Thessalonians 3:3; I Peter 1:3-9; Jude 1:24-25).*

B. You must keep in mind that, from their formation, God has given each of your children different abilities and talents according to His sovereignty *(based on Psalm 139:13-16)*. A child who has experienced a spiritual new birth has also been given at least one spiritual gift to be used in ministry for the Lord *(Romans 12:3-8, esp. verse 6a; I Corinthians 12:4-7, 11)*. You must deal with the training of each of your children according to:

    1. The way that God has worked in the life of each child *(based on Proverbs 22:6)*; and

    2. Each child's trust in the Lord for salvation *(John 1:12, 3:36; I Peter 1:3-5; I John 5:11-13)*, which will be demonstrated by faithful and loving obedience to God's Word *(based on I Samuel 15:22-23a; Psalm 112:1; John 14:15, 21; James 1:22; I John 5:3)*.

C. You are to teach your children to deny themselves daily *(Luke 9:23-25)*, to live a life of selfless dedication to the glory of the Lord *(based on Matthew 5:16; John 3:27-36, esp. verse 30; I Corinthians 10:31; Colossians 1:10; I Peter 2:12)*, and to build up others for their good *(based on Matthew 28:19-20; Romans 14:13, 19; 15:1-2; Galatians 5:13-14; 6:2, 10; Ephesians 4:15-16; Hebrews 10:23-25)*. This biblical training goes contrary to the teaching of the world, which highlights a "love for self." For this reason,

    1. You must stay alert and use every opportunity to teach your children the ways of the Lord *(Deuteronomy 6:6-9; Proverbs 25:11-12)*; and

    2. You must help them to be strong in the Lord and to stand firm against the things of the world *(I John 2:15-17)* and of Satan, who seeks to defeat them and accuses them at all times *(Ephesians 6:10-11; I Peter 5:8-9; Revelation 12:10)*.

II. **Areas of your children's lives in which biblical training is necessary through your example, instruction, and discipline**

A. In their personal lives, you must train your children through example, teaching, encouragement, support, reproof, and discipline. For example:

    1. In the area of commitment,

       a. You are to be one of the primary means by which the Good News of Jesus Christ is presented to your children, out of a deep concern for their salvation *(based on Matthew 28:19; Acts 1:8; II Corinthians 5:14-21; Ephesians 6:4)*.

       b. You are continuously to teach them God's Word and to encourage them to practice it so they, as living sacrifices to the Lord, can walk in a manner worthy of Him *(based on Deuteronomy 6:6-9; Matthew 28:20; Romans 12:1-2; Ephesians 4:1; Colossians 1:10)*. You can do this as you:

          1) Teach your children how to have a daily personal time of devotions.

          For further help in this area, refer to: **BIBLICAL BASIS FOR DAILY DEVOTIONS AND SCRIPTURE MEMORY** *(Lesson 2, Pages 9-11)*.

          2) Teach your children God's Word and its practice through the avenue of family devotions and worship

          For further help, refer to: **FAMILY DEVOTIONS AND WORSHIP (GUIDELINES AND SUGGESTIONS)** *(Lesson 17, Pages 11-15)*.

          3) Help your children begin to develop the habit of Scripture memory.

          For further help in this area, refer to: **FOUR PLANS FOR MEMORIZING SCRIPTURE** *(Lesson 2, Pages 12-13)*.

          4) Teach your children to pray on a regular basis by praying with them in the morning, at mealtimes, at bedtime, and during the day when prayer matters or needs arise, etc.

Refer to: PRAYER PROVIDES COMMUNICATION WITH GOD (Lesson 3, Pages 9-12).

5) Give your children a solid foundation for knowledge of the Scriptures by your example and by teaching them how to study God's Word for themselves

Refer to:
BIBLE STUDY AND APPLICATION FORMAT (Supplement 3) and HOW TO USE A CONCORDANCE (Supplement 5); and

6) Teach your children the importance of assembling with other believers for worship, hearing the Scriptures preached, fellowship, Bible study, and prayer. This can be accomplished through worship services, house churches, Bible study groups, home care groups, etc.

Refer to:
BIBLICAL PRINCIPLES OF STEWARDSHIP (Lesson 10, Pages 4-6) and DYING TO SELF BY SERVING OTHERS (Lesson 10, Pages 7-8).

2. In the daily practices of life, you are to teach your children to accept responsibilities and complete tasks faithfully, regardless of their feelings. Teach your believing children to please and glorify the Lord *(Psalm 115:1; II Corinthians 5:9)* and not be men-(parent-)pleasers *(based on Galatians 1:10; Ephesians 6:6-8; I Thessalonians 2:4)*. Use the following sample list to help instruct, train, and guide them in all their responsibilities. To do the above, they must learn:

a. The importance of diligently doing their work, such as household tasks or school homework *(based on I Thessalonians 4:10b-12; II Thessalonians 3:10-13).*

b. To be good stewards of all that has been entrusted to them in the following ways:

1) Using their time wisely in order to fulfill necessary tasks, to have recreational (playtime) activities, and to enjoy fellowship with the family and friends *(based on Ephesians 5:15-16);*

2) Caring for and disciplining their bodies through proper nutrition, rest, exercise, cleanliness, dressing/grooming, and sexual purity *(based on I Corinthians 6:12-20; I Thessalonians 4:3-7);*

3) Managing and caring for their material goods (such as tools, toys, household goods, money, and other personal and family items) in an unselfish manner *(based on Luke 16:10-13; II Corinthians 8:1-5; Philippians 2:3-4, 4:11-13; I Timothy 6:6, 17-19; James 2:15-16).*

Refer to: BIBLICAL PRINCIPLES OF STEWARDSHIP (Lesson 10, Pages 4-6);

4) Using their abilities (such as those used in helping parents and others with tasks), talents (such as those involving musical instruments, singing, speaking, sports, etc.), and spiritual gifts (such as helps, mercy, giving, teaching, etc.) to benefit and build up others instead of furthering their own self-centered interests or desires *(based on Matthew 25:14-30; Luke 9:23-24, 12:13-48, 16:10-13; Romans 14:19, 15:1-2; I Corinthians 4:1-2; Ephesians 5:15-17; I Peter 4:10).*

For further help, refer to:
PLEASING SELF OR PLEASING GOD (Lesson 9, Pages 10-11) and DYING TO SELF BY SERVING OTHERS (Lesson 10, Pages 7-8).

B. In their interpersonal relationships, you are to train your children to:

1. Obey and honor their parents *(Ephesians 6:1-3; Colossians 3:20);*

2. Be subject to and respectful of all authorities, at church, at school, and wherever they are *(based on Romans 13:1-5; Ephesians 6:1-8; I Peter 2:11-25)*;

3. Care for and help their brothers and sisters *(based on Matthew 22:37-39, esp. verse 39; Romans 12:9-21, 14:19, 15:1-2; I Corinthians 13:4-8a; Philippians 2:3-4; II Timothy 2:24-26)*;

4. Face interpersonal problems regularly and deal with them by first judging self, then forgiving others and seeking reconciliation *(based on Matthew 5:23-24, 7:1-5; Mark 11:25-26)*;

5. Serve others at home and within the church *(based on Galatians 6:10; Philippians 2:3-8)*;

6. Live as ambassadors of Jesus Christ before all others *(II Corinthians 5:20)*, since their lives are to be salt and light *(Matthew 5:13-16)* and a sweet aroma of Jesus Christ to everyone *(II Corinthians 2:14-17)*; and

7. Be at peace with all men, as far as it depends on them (your children) *(based on Romans 12:18)*.

UNDERSTANDING BIBLICAL DISCIPLINE

> Faithfully disciplining (training, educating, correcting) your child in a manner that pleases the Lord is an expression of biblical love. It also is a step of obedience for you as a parent and provides godly direction for your child *(based on Proverbs 13:24, 19:18, 23:13; Hebrews 12:5-13).*

I. What does discipline mean?

God's Word emphasizes that the purpose of biblical discipline is to teach one to follow God's way instead of man's way *(Hebrews 12:9-11)*. In the Old Testament, the primary word translated "discipline" is almost as frequently rendered "instruction." In the New Testament, the primary word translated "discipline" is also rendered "train" or "correct."

II. Why is discipline necessary?

A. Reproofs for discipline are God's way of keeping you and your children from straying into further sin and disobedience *(Psalm 119:67; Proverbs 5:23, 6:23, 10:17).*

B. God's discipline, which is often applied through parents to children, is for the good of individuals *(based on Hebrews 12:10)*. It keeps them from being condemned along with the world *(I Corinthians 11:32)* and produces righteous character in those who are trained by it *(Hebrews 12:10-11).*

C. Since parents are directed by God to discipline their children *(Proverbs 23:13; Ephesians 6:4)*, failing to do so is sin *(James 4:17).*

D. Without discipline, the foolishness of a child will lead to his poverty, shame, and a self-centered way of life that will bring shame to his parents *(Proverbs 13:18, 22:15, 29:15).*

III. How and when is discipline carried out?

Parental discipline is to be carried out in love *(based on Proverbs 13:24; I Corinthians 13:4-8a)*, following the example of God's loving discipline of His children. Since biblical discipline is designed to produce Christlike character *(Hebrews 12:10-11)*, parents are to practice the following:

A. Ask for God's wisdom and study His Word diligently as you make decisions on the specifics of discipline *(based on II Timothy 2:15, 3:16-17; James 1:5)*. Establish simple, clear-cut guidelines as God did in directing His people *(based on Genesis 2:16-17; Exodus 20:3-17; Deuteronomy 11:26-28).*

B. Clearly explain biblically-based standards of conduct to avoid confusion or misunderstandings *(based on Exodus 31:18, 34:1; Deuteronomy 4:13-14; Matthew 22:37-39; John 14:15).*

C. Explain the blessings of obedience *(based on Psalm 18:20-36; Matthew 5:3-12; Hebrews 5:14, 12:11; James 1:25)* and the discipline and consequences of disobedience *(based on Deuteronomy 11:26-28; Proverbs 3:12; Matthew 7:26-27; I Corinthians 11:31-32; Colossians

3:25; Hebrews 12:5-11). Remind your children that God will use trials to develop Christlike character in their lives (James 1:2-4).

D. When your children disobey, lovingly explain exactly how they disobeyed Scripture and what they are to do instead (based on Deuteronomy 6:6-7; I Corinthians 13:4-8a; Galatians 6:1-2; Colossians 3:5-17; II Timothy 3:16-17), since the purpose of discipline is restoration (based on Hebrews 12:4-13).

    1. According to your children's level of maturity and understanding (both physically and spiritually), encourage them to learn God's solutions for their current failure and begin again to do the Word (based on I Corinthians 11:31; Ephesians 6:4; II Timothy 2:15; James 1:22-25). Also, teach them to confess their sins to the Lord (I John 1:9) and to others (James 5:16a).

    2. Discipline must only become increasingly stern to turn the unrepentant one from ultimate destruction (based on Proverbs 15:10, 23:13-14). Discipline is to be done while there is still hope (Proverbs 19:18), and it is to be carried out quickly (Ecclesiastes 8:11).

    Note: If your child chooses not to repent, remember that throughout the discipline process you are to: (1) judge yourself biblically, (2) forgive him from your heart, and (3) reprove him in a spirit of gentleness.

      a. Stern discipline is specifically designed for children exhibiting foolishness (based on Proverbs 14:3, 22:15, 26:3). A child behaving in a foolish manner lacks understanding and:

        1) Uses words that are quarrelsome (Proverbs 20:3), perverse (Proverbs 19:1), ruinous (Proverbs 10:14), and slanderous (Proverbs 10:18);

        2) Displays and repeats his folly (Proverbs 13:16, 26:11), mocks at sin (Proverbs 14:9), and treats wickedness as a sport (Proverbs 10:23);

        3) Is quick-tempered (Proverbs 14:17, 29:11) and has a heart for anger (Ecclesiastes 7:9);

        4) Bases his authority in himself (Proverbs 12:15, 28:26);

        5) Despises wisdom and instruction (Proverbs 1:7), hates knowledge (Proverbs 1:22), and has no delight in understanding but only in revealing his own mind (Proverbs 18:2);

        6) Is arrogant and careless (Proverbs 14:16), displays dishonor (Proverbs 3:35), is deceitful (Proverbs 14:8); and

        7) Despises his mother (Proverbs 15:20), rejects parental discipline (Proverbs 15:5), and is a grief to his parents (Proverbs 10:1, 17:25).

      b. The sternest of parental discipline is the "rod" (Proverbs 23:13-14), which is to be applied to a child who lacks understanding (based on Proverbs 10:13) and is in need of wisdom (based on Proverbs 29:15).

      c. Since discipline produces sorrow (Hebrews 12:11), reaffirm your love after disciplining your children. If your child repents of his wrongdoings, exercise gracious compassion as God does for those who sin and repent (based on Psalm 103:10-14). Such compassion follows the example of God dealing with His children (Lamentations 3:32; II Corinthians 1:3-4) and also exemplifies the pattern of biblical restoration (II Corinthians 2:6-8).

E. Biblically evaluate your discipline with each child and modify your plans accordingly (based on Proverbs 3:5-6; 16:9; II Timothy 2:15, 3:16-17; James 1:5).

F. Since parental discipline of children is not to be associated with anger *(Ephesians 4:31-32, 6:4; Colossians 3:8)*, parents must confess to their children if they sin against them in this manner *(James 5:16)*. After confessing sin, parents must then take other necessary steps to be reconciled biblically with their children *(Matthew 5:23-24; Mark 11:25-26; Romans 12:18)*. *Even when parents seek reconciliation for a sinful manner in which they have disciplined their children in the past, discipline still must be administered, as necessary, in the present.*

Refer also to: **RECONCILIATION (REMOVING ALL HINDRANCES TO UNITY AND PEACE)** *(Lesson 12, Pages 6-8)* under **II. Confession.**

IV. What does discipline reveal?

A. A love of discipline reveals those who love true knowledge *(Proverbs 12:1)*. A rejection of discipline also reveals those who are fools *(Proverbs 1:7, 15:5)*.

B. God's discipline of His children reveals the depth of His love, because He Himself initiates their restoration *(Proverbs 3:12; Lamentations 3:32; Hebrews 12:6-8; Revelation 3:19)*. Likewise, parents exercising biblical discipline of a child reveal their love for the Lord and their child. By carrying out biblical discipline, a parent initiates and gives his child an example of loving restoration *(Proverbs 3:12, 13:24; Hebrews 12:5-11)*.

C. A parent who does not discipline his child reveals a hatred for him *(Proverbs 13:24)*.

V. What does discipline accomplish?

A. For the parent who carries out biblical discipline:

1. It provides the method by which disobedient children may be shown loving concern through restoration *(Proverbs 13:24, 19:18, 23:13-14)*;

2. It demonstrates love for the Lord and a desire to please Him, regardless of personal inconveniences or feelings you might experience *(based on John 14:15, 21; Ephesians 6:4; Colossians 1:9-10)*; and

3. It will lead you to have comfort and delight in your children who are trained by it *(Proverbs 29:17)*.

B. For the child who responds to it and is restored by it:

1. It yields the peaceful fruit of righteousness *(Hebrews 12:11)*;

2. It leads to holiness *(Hebrews 12:10)*;

3. It removes foolishness from his heart *(Proverbs 22:15)*;

4. It leads to prudence and understanding *(Proverbs 15:5, 32)*; and

5. It leads to respect for the parents *(Hebrews 12:9)*.

VI. Who is to receive discipline?

A. All children of God not faithful to His way are disciplined by the Lord *(Psalm 119:75; I Corinthians 11:29-32; Hebrews 12:5)*.

B. Disobedient children must be disciplined by their parents for their good, with a view to save them from destruction *(Proverbs 13:24, 19:18, 23:13-14)*.

FAMILY DEVOTIONS AND WORSHIP
(GUIDELINES AND SUGGESTIONS)

> In addition to teaching your children throughout the day, you must set aside specific, planned times to worship the Lord and learn His Word together. Conducting family devotions requires planning and diligence if this godly practice is to develop and be maintained in your home *(based on Deuteronomy 4:9; Psalm 95:6-7a, 145:1-7; Matthew 28:20a; John 4:23-24; Ephesians 5:15-17; Colossians 3:16; II Timothy 2:1-2, 3:14-15).*

I. **Matters to consider when planning family devotions**

   A. Because ages may vary widely among those at your family devotional times, ask the Lord to help you determine what will edify (build up) all involved *(based on Deuteronomy 6:6-7; Psalm 111:1-2, 119:30; Proverbs 1:2-9; Romans 15:1-2; Ephesians 4:29; Colossians 4:6; II Timothy 3:14-15; James 1:5).*

   B. Your family devotions should be times where teaching, praise, prayer, thanksgiving, fellowship, and encouragement take place *(based on Psalm 30:4, 33:1-3, 34:1-3; Colossians 3:16; I Thessalonians 5:16-18; Hebrews 10:24-25).*

   C. The family devotional times should teach your family to be devoted to the Lord and to one another *(similar to what happened among Christians in their homes in Acts 2:42-47, 4:32, 5:42).*

II. **Family devotions should contain all aspects of Christian development and expression**

   A. Praise *(Psalm 63:3-4)* and prayer *(Colossians 4:2)*

   1. Time should be designated for worship of the Lord by singing *(based on Ephesians 5:19; Colossians 3:16)* and speaking of His works and goodness *(based on Psalm 95:6-7a; Psalms 103, 104, and 147).*

   2. A portion of time is to be spent together in thanksgiving and intercession to the Lord for specific matters that affect individuals or the family as a whole *(based on Psalm 9:1-2; 142; Ephesians 5:19-20; Philippians 4:6-7; Colossians 4:2; I Thessalonians 5:16-18; James 5:13).*

   3. Spend time in prayer for others (government leaders, friends and teachers at school, neighbors, co-workers, your church leaders, fellow-believers in your church and community, believers in other countries, missionaries, etc.) *(based on Luke 10:2; Ephesians 6:18; Philippians 4:6-7; I Timothy 2:1-4; Hebrews 13:17-18).*

   B. Biblical instruction *(II Timothy 3:14-17)*

   1. God's Word should be studied in particular areas that are applicable to the entire family *(based on Proverbs 1:2-5; II Timothy 2:15).*

   For further assistance, refer to: **UNDERSTANDING BIBLICAL INSTRUCTION OF CHILDREN** *(Lesson 16, Pages 13-16).*

---

2. Scripture memory can be encouraged and demonstrated, with specific emphasis given to needful areas of personal or family spiritual development *(based on Psalm 119:11, 16)*.

3. When necessary and appropriate, teaching and admonishing one another should occur *(based on Matthew 7:1-5; Galatians 6:1-2; Colossians 3:16)*.

C. Fellowship *(I John 1:7)* and ministry *(I Peter 4:10)*

1. As fellow-servants of Jesus Christ *(Matthew 20:25-28; John 13:12-17)*, take time to encourage one another *(Hebrews 10:23-25)*, build up one another *(Romans 14:19, 15:1-2; Ephesians 4:29)*, confess any sins committed against one another *(James 5:16a)*, and forgive one another *(Mark 11:25-26; Ephesians 4:32)*.

2. Develop plans and follow them to help those in need *(based on II Corinthians 8:1-5, 12:15; James 1:27, 2:15-17)*.

3. Determine how your family can become personally involved in proclaiming the Good News of Jesus Christ both at home and abroad *(based on Matthew 28:18-20; Luke 10:2; Acts 1:8; I Peter 3:15)*.

4. Take time to plan for each individual's ministry and service to others as well as to plan for areas of family ministry together *(based on Romans 12:3-6a, 14:19; Ephesians 5:15-17; Hebrews 10:24-25; I Peter 4:10)*.

III. When family devotional times should take place

A. Decide upon a regular time so that all family members may plan their activities and responsibilities around this time *(based on Luke 14:28-30; Ephesians 5:15-17)*. For help in planning family devotions and worship, several suggestions follow:

1. Plan family devotions to take place at the end of a meal when the maximum number of family members may be present (usually, the morning or evening is best).

2. Plan family devotions at a time when all family members are alert and when most are free from other conflicts in schedule (for example, you may want to avoid having family devotions when young children are ready for bed and sleepy).

3. Plan reasonable amounts of time for family devotions and worship, but leave enough time at the end to allow for extra participation as needed or desired (for example, times spent in singing, in giving testimony, or in prayer may last much longer than devotions centered around study, especially for families with young children).

4. Choose days and times that are not hurried or rushed so that all may be given the opportunity to be diligent without distractions.

5. Have family devotions and worship while walking, hiking, or riding together outdoors, using God's creation to teach of His glory and majesty.

B. Family devotional times are sometimes difficult to maintain and may not occur under some circumstances (i.e., illness, emergencies, other opportunities for service, unbelieving family members prohibit it, etc.) Remember that family devotional times are not to become a legalistic requirement for spiritual growth *(based on II Corinthians 3:6)*. Family devotional times are simply to provide further opportunities for each believing family member to worship God in spirit and truth *(based on John 4:23-24)*, to build up one another in love *(Ephesians 4:14-16, esp. verse 16)*, and to serve the Lord by serving one another *(based on Romans 12:9-13)*.

IV. **Suggested topics and activities for family devotions and worship**

    A.   Family devotions that are centered around the study of God's Word should be applicable to all family members and to areas where the Lord is currently working in your lives *(based on Psalm 145:14; Philippians 1:6, 9-11; 2:12-13; Colossians 1:9-12; I Peter 3:15)*. Some examples follow:

        1.   Study how God dealt with different individuals in Scripture who faced problems (persecution, danger, temptation, etc.) and difficult decisions (whether to obey God or gain worldly prestige, whether to be faithful or follow sensual desires, whether to trust God or rely on natural wisdom and strength, etc.) This type of study is particularly useful when your family is dealing with similar problems.

        2.   Use this *Self-Confrontation* manual as a basis for doing topical studies on overcoming problems.

        3.   Investigate the biblical perspective on various subjects, such as salvation through God's grace, baptism, communion, or heaven. Examine the birth, life, crucifixion, resurrection, and imminent return of the Lord Jesus Christ. You may also study the biblical perspective on current issues of the day (i.e., abortion, divorce, homosexuality, poverty, spiritual gifts, false religions) when it is appropriate for the age level and maturity of the children. These topics are of tremendous benefit to the entire family, particularly when you study them in conjunction with upcoming or current events.

    B.   Scripture memory is a vital part of your family devotional and worship times *(based on Psalm 119:11, 16)*, especially since you can encourage one another by reciting your verses to each other *(based on Proverbs 27:17; Hebrews 10:24-25)*. In your Scripture memory times together, you may do a number of things. For example:

        1.   Have all family members memorize the same verses by learning and reciting them together. This is an effective tool in family devotional times, particularly when verses are chosen that deal with areas in which family members need instruction and growth.

        2.   As family members develop the habit of Scripture memory, have each one choose verses to memorize. Each member of the family, during the family devotional times, recites to the rest of the family what he has learned during the week. He also should explain how the portion of Scripture is applicable to his life.

        3.   Have each family member memorize verses from various training courses or activities in which each is involved (such as children's programs, the BCT I: Self-Confrontation Course, evangelism courses, etc.). Each family member then recites these verses to the others during family devotional times.

    C.   Praise, prayer, and thanksgiving are to be developed diligently within your family devotions and worship *(based on Ephesians 5:19-20; Colossians 3:16)*. Suggestions to help you establish praise, prayer, and thanksgiving as a regular part of your family devotions are as follows:

        1.   Choose one day a week for praise items and prayer requests from each family member; then, spend time praying together. You may wish to begin a family praise and prayer log book.

        2.   Have one day set aside for giving thanks for what has happened or what the Lord has done in each family member's life. To add variety, use creative and meaningful activities associated with your thanksgiving time. For example, you may determine a theme for the evening and sing songs of thanksgiving or

write a psalm of praise together. If guests are with you, they can also participate in this family devotional and worship time.

    3.   Set aside a day for singing psalms, hymns, and spiritual songs together. You may select different members to lead, or you may choose one day for favorite songs and hymns. You may choose to read one of the *Psalms* in a responsive manner, with the parents reading one verse, the children reading the next, etc. Once again, this is a particularly good activity in which guests may participate.

D.   Missions and ministry times for family devotions and worship are often neglected, but are vital patterns for believers' lives together *(based on Matthew 28:18-20; Luke 10:2; Acts 1:8)*. Some suggestions follow:

    1.   Set aside one day a week for a missions emphasis during your family devotions. Read letters from missionaries that your family supports financially or through prayer. If your family does not currently have missionaries to support, spend time determining for whom you will pray and, if possible, financially support as a family. Pray for your missionaries and others who are ministering outside of your local church family, both at home and in other lands. Develop a missions prayer log for the missionaries that your family or church supports.

    2.   As a family, do a project for your missionaries. Write a letter, put together a "care" package of goodies, or begin a "gift" fund for a missionary.

    3.   As a family, list ways that you can minister to others such as providing meals for sick people, doing chores for people who are ill or restricted, sending notes of encouragement to others, visiting shut-ins, etc. Each week, add to your list and begin prayerfully to do them once a week as a family.

E.   Worship services at home and with your local church family are beneficial for building up every member of your family *(based on Hebrews 10:23-25)*. In addition to the benefit of being personally involved with other believers in worship, your worship time can be extended and enhanced on a regular basis.

    1.   Soon after participating in worship services as part of the local body of Christ, set aside time for every member of your family to explain what they learned. Also, allow time for each to tell how he plans to respond to the Lord and others as a result of this time of worship.

    2.   Have different family members plan and conduct parts of at-home worship services. You can consider developing your own order of service. This should include Scripture reading, singing, giving toward a specific need, praying together, and even hearing a mini-sermon by a family member. Children particularly enjoy leading portions of services or serving as ushers. Home worship services are also ideal for other families to join with you, since every age group is welcomed and encouraged to participate.

V. Suggested plans and structures for family devotions and worship

A.   *Suggestion One* – Regular plan for each week:

Day 1 - Missions emphasis day
Day 2 - Scripture memory recital
Day 3 - Praise, prayer, and singing
Day 4 - Study in God's Word
Day 5 - Giving thanks, testimonies
Day 6 - Ministry "planning and doing" time
Day 7 - Worship day with "at-home" service

B. *Suggestion Two* – Set aside extended times to examine special needs or problems from a biblical perspective. For example:

   1. During the first week, investigate and study God's Word together on your chosen topic.

   2. During the second week, develop a plan to practice what your family has learned together and begin faithfully to implement it.

   3. During the third week of family devotions, each person reports on his progress in following the plan. Each family member memorizes meaningful and applicable verses, recites them during family devotions, and tells how these verses are to be applied personally.

   4. During the fourth week, return to your regular family devotions and worship schedule. On praise/prayer days, emphasize what each family member has learned. Recite learned verses on Bible memory day.

C. *Suggestion Three* – Study God's Word for a period of time (one or more weeks) as it relates to current issues and events. Record what you learned as a family.

D. *Suggestion Four* – Do a biblical character study for a week, emphasizing a particular problem or example of godliness from this person's life. The next week, rehearse and act out a specific event in this biblical character's life, encouraging each person in your family to contribute and participate.

E. *Suggestion Five* – Develop your own family plan.

VI. Conclusion about family devotions and worship

A. Family devotional and worship times can be a wonderful time of learning God's truths and biblical practice for all family members *(based on Deuteronomy 6:6-7; Psalm 111:1-2; Hebrews 10:23-25)*.

B. Ministry and discipleship are not to be separated from times of family devotions and worship *(based on Jesus' work in the lives of His disciples)*.

AN OVERALL PLAN FOR REARING CHILDREN

> Since God's Word is applicable for individuals at every age level, it is necessary that every person in a family understand that the Bible is the only standard by which each is to live. Scripture is totally sufficient to give direction for all of life, including the area of parent-child relationships. No other authority is necessary or adequate to take its place or augment its teachings (*based on Deuteronomy 6:5-7; Psalm 19:7-11; 119:89, 105, 130; Proverbs 30:5-6; Isaiah 55:6-11; I Corinthians 3:19-20; II Timothy 3:14-17; Hebrews 4:12; II Peter 1:3-4*).

I. **Carefully review the following cross references:**

   A. The foundational, biblical requirements for change (Lessons 1 and 2), recognizing the differences between living man's way and living God's way (Lessons 3 and 4);

   B. The essential elements of biblical change (Lessons 5 - 8) as you die to self and live for the Lord (Lessons 9 and 10);

   C. The necessity of biblically dealing with any anger and bitterness in your life (Lesson 11);

   D. The applicability of biblical principles to loving your neighbor (Lessons 12 and 13) and to be Christ-honoring in every relationship in the family (Lessons 14 - 17);

   E. The possible links between fear, worry, or depression in your life (Lessons 18 and 19) and problems in relationships with your children;

   F. The seriousness of life-dominating sins and their relationship to problems between parents and children (Lessons 20 and 21); and

   G. The need for you and every person in your family to establish and faithfully maintain specific standards from God's Word in every area life (Lesson 22).

NOTE: The cross-references cited above are important in dealing with parent-child relationships. In dealing with problems biblically, you must examine all aspects of your life. For example, any problem between parents and children cannot be overcome by dealing with it as an end in itself. Rather, any problem must be dealt with in light of scriptural principles for all of life in order that you may make biblical changes to be more conformed to the image of Christ. As you can see, references to previous lessons are listed in addition to those lessons not yet covered.

If you proceed in biblical counseling training, you will find that God's solutions as presented in this course apply to all problems, including those not covered in this manual.

II. **To help each of your children become aware of patterns of sin or temptations to sin in any area of life, explain to your children the importance of making a list of people, places, times, or circumstances where ongoing problems are evident in their lives.** *Parents should record information on the worksheet for each of their younger children but only as the child provides information voluntarily in judging themselves biblically.*

III. Use the VICTORY OVER FAILURES WORKSHEET (Supplement 8). To complete columns 1-3, follow the instructions given in GUIDELINES: VICTORY OVER FAILURES WORKSHEET (Supplement 7). *Parents, you must continually examine yourself biblically as you teach your children (based on Matthew 7:1-5; Romans 2:21a; II Timothy 2:15; James 3:1).*

IV. When completing column four of the VICTORY OVER FAILURES WORKSHEET (Supplement 8, Pages 1-2):

    A. You and each of your children are to develop a **basic plan** to overcome your personal sins, especially those that pertain to family relationships. In each of your plans, include deeds (thoughts, speech, and actions) that will help each person develop a Christlike manner by taking into account the following guidelines. *NOTE: The following guidelines apply only to those family members who have experienced a spiritual new birth (based on I Corinthians 2:9-14).*

        1. Think biblically

            a. Remember that God has promised to care for you and every other believer in any situation, no matter how unsettling it may seem *(Psalm 23:1-6, 37:5; Proverbs 3:25-26; Matthew 10:28-31; Romans 8:36-39; I Corinthians 10:13).*

            b. Confess all sinful thoughts to God *(I John 1:9)* and ask for His help in changing this sinful pattern *(based on I Thessalonians 5:17; Hebrews 4:15-16; James 1:5).*

            c. Rejoice *(I Thessalonians 5:16)* and give thanks in and for every situation *(Ephesians 5:20; I Thessalonians 5:18),* knowing that endurance in trials works to conform you to the image of Jesus Christ *(Romans 5:3-5; James 1:2-4).*

            d. Remember that God's forgiveness of you is the basis for you to forgive others *(Matthew 18:21-35; Ephesians 4:32; Colossians 3:13).*

            e. Remember that your love for others demonstrates the love that you have for God *(I John 2:9-11; 3:14-16; 4:7-11, 20-21).*

            f. Focus your thoughts on glorifying and pleasing God and on being a blessing to others in all situations *(based on Matthew 22:37-39; Luke 9:23-24; II Corinthians 5:9, 15; 10:5; Galatians 5:16-17; Philippians 2:3-4, 4:8; Colossians 3:2).*

            g. Within the very situation in which you find yourself, do not dwell on things that contribute to further sin. Instead discipline your mind to think on things that please the Lord *(Philippians 4:8; Colossians 3:2).* Remember to pray for those who persecute you *(Matthew 5:44).*

            h. Review psalms, hymns, and spiritual songs that you have memorized *(based on Ephesians 5:19-20; Colossians 3:16).*

            i. Think of ways you can encourage other believing family members that can stimulate them to love and good deeds *(based on Hebrews 10:23-25).*

        2. Speak biblically

            a. Confess your current sins to those whom you have failed to love in a biblical manner, including the sins of failing to complete your responsibilities. Confess any other remembered sins that you have failed to confess earlier *(based on Psalm 51:1-4; James 5:16; I John 1:9).*

            To review how to confess your sins to those you have sinned against, refer to:
            GUIDELINES: VICTORY OVER FAILURES WORKSHEET *(Supplement 7)*
            under VI. Application of biblical change, point D. and

RECONCILIATION (REMOVING ALL HINDRANCES TO UNITY AND PEACE) (Lesson 12, Pages 6-8) under **II. Confession.**

b. Do not speak about your past accomplishments *(Proverbs 27:2, 30:32; II Corinthians 10:18)*, sorrows or defeats *(Philippians 3:13-14)*, worries about the future *(Matthew 6:34)*, comparing yourself to yourself and/or others *(II Corinthians 10:12)*, or boastfully promising what you will do in the future *(Proverbs 27:1; James 4:13-16)*. Instead, edify others by thankfully speaking of the goodness of the Lord and the recent difference He has made in your life, especially in any difficulties you have encountered *(Luke 10:20; Ephesians 4:29; Colossians 4:6; Hebrews 13:15; I Peter 3:15)*.

c. Do not slander, gossip, quarrel, or use words that do not edify others *(Proverbs 10:18; Ephesians 4:29, 31; 5:4; Colossians 3:8; II Timothy 2:24; I Peter 2:1)*. Instead, let your speech be truthful and gracious, according to the need of the moment, that you may know how to answer each person *(Ephesians 4:15, 25, 29; Colossians 4:6)*.

d. Do not bring up another's sin in an accusing or vengeful manner, either to others, yourself, or to the person who has sinned *(Proverbs 10:18, 17:9, 20:19; Ephesians 4:29, 31; Colossians 3:8; I Peter 2:1)*.

e. Encourage reconciliation with God and others, being careful to follow biblical guidelines *(Matthew 5:9, 23-24; Romans 12:18; II Corinthians 2:6-8, 5:18)*.

    Refer to: *RECONCILIATION (REMOVING ALL HINDRANCES TO UNITY AND PEACE) (Lesson 12, Pages 6-8).*

f. Teach the principles of biblical instruction and discipline to every member of your family *(based on Deuteronomy 6:5-7; Ephesians 6:4)*.

    Refer to:
    UNDERSTANDING BIBLICAL INSTRUCTION OF CHILDREN (Lesson 16, Pages 13-16) and
    UNDERSTANDING BIBLICAL DISCIPLINE (Lesson 17, Pages 8-10).

    Parents: *Also confess to your children any unbiblical philosophies or statements which you have used in rearing them. Explain to them why these are unbiblical and ask their forgiveness.*

    Refer to:
    MAN'S THEORIES AND PRACTICES FOR REARING CHILDREN (Lesson 16, Pages 3-6) and
    GUIDELINES FOR REARING CHILDREN (Lesson 16, Pages 7-9).

3. Act biblically

    a. Forgive others just as God has forgiven you *(Ephesians 4:32; Colossians 3:13)*.

        Refer to: *FORGIVENESS (FORGIVING OTHERS AS GOD HAS FORGIVEN YOU) (Lesson 12, Pages 3-5) and determine if you are practicing biblical forgiveness. Make changes as necessary.*

    b. Memorize Scripture verses and study Scripture passages related to solving specific problems in your family *(based on Psalm 119:9, 11, 16; II Corinthians 10:5; Philippians 4:8; II Timothy 2:15)*. Memorize psalms, hymns, and spiritual songs that you can use at appropriate times in the future *(based on Ephesians 5:19-20; Colossians 3:16)*.

    c. Pray always with thanksgiving *(Philippians 4:6; I Thessalonians 5:17-18)* and according to God's will *(I John 5:14-15)*. Cast all your cares on the Lord *(I Peter 5:7)* and pray for those who persecute you *(Matthew 5:44)*.

    d. Identify all danger signals – such as situations, places, and personal contacts that bring temptation – and take immediate steps to eliminate, flee, or resist the temptation *(based on Psalm 1:1; Proverbs 27:12; I Corinthians 15:33; II Timothy 2:22; James 4:7; I Peter 5:8-9).*

e.   Make amends for wrongdoing and seek reconciliation with those you have offended *(based on Matthew 5:23-24).* Remember that although you have already confessed your sins *(see 2. a. above),* you need to demonstrate your determination to change.

See: **RECONCILIATION (REMOVING ALL HINDRANCES TO UNITY AND PEACE)** *(Lesson 12, Pages 6-8) under* **III. *Restitution*** *and* **IV. *The importance of reconciliation.***

Parents: Review **WAYS THAT PARENTS PROVOKE THEIR CHILDREN TO ANGER** *(Lesson 16, Pages 10-12) to determine if you have sinned or are sinning against the Lord and your children in ways similar to those listed. Confess any and all sins in this area to the Lord and to your children.*

f.   Bless others through tangible and sincere expressions of biblical love and service (this includes your daily responsibilities as a family member, student, employer, employee, roommate, etc.) *(based on Matthew 7:12; Romans 12:9-13, 15-16; 13:8-10; I Corinthians 13:4-8a; Philippians 2:3-8; I Timothy 6:17-19; I Peter 3:8-9; I John 3:18).*

For specific examples of how and when to express biblical love, even in difficult situations, refer to: **THE MEANING OF BIBLICAL LOVE** *(Lesson 13, Pages 4-6).*

Biblical love should be demonstrated:

1)   Regardless of how you feel *(based on Genesis 4:7; II Corinthians 5:14-15; Galatians 5:16-17; Philippians 4:13; James 4:17);*

2)   Especially to those who seem to be your enemies or to those who have sinned against you *(based on Matthew 5:23-24, 43-48; Mark 11:25-26; Romans 12:14, 17-21);*

3)   With kindness and tenderheartedness for the very individuals with whom you are or have been irritated *(Ephesians 4:31-32);*

4)   By taking advantage of opportunities to minister, especially in ways that keep you in a Christlike servant attitude toward others *(based on Matthew 20:25-28; Philippians 2:3-8; I Peter 4:10);* and

5)   By practicing biblical stewardship to honor the Lord and be of practical help to others *(based on Psalm 24:1; Matthew 25:14-29; I Corinthians 4:1-2; Ephesians 5:15-17; I Timothy 6:17-19; I Peter 4:10).*

   Refer to:
   BIBLICAL PRINCIPLES OF STEWARDSHIP *(Lesson 10, Pages 4-6) and* **DYING TO SELF BY SERVING OTHERS** *(Lesson 10, Pages 7-8).*

g.   Whenever necessary, conduct a "conference table" using the plan outlined in **OVERCOMING PROBLEMS THROUGH BIBLICAL COMMUNICATION (USING A CONFERENCE TABLE FOR RECONCILIATION)** (Lesson 15, Pages 6-9).

h.   Correct deficiencies in your life that exist because of a lack of discipline or neglect *(based on Colossians 3:1-17; James 4:17; I Timothy 4:7b).*

i.   Be faithful to establish and maintain a consistent time for family devotions and worship *(based on Ephesians 5:15-17).*

Refer to: **FAMILY DEVOTIONS AND WORSHIP (GUIDELINES AND SUGGESTIONS)** *(Lesson 17, Pages 11-15) for help in this area.*

j.   For each task that your child is to fulfill, especially those that are to be done on a continuing basis, train him properly using the procedures by which Jesus trained His disciples.

Refer to: **UNDERSTANDING BIBLICAL INSTRUCTION OF CHILDREN** *(Lesson 16, Pages 13-16) under* **VI. G.**

    k.   If necessary, ask a Christian friend to help you hold your child accountable to carry out his **basic** and **contingency plans** until a new pattern of godly living has been established *(Proverbs 27:17; Ecclesiastes 4:9-10; Hebrews 10:23-25).* As needed, seek biblical counsel from others *(Proverbs 11:14, 15:22).*

    l.   Be faithful in carrying out biblical discipline.

Refer to: **UNDERSTANDING BIBLICAL DISCIPLINE** *(Lesson 17, Pages 8-10).*

    m.   If a believing member of your family will not respond to the biblical restoration process after being admonished about his sin(s), continue the process of restoration as outlined in **RESTORATION/DISCIPLINE (YOUR BIBLICAL RESPONSE TO THE SIN OF ANOTHER BELIEVER)** (Lesson 13, Pages 7-8).

Review: **GUIDELINES: THE RESTORATION/ DISCIPLINE PROCESS** *(Lesson 13, Pages 9-11).*

B.   As necessary, teach your children how to develop a **"THINK AND DO" LIST** (Supplement 10) using **GUIDELINES: THE "THINK AND DO" LIST** (Supplement 9).

C.   Encourage and assist each of your children to implement his **basic plan** *(James 1:22)* and to do it heartily as unto the Lord *(Colossians 3:23-24).*

D.   Help each of your children develop a **contingency plan** to deal with unexpected situations that provide temptation to sin, especially in family relationships. Take into account the following guidelines:

    1.   Immediately ask God for help *(I Thessalonians 5:17; Hebrews 4:15-16; James 1:5).*

    2.   Review your memorized verses that deal specifically with any recognized sin(s) in your life *(based on Psalm 119:9, 11, 16).*

    3.   Immediately seek God's perspective.

        a.   Regardless of your feelings or circumstances, view this situation as an opportunity for further spiritual growth *(James 1:2-4)* because God will work out all things for good in your life *(based on Psalm 37; Proverbs 3:5-12; Romans 8:28-29; Ephesians 1:3-14; Philippians 1:6).*

           1)   Remind yourself that you can do all things through Christ who gives you strength *(Philippians 4:11-13),* since your adequacy is from God and not from any natural "inner strength" *(II Corinthians 3:5).* Remember that you can do nothing fruitful apart from Jesus Christ *(John 15:5).*

           2)   Praise and glorify God that He is sufficient even in your areas of weakness *(II Corinthians 12:9-10)* and that He will keep you from stumbling and make you stand blameless and with great joy in the presence of His glory *(Jude 1:24-25).*

        b.   Remember that God looks on your heart, not on your outward appearance *(I Samuel 16:7).* You must stand blameless before Him in your thoughts, whether others know about it or not *(based on Acts 23:1, 24:16; Romans 14:12; Ephesians 1:4, 4:1; Philippians 1:9-11; Colossians 1:21-22).*

           1)   If you even begin to think sinful thoughts in an unforeseen circumstance, confess them to the Lord *(I John 1:9).*

2) Remember that it is not the amount of time spent sinning or the immensity of the sin (by human standards) by which you should judge yourself. Rather, the fact that you stopped going God's way even momentarily is what matters *(James 2:10, 4:17)*.

4. Thank God that you are His servant in your present circumstance *(Ephesians 5:20; I Thessalonians 5:18)*. Determine how you will give glory to God *(I Corinthians 10:31; I Peter 4:11)* and seek ways to edify others by serving them in this situation *(Ephesians 4:29; Philippians 2:3-4)*.

5. Act according to your **contingency plan** as soon as you detect temptation to sin in any area of your life *(based on I Thessalonians 5:22; II Timothy 2:19-22)*. Then, begin again to do those things written in your **basic plan** *(based on Proverbs 24:16; James 1:22-25)*.

LESSON 17: HOMEWORK

> This lesson's **HOMEWORK** will help each family member demonstrate his faith in Jesus Christ by being obedient to the Bible in parent-child relationships *(based on Deuteronomy 4:9, 6:6-7; Psalm 119:105; John 14:15; Ephesians 6:1-4; Colossians 3:20-21; II Timothy 3:16-17; James 1:22-25).*

✔ *homework completed*

☐ A. * In your own words, write the meaning of *Ephesians 6:1-3*. Memorize *Ephesians 6:1-3* and begin memorizing *Genesis 4:7* and *James 1:22*. Review previous memory verses.

☐ B. * Read **BIBLICAL PRINCIPLES: PARENT-CHILD RELATIONSHIPS (PART TWO)** (Lesson 17, Pages 2-3). Highlight the referenced verses in your Bible.

☐ C. Study **TRAINING CHILDREN TO BE FAITHFUL (BIBLICAL DISCIPLESHIP IN THE HOME)** (Lesson 17, Pages 4-7). Highlight specific areas of discipleship in which you recognize how God has worked in you and other members of your family. Place these on a praise list that can be shared in your family devotions and worship *(based on Psalm 34:1-3, 115:1; I Corinthians 1:26-31).* Also highlight statements that point out changes you need to make. Complete a **VICTORY OVER FAILURES WORKSHEET** (Supplement 8) and develop a plan by which these changes will be accomplished.

☐ D. Study **UNDERSTANDING BIBLICAL DISCIPLINE** (Lesson 17, Pages 8-10). Determine a biblical plan of discipline that you will faithfully follow in your home, if you have not already done so. Set aside specific times to explain to your children God's plan of discipline that you will follow in your home. If you have failed to discipline your children biblically, confess this to the Lord and to your children *(based on I John 1:9; James 5:16)*; then, carry out steps of biblical reconciliation that may be necessary. *Refer to RECONCILIATION (REMOVING ALL HINDRANCES TO UNITY AND PEACE) (Lesson 12, Pages 6-8).*

☐ E. Read **FAMILY DEVOTIONS AND WORSHIP (GUIDELINES & SUGGESTIONS)** (Lesson 17, Pages 11-15). Highlight portions of this study that you will use in your family devotions and worship. If you do not have a specific time set aside for regular family devotions and worship, make plans to begin.

☐ F. Study **AN OVERALL PLAN FOR REARING CHILDREN** (Lesson 17, Pages 16-21). Note the common characteristics that these guidelines have with the basic steps for spiritual development in any believer's life. Highlight any statements that point out changes you need to make in bringing up your children. Make plans to begin and maintain these changes.

☐ G. * In conjunction with this lesson, answer questions 25 and 26 under **Open Book Test** (Lesson 23, Page 3).

* *The completion of assignments marked with an asterisk (*) is a prerequisite for further biblical counseling training.*

LESSON 17: STUDY GUIDE FOR DAILY DEVOTIONS
(INCLUDING SCRIPTURE MEMORY AND HOMEWORK)

> This lesson's **STUDY GUIDE** will help each family member demonstrate his faith in Jesus Christ by being obedient to the Bible in parent-child relationships *(based on Deuteronomy 4:9, 6:6-7; Psalm 119:105; John 14:15; Ephesians 6:1-4; Colossians 3:20-21; II Timothy 3:16-17; James 1:22-25*

Scripture Memory

1. * Memorize *Ephesians 6:1-3*. Begin memorizing *Genesis 4:7* and *James 1:22*.
2. Carry your memory verse cards from previous weeks along with this week's memory verses. Review your memory verses at your spare moments throughout the day.

Daily Devotional Study Guide

FIRST DAY

1. Open with prayer.
2. * Read *Principle 73* under **BIBLICAL PRINCIPLES: PARENT-CHILD RELATIONSHIPS (PART TWO)** (Lesson 17, Pages 2-3). Highlight the verses in your Bible.
3. * Write the meaning of *Ephesians 6:1-3* in your own words.
4. Study **TRAINING CHILDREN TO BE FAITHFUL (BIBLICAL DISCIPLESHIP IN THE HOME)** (Lesson 17, Pages 4-7). Highlight specific areas of discipleship in which you recognize how God has worked in you and other members of your family. Place these on a praise list that you can share in family devotions *(Psalm 34:1-3, 115:1; I Corinthians 1:26-31)*. Also highlight statements that point out changes you need to make. This is the first day of a two-day study.
5. Start a **VICTORY OVER FAILURES WORKSHEET** (Supplement 8) and begin to develop a plan by which these changes will be accomplished.
6. Close with prayer.

SECOND DAY

1. Open with prayer.
2. * Read *Principle 74* under **BIBLICAL PRINCIPLES: PARENT-CHILD RELATIONSHIPS (PART TWO)** (Lesson 17, Pages 2-3) and highlight the listed verses in your Bible if you have not already done so.
3. Complete your study of **TRAINING CHILDREN TO BE FAITHFUL (BIBLICAL DISCIPLESHIP IN THE HOME)** (Lesson 17, Pages 4-7).
4. Complete your **VICTORY OVER FAILURES WORKSHEET** (Supplement 8) that outlines the changes you need to make.
5. Close with prayer.

THIRD DAY

1. Open with prayer.
2. * Read *Principle 75* under **BIBLICAL PRINCIPLES: PARENT-CHILD RELATIONSHIPS (PART TWO)** (Lesson 17, Pages 2-3) and highlight the listed verses in your Bible.

---

3. Study **UNDERSTANDING BIBLICAL DISCIPLINE** (Lesson 17, Pages 8-10). Determine a biblical plan of discipline that you will faithfully follow in your home, if you have not already done so. If you have failed to discipline your children biblically, confess this to the Lord and to your children *(based on I John 1:9; James 5:16)*. If necessary, take steps of biblical reconciliation with your children. *Refer to:* **RECONCILIATION (REMOVING ALL HINDRANCES TO UNITY AND PEACE)** *(Lesson 12, Pages 6-8)*.

4. Close with prayer.

FOURTH DAY

1. Open with prayer.
2. * Read *Principle 4, revised from Lesson 3* under **BIBLICAL PRINCIPLES: PARENT-CHILD RELATIONSHIPS (PART TWO)** (Lesson 17, Pages 2-3).
3. Complete your study of **UNDERSTANDING BIBLICAL DISCIPLINE** (Lesson 17, Pages 8-10). Set aside a time to teach your children God's plan of discipline and explain the biblical plan of discipline you will follow in your home.
4. Close with prayer.

FIFTH DAY

1. Open with prayer.
2. * Read *Principle 76* under **BIBLICAL PRINCIPLES: PARENT-CHILD RELATIONSHIPS (PART TWO)** (Lesson 17, Pages 2-3) and highlight the listed verses in your Bible.
3. Read **FAMILY DEVOTIONS AND WORSHIP (GUIDELINES AND SUGGESTIONS)** (Lesson 17, Pages 11-15). Choose portions of this study to use in your family devotions and worship. If you do not have a specific time set aside for regular family devotions and worship, make plans to begin.
4. Close with prayer.

SIXTH DAY

1. Open with prayer.
2. * Read *Principle 77* under **BIBLICAL PRINCIPLES: PARENT-CHILD RELATIONSHIPS (PART TWO)** (Lesson 17, Pages 2-3) and highlight the listed verses in your Bible.
3. Study **AN OVERALL PLAN FOR REARING CHILDREN** (Lesson 17, Pages 16-21). Highlight any statements that point out changes you need to make in bringing up your children. This is the first day of a two-day study.
4. Close with prayer.

SEVENTH DAY

1. Open with prayer.
2. Complete your study of **AN OVERALL PLAN FOR REARING CHILDREN** (Lesson 17, Pages 16-21). Make plans to begin and maintain the changes that you need to make as a parent.
3. * In conjunction with this lesson, answer questions 25 and 26 under **Open Book Test** (Lesson 23, Page 3).
4. Close in prayer.
5. Review your memory verses and recite them to a friend or family member. Remember to explain the meaning of the verses and their application to your life.

---

*   *The completion of assignments marked with an asterisk (*) is a prerequisite for further biblical counseling training.*

LESSON 18

DEPRESSION

"If you do well, will not your countenance be lifted up? And if you do not do well, sin is crouching at the door; and its desire is for you, but you must master it."

Genesis 4:7

"But prove yourselves doers of the word, and not merely hearers who delude themselves."

James 1:22

LESSON 18: DEPRESSION

> Depression is not a disease. While there are some organic malfunctions that may trigger feelings of depression, many symptoms and maladies defined as depression (whether short-lived or chronic) are the consequences of unbiblical habits and/or sinful reactions to circumstances and other people. Depression that stems from unbiblical living can be overcome as you deal biblically with your sins and purposefully live in a manner that is pleasing to the Lord *(based on Genesis 4:3-7, esp. verse 7; Psalm 32:1-5; 42:11; 55:22; 119:28, 50, 75-77, 143, 165; John 15:10-11; II Corinthians 1:3-6; James 1:22-25).*

I. **The purposes of this lesson are:**

A. To help you understand that depression does not provide an excuse for you to live in an unbiblical manner;

B. To remind you that depression may be experienced by anyone and must be dealt with from God's perspective and not from your own perspective or any other person's philosophies;

C. To present a biblical plan to overcome depression; and

D. To provide opportunity for you to help someone deal with feelings of depression through the continuation of a case study.

II. **The outline of this lesson**

A. Self-confrontation

   1. **BIBLICAL PRINCIPLES: DEPRESSION** (Lesson 18, Pages 2-3)

   2. **UNDERSTANDING DEPRESSION** (Lesson 18, Pages 4-7)

B. Steps for spiritual growth

   1. **OVERCOMING DEPRESSION** (Lesson 18, Pages 8-13)

   2. **MY PRESENT SCHEDULE** (Supplement 14)

   3. **MY PROPOSED BIBLICAL SCHEDULE** (Supplement 15)

   4. **LESSON 18: HOMEWORK** (Lesson 18, Page 15)

   5. **STUDY GUIDE FOR DAILY DEVOTIONS** (Lesson 18, Pages 16-17)

C. Biblical counseling

   A CASE STUDY: MARY'S HUSBAND HAS LEFT HER (Lesson 18, Page 14)

BIBLICAL PRINCIPLES: DEPRESSION

> Even if you feel depressed, you are still to live biblically *(based on Psalm 19:7-11; 119:92-93, 143; John 15:8-12, 16-17; I Corinthians 13:4-8a; Philippians 4:13; Colossians 3:17; James 1:22-25; I John 2:6)*. You are to edify others and glorify God in your thoughts, words, and actions at all times instead of obeying God's Word only when you "feel like it" *(based on I Corinthians 10:31; II Corinthians 10:5; Ephesians 4:29; Philippians 2:3-4, 4:8-9; Colossians 4:6)*.

I. God's View

(Principle 78)   Symptoms defined as "depression" are sometimes precipitated by sin *(based on Genesis 4:3-14; Psalm 32:3-5, 38:1-10)*, which means you are living to please yourself instead of living to please the Lord. If you do not repent, confess your self-centeredness, and return to living in a biblical manner, you will experience even further difficulties *(based on Psalm 32:3-4, 38:1-4; Colossians 3:25; Hebrews 12:5-11)*.

(Principle 79)   To love life and see good days, you must turn from doing evil and be obedient to God's Word *(I Peter 3:10-12)*. In spite of "feeling depressed," you can live biblically because of the divine resources that God graciously provides for you *(based on Psalm 19:7-11; 34:18-19; 119:28, 105, 143; 145:14; Matthew 11:28-30; Romans 8:11-14, 26; II Corinthians 12:9-10; Philippians 4:6-7, 13; Hebrews 4:15-16)*.

Also applicable:

(Principle 16, from Lesson 6, Page 2)   The way you feel and the way you view yourself, your relationships, and your circumstances are often indications of whether you are living to please yourself or living to please God *(Genesis 4:6-7; Psalm 119:165; John 14:27, 15:10-11; Romans 14:17-18; II Corinthians 7:10; Philippians 4:6-7; I John 4:18-21)*.

II. Your hope

(Principle 80)   No matter how difficult any situation appears, the Lord Jesus Christ has overcome it *(John 16:33)*. God will not allow anything into your life that is beyond His control or beyond your ability to endure without sinning *(based on Genesis 50:20; Jeremiah 29:11; Romans 8:28-29; I Corinthians 10:13; II Corinthians 12:9-10; Philippians 4:13)*. Trials are for your good *(Romans 5:3-5; James 1:2-4; I Peter 1:6-7)*; and, as you respond biblically, give opportunity for the power of God to show forth in your life *(II Corinthians 4:7-18, 12:9-10)*.

(Principle 81)   In difficulties, God's comfort *(Psalm 119:50; II Corinthians 1:3-5, 7:6a)* and sustaining care are available to you *(Psalm 34:8, 42:11, 46:1-3, 55:22, 145:14; Lamentations 3:32; Matthew 11:28-30; Hebrews 4:15-16)*.

III. Your change

(Principle 82)   Put off disobedience to God's Word; put on living a disciplined, faithfully obedient life *(Genesis 4:7; Romans 6:11-13, 19; I Timothy 4:7-11)* out of a commitment to please God instead of yourself *(II Corinthians 5:14-15; Galatians 5:16-17).*

Also applicable:

(Principle 28, from Lesson 7, Page 2)   In order to put off sinful habits, you must first identify them by examining (judging) your life in light of God's Word *(Matthew 7:1-5; I Corinthians 11:28-31; II Timothy 3:16-17; Hebrews 4:12).* Once you have specifically identified sins in your life, you must repent of them *(Proverbs 28:13; II Corinthians 7:9-10; Revelation 2:5),* confess them *(I John 1:9),* and immediately put them aside *(Romans 6:12-13a; II Corinthians 10:5; Ephesians 4:25, 29, 31; 5:4; Colossians 3:2, 5-9).*

(Principle 29, from Lesson 7, Page 2)   As you put on righteous deeds *(Titus 2:11-12)* in the power of the Holy Spirit *(Galatians 5:16; Ephesians 3:16-21, 5:18),* you will glorify God *(I Corinthians 10:31; I Peter 4:11),* demonstrate your love for Him *(Deuteronomy 10:12; Matthew 22:37; I John 5:3; II John 1:6),* and please Him in all things *(II Corinthians 5:9; Colossians 1:10).*

IV. Your practice

(Principle 83)   Establish a biblical schedule for fulfilling your God-given responsibilities and keep the schedule regardless of any feelings of depression you may experience *(Ephesians 5:15-17; James 4:17).* Do all your responsibilities and tasks heartily as to the Lord and for His glory *(Matthew 5:16; I Corinthians 10:31; Colossians 3:17, 23-24).* If you sin, confess this to the Lord *(I John 1:9)* and, following biblical guidelines, confess your sins to those against whom you have sinned *(James 5:16).*

Also applicable:

(Principle 14, revised from Lesson 5, Page 2)   You must diligently examine yourself in a biblical manner *(Matthew 7:1-5; I Corinthians 11:31)* and obey God's Word consistently *(I John 2:3-6)* to grow increasingly into godliness *(I Timothy 4:7-8; II Peter 1:3-11)* and to realize true peace *(Psalm 119:165; John 16:33)* and joy *(John 15:10-11).*

(Principle 39, revised from Lesson 10, Page 2)   Stop living to please yourself in daily situations, responsibilities, and relationships *(Luke 9:23-24; John 3:30, 12:24-26; Romans 12:3, 14:7-8; II Corinthians 5:15)* but rather follow God's commandments *(Matthew 22:37-39).* Instead of living to please yourself, regard others as more important than yourself and be a servant to God and others *(Matthew 20:26-28; Luke 4:8; John 13:3-17, esp. verses 14-15; Romans 15:1-3; I Corinthians 9:19; 10:24, 32-33; Philippians 2:3-7; Colossians 3:23-24; I Peter 4:10).*

UNDERSTANDING DEPRESSION

> Feeling depressed is not a new phenomenon, since symptoms that are now defined as "depression" sometimes characterized people of the Bible. God's Word not only helps you face this problem but also shows you how to be an overwhelming conqueror even in the midst of feeling depressed *(based on Psalm 19:7-14, 119:165; Proverbs 16:25; I Corinthians 1:25, 3:18-20, 10:13; II Timothy 3:16-17; II Peter 1:2-10; I John 5:4-5).*

I. **What is "depression"?**

A. Many define "depression" as a condition marked by feelings of dejection and/or guilt. The result is hopelessness and cessation of activity. Often classified as a "disease" by some in the medical profession, depression is often thought to be the most prominent disorder presently observed in general medical practice. However, in spite of the prevalence of "depression," medical science admits that the causes of depression are still largely unknown.

B. In Scripture, feelings associated with being depressed are described as having a fallen countenance *(Genesis 4:7)*, having a broken spirit *(Proverbs 17:22, 18:14)*, being sad *(Proverbs 15:13)*, experiencing despair *(Psalm 42:11)*, being brokenhearted *(Psalm 147:3)*, being burdened by the weight of sin *(Psalm 38:4)*, mourning *(Psalm 38:6)*, being greatly bowed down *(Psalm 38:6)*, having grief *(Psalm 119:28)*, or losing heart (becoming faint or weary) *(Ephesians 3:13; Hebrews 12:3)*.

C. David described many of the symptoms and feelings of "being depressed" in *Psalm 38* by saying, *"...there is no soundness in my flesh because of Thine indignation; there is no health in my bones because of my sin...I am bent over and greatly bowed down; I go mourning all day long...I am benumbed and badly crushed; I groan because of the agitation of my heart...My heart throbs, my strength fails me; and the light of my eyes, even that has gone from me...I am ready to fall, and my sorrow is continually before me"* (excerpts from verses 3-17).

II. **Who can experience feelings of depression?**

A. No one is completely immune to feelings of depression *(based on I Corinthians 10:12-13)*. People in Scripture also experienced what would today be classified as "depression." As you will see in the following examples, the precipitating factor was a self-focus that led to sin, which then led to "depression":

1. Elijah reacted to Jezebel's threats by fearing for his own life, giving in to despair and fleeing, even after a great victory *(I Kings 19:1-4)*;

2. David committed sin, failed to repent, and then lost hope *(Psalm 38)*;

3. Jonah, displeased at the workings of God's sovereignty, became angry with God, which resulted in his wanting to die *(Jonah 4:1-11)*;

4. Peter denied the Lord by lying and cursing, which led him to weep bitterly *(Matthew 26:69-75)*; and

---

5.   Judas betrayed Jesus and then felt remorse. After throwing the thirty pieces of silver into the sanctuary, he committed suicide by hanging himself (*Matthew 27:1-5*).

B.   Since you may experience "depression" as a result of sinning, examples from Scripture are recorded for your instruction so you will persevere (be obedient to God's Word) and receive hope (*based on Romans 15:4*).

III.   What are possible factors that may lead to "depression"?

Any number of factors can contribute to your "being depressed." There are numerous physical factors that do not involve sin. However, you must guard against having unbiblical responses in the midst of physical problems. While the following list is not exhaustive, it indicates the importance of conducting a careful and biblical self-examination to determine what changes the Lord wants you to make in your life (*Proverbs 11:14, 18:13; Isaiah 55:8-11; Matthew 7:1-5; I Corinthians 11:31; Philippians 4:6-7; James 1:5, 22-25*).

A.   **Physical factors such as:** sickness, childbirth, surgery and the recovery process, hormonal or chemical imbalances, organic dysfunctions, sleep loss, unhealthy diet, fatigue, menstrual cycle phenomena, or physical maladies (i.e., hypoglycemia, diabetes, glandular dysfunction)

It is important that a medical diagnosis be made by a primary care physician and medical supervision be maintained with some of these conditions. At the same time, however, you must make biblical changes in your life so that you learn to live biblically in the midst of physical need and medical treatment. Remember, God is sovereign and will never allow a physical problem to come into your life that would make it impossible for you to be obedient to His Word.

B.   **Unbiblical responses to situations of life such as:** physical "handicaps" (i.e., paralysis, loss of limb, blindness, deafness), job loss, divorce, death of a loved one, loss of a relationship, financial difficulties, accidents, interpersonal conflicts, children leaving home at maturity, retirement, persecution, perceived crises, traumas, or medical treatment for yourself or your loved ones

C.   **Lack of biblical obedience with regard to:** eating disorders, overwork, insufficient rest, improper sleep habits, substance abuse (drugs, alcohol, prescribed medications), lack of exercise, failing to complete responsibilities (such as housework, yard care, assignments at work, care of children), lack of devotions, unfaithful prayer life, refusing to forgive others or be restored in personal relationships, lack of fellowship with other believers, failure to minister as part of the Body of Christ, or failure to confess sins to the Lord and to others in a faithful manner

D.   **Unbiblical thoughts and thought patterns, including:** bitterness, worry, anxiety, envy, jealousy, self-pity, a spirit of unforgiveness, impatience, procrastination, lustful thoughts, holding grudges, prideful thinking, anger, or esteeming yourself above others

Any of the above contributing factors that are not dealt with in a biblical manner may tempt you to continue in a "downward spiral," which can result in feelings of depression (see **I. B.** for biblical expressions that describe this situation).

For further information, refer to:
THE DOWNWARD SPIRAL: NEGLECTING OR REFUSING GOD'S WAY (*Lesson 5, Page 3*) *and*
THE UPWARD PATH: WALKING GOD'S WAY (*Lesson 5, Page 5*).

IV. What is the biblical perspective on factors contributing to "depression"?

A. Physical factors

1. God has fearfully and wonderfully made your body *(Psalm 139:14)*. As a believer, you have been redeemed with a price and are to exalt Christ and glorify God in your body *(I Corinthians 6:20; Philippians 1:20)*. Proper care of your body is essential in accomplishing this goal. You are to present your body as a living and holy sacrifice to God, which is your spiritual service of worship *(Romans 12:1)*.

2. Since some physical conditions (for example, hormonal imbalance or organic and glandular dysfunctions) may contribute to your feeling depressed, it is important that a medical diagnosis be made and proper care be maintained whenever this type of condition is present or suspected. However, you are still responsible to respond biblically in any difficulty regardless of your feelings *(such as Jeremiah did in Lamentations 3:31-32, 38-40; or as the Apostle Paul did in II Corinthians 12:7-10)*.

3. In the midst of physical difficulties, as you seek to be responsible (which includes seeking appropriate medical help) and are practicing biblical love in all your relationships, you will please God and will receive His strength and loving care *(based on Genesis 4:7; Psalm 34:19; 37:23-24; 119:143; 147:3, 6a; II Corinthians 12:9-10; Philippians 2:3-8; 4:13, 19; James 1:25)*.

Also applicable:

(Principle 34, revised, from Lesson 9, Page 2)   Remember who you are in Christ Jesus *(Romans 8:14-17; Ephesians 1:3-14; Colossians 2:9-12; I Peter 2:9-10)*. As a child of God, you have the assurance that your Heavenly Father, out of His grace and mercy, is involved actively in your life *(Philippians 1:6, 2:13; I Peter 2:9-10; II Peter 1:3-4)* in spite of any natural inadequacies you have *(Psalm 62:9; Isaiah 64:6; John 15:4-5; II Corinthians 3:5)*. While you are totally inadequate to live God's way in your own strength, God has chosen you to be a testimony of His power to the world *(Matthew 5:16; I Corinthians 1:26-31)*, by conforming you to the image of the Lord Jesus Christ *(Romans 8:28-29; II Corinthians 3:18)*.

(Principle 43, revised, from Lesson 10, Page 3)   Thank God for any circumstances or physical conditions that you cannot correct *(based on II Corinthians 12:7-10; Ephesians 5:20; I Thessalonians 5:18)* and correct all actual deficiencies in your life that hinder you from serving God and edifying others *(based on Matthew 22:37-39; Romans 6:19, 14:12-13; I Corinthians 10:31-33; Philippians 2:12-16; Colossians 3:2-15; Hebrews 12:1-2; James 4:8, 17)*.

B. All other factors

1. All things work together for good to those who love God and are called according to His purpose *(Romans 8:28)*. God has started and will complete His work in you *(Philippians 1:6)*, so trust Him *(Proverbs 3:5-6)*, because He intends for you to be conformed to the image of His Son *(Romans 8:29)*. He uses the trials of life to accomplish that purpose *(Romans 5:3-5; James 1:2-4)* and to prove the reality of your faith *(I Peter 1:6-7)*.

2. No matter what may occur in life, your loving obedience to God's Word *(John 14:15)* gives you an opportunity to die to self in order that you may live for Christ *(Luke 9:23-24; Galatians 2:20)*. God has promised to take care of all your

needs as you seek first His kingdom and righteousness *(Matthew 6:33),* by keeping your eyes firmly fixed on Jesus Christ·*(Hebrews 12:1-2)* and following in His steps *(Matthew 11:29; John 13:12-17; I Peter 2:21-25).*

Note: God's Word never commands you to change your feelings, but you are commanded to change your deeds (thoughts, words, and actions) by being obedient to Scripture. God's commands are not burdensome (I John 5:3). Your obedience to God's Word is based on your love for the Lord Jesus Christ instead of the unpredictability of your feelings (based on John 14:21, 23; II Corinthians 5:14-15; Galatians 5:16-17; I John 5:3).

3.   Biblical self-evaluation is necessary in every area of your life *(Matthew 7:1-5; I Corinthians 11:31),* which includes your actions *(Matthew 7:24-27; I Corinthians 13:4-8a),* your relationships with others *(Ephesians 5:21; Philippians 2:3-4),* your words *(Matthew 12:36-37; Ephesians 4:29; Colossians 4:6),* and your thought life *(II Corinthians 10:5; Colossians 3:2).* As you obey God's Word in all areas of your life, you will receive the Lord's blessing *(James 1:25).* If you are not obedient to God's Word, you will receive the Lord's corrective discipline *(I Corinthians 11:32; Hebrews 12:5-11).* Particular attention needs to be given to:

    a.   Regular confession of sins to the Lord *(I John 1:9)* and, at the appropriate time, to those against whom you have sinned *(James 5:16);*

    b.   Faithfulness in prayer *(Colossians 4:2; I Thessalonians 5:17);*

    c.   Diligence in the study of *(II Timothy 2:15),* meditation on *(Joshua 1:8; Psalm 1:2),* and memorization of God's Word *(Psalm 119:11, 16);*

    d.   Fellowship with other brothers and sisters in Christ *(Hebrews 10:23-25);* and

    e.   Consistent ministry as a servant of the Lord Jesus Christ *(I Peter 4:10).*

See: ***BIBLICAL SELF-CONFRONTATION: AN ESSENTIAL FOR DISCIPLESHIP*** *(Lesson 2, Page 6).*

OVERCOMING DEPRESSION

> While feelings of depression may result from organic malfunctioning that can be medically diagnosed and treated, a variety of other factors may contribute to this situation as well. In spite of any contributing factors, you must not base your deeds (thoughts, words, and actions) on your feelings. Instead, you are to discipline yourself for the purpose of godliness. This means you are to obey Scripture in all circumstances *(based on Matthew 5:16; 20:26-28; II Corinthians 5:14-15; Ephesians 5:15-16; Philippians 2:3-4, 14-15; 4:8-9, 11; Colossians 1:9-12, 2:6, 3:17; I Thessalonians 5:15-18; I Timothy 4:7-8; James 1:2-4).*

I. **Carefully review the following cross-references:**

   A. The foundational, biblical requirements for change (Lessons 1 and 2), recognizing the differences between living man's way and living God's way (Lessons 3 and 4);

   B. The essential elements of biblical change (Lessons 5 - 8) as you die to self and live for the Lord (Lessons 9 and 10);

   C. The necessity of biblically dealing with any anger and bitterness in your life (Lesson 11);

   D. The applicability of this situation to loving your neighbor (Lessons 12 and 13) and family relationships (Lessons 14 - 17);

   E. The possible links between fear and worry (Lesson 19) and feeling depressed;

   F. The seriousness of life-dominating sins and their relationship to your problem of feeling depressed (Lessons 20 and 21); and

   G. The need for you to establish and faithfully maintain specific standards from God's Word for every area of your life (Lesson 22).

   NOTE: *If a medical diagnosis determines organic (physiological) dysfunction, alert your doctor of your desire to follow this* **OVERCOMING DEPRESSION** *plan simultaneously while you are under medical treatment.*

The cross-references cited above are important in dealing with this specific problem area. In dealing with problems biblically, you must examine all aspects of your life. For example, the problem of depression cannot be overcome by dealing with it in isolation. Rather, any specific problem must be dealt with in light of scriptural principles for all of life. As you can see, references to previous lessons are listed in addition to those lessons not yet covered.

If you proceed in biblical counseling training, you will find that God's solutions as presented in this course apply to all problems, including those not covered in this manual.

II. **To become aware of specific times and circumstances in which you feel depressed, make a list of people, places, times, or circumstances where ongoing problems are evident in your life.**

III. Use the VICTORY OVER FAILURES WORKSHEET (Supplement 8). To complete columns 1-3, follow the instructions given in GUIDELINES: VICTORY OVER FAILURES WORKSHEET (Supplement 7).

IV. When completing column four of the VICTORY OVER FAILURES WORKSHEET (Supplement 8):

A. Develop a **basic plan** to overcome the sins you have recognized. In your plan, include deeds (thoughts, speech, and actions) that will help you develop a Christlike manner by taking into account the following guidelines:

1. Think biblically

a. Remember that God has promised to care for you in any situation, no matter how unsettling it may seem (*Psalm 23:1-6, 37:5; Proverbs 3:25-26; Matthew 10:28-31; I Corinthians 10:13; Romans 8:36-39*).

b. Confess all sinful thoughts to God (*I John 1:9*) and ask for His help in changing this sinful pattern (*based on I Thessalonians 5:17; Hebrews 4:15-16; James 1:5*). Know that all sins you have sincerely confessed to the Lord are totally forgiven in His sight (*Psalm 103:10-14; I John 1:9*).

c. Rejoice (*I Thessalonians 5:16*) and give thanks in and for every situation (*Ephesians 5:20; I Thessalonians 5:18*), knowing that endurance in trials helps conform you to the image of Jesus Christ (*based on Romans 5:3-5; James 1:2-4*).

d. Remember that God's forgiveness of you is the basis for you to forgive others (*Matthew 18:21-35; Ephesians 4:32; Colossians 3:13*).

e. Remember that your love for others demonstrates the love that you have for God (*I John 2:9-11; 3:14-16; 4:7-11, 20-21*).

f. Focus your thoughts on glorifying and pleasing God and on being a blessing to others in all situations (*based on Matthew 22:37-39; Luke 9:23-24; I Corinthians 10:31; II Corinthians 5:9, 15; 10:5; Galatians 5:16-17; Philippians 2:3-4, 4:8; Colossians 3:1-2*). Determine specific ways in which you can minister to others as a servant of Jesus Christ (*Matthew 5:16, 7:12, 20:26-28; I Peter 4:10*).

g. Within the very situation in which you find yourself, do not dwell on things that lead to sin. Instead, discipline your mind to think on things that please the Lord (*Philippians 4:8; Colossians 3:2*). Remember to pray for those who persecute you (*Matthew 5:44*).

h. Review psalms, hymns, and spiritual songs that you have memorized (*based on Ephesians 5:19-20; Colossians 3:16*).

i. Think of ways you can encourage other believers, stimulating them to love and good deeds (*Hebrews 10:23-25*).

j. Remember that when you fail to meet your responsibilities biblically, you will sense guilt (*Genesis 3:1-8, esp. verses 7-8; Romans 7:18-24*), which, when not dealt with biblically, may lead to further guilt and possible symptoms or feelings of depression (*Psalm 32:3-4*).

2. Speak biblically

a. Confess your current sins to those whom you have failed to love in a biblical manner, including the sins of failing to complete your responsibilities. Confess any other known sins that you have failed to confess earlier (*based on Psalm 51:1-4; James 4:17, 5:16; I John 1:9*).

To review how to confess your sins to those you have sinned against, refer to:
***GUIDELINES: VICTORY OVER FAILURES WORKSHEET** (Supplement 7)
under **VI. Application of biblical change**, point D. and*
***RECONCILIATION (REMOVING ALL HINDRANCES TO UNITY AND
PEACE)** (Lesson 12, Pages 6-8) under II. Confession.*

 b. Do not complain about your present situation or about feelings of depression *(Philippians 2:14-15)*. Do not speak about your past accomplishments *(Proverb 27:2, 30:32; II Corinthians 10:18)*, sorrows or defeats *(Philippians 3:13-14)*, worries about the future *(Matthew 6:34)*, comparing yourself to yourself and/or others *(II Corinthians 10:12)*, or boastfully promising what you will do in the future *(Proverbs 27:1; James 4:13-16)*. Instead, edify others by thankfully speaking of the goodness of the Lord and the recent difference He has made in your life in this situation *(Luke 10:20; Ephesians 4:29; Colossians 4:6; Hebrews 13:15; I Peter 3:15)*.

 c. Do not slander, gossip, quarrel, or use words that do not edify others *(Proverbs 10:18; Ephesians 4:29, 31; 5:4; Colossians 3:8; II Timothy 2:24; I Peter 2:1)*. Instead, let your speech be truthful and gracious, according to the need of the moment, that you may know how to answer each person *(Ephesians 4:15, 25, 29; Colossians 4:6)*.

 d. Do not bring up another's sin in an accusing or vengeful manner, either to others, yourself, or to the person who has sinned *(Proverbs 10:18, 17:9, 20:19; Ephesians 4:29, 31; Colossians 3:8; I Peter 2:1)*.

 e. Initiate and encourage others to be reconciled with God and yourself, being careful to follow biblical guidelines *(Matthew 5:9, 23-24; Romans 12:18; II Corinthians 2:6-8, 5:18)*.

 *Refer to: **RECONCILIATION (REMOVING ALL HINDRANCES TO UNITY AND PEACE)** (Lesson 12, Pages 6-8).*

3. Act biblically

 a. Since symptoms and feelings of depression can result from any number of factors, gather information to discover what may have contributed to your present situation *(Proverbs 18:15; I Corinthians 11:31; James 1:5)*. *For the following, refer to: **GOD'S STANDARDS FOR YOU** (Lesson 22, Pages 4-6) under **III. Incorporating God's standards into your life**.*

  1) Read **UNDERSTANDING DEPRESSION** (Lesson 18, Pages 4-7). Keep track of all you do this week by using **MY PRESENT SCHEDULE** (Supplement 14). At the end of the week, evaluate your activities and then decide which ones need to be eliminated.

  2) Also determine which biblical tasks and responsibilities have been neglected and need to be incorporated into your next week's schedule.

  3) Use **MY PROPOSED BIBLICAL SCHEDULE** (Supplement 15) to construct your plans as unto the Lord for the coming week.

 b. Forgive others just as God has forgiven you *(Ephesians 4:32; Colossians 3:13)*.
 *Refer to: **FORGIVENESS (FORGIVING OTHERS AS GOD HAS FORGIVEN YOU)** (Lesson 12, Pages 3-5) and determine if you are practicing biblical forgiveness. Make changes as necessary.*

 c. Memorize Scripture verses and study Scripture passages specifically related to feeling depressed, your responsibilities, disciplined living, and God's care and sovereign plan for you *(based on Psalm 119:9, 11, 16; II Corinthians 10:5; Philippians 4:8; II Timothy 2:15)*. *For specific verses to memorize, refer to verses listed in **BIBLICAL PRINCIPLES: DEPRESSION** (Lesson 18, Pages 2-3).*

d.   Memorize psalms, hymns, and spiritual songs to be used at appropriate times, especially when you feel depressed *(based on Ephesians 5:19-20; Colossians 3:16)*.

e.   Pray always with thanksgiving *(Philippians 4:6; I Thessalonians 5:17-18)* and according to God's will *(I John 5:14-15)*. Cast all your cares on the Lord *(I Peter 5:7)*, be anxious for nothing *(Philippians 4:6-7)*, and pray for those who persecute you *(Matthew 5:44)*. A constant practice of prayer helps you not to lose heart *(Luke 18:1)*.

    Refer to: **PRAYER PROVIDES COMMUNICATION WITH GOD** *(Lesson 3, Pages 9-12)*.

f.   Identify all danger signals – such as situations, places, and personal contacts that bring temptation – and take immediate steps to eliminate, resist, or flee the temptation *(based on Psalm 1:1; Proverbs 27:12; I Corinthians 10:13, 15:33; II Timothy 2:22; James 4:7; I Peter 5:8-9)*.

g.   Make amends for wrongdoing and seek reconciliation with those you have offended *(based on Matthew 5:23-24)*. Remember that although you have already confessed your sins *(see 2. a. above)*, you need to demonstrate your serious intent to change.

    See: **RECONCILIATION (REMOVING ALL HINDRANCES TO UNITY AND PEACE)** *(Lesson 12, Pages 6-8)* **under III. Restitution and IV. The importance of reconciliation.**

h.   Bless others through tangible and genuine expressions of biblical love and service (this includes your daily responsibilities as a family member, student, employer, employee, roommate, etc.) *(based on Matthew 7:12; Romans 12:9-13, 15-16; 13:8-10; I Corinthians 13:4-8a; Philippians 2:3-8; I Timothy 6:17-19; I Peter 3:8-9; I John 3:18)*. You are to do this:

1)   Regardless of how you feel *(based on Genesis 4:7; II Corinthians 5:14-15; Galatians 5:16-17; Philippians 4:13; James 4:17)*;

2)   Especially to those who seem to be your enemies or to those against whom you have sinned *(based on Matthew 5:23-24, 43-48; Mark 11:25-26; Romans 12:14, 17-21)*;

3)   With kindness and tenderheartedness for the very individuals with whom you are or have been irritated *(Ephesians 4:31-32)*;

4)   By taking advantage of opportunities to minister, especially in ways that keep you in a Christlike servant attitude towards others *(based on Matthew 20:25-28; Philippians 2:3-8; I Peter 4:10)*; and

5)   By practicing biblical stewardship to honor the Lord and to be of practical help to others *(based on Psalm 24:1; Matthew 25:14-29; I Corinthians 4:1-2; Ephesians 5:15; I Timothy 6:17-19; I Peter 4:10)*.

    Refer to:
    BIBLICAL PRINCIPLES OF STEWARDSHIP *(Lesson 10, Pages 4-6)* and **DYING TO SELF BY SERVING OTHERS** *(Lesson 10, Pages 7-8)*.

    For specific examples of how and when to express biblical love, even in difficult situations, refer to: **THE MEANING OF BIBLICAL LOVE** *(Lesson 13, Pages 4-6)*.

i.   Whenever necessary, conduct a "conference table" using the plan outlined in **OVERCOMING PROBLEMS THROUGH BIBLICAL COMMUNICATION (USING A CONFERENCE TABLE FOR RECONCILIATION)** (Lesson 15, Pages 6-9).

j.   Correct deficiencies in your life that exist because of a lack of discipline or neglect *(based on Colossians 3:1-17; I Timothy 4:7b; James 4:17)*.

k. Begin to do what you know God wants you to do in order to please Him, whether you feel like it or not (*Genesis 4:6-7; Ephesians 4:1; Colossians 1:10; James 4:17*). Review your biblical tasks and responsibilities that you have scheduled on **MY PROPOSED BIBLICAL SCHEDULE** (Supplement 15) and maintain this schedule in a diligent manner during the coming week (*based on Ephesians 5:15-17; Colossians 3:17, 23-24*).

NOTE: God will bless your obedience to His Word (James 1:25). However, enthusiasm may or may not follow your obedience to Him; nevertheless, you are to obey first, not waiting for your feelings to change. If you wait for your feelings to change you may never begin, let alone finish, your responsibilities. Also, do not try to change your feelings; you can't. God never commands you to feel a certain way, but you are to live a life of obedience to Scripture (John 14:15, 21; I John 5:3; II John 1:6).

l. If you need help, ask a Christian friend to hold you accountable for carrying out your **basic and contingency plans** until you have established a new pattern of godly living (*Proverbs 27:17; Ecclesiastes 4:9-10; Hebrews 10:23-25*). If necessary, seek biblical counsel from others (*Proverbs 11:14, 15:22*).

B. As necessary, develop a **"THINK AND DO" LIST** (Supplement 10) using **GUIDELINES: THE "THINK AND DO" LIST** (Supplement 9).

C. Implement your **basic plan** (*James 1:22*) and do it heartily for the Lord (*Colossians 3:23-24*).

D. Develop a **contingency plan** to deal with unusual situations that provide temptation for you to sin by failing to fulfill responsibilities or by neglecting to confess your sins to God and to those against whom you have sinned (*based on Psalm 1:1; Proverbs 27:12; II Timothy 2:22; James 4:17, 5:16; I John 1:9*). Take into account the following guidelines:

1. Immediately ask God for help (*I Thessalonians 5:17; Hebrews 4:15-16; James 1:5*).

2. Review your memorized Scripture verses that deal specifically with God's provision in this situation to avoid a sinful focus on self (*based on Psalm 119:9, 11, 16*).

3. Immediately seek God's perspective.

a. Your peace and joy must be in the Lord and must not be dependent on other persons or circumstances in your life (*Psalm 119:165; Isaiah 26:3; John 14:27, 15:11, 16:33; Romans 14:17*).

b. Regardless of your feelings or circumstances, view this situation as an opportunity for further spiritual growth (*James 1:2-4*) because God will work all things together for good in your life (*based on Psalm 37; Proverbs 3:5-12; Romans 8:28-29; Ephesians 1:3-14; Philippians 1:6*).

1) Remind yourself that you can do all things through Christ who gives you strength (*Philippians 4:11-13*), since your adequacy is from God and not from any natural "inner strength" (*II Corinthians 3:5*). Remember that you can do nothing fruitful apart from Jesus Christ (*John 15:5*).

2) Praise and glorify God that He is sufficient in your areas of weakness (*II Corinthians 12:9-10*) and that He will keep you from stumbling and make you stand blameless and with great joy in the presence of His glory (*Jude 1:24-25*).

c. Remember that God looks on your heart, not on your outward appearance (*I Samuel 16:7*). You must stand blameless before Him in your thoughts, whether others know about it or not *(based on Acts 23:1, 24:16; Romans 14:12; Ephesians 1:4, 4:1; Philippians 1:9-11; Colossians 1:21-22).*

1) If you even begin to think sinful thoughts in this unforeseen circumstance (such as doubting God's loving care or spending time in self-pity), confess them to the Lord *(I John 1:9).*

2) Remember that it is not the amount of time spent sinning or the immensity of the sin (by human standards) by which you should judge yourself. Rather, the fact that you stopped going God's way even momentarily is what matters *(James 2:10, 4:17).*

4. Thank God that you are His servant in your present circumstance *(based on Ephesians 5:20; I Thessalonians 5:18).* Determine how you will give glory to God *(I Corinthians 10:31; I Peter 4:11)* and seek ways to edify others by serving them or by speaking wholesome, uplifting words, no matter how you may feel *(Ephesians 4:29; Philippians 2:3-4).*

5. Follow your contingency plan as necessary. Then, begin again to do those things written in your **basic plan** *(based on Proverbs 24:16; James 1:22-25).*

A CASE STUDY: MARY'S HUSBAND HAS LEFT HER

Mary enters the room for her next counseling session with her head down. She walks much slower than she has in previous weeks.

Counselor: "MARY, YOU LOOK A BIT PALE TODAY, AND YOU DON'T LOOK AS JOYFUL AS YOU DID THE LAST TIME WE MET. WHERE IS TOM?"

Mary: "TOM IS UPSET WITH ME, AND HE'S NOT COMING ... BUT I DON'T SEE HOW IT COULD BE MY FAULT. I WAS SICK THIS WEEK WITH A HIGH FEVER FOR ABOUT FOUR DAYS. I SPENT A LOT OF TIME IN BED SO I DIDN'T HAVE THE OPPORTUNITY TO DO MUCH AROUND THE HOUSE. WHEN I FINALLY WAS ABLE TO GET OUT OF BED, I WAS MET WITH DISASTER! THE KIDS AND TOM HAD TOTALLY DESTROYED THE HOUSE. FOOD WAS EVERYWHERE, CLOTHES AND PAPERS WERE ALL OVER THE FLOOR...NOT TO MENTION THE NORMAL OVERFLOW OF TOM'S SHIRTS THAT NEEDED TO BE IRONED! I COULDN'T FIND ANYTHING BECAUSE DIRTY CLOTHES AND MISPLACED ITEMS WERE FROM ONE END OF THE HOUSE TO THE OTHER."

Counselor: "HOW DID YOU RESPOND?"

Mary: "I COULDN'T FACE THE MESS SO I TURNED AROUND AND WENT BACK TO BED. AFTER ALL THE WORK I HAD DONE PREVIOUSLY WITH MY SCHEDULE AND LISTS OF PRIORITIES, I JUST COULDN'T HANDLE THE THOUGHT OF STARTING ALL OVER AGAIN! I HAVEN'T SLEPT WELL FOR THE LAST TWO NIGHTS EITHER, THINKING ABOUT HOW I AM EVER GOING TO GET THINGS BACK TO NORMAL. WHEN I WAKE UP IN THE MORNING, I JUST DON'T FEEL LIKE TACKLING IT. THIS MORNING I CAME INTO THE KITCHEN FOR A CUP OF TEA AND THERE WASN'T A CLEAN CUP IN THE HOUSE. DISHES WERE PILED UP, THE BABY HAD GOTTEN INTO THE GARBAGE AND TRASH WAS ALL OVER THE FLOOR. I'VE BEEN LYING DOWN ALL MORNING. I CAN'T CLEAN UP THAT HOUSE! IT'S TOO MUCH FOR ME! I DON'T KNOW WHERE TO START AND I CAN'T SEEM TO GET MOTIVATED TO START. I DREAD GOING BACK TO THAT MESS AFTER I LEAVE THIS SESSION. I THINK I'LL JUST GO BACK TO BED AND HOPE IT ALL DISAPPEARS. IT MUST BE ALL A BAD DREAM!"

How will you counsel Mary by helping her: (1) to become aware of her own sinful self-focus? (2) to see the consequences of her sin and the further difficulties she will inevitably encounter? and (3) to confront other family members biblically for their unloving actions and lack of faithfulness in completing responsibilities?

What verses could give Mary the biblical hope that she needs in this situation?

What homework would you assign so Mary could take the necessary steps to accomplish these biblical changes?

What will you do to respond biblically to Tom?

LESSON 18: HOMEWORK

> This lesson's **HOMEWORK** will help you realize that there
> is hope in any situation (even during times of depression)
> as you live to please the Lord instead of yourself (based on
> *Psalm 145:14; John 16:33; II Corinthians 4:16-18;*
> *Ephesians 5:15-17; Colossians 1:9-12; I Timothy 4:7-11;*
> *Hebrews 4:15-16; James 1:2-4, 2:22-25).*

✔ *homework completed*

☐ A. * In your own words, write the meaning of *Genesis 4:7* and *James 1:22*. Memorize *Genesis 4:7* and *James 1:22* and begin memorizing *Matthew 6:33-34* and *I John 4:18*. Review previous memory verses.

☐ B. * Read **BIBLICAL PRINCIPLES: DEPRESSION** (Lesson 18, Pages 2-3). Highlight listed verses that you have not marked in your previous studies.

☐ C. * Study **UNDERSTANDING DEPRESSION** (Lesson 18, Pages 4-7). Notice how God's Word gives you hope and provides direction during those times in which you may feel depressed. Even if you are under medical care, you can still live biblically (no matter how you feel) as you obey God's Word. Highlight applicable verses.

☐ D. * Study **OVERCOMING DEPRESSION** (Lesson 18, Pages 8-13). If applicable, use a **VICTORY OVER FAILURES WORKSHEET** (Supplement 8) and begin to take the necessary steps to overcome depression (especially in relation to the problem that the Lord wants you to work on during this course).

☐ E. * Read **A CASE STUDY: MARY'S HUSBAND HAS LEFT HER** (Lesson 18, Page 14). Answer the questions which follow.

☐ F. * In conjunction with this lesson, answer question 27 under **Open Book Test** (Lesson 23, Page 3).

* *The completion of assignments marked with an asterisk (*) is a prerequisite for further biblical counseling training.*

LESSON 18: STUDY GUIDE FOR DAILY DEVOTIONS
(INCLUDING SCRIPTURE MEMORY AND HOMEWORK)

> This week's **STUDY GUIDE** will help you realize that there is hope in any situation (even during times of depression) as you live to please the Lord instead of yourself *(based on Psalm 145:14; John 16:33; II Corinthians 4:16-18; Ephesians 5:15-17; Colossians 1:9-12; I Timothy 4:7-11; Hebrews 4:15-16; James 1:2-4, 2:22-25).*

Scripture Memory

1. * Memorize *Genesis 4:7* and *James 1:22*. Begin memorizing *Matthew 6:33-34* and *I John 4:18.*
2. Carry your memory verse cards from previous weeks along with this week's memory verses. Review your memory verses during spare moments throughout the day.

Daily Devotional Study Guide

FIRST DAY

1. Open with prayer.
2. * Read *Principle 78* under **BIBLICAL PRINCIPLES: DEPRESSION** (Lesson 18, Pages 2-3). Highlight the listed verses in your Bible.
3. * Write the meaning of *Genesis 4:7* and *James 1:22* in your own words.
4. Close with prayer.

SECOND DAY

1. Open with prayer.
2. * Read *Principle 79* under **BIBLICAL PRINCIPLES: DEPRESSION** (Lesson 18, Pages 2-3). Highlight the listed verses in your Bible. *Also review and note the applicability of Principle 16 (Lesson 6, Page 2) to this problem.*
3. * Study **UNDERSTANDING DEPRESSION** (Lesson 18, Pages 4-7). This is the first day of a two-day study. Mark any statements that point out changes that you need to make in your life. Highlight any verses that are especially applicable to you.
4. Close with prayer.

THIRD DAY

1. Open with prayer.
2. * Read *Principle 80* under **BIBLICAL PRINCIPLES: DEPRESSION** (Lesson 18, Pages 2-3). Highlight the listed verses in your Bible.
3. * Complete your study of **UNDERSTANDING DEPRESSION** (Lesson 18, Pages 4-7).
4. Close with prayer.

FOURTH DAY

1. Open with prayer.
2. * Read *Principle 81* under **BIBLICAL PRINCIPLES: DEPRESSION** (Lesson 18, Pages 2-3). Highlight the listed verses in your Bible.

3. * Study **OVERCOMING DEPRESSION** (Lesson 18, Pages 8-13). If applicable, use a **VICTORY OVER FAILURES WORKSHEET** (Supplement 8) and begin to take the necessary steps to overcome depression (especially in relation to the problem that the Lord wants you to work on during this course). This is the first day of a three-day study.
4. Close with prayer.

FIFTH DAY

1. Open with prayer.
2. * Read *Principle 82* under **BIBLICAL PRINCIPLES: DEPRESSION** (Lesson 18, Pages 2-3). Highlight the listed verses in your Bible. *Also review Principles 28 and 29 (Lesson 7, Page 2) and note their applicability to your life.*
3. * Continue your study of **OVERCOMING DEPRESSION** (Lesson 18, Pages 8-13).
4. Close with prayer.

SIXTH DAY

1. Open with prayer.
2. * Read *Principle 83* under **BIBLICAL PRINCIPLES: DEPRESSION** (Lesson 18, Pages 2-3). Highlight the listed verses in your Bible.
3. * Complete your study of **OVERCOMING DEPRESSION** (Lesson 18, Pages 8-13).
4. Close with prayer.

SEVENTH DAY

1. Open with prayer.
2. * Review *Principle 14, revised from Lesson 5, Page 2* and *Principle 39, revised from Lesson 10, Page 2.* Both of these revised principles are on Page 3 of Lesson 18.
3. * Read **A CASE STUDY: MARY'S HUSBAND HAS LEFT HER** (Lesson 18, Page 14). Answer the questions which follow.
4. * In conjunction with this lesson, answer question 27 under **Open Book Test** (Lesson 23, Page 3).
5. Close in prayer.
6. Ask a friend to listen to you recite this week's memory verses. Explain how these verses have application to your life.

*   *The completion of assignments marked with an asterisk (*) is a prerequisite for further biblical counseling training.*

LESSON 19

FEAR AND WORRY

"But seek first His kingdom and His righteousness; and all these things shall be added to you. Therefore do not be anxious for tomorrow; for tomorrow will care for itself. Each day has enough trouble of its own."

Matthew 6:33-34

"There is no fear in love; but perfect love casts out fear, because fear involves punishment, and the one who fears is not perfected in love."

I John 4:18

LESSON 19: FEAR AND WORRY

> The temptations to fear and to worry are common but can be overcome as you trust God for all things and in all circumstances. As you remain obedient to Scripture, you will not be hampered by fear and worry. Instead, you will experience the peace and joy that God provides through the Lord Jesus Christ *(based on Psalm 37:1-5, 56:11; Matthew 6:33-34; John 14:27, 15:10-11, 16:33; I Corinthians 10:13, 31; Romans 8:28-29; Philippians 4:6-9; I Peter 3:13-16; I John 4:18, 5:4-5).*

I. **The purposes of this lesson are:**

   A. To remind you of God's resources to help you overcome fear and worry;

   B. To alert you to situations in which you may be tempted to fear and worry;

   C. To show how Christlike love, obedient living, and purposeful prayer all contribute to overcoming fear and worry;

   D. To present a scriptural plan for you to overcome fear and worry; and

   E. To provide opportunity for you to help someone overcome fear and worry through the continuation of a case study.

II. **The outline of this lesson**

   A. Self-confrontation

      1. **BIBLICAL PRINCIPLES: FEAR AND WORRY** (Lesson 19, Pages 2-3)

      2. **TEMPTATIONS TO FEAR AND WORRY** (Lesson 19, Pages 4-5)

      3. **LOVE VERSUS FEAR (GOD'S WAY VERSUS MAN'S WAY)** (Lesson 19, Pages 6-7)

   B. Steps for spiritual growth

      1. **OVERCOMING FEAR AND WORRY** (Lesson 19, Pages 8-12)

      2. **LESSON 19: HOMEWORK** (Lesson 19, Page 14)

      3. **STUDY GUIDE FOR DAILY DEVOTIONS** (Lesson 19, Pages 15-16)

      4. **GUIDELINES: FREEDOM FROM ANXIETY (BIBLICAL ACTION AND PRAYER PLAN)** (Supplement 16)

      5. **FREEDOM FROM ANXIETY (BIBLICAL ACTION AND PRAYER PLAN)** (Supplement 17)

   C. Biblical counseling

      A CASE STUDY: MARY'S HUSBAND HAS LEFT HER (Lesson 19, Page 13)

BIBLICAL PRINCIPLES: FEAR AND WORRY

> Fear, worry, and anxiety are sins which can paralyze your mind, immobilize your body, and hinder your growth in Christ. Adam and Eve initially committed these sins in the Garden of Eden after believing Satan's lies and subsequently choosing to disobey God. Satan, not God, is behind these obstacles to spiritual maturity; but God has graciously given you all that is necessary to overcome them *(based on Genesis 3:9-10; Matthew 6:25-34; Philippians 4:6-9; II Timothy 1:7; I John 4:18, 5:4-5).*

I. God's View

(Principle 84) Overwhelming fear and worry result from living to please yourself instead of living to please the Lord *(based on Matthew 6:25-34; 25:14-30, esp. verses 25-26; Luke 12:4; I Peter 3:13-16; I John 4:15-19).* Instead of a sinful self-focus, you are to fear (reverence) God *(Deuteronomy 5:29, 13:4; Psalm 25:14, 33:8, 147:11; Proverbs 10:27; Luke 1:50, 12:5; II Corinthians 7:1; I Peter 2:17)* and have a responsive concern (care) for others *(based on I Corinthians 12:25; II Corinthians 11:24-30, esp. verse 28; Philippians 4:10).*

II. Your hope

(Principle 85) God has not given you a spirit of timidity (fear) but of power and love and discipline (sound judgment) *(II Timothy 1:7).*

(Principle 86) God has promised to provide all the necessities of life as you seek to please Him *(Proverbs 3:5-10; Luke 12:22-34; Philippians 4:19).* God is always available to help you *(Psalm 55:22, 94:17-19, 145:14),* and He is firmly in control of every aspect of your life *(based on Psalm 139:1-18; Jeremiah 17:7-8, 29:11; Lamentations 3:32; Romans 8:28-29, 35-39).*

III. Your change

(Principle 87) Put off timid, fearful, and troubled thinking. Put on love and sound judgment in the power of the Holy Spirit *(based on II Timothy 1:7; I John 4:9-19, esp. verse 18).* Recognize that in Christ Jesus you have peace *(John 14:27, 16:33).*

(Principle 88) Put off self-centered concern about the future *(Matthew 6:25, 34; Luke 12:22-34, esp. verses 22-23).* Put on "doing the Word" *(based on Psalm 119:165; Matthew 6:33-34; Philippians 4:9; Hebrews 5:14; James 1:22-25),* with special emphasis given to prayer with thanksgiving *(Philippians 4:6-7; I Thessalonians 5:17-18)* and dwelling on the things of God *(Philippians 4:8; Colossians 3:2).*

IV. **Your practice**

(Principle 89)   In order to deal biblically with fear, you must confess your self-centered fear to the Lord *(I John 1:9)* and fulfill your responsibilities in Christlike love *(I Corinthians 13:4-8a; Colossians 3:12-14)*, regardless of your feelings *(based on II Corinthians 5:14-15; Philippians 4:6-9; I John 4:18)*.

(Principle 90)   To overcome worry, make a plan to accomplish today's tasks and do each task heartily as unto the Lord *(Proverbs 16:9; Ephesians 5:15-17; Philippians 4:6-9; Colossians 3:17, 23-24)*.

TEMPTATIONS TO FEAR AND WORRY

> When you live to please yourself, circumstances that God designs to teach you to trust and obey Him instead become temptations for you to fear and worry *(based on Psalm 31:1-5, 13-15; 56:4, 11; Isaiah 12:2; Lamentations 3:22-24; Luke 12:29-31; Philippians 4:6-9; James 1:2-4; I Peter 5:5-7).*

I. **Situations that tempt you to fear and worry (sample lists – to be read downward)**

Circumstances of life	Mental/Spiritual
Impending death	Refusing salvation in Christ Jesus
Unexpected bills	Planning to sin or hiding past sins
Reduction or loss of income	Procrastination, indecision
Crippling injury, prolonged illness	Lack of prayer
Imminent surgery	Not knowing the future
Perceived loss of a relationship	Focusing on changing others
Searching for a new church, job, home, etc.	Failing to deal with another's sin in a biblical manner
Persecution, threats	Refusing to forgive another
Children leaving home	Always wanting your own way
Difficult job or home situation	Expecting perfection in others

II. **Your biblical response to situations that tempt you to fear and worry**

A. You are to fear (reverence) God *(Psalm 33:8; Proverbs 23:17; Ecclesiastes 12:13; Matthew 10:28)*, which will result in (a sample list):

1. Salvation *(Psalm 85:9);*
2. Wisdom and knowledge *(Psalm 111:10; Proverbs 1:7, 2:5; Isaiah 33:6);*
3. Steadfastness *(Psalm 112:7);*
4. Improved health *(Proverbs 3:7-8);*
5. Prolonged life *(Proverbs 10:27);*
6. Vitality (fountain of life) *(Proverbs 14:27);*
7. God's goodness and lovingkindness toward you *(Psalm 31:19; 103:11, 13, 17);*
8. Eternal reward *(Revelation 11:18);*
9. God's watchfulness and protection over your life *(Psalm 33:18-22; 34:7, 9);*
10. Blessing from the Lord *(Psalm 115:13);*

11. Obedience and a motivation to serve Him *(Deuteronomy 10:12; II Corinthians 7:1)*;

12. Satisfied sleep *(Proverbs 19:23)*; and

13. Strong confidence *(Proverbs 14:26)*.

B. You are not to fear what man might do to you *(Numbers 14:9; Deuteronomy 1:16-17; Psalm 46:1-3; Proverbs 3:25-26; Matthew 10:24-28)*. Instead, you are to trust God *(Psalm 23:4, 56:11, 118:6)* and respond with actions motivated by loving concern *(for example: I Samuel 17:11, 24, 32; Esther 4:11-5:2; Acts 16:19-32; II Corinthians 11:23-29, esp. verses 28-29)*.

C. You are not to worry (be anxious) since this reveals a lack of trust in God and will prohibit you from being spiritually fruitful *(based on Matthew 6:25-34; Luke 8:14)*.

Refer to: **PLEASING SELF OR PLEASING GOD** *(Lesson 9, Pages 10-11) to be reminded that it is not the intensity of an emotion that determines its correctness. Instead, the key issue is whether your response reveals that you are living for self or living for the Lord.*

LOVE VERSUS FEAR
(GOD'S WAY VERSUS MAN'S WAY)

> Man often fears the consequences of his actions and the "punishment" of life in general because he is not perfected (matured, completed) in the love of God. God's love is perfected in you when you sincerely believe in the Lord Jesus Christ, remain obedient to God's Word, and love others in the Body of Christ. Love that is perfected in this manner casts out all your fear *(based on Romans 8:35-39; I Corinthians 13:4-8a; I John 2:3-5; 4:7-8, 12, 15-21).*

I. **The contrast between love and fear (sample list)**

GOD'S WAY (LOVE)	MAN'S WAY (FEAR)
A. Love looks for opportunities to give *(John 3:16; I John 3:16-18).*	Fear keeps a wary eye on possible consequences of involvement.
B. Love lays down its life for others *(I John 3:16).*	Fear will not take personal risks to help another.
C. Love believes all things *(I Corinthians 13:7).*	Fear is highly suspicious.
D. Love never fails *(I Corinthians 13:8a).*	Fear occasions greater fear – failure to assume responsibilities brings more fear of consequences of acting irresponsibly.

Review: **THE MEANING OF BIBLICAL LOVE** *(Lesson 13, Pages 4-6). Notice that for each element of biblical love, self-focused fear tells you to do just the opposite.*

II. **The powerful love of Jesus Christ disarms fear**

A. By conquering death, the Lord Jesus has delivered those who trust (believe in) Him from the fear of death and has broken their slavery to sin and Satan *(based on Romans 6:5-7; Hebrews 2:14-15).*

B. God's love for you, demonstrated by His Son's death on the cross for your sins, can bring you into His eternal family through Jesus Christ and thus lead you out of fear *(Romans 5:8, 8:15).*

C. Christ's love empowers you to be an overwhelming conqueror in any situation of life *(Romans 8:35-39),* as you exercise your faith in and through Him *(I John 5:4-5).*

D. Through Jesus Christ, God has granted you power and love and discipline (sound judgment), which cannot exist with a spirit of fear *(II Timothy 1:7).*

III. **Perfect love casts out fear**

A. Perfect love is demonstrated in God's gift of His only Son, Jesus Christ *(based on John 3:16-17; Romans 5:8; I John 3:1, 16; 4:9-10).*

---

1. Your ability to love others is based in God's love to you through the Lord Jesus Christ *(John 13:34-35, 15:12; I John 4:7-11, 19-21).*

2. You are to follow the example of your Heavenly Father and practice perfect love towards others, even in difficult circumstances *(based on Matthew 5:43-48).*

3. Your loving response to God for His great love to you through Jesus is demonstrated by obeying His Word in all things *(John 14:15, 21, 23-24; I John 5:3; II John 1:6)* and by loving others *(I John 3:10-18; 4:7-8, 20-21).*

B. God's love through Jesus Christ is perfected (matured, completed) in you as you abide in Him *(I John 4:15-17).* You can be assured you are abiding in Him when you:

1. Confess Jesus as the Son of God *(I John 2:22-25; 4:9, 14-15),*

2. Keep (obey) the Word of God *(I John 2:5, 3:24),* and

3. Practice biblical love toward others *(I John 4:12).*

    Refer to: **THE MEANING OF BIBLICAL LOVE** *(Lesson 13, Pages 4-6).*

C. To the extent that God's love is perfected within you (see **III.** B. above), you will be able to conquer fear *(based on I John 4:18).*

OVERCOMING FEAR AND WORRY

> In all circumstances of life, you can choose to follow man's way (trusting in yourself and natural wisdom) or God's way (trusting in God and His wisdom). To overcome any problem, including fear and worry, you must discipline yourself for the purpose of godliness *(based on I Corinthians 3:19-20; Philippians 4:6-9; I Timothy 4:7-8; II Timothy 1:7; James 1:22-25, 4:17; I John 4:18).*

I. **Carefully review the following cross-references:**

A. The foundational, biblical requirements for change (Lessons 1 and 2), recognizing the differences between living man's way and living God's way (Lessons 3 and 4);

B. The essential elements of biblical change (Lessons 5 - 8) as you die to self and live for the Lord (Lessons 9 and 10);

C. The necessity of biblically dealing with any anger and bitterness in your life (Lesson 11);

D. The applicability of this situation to loving your neighbor (Lessons 12 and 13) and family relationships (Lessons 14 - 17);

E. The possible link between feeling depressed (Lesson 18) and fear and worry;

F. The seriousness of life-dominating sins and their relationship to fear and worry (Lessons 20 and 21); and

G. The need for you to establish and faithfully maintain specific standards from God's Word for every area of your life (Lesson 22).

NOTE: The cross-references cited above are important in dealing with fear and worry. In dealing with problems biblically, you must examine all aspects of your life. For example, the problem of fear cannot be overcome by dealing with it as an end in itself. Rather, any specific problem must be dealt with in light of scriptural principles for all of life. As you can see, references to previous lessons are listed in addition to those lessons not yet covered.

If you proceed in biblical counseling training, you will find that God's solutions as presented in this course apply to all problems, including those not covered in this manual.

II. **To become aware of the patterns of sin or temptations in regard to fear and worry, make a list of people, places, times, or circumstances where ongoing problems are evident in your life.**

III. **Use the VICTORY OVER FAILURES WORKSHEET (Supplement 8). To complete columns 1-3, follow the instructions given in GUIDELINES: VICTORY OVER FAILURES WORKSHEET (Supplement 7).**

IV. **When completing column four of the VICTORY OVER FAILURES WORKSHEET (Supplement 8):**

A. Develop a **basic plan** to overcome the sins you have recognized. In your plan, include deeds (thoughts, speech, and actions) that will help you develop a Christlike manner by taking into account the following guidelines:

1. Think biblically

    a. Remember that God has promised to care for you in any situation, no matter how unsettling it may seem *(Psalm 23:1-6, 37:5; Proverbs 3:25-26; Matthew 10:28-31; I Corinthians 10:13; Romans 8:36-39)*.

    b. Confess all sinful thoughts to God *(I John 1:9)* and ask for His help in changing this sinful pattern *(based on I Thessalonians 5:17; Hebrews 4:15-16; James 1:5)*.

    c. Rejoice *(I Thessalonians 5:16)* and give thanks in and for every situation *(Ephesians 5:20; I Thessalonians 5:18)*, knowing that endurance in trials helps conform you to the image of Christ *(based on Romans 5:3-5; James 1:2-4)*.

    d. Remember that God's forgiveness of you is the basis for you to forgive others *(Matthew 18:21-35; Ephesians 4:32; Colossians 3:13)*.

    e. Remember that your love for others demonstrates the love that you have for God *(I John 2:9-11; 3:14-16; 4:7-11, 20-21)*.

    f. Focus your thoughts on glorifying and pleasing God and on being a blessing to others in all situations *(based on Matthew 22:37-39; Luke 9:23-24; II Corinthians 5:9, 15; 10:5; Galatians 5:16-17; Philippians 2:3-4, 4:8; Colossians 3:1-2)*.

    g. Within the very situation in which you find yourself, do not dwell on things that lead to sin. Instead, discipline your mind to think on things that please the Lord *(Philippians 4:8; Colossians 3:2)*. Remember to pray for those who persecute you *(Matthew 5:44)*.

    h. Review psalms, hymns, and spiritual songs that you have memorized *(based on Ephesians 5:19-20; Colossians 3:16)*.

    i. Think of ways you can encourage other believers that can stimulate them to love and good deeds *(Hebrews 10:23-25)*.

2. Speak biblically

    a. Confess to the Lord your sins of fear and worry. Confess your sins to those whom you have failed to love in a biblical manner, including the sins of failing to complete your responsibilities. Confess any other remembered sins that you have failed to confess earlier *(based on Psalm 51:1-4; James 5:16; I John 1:9)*.

        To review how to confess your sins to those you have sinned against, refer to:
        GUIDELINES: VICTORY OVER FAILURES WORKSHEET *(Supplement 7)*
            under **VI. Application of biblical change**, *point D. and*
        RECONCILIATION (REMOVING ALL HINDRANCES TO UNITY AND PEACE) *(Lesson 12, Pages 6-8) under II. Confession.*

    b. Do not speak about your past accomplishments *(Proverbs 27:2, 30:32; II Corinthians 10:18)*, sorrows or defeats (especially those linked to fear and worry) *(Philippians 3:13-14)*, anxiety about the future *(Matthew 6:34)*, comparing yourself to yourself and/or others *(II Corinthians 10:12)*, or boastfully promising what you will do in the future *(Proverbs 27:1; James 4:13-16)*. Instead, edify others by thankfully speaking of the goodness of the Lord and the recent difference He has made in your life *(Luke 10:20; Ephesians 4:29; Colossians 4:6; Hebrews 13:15; I Peter 3:15)*.

c. Do not slander, gossip, quarrel, or use words that do not edify others *(Proverbs 10:18; Ephesians 4:29, 31; 5:4; Colossians 3:8; II Timothy 2:24; I Peter 2:1).* Instead, let your speech be truthful and gracious, according to the need of the moment, that you may know how to answer each person *(Ephesians 4:15, 25, 29; Colossians 4:6).*

d. Do not bring up another's sin in an accusing or vengeful manner, either to others, yourself, or to the person who has sinned *(Proverbs 10:18, 17:9, 20:19; Ephesians 4:29, 31; Colossians 3:8; I Peter 2:1).*

e. Encourage reconciliation with God and others, following biblical guidelines *(Matthew 5:9, 23-24; Romans 12:18; II Corinthians 2:6-8, 5:18).*

   Refer to: **RECONCILIATION (REMOVING ALL HINDRANCES TO UNITY AND PEACE)** *(Lesson 12, Pages 6-8).*

3. Act biblically

a. Forgive others just as God has forgiven you *(Ephesians 4:32; Colossians 3:13).*

   Refer to: **FORGIVENESS (FORGIVING OTHERS AS GOD HAS FORGIVEN YOU)** *(Lesson 12, Pages 3-5) and determine if you are practicing biblical forgiveness. Make changes as necessary.*

b. Memorize Scripture verses and study Scripture passages specifically related to fear, worry, biblical love, abiding in God, and trusting in Him *(based on Psalm 119:9, 11, 16; II Corinthians 10:5; Philippians 4:8; II Timothy 2:15).* Memorize psalms, hymns, and spiritual songs that can be used whenever you are tempted to fear or worry *(based on Ephesians 5:19-20; Colossians 3:16).*

   Many promises of Scripture applicable to someone who is depressed are also beneficial to help overcome fear and worry. For specific verses to memorize, refer to:
   BIBLICAL PRINCIPLES: DEPRESSION *(Lesson 18, Pages 2-3) and*
   BIBLICAL PRINCIPLES: FEAR AND WORRY *(Lesson 19, Pages 2-3).*

c. Pray always with thanksgiving *(Philippians 4:6; I Thessalonians 5:17-18)* and according to God's will *(I John 5:14-15).* Humbly submit to fellow-believers *(I Peter 5:5)* and to the Lord *(I Peter 5:6),* cast all your cares on Him *(I Peter 5:7),* and pray for those who persecute you *(Matthew 5:44).*

   Refer to:
   GUIDELINES: FREEDOM FROM ANXIETY (BIBLICAL ACTION AND PRAYER PLAN) *(Supplement 16) and*
   FREEDOM FROM ANXIETY (BIBLICAL ACTION AND PRAYER PLAN) *(Supplement 17).*

d. Identify all danger signals – such as situations, places, and personal contacts that bring temptation – and take immediate steps to eliminate, flee, or resist the temptation *(based on Psalm 1:1; Proverbs 27:12; I Corinthians 15:33; II Timothy 2:22; James 4:7; I Peter 5:8-9).*

e. Make amends for wrongdoing and seek reconciliation with those you have offended *(based on Matthew 5:23-24).* Remember that although you have already confessed your sins *(see 2. a. above),* you need to demonstrate your serious intent to change.

   See: **RECONCILIATION (REMOVING ALL HINDRANCES TO UNITY AND PEACE)** *(Lesson 12, Pages 6-8) under III. Restitution and IV. The importance of reconciliation.*

f. Bless others through tangible and genuine expressions of biblical love and service (this includes your daily responsibilities as a family member, student, employer, employee, roommate, etc.) *(based on Matthew 7:12; Romans 12:9-13, 15-16; 13:8-10; I Corinthians 13:4-8a; Philippians 2:3-8; I Timothy 6:17-19; I Peter 3:8-9; I John 3:18).* You are to do this:

1) Regardless of how you feel *(based on Genesis 4:7; II Corinthians 5:14-15; Galatians 5:16-17; Philippians 4:13; James 4:17);*

2) Especially to those who seem to be your enemies or to those against whom you have sinned *(based on Matthew 5:23-24, 43-48; Mark 11:25-26; Romans 12:14, 17-21);*

3) With kindness and tenderheartedness for the very individuals with whom you are or have been irritated *(Ephesians 4:31-32);*

4) By taking advantage of opportunities to minister, especially in ways that keep you in a Christlike servant attitude toward others *(based on Matthew 20:25-28; Philippians 2:3-8; I Peter 4:10);* and

5) By practicing biblical stewardship to honor the Lord and to be of practical help to others *(based on Psalm 24:1; Matthew 25:14-29; I Corinthians 4:1-2; Ephesians 5:15-17; I Timothy 6:17-19; I Peter 4:10).*

Refer to:
***BIBLICAL PRINCIPLES OF STEWARDSHIP** (Lesson 10, Pages 4-6) and **DYING TO SELF BY SERVING OTHERS** (Lesson 10, Page 7-8).*

For specific examples of how and when to express biblical love, even in difficult situations, refer to: **THE MEANING OF BIBLICAL LOVE** *(Lesson 13, Pages 4-6).*

g. Whenever necessary, conduct a "conference table" using the plan outlined in **OVERCOMING PROBLEMS THROUGH BIBLICAL COMMUNICATION (USING A CONFERENCE TABLE FOR RECONCILIATION)** (Lesson 15, Pages 6-9).

h. Correct deficiencies in your life that exist because of a lack of discipline or neglect *(based on Colossians 3:1-17; I Timothy 4:7b; James 4:17).*

i. If you need help, ask a Christian friend to hold you accountable in carrying out your **basic and contingency plans** until you have established a new pattern of godly living *(Proverbs 27:17; Ecclesiastes 4:9-10; Hebrews 10:23-25).* If necessary, seek biblical counsel from others *(Proverbs 11:14, 15:22).*

j. Quickly fill the many voids created by putting off the old patterns of fear and worry with a vigorous program of living righteously and spending much time with other believers *(II Timothy 2:22; Hebrews 10:23-25).*

For the following three points, refer to: **GOD'S STANDARDS FOR YOU** *(Lesson 22, Pages 4-6) under* **III. Incorporating God's standards into your life.**

k. Keep track of all you do this week by using **MY PRESENT SCHEDULE** (Supplement 14). At the end of the week, evaluate your activities and then decide which ones need to be eliminated.

l. Determine which biblical tasks and responsibilities have been neglected and need to be incorporated into your next week's schedule.

m. Use **MY PROPOSED BIBLICAL SCHEDULE** (Supplement 15) to construct your plans as unto the Lord for the coming week.

B. As necessary, develop a **"THINK AND DO" LIST** (Supplement 10) using **GUIDELINES: THE "THINK AND DO" LIST** (Supplement 9).

C. Implement your **basic plan** *(James 1:22)* and do it heartily as unto the Lord *(Colossians 3:23-24).*

D. Develop a **contingency plan** to deal with unusual situations that tempt you to fear or worry. Take into account the following guidelines:

1. Immediately ask God for help *(Hebrews 4:15-16; James 1:5)*.

2. Review your memorized Scripture verses that deal specifically with fear or worry *(based on Psalm 119:9, 11, 16)*.

3. Immediately seek God's perspective.

   a. Regardless of your feelings or circumstances, view this situation as an opportunity for further spiritual growth *(James 1:2-4)* because God will work all things together for good in your life *(based on Psalm 37; Proverbs 3:5-12; Romans 8:28-29; Ephesians 1:3-14; Philippians 1:6)*.

      1) Remind yourself that you can do all things through Christ who gives you strength *(Philippians 4:11-13)*, since your adequacy is from God and not from any natural "inner strength" *(II Corinthians 3:5)*. Remember that you can do nothing fruitful apart from Jesus Christ *(John 15:5)*.

      2) Praise and glorify God that He is sufficient in your areas of weakness *(II Corinthians 12:9-10)* and that He will keep you from stumbling and make you stand blameless and with great joy in the presence of His glory *(Jude 1:24-25)*.

   b. Remember that God looks on your heart, not on your outward appearance *(I Samuel 16:7)*. You must stand blameless before Him in your thoughts (including thoughts which dwell on fear and worry) whether others know about it or not *(based on Acts 23:1, 24:16; Romans 14:12; Ephesians 1:4, 4:1; Philippians 1:9-11; Colossians 1:21-22)*.

      1) If you even begin to think sinful thoughts (especially of fear or worry) in this unforeseen circumstance, confess them to the Lord *(I John 1:9)*.

      2) Remember that it is not the amount of time spent sinning or the immensity of the sin (by human standards) by which you should judge yourself. Rather, the fact that you stopped going God's way even momentarily is what matters *(James 2:10, 4:17)*.

4. Thank God that you are His servant in your present circumstance *(based on Ephesians 5:20; I Thessalonians 5:18)*. Determine how you will give glory to God instead of being fearful or worrying *(based on I Corinthians 10:31; I Peter 4:11)*. Seek ways to edify and serve others, especially those about whom you are tempted to fear or worry *(Ephesians 4:29; Philippians 2:3-4)*.

5. Act according to your **contingency plan** as soon as you detect temptation to fear or worry. Then, begin again to do those things written in your **basic plan** *(based on Proverbs 24:16; James 1:22-25)*.

A CASE STUDY: MARY'S HUSBAND HAS LEFT HER

> Remember the faithfulness of God and His forgiveness of
> your sins whenever you fail to obey His Word
> (*II Timothy 2:11-13, esp. verse 13; I John 1:9*).

This week both Mary and her husband Tom come to the session. After both enter the room, Tom begins to speak.

Tom: "I HAVE ALREADY ASKED THE LORD AND MARY TO FORGIVE ME FOR MY FAITHLESSNESS IN NOT ATTENDING OUR LAST SESSION TOGETHER. BOTH HAVE FORGIVEN ME. NOW, I ASK YOUR FORGIVENESS FOR MY SELF-CENTERED BEHAVIOR IN FAILING TO ATTEND THE LAST SESSION."

Each member of the counseling team verbally grants forgiveness to Tom. The lead counselor continues:

Counselor: "YOU HAVE TAKEN A BIBLICAL STEP IN CONFESSING YOUR SINS TO THE LORD AND OTHERS. LET'S TAKE TIME TO REVIEW THE STEPS THAT YOU ARE TO TAKE TO DEMONSTRATE YOUR WILLINGNESS TO BE RECONCILED TO THE LORD AND TO MARY."

The counselor reviews the steps of reconciliation that demonstrate Tom's renewed commitment to live again to please the Lord. Tom very excitedly expresses how he has already obeyed God's Word in this regard, and Mary confirms his testimony but in a subdued manner. She lowers her head and begins to speak rather haltingly.

Mary: "I'VE BEEN PRAYING FOR US TO HAVE A CHRISTIAN HOME FOR A LONG TIME. . . I REALLY DON'T KNOW. WHAT HAPPENS IF THIS DOESN'T LAST AND THINGS DON'T WORK OUT? SUPPOSE TOM BECOMES A MORE LOVING HUSBAND AND THEN GOES BACK TO HIS OLD WAYS? WHAT IF HE DECIDES LATER ON TO SIN CONTINUALLY AND THEN CONFESS HIS SINS LIKE HE HAS DONE NOW BUT REALLY DOESN'T CHANGE? I AM AFRAID OF WHAT MAY HAPPEN IN OUR HOME IN THE FUTURE."

How do you counsel Mary at this point?

How can you help Mary see her self-focus which is leading her to fear?

What verses can give Mary hope?

What homework should Mary be assigned?

LESSON 19: HOMEWORK

> This week's **HOMEWORK** teaches you how to overcome
> fear and worry according to biblical principles *(based on
> Psalm 118:6; Proverbs 3:7; Lamentations 3:22-24, 32-33;
> Matthew 6:25-34; Philippians 4:6-9; II Timothy 1:7; I Peter 5:6-7;
> I John 4:18, 5:4-5).*

✔ *homework completed*

☐ A. * In your own words, write the meaning of *Matthew 6:33-34* and *I John 4:18*. Memorize *Matthew 6:33-34* and *I John 4:18* and begin memorizing *Romans 6:22* and *Ephesians 6:10-11.*

☐ B. * Read **BIBLICAL PRINCIPLES: FEAR AND WORRY** (Lesson 19, Pages 2-3). Mark the listed verses in your Bible that you have not previously marked.

☐ C. * Study **OVERCOMING FEAR AND WORRY** (Lesson 19, Pages 8-12). If applicable, use a **VICTORY OVER FAILURES WORKSHEET** (Supplement 8) and begin to take the necessary steps to overcome fear and worry (especially in relation to the problem that the Lord wants you to work on during this course).

☐ D. Read **TEMPTATIONS TO FEAR AND WORRY** (Lesson 19, Pages 4-5). Place a check beside any statements which describe situations that tempt you to fear or worry. Add to this list any other situations in which you experience fear or worry and develop biblical plans to be an overcomer in these areas. *Review* **OVERCOMING FEAR AND WORRY** *(Lesson 19, Pages 8-12) as necessary.*

☐ E. Study **LOVE VERSUS FEAR (GOD'S WAY VERSUS MAN'S WAY)** (Lesson 19, Pages 6-7). As you review the contrasts between biblical love and fear, especially note how fear is cast out by perfect love and how abiding in Christ is related to overcoming fear.

☐ F. Study **GUIDELINES: FREEDOM FROM ANXIETY (BIBLICAL ACTION AND PRAYER PLAN)** (Supplement 16) and, if necessary, begin to use the plan outlined in **FREEDOM FROM ANXIETY (BIBLICAL ACTION AND PRAYER PLAN)** (Supplement 17) as part of your daily devotional time.

☐ G. * Read **A CASE STUDY: MARY'S HUSBAND HAS LEFT HER** (Lesson 19, Page 13). Answer the questions following the case study.

☐ H. * In conjunction with this lesson, respond to statement 28 under **Open Book Test** (Lesson 23, Page 3).

---

* *The completion of assignments marked with an asterisk (*) is a prerequisite for further biblical counseling training.*

LESSON 19: STUDY GUIDE FOR DAILY DEVOTIONS
(INCLUDING SCRIPTURE MEMORY AND HOMEWORK)

> This week's **STUDY GUIDE** teaches you how to overcome fear and worry according to biblical principles *(based on Psalm 118:6; Proverbs 3:7; Lamentations 3:22-24, 32-33; Matthew 6:25-34; Philippians 4:6-9; II Timothy 1:7; I Peter 5:6-7; I John 4:18, 5:4-5).*

Scripture Memory

1. * Memorize *Matthew 6:33-34* and *I John 4:18*. Begin memorizing *Romans 6:22* and *Ephesians 6:10-11.*
2. Carry your memory verse cards from previous weeks along with this week's memory verses. Review your memory verses during spare moments throughout the day.

Daily Devotional Study Guide

FIRST DAY

1. Open with prayer.
2. * Read *Principle 84* under **BIBLICAL PRINCIPLES: FEAR AND WORRY** (Lesson 19, Pages 2-3). Highlight the listed verses in your Bible.
3. * Write the meaning of *Matthew 6:33-34* and *I John 4:18* in your own words.
4. Close with prayer.

SECOND DAY

1. Open with prayer.
2. * Read *Principle 85* under **BIBLICAL PRINCIPLES: FEAR AND WORRY** (Lesson 19, Pages 2-3). Highlight the listed verses in your Bible.
3. * Study **OVERCOMING FEAR AND WORRY** (Lesson 19, Pages 8-12). If applicable, use a **VICTORY OVER FAILURES WORKSHEET** (Supplement 8) and begin to take the necessary steps to overcome fear and worry (especially in relation to the problem that the Lord wants you to work on during this course). This is the first day of a three-day study.
4. Close with prayer.

THIRD DAY

1. Open with prayer.
2. * Read *Principle 86* under **BIBLICAL PRINCIPLES: FEAR AND WORRY** (Lesson 19, Pages 2-3). Highlight the listed verses in your Bible.
3. * Continue your study of **OVERCOMING FEAR AND WORRY** (Lesson 19, Pages 8-12). Be diligent to develop a biblical plan that will help you overcome these problems in your life.
4. Close with prayer.
5. Are you remaining faithful to memorize Scripture? Make adjustments in your schedule as necessary. *Use MY PROPOSED BIBLICAL SCHEDULE (Supplement 15) to help you be more disciplined in this area of spiritual development.*

FOURTH DAY

1. Open with prayer.
2. * Read *Principle 87* under **BIBLICAL PRINCIPLES: FEAR AND WORRY** (Lesson 19, Pages 2-3). Highlight the listed verses in your Bible.
3. * Complete your study of **OVERCOMING FEAR AND WORRY** (Lesson 19, Pages 8-12). As you review your biblical plan, prayerfully determine the specific steps that you should initially take to overcome fear or worry.
4. Close with prayer.

FIFTH DAY

1. Open with prayer.
2. * Read *Principle 88* under **BIBLICAL PRINCIPLES: FEAR AND WORRY** (Lesson 19, Pages 2-3). Highlight the listed verses in your Bible.
3. Read **TEMPTATIONS TO FEAR AND WORRY** (Lesson 19, Pages 4-5). Place a check beside any statements which describe situations that tempt you to fear or worry. Add to this list any other situations in which you experience fear or worry and develop biblical plans to be an overcomer in these areas. *Review OVERCOMING FEAR AND WORRY (Lesson 19, Pages 8-12) as necessary.*
4. Close with prayer.

SIXTH DAY

1. Open with prayer.
2. * Read *Principle 89* under **BIBLICAL PRINCIPLES: FEAR AND WORRY** (Lesson 19, Pages 2-3). Highlight the listed verses in your Bible.
3. Study **LOVE VERSUS FEAR (GOD'S WAY VERSUS MAN'S WAY)** (Lesson 19, Pages 6-7). As you review the contrasts between biblical love and fear, especially note how fear is cast out by perfect love and how abiding in Christ is related to overcoming fear.
4. Close with prayer.

SEVENTH DAY

1. Open with prayer.
2. * Read *Principle 90* under **BIBLICAL PRINCIPLES: FEAR AND WORRY** (Lesson 19, Pages 2-3). Highlight the listed verses in your Bible.
3. * Read **A CASE STUDY: MARY'S HUSBAND HAS LEFT HER** (Lesson 19, Page 13). Answer the questions which follow the case study.
4. Study **GUIDELINES: FREEDOM FROM ANXIETY (BIBLICAL ACTION AND PRAYER PLAN)** (Supplement 16) and, if necessary, begin to use the plan outlined in **FREEDOM FROM ANXIETY (BIBLICAL ACTION AND PRAYER PLAN)** (Supplement 17) as part of your daily devotional time.
5. * In conjunction with this lesson, respond to statement 28 under **Open Book Test** (Lesson 23, Page 3).
6. Close in prayer.
7. Ask a friend to listen to you recite this week's memory verses. Explain how these verses apply to your life.

---

*   *The completion of assignments marked with an asterisk (*) is a prerequisite for further biblical counseling training.*

LESSON 20

LIFE-DOMINATING SINS (PART ONE)

"But now having been freed from sin and enslaved to God, you derive your benefit, resulting in sanctification, and the outcome, eternal life."

Romans 6:22

"Finally, be strong in the Lord, and in the strength of His might. Put on the full armor of God, that you may be able to stand firm against the schemes of the devil."

Ephesians 6:10-11

LESSON 20: LIFE-DOMINATING SINS (PART ONE)

> When you willingly or unknowingly are under the control
> of any power other than God's Holy Spirit (e.g., drugs,
> alcohol, sex, another person, your peer group, a false
> religion, a self-centered habit such as gossip or laziness, or
> a self-oriented desire for power, food, or wealth), you are
> in bondage to sin. However, God has broken the power of
> sin through the Lord Jesus Christ, and you can overcome
> sinful habits by depending on His strength and being
> obedient to His Word *(based on John 8:34-36; Romans 6:1-7,
> 11-22; 8:11-15; Galatians 5:16; II Peter 2:19b;
> I John 3:23-24, 5:1-5).*

I.   **The purposes of this lesson are:**

A.   To help you recognize life-dominating sins;

B.   To list some of man's inadequate theories and solutions for dealing with life-dominating sins;

C.   To illustrate how a life-dominating sin affects every area of a person's life; and

D.   To contrast God's conquering power over sin with Satan's vanquished power that tries to enslave you to sin.

II. **The outline of this lesson**

A.   Self-confrontation

1.   **BIBLICAL PRINCIPLES: LIFE-DOMINATING SINS (PART ONE)** (Lesson 20, Page 2)

2.   **RECOGNIZING LIFE-DOMINATING SINS** (Lesson 20, Pages 3-7)

3.   **THE EFFECTS OF LIFE-DOMINATING SINS (THE CIRCLE OF LIFE)** (Lesson 20, Page 8)

4.   **GOD HAS BROKEN SATAN'S POWER** (Lesson 20, Pages 9-11)

B.   Steps for spiritual growth

1.   **LESSON 20: HOMEWORK** (Lesson 20, Page 12)

2.   **STUDY GUIDE FOR DAILY DEVOTIONS** (Lesson 20, Pages 13-14)

C.   Biblical counseling

(Case study resumes in Lesson 21)

BIBLICAL PRINCIPLES: LIFE-DOMINATING SINS
(PART ONE)

> Whenever you practice a particular sin, you place yourself under its control. While enslaved by that sin, you cannot legitimately claim to be wholeheartedly following Jesus Christ. If you persistently continue to practice this sin and do not take biblical steps to overcome it, you have reason to doubt the genuineness of your salvation. In spite of your own inherent inability to overcome the bondage of a life-dominating sin, God's grace, mercy, and power have been provided for you, as a sincere believer in Jesus Christ, to overcome any sin. Furthermore, as you overcome sin's power by God's enablement, the character of Christ is developed in your life *(based on Psalm 119:9-11; Romans 6:1-14, 8:2; I Corinthians 6:9-20; Ephesians 2:1-10; II Timothy 2:22; Hebrews 10:26-27; II Peter 1:2-10; I John 1:6 - 2:6; 3:4-10; 4:4; 5:5).*

I. **God's View**

(Principle 91) God holds you responsible for all your deeds (thoughts, words, and actions), including those that are life-dominating or those that are thought to be "genetically predisposed" or "addictive" *(based on Ecclesiastes 12:13-14; Ezekiel 18:2-20, esp. verse 20; Matthew 12:35-37; Romans 2:1-11; I Corinthians 3:8; II Corinthians 5:10; Colossians 3:23-25; I Peter 1:17; Revelation 22:12).* You become a slave to whatever controls you *(Romans 6:16-18; II Peter 2:19b).*

II. **Your Hope**

(Principle 92) No matter how serious or long-standing your sin, it can be overcome completely and in a very short period of time as you follow God's plan for all of life *(based on Romans 6:17-18; I Corinthians 6:9-11, esp. verse 11; 10:13; II Corinthians 5:17; II Timothy 3:16-17; I John 5:3-5).*

Also applicable:

Principles 20-26 in **BIBLICAL PRINCIPLES: BIBLICAL BASIS FOR CHANGE** *(Lesson 6, Pages 2-3), under* **II. Your hope in the midst of trials.**

*(**NOTE:** from Lesson 9, Page 3)* Your Heavenly Father, the Sovereign God of the universe, has your best interests at heart *(Jeremiah 29:11; Romans 8:28),* and will accomplish His purposes in your life *(Isaiah 46:9-11; Romans 8:29; Philippians 1:6, 2:13).* He promises to equip you fully for every good work *(I Corinthians 12:7; II Timothy 3:16-17; I Peter 4:9-10)* and to be with you through every circumstance of life *(Psalm 23:1-6, 121:1-8; II Timothy 4:18; I John 5:18).*

RECOGNIZING LIFE-DOMINATING SINS

> Only after you experience a spiritual new birth and then
> continually obey Scripture will you be able to recognize
> and overcome a life-dominating sin in a manner that
> pleases and glorifies the Lord *(based on Romans 6:6-7, 11,
> 16-18; 8:8; I Corinthians 2:14; 6:9-12, 19-20;
> I Thessalonians 4:1-8; Hebrews 5:14, 13:20-21; James 1:21-25;
> I Peter 2:2-3, 12; II Peter 1:2-11).*

I. **Characteristics of a life-dominating sin**

A. You practice this sin even though you have tried repeatedly to stop *(disregarding Romans 6:1-2, 6-7, 11-13; I Corinthians 6:12, 19-20; Galatians 5:16-17).*

B. You practice this sin and blame others or circumstances for your failure to stop *(disregarding Ezekiel 18:4, 20; Mark 7:20-23; Romans 14:12; II Corinthians 5:10).*

C. You deny that what you are doing is sin *(disregarding I Peter 1:16; I John 1:8).*

D. You convince yourself that you are not enslaved to this sin and "can stop at any time," even though you continue in this sin *(disregarding John 8:34; Romans 6:1-2, 16; II Timothy 2:22; James 2:10, 4:17; I John 3:3).*

E. You convince yourself that this sin has no power over you since you do not commit this sin as much as you once did *(disregarding John 14:15; Romans 6:12-16; I Corinthians 6:12; I Thessalonians 4:7, 5:22; II Timothy 2:22).*

F. You repeat the sin even though any pleasure or satisfaction to yourself is short-lived while the harm to yourself and others is considerable and long term *(disregarding Romans 6:16, 21; 14:7-8, 19; 15:2; I Corinthians 6:19-20; II Corinthians 5:15; Galatians 5:16-17; James 1:14-15; I Peter 4:3-6).*

G. You seek to hide your sin *(disregarding Psalm 32:1-5; John 3:19-21; Ephesians 5:8-17; James 5:16)* by:

1. Having separate "sets" of friends or acquaintances (i.e., you lead a "double life"), taking care not to let either know about the other *(disregarding Matthew 5:13-16; Romans 12:9; I Corinthians 15:33; II Corinthians 6:14-18; Ephesians 5:11);*

2. Lying on a regular basis to cover up your sin *(disregarding Proverbs 6:16-19, 12:22, 28:13; Colossians 3:9-10);*

3. Trying to make others think that you are living God's way *(disregarding Proverbs 6:12-15; Mark 7:20-23, esp. verse 22; II Timothy 3:13; James 3:17; I Peter 2:1-3);*

4. Acting indignant or surprised when someone finds inconsistencies in your life that lead them to suspect your problem *(disregarding Proverbs 14:8, 27:6a, 29:9; James 1:22-24);* or

5. Being contentious and seeking to develop factions among believers by encouraging others to take up your cause against others in the body of Christ *(disregarding Romans 16:17-18; Ephesians 4:1-3; Hebrews 12:14).*

H. You revile or slander the very people who are seeking to restore you to the Lord and others *(disregarding Psalm 15:1-3; Proverbs 10:16-17, 16:28; Matthew 15:19; Mark 7:20-23, esp. verse 22; Ephesians 4:31-32; James 5:9; I Peter 2:1-3).*

I. You continue in this sin although you know that it is not edifying to do so *(disregarding Romans 15:2; I Corinthians 6:12, 10:23-24).*

J. You still commit this sin although you know that it obscures the testimony of Jesus Christ in your life and is a stumbling block to others *(disregarding Matthew 5:16; Romans 14:13; I Peter 2:11-12, 24; 3:15-16).*

K. You continue in this sin despite the knowledge that God's Word tells you to stop sinning and that God's provisions are sufficient to release you from this bondage *(disregarding Romans 6:5-7, 12-14, 22; I Corinthians 10:13; Galatians 5:16-17; II Timothy 3:16-17; James 4:17; I John 4:4).*

L. You repeatedly commit this sin while knowing that this does not please the Lord nor bring glory to God *(disregarding I Corinthians 6:20, 10:31; II Corinthians 5:9; Colossians 1:10; I Peter 2:11-12).*

M. You continue in this sin even though you realize that your deeds (thoughts, words, and actions) do not conform to the character of Christ *(disregarding II Corinthians 10:5; Galatians 2:20, 5:22-24; Colossians 3:1-11; I Peter 1:14-16; I John 3:2-3).*

II. Man's view of life-dominating sins

A. The philosophy of this world often teaches that "undesirable behavior" (what the Bible names as sin) is caused by a "disease" or "predisposition" with which you must learn to live ("to cope"). Helping you "cope" often involves drug therapy, psychoanalysis, or even encouragement to accept an "alternative lifestyle." Thus, we see that man's natural wisdom tries to deal with problems of life by "redefining" sin and/or encouraging acceptance of sin. As a result, God's Word is rejected as the authority for all of life, thus leading many to increasing heartache, misery, and delusion.

B. The world recognizes that some life-dominating problems are detrimental to one's life (e.g., criminal acts, procrastination and laziness, "phobias"), and people are encouraged to deal with them. However, plans for overcoming these problems are based on natural wisdom, disregarding God's power and the guidelines of His Word. "Solutions" such as these exalt man and do not teach a person to please the Lord in all things.

III. Some of man's erroneous explanations for life-dominating sins

A. Certain individuals have a genetic pre-disposition to certain "preferences" and cannot help themselves and, thus, are not responsible for their subsequent deeds *(often used to explain homosexuality).*

B. Certain problems that control individuals are "diseases," and must be treated as such *(often used to explain depression, fears or "phobias," drug or alcohol abuse, "personality disorders").*

C. Because of the "personality type" of an individual, he will tend to act in certain ways; it is just part of his unique make-up *(often used to explain extreme anger, depression, worry, fear, "mood swings").*

D.   Enslavement to the problem is simply an expression of the person's extremely low "self-esteem" (*often used to explain anorexia, bulimia, depression, adultery, gang violence, robbery, murder, fornication as displayed through involvement in pornography, prostitution, or sexual perversion*).

E.   An individual may be enslaved to a problem because of the way he was treated as a child; if he was treated a certain way by his parents or other adults responsible for him, he will often treat others the same way (*often used to explain physical violence, violent verbal outbursts of anger, lying, stealing, child abuse, vandalizing other people's goods*).

F.   Enslavement to the problem may be the person's way of reacting to or seeking to get even for extreme wrongs done to him in the past (*often used to explain murders, rape, adultery, sexual abuse of children, reverting to child-like behavior, or withdrawal from responsibilities in life such as "catatonia," simply staying in bed, or not starting tasks*).

IV. **Some of man's attempts to deal with problems that enslave individuals**

A.   The "ill" person is admitted to a treatment center that specializes in treating his "disease." (The program will often include extensive psychotherapy, open antagonism to God's Word, unbiblical communication, and numerous unscriptural approaches to problems that highlight the wisdom of man over the wisdom of God.)

Note: Some facilities that specialize in treating a specific "disease" do help a person stop giving in to this particular sin (such as drug or alcohol abuse). However, exercising self-control in one area of life does not deal with the problem of a person's heart before God and, thus, cannot help a person live in a manner that pleases the Lord in all things. (Review Lessons 1 and 2.)

B.   Some programs use "spiritual" principles found in God's Word to help people from being controlled by a life-dominating problem but seek not to "offend" anyone by acknowledging the Bible as the source of these principles.

Note: Various treatment or recovery plans follow principles found in God's Word (often without realizing it) to try and help people stop being controlled by a life-dominating problem or habit (sin). These programs use terms found in the Bible, such as "being powerless," "forgiveness of others," "confession of wrongs," "restitution or making amends," and "fellowship with others." However, these "spiritual programs" do not acknowledge the Bible as the authority for all of life's problems and also allow those within the programs to choose their own god (their "higher power"). As a result, these recovery plans minimize or oppose the eternally significant need to have a personal relationship with God through the Lord Jesus Christ and, thus, cannot teach one to be obedient to God's Word in every area of life. When someone seeks to deal with a problem for a self-serving purpose rather than to please God, God's resources and His accompanying peace and joy are unavailable to him. (Review Lessons 1 - 4.)

C.   Prescribe drugs to alter moods to help the individual "feel better" about his problem (i.e., relieve the symptoms) and simultaneously provide "professional counseling" to help a person "understand his problem" and learn "less stressful" and "more beneficial" ways to live.

Note: Some physiological dysfunctions (organic and glandular) must be treated medically and may involve the use of prescribed medication under the supervision of a primary care medical doctor. However, any guidance for thinking and living based on the wisdom of man instead of the wisdom of God as revealed in Jesus Christ and God's Word is inadequate and is to be avoided. (Review Lessons 3 - 8.)

D. Have the individual join a secular "support group" composed of individuals who have experienced the same problem, because they can understand what the individual is going through better than anyone else.

Note: While those in a non-Christian "support group" are usually aware of the consequences of their bad (sinful) behavior and can warn others accordingly, the "understanding" and subsequent "help" come from people in the group instead of Jesus Christ (see Hebrews 4:15-16) and God's Word (see II Timothy 3:16-17; Hebrews 4:12). Without biblical guidelines, the "communication" in such groups often is composed of sinful expressions of emotion, wrathful confrontations, remembrances of past sins, gossip, blasphemy, and unbiblical "solutions" to problems. In addition, a self-focus is often of primary importance in "making progress" as a member of a secular support group. (Review Lessons 4 - 13.)

E. Teach the individual to like himself and to be his own best friend (i.e., develop a "good self-image"). By doing this, you will help him to face and deal with his problem for his own best interests. *(Review Lesson 4 and Lessons 9 - 10.)*

F. Help the individual find other emotional outlets ("releases") for the same problem. This type of "therapy" is often accomplished through "professional counseling" and/or "reward" and "punishment" techniques.

Note: This "therapy" may redirect behavior, at least temporarily, to that which would be less detrimental to a person or those around him; but it fails to deal with the basic problem of the lack of a wholehearted commitment to God through Jesus Christ. Without a personal relationship to the Lord, obedience to Scripture is impossible; and "new directions or expressions" of the problem are often sinful themselves. This approach to dealing with problems fails to deal with the larger challenge of dying to self in order to please the Lord in all things and edify others through ministry and expressions of biblical love. (Review Lessons 4 - 10.)

G. Teach the individual that although his "disease" or "genetic predisposition" will never change, he may stop various activities that are associated with it.

Note: This emphasis on personal responsibility is in itself a biblical perspective, although its link to Scripture is usually unknown or purposefully avoided. Often associated with this method of dealing with problems is accountability to others. This, too, is based on scriptural principles; but the foundation of God's Word is usually overlooked or denied. This approach often emphasizes that one doesn't have enough natural strength to be responsible or accountable (another biblical perspective that usually fails to receive proper credit), but the "needed strength or power" comes from the support of others or another variably defined "god source." Although stopping sinful activities is commendable, the basic focus is on man, not God. The complete and supernatural change that can only be accomplished through the power of Jesus Christ (see II Corinthians 5:17) cannot be realized or emphasized. Without a spiritual new birth, a person will not be empowered to change by the Holy Spirit and cannot understand God's Word. (Review Lessons 1 - 8.)

H. Learn how to "separate yourself" from the life-dominating problem of another (i.e., cease being a "co-dependent").

Note: Programs designed for "co-dependents" rightfully point out the mistake of adapting to the "sick" (sinful) behavior of a person enslaved by a life-dominating problem. However, the "co-dependent" person is also defined as "sick" for remaining in the relationship with the one enslaved to a life-dominating problem. Usually, these programs emphasize concentrating on your own life and not covering up or participating in the "sick" behavior of another. While the basic thrust of this emphasis may be similar to biblical principles, the manner of concentrating on your own life and refusing to condone or adapt to the sins of another is based on the wisdom of man and is contrary to Scripture. For example, at the heart of most secular programs for "co-dependents" is an emphasis on "self" (i.e., "you do this for you and not for anyone else"). To their credit, secular programs for "co-dependents" promote "support" between its members and do not allow blameshifting. However, learning to live for God and edifying others biblically is not an emphasis in these programs (see I Corinthians 2:14). Numerous other specific violations of Scripture are often allowed and, sometimes, even encouraged (for example, angry outbursts, remembrances of past sins, gossip, encouragement of marriage dissolution, expressions of bitterness, lack of biblical forgiveness, or not practicing biblical love). (Review all lessons.)

V. Some results of remaining enslaved by sin

A. God does not assure you that He will hear or answer your prayers *(based on Psalm 66:18; Proverbs 15:29, 28:9; Isaiah 59:1-2; I Peter 3:12).*

B. You will bear spiritual as well as physical consequences *(based on Psalm 32:3-5, 38:1-10, 51:3; I Corinthians 5:3-5, 11:28-30; Colossians 3:25; Hebrews 12:5-11).*

C. You will lose the joy of your salvation *(based on Psalm 51:8-12; I John 1:4)* and may doubt that you have a regenerative relationship with the Lord (i.e., that you are a believer) *(based on I Corinthians 6:9-10; I John 2:4; 3:4-10).*

D. You will become increasingly more miserable, and life will become more difficult *(based on Proverbs 1:24-32; 13:15, 21a; 28:13-14),* since you are giving Satan an advantage in your life *(based on II Corinthians 2:10-11, 10:5; Ephesians 4:26-27, esp. verse 27; II Peter 2:19b-22; I John 3:4-9).*

E. You place yourself under the corrective discipline of the Lord *(Hebrews 12:5-11),* and the sternness of the discipline to restore you to the Lord and others will increase *(based on Proverbs 15:10; Matthew 18:15-20).*

F. You, through your own deeds, will hinder all true fellowship with those in the body of Christ *(based on I Corinthians 5:9-11; II Thessalonians 3:11-15).*

G. You remain in spiritual delusion because you are merely a hearer of the Word and not a doer *(based on James 1:22-24),* and you cannot discern clearly between good and evil *(based on Hebrews 5:14).*

THE EFFECTS OF LIFE-DOMINATING SINS
(THE CIRCLE OF LIFE)

To determine the effects of a life-dominating sin, you must examine the way it is demonstrated in all areas of life. If you practice a life-dominating sin, it will eventually affect all relationships and responsibilities. Other life-dominating sins are often developed and practiced to "cover up" (practice deceit) for a primary life-dominating sin *(based on Psalm 36:1-4; Proverbs 1:24-32, 2:11-15, 4:19, 5:22-23, 12:20a, 13:6, 14:14a; Romans 6:16; Galatians 5:16-21; James 1:22-24; II Peter 2:20-22; I John 3:4-9).*

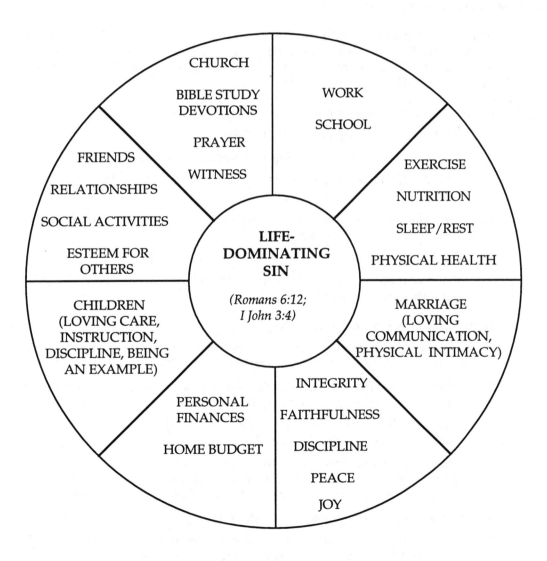

GOD HAS BROKEN SATAN'S POWER

> Satan, the primary adversary of God and man, has great and evil power as the prince of this world. Part of his diabolical plan is to deceive all mankind, to accuse believers before the Lord, and to cripple God's children by encouraging them to sin. Jesus Christ, through His redemptive death and victorious resurrection, has overcome the power of Satan. This victory has been given and is readily available to those who are in Christ (believers) *(based on Romans 6:5-6; II Corinthians 4:4; Ephesians 2:2, 6:12; I Thessalonians 3:5; Hebrews 2:14-15; I Peter 5:8; I John 3:8; 4:4; 5:4-5, 18-19; Revelation 12:10).*

I. **Satan's characteristics and power**

   A. Satan (also named in Scripture as the Devil, Adversary, Enemy, Destroyer, Dragon, Accuser, Serpent, and Tempter) is the chief of the fallen heavenly beings and is the arch-enemy of God and man *(based on Job 1:6-11, 2:1-7; Zechariah 3:1; Matthew 25:41; Ephesians 6:11-12; I Peter 5:8; Revelation 12:7-9).*

   B. Satan is described in Scripture as:

      1. Sinning from the beginning *(I John 3:8);*

      2. A murderer from the beginning and the father of lies *(John 8:44);*

      3. An imposter, appearing as an angel of light *(II Corinthians 11:14)* but full of evil *(John 17:15; I John 2:13-14, 5:18-19);*

      4. The tempter *(Matthew 4:3; I Thessalonians 3:5),* who is diabolically crafty *(II Corinthians 11:3; Ephesians 6:11);*

      5. The instigator of the fall of man *(Genesis 3:1-6);* and

      6. Like a roaring lion *(I Peter 5:8),* a serpent *(Genesis 3:1-4; Revelation 12:9, 20:2),* and a dragon *(Revelation 12:3, 7, 9).*

   C. Satan's power is enormous, since he:

      1. Rules a vast kingdom of fallen angels and demonic beings *(based on Matthew 12:26-29, 25:41; Ephesians 6:12; Revelation 12:4, 7, 9);*

      2. Is the prince of the power of the air *(Ephesians 2:2)* and has the whole world (its system or order) in his power *(I John 5:19b);*

      3. Is the god *(II Corinthians 4:4),* ruler *(John 12:31, 14:30, 16:11),* and deceiver of the whole world (Revelation 12:9, 20:3);

      4. Has every person who is not "in Christ" (a believer) as "his child" *(Matthew 13:24-30, 36-42, esp. verse 38; Ephesians 2:2-3; I John 3:7-10, esp. verse 10)* and under his power *(Ephesians 2:2-3; II Timothy 2:24-26, esp. verse 26);* and

      5. Has always opposed and will continue to oppose God's work by:

         a. Taking away God's Word from the hearts of unbelievers so that they will not believe in the Lord Jesus Christ and be saved *(Luke 8:11-12);*

  b. Blinding the minds of the unbelieving that they might not see the light of the Good News of Jesus Christ *(II Corinthians 4:4)*;

  c. Using false messengers (false prophets, false apostles, false teachers, false Messiahs) who can demonstrate great signs and wonders *(based on Matthew 7:15-23; Matthew 24:4-5, 11, 23-24; Mark 13:6, 21-22; II Corinthians 11:13-15; II Thessalonians 2:8-10; II Peter 2:1-3, 12-22; I John 4:1)*;

  d. Distorting God's Word *(based on Genesis 3:1-5; Matthew 4:3, 6; II Peter 1:20 - 2:1)*;

  e. Using demonic power to enslave unbelievers in false worship *(based on Psalm 106:34-39, esp. verse 37; I Corinthians 10:19-20; I Timothy 4:1; Revelation 9:20)* and to afflict them physically *(based on Matthew 9:32, 12:22, 17:15-18; Mark 5:1-5, 9:17-22)*;

  f. Sowing tares (false believers) among those in the Body of Christ *(based on Matthew 13:24-30, 36-43)*;

  g. Tempting believers to commit sin *(based on Acts 5:3; I Corinthians 7:5; I Thessalonians 3:5)*;

  h. Accusing believers before God continually *(Revelation 12:10)*;

  i. Scheming against and trying to mislead the children of God *(based on Matthew 24:24; II Corinthians 11:3; Ephesians 6:11; I Thessalonians 2:18)*; and

  j. Bringing suffering into the lives of God's children (but always under the limitations imposed by God) *(based on Job 1:8-12, esp. verse 12; 2:3-6, esp. verse 6; Luke 22:31-32; Revelation 2:10)*.

II. Satan's limitations and judgment

A. Satan's power and abilities are not co-equal with God, since Satan is a created being *(based on Colossians 1:13-17, esp. verse 16)*. Everything that has been created, no matter how powerful, is under subjection to the power of the risen Lord Jesus Christ *(Matthew 28:18; Ephesians 1:19-23, esp. verses 21-22; Colossians 1:16; 2:9-10, esp. verse 10)*.

B. Satan can do and can have only what God allows *(based on Job 1:7-12, 2:1-7; Luke 4:6, 22:31-32; II Thessalonians 2:1-12, esp. verse 7; Revelation 2:10)*.

C. Satan has been cursed by God *(Genesis 3:14-15)*, has already been judged *(John 12:31; 16:7-11, esp. verse 11)*, and will eventually be cast into eternal fire with his angels *(Matthew 25:41)*, his other deceivers *(Revelation 20:10)*, and unbelievers *(Revelation 20:15)*.

D. Jesus appeared on earth that He might publicly destroy (make inoperative, to loose or dissolve) the works of the devil *(based on Genesis 3:15; I John 3:8)* and disarm the powers of the rulers and authorities who are under Satan's control *(based on Luke 10:17-19; Colossians 2:13-15, esp. verse 15)*.

  1. Jesus was completely victorious over Satan's temptations *(Matthew 4:1-11; Luke 4:1-13)*.

  2. While on earth, Jesus also demonstrated His defeat of Satan *(Mark 3:22-27, esp. verse 27)* by exercising power over demons *(Matthew 9:32-33, 12:22, 17:14-18; Mark 5:1-13, esp. verses 8 and 13; Mark 9:17-27, esp. verse 25; Luke 11:14, 20)*, with demons recognizing the authority that He has over them *(Mark 5:7-12, esp. verses 7, 10, 12)*.

E.   By His sacrificial death, Jesus took away Satan's power of death and gave deliverance to those who were in bondage to Satan *(Acts 26:14-18, esp. verse 18; Hebrews 2:14-15)*, cancelling their debt of sin *(Colossians 2:13-14)*, giving them eternal life, and bringing them under His protective care *(John 10:27-29)*.

F.   Although Satan can tempt a believer to sin *(I Corinthians 7:5; I Thessalonians 3:5)*, a believer has the insurmountable power of the risen Jesus Christ within *(I John 4:4)* and, thus, is able to defeat Satan in every temptation by not sinning *(Romans 6:6-14, 17-18; 8:9-18; I Corinthians 10:13; I Peter 2:24-25)*.

   1.   In spite of Satan's phenomenal power, a believer who is depending on the Lord's power, resources, and already established victory over Satan, can be aware of the schemes of the devil *(II Corinthians 2:11)* and can stand firm against them *(Ephesians 6:10-18)*.

   2.   A believer who is submitting to God can resist the devil and can be an overwhelming conqueror in Christ Jesus *(Romans 8:31-39; James 4:7; I Peter 5:8-10; Revelation 12:10-11, esp. verse 11)*.

G.   Followers of Jesus Christ will be opposed by Satan, especially as they proclaim the liberating message of the Good News of Jesus Christ. However, even if they face the formidable opposition of demonic powers, true disciples of Christ have been given His authority over these hellish servants of Satan *(based on Matthew 10:1; Mark 9:38-40, 16:15-18; Luke 10:17-20; Acts 5:12-16, esp. verse 16; 8:4-8; 16:16-18; Romans 6:16-19, 8:35-39; II Corinthians 12:7-10; I John 4:4)*.

III. **Satanic associations are to be discarded from your life**

A.   The worship of Satan or involvement in any related depraved practice is abhorrent to God and has been forbidden by Him *(based on Leviticus 17:7, 19:31, 20:6; Deuteronomy 18:9-14; II Kings 21:1-6, esp. verse 6; I Chronicles 10:13-14; Psalm 106:34-40; Matthew 4:8-10; I Corinthians 10:19-21; I Timothy 4:1; Revelation 21:8)*.

   1.   You are to destroy all memorabilia, artifacts, trinkets, literature, implements, pictures or any other reminders of Satanic worship, demonism, spiritism, or other occult practices that are in your possession *(based on I Kings 15:12; II Kings 10:18-31, esp. verses 25-28; 23:4-20; Jeremiah 4:1; Acts 19:18-20, esp. verse 19; I Corinthians 10:14, 19-20, 23; Philippians 4:8; Colossians 3:2)*.

   2.   You are not to associate with those involved in Satanic practices *(based on I Corinthians 15:33; II Corinthians 6:15-18; Ephesians 5:11-12; II John 1:7-11)*.

B.   Simply removing yourself from any attachment to Satanic practices does not empower you to be free from sin or experience change in your life. That empowerment comes solely from a spiritual new birth *(John 3:3)*, a constant reliance on Jesus Christ *(John 15:5; I John 4:4)*, and faithful obedience to the Word of God *(Psalm 19:7-11; II Timothy 3:16-17; II Peter 1:2-11) (see **II.** above)*.

Refer also to:
***BIBLICAL PERSPECTIVE ON TESTS AND TEMPTATIONS** (Lesson 8, Pages 3-7),*
***PRACTICAL STEPS FOR ACHIEVING BIBLICAL CHANGE** (Lesson 8, Pages 8-10),*
***PUTTING ON THE FULL ARMOR OF GOD** (Lesson 21, Pages 4-12), and*
***OVERCOMING LIFE-DOMINATING SINS** (Lesson 21, Pages 13-19).*

LESSON 20: HOMEWORK

> This week's **HOMEWORK** provides encouragement as you are reminded that God has provided sufficient resources and power for you to overcome any life-dominating sin through the Lord Jesus Christ *(based on Romans 6:1-7, 8:11-18; II Timothy 3:16-17; Hebrews 2:14-15; II Peter 1:2-11; I John 4:4; 5:4-5, 18)*.

✔ *homework completed*

☐ A. * In your own words, write the meaning of *Romans 6:22* and *Ephesians 6:10-11*. Memorize *Romans 6:22* and *Ephesians 6:10-11* and begin memorizing *Ephesians 5:18* and *6:12-13*. Review previous memory verses.

☐ B. * Read **BIBLICAL PRINCIPLES: LIFE-DOMINATING SINS (PART ONE)** (Lesson 20, Page 2). Highlight listed verses in your Bible.

☐ C. * Study **RECOGNIZING LIFE-DOMINATING SINS** (Lesson 20, Pages 3-7). Review the characteristics of a life-dominating sin and prayerfully examine yourself in this regard. Note the natural man's explanations and attempts to deal with life-dominating problems (sins). Place a check beside those which you have accepted as being "truth." Especially note the results that occur when one continues to practice a life-dominating sin.

If you recognize a life-dominating sin in your own life and do not have it listed as the problem that the Lord wants you to overcome in this course, confess it as sin to the Lord and immediately take biblical steps to overcome it. *Review Lessons 5 - 8.*

☐ D. * Review **THE EFFECTS OF LIFE-DOMINATING SINS (THE CIRCLE OF LIFE)** (Lesson 20, Page 8). If you recognize that any sin has affected specific areas of your life, take the necessary biblical steps to be restored to the Lord and to others in those areas.

Refer also to:
THE UPWARD PATH: WALKING GOD'S WAY (Lesson 5, Page 5),
PRACTICAL STEPS FOR ACHIEVING BIBLICAL CHANGE (Lesson 8, Pages 8-10),
INTERPERSONAL PROBLEMS (PARTS ONE AND TWO) (Lessons 12 and 13), and
GUIDELINES: VICTORY OVER FAILURES WORKSHEET (Supplement 7).

☐ E. * Study **GOD HAS BROKEN SATAN'S POWER** (Lesson 20, Pages 9-11). Note the manner in which Satan tries to thwart the work of God. Thoroughly review the referenced passages of Scripture that list Satan's limitations and judgment. Mark the verses that tell how God has completely overcome Satan's power in the life of a believer.

☐ F. * In conjunction with this lesson, respond to statement 29 under **Open Book Test** (Lesson 23, Page 3).

   *   *The completion of assignments marked with an asterisk (*) is a prerequisite for further biblical counseling training.*

LESSON 20: STUDY GUIDE FOR DAILY DEVOTIONS
(INCLUDING SCRIPTURE MEMORY AND HOMEWORK)

> This week's **STUDY GUIDE** provides encouragement as
> you are reminded that God has provided sufficient
> resources and power for you to overcome any
> life-dominating sin through the Lord Jesus Christ *(based on
> Romans 6:1-7, 8:11-18; II Timothy 3:16-17; Hebrews 2:14-15;
> II Peter 1:2-11; I John 4:4; 5:4-5, 18).*

Scripture Memory

1. * Memorize *Romans 6:22* and *Ephesians 6:10-11* and begin memorizing *Ephesians 5:18* and *6:12-13*. Review previous memory verses.
2. Carry your memory verse cards from previous weeks along with this week's memory verses. Review your memory verses during spare moments throughout the day.

Daily Devotional Study Guide

FIRST DAY

1. Open with prayer.
2. * Read *Principle 91* under **BIBLICAL PRINCIPLES: LIFE-DOMINATING SINS (PART ONE)** (Lesson 20, Page 2). Highlight the listed verses in your Bible.
3. * Write the meaning of *Romans 6:22* and *Ephesians 6:10-11* in your own words.
4. Close with prayer.

SECOND DAY

1. Open with prayer.
2. * Read *Principle 92* under **BIBLICAL PRINCIPLES: LIFE-DOMINATING SINS (PART ONE)** (Lesson 20, Page 2). Highlight the listed verses in your Bible.
3. * Begin your study of **RECOGNIZING LIFE-DOMINATING SINS** (Lesson 20, Pages 3-7). Today, review the characteristics of a life-dominating sin and prayerfully examine yourself in this regard. This is the first day of a three-day study.
4. Close with prayer.

THIRD DAY

1. Open with prayer.
2. * Review *Principles 20 - 26* under **BIBLICAL PRINCIPLES: BIBLICAL BASIS FOR CHANGE** (Lesson 6, Pages 2-3).
3. * Continue your study of **RECOGNIZING LIFE-DOMINATING SINS** (Lesson 20, Pages 3-7). Note the natural man's explanations and attempts to solve life-dominating problems (sins), placing a check beside those which you have accepted as "truth." Especially note the results that occur when one continues to practice a life-dominating sin. If you recognize a life-dominating sin in your own life and do not have it listed as the problem that the Lord wants you to overcome in this course, confess it as sin to the Lord and immediately take biblical steps to overcome it. *Review Lessons 5 - 8.*
4. Close with prayer.
5. Are you being faithful to memorize God's Word this week?

FOURTH DAY

1. Open with prayer.
2. * Review the *NOTE from Lesson 9, Page 3* that is reprinted under **BIBLICAL PRINCIPLES: LIFE-DOMINATING SINS (PART ONE)** (Lesson 20, Page 2).
3. * Complete your study of **RECOGNIZING LIFE-DOMINATING SINS** (Lesson 20, Pages 3-7). Take biblical steps to overcome all life-dominating sins in your life.
4. Close with prayer.

FIFTH DAY

1. Open with prayer.
2. * Review **THE EFFECTS OF LIFE-DOMINATING SINS (THE CIRCLE OF LIFE)** (Lesson 20, Page 8). If you recognize that any sin has affected specific areas of your life, take the necessary biblical steps to be restored to the Lord and to others in those areas.
    Refer also to:
    THE UPWARD PATH: WALKING GOD'S WAY (Lesson 5, Page 5),
    PRACTICAL STEPS FOR ACHIEVING BIBLICAL CHANGE (Lesson 8, Pages 8-10),
    INTERPERSONAL PROBLEMS (PARTS ONE AND TWO) (Lessons 12 and 13), and
    GUIDELINES: VICTORY OVER FAILURES WORKSHEET (Supplement 7).
3. * Begin your study of **GOD HAS BROKEN SATAN'S POWER** (Lesson 20, Pages 9-11). This is the first in a three-day study. In today's study, especially note the manner in which Satan tries to thwart the work of God under **I. C. 5.**
4. Close with prayer.

SIXTH DAY

1. Open with prayer.
2. * Continue your study of **GOD HAS BROKEN SATAN'S POWER** (Lesson 20, Pages 9-11). Thoroughly review the passages of Scripture that describe Satan's limitations and judgment under **II.** Mark the verses that tell how God has completely overcome Satan's power in the life of a believer.
3. Take the necessary biblical steps to overcome all life-dominating sins in your life.
4. Close with prayer.

SEVENTH DAY

1. Open with prayer.
2. * Complete your study of **GOD HAS BROKEN SATAN'S POWER** (Lesson 20, Pages 9-11). Under **III.**, review the importance of removing yourself from anything or anyone associated with Satanic practices.
3. Take the necessary biblical steps to overcome all life-dominating sins in your life.
4. * In conjunction with this lesson, respond to statement 29 under **Open Book Test** (Lesson 23, Page 3).
5. Close in prayer.
6. Ask a friend to listen to you recite this week's memory verses. Explain how these verses have application to your life.

*   *The completion of assignments marked with an asterisk (*) is a prerequisite for further biblical counseling training.*

LESSON 21

LIFE-DOMINATING SINS (PART TWO)

"And do not get drunk with wine, for that is dissipation, but be filled with the Spirit."

Ephesians 5:18

"For our struggle is not against flesh and blood, but against the rulers, against the powers, against the world forces of this darkness, against the spiritual forces of wickedness in the heavenly places. Therefore, take up the full armor of God, that you may be able to resist in the evil day, and having done everything, to stand firm."

Ephesians 6:12-13

LESSON 21: LIFE-DOMINATING SINS (PART TWO)

> If you have experienced a spiritual new birth, thus becoming a believer in the Lord Jesus Christ, you are no longer under bondage to Satan. Jesus has given you eternal life and has placed you under His care. Since victory over Satan has already been provided by the death, burial, and resurrection of Jesus Christ, you are to use all the resources that God has given you and be an overwhelming conqueror in Christ *(based on John 8:34-36, 10:27-29; Romans 8:31-39; Ephesians 6:10-18; Hebrews 2:14-15; James 4:7; I John 3:8, 5:1-5).*

I.   **The purposes of this lesson are:**

   A.   To review the resources God has provided for you to overcome Satan in every dimension of your life;

   B.   To present the various parts of the full armor of God and show how they apply to your life;

   C.   To provide a biblical plan for overcoming life-dominating sins;

   D.   To present scriptural guidelines for responding to someone who is practicing a life-dominating sin; and

   E.   To continue the development of a case study in biblical counseling.

II. **The outline of this lesson**

   A.   Self-confrontation

   1.   **BIBLICAL PRINCIPLES: LIFE-DOMINATING SINS (PART TWO)** (Lesson 21, Pages 2-3)

   2.   **PUTTING ON THE FULL ARMOR OF GOD** (Lesson 21, Pages 4-12)

   3.   **OVERCOMING LIFE-DOMINATING SINS** (Lesson 21, Pages 13-19)

   4.   **BIBLICALLY RESPONDING TO SOMEONE WITH A LIFE-DOMINATING SIN** (Lesson 21, Pages 20-23)

   B.   Steps for spiritual growth

   1.   **LESSON 21: HOMEWORK** (Lesson 21, Page 26)

   2.   **STUDY GUIDE FOR DAILY DEVOTIONS** (Lesson 21, Pages 27-28)

   C.   Biblical counseling

   A CASE STUDY: MARY'S HUSBAND HAS LEFT HER (Lesson 21, Pages 24-25)

BIBLICAL PRINCIPLES: LIFE-DOMINATING SINS
(PART TWO)

> God has defeated Satan through the death and resurrection
> of the Lord Jesus Christ. Through this overwhelming
> victory, God has also empowered you to overcome any
> temptation to sin and has provided sufficient resources for
> you to respond biblically to any problem of life. By relying
> on God's power and being obedient to His Word, you can
> be an overcomer in any situation *(based on Romans 6:1-7;*
> *8:31-39, esp. verse 37; I Corinthians 10:13; Colossians 1:13,*
> *19-23; 2:9-15; II Timothy 3:16-17; Hebrews 2:13-14, 4:15-16;*
> *II Peter 1:2-11; I John 4:4, 5:4-5).*

III. **Your Change** (outline continues from Lesson 20, Page 2)

(Principle 93)　　You are immediately to stop (put off) yielding to or placing yourself under the control of any sin that has you enslaved. Instead, determine to place yourself under the powerful control of the Holy Spirit and wholeheartedly commit to obey God's Word (put on) in every area of your life *(Romans 6:11-18, 22; 8:2-16, esp. verses 2, 5-6, 14; Galatians 5:16-17; Ephesians 5:18; II Timothy 3:16-17; I Peter 2:11; II Peter 1:2-11).*

IV. **Your Practice**

(Principle 94)　　Since God's Word teaches that those who continually practice sin shall not inherit the Kingdom of God *(I Corinthians 6:9-10; Galatians 5:19-21; I John 3:6-9),* make a thorough examination of yourself to determine if you are in the faith (i.e., whether you are truly a believer in Jesus Christ) *(based on John 3:3, 16-21, 36; Romans 10:8-11; II Corinthians 13:5; I John 2:3-6, 3:4-9, 5:11-13).*

　　　　Also refer to: **YOU CAN CHANGE BIBLICALLY (PART ONE)** *(Lesson 1, Pages 3-7).*

(Principle 95)　　Make a thorough biblical evaluation of when, where, how, and with whom you commit the sin by which you are being dominated *(based on Psalm 139:23-24; Matthew 7:1-5; I Corinthians 11:31)* and develop a biblical plan to be an overcomer in all of these situations by putting on the full armor of God *(based on Romans 6:12-13; I Corinthians 6:9-12; Ephesians 2:10; 4:1-3, 25-32; 6:10-18; Colossians 2:6, 3:1-17).*

Also applicable:

(Principle 13, revised from Lesson 5, Page 2)　　To appropriate God's gracious wisdom in facing and dealing with your problems, you must ask in faith *(Hebrews 4:16; James 1:5-8),* live according to God's Word *(James 1:22-25),* and depend on His power *(II Corinthians 3:4-5; Philippians 4:13).*

*Principles 27-29 under **BIBLICAL PRINCIPLES: BIBLICAL STRUCTURE FOR CHANGE** (Lesson 7, Page 2)*

Also refer to:
YOU CAN CHANGE BIBLICALLY (PART TWO) *(Lesson 2, Pages 2-5);*
SCRIPTURE IS YOUR AUTHORITY *(Lesson 3, Pages 3-5);*
THE HOLY SPIRIT EMPOWERS YOU TO SOLVE YOUR PROBLEMS *(Lesson 3, Pages 6-8);*
PRAYER PROVIDES COMMUNICATION WITH GOD *(Lesson 3, Pages 9-12);*
THE BIBLICAL VIEW OF SELF *(Lesson 4, Pages 5-10), under **IV., V., and VI.**; and*
BIBLICAL CHANGE IS A PROCESS *(Lesson 7, Pages 3-4).*

(Principle 96)   Take immediate steps to eliminate, resist, or flee from temptations that arise unexpectedly, especially in the area of your life-dominating sin *(based on Psalm 1:1; Proverbs 4:14-19, 27:12; I Corinthians 15:33; II Timothy 2:22; James 4:7; I Peter 5:8-9).*

(Principle 97)   Continually be a faithful doer of the Word in every area of your life. Be especially diligent to follow your biblical plan to overcome your life-dominating sin(s) so that you can mature in Christlikeness in all your deeds (thoughts, words, and actions) *(based on Psalm 19:7-11; II Timothy 3:16-17; Hebrews 5:14; James 1:22-25; I Peter 1:13-22; II Peter 1:2-11).*

REMEMBER: As a child of God, you are not your own; you have been bought with the precious sacrifice of Jesus Christ and are a temple of the Holy Spirit (I Corinthians 6:19-20; Ephesians 1:7; I Peter 1:17-19). In light of that fact, you are to please and glorify the Lord in all your deeds (thoughts, words, and actions) (based on Matthew 5:16; Romans 12:1-2; I Corinthians 10:31; II Corinthians 5:9; Colossians 1:10; Hebrews 9:14; I Peter 1:13-16, 2:9-12).

Also refer to:
THE UPWARD PATH: WALKING GOD'S WAY *(Lesson 5, Page 5);*
THE IMPORTANCE OF DOING THE WORD *(Lesson 5, Pages 6-9);*
BIBLICAL PERSPECTIVE ON TESTS AND TEMPTATIONS *(Lesson 8, Pages 3-7);*
PRACTICAL STEPS FOR ACHIEVING BIBLICAL CHANGE *(Lesson 8, Pages 8-10) under **I. Respond immediately to your need for biblical change**; and*
OVERCOMING LIFE-DOMINATING SINS *(Lesson 21, Pages 13-19).*

PUTTING ON THE FULL ARMOR OF GOD

> As an obedient believer, you are to stand firm in the strength of the Lord, to be sober in spirit, and to remain alert in order to resist the schemes of the devil. However, in all areas of your walk as a believer, you are incapable in your own strength and insufficient in your own resources to overcome the wiles and temptations of Satan. Therefore, you must put on the full armor of God to be an overwhelming conqueror in your continuing spiritual battle against the forces of hell *(based on Ephesians 6:10-18; James 4:7; I Peter 5:8-10; Revelation 12:11).*

I. **The purposes of the armor of God**

   A. Taking up the full armor of God prepares you to resist the schemes of the devil *(Ephesians 6:11).*

   B. Putting on the full armor of God enables you stand firm in the strength of the Lord *(Ephesians 6:10-11, 13).*

   C. Being protected by all parts of the full armor of God helps you to be equipped for walking daily in confidence in the Lord *(Ephesians 6:13-17).*

II. **The need for putting on the armor of God**

   A. As a believer in Christ, your struggle is not merely in the physical realm. You are also in a massive spiritual battle against rulers, powers, the world forces of darkness, and spiritual forces of wickedness *(Ephesians 6:12).*

   B. Your adversary, the devil, tempts you to sin so that your effectiveness as a believer in Christ will be destroyed *(based on I Thessalonians 3:5; I Peter 5:8-10).*

   C. Satan, as the ruler and deceiver of this world *(John 12:31; Revelation 12:9)*, diligently schemes to take advantage of you and all other believers in Christ *(based on II Corinthians 2:11).*

   D. Satan, through his false messengers, continually tries to mislead you as a believer in Christ *(based on Matthew 24:24; II Corinthians 11:3-4; Titus 1:10-16; I John 2:21-26).*

   See also: **GOD HAS BROKEN SATAN'S POWER** *(Lesson 20, Pages 9-11)* under **I.**

III. **Your confidence in the spiritual battle**

   A. As a believer, you are a new creation *(II Corinthians 5:17)* and are established in your position in Christ *(Romans 8:14-17; I Corinthians 1:30; Galatians 4:4-7; Ephesians 2:5-7; Philippians 3:20; Colossians 2:9-10).*

   Refer to:
   YOU CAN CHANGE BIBLICALLY (PART ONE) *(Lesson 1, Pages 3-7)*, **VII. C.** and
   YOU CAN CHANGE BIBLICALLY (PART TWO) *(Lesson 2, Pages 3-5)*, **I. A.**

B. Because of the death and resurrection of the Lord Jesus Christ, you, as a believer, can be more than a conqueror *(Romans 8:31-39, esp. verse 37; I John 4:4, 5:4-5)*, since you no longer need be enslaved by sin *(Romans 6:5-14, 17-18; Hebrews 2:14-15)*.

Refer to:
YOU CAN CHANGE BIBLICALLY (PART ONE) *(Lesson 1, Pages 3-7), III. and*
GOD HAS BROKEN SATAN'S POWER *(Lesson 20, Pages 9-11), II. D., E., and F.*

C. As a believer, you have free access to the mercy, grace, wisdom, and power of God in Jesus Christ through prayer *(based on Matthew 26:41; Luke 22:40; John 16:23-24; II Thessalonians 3:1-3; Hebrews 4:15-16; James 1:5; I John 5:14-15)*.

Refer to: ***PRAYER PROVIDES COMMUNICATION WITH GOD*** *(Lesson 3, Pages 9-12)*.

D. Through the indwelling of the Holy Spirit *(based on John 14:16-17; Romans 8:9, 14; I Corinthians 3:16, 6:19; Galatians 4:6-7; II Timothy 1:14)*, you are enabled to discern between truth and error *(I John 2:18-27, esp. verses 20 and 27)* and can receive divine guidance *(I Corinthians 2:9-13)*. Additionally, the Holy Spirit can keep you from fulfilling the desires of the flesh *(Galatians 5:16-17)*.

Refer to:
YOU CAN CHANGE BIBLICALLY (PART TWO) *(Lesson 2, Pages 3-5), I. B. and*
THE HOLY SPIRIT EMPOWERS YOU TO SOLVE YOUR PROBLEMS *(Lesson 3, Pages 6-8)*.

E. God has given you His Word (the Bible) as the sole authority to guide you in every aspect of your life *(based on Psalm 19:7-11; 119:11, 105; II Timothy 3:16-17; Hebrews 4:12; II Peter 1:2-11)*.

Refer to:
YOU CAN CHANGE BIBLICALLY (PART TWO) *(Lesson 2, Pages 3-5),* ***I. B., C., D.*** *and*
SCRIPTURE IS YOUR AUTHORITY *(Lesson 3, Pages 3-5)*.

IV. **Your responsibility to put on the full armor of God**

A. Since each piece of God's armor is designed to protect you in specific ways in your spiritual battles, you remain vulnerable to defeat if you put on some parts of the armor and neglect to put on other parts. Remember, God's armor is totally sufficient for you to resist the devil and to stand firm against him, but it is your responsibility to put on the **full** armor of God *(based on Ephesians 6:10-17)*.

1. *"... having girded your loins with truth ..." (Ephesians 6:14)*

   a. Just as a belt held a Roman soldier's tunic out of the way for ease of movement in battle, so should your use of biblical truth allow you to move about freely in everyday life, unhindered and unentangled by sin, ready to do spiritual battle.

   b. Truth that comes solely from God's Word *(Psalm 119:160; John 17:17)* emphasizes a correct understanding of the Lord Jesus Christ *(John 14:6)* and your relationship with Him *(John 8:31-32, 36)*. Biblical truth also emphasizes that you are to be truthful as you confront yourself biblically *(based on Psalm 51:6; Matthew 7:1-5; Luke 6:39-45)* and your relationships with others *(John 13:35; Romans 12:9; I Corinthians 13:4-8a; Ephesians 4:15, 25)*. It is especially important that you recognize the areas in which you are most vulnerable to the attacks of Satan. With determined truthfulness, develop a biblical plan to overcome these specific areas of weakness or temptation and be alert *(based on Psalm 119:11; I Corinthians 11:31; I Thessalonians 5:6; Hebrews 12:1-2; I Peter 5:8).*

2. *"... having put on the breastplate of righteousness," (Ephesians 6:14)*

    a. Just as a breastplate protected a Roman soldier from receiving severe wounds in hand-to-hand combat, your obedience to God's Word in all your deeds (thoughts, words, actions) will equip you to stand firm and not be overcome by any of Satan's diabolical attacks or crafty schemes in your everyday life.

    b. Your "breastplate of righteousness," as demonstrated in your Christlike thoughts, words, and actions, cannot be separated from your faith in the Lord Jesus Christ *(Romans 1:17, 3:21-22; II Corinthians 5:7; Philippians 3:7-11, esp. verse 9).*

    Note: Faith in Christ and subsequent demonstrations of Christlike love can also be described as a "breastplate" (I Thessalonians 5:8a).

    c. As a believer, the righteousness of Jesus Christ was "put on" you by God as a result of your spiritual new birth *(I Corinthians 1:30; II Corinthians 5:21).* This righteousness is demonstrated by living to please the Lord in every area of your life instead of living to please yourself by following your own desires, "common sense," or the world's wisdom *(based on I Corinthians 3:18-20; II Corinthians 5:9, 14-15).* In other words, does your practice of everyday righteousness (i.e., living in obedience to God's Word in your thoughts, words, and actions) reflect the position of righteousness that is yours by being in Christ?

    Note: God has been, is, and always will be righteous (Psalm 116:5, 145:17); however, He also is described as "putting on" a breastplate of righteousness when responding to a specific situation (Isaiah 59:9-21, esp. verse 17).

3. *"and having shod your feet with the preparation of the gospel of peace;" (Ephesians 6:15)*

    a. Just as a Roman soldier's "sandal-boot" was made to protect his feet from injury, to enable him to take long marches over rough terrain, and to keep him from slipping, so should you be equipped spiritually by the liberating message of Jesus Christ.

    b. Being equipped (prepared) by the gospel of peace gives you, as a believer in Jesus Christ, great encouragement and assurance because you have been reconciled to (are at peace with) God through Jesus Christ, who is our peace *(Ephesians 2:11-18, esp. verses 14-15, 17; Colossians 1:19-23).* No matter what tribulations may arise, you can be at peace in Christ Jesus since He has overcome the world *(John 16:33).* Knowing that Satan has already been defeated through Christ Jesus, you can be confidently at peace when you face any spiritual battle on the way to final victory *(Romans 16:20).*

    c. As a believer, you are to be ready to tell others how they also can be reconciled to God (be at peace) *(II Corinthians 5:18-20; Colossians 4:5-6; I Peter 3:15).*

4. *"in addition to all, taking up the shield of faith with which you will be able to extinguish all the flaming missiles of the evil one." (Ephesians 6:16).*

    a. Just as a Roman soldier trusted in the sufficiency of his large "body-shield," even while flaming arrows rained down on him, so should you be confident of God's protective care and sufficiency through Christ Jesus and God's Word in any situation of life.

b.   Remember that you are never adequate in your own strength to win any spiritual battle with Satan, but you are to depend totally on the Lord *(Proverbs 30:5; II Corinthians 3:5-6)*.

c.   Your faith (trust) in God rests on the sure foundation of the Lord Jesus Christ *(Galatians 2:20)*, and it overcomes the world *(I John 5:4-5)*. However, "faith" is not simply belief in correct facts; biblical faith results in action that conforms to the Word of God and brings glory to the Lord *(based on I Thessalonians 1:2-3; II Thessalonians 1:11-12; Hebrews 11:1-12:3; James 2:14-26; I Peter 1:6-7; II Peter 1:5-8)*.

Note: Roman soldiers protected one another as a unit by enclosing themselves behind overlapping shields when under severe attack. Since Satan's attacks on the Body of Christ never cease, it is obvious that members of the Body of Christ are to be linked with one another in their common faith in the Lord Jesus Christ, which results in faithful and loving obedience to God's Word (based on Proverbs 24:6; Ecclesiastes 4:9-12; Ephesians 4:16; Hebrews 10:23-25).

5.   *"And take the helmet of salvation ..." (Ephesians 6:17)*

a.   Just as a Roman soldier's helmet protected his head from crushing blows from the enemy, so should your reliance on the completeness and certainty of your salvation protect you from thoughts that would hinder you from becoming more like Jesus Christ.

b.   Realizing that the penalty for your sins has been paid *(Colossians 2:13-14; Hebrews 10:10-14; I Peter 3:18)* and that God is presently working to conform you to the character of His Son, Jesus Christ *(based on Romans 8:28-29; II Corinthians 3:18; Philippians 1:6, 3:12-14)*, you have no need to fear as you remain obedient to the Word of God in anticipation of seeing Jesus face to face *(based on I Thessalonians 2:13; Titus 2:11-14; I Peter 1:13; I John 3:3)*.

c.   Because of your salvation in Jesus Christ, you are able to bring your thoughts into subjection and concentrate on being obedient to Christ *(based on II Corinthians 10:5; Colossians 3:2)* as God continually renews your mind, changing you into the image of Christ *(Romans 12:1-2, esp. verse 2; II Corinthians 3:18; Ephesians 4:22-24, esp. verse 23; Colossians 3:10)*.

6.   *"... and the sword of the Spirit, which is the word of God." (Ephesians 6:17)*

a.   Just as a Roman soldier knew how to use his sword effectively in hand-to-hand combat, so should you know how to use God's Word effectively to thwart temptations to sin and other Satanic attacks that will inevitably come your way.

b.   Just as the Word of God gives you wisdom that leads to salvation *(II Timothy 3:15)*, it also continues to accomplish spiritual results after your spiritual new birth *(Hebrews 4:12)*, being very powerful *(Jeremiah 23:29)* and totally sufficient for every situation in life *(Psalm 19:7-11; II Timothy 3:16-17; II Peter 1:3-4)*. You are to handle it accurately *(based on II Timothy 2:15)* by being a consistent and faithful doer of the Word, since this keeps you from spiritual delusion and enables you to discern good and evil clearly *(James 1:22-25; Hebrews 5:14)*. Your constant love for (obedience to) God's Word will give you great peace, and nothing can cause you to stumble *(Psalm 119:165; II Peter 1:2-10, esp. verse 10)*.

c.   The Word of God is more than adequate to cause Satan to flee, but it must be specifically applied in order to be used effectively to combat temptations *(based on Psalm 119:11, 24, 41-42, 133; Matthew 4:1-11, esp. verses 4, 7, 10; II Timothy 2:15, 3:16-17; Hebrews 4:12)*.

B.   After you have put on the full armor of God, you are to stand firm and resist the devil *(Ephesians 6:11, 13; James 4:7; I Peter 5:8-9).* From this victorious position in Christ (fully covered by God's armor), you are to pray at all times by means of God's Spirit, especially praying for others in the Body of Christ *(based on Romans 8:26-27; Ephesians 6:18).*

V.   **Practical help for putting on the full armor of God**

A.   *"... having girded your loins with truth ..." (Ephesians 6:14).* In order to gird up your loins with truth:

1.   Set aside time to study what Jesus Christ has done for you through His death and resurrection by placing you in Him and disarming Satan's power.

Refer to:
YOU CAN CHANGE BIBLICALLY (PART ONE) (Lesson 1, Pages 2-7);
YOU CAN CHANGE BIBLICALLY (PART TWO) (Lesson 2, Pages 2-5); and
GOD HAS BROKEN SATAN'S POWER (Lesson 20, Pages 9-11).

2.   Make a list of Bible verses and passages that have been of special meaning in your life; also list those that will give you specific help in times of temptation. Choose Bible verses that deal with your area of temptation, listing them in order of their relevance to your particular problem. Then determine how many verses you will memorize each week and how many you will review periodically.

In addition, memorize verses that will give others hope or specific help in facing and dealing with problems in a biblical manner.

Refer to:
BIBLICAL BASIS FOR DAILY DEVOTIONS AND SCRIPTURE MEMORY
      (Lesson 2, Pages 9-11) and
FOUR PLANS FOR MEMORIZING SCRIPTURE (Lesson 2, Pages 12-13) with
      each lesson's memory verses in this course.

3.   Remain faithful and consistent in your daily devotions, in order to abide in the Lord and in His Word. In planning your daily devotions, keep a list of topics that you need to study in more depth. You may discover these topics through your regular personal Bible study, sermons you hear, or questions about the Scriptures you are asked by others.

Refer to:
BIBLICAL BASIS FOR DAILY DEVOTIONS AND SCRIPTURE MEMORY
      (Lesson 2, Pages 9-11).

B.   *"... having put on the breastplate of righteousness," (Ephesians 6:14).* In order to put on the breastplate of righteousness:

1.   Identify areas of your life in which you are weak and are still learning to overcome temptation. Make a list of circumstances (such as times of the month, locations, relationships) in which you are most tempted to allow the practices of the old nature to take over your life (in thoughts, speech, or actions). In this way, you will become alert to attacks from Satan in his attempts to defeat you.

Refer to:
EXAMPLES OF MAN'S WAY COMPARED TO GOD'S WAY (Lesson 4,
      Pages 12-13);
THE DOWNWARD SPIRAL: NEGLECTING OR REFUSING GOD'S WAY
      (Lesson 5, Page 3);
THE UPWARD PATH: WALKING GOD'S WAY (Lesson 5, Page 5);

BIBLICAL PERSPECTIVE ON TESTS AND TEMPTATIONS (Lesson 8, Pages 3-7);
RECOGNIZING LIFE-DOMINATING SINS (Lesson 20, Pages 3-7), under I. Characteristics of a life-dominating sin;
GUIDELINES: VICTORY OVER FAILURES WORKSHEET (Supplement 7);
VICTORY OVER FAILURES WORKSHEET (Supplement 8);
GUIDELINES: THE "THINK AND DO" LIST (Supplement 9); and
"THINK AND DO" LIST (Supplement 10).

2.   Learn to judge yourself in a biblical manner. Develop and faithfully maintain a biblical plan for living that will please the Lord in all things and be a blessing to others, especially in your daily responsibilities and specific areas of service and ministry. As part of your biblical plan for life, include a contingency plan that will help you overcome unexpected temptations.

Refer to:
BEGINNINGS OF BIBLICAL CHANGE (Lesson 5, Page 4);
BIBLICAL CHANGE IS A PROCESS (Lesson 7, Pages 3-4);
PRACTICAL STEPS FOR ACHIEVING BIBLICAL CHANGE (Lesson 8, Pages 8-10);
BIBLICAL PRINCIPLES OF STEWARDSHIP (Lesson 10, Pages 4-6);
DYING TO SELF BY SERVING OTHERS (Lesson 10, Pages 7-8);
GOD'S STANDARDS FOR YOU (Lesson 22, Pages 4-6);
GUIDELINES: VICTORY OVER FAILURES WORKSHEET (Supplement 7);
VICTORY OVER FAILURES WORKSHEET (Supplement 8); and
The "OVERCOMING" plans for each problem (Lessons 10, 11, 13, 18, 19, and 21).

3.   Evaluate the opportunities you have to put specific steps of your plans into practice.

As you go through each instance, answer the following questions:

a.   What happened this time?

b.   What did I do?

c.   What should I have done?

If you did what was biblical and pleasing to the Lord, the second and third answers should be the same. (If the answers to the second and third questions differ, make the necessary adjustments in your plan and renew your commitment to be faithful in practicing your biblical plan for living).

Refer to:
GUIDELINES: VICTORY OVER FAILURES WORKSHEET (Supplement 7);
VICTORY OVER FAILURES WORKSHEET (Supplement 8);
MY PRESENT SCHEDULE (Supplement 14); and
MY PROPOSED BIBLICAL SCHEDULE (Supplement 15).

C.   *"and having shod your feet with the preparation of the gospel of peace;" (Ephesians 6:15).*
In order to be equipped by the gospel of peace:

1.   Remember that you are no longer under the wrath of God but instead are at peace (reconciled) with Him through Jesus Christ.

Refer to:
YOU CAN CHANGE BIBLICALLY (PART ONE) (Lesson 1, Pages 3-7);
YOU CAN CHANGE BIBLICALLY (PART TWO) (Lesson 2, Pages 3-5);
BIBLICAL BASIS FOR PEACE AND JOY (Lesson 6, Pages 8-10); and
GOD HAS BROKEN SATAN'S POWER (Lesson 20, Pages 9-11).

2. Enroll, if needed, in evangelism training that may be available in your church or in your local area. Know the biblical reason for the hope within you and continue to update your testimony of what God is doing in your life. Be ready to tell others of the grace of God in Christ Jesus as opportunities are given you by the Lord.

   Refer to:
   YOU CAN CHANGE BIBLICALLY (PART ONE) (Lesson 1, Pages 3-7) and
   PREPARING A PERSONAL TESTIMONY (Supplement 4).

D. *"in addition to all, taking up the shield of faith with which you will be able to extinguish all the flaming missiles of the evil one." (Ephesians 6:16).* In order to take up the shield of faith:

   1. Remember that the circumstances and relationships in which you have the most intense trials are the ones in which you especially need to take up the shield of faith. God uses these trials to develop Christlike character in your life, and they give you an opportunity to die to self in order to live for Jesus Christ.

      Refer to:
      YOU CAN CHANGE BIBLICALLY (PART TWO) (Lesson 2, Pages 3-5);
      SCRIPTURE IS YOUR AUTHORITY (Lesson 3, Pages 3-5);
      THE HOLY SPIRIT EMPOWERS YOU TO SOLVE YOUR PROBLEMS (Lesson 3, Pages 6-8);
      PRAYER PROVIDES COMMUNICATION WITH GOD (Lesson 3, Pages 9-12);
      BIBLICAL HOPE (Lesson 6, Pages 6-7); and
      BIBLICAL PERSPECTIVE ON TESTS AND TEMPTATIONS (Lesson 8, Pages 3-7).

   2. You are to respond to difficulties in a manner that pleases the Lord instead of focusing on your own self-interests.

      Refer to:
      PLEASING SELF OR PLEASING GOD (Lesson 9, Pages 10-11);
      OVERCOMING A PREOCCUPATION WITH SELF (Lesson 10, Pages 9-12);
      UNBIBLICAL RESPONSES TO ANGER AND BITTERNESS (Lesson 11, Pages 4-5);
      A BIBLICAL VIEW OF ANGER (Lesson 11, Pages 6-9);
      A BIBLICAL VIEW OF BITTERNESS (Lesson 11, Pages 10-11);
      OVERCOMING ANGER AND BITTERNESS (Lesson 11, Pages 12-16);
      OVERCOMING INTERPERSONAL PROBLEMS (Lesson 13, Pages 19-23);
      OVERCOMING PROBLEMS THROUGH BIBLICAL COMMUNICATION (Lesson 15, Pages 6-9);
      AN OVERALL PLAN FOR REARING CHILDREN (Lesson 17, Pages 16-21);
      OVERCOMING DEPRESSION (Lesson 18, Pages 8-13);
      TEMPTATIONS TO FEAR AND WORRY (Lesson 19, Pages 4-5);
      OVERCOMING FEAR AND WORRY (Lesson 19, Pages 8-12); and
      OVERCOMING LIFE-DOMINATING SINS (Lesson 21, Pages 13-19).

E. *"And take the helmet of salvation ..." (Ephesians 6:17).* To take up the helmet of salvation:

   1. Know thoroughly the completeness and certainty of your salvation in Jesus Christ.

      Refer to:
      YOU CAN CHANGE BIBLICALLY (PART ONE) (Lesson 1, Pages 3-7);
      YOU CAN CHANGE BIBLICALLY (PART TWO) (Lesson 2, Pages 3-5);
      THE BIBLICAL MODEL OF MAN'S FAILURE (Lesson 4, Pages 3-4);
      THE BIBLICAL VIEW OF SELF (Lesson 4, Pages 5-10); and

> *KNOWING THE DIFFERENCE BETWEEN MAN'S WAY AND GOD'S WAY*
> *(Lesson 4, Page 14).*

2. Discipline your thoughts to concentrate on pleasing the Lord and becoming more Christlike. Remember that you will soon see Him face to face.

   Refer to:
   BIBLICAL BASIS FOR DAILY DEVOTIONS AND SCRIPTURE MEMORY
       (Lesson 2, Pages 9-11);
   FOUR PLANS FOR MEMORIZING SCRIPTURE *(Lesson 2, Pages 12-13);*
   THE EFFECTS OF UNBIBLICAL THOUGHTS, SPEECH, AND ACTIONS
       (Lesson 7, Page 5);
   RENEWING YOUR MIND *(Lesson 7, Pages 6-7);*
   GUIDELINES: THE "THINK AND DO" LIST *(Supplement 9); and*
   "THINK AND DO" LIST *(Supplement 10).*

F. *"... and the sword of the Spirit, which is the word of God." (Ephesians 6:17).* To use the Word of God effectively:

   1. Be a student of Scripture.

      Refer to:
      BIBLICAL BASIS FOR DAILY DEVOTIONS AND SCRIPTURE MEMORY
          (Lesson 2, Pages 9-11) and
      SCRIPTURE IS YOUR AUTHORITY *(Lesson 3, Pages 3-5).*

   2. Be a doer of the Word.

      Refer to: ***THE IMPORTANCE OF DOING THE WORD*** *(Lesson 5, Pages 6-9).*

   3. Know how to combat the schemes of Satan with the Word of God.

      Refer to:
      BASIC APPROACHES TO SOLVING PERSONAL PROBLEMS *(Lesson 4,*
          Page 11);
      EXAMPLES OF MAN'S WAY COMPARED TO GOD'S WAY *(Lesson 4,*
          Pages 12-13);
      KNOWING THE DIFFERENCE BETWEEN MAN'S WAY AND GOD'S WAY
          (Lesson 4, Page 14);
      THREE LEVELS OF PROBLEMS *(Lesson 6, Pages 4-5);*
      BIBLICAL PERSPECTIVE ON TESTS AND TEMPTATIONS *(Lesson 8,*
          Pages 3-7); and
      GOD HAS BROKEN SATAN'S POWER *(Lesson 20, Pages 9-11).*

G. Having put on the full armor of God, be faithful to pray regularly and fervently. In order to do this:

   1. You should have a regular pattern and plan of prayer.

      Refer to:
      BIBLICAL BASIS FOR DAILY DEVOTIONS AND SCRIPTURE MEMORY
          (Lesson 2, Pages 9-11);
      PRAYER PROVIDES COMMUNICATION WITH GOD *(Lesson 3, Pages 9-12);*
      MY PROPOSED BIBLICAL SCHEDULE *(Supplement 15);*
      GUIDELINES: FREEDOM FROM ANXIETY (BIBLICAL ACTION AND
          PRAYER PLAN) *(Supplement 16); and*
      FREEDOM FROM ANXIETY (BIBLICAL ACTION AND PRAYER PLAN)
          (Supplement 17).

   2. In your prayer life, ask for His continued wisdom in judging yourself biblically in all situations and rely on His leading and sovereignty in your daily activities.

Refer to:
THE HOLY SPIRIT EMPOWERS YOU TO SOLVE YOUR PROBLEMS
(Lesson 3, Pages 6-8), **II. B.;**
PRAYER PROVIDES COMMUNICATION WITH GOD *(Lesson 3, Pages 9-12);*
BEGINNINGS OF BIBLICAL CHANGE *(Lesson 5, Page 4);*
THE UPWARD PATH: WALKING GOD'S WAY *(Lesson 5, Page 5);*
PRACTICAL STEPS FOR ACHIEVING BIBLICAL CHANGE *(Lesson 8, Pages 8-10);*
GUIDELINES: VICTORY OVER FAILURES WORKSHEET *(Supplement 7); and*
VICTORY OVER FAILURES WORKSHEET *(Supplement 8).*

OVERCOMING LIFE-DOMINATING SINS

> You do not have to be controlled by sin, since sin's power has been broken in a believer's life through the Lord Jesus Christ. Relying solely on God's resources, you can be more than a conqueror in Jesus Christ, even in the areas in which you have been enslaved to sin for a very long time *(based on Romans 6:5-7, 12-18; 8:31-39; I Corinthians 10:13; Ephesians 6:10-18; II Timothy 3:16-17; Hebrews 2:14-15; I Peter 2:24-25, 5:8-10; I John 3:8, 4:4).*

I.   Carefully review the following cross-references:

A.   The foundational, biblical requirements for change (Lessons 1 and 2), recognizing the differences between living man's way and living God's way (Lessons 3 and 4);

B.   The essential elements of biblical change (Lessons 5 - 8) as you die to self and live for the Lord (Lessons 9 and 10);

C.   The necessity of biblically dealing with any anger and bitterness in your life (Lesson 11);

D.   The applicability of this situation to loving your neighbor (Lessons 12 and 13) and family relationships (Lessons 14 - 17);

E.   The possible links between fear, worry, or depression in your life (Lessons 18 and 19) and this problem; and

F.   The need for you to establish and faithfully maintain specific standards from God's Word in every area of your life (Lesson 22).

NOTE: The cross-references cited above are important in dealing with life-dominating sins. In dealing with problems biblically, you must examine all aspects of your life. For example, sins such as homosexuality, chronic laziness, occult practices, or chemical abuse (drugs or alcohol), cannot be overcome by dealing with them as an end in themselves. Rather, any specific problem must be dealt with in light of scriptural principles for all of life.

If you proceed in biblical counseling training, you will find that God's solutions as presented in this course apply to all problems, including all those not covered in this manual.

II. To become aware of the patterns of sin or temptations in regard to this particular problem, make a list of people, places, times, or circumstances where ongoing problems are evident in your life.

III. Use the VICTORY OVER FAILURES WORKSHEET (Supplement 8). To complete columns 1-3, follow the instructions in GUIDELINES: VICTORY OVER FAILURES WORKSHEET (Supplement 7).

IV. When completing column four of the VICTORY OVER FAILURES WORKSHEET (Supplement 8):

A. Develop a **basic plan** to overcome the sins you have recognized. In your plan, include deeds (thoughts, speech, and actions) that will help you develop a Christlike manner by taking into account the following guidelines:

1. Think biblically

   a. Consider thoroughly the issue of your salvation *(based on I Corinthians 6:9-10; II Corinthians 13:5; Galatians 5:19-21; I John 2:3-6, 3:7-10).*

   If necessary, refer to: **YOU CAN CHANGE BIBLICALLY (PART ONE)** *(Lesson 1, Pages 3-7). If you are a believer in Jesus Christ, then the remainder of this plan to overcome life-dominating sins is applicable to you. If you realize you have not made a commitment to Jesus Christ for salvation, review: Lesson 1, Page 5,* **V. By faith, you can take the first step of biblical change.**

   b. As a believer, remember that God has promised to care for you in any situation, no matter how unsettling it may seem *(Psalm 23:1-6, 37:5; Proverbs 3:25-26; Matthew 10:28-31; I Corinthians 10:13; Romans 8:28-29, 36-39).*
   Review: **BIBLICAL HOPE** *(Lesson 6, Pages 6-7).*

   c. Remember that God, through the death and resurrection of Jesus Christ, has broken Satan's power *(based on Acts 26:14-18, esp. verse 18; Hebrews 2:14-15; I John 3:8),* and you no longer have to be enslaved by sin *(based on Romans 6:6-14, 17-18; 8:9-18; I Corinthians 10:13; I Peter 2:24-25; I John 4:4).*
   Review: **GOD HAS BROKEN SATAN'S POWER** *(Lesson 20, Pages 9-11).*

   d. Confess all sinful thoughts to God *(I John 1:9)* and ask for His help in overcoming this sinful pattern *(based on I Thessalonians 5:17; Hebrews 4:15-16; James 1:5).*

   e. Rejoice *(I Thessalonians 5:16)* and give thanks in and for every situation *(Ephesians 5:20; I Thessalonians 5:18),* knowing that endurance in trials helps conform you to the image of Christ *(based on Romans 5:3-5; James 1:2-4).*
   Review: **BIBLICAL BASIS FOR PEACE AND JOY** *(Lesson 6, Pages 8-10).*

   f. Remember that God's forgiveness of you is the basis for you to forgive others *(Matthew 18:21-35; Ephesians 4:32; Colossians 3:13).*
   Review: **FORGIVENESS (FORGIVING OTHERS AS GOD HAS FORGIVEN YOU)** *(Lesson 12, Pages 3-5).*

   g. Remember that your love for others demonstrates the love that you have for God *(I John 2:9-11; 3:14-16; 4:7-11, 20-21).* Remember to pray for those who persecute you *(Matthew 5:44).*
   Review: **THE MEANING OF BIBLICAL LOVE** *(Lesson 13, Pages 4-6).*

   h. Focus your thoughts on glorifying and pleasing God and on being a blessing to others in all situations *(based on Matthew 22:37-39; Luke 9:23-24; II Corinthians 5:9, 15; 10:5; Galatians 5:16-17; Philippians 2:3-4, 4:8; Colossians 3:2).*

   i. Within the very situation in which you find yourself, do not dwell on things that lead to further sin. Instead, discipline your mind to think on things that please the Lord *(Philippians 4:8; Colossians 3:2).*
   Review:
   THE EFFECTS OF UNBIBLICAL THOUGHTS, SPEECH, AND ACTIONS *(Lesson 7, Page 5) and*
   RENEWING YOUR MIND *(Lesson 7, Pages 6-7).*

   j. Review psalms, hymns, and spiritual songs that you have memorized *(based on Ephesians 5:19-20; Colossians 3:16).*

   k. Think of ways to encourage other believers, stimulating them to love and good deeds *(Hebrews 10:23-25).*

2.   Speak biblically

     a.   Confess your current sins to the Lord and to those whom you have failed to love in a biblical manner, including sins of failing to fulfill your responsibilities. Confess past sins that you have failed to confess earlier *(based on Psalm 51:1-4; James 5:16; I John 1:9).*

         To review how to confess your sins to those you have sinned against, refer to: **GUIDELINES: VICTORY OVER FAILURES WORKSHEET** *(Supplement 7)* *under VI. Application of biblical change, point D. and* **RECONCILIATION (REMOVING ALL HINDRANCES TO UNITY AND PEACE)** *(Lesson 12, Pages 6-8) under II. Confession.*

     b.   Do not speak about your past accomplishments *(Proverbs 27:2, 30:32; II Corinthians 10:18),* sorrows, or defeats *(Philippians 3:13-14),* worries about the future *(Matthew 6:34),* comparing yourself to yourself and/or others *(II Corinthians 10:12),* or boastfully promising what you will do in the future *(Proverbs 27:1; James 4:13-16).* Instead, edify others by thankfully speaking of the goodness of the Lord and what He has done for you in this situation *(based on Mark 5:19-20; Luke 10:20; Ephesians 4:29; Colossians 4:6; Hebrews 13:15; I Peter 3:15).*

     c.   Do not slander, gossip, quarrel, or use words that do not edify others *(Proverbs 10:18; Ephesians 4:29, 31; 5:4; Colossians 3:8; II Timothy 2:24; I Peter 2:1).* Instead, let your speech be truthful and gracious, according to the need of the moment, that you may know how to answer each person *(Ephesians 4:15, 25, 29; Colossians 4:6).*

     d.   Do not bring up another's sin in an accusing or vengeful manner, either to others, yourself, or to the person who has sinned *(Proverbs 10:18, 17:9, 20:19; Ephesians 4:29, 31; Colossians 3:8; I Peter 2:1).* *Review:* **FORGIVENESS (FORGIVING OTHERS AS GOD HAS FORGIVEN YOU** *(Lesson 12, Pages 3-5), especially* **II. Responding to God's forgiveness.**

     e.   Encourage reconciliation with God and others, following biblical guidelines *(Matthew 5:9, 23-24; Romans 12:18; II Corinthians 2:6-8, 5:18).* *Refer to:* **RECONCILIATION (REMOVING ALL HINDRANCES TO UNITY AND PEACE)** *(Lesson 12, Pages 6-8).*

3.   Act biblically

     a.   Identify all danger signals (e.g., situations, places, times, and personal contacts that bring temptation) and take immediate steps to eliminate, flee, or resist the temptation *(based on Psalm 1:1; Proverbs 27:12; I Corinthians 10:13, 15:33; II Timothy 2:22; James 4:7; I Peter 5:8-9).* *Review:* **BIBLICAL PERSPECTIVE ON TESTS AND TEMPTATIONS** *(Lesson 8, Pages 3-7).*

     b.   Halt all activities, cut off all contacts, stop all associations, and destroy all items and paraphernalia which have to do with the particular sin that has enslaved you *(based on Romans 6:12-13, 21; I Corinthians 15:33; II Corinthians 6:14 - 7:1; Ephesians 5:11-17, esp. verses 11-12; Philippians 3:16-20; I Thessalonians 5:22; II Timothy 2:22).* Quickly fill the many voids created by putting off the old ways with a vigorous plan of living righteously, putting on the new ways *(Titus 2:11-14).* *Review: Lessons 5 - 8 and* **GUIDELINES: VICTORY OVER FAILURES WORKSHEET** *(Supplement 7).*

         Note: If necessary, seek and remain under the supervision of a primary care physician while you are taking steps to overcome any sin in your life which has affected your physical health (e.g., in severe instances, you may be admitted to a detoxification center because your body is dangerously depleted and must adjust to withdrawing from an habitual use of drugs or alcohol). Your medical doctor should closely monitor your withdrawal to allow your body sufficient time to adjust to being drug-free. The counseling team must be prepared to work closely with the physician in such cases.

c. If you have any artifacts, trinkets, jewelry, pictures, literature, or any other memorabilia associated with the occult, destroy them. Also, you are to cease being associated in any way with people involved in Satanic practices.
Refer to: **GOD HAS BROKEN SATAN'S POWER**, *Lesson 20, Pages 9-11, under III.* **Satanic associations are to be discarded from your life.**

d. Spend much time with other believers *(Hebrews 10:23-25)* and wholeheartedly put on the full armor of God in order to stand firm against the devil *(Ephesians 6:10-17)*.
See: **PUTTING ON THE FULL ARMOR OF GOD** *(Lesson 21, Pages 4-12)*.

e. Forgive others just as God has forgiven you *(Ephesians 4:32; Colossians 3:13)*.
Refer to: **FORGIVENESS (FORGIVING OTHERS AS GOD HAS FORGIVEN YOU)** *(Lesson 12, Pages 3-5) and determine if you are practicing biblical forgiveness. Make changes as necessary.*

f. Memorize Scripture verses and study Scripture passages specifically related to facing and dealing with this particular problem *(based on Psalm 119:9, 11, 16; II Corinthians 10:5; Philippians 4:8; II Timothy 2:15)*. Especially memorize verses that tell of the overcoming power that is yours in Christ Jesus *(Refer to:* **GOD HAS BROKEN SATAN'S POWER**, *Lesson 20, Pages 9-11, under II.* *D., E., F., and G.)*. Also memorize psalms, hymns, and spiritual songs that can be used at appropriate times *(based on Ephesians 5:19-20; Colossians 3:16)*.
Review:
BIBLICAL BASIS FOR DAILY DEVOTIONS AND SCRIPTURE MEMORY *(Lesson 2, Pages 9-11) and*
FOUR PLANS FOR MEMO5RIZING SCRIPTURE *(Lesson 2, Pages 12-13)*.

g. Pray always with thanksgiving *(Philippians 4:6; I Thessalonians 5:17-18)* and according to God's will *(I John 5:14-15)*. Cast all your cares on the Lord *(I Peter 5:7)*.
Review:
PRAYER PROVIDES COMMUNICATION WITH GOD *(Lesson 3, Pages 9-12) and*
GUIDELINES: FREEDOM FROM ANXIETY (BIBLICAL ACTION AND PRAYER PLAN) *(Supplement 16)*.

h. Make amends for wrongdoing and seek reconciliation with those you have offended *(based on Matthew 5:23-24)*. Remember that although you have already confessed your sins *(see 2. a. above)*, you need to demonstrate actively your serious intent to change.
See: **RECONCILIATION (REMOVING ALL HINDRANCES TO UNITY AND PEACE)** *(Lesson 12, Pages 6-8) under III.* **Restitution** *and IV.* **The importance of reconciliation.**

i. Bless others through tangible expressions of biblical love and service (this includes your daily responsibilities as a family member, student, employer, employee, roommate, etc.) *(based on Matthew 7:12; Romans 12:9-13, 15-16; 13:8-10; I Corinthians 13:4-8a; Philippians 2:3-8; I Timothy 6:17-19; I Peter 3:8-9; I John 3:18)*. You are to do this:

    1) Regardless of how you feel *(based on Genesis 4:7; II Corinthians 5:14-15; Galatians 5:16-17; Philippians 4:13; James 4:17);*

    2) Especially to those who seem to be your enemies or to those against whom you have sinned *(based on Matthew 5:23-24, 43-48; Mark 11:25-26; Romans 12:14, 17-21);*

    3) With kindness and tenderheartedness for the very individuals with whom you are or have been irritated *(Ephesians 4:31-32);*

    4) By taking advantage of opportunities to minister in ways that keep you in a Christlike servant attitude toward others *(based on Matthew 20:25-28; Philippians 2:3-8; I Peter 4:10);* and

    5) By practicing biblical stewardship to honor the Lord and to be of practical help to others *(based on Psalm 24:1; Matthew 25:14-29; I Corinthians 4:1-2; Ephesians 5:15-17; I Timothy 6:17-19; I Peter 4:10).*
Refer to:
BIBLICAL PRINCIPLES OF STEWARDSHIP *(Lesson 10, Pages 4-6)*
and
DYING TO SELF BY SERVING OTHER *(Lesson 10, Page 7-8).*

To learn how and when to express biblical love, even in difficult situations, refer to:
THE MEANING OF BIBLICAL LOVE *(Lesson 13, Pages 4-6).*

    j. Whenever necessary, conduct a "conference table." *Refer to the plan outlined in:* **OVERCOMING PROBLEMS THROUGH BIBLICAL COMMUNICATION (USING A CONFERENCE TABLE FOR RECONCILIATION)** *(Lesson 15, Pages 6-9).*

    k. Correct deficiencies in your life that exist because of a lack of discipline or neglect *(based on Colossians 3:1-17; I Timothy 4:7b; James 4:17).*
Refer to: **GUIDELINES: VICTORY OVER FAILURES WORKSHEET** *(Supplement 7) and review Lessons 5 - 8 if necessary.*

    l. If you need help, ask Christian friends to hold you accountable to carry out your **basic and contingency plans** until you have established a new pattern of godly living *(Proverbs 27:17; Ecclesiastes 4:9-10; Hebrews 10:24).* If necessary, seek biblical counsel from others *(Proverbs 11:14, 15:22).*

B. As necessary, develop a **"THINK AND DO" LIST** (Supplement 10) using **GUIDELINES: THE "THINK AND DO" LIST** (Supplement 9).

C. Implement your **basic plan** *(James 1:22)* and do it heartily for the Lord *(Colossians 3:23-24).*

D. Develop a **contingency plan** to deal with unusual situations that tempt you to sin, especially in those areas where a particular sin has dominated your life. Take into account the following guidelines:

    1. Immediately ask God for help *(I Thessalonians 5:17; Hebrews 4:15-16; James 1:5).*

    2. Review memorized Scripture verses that deal specifically with God's resources that are available for you to overcome sin *(based on Psalm 119:9, 11, 16).* As appropriate, sing the psalms, hymns, and spiritual songs that you have memorized for such occasions *(based on Ephesians 5:19-20; Colossians 3:16).*

    3. Immediately seek God's perspective.

        a. Regardless of your feelings or circumstances, view this situation as an opportunity for further spiritual maturity *(James 1:2-4)* because God works out all things for good in the lives of His children *(based on Psalm 37; Proverbs 3:5-12; Romans 8:28-29; Ephesians 1:3-14; Philippians 1:6).*

1) Remind yourself that you can do all things through Christ who gives you strength *(Philippians 4:11-13)*, since your adequacy is from God and not from any natural "inner strength" *(II Corinthians 3:5)*. Remember that you can do nothing fruitful apart from Jesus Christ *(John 15:5)*.

2) Praise and glorify God that He is sufficient even in your areas of weakness *(II Corinthians 12:9-10)* and that He will keep you from stumbling and make you stand blameless and with great joy in the presence of His glory *(Jude 1:24-25)*.

b. Remember that God looks on your heart, not on your outward appearance *(I Samuel 16:7)*. You must stand blameless before Him in your thoughts, whether others know about it or not *(based on Acts 23:1, 24:16; Romans 14:12; Ephesians 4:1; Philippians 1:9-11; Colossians 1:21-22)*.

1) If you even begin to think sinful thoughts in an unforeseen circumstance, confess them to the Lord *(I John 1:9)*.

2) Remember that it is not the amount of time spent sinning or the immensity of the sin (by human standards) by which you should judge yourself. Rather, the fact that you stopped going God's way even momentarily is what matters *(James 2:10, 4:17)*.

4. Thank God that you are His servant in your present circumstance *(based on Ephesians 5:20; I Thessalonians 5:18)*. Determine how you will give glory to God *(I Corinthians 10:31; I Peter 4:11)* and seek ways to edify others by serving them in this situation *(Ephesians 4:29; Philippians 2:3-4)*.

E. Act according to your **contingency plan** as soon as you detect a temptation to sin *(based on I Thessalonians 5:22; II Timothy 2:19-22)*. Then, begin again to do those things written in your **basic plan** *(based on Proverbs 24:16; James 1:22-25)*.

F. If you fall to temptation by choosing to gratify your fleshly desires instead of choosing to obey the Word of God, you will often experience painful consequences and the discipline of the Lord *(based on Deuteronomy 11:26-28; Proverbs 1:22-32; Romans 6:16; Colossians 3:25; Hebrews 12:5-13; James 1:14-15; II Peter 2:19b)*, as has been illustrated in the lives some in the Bible *(Joshua 7:1-5, 20-26; Judges 16:15-21; II Samuel 12:14-18)*.

1. Even though you may fall to temptation, you can be restored by the power of God *(Psalm 37:23-24, 145:14; Proverbs 24:16; Micah 7:7-9)*, begin again to be a doer of the Word *(James 1:25)*, and continue onward in your walk in the Lord Jesus Christ *(Ephesians 4:1; Philippians 3:12-14)*.

a. The first step in this process is to recognize and confess your failures to the Lord so you can receive His pardon and cleansing *(based on Psalm 51:1-4; I John 1:9; Revelation 2:5)*.

b. Confess your sins to those against whom you have sinned *(James 5:16)*, thus facilitating the possibility for reconciliation and the restoration of relationships *(Romans 12:18)*.

Note: Some relationships cannot and should not be restored if they provide temptation to sin (I Thessalonians 5:21-23; II Timothy 2:22) or if they do not bring glory to God (I Corinthians 10:31-33). To determine biblically if a relationship should be restored, refer to: PRACTICAL STEPS FOR ACHIEVING BIBLICAL CHANGE (Lesson 8, Pages 8-10) and answer the questions under I. F. 7.

c. Revise your contingency plan, as necessary, to be more effectively prepared to overcome any future temptations *(based on II Timothy 2:15; II Peter 1:2-10)*.

Review:
THE UPWARD PATH: WALKING GOD'S WAY *(Lesson 5, Page 5)* and
THE IMPORTANCE OF DOING THE WORD *(Lesson 5, Pages 6-9).*

2. As you return to the divine resources that God has made available to you, you are promised God's comfort *(Psalm 119:50; Lamentations 3:22-23; II Corinthians 1:3-4)*, His guidance *(Psalm 119:105, 133, 143; Romans 8:14; II Timothy 3:16-17)*, and His divine strength to continue in His way *(Psalm 119:28, 156; Romans 8:10-13; Philippians 4:13).*

3. As a true believer in Jesus Christ, you can again experience biblical hope since:

    a. The discipline of the Lord, while sorrowful *(Hebrews 12:11)*, is an expression of His love for you *(Hebrews 12:5-6);*

    b. God has promised to continue His work in you *(Philippians 1:6, 2:13; I Thessalonians 5:23-24)* and is able to keep you from stumbling and to make you stand in His presence without blame and with great joy *(Jude 1:24);* and

    c. He will confirm (make firm, establish) you to the end *(I Corinthians 1:4-9).*

    Review: **BIBLICAL HOPE** *(Lesson 6, Pages 6-7).*

4. In spite of your failures, God has promised to work out all things for good *(Romans 8:28).* You are to begin again to demonstrate your love for Him by being obedient to His Word *(John 14:15; I John 5:3; II John 1:6)* in light of your calling to be conformed to the image of the Jesus Christ *(Romans 8:29; II Corinthians 3:18).*

BIBLICALLY RESPONDING TO SOMEONE WITH A LIFE-DOMINATING SIN

> Among your friends, family, or acquaintances, you may know someone who is enslaved by a life-dominating sin. As a faithful, loving believer, you have the unique opportunity to help reconcile this person to the Lord (if an unbeliever) or help restore him to a life of peace, joy, and righteousness (if a believer) *(based on II Corinthians 5:14-20; Galatians 6:1-5).*

I. **Life-dominating sins of others give you an opportunity to examine yourself biblically.**

   A. Before attempting to deal with another's person's sins, you are to examine your own life before the Lord *(Matthew 7:1-5).*
   Refer to:
   BIBLICAL SELF-CONFRONTATION: AN ESSENTIAL FOR DISCIPLESHIP *(Lesson 2, Page 6)* and
   BIBLICAL SELF-CONFRONTATION: A PREREQUISITE FOR HELPING OTHERS BIBLICALLY *(Lesson 2, Pages 7-8).*

   B. You are to be a faithful doer of the Word in all things *(James 1:25),* since your obedience to Scripture is based on your love for the Lord *(John 14:15; I John 5:3; II John 1:6)* and not on another's behavior.

      1. As a doer of the Word, you are to treat others in the same manner that you would like them to treat you *(Matthew 7:12).*

      2. As a doer of the Word, you are to show biblical love at all times and to esteem others as more important than yourself *(based on Luke 10:25-37; I Corinthians 13:4-8a; Philippians 2:3-4).*
      Refer to: ***THE MEANING OF BIBLICAL LOVE*** *(Lesson 13, Pages 4-6), especially under IV. E.*

      3. As a doer of the Word, you are to practice biblical forgiveness and to encourage biblical reconciliation at all times *(based on Matthew 5:23-24; Mark 11:25-26; Luke 17:3-4; Ephesians 5:32).*
      Refer to:
      FORGIVENESS (FORGIVING OTHERS AS GOD HAS FORGIVEN YOU) *(Lesson 12, Pages 3-5),*
      RECONCILIATION (REMOVING ALL HINDRANCES TO UNITY AND PEACE) *(Lesson 12, Pages 6-8),*
      THE IMPORTANCE OF DOING THE WORD *(Lesson 5, Pages 6-9), and*
      BIBLICAL BASIS FOR PEACE AND JOY *(Lesson 6, Pages 8-10).*

II. **Believers or unbelievers need to learn the effects of their life-dominating sin.**

   A. A person with a life-dominating sin cannot know the full effects of his sinful practice in his own life or the lives of others, because:

      1. He is focused on gratifying self-centered desires *(based on I Corinthians 6:9-12; Galatians 5:19-21; James 1:14-15);*

---

2.   He is spiritually deluded and does not know the kind of person he really is *(based on James 1:22-24)*; and

3.   He cannot clearly discern between good and evil *(based on I Corinthians 2:14; Hebrews 5:14)*.

B.   Out of your commitment to the Lord and your biblical love for someone enslaved to sin, you are to avoid quarreling *(II Timothy 2:24-26)* and blameshifting *(Ezekiel 18:4, 20; Romans 14:12)*. Instead, speak the truth in love by telling the person of the detrimental effects his sin will have on himself and others *(based on Romans 6:16, 13:11-14; Ephesians 4:25, 5:11-14; James 1:14-15, esp. verse 15)*. *Follow guidelines in:*
BIBLICAL COMMUNICATION *(Lesson 13, Pages 12-14)*.

1.   If the person with a life-dominating sin is a believer, use biblical restoration procedures *(Matthew 18:15-17; Galatians 6:1)*. *Note 2. a. and 2. b. below.*
Review:
RESTORATION/DISCIPLINE (YOUR BIBLICAL RESPONSE TO THE SIN OF ANOTHER BELIEVER) *(Lesson 13, Pages 7-8) and*
GUIDELINES: THE RESTORATION/DISCIPLINE PROCESS *(Lesson 13, Pages 9-11)*.

2.   If the person is an unbeliever, remember that he cannot understand the things of God *(I Corinthians 2:14)*. However, he sometimes will realize that his actions are "wrong" *(Romans 1:18-23, esp. verse 19)*. In spite of his enslavement and delusion, an unbeliever can often be helped to understand the magnitude and effects of his present sinful behavior in every area of his life *(Proverbs 13:15b; Colossians 3:25; I John 3:4) Refer also to:* **THE EFFECTS OF LIFE-DOMINATING SINS (THE CIRCLE OF LIFE)** *(Lesson 20, Page 8)*.

a.   A person enslaved by sin will often try to excuse his sinful behavior. However, even one involved in the sin cannot overlook these consequences since they deal with observable, measurable facts (e.g., lying, pregnancy out of wedlock, venereal diseases or AIDS, hiding money or not being willing to account for money spent, encouraging others to participate with him in sin, asking others to "cover up" for him, failing to be at work on time, hiding drugs or alcohol, not completing household responsibilities, etc.).

b.   It is sometimes necessary to keep a record of the many effects and consequences of another's sinful behavior in order to present this evidence to the one who is enslaved by sin. This is not done in order to "remember wrongs suffered against you," which would be a violation of biblical love *(I Corinthians 13:5)*; but it is done with the purpose of lovingly teaching another of his focus on self and his lack of love for God and others *(based on Ephesians 4:25, 5:11-12)*. *Refer also to:* **FORGIVENESS (FORGIVING OTHERS AS GOD HAS FORGIVEN YOU)** *(Lesson 12, Pages 3-5, under II. 5)*.

c.   Always be ready to present the liberating message of Jesus Christ to someone who is under Satan's dominion and is enslaved by sin *(I Peter 3:15-16)*.
Refer to:
YOU CAN CHANGE BIBLICALLY (PART ONE) *(Lesson 1, Pages 3-7), and*
GOD HAS BROKEN SATAN'S POWER *(Lesson 20, Pages 9-11)*.

3.   If a person with a life-dominating sin breaks a law that must be reported to governmental authorities (for example: child abuse or child endangerment, drug use, drug sales or purchases, robbery, assault and battery, etc.), he is to be dealt with by those authorities *(Romans 13:1-7; I Peter 2:13-16)*.

Note: Friends or family members of a person mastered by sin often know that he has broken the law. However, in a misguided effort to "help him" or "not cause him any more trouble," they will not contact governmental authorities to deal with the matter. Friends or family members thus "cover up" for a person breaking the law and, often without realizing it, help to forestall the needed consequences of sin and/or the discipline of the Lord.

III. **You are to use all biblical resources and to remain obedient to Scripture in every dimension when dealing with a person enslaved by sin.**

    A.   You are not responsible to change a person who is mastered by sin, nor are you able to do so. Lasting change in anyone's life is the work of the Holy Spirit that is linked to one's obeying the Word of God *(II Corinthians 3:18; Galatians 5:22-23; I Thessalonians 2:13; Titus 3:5; II Peter 1:2-11).*
Review:
***SCRIPTURE IS YOUR AUTHORITY** (Lesson 3, Pages 3-5);*
***THE HOLY SPIRIT EMPOWERS YOU TO SOLVE YOUR PROBLEMS** (Lesson 3, Pages 6-8) under II.*
***BIBLICAL CHANGE IS A PROCESS** (Lesson 7, Pages 3-4); and*
***PRACTICAL STEPS FOR ACHIEVING BIBLICAL CHANGE** (Lesson 8, Pages 810).*

    B.   Even though you are to bear the weaknesses of those without strength and are to please others for their edification *(Romans 15:1-2),* you are not to hide failures or assume responsibilities of those who have a life-dominating sin *(based on Proverbs 26:5; Romans 14:12; Ephesians 5:11-12).*

        Note: Sometimes, well-meaning but misguided friends or family members "cushion" a person from the effects of his life-dominating sin. Thus, he is shielded from the usual, far-reaching consequences of his sinful behavior and does not personally experience the discipline of the Lord to an effective degree. As a result, he may continue to practice sin because he has been denied the consequences that the Lord wants to use to turn him from his sinful ways (based on Proverbs 1:22-32; Hebrews 12:5-13, esp. verses 10-11).

    C.   After biblically confronting someone with a life-dominating sin, do not shun or avoid him until he "proves himself." The restoration and reconciliation process requires your consistent and faithful involvement in his life, in a spirit of gentleness *(based on Proverbs 17:17; 27:5-6, 17; Matthew 18:15-17; Luke 17:3-4; II Corinthians 5:17-21; Galatians 6:1-2).*

    D.   No matter what adverse effects another's life-dominating sin has had on you, you are to forgive him from your heart *(Matthew 18:21-35, esp. verse 35),* even if it is necessary to keep aloof from him *(II Thessalonians 3:6).*
Review:
***FORGIVENESS (FORGIVING OTHERS AS GOD HAS FORGIVEN YOU)** (Lesson 12, Pages 3-5),*
***RECONCILIATION (REMOVING ALL HINDRANCES TO UNITY AND PEACE)** (Lesson 12, Pages 6-8), and*
***QUESTIONS AND ANSWERS ABOUT BIBLICAL FORGIVENESS** (Lesson 12, Pages 9-13).*

    E.   You are not to gossip about someone with a life-dominating sin *(based on Leviticus 19:16; Proverbs 17:9, 18:8; Romans 1:28-32, esp. verse 29; II Corinthians 12:20);* instead you are to seek biblical counsel, as necessary, to determine how you should respond to someone in this condition. This biblical counsel should come only from those who are mature enough to help you face and deal with the problem in a biblical manner *(based on Proverbs 11:14, 15:22).*

Review: **BIBLICAL COMMUNICATION** *(Lesson 13, Pages 12-14).*

Note: Gossip is not a matter of information being true or false. Even though the information is true, it is gossip whenever you pass on information that is not edifying about another simply for "information's sake" instead of it being integral to the restoration process (based on Matthew 7:12; Romans 15:2; Ephesians 4:29).

F.   In dealing with a believer about his life-dominating sin, encourage him to examine his thoughts *(Matthew 15:19; Mark 7:20-23)*, speech *(Matthew 12:34; Luke 6:45)*, and actions *(Matthew 15:18-20; Mark 7:20-23)*, biblically, especially as to how these relate to overcoming the sin that has dominated his life.

Note: Feelings, good or bad, that are associated with overcoming a life-dominating sin are not to be the focus of attention. Instead, encourage the individual to concentrate on pleasing the Lord and bringing glory to Him by being obedient to His Word (based on John 14:15, 15:8; II Corinthians 5:9; Colossians 1:9-12; I John 5:3) in thought (II Corinthians 10:5; Philippians 4:8), speech (Ephesians 4:29; Colossians 4:6), and actions (Matthew 5:16; I Corinthians 10:31; Philippians 4:9; Colossians 3:17). Remember that lasting peace and joy are promised to a believer who is obedient to Scripture (based on Psalm 119:165-168; John 15:10-11; Romans 14:17; Philippians 4:6-7).
Refer to:
THREE LEVELS OF PROBLEMS *(Lesson 6, Pages 4-5) and*
BIBLICAL BASIS FOR PEACE AND JOY *(Lesson 6, Pages 8-10).*

G.   Throughout the process of dealing with someone with a life-dominating sin, be diligent to:

1.   Examine yourself biblically *(Matthew 7:1-5; I Corinthians 11:31)*. Regularly and diligently confess your sins to the Lord *(I John 1:9)* and, at the appropriate time, to those against whom you have sinned *(James 5:16)*.

2.   Be faithful in maintaining your own daily devotions, Scripture memory and prayer life *(Psalm 1:1-3, 119:11; Colossians 4:2)*.
Refer to:
BIBLICAL BASIS FOR DAILY DEVOTIONS AND SCRIPTURE MEMORY *(Lesson 2, Pages 9-11)*,
PRAYER PROVIDES COMMUNICATION WITH GOD *(Lesson 3, Pages 9-12), and*
GUIDELINES: FREEDOM FROM ANXIETY (BIBLICAL ACTION AND PRAYER PLAN) *(Supplement 16).*

3.   Practice biblical love and biblical communication at all times, being especially careful not to return evil for evil but to overcome evil with good. Remember that your life is to be salt and light in all situations in order to give glory to God *(Matthew 5:13-16; Romans 12:21; I Corinthians 13:4-8a; Ephesians 4:25, 29; Colossians 4:6; I Peter 3:8-9)*.
Refer to: **THE MEANING OF BIBLICAL LOVE** *(Lesson 13, Pages 4-6) and*
BIBLICAL COMMUNICATION *(Lesson 13, Pages 12-14).*

4.   Be a biblical steward in every area of your life *(I Corinthians 4:2)*.
Refer to: **BIBLICAL PRINCIPLES OF STEWARDSHIP** *(Lesson 10, Pages 4-6).*

5.   Trust God in this situation, knowing that He will work all things out for good in your life as you continue to obey His Word *(Romans 8:28-29)*. Remember that trials are designed to mature you in Christ *(based on Romans 5:3-5; James 1:2-4)*.

A CASE STUDY: MARY'S HUSBAND HAS LEFT HER

> After receiving a spiritual new birth through the Lord Jesus Christ, a believer is provided with God's power and resources to overcome any life-dominating sin. Sometimes, the first major test that he faces is to rely *solely* on God's power and His Word to overcome the enslavement of a life-dominating sin *(based on Romans 6:1-23, 8:5-18; I Corinthians 6:9-11; II Corinthians 5:14-17; Galatians 2:20, 5:16-25; I John 2:15-17, 5:2-5).*

Both Tom and Mary come to the session. After the opening prayer, the counselor speaks.

Counselor:	"TOM , IT IS GOOD TO HAVE YOU BACK WITH US AGAIN."
Tom:	*(He seems interested in being there)* "THANKS."
Counselor:	"SO, MARY, HOW DID YOUR WEEK GO?"
Tom:	*(Interrupts before Mary can answer.)* "EXCUSE ME, BUT I WOULD LIKE TO ANSWER THAT QUESTION BEFORE MARY DOES. I THINK HER WEEK HAS BEEN GREAT! I NEVER THOUGHT I WOULD SAY THIS, BUT MARY HAS REALLY CHANGED! SHE DOESN'T NAG ME ANYMORE, THE HOUSE LOOKS GREAT, DINNER IS ON TIME – AND DELICIOUS, I MIGHT ADD – AND THE CHILDREN ARE RESPONDING TO HER INSTEAD OF HIDING IN THEIR ROOMS AT NIGHT."
Counselor:	"THAT'S A WONDERFUL REPORT! HOW DID YOUR WEEK GO, TOM?"
Tom:	"TO TELL YOU THE TRUTH, MY WEEK DIDN'T GO AS WELL AS MARY'S DID. I HAVE A DRINKING PROBLEM. ACTUALLY IT HAS ME. MOST OF OUR MONEY HAS BEEN GOING FOR LIQUOR, AND I CAN'T SEEM TO OVERCOME IT. I MUST HAVE INHERITED IT FROM MY FATHER WHO WAS AN ALCOHOLIC. I CAN SEE MYSELF GOING DOWN THE SAME ROAD. I WANT TO STOP, BUT I JUST DON'T THINK I CAN. I GUESS I NEED TO GET PROFESSIONAL HELP, BUT WE JUST CAN'T AFFORD IT RIGHT NOW."

Since Tom needs biblical hope, how can you help him? (Remember, he is a new believer in Christ). Suggestions:

(1) He needs to be taught how God has broken Satan's power in a life-dominating sin.

Refer to:
YOU CAN CHANGE BIBLICALLY (PART TWO) *(Lesson 2, Pages 3-5) and*
GOD HAS BROKEN SATAN'S POWER *(Lesson 20, Pages 9-11).*

(2) Ask Tom further questions to help him understand how his life-dominating sin has affected every area of his life.

> *Refer to:* **THE EFFECTS OF LIFE-DOMINATING SINS (THE CIRCLE OF LIFE)** *(Lesson 20, Page 8)*.

(3) He needs to make a commitment to please God in all aspects of his life and make immediate plans to change biblically.

> *Refer to:*
> **PRACTICAL STEPS ON ACHIEVING BIBLICAL CHANGE** *(Lesson 8, Pages 8-10)*
>   *and*
> **GUIDELINES: VICTORY OVER FAILURES WORKSHEET** *(Supplement 7)*.

(4) Assign extensive homework, since a total life change is an immediate necessity.

> *Refer to:*
> **PUTTING ON THE FULL ARMOR OF GOD** *(Lesson 21, Pages 4-12) and*
> **OVERCOMING LIFE-DOMINATING SINS** *(Lesson 21, Pages 13-19)*.

Remember that Mary still needs to continue her own growth in Christ no matter what Tom does *(Matthew 7:1-5; I Corinthians 11:31)*. How would you help her from Scripture? Suggestions:

(1) Remind her that her peace and joy comes from being obedient to God's Word out of her love for Jesus Christ.

> *Refer to:* **BIBLICAL BASIS FOR PEACE AND JOY** *(Lesson 6, Pages 8-10)*.

(2) Remind her that she is responsible only for her own growth in Christ.

> *Refer to:*
> **BIBLICAL SELF-CONFRONTATION: AN ESSENTIAL FOR DISCIPLESHIP** *(Lesson 2, Page 6) and*
> **GUIDELINES: VICTORY OVER FAILURES WORKSHEET** *(Supplement 7)*.

(3) She is not to try to change Tom, since Tom's biblical changes are solely between him and the Lord.

> *Refer to:*
> **THE IMPORTANCE OF DOING THE WORD** *(Lesson 5, Pages 6-9) and*
> **BIBLICALLY RESPONDING TO SOMEONE WITH A LIFE-DOMINATING SIN** *(Lesson 21, Pages 20-24)*.

Since Tom and Mary and their children still have biblical changes to make in their home, how could you encourage them to do so?

Suggestion: Remind them that they should continue to have regularly scheduled conference tables.

> *Refer to:* **OVERCOMING PROBLEMS THROUGH BIBLICAL COMMUNICATION** *(Lesson 15, Pages 6-9)*.

LESSON 21: HOMEWORK

This week's **HOMEWORK** gives you biblical steps to overcome any life-dominating sin and to be equipped to help others who may be mastered by a particular sin *(based on Romans 6:1-7; I Corinthians 6:9-12; Galatians 5:16-17, 6:1-2; Ephesians 6:10-18; Hebrews 2:14-15; I John 4:4, 5:4-5).*

✔ *homework completed*

☐ A. * In your own words, write the meaning of *Ephesians 5:18* and *6:12-13.* Memorize *Ephesians 5:18* and *6:12-13* and begin memorizing *Galatians 5:22-25.*

☐ B. * Read **BIBLICAL PRINCIPLES: LIFE-DOMINATING SINS (PART TWO)** (Lesson 21, Pages 2-3). Mark the listed verses in your Bible that you have not marked previously.

☐ C. * Study **PUTTING ON THE FULL ARMOR OF GOD** (Lesson 21, Pages 4-12). You can use this practical guide, not only in your own walk in Christ, but also to help others stand firm against the schemes of Satan.

☐ D. * Study **OVERCOMING LIFE-DOMINATING SINS** (Lesson 21, Pages 13-19). Observe how a biblical plan to overcome life-dominating sins must encompass every area of one's life and must be diligently maintained on a daily basis.

☐ E. * Study **BIBLICALLY RESPONDING TO SOMEONE WITH A LIFE-DOMINATING SIN** (Lesson 21, Pages 20-23). Especially note that you are not responsible to make changes in another's life – that is the work of the Holy Spirit. However, you are to use all resources to help someone understand the damaging effects of his sin and how his present behavior shows a lack of love for God and others.

☐ F. * Read **A CASE STUDY: MARY'S HUSBAND HAS LEFT HER** (Lesson 21, Pages 24-25). Even though Tom has admitted to having a life-dominating sin, note how each member of the family must continue to concentrate on pleasing the Lord in their own lives and not base their peace and joy on Tom's actions.

☐ G. * In conjunction with this lesson, respond to statement 30 under **Open Book Test** (Lesson 23, Page 3).

* *The completion of assignments marked with an asterisk (*) is a prerequisite for further biblical counseling training.*

LESSON 21: STUDY GUIDE FOR DAILY DEVOTIONS
(INCLUDING SCRIPTURE MEMORY AND HOMEWORK)

> This week's **STUDY GUIDE** gives you biblical steps to overcome any life-dominating sin and to be equipped to help others who may be mastered by a particular sin *(based on Romans 6:1-7; I Corinthians 6:9-12; Galatians 5:16-17, 6:1-2; Ephesians 6:10-18; Hebrews 2:14-15; I John 4:4, 5:4-5).*

Scripture Memory

1. * Memorize *Ephesians 5:18* and *6:12-13* and begin memorizing *Galatians 5:22-25.*
2. Carry your memory verse cards from previous weeks along with this week's memory verses. Review your memory verses during spare moments throughout the day.

Daily Devotional Study Guide

FIRST DAY

1. Open with prayer.
2. * Read *Principles 93 and 94* in **BIBLICAL PRINCIPLES: LIFE-DOMINATING SINS (PART TWO)** (Lesson 21, Pages 2-3). Highlight the listed verses in your Bible.
3. * Write the meaning of *Ephesians 5:18* and *6:12-13* in your own words.
4. Close with prayer.

SECOND DAY

1. Open with prayer.
2. * Read *Principle 95* under **BIBLICAL PRINCIPLES: LIFE-DOMINATING SINS (PART TWO)** (Lesson 21, Pages 2-3). Highlight listed verse in your Bible. Also review *Principle 13, from Lesson 5, Page 2,* and *Principles 27-29, from Lesson 7, Page 2.*
3. * Begin to read **PUTTING ON THE FULL ARMOR OF GOD** (Lesson 21, Pages 4-12). The length and detail of this study prohibits in-depth review during this week. However, this reference tool should be closely studied in the future. During the next two days, become aware of the subjects covered in this study. Place a check mark by the parts of the armor of God that you especially need to "put on" in your own life. This is the first day of a two-day study.
4. Close with prayer.

THIRD DAY

1. Open with prayer.
2. * Read *Principles 96 and 97* in **BIBLICAL PRINCIPLES: LIFE-DOMINATING SINS (PART TWO)** (Lesson 21, Pages 2-3). Highlight the listed verses in your Bible.
3. * Complete your overview of **PUTTING ON THE FULL ARMOR OF GOD** (Lesson 21, Pages 4-12). Remember to place a check mark beside the parts of the armor of God that need to be more effectively "put on" in your own life.
4. Close with prayer.

FOURTH DAY

1. Open with prayer.
2. * Study **OVERCOMING LIFE-DOMINATING SINS** (Lesson 21, Pages 13-19). Observe how a biblical plan to overcome life-dominating sins must encompass every area of one's life and must be diligently maintained on a daily basis. This is the first day of a three-day study.
3. Close with prayer.
4. Are you remaining faithful to memorize Scripture? Make adjustments in your schedule as necessary. *Use MY PROPOSED BIBLICAL SCHEDULE (Supplement 15) to help you become more disciplined in this area of spiritual development.*

FIFTH DAY

1. Open with prayer.
2. * Continue your study of **OVERCOMING LIFE-DOMINATING SINS** (Lesson 21, Pages 13-19). If you are mastered by a particular sin, highlight the steps that you are not doing and begin immediately to practice them on a regular basis.
3. Close with prayer.

SIXTH DAY

1. Open with prayer.
2. * Complete your study of **OVERCOMING LIFE-DOMINATING SINS** (Lesson 21, Pages 13-19). Faithfully implement each step of this plan to help you overcome any sin that has mastery over you.
3. * Read **BIBLICALLY RESPONDING TO SOMEONE WITH A LIFE-DOMINATING SIN** (Lesson 21, Pages 20-23). Especially note that you are not responsible to make changes in another's life – that is the work of the Holy Spirit. However, you are to use all resources to help someone understand the damaging effects of his sin and how his present behavior shows a lack of love for God and others. *This plan needs more in-depth study than can be accomplished in a day or two. Mark those parts of this study that you will examine in more detail in the future.* If you know someone who has a life-dominating sin, begin to make plans to confront him biblically in love and in a spirit of gentleness.
4. Close with prayer.

SEVENTH DAY

1. Open with prayer.
2. * Read **A CASE STUDY: MARY'S HUSBAND HAS LEFT HER** (Lesson 21, Pages 24-25). Even though Tom has admitted to a life-dominating sin, note how each member of the family must still concentrate on pleasing the Lord in their own lives and not base their peace and joy on Tom's actions. Learn how to respond scripturally to every area of this family's problems by answering the questions at the conclusion of the case study.
3. * In conjunction with this lesson, respond to statement 30 under **Open Book Test** (Lesson 23, Page 3).
4. Close in prayer.
5. Ask a friend to listen to you recite this week's memory verses. Explain how these verses have application to your life.

*   *The completion of assignments marked with an asterisk (*) is a prerequisite for further biblical counseling training.*

LESSON 22

GOD'S STANDARDS FOR LIFE

"But the fruit of the Spirit is love, joy, peace, patience, kindness, goodness, faithfulness, gentleness, self-control; against such things there is no law. Now those who belong to Christ Jesus have crucified the flesh with its passions and desires. If we live by the Spirit, let us also walk by the Spirit."

Galatians 5:22-25

LESSON 22: GOD'S STANDARDS FOR LIFE

> God has begun His good work in you and purposes to mature (perfect) you throughout your life *(based on Romans 8:28-29; I Corinthians 1:4-9; Philippians 1:6; James 1:2-4)*. You are responsible to walk in God's way and to cooperate with His work in your life *(based on Romans 12:1-2; Ephesians 4:1-3; Philippians 2:12-13; Colossians 1:10, 2:6-7)*.

I. **The purposes of this lesson are:**

   A. To help you gain a godly perspective on every aspect of your life, not just those areas where you are experiencing problems;

   B. To help you establish a set of biblical standards for yourself (and, if applicable, for your children) that will promote maturity in Christ;

   C. To illustrate how a faithful pattern of biblical living is to be established through a continuation of a case study; and

   D. To encourage you to complete the **COURSE EXAM** (Lesson 23) and to be prepared to give your testimony in the next class session.

II. **The outline of this lesson**

   A. Self-confrontation

      1. **BIBLICAL PRINCIPLES: GOD'S STANDARDS FOR LIFE** (Lesson 22, Pages 2-3)

      2. **GOD'S STANDARDS FOR YOU** (Lesson 22, Pages 4-6)

   B. Steps for spiritual growth

      1. **LESSON 22: HOMEWORK** (Lesson 22, Page 9)

      2. **STUDY GUIDE FOR DAILY DEVOTIONS** (Lesson 22, Pages 10-11)

   C. Biblical counseling

      A CASE STUDY: MARY'S HUSBAND HAS LEFT HER (Lesson 22, Pages 7-8)

BIBLICAL PRINCIPLES: GOD'S STANDARDS FOR LIFE

> God, who has begun His good work in you, purposes to mature (complete, perfect) you throughout the rest of your life *(based on Romans 8:28-29; I Corinthians 1:4-9; Philippians 1:6; James 1:2-4)*. You are responsible to fear (reverence) God and keep His commandments in all dimensions of your life (thoughts, words, and actions) *(based on Ecclesiastes 12:13-14)*.

I. God's View

(Principle 98)   God's standards are always consistent and are never subject to the whim of the moment. His commands are changeless *(Isaiah 40:8; I Peter 1:25)*; they do not fluctuate with the age in which you live *(based on Psalm 19:7-11; 119:89, 160; Proverbs 30:5-6)* because God Himself is changeless *(based on Exodus 3:14-15; Malachi 3:6; John 8:57-58; Hebrews 1:10-12, 13:8)*.

(Principle 99)   God's standards are the same for all individuals, in all cultures, and at all age levels, regardless of personality or background *(based on II Chronicles 19:7; Proverbs 20:11; Acts 10:34-35; Romans 1:16, 2:2-11, 3:21-30; Galatians 3:26-29; Ephesians 6:9; Colossians 3:25; II Timothy 3:14-15)*. Therefore, no "double standard" exists for adults, children, the rich, the poor, nationalities, different occupations, either gender, or any other distinction.

(Principle 100)   The key to fruitfulness in your life is to fear (have reverence for) God *(Psalm 111:10, 145:19; Proverbs 1:7, 3:7-8, 9:10, 14:27, 19:23; Ecclesiastes 8:12-13, 12:13-14)* and consistently keep His commandments in every aspect of your life (be a doer of the Word) *(based on Exodus 20:1-17; Deuteronomy 11:26-28; Matthew 7:24-27; John 14:21, 23; 15:10-11; James 1:25; I John 3:22)*.

II. Your Hope

(Principle 101)   God's plans for you are for your benefit *(based on Psalm 145:17; Jeremiah 29:11-13; Romans 8:28)* and have as their goal your maturity in Christ *(based on Romans 8:29; II Corinthians 3:18)*. If you keep God's commandments, He will bless you; if you do not keep them, He will judge you with a view to discipline *(Deuteronomy 11:8-9, 13-17, 26-28; Psalm 32:3-5; I Corinthians 11:31-32; Hebrews 12:5-11; James 1:22-25)*.

(Principle 102)   God's standards are not burdensome *(Matthew 11:28-30)* for He will strengthen, uphold, and keep you from stumbling as you walk in His way, cooperating with the change He is accomplishing in your life *(based on Joshua 1:8-9; Psalm 103:1-5, 121:1-8; Proverbs 3:5-6; Isaiah 40:29-31; Matthew 28:18-20; John 6:37; Ephesians 1:13-14; Philippians 2:12-13; Colossians 2:6-7; II Peter 1:10; Jude 1:24-25)*.

III. Your Change

(Principle 103)   Put off the deeds of darkness; put on the Lord Jesus Christ and make no provision for fleshly lusts *(Romans 13:12-14)*. Put on the full armor of God to withstand the schemes of the devil *(Ephesians 6:10-18)*.

(Principle 104)   Do not be surprised at trials, even if they seem fiery; instead, rejoice in them because God uses them to develop Christlike maturity in your life *(based on Romans 5:3-5; II Corinthians 4:7-18; James 1:2-4; I Peter 4:12-13)*. Be prepared to be reviled and to suffer persecution because of your commitment to Jesus Christ and your faithfulness in being obedient to God's Word *(based on Matthew 5:10-12, 10:16-28; II Timothy 3:12; I Peter 4:12-19)*. If you should endure suffering for the sake of righteousness, you are blessed of the Lord *(based on Matthew 5:10-12; Luke 6:22-23; James 5:10-11; I Peter 3:13-17, esp. verse 14; I Peter 5:6-10)*.

IV. Your Practice

(Principle 105)   Establish and maintain biblical standards that will encourage you and your children (if any) toward godliness. Identify godly traits that need to be developed within you, along with corresponding biblical responsibilities and activities which will demonstrate Christlikeness *(based on Galatians 5:22-23; Ephesians 1:4, 4:1, 4:17 - 6:9; Philippians 2:12-13; Colossians 3:12-24; I Timothy 4:7-8; II Peter 1:2-10)*.

GOD'S STANDARDS FOR YOU

> In every relationship and in every situation, you are to exhibit the character of Jesus Christ through your obedience to God's Word *(based on Matthew 5:13-16; John 15:1-10; II Corinthians 2:14-17; Colossians 2:6-7; Titus 2:11-14; II Peter 1:2-10).*

I. **What you are to do (a sample list)**

A. As a believer in the Lord Jesus Christ, you are to:

1. Love God wholeheartedly by responding in loving obedience to His Word, regardless of how you feel *(based on I Samuel 15:22-23; Matthew 22:37-40; John 14:15, 21; Galatians 5:16-17; I John 5:3);*

2. Worship the Lord *(Deuteronomy 6:13; Psalm 2:11, 29:2; Matthew 4:10),* both individually and with other believers *(Psalm 1; Psalm 47; Acts 2:42-46, 5:42; Colossians 3:16; Hebrews 10:23-25);*

3. Preserve the unity of the body of Christ *(I Corinthians 1:10, 12:22-26; Ephesians 4:1-3; Philippians 2:1-4);*

4. Study and memorize God's Word *(Psalm 1:1-3, 119:11; II Timothy 2:15);*

5. Receive (accept) and heed (take seriously) reproof and instruction *(Proverbs 1:2-5, 3:11-12, 9:7-9; Hebrews 12:5-6);*

6. Be an example to others *(Matthew 5:16; I Corinthians 11:1; I Timothy 4:12);*

7. Be faithful *(I Corinthians 4:2; Galatians 5:22);*

8. Be gentle in correcting others *(Galatians 6:1; II Timothy 2:24-26)* and restore those caught up in sin to the Lord, to others, and to usefulness in the body of Christ *(Matthew 18:15-20; Luke 17:3-4; Romans 15:14; Galatians 6:1-5);*

9. Be honest/truthful *(Ephesians 4:15, 25)* and speak in an edifying manner *(Ephesians 4:29; Colossians 4:6),* which includes returning a blessing when reviled *(Romans 12:14; I Peter 3:8-9);*

10. Be a peacemaker/live at peace with others *(Matthew 5:9; Romans 12:18)* and reconcile with anyone who has something against you *(Matthew 5:23-24);*

11. Deny yourself and consider others as more important than yourself *(Luke 9:23-25; Philippians 2:3-8),* serving them as Jesus did *(Matthew 20:26-28; John 13:12-17; Ephesians 6:7-8);*

12. Do your own work and whatever you do, do it heartily as for the Lord *(Colossians 3:23-24; I Thessalonians 4:11-12; II Thessalonians 3:10-12);*

13. Exercise self-control/discipline *(II Corinthians 5:14-15; Galatians 5:23; I Timothy 4:7-8);*

14. Forgive from the heart (before the Lord) anyone who has sinned against you and be ready to grant forgiveness to anyone who asks you *(Matthew 18:21-22, 35; Mark 11:25-26; Luke 17:3-4);*

15. Practice biblical love in all your relationships *(Matthew 5:44; John 13:34-35; Romans 13:8, 10; I Corinthians 13:4-8a; Ephesians 5:25; Titus 2:3-4);*

16.   Practice good stewardship of:

   a.   Your body *(I Corinthians 6:19-20)*;

   b.   Your time *(Ephesians 5:15-17)*;

   c.   Material goods *(II Corinthians 9:6-12; Ephesians 4:28; I Timothy 6:17-19; James 2:15-16)*;

   d.   Your abilities, talents, and spiritual gifts *(based on Matthew 25:14-30; Romans 12:3-8; I Corinthians 12:7; Ephesians 4:11-12, 15-16; I Peter 4:10-11)*; and

17.   Rejoice always, even in the midst of trials *(Philippians 4:4; I Thessalonians 5:16; James 1:2-4)*.

B.   As a believing husband, you are to:

   1.   Love your wife as Christ loved the church *(Ephesians 5:25-33)*,

   2.   Live with your wife in an understanding way *(I Peter 3:7)*, and

   3.   Provide for your household *(I Timothy 5:8)*.

C.   As a believing wife, you are to:

   1.   Be a helper fit (suitable) for your husband *(Genesis 2:18)*;

   2.   Respect, love, and be submissive to your husband *(Ephesians 5:22-24, 31, 33; Titus 2:4-5; I Peter 3:1-6)*; and

   3.   Take care of needs in your household *(Proverbs 31:10-27; I Timothy 5:14; Titus 2:5)*.

D.   As a believing husband/wife team, you are to:

   1.   Submit to one another *(Ephesians 5:21)* and

   2.   Maintain unity in your relationship with one another; that is, act as one flesh *(Genesis 2:22-24; Matthew 19:4-6; Ephesians 5:31)*.

E.   As a believing parent, you are to:

   1.   Lovingly train your children through instruction, discipline, and example *(Deuteronomy 6:6-9; Ephesians 6:4; Titus 2:4)* and

   2.   Avoid exasperating (provoking) your children *(Ephesians 6:4)*.

F.   As a believing child, you are to:

   1.   Obey your parents while under their authority and training *(Ephesians 6:1)*;

   2.   Honor your parents *(Exodus 20:12; Deuteronomy 5:16; Ephesians 6:2)*; and

   3.   Heed and remember (listen to and take seriously) the teachings of your parents *(Proverbs 1:8-9)*.

G.   As a believing employee, you are to:

   1.   Be obedient and submissive to your employer *(based on Ephesians 6:5-8; Colossians 3:22; I Timothy 6:1-2; Titus 2:9; I Peter 2:18)*;

   2.   Honor your employer *(I Timothy 6:1-2)*; and

   3.   Be honorable in all your dealings with your employer *(I Timothy 6:2; Titus 2:10)*.

H.   As a believing employer, you are to:

   1.   Act in fairness and with justice toward your employees *(Colossians 4:1)* and

   2.   Give up threatening your employees *(Ephesians 6:9)*.

I.   As a scripturally qualified church leader, you are to:

    1.   Be worthy of the trust placed in you *(based on I Timothy 3:1-15; Titus 1:6-9, 2:7-8; I Peter 5:1-3)*, discipling others so that they will be able to teach others also *(II Timothy 2:2)* and

    2.   Correct (admonish, instruct) others in gentleness, always seeking to restore them to the Lord *(based on Matthew 18:15-20; Galatians 6:1-2; II Timothy 2:24-26)*.

II.   How you are to obey God's standards

A.   Do all things heartily as for the Lord *(Colossians 3:23-24)*, with good will *(Ephesians 6:7-8)* and zeal *(Titus 2:14; I Peter 3:13)*.

B.   Be unselfish *(Philippians 2:3)* and do not grumble, dispute, or argue *(Philippians 2:14-16; II Timothy 2:24; Titus 2:9, 3:9)*.

C.   Respond with tenderness *(based on Ephesians 4:32; I Thessalonians 2:7-8)* and wisdom *(Ephesians 5:15; Colossians 4:5; James 3:15-18)*.

D.   Reverence the Lord with fear (awe) and trembling *(based on II Corinthians 5:10-11; Philippians 2:12-13)*.

E.   Respond with joy *(based on Philippians 2:17-18)*, giving glory to God and not offending anyone *(based on I Corinthians 10:31-33)*.

III. Incorporating God's standards into your life

A.   Record all your typical weekly activities by using **MY PRESENT SCHEDULE** (Supplement 14).

B.   Place a line through every activity that should not be continued. Use the following questions to determine what activities need to be eliminated *(reviewed from Lesson 8, Page 9)*:

    1.   Is this profitable *(I Corinthians 6:12, 10:23a)*?

    2.   Am I controlled by this in any way *(I Corinthians 6:12)*?

    3.   Is this a stumbling block in my life *(Matthew 5:29-30, 18:8-9)*?

    4.   Could this lead another believer to stumble *(Romans 14:13; I Corinthians 8:9-13)*?

    5.   Does this edify (build up) others *(Romans 14:19; I Corinthians 10:23-24)*?

    6.   Does this glorify God *(Matthew 5:16; I Corinthians 10:31)*?

C.   List on a separate sheet all activities and responsibilities that should be started. *Refer back to* **I. What you are to do (a sample list)**.

D.   Develop a plan to live in a manner that pleases the Lord and record your new schedule on **MY PROPOSED SCHEDULE** (Supplement 15).

A CASE STUDY: MARY'S HUSBAND HAS LEFT HER

> *"The conclusion, when all has been heard, is: fear God and keep*
> *His commandments, because this applies to every person.*
> *Because God will bring every act to judgment, everything which*
> *is hidden, whether it is good or evil." (Ecclesiastes 12:13-14)*

Tom and Mary have been faithful doers of the Word for many weeks. Tom has taken biblical steps to overcome his addiction to alcohol. Mary has continued her own growth in Christ by concentrating on her responsibilities before the Lord instead of looking to Tom for her peace and joy. They have had "family conference tables" regularly and have included their children in this pattern of biblical communication. As a result, their children have begun to be doers of the Word themselves. For a number of weeks, the entire family has participated in family devotions, and each member has become involved in their church. While most of these godly practices were originally homework assignments from their counseling sessions, Tom and Mary now have incorporated them as a normal part of their life in Christ. Whenever a new challenge occurs in their home or in their personal lives, they have begun to help one another discover how God's Word applies to the situation.

With these biblical practices established, they come to their final counseling session to present their biblical plan for continuing growth in Christ. After greetings are exchanged, the lead counselor speaks.

Counselor: "WE HAVE BEEN LOOKING FORWARD TO THIS SESSION FOR A NUMBER OF WEEKS. AS YOUR HOMEWORK ASSIGNMENT INDICATED, THE PURPOSE OF THIS SESSION IS TO GIVE YOU BOTH AN OPPORTUNITY TO PRESENT BIBLICAL PLANS FOR CONTINUED GROWTH IN CHRIST. LET'S TAKE TIME TO THANK GOD FOR HIS WORD AND HIS FAITHFULNESS IN ALL OF OUR LIVES."

During prayer, each person thankfully speaks of God's faithfulness and the total sufficiency of His Word. After the lead counselor concludes in prayer, he addresses Tom and Mary.

Counselor: "WE KNOW YOU HAVE BEEN FAITHFUL IN COMPLETING PAST HOMEWORK ASSIGNMENTS. NOW, WHAT HAVE YOU DECIDED UPON AS YOUR FUTURE PLAN FOR GROWTH?"

Tom: "IT HAS BEEN BEYOND OUR EXPECTATIONS TO FIND THE GREATEST REASON FOR LIVING, WHICH IS TO LIVE FOR JESUS CHRIST."

Mary: "I AGREE WITH THAT! IT SEEMS SO LONG AGO THAT I WAS WITHOUT HOPE AND UNABLE TO REALIZE THAT GOD HAD A PLAN FOR MY LIFE."

Both Tom and Mary then present their biblical plans for continued growth in Christ. They make commitments to continue their present patterns of personal and family devotions, Scripture memory, worship service and Bible study attendance, fellowship with other believers, family conference tables, scheduling of responsibilities (highlighting specific ways to serve one another), and continual self-confrontation in a biblical manner. In addition to continuing their present godly behavior, they present plans to become personally involved in their church's ministry and to have family projects designed to help others. They express a desire to be trained in biblical counseling and make commitments to enroll in the next Self-Confrontation course.

After explaining their future plans for continuing faithfulness in their biblical walk, Tom and Mary review the homework assignments that were especially beneficial in helping them put off their self-focus in order to live for the Lord. Both mentioned the encouragement found in Romans 8:28-29 and I Corinthians 10:13 in the early stages of their counseling. They also tell of their initial surprise at learning how unloving they were, which became evident to them through their study of I Corinthians 13:4-8a. When they conclude, the lead counselor speaks.

Counselor: "TO HEAR YOU SPEAK OF THE DIFFERENCE THAT JESUS CHRIST HAS MADE IN YOUR LIVES THROUGH YOUR OBEDIENCE TO SCRIPTURE HAS ENCOURAGED ALL OF US. NOT ONLY HAVE WE BEEN PRIVILEGED TO SEE GOD WORK IN ALL OF OUR LIVES, BUT WE HAVE GAINED YOU AS FRIENDS IN CHRIST FOR YEARS TO COME. EVEN THOUGH OUR COUNSELING SESSIONS CONCLUDE, WE WANT TO BE AVAILABLE TO YOU IN THE COMING MONTHS AND DESIRE TO HEAR MORE ABOUT GOD'S DEALINGS IN YOUR LIFE."

The counselor then explains that he and the other counselors would welcome regular contact with them in the coming months. It is explained that one of the counselors will contact Tom and Mary at least once a month in the coming year to encourage them in their growth in Christ. After this explanation of follow-up and accountability is given, the session is closed in prayer.

LESSON 22: HOMEWORK

This week's **HOMEWORK** reviews the foundational
guidelines in God's Word that are your standards for life.
As you faithfully and wholeheartedly put these standards
into practice, you will experience the blessings of the Lord,
and the characteristics of Jesus Christ will be developed
within you *(based on Romans 8:28-29, 12:1-2;*
II Corinthians 3:18; Philippians 2:12-16; James 1:25;
II Peter 1:2-11).

✔ *homework completed*

☐ A. * In your own words, write the meaning of *Galatians 5:22-25*. Memorize *Galatians 5:22-25* and begin memorizing *I John 5:3-5.*

☐ B. * Read **BIBLICAL PRINCIPLES: GOD'S STANDARDS FOR LIFE** (Lesson 22, Pages 2-3). Mark the listed verses in your Bible that you have not marked previously.

☐ C. * Study **GOD'S STANDARDS FOR YOU** (Lesson 22, Pages 4-6). Mark any statements that point out areas of needed spiritual growth in your life. Include these as part of your **VICTORY OVER FAILURES WORKSHEET** (Supplement 8) or **MY PROPOSED BIBLICAL SCHEDULE** (Supplement 15).

☐ D. Develop a plan to complete all biblical activities and responsibilities by following the instructions given in **GOD'S STANDARDS FOR YOU** (Lesson 22, Page 6) under **III. Incorporating God's standards into your life.**

☐ E. * Read **A CASE STUDY: MARY'S HUSBAND HAS LEFT HER** (Lesson 22, Pages 7-8). Observe how establishing God's standards in your life not only solves any problems you might have, but it provides a foundation for all of life.

☐ F. * Complete your **COURSE EXAM** (Lesson 23). If applicable, turn it in to your instructor at the next class session.

☐ G. Complete your personal testimony about the biblical changes that have occurred in your life during this course. *Refer to **COURSE EXAM** (Lesson 23, Page 3) under **Your Testimony of Self-Confrontation Results** for guidance in preparing your testimony.* Also, be prepared to give your testimony verbally in class.

* *The completion of assignments marked with an asterisk (*) is a prerequisite for further biblical counseling training.*

Lesson 22, Page 9   © Biblical Counseling Foundation

LESSON 22: STUDY GUIDE FOR DAILY DEVOTIONS
(INCLUDING SCRIPTURE MEMORY AND HOMEWORK)

> This week's **STUDY GUIDE** reviews the foundational
> guidelines in God's Word that are your standards for life.
> As you faithfully and wholeheartedly put these standards
> into practice, you will experience the blessings of the Lord,
> and the characteristics of Jesus Christ will be developed
> within you *(based on Romans 8:28-29, 12:1-2;*
> *II Corinthians 3:18; Philippians 2:12-16; James 1:25;*
> *II Peter 1:2-11).*

Scripture Memory

1.   * Memorize *Galatians 5:22-25* and begin memorizing *I John 5:3-5.*
2.   Carry your memory verse cards from previous weeks along with this week's memory verses. Review your memory verses during your spare moments throughout the day.

Daily Devotional Study Guide

FIRST DAY

1. Open with prayer.
2. * Read *Principle 98* under **BIBLICAL PRINCIPLES: GOD'S STANDARDS FOR LIFE** (Lesson 22, Pages 2-3). Highlight the listed verses in your Bible.
3. * Write the meaning of *Galatians 5:22-25* in your own words.
4. Close with prayer.

SECOND DAY

1. Open with prayer.
2. * Read *Principle 99* under **BIBLICAL PRINCIPLES: GOD'S STANDARDS FOR LIFE** (Lesson 22, Pages 2-3). Highlight the listed verses in your Bible.
3. * Study **GOD'S STANDARDS FOR YOU** (Lesson 22, Pages 4-6). Mark any statements that point out areas of needed spiritual growth in your life. Include these as part of your **VICTORY OVER FAILURES WORKSHEET** (Supplement 8) or **MY PROPOSED BIBLICAL SCHEDULE** (Supplement 15). This is the first day of a two-day study.
4. Work on the **COURSE EXAM** in Lesson 23. Take special note of the last portion entitled **Your testimony of Self-Confrontation results.**
5. Close with prayer.

THIRD DAY

1. Open with prayer.
2. * Read *Principle 100* under **BIBLICAL PRINCIPLES: GOD'S STANDARDS FOR LIFE** (Lesson 22, Pages 2-3). Highlight the listed verses in your Bible.
3. * Complete your study of **GOD'S STANDARDS FOR YOU** (Lesson 22, Pages 4-6). As you note those areas of your life in which you are being obedient to God's standards, take time today to give Him praise for the work He is accomplishing in your life *(Romans 8:29; II Corinthians 3:18; Philippians 1:6, 2:12-13; I Thessalonians 5:18).* In areas where you need to incorporate biblical standards into your life,

---

make plans for specific change and faithfully carry out those plans (as outlined in Lesson 22, Page 6, under **III. Incorporating God's standards into your life**).

4. Work on the **COURSE EXAM** (Lesson 23). Prepare your testimony following the guidelines under **Your testimony of Self-Confrontation results** (Lesson 23, Page 3).

5. Close with prayer.

FOURTH DAY

1. Open with prayer.
2. * Read *Principle 101* under **BIBLICAL PRINCIPLES: GOD'S STANDARDS FOR LIFE** (Lesson 22, Pages 2-3). Highlight the listed verses in your Bible.
3. Continue work on the **COURSE EXAM** (Lesson 23) and your testimony for the next class session.
4. Close with prayer.

FIFTH DAY

1. Open with prayer.
2. * Read *Principle 102* under **BIBLICAL PRINCIPLES: GOD'S STANDARDS FOR LIFE** (Lesson 22, Pages 2-3). Highlight the listed verses in your Bible.
3. Continue work on the **COURSE EXAM** (Lesson 23) and your testimony.
4. Close with prayer.

SIXTH DAY

1. Open with prayer.
2. * Read *Principles 103 and 104* under **BIBLICAL PRINCIPLES: GOD'S STANDARDS FOR LIFE** (Lesson 22, Pages 2-3). Highlight the listed verses in your Bible.
3. * Read **A CASE STUDY: MARY'S HUSBAND HAS LEFT HER** (Lesson 22, Pages 7-8). Note how biblical standards are to be applied to every area of life.
4. Continue work on the **COURSE EXAM** (Lesson 23) and your testimony.
5. Close with prayer.

SEVENTH DAY

1. Open with prayer.
2. * Read *Principle 105* under **BIBLICAL PRINCIPLES: GOD'S STANDARDS FOR LIFE** (Lesson 22, Pages 2-3). Highlight the listed verses in your Bible.
3. Complete work on the **COURSE EXAM** that is presented in Lesson 23.
4. Ask a friend to hear you recite this week's memory verses. Explain how these verses apply to your life.
5. Complete your personal testimony about the biblical changes that have occurred in your life during this course. *Refer to* **COURSE EXAM** *(Lesson 23, Page 3) under* **Your Testimony of Self-Confrontation Results** *for further guidance in preparing your testimony.* Also, be prepared to give your testimony verbally in class.
6. Close in prayer.

*   *The completion of assignments marked with an asterisk (*) is a prerequisite for further biblical counseling training.*

LESSON 23

COURSE EXAM

LESSON 23: COURSE EXAM

> This exam will help you determine the extent to which you
> have learned the biblical principles and corresponding
> solutions to problems that are presented in this course.
> May you further realize God's sufficiency to face and deal
> with all of life's challenges through His Son, His Word, and
> His Spirit as you complete this examination.

General Directions

This exam consists of three sections: **Memory Verse Evaluation, Open Book Test,** *and* **Your Testimony of Self-Confrontation Results.** *When completing this exam, do not write on these pages. Instead, record your answers as completely as possible on your own paper, keeping your answers directly applicable to the questions asked. Whenever a Scripture reference is called for, list the* **book, chapter,** *and* **verse(s).** *If a verse needs to be written in its entirety, you will be asked specifically to do so.*

Memory Verse Evaluation

1. Grade yourself on the memory verses assigned in this course by writing the appropriate response, according to the categories listed below:

   a. **Excellent**: I memorized the verses and can recite them with very few errors.

   b. **Very Good**: I memorized all but four or five of the verses.

   c. **Good**: I memorized all but six or seven of the verses.

   d. **Fair**: I memorized half of the verses.

   e. **Not very well**: I need more study to memorize the verses.

   f. I plan to continue memorizing/reviewing these and other verses. *(This category may apply to all the above.)*

2. List the references for at least three verses or passages that were the most meaningful to you as you progressed through this course. Beside each reference, tell how the Lord used this verse or passage in your life.

Open Book Test

This "Open Book" test, in which you may use your Bible and this manual, is designed to be a time of spiritual refreshment for you. It will give you an opportunity to review and put in your own words what you have learned.

1. Write one verse in its entirety (and reference) that shows a person's hopelessness apart from salvation provided through Jesus Christ. (Lesson 1, Pages 2-4)

2. Explain how a person can receive the gift of eternal life, citing at least three Scripture references to support your explanation. (Lesson 1, Page 4)

3. List one Scripture reference that specifically states you should judge yourself first before dealing with the problems of someone else. (Lesson 2, Pages 2, 7-8)

4. List three Scripture references that tell of the total sufficiency of Scripture. (Lesson 3, Pages 2-5)

5. In your own words, explain how you would tell a fellow-believer that God's Word is all that is necessary to solve any problem. (Lesson 3, Pages 3-5)

6. How does the Holy Spirit help you face and deal with your problems? List at least three Scripture references to support your explanation. (Lesson 3, Pages 2, 6-8)

7. List five reasons (with Scripture references) for the importance of prayer. (Lesson 3, Pages 2, 9-12)

8. List three reasons (with Scripture references) why, under certain circumstances, you may not receive what you ask for in prayer. (Lesson 3, Pages 9-12)

9. List three reasons (with Scripture references) why the natural man cannot please God. (Lesson 4, Pages 2, 6, 11)

10. List five Scripture references that emphasize the importance of being a "doer of the Word." (Lesson 5, Pages 6-9)

11. What are the three levels in which problems are revealed? (Lesson 6, Pages 2, 4-5)

12. List at least three "statements of hope" in *I Corinthians 10:13*. Then explain each of these statements as though you were telling someone how to have hope in any situation. Also explain how you would use this verse with an unbeliever.

13. *Romans 5:3-5* and *James 1:2-4* state that trials are for a believer's good. In a brief paragraph, describe how you would explain this spiritual truth to someone who has lost hope in an extremely difficult trial. (Lesson 6, Page 3)

14. What does it mean to "put off the old" and "put on the new?" *(Refer to Romans Chapter 6; Ephesians 4:22-24; Colossians 3:5-15.)* (Lesson 1, Page 6; Lesson 4, Page 7; Lesson 7, Pages 2-3)

15. List at least five biblical steps that must be taken in order to walk again in a manner worthy of the Lord after a person has sinned and has recognized it. (Give the supporting Scripture verses). (Lesson 8, Pages 8-10)

16. What is the primary problem with a believer emphasizing the "need" to have a "good self-esteem" or "positive self-image?" List at least five reasons (with supporting Scriptures) why a focus on self in any dimension is contrary to God's Word. (Lesson 4, Pages 5-11; Lesson 9, Pages 4-5)

17. List five statements (along with supporting verse references) that emphasize the need for a believer to be a faithful steward of the Lord. (Lesson 10, Pages 4-8)

18. List five ways in which you can know if your anger is a violation of Scripture. List verse references. (Lesson 11, Pages 6-11)

19. Name at least five biblical truths you could tell a fellow believer who said that he "couldn't forgive another." List Scripture references. (Lesson 12, Pages 3-5, 10-13)

20. What steps must be taken to be completely reconciled with another? List Scripture references. (Lesson 12, Pages 6-8)

21. Name at least ten characteristics of biblical love. Cite Scripture references. (Lesson 13, Pages 4-6)

22. Name at least five characteristics of biblical communication. Cite Scripture references. (Lesson 13, Pages 12-14)

23. What are at least five major elements in a biblical marriage? Cite Scripture references. (Lesson 14, Pages 3-4)

24. Write a short outline, with Scripture references, of biblical truths to guide your discussion with someone who tells you that love is dead in his marriage. (Lessons 14 - 15)

25. What are important biblical guidelines for Christian parents to follow in training up their children? Cite supporting Scripture. (Lessons 16 and 17)

26. What is the purpose of discipline? When is it necessary to discipline a child? Cite Scripture references for your answers. (Lesson 17, Pages 8-10)

27. What are five key areas for discussion with someone suffering from depression? Cite Scripture references. (Lesson 18, Pages 2-3)

28. List five specific steps of biblical action a person suffering from fear and worry should take. Cite Scripture references. (Lesson 19, Pages 10-12)

29. Write a brief paragraph (with Scripture references) describing how God has broken Satan's power. (Lesson 20, Pages 9-11)

30. List a least twenty specific biblical steps a person should take to overcome a life-dominating sin. (Lessons 21, Pages 13-19)

Your Testimony of Self-Confrontation Results

This section will help you prepare your testimony which is to be given either in this or the next class session. Use the following questions as a guide:

1. Describe what you have learned about the problem you chose to work on during this course by answering the following:

    a. What biblical habits have been established in your life?

    b. What biblical habits do you still need to develop?

    c. What problems did you discover of which you were not previously aware?

    d. Was the problem on which you chose to work the actual source of your difficulty or did a more important problem surface? Describe.

    e. What did you learn about yourself and your responses within the problem?

2. How have biblical principles, topical studies, and homework in this course helped you in your personal walk with the Lord Jesus Christ?

3. How has this training helped you minister to others?

415

LESSON 24

INTRODUCTION TO COURSE II:
BIBLICAL COUNSELING TRAINING

"For this is the love of God, that we keep His commandments; and His commandments are not burdensome. For whatever is born of God overcomes the world; and this is the victory that has overcome the world – our faith. And who is the one who overcomes the world, but he who believes that Jesus is the Son of God?"

I John 5:3-5

LESSON 24: INTRODUCTION TO COURSE II: BIBLICAL COUNSELING TRAINING

> This course has endeavored to teach you how to confront yourself in a biblical manner. As you obey the Lord in your own spiritual growth, you become better equipped to help others in a manner that brings glory to God *(based on Matthew 5:16, 7:1-5; I Corinthians 10:31; II Corinthians 1:3-5; Galatians 6:1-2; II Timothy 3:16-17; Hebrews 5:14; James 1:22-25).*

I. **The purposes of this lesson are:**

   A. To review the purposes of biblical counseling and the need for believers to counsel biblically;

   B. To present basic biblical counseling procedures that you can use to help others to solve their problems in a biblical manner;

   C. To encourage you to continue the biblical habits that you have developed during this course; and

   D. To provide an opportunity for you to give your testimony of the changes the Lord has made in your life during this course.

II. **The outline of this lesson**

   A. Biblical counseling

   1. **INTRODUCTION TO COURSE II: BIBLICAL COUNSELING TRAINING** (Lesson 24, Pages 2-3)

   2. **BASIC BIBLICAL COUNSELING PROCEDURES** (Lesson 24, Pages 4-6)

   B. Steps for spiritual growth

   LESSON 24: HOMEWORK (Lesson 24, Page 7)

INTRODUCTION TO COURSE II:
BIBLICAL COUNSELING TRAINING

> The responsibility and privilege of offering solutions to overcome problems of life belong to the Body of Christ *(based on Matthew 7:1-5, 18:15-20; Romans 15:14; II Corinthians 5:14-20; Galatians 6:1-2; II Timothy 3:16-17).*

I. **What is biblical counseling?**

Refer also to:
WHAT MAKES COUNSELING BIBLICAL? (Supplement 1) and
FACTS ABOUT BIBLICAL COUNSELING (Supplement 11).

A. Biblical counseling is the restoration of those who have fallen and is done with concern, in gentle confrontation, and with the goal of change *(based on Matthew 18:15; Romans 15:14; Galatians 6:1-2)* using the Bible as the only authoritative guide *(Psalm 19:7-14; II Timothy 3:16-17; Hebrews 4:12; II Peter 1:3-4).*

B. Biblical counseling involves training in righteousness ("in-depth discipleship") so that the counselee will not stumble *(II Peter 1:2-11, esp. verse 10)*, will bear his own load *(Galatians 6:5)*, will be adequate to handle all of life's problems *(II Timothy 3:16-17)*, and will be able to help others biblically *(II Corinthians 1:3-5).*

II. **Why train believers to counsel biblically?**

A. God's Word is the only authority for faith and conduct and is the sole, legitimate standard by which all aspects of living are evaluated. It is totally sufficient to provide guidance for every problem of life *(Psalm 19:7-11; Proverbs 30:5-6; Colossians 2:8; II Timothy 3:16-17; Hebrews 4:12; II Peter 1:2-4).*

B. Problems occur within the Body of Christ that must be dealt with in a biblical manner *(e.g., I Corinthians 6:1-8, 11:17-22; Galatians 1:6, 3:1; II Thessalonians 3:10-15; I Timothy 5:19-20; Titus 3:10-11).*

C. Unbelievers have great needs that can only be met through Jesus Christ and living by the Word of God *(e.g., Romans 8:6-8; I Corinthians 2:14; II Corinthians 4:3-4; Galatians 5:19-21; Ephesians 2:1-3; II Timothy 3:13).*

D. Biblical counseling helps remove obstacles to a counselee's growth (sanctification). Every believer needs to be made aware of:

1. God's plan for him to become more Christlike *(Romans 8:29);*

2. Spiritual battles *(Galatians 5:17; Ephesians 6:10-18)* and God's method of using trials to make biblical changes in his life *(James 1:2-4);* and

3. The danger of false teachers in the church, especially those who deny Jesus Christ or present unbiblical ways to solve problems *(based on II Corinthians 11:12-15; Colossians 2:4, 7-8; II Timothy 2:15-16; I John 4:1-3).*

E. All spiritual believers (those who walk by the Spirit and are faithful in confronting themselves) are adequate to admonish (counsel) one another and are commanded by God to restore (mend) others *(based on Matthew 7:1-5, 18:15; Romans 15:14; Galatians 5:25 - 6:1).*

F.   Training in biblical counseling significantly improves a person's ability to evangelize *(based on Proverbs 18:13, 20:5; John 4:7-26)* and to make disciples *(based on Matthew 28:19-20)*. Like a physician diagnosing an illness, you will be able to show the relevance of the Good News of Jesus Christ and the application of Scripture as you take time to understand the problem and analyze the situation.

G.   The pastor's primary function is to equip believers to do the work of ministry *(Ephesians 4:11-12)*. When a pastor trains his flock (believers) to counsel biblically, the believers:

     1.   Relieve the pastor from shouldering counseling responsibilities alone *(based on Exodus 18:13-26; Matthew 18:15-16; Romans 15:14; Galatians 6:1-2)*;

     2.   Become mature by learning to confront themselves in a biblical manner *(Matthew 7:5)* as they discover the total sufficiency of God's Word to deal with any problem of life *(II Timothy 3:14-17; Hebrews 4:12; II Peter 1:2-11)*;

     3.   Are given opportunities to comfort others *(II Corinthians 1:3-5)* and be blessed through giving *(based on Acts 20:35)*; and

     4.   Will be able to teach (train) others also *(based on Matthew 28:19-20; John 20:21; II Timothy 2:2)*.

III. What can you do to prepare yourself for further training in biblical counseling?

A.   Complete a training course in personal evangelism and, if possible, attend BCT II: Biblical Counseling Basic Course in your local area or at a Concentrated Course in Biblical Counseling. *Review:* **BIBLICAL COUNSELING TRAINING OVERVIEW** *(Supplement 2, Page 6)*.

B.   What you have learned in this course can be applied in step-by-step biblical counseling procedures to help others deal with their problems in a biblical manner. Your counseling procedures must be based on Scripture, since in the words of Jesus, *"That which is born of the flesh is flesh; and that which is born of the Spirit is spirit"* *(John 3:6)*.

     1.   "That which is born of the flesh" pertains to the natural man. "That which is born of the Spirit" pertains to your spiritual new birth and the spiritual dimension of your life. Your new birth, provided by the Holy Spirit of God, allows you to grow for the purpose, not of death, but of life eternal.

     2.   The things of the Spirit of God cannot be understood by the natural man because they are spiritually discerned *(I Corinthians 2:14)*. Therefore, instead of procedures established by the wisdom of man, spiritual procedures must be established that are based on the truths of Scripture.

C.   Those who counsel others in a biblical manner must have specific steps to follow just as a medical doctor must follow basic steps to accomplish his purposes.

     1.   Note **BASIC BIBLICAL COUNSELING PROCEDURES** (Lesson 24, Pages 4-6). Elements listed are referenced to lessons and supplements.

     2.   A more detailed Diagnostics Chart for Biblical Counseling (In-Depth Discipleship) is introduced in BCT II: The Biblical Counseling Basic Course.

D.   As you review **BASIC BIBLICAL COUNSELING PROCEDURES** (Lesson 24, Pages 4-6), compare these steps with the counseling procedures that were followed throughout this course with Tom and Mary in **A CASE STUDY: MARY'S HUSBAND HAS LEFT HER.**

BASIC BIBLICAL COUNSELING PROCEDURES

"That which is born of the flesh is flesh; and
that which is born of the spirit is spirit." (John 3:6)

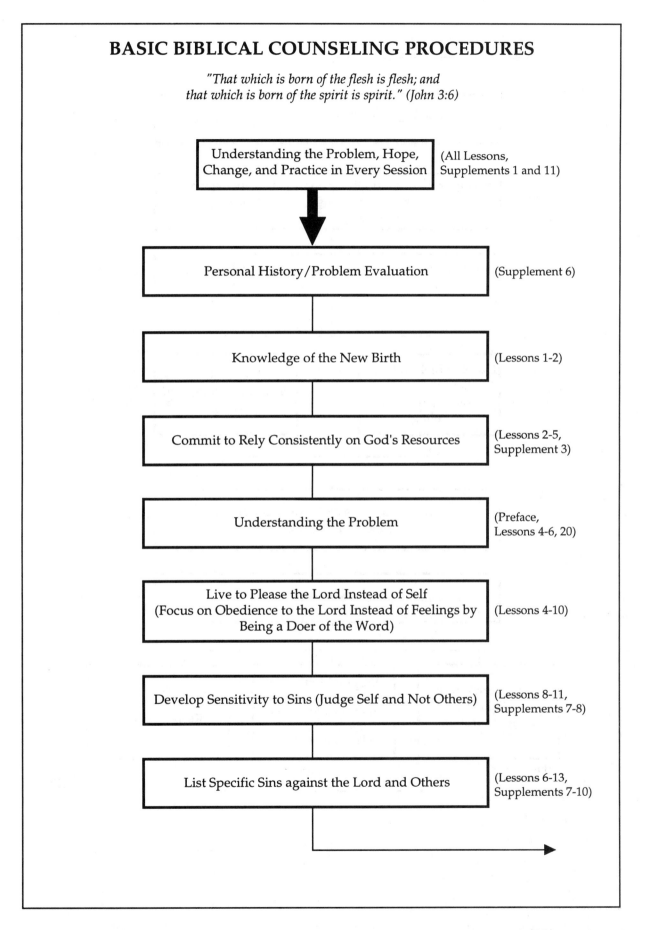

Understanding the Problem, Hope, Change, and Practice in Every Session	(All Lessons, Supplements 1 and 11)
Personal History/Problem Evaluation	(Supplement 6)
Knowledge of the New Birth	(Lessons 1-2)
Commit to Rely Consistently on God's Resources	(Lessons 2-5, Supplement 3)
Understanding the Problem	(Preface, Lessons 4-6, 20)
Live to Please the Lord Instead of Self (Focus on Obedience to the Lord Instead of Feelings by Being a Doer of the Word)	(Lessons 4-10)
Develop Sensitivity to Sins (Judge Self and Not Others)	(Lessons 8-11, Supplements 7-8)
List Specific Sins against the Lord and Others	(Lessons 6-13, Supplements 7-10)

420

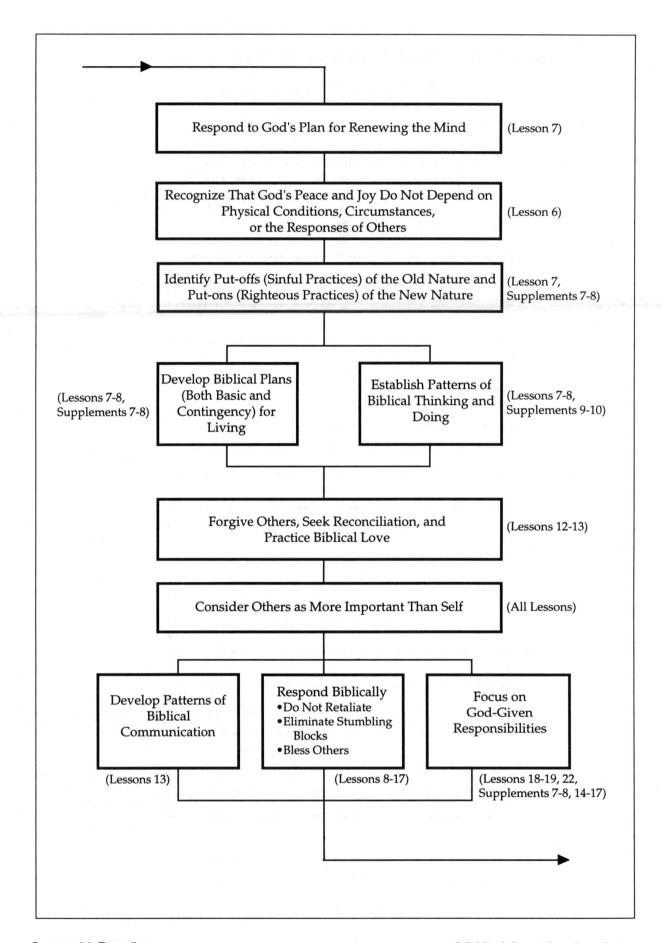

Respond to God's Plan for Renewing the Mind (Lesson 7)

Recognize That God's Peace and Joy Do Not Depend on Physical Conditions, Circumstances, or the Responses of Others (Lesson 6)

Identify Put-offs (Sinful Practices) of the Old Nature and Put-ons (Righteous Practices) of the New Nature (Lesson 7, Supplements 7-8)

(Lessons 7-8, Supplements 7-8)

Develop Biblical Plans (Both Basic and Contingency) for Living

Establish Patterns of Biblical Thinking and Doing (Lessons 7-8, Supplements 9-10)

Forgive Others, Seek Reconciliation, and Practice Biblical Love (Lessons 12-13)

Consider Others as More Important Than Self (All Lessons)

Develop Patterns of Biblical Communication

Respond Biblically
• Do Not Retaliate
• Eliminate Stumbling Blocks
• Bless Others

Focus on God-Given Responsibilities

(Lessons 13)

(Lessons 8-17)

(Lessons 18-19, 22, Supplements 7-8, 14-17)

Lesson 24, Page 5

© Biblical Counseling Foundation

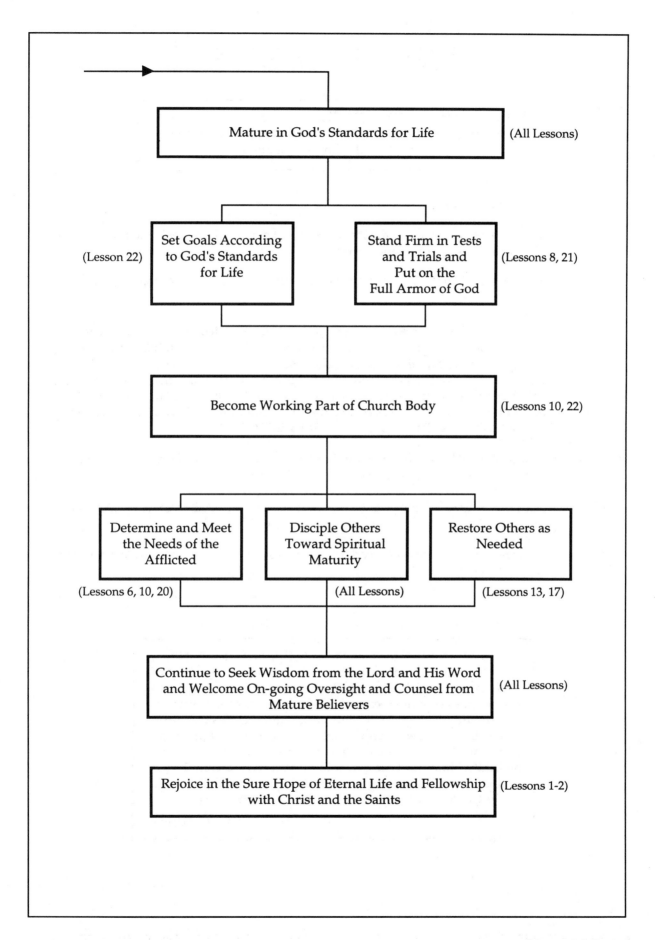

Mature in God's Standards for Life — (All Lessons)

(Lesson 22) — Set Goals According to God's Standards for Life

Stand Firm in Tests and Trials and Put on the Full Armor of God — (Lessons 8, 21)

Become Working Part of Church Body — (Lessons 10, 22)

Determine and Meet the Needs of the Afflicted
(Lessons 6, 10, 20)

Disciple Others Toward Spiritual Maturity
(All Lessons)

Restore Others as Needed
(Lessons 13, 17)

Continue to Seek Wisdom from the Lord and His Word and Welcome On-going Oversight and Counsel from Mature Believers — (All Lessons)

Rejoice in the Sure Hope of Eternal Life and Fellowship with Christ and the Saints — (Lessons 1-2)

LESSON 24: HOMEWORK

> This week's **HOMEWORK** allows you to preview further
> training in biblical counseling that is provided by the
> Biblical Counseling Foundation.

✔ *homework completed*

☐ A.   * In your own words, write the meaning of *I John 5:3-5.* This week, memorize *I John 5:3-5* and review past memory verses.

☐ B.   * Read **INTRODUCTION TO COURSE II: BIBLICAL COUNSELING TRAINING** (Lesson 24, Pages 2-3).

☐ C.   * Review **BASIC BIBLICAL COUNSELING PROCEDURES** (Lesson 24, Pages 4-6). This is an abbreviated version of the Diagnostics Chart for Biblical Counseling (In-Depth Discipleship) that is presented in BCT II: Biblical Counseling Basic Course. Notice the step-by-step procedures that you can use to help others face and deal with their problems in a biblical manner. As you study this plan, compare these steps with the counseling procedures that were followed with Tom and Mary in **A CASE STUDY: MARY'S HUSBAND HAS LEFT HER.**

☐ D.   Continue to deal biblically with any problems in your life in order to please the Lord in all things and to demonstrate your love for Him.

☐ E.   Determine if there are subjects in this course that you need to review. Develop a plan for further study and schedule accordingly.

*   *The completion of assignments marked with an asterisk (*) is a prerequisite for further biblical counseling training.*

> You have completed the manual for BCT I: Self-Confrontation. You should now understand the importance and necessity of confronting yourself biblically if you are to enjoy the full peace and joy that accompanies an abundant life in Jesus Christ. If you decide to take BCT II: Biblical Counseling Basic Course, you will learn how to apply biblical principles in a practical, systematic manner to help others face and deal with problems biblically. May God bless you in all you have accomplished in this course. I encourage you to seek God's strength as you apply God's Word to your life and personal ministry.
>
> John C. Broger

SUPPLEMENTS AND PRACTICAL HELPS

424

WHAT MAKES COUNSELING BIBLICAL?

Most people agree with the statement found in *Job 5:7* which says, *"For man is born for trouble as the sparks fly upward."* For centuries, mankind has been searching for explanations and solutions to the complex problems of living in a fallen world.

Man's search for ways to explain and to "cope" with his problems has produced many interesting and often conflicting theories such as: man is basically good and is able to live up to this potential; man has been victimized by his conscience, leaving him insecure and in need of resocialization; man is just a high-level animal who has been conditioned by his environment and needs to be reprogrammed; man's basic problem is a lack of self-esteem and an inability to love himself.

These are only a few of the most popular theories currently being used in the counseling field. All of these theories are predictably contrary to God's Word, since they have been devised by man operating outside the divine revelation of God *(I Corinthians 2:14).*

DEPENDING ON THE BIBLE

Is it necessary to turn to these worldly counseling theories and techniques to solve problems of living? Isn't it possible that understanding and overcoming life's problems can be accomplished by applying biblical truths?

The Bible itself states that the truths contained within it are entirely sufficient to enable a person to live a life pleasing to God *(II Peter 1:3-4).* It provides all the needed principles and guidance for understanding our mental processes, analyzing our emotional responses, and exercising control over our behavior. The laws, testimonies, precepts, commandments, judgments, and principles in the Old and New Testaments provide the only authoritative guide for man's thoughts, words, and actions *(Psalm 19:7-14; Hebrews 4:12).*

The promises and authority of God contained in His Word offer the basis for a vital and abundant life. The Scripture contains the solutions to every problem of attitude, relationship, communication, conduct, and behavior *(II Timothy 3:16-17).*

DEVELOPING BIBLICAL HABITS

In order to establish a scriptural base for biblical counseling, 105 biblical principles and their supporting verses are presented in the BCF Self-Confrontation course. These biblical principles can be applied in a systematic manner to overcome any problem of life and are not a mixture of man-contrived theories sprinkled with a few Bible verses unrelated to problem solving. Instead, these biblical principles provide the essential foundation for any person to change his unbiblical patterns of living and establish new habits of biblical behavior. While extensive and unalterable, these biblical principles are not meant to be all inclusive due to the living and active characteristics of God's Word *(Hebrews 4:12).*

In counseling that is true to God's Word, a biblical counselor will collect enough information to enable him to recognize and understand the problem in order to formulate the biblical solution. Counselees are encouraged to confront the failures and shortcomings of their personal lives from a biblical point of view *(Matthew 7:1-5).* In doing this, they should begin to see the necessity of turning their focus away from their own desires *(II Corinthians 5:14-15; Galatians 5:17, 19-21; James 4:1-3)* and should determine to live in a manner pleasing to God *(II Corinthians 5:9; Ephesians 4:1-3; Colossians 1:10-12).*

In order for biblical counseling to be effective, both the counselor and the counselee must be deeply committed to the Lordship of Jesus Christ and the authority of God's

Word. They must be continually committed to *"walk in a manner worthy of the Lord, to please Him in all respects, bearing fruit in every good work and increasing in the knowledge of God"* (Colossians 1:10). This commitment will change a person's focus from loving self to a focus on loving God and loving others in response to God's gracious love demonstrated in Jesus Christ *(Matthew 18:21-35; Romans 5:8; Ephesians 4:32; I John 4:11)*.

CONSTANT APPLICATION OF BIBLICAL PRINCIPLES

Even if the counselee has little or no concept of a biblical relationship with God and a limited knowledge of what is meant by a sincere commitment to Christ, biblical counseling can be extremely effective. As the biblical counselor continually focuses the counselee's attention on the authority and sufficiency of Scripture and explores the counselee's problems from a biblical standpoint, the necessity for a wholehearted commitment to Christ will be repeatedly presented.

As the counselee begins to view his problems from a biblical standpoint, he will begin to understand that the peace and joy promised by God do not depend on his financial situation, his work environment, the behavior of his spouse, or on any other external circumstance. A discouraged or despondent counselee can gain great hope as he learns from Scripture that God's peace and joy can be his as he depends solely on his relationship with God through Jesus Christ *(John 14:27, 16:33)*.

PRESUPPOSITIONS OF BIBLICAL COUNSELING

In His Word, God has given us everything we need to live in a manner that pleases Him *(II Peter 1:3-4)*. We must not integrate man's theories with biblical truth in order to solve our problems and live a victorious life. As a matter of fact, Scripture promises us that when we seek to place God's Word on a level with man's thinking, serious consequences occur *(Proverbs 1:22-32, 14:12, 30:5-6; Isaiah 5:20-21; Romans 8:6-8; I Corinthians 3:19-20)*.

Biblical counseling is based upon the biblical teaching that we will each give an account of ourselves to God *(Romans 14:12; II Corinthians 5:10)*. Even though believers in Christ will not be condemned by their sins in eternity *(Romans 8:1; Hebrews 9:27-28, 10:10-18)* as will non-believers *(Revelation 20:15)*, there are consequences for sins *(Ezekiel 18:20; Colossians 3:25)*. Counselees are shown that they are responsible before God solely for their own thoughts, words, and actions and that they are not responsible for changing anyone else's life.

In learning to assume responsibility for one's own behavior, a counselee needs to understand the conflict between his old self and his new nature in Christ *(Romans chapter 6; II Corinthians 5:17; Galatians 5:16)*. A counselee must determine, by an act of his will, to lay aside his old way of life with its lusts and deception and to begin to act in a way that reflects the new Christlike nature God has given him *(Ephesians 4:22-24; Colossians 3:5-17)*. A counselee must develop godly thought patterns *(II Corinthians 10:5; Philippians 4:8)* if he is to have a renewed mind and be successful in living a life that corresponds to the new nature which is created by God in holiness of the truth *(Romans 12:2; Ephesians 4:23-24)*.

Any changes that a counselee makes must be done in order to please God and not to gratify himself or please his parents, his spouse, or anyone else *(II Corinthians 5:9, 15; Colossians 1:10; I Thessalonians 2:4, 6)*. This requires a commitment to obey God's Word and not to depend on or be ruled by feelings, regardless of how strong or persuasive they may be *(II Corinthians 5:14-15; Galatians 5:16-17)*.

Biblical counseling is based upon these basic presuppositions which have been verified by years of application, observation, and testimony. These principles are not only verifiable, but they are also effective in every part of the world, in every culture, with all age groups, and in all levels of society. Biblical principles are based on the inerrant Word of God which transcends all man-made distinctions between people.

ESSENTIAL ELEMENTS OF BIBLICAL COUNSELING

In every biblical counseling session, four elements are emphasized:

1. UNDERSTANDING THE PROBLEM. Gaining God's perspective on any difficulty is important for those involved in solving problems biblically *(Proverbs 3:5-6; Isaiah 55:8-9; Romans 5:3-5, 8:28-29; James 1:2-4)*. You must begin to look honestly at yourself in light of God's Word *(Matthew 7:1-5; Luke 6:42-49; I Corinthians 11:31)*. Understanding a problem requires that biblical inquiry be made *(Proverbs 18:13, 17; II Timothy 3:16-17; James 1:19)* and truthful answers be given *(Ephesians 4:15, 25)*, in order for the total spectrum of the problem to be revealed *(Mark 7:20-23; James 1:22-25, 4:17)* (see next section: **BIBLICAL ANALYSIS OF A PROBLEM**).

2. HOPE. In His Word, God has promised that He will not let you be tried or tempted, suffer "stress" or anxiety, or face any problem beyond your endurance. Instead He will provide ample help and direction in every situation as you deal with the problem His way *(I Corinthians 10:13; Hebrews 4:15-16)*.

3. CHANGE. You must learn how to lay aside (or "put off") the old self-centered habits and destructive thoughts (such as anxiety, bitterness, and resentment). Instead, you are to "put on" biblical patterns of thought, words, and action *(Romans 6:6-7, 12-13; Ephesians 4:22-32; Philippians 4:6-9; Colossians 3:5-17)*.

4. PRACTICE. You must take action to put God's solutions into practice in your everyday activities. If you hear the Word and do not put it into practice, you deceive yourself and your problems become worse. But if you become a doer of the Word, God has promised that you will be blessed and will experience His peace and joy in spite of any turmoil around you *(Psalm 85:8-10; Isaiah 32:17; John 15:10-12, 16:33; Hebrews 5:14; James 1:22-25, 3:14-18; I Peter 3:8-12)*.

BIBLICAL ANALYSIS OF A PROBLEM

In analyzing problems from a scriptural perspective, biblical counselors recognize three levels of every problem.

1. THE FEELING OR PERCEPTION LEVEL. A person will often seek counseling when there is a disruption or discomfort of feelings, most notably a lack of peace and joy. Following a scriptural pattern, biblical counselors carefully explore the feeling level of a problem in order to define the nature of the problem being presented (the **what, when, where,** and **how** of the problem as depicted in *Genesis 3:8-13, 4:6; I Kings 19:9-14; Proverbs 18:13, 17; Luke 24:13-35; John 20:11-18)*.

2. THE DOING LEVEL. Biblical counselors attempt to help the counselee identify specific thoughts, words, and actions which violate biblical injunctions. A person focused on self tends to allow his feelings to dictate his behavior, regardless of what effect this may have on others. Living by one's feelings inevitably leads to doing the wrong things, which leads to more problems and further violations of biblical principles. For our instruction *(Romans 15:4)*, numerous examples of this self-centered pattern of behavior are given in Scripture *(Genesis 3:6-13, 4:5-8, 37:11-33; II Samuel 11:1-27, 13:1-33; II Chronicles 26:16-21)*.

   However, God's Word says that all of one's thoughts, words, and actions should result from a commitment to please God by obeying Him *(John 14:15; II Corinthians 5:9-15; Colossians 1:10)*. When a counselee begins to obey God, regardless of his feelings *(Romans 6:12-13; II Corinthians 5:15; Galatians 5:17)*, then God's promised blessings are available to him *(Genesis 4:7; James 1:25)*. Foremost among these blessings are lasting peace, joy, and righteousness *(Romans 14:17)*.

3.   THE HEART LEVEL. Scripture tells us that out of the heart come anger, bitterness, resentment, and all other evils that are defiling *(Matthew 15:18-20)*. The way a person responds to his problems reflects the condition of his heart *(Mark 7:21-23)*. No human being (including a biblical counselor) can fully understand the heart of any other person *(Jeremiah 17:9)*, but God examines each heart thoroughly *(I Samuel 16:7; Jeremiah 17:10)*. In biblical counseling, the counselor presents the counselee with the truths found in the Word of God, knowing it is the work of the Holy Spirit to convict the counselee of his sin and teach him the way to live a life pleasing to God *(John 16:8-13; Galatians 5:16-17; Hebrews 4:12-13)*. A biblical counselor discourages the counselee from looking to human counselors as the authority. The counselor teaches that the authority is the Word of God *(II Timothy 3:16-17)*, and the true Counselor is the Holy Spirit *(I Corinthians 2:10-13)*.

In the biblical counseling process, the counselor will help the counselee examine himself *(Matthew 7:5; I Corinthians 11:31; II Corinthians 13:5)* so that he will have a pure heart before the Lord *(I Samuel 16:7; Psalm 51:10, 17; 139:23-24; I Thessalonians 2:3-4; Hebrews 10:19-22)*, that it might be well with him *(Deuteronomy 5:29)* and that he may be blessed *(Matthew 5:8)*.

PROBLEMS CAN BE OVERCOME

While trials and tribulations are a part of life, God has a purpose for all of them *(Romans 5:3-5, 8:28; James 1:2-4)*. No matter what difficulties arise, God has promised that a believer in Christ can be an overcomer in every situation *(Romans 8:35-37; I Corinthians 10:13; I John 5:4-5)* as he responds in obedience to God's Word *(James 1:25)*. Even though obedience to God may not be easy *(Romans 7:18-19)*, it can be done as a response of love for what Jesus Christ has accomplished for a believer *(John 14:15; Romans chapter 6; I John 5:3; II John 1:6)*. Following the example of our Lord Jesus Christ, a child of God is to remain obedient even during times of suffering *(Hebrews 5:8; I Peter 2:20-21)*, looking beyond present circumstances to the glory that will be revealed *(Romans 8:18; II Corinthians 4:16-18)*.

Today, there is a critical need in the Body of Christ to return to the exclusive use of God's Word in overcoming personal problems and counseling others to do likewise in their difficulties *(II Corinthians 1:3-5)*. The biblical principles contained in the courses of study prepared by the Biblical Counseling Foundation (BCF) are based solely on the Word of God and not on human assumptions, opinions, experiences, theories, or any other secular philosophies.

THE BCF BIBLICAL COUNSELING TRAINING PROGRAM

BIBLICAL COUNSELING OFFERS GOD'S SOLUTIONS

The Bible deals with all of life's problems by identifying causes and providing authoritative solutions. As *II Timothy 3:16-17* states, *"All Scripture is inspired by God and profitable for teaching, for reproof, for correction, for training in righteousness; that the man of God may be adequate, equipped for every good work."* The responsibility and privilege of offering solutions to overcome life-dominating sins, broken hearts, and life's troubles belong to the Church.

WHAT IS A BIBLICAL COUNSELOR?

A biblical counselor is a committed, maturing believer who is trained to apply biblical principles to deal with the problems of everyday living. He is committed to the position that God's Word is the only authoritative standard for faith and conduct. He does not base his counseling knowledge on human assumptions, opinions, experience, or other concepts of behavior. Instead, he uses the full range of biblical principles and precepts to help the counselee face and deal with his problems in a biblical manner. He holds to the essential truths of Scripture without any particular theological emphasis or any practice not specifically advocated in the Scriptures.

TRAINING THE BIBLICAL COUNSELOR

As explained in Supplement 1, Page 3, biblical counseling consists of four essential components: understanding the problem, hope, change, and practice. From the training standpoint:

First: A biblical counselor asks questions and listens carefully to the responses so sufficient facts can be gathered to *understand the problem.* God's solutions are practical and personally applicable to every person's problems, so it is necessary to address the true problem – not merely "fix the feeling" or manipulate circumstances *(Proverbs 18:2, 13; James 1:19).*

Second: The biblical counselor can assure the counselee with confidence that there is *hope* in every situation. In Scripture, God has promised that He will not let you be tried or tempted, suffer "stress" or anxiety, or face any problem beyond your endurance. Instead, He will provide the solution in every circumstance or situation as you deal with the problem His way *(I Corinthians 10:13; Hebrews 4:15-16).* The counselor demonstrates this hope in numerous ways from the Scripture whenever the counselee needs the reinforcement of that hope.

Third: The biblical counselor teaches the counselee how to *change* by learning how to lay aside the old sinful and self-centered thoughts, words, actions, and destructive anxieties. Then, the counselee must learn the new biblical ways of thinking and living *(Romans 6:6-7, 12-13; Ephesians 4:22-32; Philippians 4:6-9; Colossians 3:5-17).*

Fourth: The biblical counselor must show that God's solutions are to be put into *practice* on a daily basis. If one hears God's Word but does not change in accord with its principles and precepts, that person deludes and deceives himself and his problems get worse. On the other hand, if a person is a doer of the Word, God has promised His peace, joy, and other blessings in spite of any situation *(John 15:10-11, 16:33, 17:13; James 1:22-25; I Peter 3:8-12).*

WHO IS TO COUNSEL?

Scripture tells us that the pastor-teacher is "to equip the saints for the work of service" *(Ephesians 4:11-12).* In addition, all believers – pastors and laymen alike – are commanded to instruct, reprove, and restore one another *(Matthew 18:15; 28:19-20; Romans 15:14; Galatians 6:1)*. Counseling, admonishing, and instructing were a major part of service in the first century New Testament Church. Likewise today, trained biblical counselors, composed of lay men and women within a church family, can assist the pastor-teacher to meet the needs of the church and the surrounding community.

HOW DOES ONE BECOME A BIBLICAL COUNSELOR?

To help meet the need for biblical counseling, the Biblical Counseling Foundation has developed a training program based completely on the Bible as the only authoritative standard for faith and conduct.

The overall objective is to have members of the church body equipped to live in a manner worthy of their calling in today's world *(Ephesians 4:1)*. There are two basic purposes in being trained as a biblical counselor:

1. To be able to face and deal with your own problems biblically *(Matthew 7:1-5; I Corinthians 10:13, 11:31; Galatians 6:4-5; Ephesians 4:22-24; Hebrews 4:12; II Peter 1:3-10)*, and

2. To know how to counsel others biblically through a proper application of biblical principles *(Romans 15:14; II Corinthians 1:3-4; Galatians 6:1-2; II Timothy 3:16-17)*.

WHAT IS THE BIBLICAL COUNSELING FOUNDATION?

The Biblical Counseling Foundation (BCF) began training believers to counsel in 1973 and was incorporated in the Commonwealth of Virginia in 1977 as a non-profit institution for the purpose of promoting, encouraging, and providing biblical counseling training. Its objective is to minister and teach. It is not a business or a profit-oriented organization. Its purpose is to assist and minister to those who need help dealing with problems, both in their lives and in the lives of others. Counselors associated with BCF provide their services as a ministry of the church without any charge or fee or any financial obligation, actual or implied. The BCF seeks to support and enhance the ministry of the local church. Therefore, the counselors are under the supervision of the sponsoring church or Christian organization. The BCF is a member of the National Association of Evangelicals (NAE).

The BCF office staff in Palm Desert, California responds to inquiries and administrative matters which arise from the expanding national and overseas outreach of BCF. The BCF office provides oversight and helps to coordinate the annual Concentrated Courses in Biblical Counseling. These five-day courses are taught at least four times each year in convenient locations in the United States. Additionally, the BCF office staff help to coordinate the three-week international intensive training courses conducted in various countries of the world.

WHAT RESOURCES ARE AVAILABLE?

The Biblical Counseling Foundation has developed two foundational training courses, the first of which you are now taking. These two courses are followed by three levels of training which consist of classroom instruction and actual counseling experience. Each stage of training has been planned to equip believers to become effective biblical counselors.

The first two courses *(BCT I: Self-Confrontation Course* and *BCT II: Biblical Counseling Basic Course)* are designed to be taught in weekly lessons of two hours each. Students should plan to spend *at least* five hours weekly on each lesson's homework. These courses illustrate how biblical truth may be personally and practically applied in dealing with your own problems in addition to equipping you to help others overcome their problems in a manner that pleases the Lord.

The three advanced courses provide practical counseling training at increasing levels of responsibility as a local counseling ministry grows.

WHERE DO YOU BEGIN?

BCT I: Self-Confrontation Course trains individuals in the basics of biblical living and counseling. The course may be taken by yourself or with others in a class of any size. There are no prerequisites for the Self-Confrontation Course. The only items needed are a Bible, the *Self-Confrontation* manual, and a concordance, coupled with a will to learn and apply the Word of God to each problem of everyday living. You are encouraged to start this study with high expectations for making biblical changes that will lead to continuing spiritual maturity. This manual is intended to be used as a practical guide to help you face and deal with your problems biblically and is not a theoretical, theological treatise. It will help you learn how to apply scriptural principles in your daily life. As a doer of the Word you will find blessing and rich reward *(James 1:25)*.

BCT II: Biblical Counseling Basic Course is designed to be taught in a class of limited size (usually less than fifteen students). *BCT III: Beginning to Counsel* may be conducted with any size class. As the counseling ministry within the church and community grows, *BCT IV: Training Others to Counsel* and *BCT V: Developing and Overseeing the Counseling Ministry* may be added. In addition, BCF offers a *Self-Study Bible Course in Counseling*, as part of *Biblical Counseling (Volume II)*. The Self-Study Bible Course may be completed in conjunction with the counseling training courses. Brief descriptions of all levels of training are provided in the next section titled, **"ON-GOING LOCAL TRAINING."**

Pastors and other church leaders will find the annual Concentrated Courses in Biblical Counseling extremely helpful for starting and maintaining a counseling ministry with their churches and communities.

The following descriptions and diagram provide an overview of the total training program. For further help, please write to the Administrative Office of the Biblical Counseling Foundation (address listed on Page 8 below).

ON-GOING LOCAL TRAINING

Basic Evangelism

Basic evangelism training is fundamental to the ministry of biblical counseling. The biblical counselor's first responsibility in a counseling situation is to determine if the counselee has a personal relationship with the only One – God Himself – who can provide true solutions to life's problems. Thus, a biblical counselor must know how to present the Gospel – the Good News of salvation provided through the Lord Jesus Christ.

Students who plan to minister as biblical counselors should enroll in an evangelism course which provides at least 10 hours of instruction and 10 hours of home visitation or on-the-job training. Some churches provide a full year of instruction, one night a week, including home visitation. You will find a number of excellent courses available.

BCT I: Self-Confrontation Course

This 24-week course teaches the essential biblical principles necessary for victorious living. Each individual needs to confront the failures and shortcomings in his own life from a biblical viewpoint before attempting to help anyone else *(Matthew 7:1-5; Luke 6:41-42)*. The basic scriptural principles for addressing the problems of life, as presented in the *Self-Confrontation* manual, comprise the foundation for the remaining courses in the Biblical Counseling Training series.

Instructor's Guide: BCT I – Self-Confrontation Course

Regardless of the instructor's previous teaching experience, the Instructor's Guide for *BCT I: Self-Confrontation Course* is a valuable tool for consistency in teaching how to confront one's self in a biblical manner and how to help others deal with their problems in a manner pleasing to the Lord. Contained in the Guide are teaching outlines, suggested time allocations for teaching points, illustrations, and suggestions for the evaluation of student homework and examinations. Teaching tapes of actual course sessions may also be purchased.

BCT II: Biblical Counseling Basic Course

The biblical principles and precepts presented in the *Self-Confrontation* manual are further applied in *Biblical Counseling (Volumes I and II)*. This is accomplished in a twenty-four week course through practical case studies, role-plays, and the diagnostics chart for biblical counseling. In *BCT II: Biblical Counseling Basic Course*, the student learns how to plan for counseling sessions and also practices how to explain and apply biblical principles for helping others to overcome their problems. The role-plays are designed to teach the biblical concepts of team counseling, understanding the problem from God's perspective, and the development of hope, change, and practice. Scriptural solutions are personalized through biblical homework assignments. Also, portions of the *BCF Self-Study Bible Course in Counseling*, described below, are incorporated as homework assignments.

Instructor's Guide – BCT II: Biblical Counseling (Volumes I and II)

The Instructor's Guide for BCT II contains lecture outlines with corresponding illustrations, role-play agendas, completed role-play case outlines, tools for evaluation of students in the course, and guidelines for determining and developing biblical homework.

Since actual counselor training is begun in this course, the instructor for BCT II should be an experienced biblical counselor in order to give scriptural answers to students' questions about actual counseling cases and the lesson's role-play. Instructor qualifications are included in the Instructor's Guide.

BCT III: Beginning to Counsel

Advanced training begins with active participation in actual counseling cases. The student counselor is closely supervised and discipled while assuming the responsibilities of an assistant counselor. At this point in training, each student should continue intensive work on the *BCF Self-Study Bible Course in Counseling*.

The classroom sessions consist of topics related to conduct of cases and evaluation of a counselee's progress in becoming a doer of the Word. In addition, the assistant counselor learns to plan counseling sessions and gradually begins to lead portions of counseling cases. He also learns how to disciple a counselee between the counseling sessions. *Biblical Counseling (Volumes I and II)* are used extensively at this level of training.

BCT IV: Training Others to Counsel

At this level, the counselor continues casework and begins to train and evaluate assistant counselors. He also completes work on the *BCF Self-Study Bible Course in Counseling*, which becomes his own "case reference" guide.

Classroom sessions for BCT IV consist of training in cases with multiple counselees, marriage problems, and parent-child difficulties. *Biblical Counseling (Volumes I and II)* continue to be used as valuable references throughout this training level.

BCT V: Developing and Overseeing the Counseling Ministry

At this level, the biblical counselor is trained to disciple, supervise, and evaluate counselors. Classroom instruction addresses topics involving administrative matters in a biblical counseling ministry, instructor training for biblical counseling courses, and more complicated problems in counseling such as church discipline matters, abortion, terminal diseases, etc. *Biblical Counseling (Volume II)* remains a basic reference guide for those at this level of training and ministry.

Specialized Training: The BCF Self-Study Bible Course in Counseling

Since no one can counsel biblically without a reasonable grasp of Scripture, the *BCF Self-Study Bible Course in Counseling* is designed to acquaint the prospective counselor with principles and precepts from the Old and New Testaments which apply to dealing with problems and achieving maturity in Christ. Completion of this course is sometimes required by local churches and missions organizations for certification as a biblical counselor. The Self-Study Bible Course typically takes 400-600 hours to complete and is usually completed in conjunction with BCT II, BCT III, and BCT IV (see diagram on following page).

The *BCF Self-Study Bible Course in Counseling* consists of four major sections:

1. *A study of twelve key scriptural doctrines that have direct application to biblical counseling.* A comprehensive concordance is needed to complete this study. Each student begins to compile his own list and explanation of meaningful verses and passages that can be used to give counselees hope, to show the need for biblical change, and to support biblical homework that is assigned.

2. *A study of 24 Old Testament biblical characters from a biblical counselor's perspective.* In this section, the student analyzes the life of a biblical character as though this biblical personality was coming for counseling to seek answers for the problems in his life. The student, using only the information given him about the character in the Scriptures, develops a case agenda (using both the Old and New Testaments) and describes how he would counsel each of these persons in Scripture with principles from God's Word.

3. *A biblical counseling perspective of the poetic and prophetic books in the Old Testament.* In this portion, the student analyzes and identifies biblical counseling principles found in *Psalms, Proverbs, Ecclesiastes,* and in a number of the prophetic books of the Old Testament.

4. *A counseling overview, consisting of two parts:*

   a. *Part one* asks a variety of questions concerning counseling topics, development of reference materials for cases, etc.

   b. *Part two* studies the way that Jesus counseled. The student looks at how the Lord Jesus understood problems in the lives of others, the manner in which He gave hope, the directions for change that He outlined to others, and the assignments (practice) that He gave to specific people.

STANDARDS OF CONDUCT AND CODE OF ETHICS

Certain standards that apply to the biblical counselor are inherent in the Scriptures. These standards of conduct and code of ethics for biblical counselors are contained in *Biblical Counseling (Volume II)*, which is the primary reference manual for courses II through V. All biblical counselors should agree with and abide by these standards.

BIBLICAL COUNSELING TRAINING OVERVIEW

The following chart illustrates the progression of the Biblical Counseling Training (BCT) developed by the Biblical Counseling Foundation (BCF).

The BCF also offers one-week Concentrated Courses and three-week international intensive courses in biblical counseling to train and assist pastors, Christian leaders, teachers, missionaries, educators, medical professionals, administrators, personnel managers, and other believers in developing a biblical counseling ministry in their churches, schools, missions organizations, and vocations.

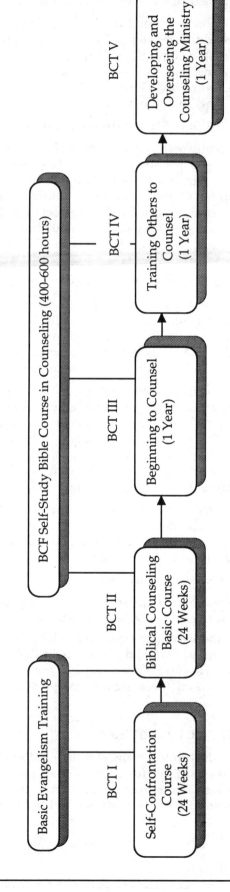

SUMMARY OF COUNSELING TRAINING HOURS

Course Name	Hours In Class	Hours Individual Study*	Hours In Case Sessions*
Basic Evangelism Training (through local church)	10	10	
BCT I: Self Confrontation Course	48	120	
BCT II: Biblical Counseling Basic Course	48	120	
BCT III: Beginning to Counsel	40	100	100
BCT IV: Training Others to Counsel	40	100	100
BCT V: Developing and Overseeing the Counseling Ministry	40	100	100
Self-Study Bible Course in Counseling		500	
TOTALS*	226	1,050	300

*Please note that the training hours are approximate, and will vary (especially in individual and casework times) with each person, according to training needs.

SPECIAL TRAINING FOR PASTORS, CHRISTIAN LEADERS, AND PROFESSIONALS

Concentrated Course in Biblical Counseling

The Biblical Counseling Foundation also offers a five-day concentrated training course in biblical counseling for three specific purposes: (1) to help believers in Christ face and deal with their own problems in a biblical manner; (2) to equip pastors, teachers, missionaries, medical professionals, administrators, personnel managers, Christian leaders, and other believers to counsel others in a biblical manner; and (3) to help those interested to initiate and maintain a biblical counseling ministry in their own churches, schools, missions organizations, or vocations.

Three-week Intensive Course for Internationals

The Biblical Counseling Foundation offers intensive three-week courses for internationals. The purpose of this training is to prepare indigenous training teams for in-depth discipleship and biblical counseling in their own countries or regions of the world. The first, or primary, three-week course is taught by BCF instructors and includes BCT I (35 hours), BCT II (50 hours), and how to develop training courses in national and local areas (10 hours). Those international ministry leaders completing the three-week training then sponsor and assist BCF instructors in a second three-week course covering the same subjects in their own countries. These indigenous courses are conducted some time later in designated countries after appropriate planning and preparation by the ministry leaders.

In these courses, several sequential training tracks provide opportunities for continuing development of skills in biblical counseling and provide help in establishing and administering a biblical counseling ministry. The three initial tracks cover the following curriculum:

Track I: Principles and Practices

Curriculum:

A. Presentation of Principles and Precepts of Biblical Counseling
- Man's Need and God's Provision
- Biblical Principles for Change
- Problem Development, Identification, and Solution
- Specific and Lasting Biblical Change
- Self-Centeredness, Depression
- The Christian Home, Marriage
- Envy, Covetousness, Jealousy, Greed
- Anger, Resentment, and Bitterness
- Fear, Worry, and Anxiety
- Continuing Christian Growth

B. Question and Answer Sessions

Track II: Processes and Procedures

Prerequisites:
- Completion of Track I in a previous BCF Concentrated Course or successful completion of the Self-Confrontation course

Curriculum:
- Lectures and Role-Plays in Counseling Procedures
- Understanding and Analysis of the Problems

- Assigning Biblical Homework
- How to Counsel Individuals with Problems of:
  Anger/Bitterness
  Depression
  Fear and Worry
  Poor Communications
  Poor relationships with family/others
- Developing Biblical Agendas
- Establishing and Evaluating Commitment
- Giving Biblical Hope, Effecting Change

Track III: Problems and Program

Prerequisites:

- Completion of Track II in a previous BCF Concentrated Course or successful completion of the Biblical Counseling Basic Course (BCT II).
- Successful completion of a written exam on biblical counseling (sent to you upon pre-registration).
- Special note to those registering for Track III: At least three difficult or complicated counseling situations you have encountered are to be typed out and submitted with your registration form. These counseling situations will be addressed, and biblical solutions will be given during the week.

Curriculum:

A. Training in:
- Establishing a Church Counseling Ministry
- Assigning, Conducting, and Following-up Cases
- Discipling and Evaluating Counselors and Supervisors
- Conducting Biblical Counseling Courses
  Student Commitment, Instructor Training, Course Content

B. Teaching on and Help with Complicated Cases
- Alcohol, Drug, and Substance Abuse
- Terminal Illnesses
- Physical Handicaps
- Homosexuality
- Spouse Beating
- Bizarre Behavior

The Concentrated Courses are held annually in Rancho Mirage, California, the Washington, D.C. area, and Santa Barbara, California. Others are held periodically in other parts of the United States and other countries. Currently, the Rancho Mirage, California seminar is held in February of each year. The Washington, D.C. seminar is held in April. The Santa Barbara, California seminar is conducted in August.

If you are interested in acquiring materials, receiving further information, or attending future courses to assist you in the biblical counseling ministry of your church, you may contact the Biblical Counseling Foundation as follows:

Postal Address:	**42-600 Cook Street, Suite 100**
	Palm Desert, CA 92211-5143 USA
Telephone:	**(760) 773-2667**
FAX:	**(760) 340-3778**
Email for orders:	**orders@bcfministries.org**
Email for correspondence:	**admin@bcfministries.org**
BCF Website:	**http://www.bcfministries.org**

BIBLE STUDY AND APPLICATION FORMAT

(based on II Timothy 3:16-17)

Biblical Reference	Teaching — What is the commandment or principle?	Reproof — How have I failed to live by it?	Correction — What do I need to do?	Training in Righteousness — What is my specific plan - how will I do it?
1 SAMUEL 12:23	PRAY FOR OTHERS	BY NOT PRAYING OFTEN	PRAY FOR THEM IMMEDIATELY	TO REMEMBER TO PRAY FOR OTHERS FIRST
MATTHEW 7:1-5	DO NOT JUDGE	BY TALKING OF OTHERS	JUDGE SELF FIRST	LOOK AT SELF FIRST

BIBLE STUDY AND APPLICATION FORMAT (EXAMPLE 1)

(based on II Timothy 3:16-17)

Biblical Reference	Teaching	Reproof	Correction	Training in Righteousness
	What is the commandment or principle?	How have I failed to live by it?	What do I need to do?	What is my specific plan - how will I do it?
		Example of an incorrectly done worksheet		
I John 3:17	We don't demonstrate God's love in us if we are not willing to share with others.	I tend to be very selfish and to take care only of my own needs. I stockpile for the future instead of sharing.	I need to learn to be more generous and be more willing to share.	I will read verses on generosity. I will ask God to give me a generous nature. I will love my neighbor!
		Example of a correctly done worksheet		
I John 3:17	We don't demonstrate God's love in us if we are not willing to share our lives as well as material goods with others.	I became aware of a woman at church whose children needed new winter coats. Her husband is disabled and unable to work and cannot afford to buy coats. Even though I knew that our family could help, I reasoned that my kids and I also needed new coats. After all, I can't be responsible for everyone.	In reality, only one of my children really needs a coat. The others only want new ones of a more current style. I need to buy the one needed coat for my child and use the rest of the money to buy coats for this family in need.	1. Pray for God's guidance and strength in carrying out a plan to help this family. 2. Call a family meeting. Explain the need to my family, present my plans to help another family, and get my family's ideas on how we can help. 3. With my family, review verses on sharing and pray for our part in meeting this need. 4. Contact the leaders in my church to alert them of the needs of the other family and tell of my family's plans to help. 5. Call the woman in need. Explain to her how my sharing shows my love to the Lord and provides a blessing for her family as well as my own. 6. Schedule a shopping trip so her family can pick out the coats they need. 7. Perhaps take their family to lunch as part of the shopping trip.

BIBLE STUDY AND APPLICATION FORMAT (EXAMPLE 2)

(based on II Timothy 3:16-17)

Biblical Reference	Teaching	Reproof	Correction	Training in Righteousness
	What is the commandment or principle?	How have I failed to live by it?	What do I need to do?	What is my specific plan – how will I do it?
		Example of an incorrectly done worksheet		
Psalm 119:11	I should treasure God's Word in my heart (or mind).	I haven't been memorizing God's Word.	I need to start memorizing Scripture.	I will ask God to help me start memorizing Scripture and will memorize one verse a week.
		Example of a correctly done worksheet		
Psalm 119:11	I should treasure God's Word in my heart (or mind).	Instead of having a plan of regular Scripture memory, I am watching more than three hours of television daily. I have not even tried to develop a plan of memorizing Scripture. In fact, I have been lazy, saying that any memory work is too hard for me. I have made excuses for my failure to the Lord.	In the next four weeks, I will memorize four verses on the subject of obedience. While I am memorizing the four verses, I will seek to develop a plan for Scripture memory for the rest of the year.	1. I will pray daily for God's help in memorizing His Word. 2. Using a concordance, I will find four verses on obedience that are significant to my life and write them on small cards. 3. The first week, I will carry one memory verse card with me and use it in spare moments to memorize this verse (for example, standing in line, walking alone, waiting for and riding on the bus). 4. I will tell my family of my plan and request that they ask me to recite my verse(s) every day. 5. I will add one new memory verse card each week that I will carry with me and memorize during my spare moments (I will review my previous verses). 6. During this month, I will also choose four verses on the subject of salvation for the next month's memory work. I will also review my four verses on obedience during the next month.

PREPARING A PERSONAL TESTIMONY

> One of the greatest privileges you have is presenting the Good News of Jesus Christ to others. You need to be prepared to give your testimony to others *(based on I Peter 3:15).*

The Apostle Paul provided a good example for you to follow when he gave his testimony of conversion before King Agrippa in *Acts 26:1-23.*

Life Before Conversion (Acts 26:4-11)
A religious life but opposed to God

Conversion (Acts 26:12-18)
A recognition of a need for Christ and a commitment to Christ

Life After Conversion (Acts 26:19-23)
A changed life and a witness for Christ

Few believers have as dramatic a testimony as Paul, but all believers can follow the same general outline: *Life Before Conversion, Conversion, Life After Conversion.*

To implant this testimony outline firmly in your mind, you should develop a "ten second" testimony that forms the basis for a more complete testimony. For example:

(Life Before Conversion) There was a time in my life when I was hopeless and confused; *(Conversion)* then I had an encounter with Jesus Christ that changed my life. *(Life After Conversion)* Ever since then, I have had a purpose for living.

Another example would be: *(Life Before Conversion)* I always thought I wasn't that bad and would go to heaven no matter what. *(Conversion)* However, God had a different plan to which I responded. *(After Conversion)* I know now I'll go to heaven.

Life before conversion: Try to use descriptive words that a non-believer will understand which would characterize your life prior to knowing Christ *(examples: selfish, no meaning, guilty, troubled, without hope, full of anxiety, always trying to be #1, etc.).*

Conversion: Then describe your conversion in terms that a non-believer will readily understand. Phrases such as "got saved" or "had my sins covered by the blood" or "knelt at Calvary," while meaningful to believers, will probably not be understood by a non-believer. You might describe your conversion experience with phrases such as: "I discovered God loved me" or "I realized Jesus was God's Son" or "Someone told me that God had a plan for my life."

Life after conversion: Use words familiar to a non-believer to describe your life now *(examples: I stopped worrying. I found peace. My guilt is gone. I have found the only way to real living).*

Remember to keep your "ten second" testimony simple without going into detail. *Details are reserved for your "expanded testimony" to be developed in future lessons. Examples of "expanded testimonies" are given on Page 2 of Supplement 4.*

TEN SECOND ... THIRTY SECOND ... SIXTY SECOND TESTIMONIES (EXAMPLES)

Example of a ten-second testimony:

(before)   "There was a time in my life when I had no lasting peace and joy, but someone told me that was because I didn't have a personal relationship with Jesus Christ.

(conversion)   After my relationship with God was established,

(after)   I discovered the reality of true peace and joy."

The above ten-second testimony expanded into a thirty-second testimony:

(before)   "When I was younger, I couldn't find lasting peace and joy in anything or anyone. My friends and activities could not fill that emptiness in my life."

(conversion)   "One day, a friend of mine told me how Jesus had died so that my life could have meaning and direction. I then realized that I was a sinner in need of God's forgiveness. So I asked God to forgive me, and genuinely believed in Jesus as my Savior, receiving Him into my life."

(after)   "Since turning my life over to Jesus, I have discovered that the Bible provides all the answers I need. No matter what comes along, God's peace and joy are mine forever."

The above thirty-second testimony expanded into a sixty-second testimony:

(before)   "When I was younger, I couldn't find lasting peace or joy in anything or anyone. Even though my friends and I always were on the move, it seemed there should be more to life than what I was experiencing. My friends even agreed with that."

(conversion)   "One day, a friend and I were talking about some problems I was having; and he explained that my biggest problem was not having a personal relationship with Jesus Christ. He showed me that no one was perfect, which means that all have sinned, as the Bible says in Romans 3:23. And, I learned that the Bible, in Romans 6:23, says my sins had earned a definite wage for me, which was death. However, God didn't leave me in that position. Jesus died for me so my sins could be forgiven, and I could enjoy a relationship with God and receive His gift of eternal life."

"All I had to do was to believe genuinely that Jesus died to pay the penalty for my sins and that He rose from the dead so I could have a new life. My next step of commitment was to ask Him to forgive me of my sins. My prayer was simple; I said, 'God, please forgive me for my sins. Thank you for sending your Son, Jesus, to die for me and to live so I could have eternal life. Please save me from my sins, and take control of my life, Lord Jesus.' "

(after)   "Since turning my life over to Jesus, God's lasting peace and joy have been mine as I have obeyed God's Word to overcome problems. I don't mean that I don't have trials, but I am now confident that God will help, guide, and strengthen me when problems come. Have you ever considered the difference that Jesus Christ could make in your life?"

HOW TO USE A CONCORDANCE

A concordance is a helpful tool that will enable you to locate verses in the Bible in which particular words are used. The words contained in a concordance are arranged alphabetically like a dictionary and are followed by a listing of biblical passages where that word is used.

For example, if you were to look up the word, "doers," you would find:

There the *d* of iniquity have fallen	*Psalm 36:12*
will lead them away with the *d* of iniquity	*Psalm 125:5*
not only are the *d* of wickedness built up	*Malachi 3:15*
but the *d* of the Law will be justified	*Romans 2:13*
But prove yourselves *d* of the word	*James 1:22*

In a concordance, only portions of a verse are listed and the first letter of the word being examined is sometimes printed instead of the entire word.

You can use a concordance to discover what God's Word says about a particular subject by following these suggestions. For illustrative purposes, "Bible" is our subject.

1. Look up the subject itself to discover if there is a listing. In the case of "Bible," there is no listing.

2. Select biblical words that are good synonyms for your subject.

   EXAMPLE: Word of God, Scripture, Law

   Look up these words in the concordance. After discovering the verses that give you insight into your subject, you could highlight the verse in your Bible, write out the verse for your continuing study, or perhaps give a summary of the verse's truth. As an illustration, if you were to look up "Word of God," you might do the following.

   EXAMPLE: *Hebrews 4:12, "For the Word of God is living and active and sharper than any two-edged sword, and piercing as far as the division of soul and spirit, of both joints and marrow, and able to judge the thoughts and intentions of the heart."*

   A summary of this verse might be: "The Word of God is living, active, and able to discern the thoughts and intentions of the heart."

   Looking up "Scripture,"

   EXAMPLE: *II Timothy 3:16-17, "All Scripture is inspired by God and is profitable for teaching, for reproof, for correction, for training in righteousness; that the man of God may be adequate, equipped for every good work."*

   A summary statement might be: "The Word of God teaches me how to live biblically, corrects me when I fail, and helps me to recover so I can be an effective doer of the Word."

3. Modifying a word form may also be helpful.

   EXAMPLE: "Scripture" – writings, written, wrote, write

   Looking up "writings,"

   EXAMPLE: *II Timothy 3:15, "... the sacred writings which are able to give you the wisdom that leads to salvation through faith which is in Christ Jesus."*

   A summary statement might be: "God's Word leads me to salvation through Christ Jesus."

4.   You might also refer to words that have a close association with your subject or word.

    EXAMPLE: voice of the Lord, teachings

    Looking up "voice,"

    EXAMPLE: *Psalm 29:4, "The voice of the Lord is powerful, The voice of the Lord is majestic."*

    A summary statement in this case might parallel the actual words of the text such as, "The voice of the Lord is powerful and majestic."

While a complete concordance may look intimidating due to its volume of material and physical size, do not hesitate to use it. Using a concordance to find a particular word, verse, or subject in the Bible can enrich your understanding of the truths of God's Word.

PERSONAL HISTORY/PROBLEM EVALUATION

BASIC INFORMATION ABOUT THE PROBLEM

DATE: _____

PERSONAL INFORMATION

NAME: _____ PHONE #: _____ FAX # _____

ADDRESS: _____

OCCUPATION: _____ BUSINESS PHONE #: _____

GENDER: _____ BIRTH DATE: _____ AGE: _____ EMAIL ADDRESS: _____

MARITAL STATUS:

Single ❑   Engaged ❑   Married ❑   Separated ❑   Divorced ❑   Widowed ❑

EDUCATION: Last Grade Completed (Prior to college) _____ Other Education (List type and years) _____

_____ RECOMMENDED BY: _____

NAME OF SPOUSE: _____ OCCUPATION: _____

SPOUSE'S ADDRESS (If different from yours): _____

THE BASIC PROBLEM AS YOU UNDERSTAND IT:

Briefly complete the following (please use the back if necessary):

1. PLEASE DESCRIBE THE CURRENT PROBLEM.

2. WHAT HAVE YOU DONE ABOUT IT?

3. WHAT HELP ARE YOU SEEKING?

4. WHAT LED YOU TO SEEK HELP NOW?

DETAILED INFORMATION RELATED TO THE PROBLEM

INFORMATION ABOUT SPIRITUAL LIFE

DENOMINATIONAL PREFERENCE: _____ CHURCH NAME: _____

CHURCH ADDRESS: _____ PASTOR'S NAME: _____

CHURCH ATTENDANCE: Frequency of attendance _____Times per month

WHAT ARE YOU LEARNING THROUGH THE SERMONS/MESSAGES/BIBLE STUDIES AT YOUR CHURCH?

_____

PLEASE LIST MINISTRY INVOLVEMENT: _____

CHURCH ATTENDED IN CHILDHOOD: _____

HAVE YOU BEEN BAPTIZED?   Yes ❑   No ❑   WHEN? _____

IF MARRIED, RELIGIOUS BACKGROUND OF SPOUSE: _____

(ONLY IF APPLICABLE) SPOUSE'S CHURCH ATTENDANCE:

Spouse's church name _____ Frequency of attendance _____ Times per month

DO YOU PRAY TO GOD?   Never ❑ Occasionally ❑ Often ❑   How often? _____

WHAT DO YOU PRAY ABOUT? _____

HAVE YOU COME TO TO THE PLACE IN YOUR SPIRITUAL LIFE WHERE YOU KNOW WITH CERTAINTY THAT IF YOU WERE TO DIE TONIGHT YOU WOULD GO TO HEAVEN?

Yes ❑   No ❑   Uncertain ❑

IF YES, WHAT IS YOUR BASIS FOR ANSWERING THE ABOVE QUESTION AS YOU DID? _____

_____

HAVE YOU RECEIVED JESUS CHRIST PERSONALLY AS YOUR SAVIOR?

Yes ❑   No ❑   Uncertain ❑   Don't Know What You Mean ❑

IF YES, HOW DO YOU KNOW THAT JESUS CHRIST IS YOUR SAVIOR? _____

_____

IF YOU HAVE RECEIVED CHRIST AS SAVIOR, WHAT CHANGES TOOK PLACE IN YOUR LIFE WHEN YOU BECAME A BELIEVER? _____

_____

IF YOU HAVE RECEIVED CHRIST AS SAVIOR, HAVE YOU TOLD HOUSEHOLD/FAMILY MEMBERS ABOUT RECEIVING JESUS AS SAVIOR?   Yes ❑   No ❑

WHOM HAVE YOU TOLD? _____

DO YOU READ THE BIBLE? Never ❑ Occasionally ❑ Often ❑ How often? _____

DO YOU HAVE PERSONAL DEVOTIONS? Never ❑ Occasionally ❑ Often ❑ How often? _____

DESCRIBE YOUR PERSONAL DEVOTIONS: _____

_____

DO YOU HAVE FAMILY DEVOTIONS? Never ❑ Occasionally ❑ Often ❑ How often? _____

DESCRIBE YOUR FAMILY DEVOTIONS: _____

_____

EXPLAIN ANY RECENT CHANGES IN YOUR SPIRITUAL LIFE: _____

INFORMATION ABOUT PRIOR COUNSELING

HAVE YOU HAD ANY COUNSELING BEFORE?   Yes ❑   No ❑

COUNSELOR NAME(S)	DATES From To	MEDICATION PRESCRIBED	OUTCOME

INFORMATION ABOUT PERSONAL HABITS AND HEALTH

APPROXIMATELY HOW MANY HOURS OF SLEEP DO YOU GET EACH NIGHT? _____

WHEN DO YOU NORMALLY: go to bed? _____ fall asleep? _____ wake up? _____ get out of bed? _____

IF THERE IS A LENGTH OF TIME BETWEEN YOUR GOING TO BED AND FALLING ASLEEP, WHAT DO YOU DO DURING THAT TIME? _____

_____

IF THERE IS A LENGTH OF TIME BETWEEN YOUR WAKING UP AND GETTING OUT OF BED, WHAT DO YOU DO DURING THAT TIME? _____

_____

DESCRIBE ANY RECENT CHANGES IN SLEEP HABITS: _____

_____

STATE OF HEALTH: Very Good ❑   Good ❑   Average ❑   Declining ❑   Other ❑

DATE OF LAST MEDICAL EXAMINATION: _____ RESULTS: _____

ARE YOU PRESENTLY TAKING MEDICATION? Yes ❑   No ❑   WHAT? _____ DOSAGE? _____

FOR WHAT REASON DO YOU TAKE THIS MEDICATION? _____

_____

HAVE YOU USED DRUGS FOR OTHER THAN MEDICAL PURPOSES? Yes ❑   No ❑   WHEN? _____

WHAT? _____ AMOUNTS/DOSAGES? _____

DO YOU DRINK ALCOHOLIC BEVERAGES?   Yes ❑   No ❑   WHEN? _____ HOW MUCH? _____

MARRIAGE AND FAMILY INFORMATION:

NAME OF SPOUSE: _____ ADDRESS: _____

PHONE #:_____ OCCUPATION: _____BUSINESS PHONE #:_____

YOUR SPOUSE'S AGE: _____ EDUCATION (In years): _____ RELIGION: _____

IS SPOUSE WILLING TO COME WITH YOU?   Yes ☐   No ☐   Have not asked yet ☐   Not certain ☐

ARE YOU CURRENTLY SEPARATED?   Yes ☐   No ☐   Since when? _____

HAVE YOU EVER BEEN SEPARATED IN THE PAST?   Yes ☐   No ☐   No. of times _____

HAS EITHER OF YOU EVER FILED FOR DIVORCE?   Yes ☐   No ☐   When? _____ Who? _____

DATE OF MARRIAGE: _____ YOUR AGES WHEN MARRIED: Husband _____ Wife _____

HOW LONG DID YOU KNOW YOUR SPOUSE BEFORE MARRIAGE?_____

LENGTH OF STEADY DATING WITH SPOUSE:_____ LENGTH OF ENGAGEMENT: _____

HAVE YOU BEEN MARRIED BEFORE?   Yes ☐   No ☐

IF YES, HOW MANY TIMES?   Husband _____ Wife _____

IF YOU WERE MARRIED BEFORE, HOW DID THE MARRIAGE(S) END?   _____

CHILDREN'S NAMES	AGES	GENDER	LIVING? Yes	No	EDUCATION IN YEARS	MARITAL STATUS	*PM

*CHECK THIS COLUMN IF CHILD IS BY PREVIOUS MARRIAGE

IF YOU WERE REARED BY ANYONE OTHER THAN YOUR OWN PARENTS, BRIEFLY EXPLAIN: _____

NO. OF OLDER   Brothers _____ Sisters _____ NO. OF YOUNGER   Brothers _____ Sisters _____

GUIDELINES: VICTORY OVER FAILURES WORKSHEET

> The **VICTORY OVER FAILURES WORKSHEET** is a useful tool that will help you implement biblical change into your life and, as the situation warrants, teach others to do the same in their lives *(based on Matthew 7:1-5; II Corinthians 1:3-5, 13:5; Galatians 6:1-5; II Timothy 3:16-17).*

I. Purposes of the VICTORY OVER FAILURES WORKSHEET

A. To help you examine (judge) yourself biblically *(Psalm 139:23-24; Matthew 7:1-5; I Corinthians 11:31; Galatians 6:4);*

B. To help you recognize specific biblical put-offs/put-ons for daily living *(for example: Ephesians 4:22-32; Colossians 3:5-17);*

C. To help you develop and act upon specific plans for biblical change *(James 1:22-25);* and

D. To help you make your specific biblical changes part of a scriptural plan for every area of your life *(Romans 6:12-13, 8:28-29; Colossians 2:6, 3:2-17; II Timothy 3:16-17; I Peter 1:14-16).*

II. Procedures for biblical change

A. Commit yourself to God's sovereignty and rule in your life.

1. Receive Jesus Christ as Lord and Savior *(John 1:12; Romans 10:9-11; I Corinthians 15:1-4; Ephesians 2:8-10).*

2. Determine to walk daily in a manner that pleases God *(II Corinthians 5:9; Ephesians 4:1; Colossians 1:10, 3:17).*

B. Determine the specific ways you have sinned against God. Repent of your sinful ways; they are contrary to Scripture and displeasing to God *(Proverbs 28:13; Revelation 2:5, 3:19).* Confess these sins to Him *(I John 1:9).*

C. Ask God for wisdom to know what changes to make and how to make them *(Psalm 139:23-24; James 1:5).* Ask with faith that He will answer *(Hebrews 11:6; James 1:5-8).*

D. Forgive others that have sinned against you *(Mark 11:25-26; Ephesians 4:31-32)* with a goal of reconciling with them *(Matthew 5:23-24; Romans 12:18).* Following biblical guidelines, confess to other individuals the sins you have committed against them *(James 5:16).*

E. Diligently study God's Word on a regular basis *(Joshua 1:8; Psalm 1:2; II Timothy 2:15, 3:16-17)* and memorize Scripture to store His truth in your heart *(Psalm 119:11, 16).*

F. Pray always in every circumstance and do not lose heart *(Luke 18:1; Philippians 4:6-7; I Thessalonians 5:17).*

G. Do what God says to do *(Matthew 7:24-26; James 1:22-25)* regardless of your feelings *(Genesis 4:6-7; Romans 13:14; Galatians 5:16-17; I Peter 4:2)* in order to glorify Him

(Matthew 5:16; I Corinthians 10:31), staying under the control and guidance of the Holy Spirit *(John 14:26, 16:13; Romans 8:14; Ephesians 4:30, 5:18)*.

III. God's promises concerning biblical change in your life

A. In Christ, you have assurance of victory over failures *(Romans 8:37-39; II Corinthians 2:14, 10:4; I John 5:4-5, 18)*.

B. As an overcomer, you are assured of final rewards *(Revelation 2:7, 11, 17, 26; 3:5, 12, 21; 21:6-7)*.

IV. Perspective for biblical change

A. Scripture is the sole standard and authority for your life *(Psalm 19:7-11; 119:24, 105; Romans 15:4; II Timothy 3:16-17; Hebrews 4:12; II Peter 1:3-4)*.

B. The only lasting hope is promised in the Scriptures. *(The following is reprinted from: BIBLICAL PRINCIPLES: BIBLICAL BASIS FOR CHANGE, Lesson 6, Pages 2-3, under II. Your hope in the midst of trials)*.

1. Those in Christ are freed from the power and penalty of sin *(Romans 6:6-7, 14, 18, 23)*.

2. God will not allow believers to be tested or tempted beyond what they can bear. He gives you His grace and strength to endure every test and resist every temptation so that you never have to sin *(Romans 8:35-39; I Corinthians 10:13; II Corinthians 4:7-10, 12:9-10; Philippians 4:13; Hebrews 4:15-16; II Peter 2:4-9)*.

3. Our Lord Jesus Christ will grant mercy and provide grace to help in every need. As your advocate, He constantly intercedes for you to God the Father and fully understands your weaknesses *(Hebrews 2:18, 4:15-16, 7:25; I John 2:1)*.

4. Trials and testings will develop and mature you in Christ if you respond to them in God's way *(Romans 5:3-5; James 1:2-4)*. He never devises evil or harm for you; rather His plans for you are for your good *(Genesis 50:20; Deuteronomy 8:2, 5, 16; Psalm 145:17; Ecclesiastes 7:13-14; Jeremiah 29:11-13; Romans 8:28-29; James 1:13-17)*.

5. God's peace and joy are available to believers regardless of others, possessions, or circumstances *(Psalm 119:165; Matthew 5:3-12; John 14:27, 15:11, 16:33, 17:13; Romans 14:17; Philippians 4:4-7; I Peter 1:6-9)*.

6. Only God can change people *(Ezekiel 36:26-27; Philippians 1:6, 2:13)*, so you cannot and are not responsible for changing them. You are accountable to God solely for your own deeds *(Jeremiah 17:10; Ezekiel 18:1-20, especially verse 20; Matthew 16:27; Romans 2:5-10; Colossians 3:23-25; I Peter 1:17)* and are to do your part in living at peace with others *(Matthew 5:23-24; Mark 11:25; Romans 12:9-21, 14:19; I Peter 3:8-9, 4:8)*.

7. When you confess your sins, God forgives and cleanses you *(I John 1:9)*.

V. Procedures for biblical change using the VICTORY OVER FAILURES WORKSHEET.

A. To develop a pattern of victory over failures, complete the four columns on the worksheet, referring to key passages of Scripture to determine possible areas of failure *(for example, Romans chapters 12-14; I Corinthians 13:4-8a; Ephesians 4:22 - 6:9; Colossians chapter 3; I Peter 2:11 - 3:17)*.

1. In column 1, begin to make a list of all the ways you have failed to act in a biblical manner *(Matthew 7:5)*. To avoid confusion, make one worksheet for problems

---

that involve only you and the Lord and use a separate worksheet for each person you have sinned against (for example: a family member, a roommate, a co-worker, a neighbor, or a friend).

2.   In completing columns 2 and 3, study God's Word diligently and extensively to discover as many "put-offs" and related "put-ons" as possible, in order to deal biblically with the sinful deeds listed in column 1. "Put-offs" and "put-ons" should be in the same passage of Scripture to keep them relevant to each other.

    a.   List each "put-off" and corresponding "put-on", along with the associated Scripture passage, directly across from each other in columns 2 and 3.

    b.   Be sure to list all the "put-offs" and "put-ons" that apply to each incident in column 1.

3.   Next, look for "put-offs" and "put-ons" that occur repeatedly in columns 2 and 3 (i.e., areas in which you repeatedly stumble, such as anger, bitterness, unwholesome words, etc.). Then, list each pattern at the top of column 4.

4.   Finally, in completing column 4, develop a specific plan to deal biblically with each "put-off" and "put-on" pattern. Refer to the lessons that deal with your specific problem areas for help in making your plans.

5.   Use the format on the following page as a suggested guideline to gain victory over failures in any area of your life:

(1) My specific, biblical failure (thoughts, words, actions) *(Matthew 7:1-5)*	(2) Put-off & biblical reference(s) *(Ephesians 4:22; Colossians 3:5-9)*	(3) Put-on & biblical reference(s) *(Ephesians 4:24; Colossians 3:10-17)*	(4) My plan not to repeat this sin and to respond biblically instead *(Titus 2:11-14)*
In this column list specific unbiblical thoughts, words, and actions – not merely emotions or attitudes *(refer to Matthew 15:18-20, 22:37-39; I Corinthians 6:9-10; Galatians 5:19-21; Ephesians 4:15, 25-32).*	In this column, identify sinful patterns of thoughts, words, or actions from the items that are repeated in column 1.	In this column, list the biblical "put-on" (with its Scripture references) for each sinful pattern ("put-off") listed in column 2. Remember that some "put-ons" do not have associated "put-offs".	In this column, list SPECIFIC THOUGHTS, SPEECH, AND ACTIONS that will replace the sinful patterns described in columns 2 and 3 *(in obedience to James 1:22).*
Also, take care not to place blame on anyone else for your failures *(in light of Ezekiel 18:20; Matthew 7:5).*	For each pattern, list one or more verses that identify the pattern(s) as sin ("put-off"). You may list a variety of scriptural references, but good starting points are *I Corinthians 13:4-8a; Ephesians 4:15, 25-32; and Colossians chapter 3.* Make sure that the "put-off" and "put-on" come from the same portion of Scripture to keep them relevant to each other.		Also identify specific steps of biblical response when you are confronted with temptation, especially in a crisis. When you go to another to ask forgiveness *(based on Matthew 5:23-24),* be sure to tell the person your intention is to change to God's way. Describe your plan to avoid repeating the sin and ask for help as needed.

This biblical pattern for gaining victory over failures should be practiced on a regular basis throughout your Christian life.

6. Spend as much time as you need to complete your **VICTORY OVER FAILURES WORKSHEET** (Supplement 8, Page 1), so that you begin to see and understand what God says about your thoughts, words, and actions *(Jeremiah 17:9-10)*. Ask God to help you *(Psalm 139:23-24; James 1:5)*.

    a. Start with one of your specific failures and go through the four columns from left to right. **Remember that this worksheet is merely a tool for keeping short accounts and dealing with your sins on a daily/regular basis *(Proverbs 28:13; Ephesians 4:1; James 4:17)*. It is neither designed nor intended to limit or substitute for the Holy Spirit's convicting power in your life.**

    b. You may not get all four columns completed the first week for each of your failures, but at least work on the first three columns.

B. During subsequent weeks, continue working on your worksheet, concentrating on the following areas:

    1. Becoming more specific in listing your unbiblical deeds (thoughts, words, and actions) *(Ephesians 4:15-32)*;

    2. Accepting responsibility for your own behavior *(Matthew 7:5)*; and

    3. Refining the plans you have listed in column 4 so that your thoughts, words, and actions will be more conformed to Scripture and the character of Christ *(I Corinthians 11:31; Philippians 3:12-14)*.

    An expansion of column 4 is provided on Supplement 8, Page 2, because typically, your specific plan will be much longer than the items in columns 1-3. This extra page allows you to have adequate space to write your plan to live biblically.

VI. Application of biblical change

A. As you are completing the **VICTORY OVER FAILURES WORKSHEET** (Supplement 8), repent and confess your sins to God *(I John 1:8-10)*.

B. Recognize that God forgives your sins; therefore, you should not dwell upon sins which God has forgiven *(based on Psalm 103:12; Jeremiah 31:34; Philippians 3:12-14, 4:8-9; Hebrews 10:17; I John 1:9)*.

C. Instead, dwell on and put into practice the new, righteous deeds (thoughts, words, and actions) that you have planned in column 4 *(Philippians 4:8-9; Colossians 3:2, 23-24; 4:6; James 4:17)*.

D. Now, plan for and practice reconciliation with the ones against whom you have sinned *(Matthew 5:23-24; Romans 12:18)*.

    1. When you ask another person to forgive you, be sure to communicate the following, in your own words *(based on Ephesians 4:15, 25)*:

        "I recognize that I have sinned against the Lord and you by (name the specific sin). It is my intention never again to repeat this offense against you or anyone else. I repent and will change by doing the following. (Explain your specific plan for change). I have asked the Lord to forgive me, and I want you to know that I desire your forgiveness as well. Will you please forgive me?"

    2. Practice asking for forgiveness by first writing it, then, by saying it out loud. Prepare yourself for various responses from the other person and plan how to

respond biblically *(Ephesians 4:15-32; I Peter 2:20-21; 3:13-17)*. Be careful to remain lovingly honest when writing how you will respond to others' replies *(Ephesians 4:15, 25)*. Also, make sure you communicate your seriousness to change and to be reconciled with them. To do otherwise would be to practice love with hypocrisy *(Romans 12:9)*.

Write and rehearse what you would do and say if the other person replies with statements such as "Oh, that's all right," (minimizing sin) or "Don't worry about it," (avoiding a commitment to forgive) or "People do that all the time," (minimizing or making excuses for sin) or "I won't forgive you," (lack of forgiveness) or "I'll forgive you but I won't forget it" (lack of forgiveness; harboring a grudge).

   a.   For example, in response to "Oh, that's all right" or "Don't worry about it" or "People do that all the time," you might say, "Even though my actions may not have bothered you or offended you, I recognize that my actions towards you were unloving, contrary to Scripture, and not pleasing to God. Since my desire is to be a Christlike person and to love you God's way, I ask for and would like your forgiveness" *(based on Romans 12:18; I Corinthians 13:4-8a; Ephesians 4:1; James 4:17)*.

   b.   If the offended person says, "I won't forgive you," you might respond with, "I am deeply sorry (i.e., sorrowful) that I have so offended you. I regret being unloving to you and not living in a biblical manner. I have made a commitment and am serious about living in a more Christlike manner in our relationship and will be praying that our relationship can be restored" *(based on Matthew 5:16; Romans 12:18; Ephesians 4:25, 29; Colossians 2:6)*.

   c.   If you ask for forgiveness and hear a response similar to, "I'll forgive you but I won't forget it," you might say, "I regret being part of such a painful memory in your life. My behavior was contrary to biblical love. I commit to act and speak in such a way that our future relationship will, hopefully, be surrounded by much better remembrances" *(based on Matthew 5:5, 9, 16; Romans 12:18; I Corinthians 13:4-8a; Ephesians 4:1, 15, 29; James 3:17-18; I John 4:11)*.

Review: **RECONCILIATION (REMOVING ALL HINDRANCES TO UNITY AND PEACE)** *(Lesson 12, Pages 6-8)*.

E.   After determining how you will reconcile with those who have something against you *(Matthew 5:23-24)* or with those against whom you have sinned *(James 5:16)*, go to each individual in the following manner:

   1.   At a time when the other person is not busy or occupied *(Proverbs 25:11; Philippians 2:4)*, ask if you may talk with him about your failure in the relationship *(Proverbs 25:11; Ephesians 4:25)*. If that time is not appropriate for the other person, ask if you may set an appointed time to meet with him and confess your own failures that you have committed against him *(Proverbs 25:11; James 5:16)*.

   2.   When you meet with the one sinned against, confess your sin *(James 5:16)* and ask for forgiveness in order to be reconciled (at peace) with that person *(Romans 12:18, 14:19)*.

F.   Continue to change biblically according to your plan listed in column 4 *(I Corinthians 4:2; Philippians 2:12-16)*.

G.   If you should fail again:

   1.   Confess your sins to God and, at an appropriate time, confess your sins to others *(I John 1:9; James 5:16)*.

2. Modify your plan for biblical change by taking into account your recent failure *(Matthew 7:1-5; I Corinthians 11:31; Philippians 2:12-13, 3:12-14)*.

3. Read again the verses listed in **III. God's promises concerning biblical change in your life** (Page 2).

4. Begin to change biblically using your revised plan *(Isaiah 40:29; Romans 12:21; Philippians 4:13; Hebrews 5:14; I John 4:4)*.

454

VICTORY OVER FAILURES WORKSHEET (1 John 5:4-5)

Page _____ of _____

(if applicable) Name of person I have failed to love God's way _____

(1) My specific unbiblical thoughts, words, and actions (Matthew 7:1-5)	(2) "Put off" and biblical reference(s) (Ephesians 4:22; Colossians 3:5-9)	(3) "Put on" and biblical reference(s) (Ephesians 4:23-24; Colossians 3:10-17)	(4) My plan not to repeat this sin and to respond biblically instead (Titus 2:11-14)

VICTORY OVER FAILURES WORKSHEET (1 John 5:4-5)

Column (4) Expansion

Page _____ of _____

Column (4) - My plan not to repeat this sin and to respond biblically instead (*Titus 2:11-14*)

Supplement 8, Page 2

VICTORY OVER FAILURES WORKSHEET (1 John 5:4-5) - EXAMPLE

(if applicable) Name of person I have failed to love God's way _my children_

(1) My specific unbiblical thoughts, words, and actions (Matthew 7:1-5)	(2) "Put off" and biblical reference(s) (Ephesians 4:22; Colossians 3:5-9)	(3) "Put on" and biblical reference(s) (Ephesians 4:23-24; Colossians 3:10-17)	(4) My plan not to repeat this sin and to respond biblically instead (Titus 2:11-14)
My children constantly annoy me by nagging me about all kinds of things, and they always want money. I told them to "shut up" or they'd end up just like their father.	Retaliation (I Peter 2:23) Unkindness (I Corinthians 13:4)	Entrust self to God (I Peter 2:23) Speak the truth in love (Ephesians 4:15)	When I get harassed by the children again, I will: 1. Pray (I Thessalonians 5:17) 2. Study Scripture (II Timothy 2:15) 3. Work on memory verses (Psalm 119:11) 4. Evaluate myself in the situation (Matthew 7:1-5) 5. Do the responsible thing (Genesis 4:7) a. Trust God (I Peter 2:23) b. Speak the truth in love (Ephesians 4:15) 6. Flee temptation (II Timothy 2:22) 7. Get help from biblical counselors (Galatians 6:1-2) 8. Confess to God any failure to keep this plan (I John 1:9)

Example of an incorrectly done worksheet

Supplement 8, Page 3

VICTORY OVER FAILURES WORKSHEET (1 John 5:4-5) - EXAMPLE

Page __1__ of __3__

(if applicable) Name of person I have failed to love God's way ___my children___

Example of a correctly done worksheet

(1) My specific unbiblical thoughts, words, and actions (Matthew 7:1-5)	(2) "Put off" and biblical reference(s) (Ephesians 4:22; Colossians 3:5-9)	(3) "Put on" and biblical reference(s) (Ephesians 4:23-24; Colossians 3:10-17)	(4) My plan not to repeat this sin and to respond biblically instead (Titus 2:11-14)
A. When my children asked for some money, I told them I didn't have any and blamed their father for the lack of funds.	A. Gossip (Proverbs 17:9b) Division (I Corinthians 1:10) Judging others (Matthew 7:1-4; Romans 2:1, 14:13)	A. Covering the transgression (Proverbs 17:9a) Unity (I Corinthians 1:10; Ephesians 4:3) Judging self (Matthew 7:5)	**PATTERNS:** Anger, gossip, unwholesome words, and judging **My basic plan for overcoming anger is to think, speak, and act biblically.** **Think biblically.** *In my devotions, I will pray for God's help to overcome my anger, to understand His Word, and to apply these truths specifically to my life. I will also confess all my known sins to the Lord during my devotional time and will pray for His strength and wisdom on three separate occasions each day (morning, afternoon, and evening).*
B. When my children asked for money again that afternoon, I became angry, glared at them, and yelled at them. I said, "Leave me alone. If you don't stop nagging me, you'll have more to regret than not having money. You're going to end up just like your father...", and then I proceeded to speak critically of their father in front of them.	B. Gossip (Proverbs 17:9b) Anger, malice, slander (Ephesians 4:31) Yelling (Proverbs 15:1) Unwholesome (tearing down) words (Ephesians 4:29) Judging others (Matthew 7:1-4; Romans 2:1, 14:13)	B. Covering the transgression (Proverbs 17:9a) Kindness, compassion, and forgiveness (Ephesians 4:32) Gentle answer (Proverbs 15:1) Edifying words (Ephesians 4:29) Judging self (Matthew 7:5)	*I will make a list this week of ways I can bless my husband and children. I will then dwell on these blessings every day rather than on the perceived wrongs committed against me.* *I will thank God for my husband and children and the Lord's use of these trials I am experiencing to make me more Christlike. I will repeat my prayers of thankfulness every day in the future.*
C. I then told them to get out of my sight and pushed them out of the room.	C. Anger, malice, slander (Ephesians 4:31) Impatient, unkind (I Corinthians 13:4) Unwholesome words (Ephesians 4:29)	C. Kindness, compassion, and forgiveness (Ephesians 4:32) Believing, hoping, and enduring all things (I Corinthians 13:7) Edifying words (Ephesians 4:29)	*When my kids repeat requests of me, I will try to see things from their perspective. Before I make any response, I will evaluate my response by asking myself the following questions:*

VICTORY OVER FAILURES WORKSHEET (1 John 5:4-5)

Column (4) Expansion

Column (4) - My plan not to repeat this sin and to respond biblically instead (Titus 2:11-14)

Is this profitable; or in other words, does my response contribute toward the development of godly traits or help to accomplish biblical responsibilities in my children's lives (I Corinthians 6:12, 10:23a)?

Does my response bring me back under the control of sin in any way (I Corinthians 6:12)?

Does my response reveal an area of spiritual weakness (a stumbling block) in my life (Matthew 5:29-30, 18:8-9)?

Could this lead another believer in Christ to stumble (Romans 14:13; I Corinthians 8:9-13)?

Does this edify (build up) others or (stated in another way), is this a biblically loving thing to do (Romans 14:19; I Corinthians 10:23-24)?

Does this glorify God (Matthew 5:16; I Corinthians 10:31)?

Speak biblically.

Rather than threaten the kids and slander my husband, I will:

Be slow to speak by thinking about what I will say before saying it.

Look for ways to bless the kids. Rather than threaten them I will show them how God is building His likeness into them and me through this situation.

When the kids repeat requests of me, I will respond with a soft and gentle voice.

I will ask my husband and my children to pray for me and to remind me gently of my plan and my commitment to change as they see the need. This will both bless them and show them that Christ is our model for living and not other people.

I will speak only those things that give biblical honor and respect to my husband instead of calling him names that tear him down. I will verbally support my husband biblically in front of the kids without making excuses for him.

Act biblically.

In my study of God's Word:

*I will use a concordance to study "forgiveness" and "kindness". For one week, I will use the **BIBLE STUDY AND APPLICATION FORMAT** (Supplement 3) as a study guide to help me understand one verse a day on these subjects.*

In week two, I will find at least two biblical characters who exhibit forgiveness and kindness and will study their lives to see how I can better live as a kind and forgiving person.

In week three, I will study Proverbs 31 and I Peter 2:18-3:16 to discover how I can be a more godly wife and mother. I will use these passages as a foundation for examining myself and developing a basic plan for biblical living.

In my Scripture memory, I will memorize I Corinthians 13:4-8a and Ephesians 4:29-32. To do this I will write out both passages on three index cards. I will post one on my bathroom mirror. The second I will post on the dash of my car for review while I am waiting in traffic or whenever I stop. The third card will be carried with me for review at spare moments throughout the day.

I will teach my children what I have learned about biblical forgiveness and will ask my children to forgive me for:

Saying unwholesome words about their father,
Being unkind and impatient with them when I shoved them,
Failing to speak the truth in love,
Judging them,
Creating division in the family,
Acting in an unloving manner by wanting my own way, and
Yelling and getting angry with them.

VICTORY OVER FAILURES WORKSHEET (1 John 5:4-5)– EXAMPLE

Page ___3___ of ___3___

Column (4) Expansion

Column (4) - My plan not to repeat this sin and to respond biblically instead *(Titus 2:11-14)*

I will lovingly seek to solve any problems that come up. I will find ways to demonstrate a loving relationship when we're alone as well as when we're in front of the children.

I will seek help from fellow-believers and biblical counselors to hold me accountable and, when needed, to help me revise this plan.

My contingency plan for overcoming anger:

As soon as I recognize that I am angry, I will:

Ask for God's help and seek His perspective on the situation.
Confess all sinful thoughts and ask God for his wisdom.
Thank God that I am His servant in the present circumstance.
Review the Scripture verses that I have memorized on anger.

Determine to overcome anger in a biblical manner by being:

Quick to hear:
I will listen carefully, ask questions, get the facts related to the circumstances in which anger rose within me and will make no pre-judgments or hasty decisions.

Slow to speak:
When I speak, I will discuss biblical solutions to the problem and will speak only words that edify instead of those that are critical or harmful to others.

Slow to anger:
With my children, I will deal with performance, not motive.
With myself, I will deal with my motives and change my sinful thoughts, words, and actions to biblical ones instead.

Act vigorously on the above contingency plan as soon as I detect temptation to be focused on self. Then, I will begin again to do those things written in my basic plan.

If I fail to keep my plan:

I will evaluate my unbiblical steps that led to my failure and adjust the plan accordingly.
I will confess known sins to the Lord and also to those against whom I have sinned (James 5:16; I John 1:9).
I will begin to implement the plan again, regardless of how I feel.

GUIDELINES: THE "THINK AND DO" LIST

Renewing your mind is accomplished by God *(Philippians 2:13)* and is essential for you to mature in Christ *(Romans 12:1-2; Ephesians 4:22-24; Colossians 3:10)*. You should endeavor to view every situation from God's perspective *(Philippians 4:4-9; Colossians 3:1-3, 15-16)* and to be obedient to God's Word in every circumstance *(John 14:23-24; Philippians 4:8-9; Colossians 3:17; James 1:25)*. Renewing your mind is linked to putting off the practices of the old self, with its sinful actions and desires and, in its place, putting on the new self which leads to maturity in Christ *(Ephesians 4:22-24; Colossians 3:8-10)*. Remember that your thoughts, speech, and actions are all deeds (part of the "doing level" of your problems) and are indicators of what is in your heart *(Matthew 15:18-20a; Mark 7:20-23)*.

For further teaching on renewing your mind, see: RENEWING YOUR MIND (Lesson 7, Pages 6-7).

The purpose of the **"THINK AND DO" LIST** (Supplement 10) is to help you plan *now* to have a biblical thought life and to have a biblical plan to overcome temptation. In essence, this list is a supplement to the **VICTORY OVER FAILURES WORKSHEET** (Supplement 8) as it applies to your sinful thoughts and resultant actions. It is a contingency plan designed to help you deal with your thought life. Listed below are some guidelines to help you develop your personal **"THINK AND DO" LIST**.

I.   **It is important to develop a "THINK AND DO" LIST in order to:**

A.   Establish a new, biblical pattern for thoughts and actions in areas where you have been tempted and have previously sinned *(e.g., anger, worry, disagreements, child-discipline situations, being unfaithful in daily responsibilities, etc.) (Romans 6:13; II Corinthians 10:5; Colossians 3:2, 5-15; Titus 2:11-12)*.

B.   Plan ahead for times when you know that trials (temptations or tests) may very well come *(e.g., upcoming major surgery, major events, or decisions in your life, projected absences from your normal responsibilities of daily life, etc.) (Proverbs 3:5-6, 16:3; I Corinthians 10:13)*.

C.   Live blamelessly before God and others rather than for self, even in the areas sometimes unseen by men *(Psalm 44:20-21; Jeremiah 17:9-10; Matthew 5:16; Philippians 2:12-16; I Peter 2:12)*.

II. **As you develop your "THINK AND DO" LIST, include the following:**

A.   Recognize the circumstances, responsibilities, and relationships in which you have developed a habit of unbiblical thoughts and actions.

1.   **In the left-hand column *(Labelled "My Temptations and Sinful Thoughts")* –** List the time(s) of day or circumstances when you know you are tempted to sin in your thought life. Remember that even the smallest amount of time that you do not think biblically is still sin *(James 4:17)*. It is not a matter of degree or length of time that determines whether you sin; rather, it is anything that is not done God's way *(i.e., not according to the Scriptures) (I John 3:4b, 5:17a)*.

2.   **In the center column *(Labelled "What I Should Be Thinking In This Situation")* –** Corresponding to all the qualities listed in *Philippians 4:8*, list specific thoughts that you ought to have in your times of temptation. This means that instead of dwelling only on the temptation or on the problem, you must think about the solutions that God's Word gives to deal with your present

circumstance. Do not merely list "nice, good" things to think about that ignore the problem; instead, list specific things you should be thinking in this particular circumstance. List the specific truths from Scripture that apply in this situation for hope and change. Also list what God's Word tells you is true about the Lord, His provision, and His work in your life within this particular circumstance *(Psalm 19:14; 119:9, 50, 92, 101, 105, 143; I Corinthians 10:13; Philippians 4:8-9; James 1:2-4).*

3. **In the right-hand column** *(Labelled "What I Should Be Doing As A Result of My New Biblical Thinking")* – Based on the biblical perspective gained from your study in the center column, develop a specific plan of action to deal with this situation. Remember, it is not your responsibility to change others or to manipulate the situation *(Ezekiel 18:20; Romans 12:9a)*; rather, you are to do your own responsibilities to glorify the Lord *(Colossians 3:17, 23-24)* and to bless others *(Romans 12:9-21; Colossians 4:5-6; I Peter 3:8-12).*

B. Carry your **"THINK AND DO" LIST** with you as long as necessary to help you develop a pattern of dealing with temptations in a biblical manner.

C. The moment you recognize temptation, begin to practice your biblical plan for dealing with your thoughts. If necessary, pull out your **"THINK AND DO" LIST** to help you remember your plan.

462

"THINK AND DO" LIST

Problem: _____

Page _____ of _____

My Temptations and Sinful Thoughts (Matthew 15:19; James 1:14-15)	What I Should Be Thinking in This Situation (Psalm 19:14; Philippians 4:8)	What I Should Be Doing As a Result of My New Biblical Thinking (Philippians 4:9)

© Biblical Counseling Foundation

Permission is granted to reproduce this form for personal or ministry use

"THINK AND DO" LIST– EXPLANATION   Page _____ of _____

Problem: _____

My Temptations and Sinful Thoughts
(Matthew 15:19; James 1:14-15)
On a blank "THINK AND DO" LIST, follow the instructions below.

The Temptation of Sinful Thoughts:
In this column, list the sinful thoughts you are tempted to think or ways in which you sinned in your thought life *(I Corinthians 11:31)* and confess them as sin to the Lord *(I John 1:9)*.

The Incident(s) in Which I Sinned:
Describe the incident or occasion in which you sinned in your thoughts. List people involved, where you were, time of day, how long the incident lasted, and any other pertinent information. Remember to take full responsibility for your thoughts and not blame others. This will help you gain God's perspective on how your thinking influences your actions *(based on Ezekiel 18:20; I Corinthians 11:31; Ephesians 4:15; James 1:13-14)*.

What I Did As a Result of My Sinful Thoughts:
Describe what you did (how you spoke and acted) as a result of your sinful thinking *(based on I Peter 1:14-17)*.

The Times of Day or Occasions That I Am Repeatedly Tempted in This Way:
If this is part of a repeated pattern, list times, locations, people, etc., when you are tempted and frequently sin in your thought life *(based on I Corinthians 11:31; I Peter 5:8)*.

What I Should Be Thinking in This Situation
(Psalm 19:14; Philippians 4:8)
On a blank "THINK AND DO" LIST, list what you should think in all areas below.

a) **True:** What is true of this situation and about yourself, from a biblical perspective? *(refer to I Corinthians 10:13; Galatians 5:17; Philippians 4:19; James 1:13)*.

b) **Honorable:** What can you do that will give most honor to the Lord? *(refer to I Corinthians 10:31; Colossians 1:10; I Thessalonians 5:17, 22; Hebrews 4:14-16)*

c) **Right:** What is the right way for you to respond to the temptation? *(refer to Psalm 119:11; Matthew 4:4-10)*

d) **Pure:** What must you do to keep yourself pure in this situation? What steps should you take to flee from this temptation? *(refer to II Timothy 2:22; I Peter 3:8-16; I John 3:3)*

e) **Lovely:** What lovely thing could the Lord be doing in your life through this very situation? What opportunities is God giving you to show His character to others? *(refer to Romans 8:28-29)*

f) **Of good repute:** How can you follow the example of Christ in this situation as His ambassador? *(refer to II Corinthians 5:20; I Peter 2:21-23)*

g) **Excellent:** What can you do to keep a clear conscience and show yourself blameless right now? *(refer to II Corinthians 1:12; Philippians 2:14-16, 3:13-16)*

h) **Worthy of praise:** In this situation, for what can you praise the Lord? *(refer to II Corinthians 1:3-5; Colossians 3:16-17; Hebrews 13:15)*

What I Should Be Doing As a Result of My New Biblical Thinking *(Philippians 4:9)*

In this column, write a specific step-by-step plan for doing all the things you determined to do in the second column. List even the simplest steps, such as:

- what to pray at the very time of temptation *(based on I Thessalonians 5:17; James 1:5)*
- what verses to review for hope and perspective *(based on Psalm 119:11; Romans 15:4)*
- what steps to take in solving the problem *(based on James 1:22-25)*
- what you will do to get the focus off yourself *(based on Luke 9:23-24; II Corinthians 5:14-15; Galatians 5:16-17)*
- what to do to bless the very people who are part of this situation *(based on Romans 12:14; Ephesians 4:29; I Peter 3:8-9)*
- what you will say to give praise and give thanks to the Lord for His work in your life through this circumstance *(based on Psalm 34:1, 71:5-8; Ephesians 5:20; I Thessalonians 5:18)*
- how you will do any correction in gentleness and what you will say that will be focused on restoration, not condemnation *(based on Romans 12:18; Galatians 6:1-4)*

© Biblical Counseling Foundation

"THINK AND DO" LIST– EXAMPLE

Problem: _____ My husband comes home late on Thursday evenings _____

My Temptations and Sinful Thoughts (Matthew 15:19; James 1:14-15)	What I Should Be Thinking in This Situation (Psalm 19:14; Philippians 4:8)	What I Should Be Doing As a Result of My New Biblical Thinking (Philippians 4:9)

The Temptation of Sinful Thoughts:

I tore down my husband in my thoughts, thought of revenge against him, judged him, and had thoughts of self-pity about my rights.

The Incident(s) in Which I Sinned:

My husband came home late again this past Thursday night. This seems to be a pattern on Thursdays, and I have not really talked with him about why he is late. (I have fretted, worried, fumed, and reviled my husband in my thoughts most of the past twenty times he's been late).

What I Did As a Result of My Sinful Thoughts:

I burned his dinner to "show him that I'm not a maid to cater to his whims." I snapped at him when he walked in the door, refused to kiss him, and gave him the silent treatment the rest of the evening. I criticized him openly in front of the children. I've asked his forgiveness, and I have greeted him kindly, (as per my plan in the VICTORY OVER FAILURES WORKSHEET). However, I still become upset and am tempted to give him the silent treatment. I really have a hard time for the 3 hours before he gets home.

The Times of Day or Occasions That I Am Repeatedly Tempted in This Way:

Every Thursday evening for two months and often during the week. I have made excuses to my

---

TRUE– *It is true that my husband comes home late regularly on Thursday evenings. However, instead of just getting angry and judging my husband, I need to plan to discuss with him the reason for this lateness (Ephesians 4:25-26).*

HONORABLE – *I need to formulate a plan for how I will ask him, so that I will have a forgiving spirit and not blow up at him while trying to solve the lateness problem (Mark 11:25; Ephesians 4:29; Colossians 4:6).*

RIGHT – *Begin to deal with my thoughts when the temptation begins – 3 hours before my husband's arrival and not just before he walks in the door. Plan how I will greet him when he walks in by blessing him instead of tearing him down in my mind. (I Peter 3:8-12).*

PURE/WORTHY OF PRAISE– *Review my memorized Scriptures to gain perspective of what the Lord is doing in me. This will keep my mind pure with the Word, not just with my opinion of the situation (Psalm 19:8; 119:9,11). When possible, think of songs of praise to the Lord or listen to Christian music (Ephesians 5:19; Colossians 3:16). To avoid lying to the children about why their father is not home on Thursday evenings, I will plan how to tell them their father is late in a loving manner without bitterness or being critical of their father (Romans 14:10, 13; Ephesians 4:15, 31).*

LOVELY/OF GOOD REPUTE – *Plan how to show my husband a different response – one of patience, kindness, and loving concern – rather than the unkind one he has been receiving when he comes in (I Corinthians 13:4-5).*

When I realize that my husband will be late or when I think about it during the week:

* Pray. Ask God to help me control my thoughts, to give me the wisdom and grace to deal with this situation without sinning against God or my husband. Thank the Lord for His provision of strength to handle this opportunity.

* Write what I will say to my husband when he arrives to avoid manipulating him or being unloving in my speech.

* Sing Scripture set to music to remind myself of God's work in my life. Recite verses I have been memorizing lately (for example: Ephesians 4:29-32; Colossians 4:6; I Peter 3:8-12).

* Write how I will ask my husband for help in solving the problem of his Thursday schedule. Ask if the lateness will be a regular occurrence on Thursdays. Ask the reasons for his lateness on Thursdays. Would it be possible to call me if he will be later than usual? Make alternate plans for Thursdays in the event that my husband's schedule will not change (I could feed the children earlier, and he and I can eat later).

* If my husband is still not home, begin to do some extra responsibilities that I don't complete at other times (such as ironing, needlework, writing letters to relatives, etc.) I will also complete responsibilities that will bless my husband (such as housecleaning, ironing his clothes, etc.).

* If appropriate this evening (after my husband has had time to eat his dinner and relax from his trip home), ask him if we can talk about what we can do together to

---

Supplement 10, Page 3a

"THINK AND DO" LIST

Problem: <u>My husband comes home late on Thursday evenings</u>

My Temptations and Sinful Thoughts (Matthew 15:19; James 1:14-15)	What I Should Be Thinking in This Situation (Psalm 19:14; Philippians 4:8)	What I Should Be Doing As a Result of My New Biblical Thinking (Philippians 4:9)
children about their father's lateness. Now I even criticize him openly in front of the children.	***EXCELLENT*** *– Plan how to redeem time wisely while waiting for husband to come home (Ephesians 5:16). I will set aside time to pray for him (Philippians 4:6-7). Plan how to be the mother I ought to be to train my children in the ways of the Lord (Proverbs 22:6; II Timothy 3:16-17; Hebrews 5:14, 12:11).*	*solve the situation that seems to lead to an unusual schedule on Thursdays. Ask questions to determine if our family schedule needs to be altered to allow for more flexibility on Thursdays. Work at solving the problem; don't attack husband.* *Every evening before bedtime, I will thank God for my husband, listing the blessings that are being provided for our family. During this prayer time, I will also thank God for giving me this opportunity to grow into a more Christlike wife.* *Ask God to help me use this experience to be the Christlike example to my children that I ought to be in word and action.*

FACTS ABOUT BIBLICAL COUNSELING

1. **BIBLICAL COUNSELING: A MINISTRY** – Biblical counseling is a ministry that all committed believers within the body of Christ are to have toward all who have need *(based on Matthew 28:19-20; Romans 15:14; Galatians 6:1-5)*. The range of problems with which biblical counselors deal is very wide. It includes broken marriages, parent-child relationships, depression, alcohol and drug abuse, tension, turmoil, anxiety, fear, worry, and any number of other problems resulting in mental and physical distress.

2. **TRAINING OF THE BIBLICAL COUNSELOR** – The biblical counselor is trained in the use of the Scripture and the principles of biblical counseling. He is committed to the position that the Scriptures are the *only* authoritative standard for faith and conduct *(II Timothy 3:16-17)*. He does not base his counseling knowledge on his own or others' opinions, experience, or concepts of behavior *(Isaiah 55:8-11)*; but, instead, he seeks to marshal the full range of biblical truth to bear on the counselee's need *(Hebrews 4:12)*. In counseling sessions, he will hold to the essential truths of Scripture without particular theological emphasis on any practice not specifically advocated in the Scriptures *(Titus 2:1)*.

3. **THE FOCUS OF THE BIBLICAL COUNSELOR** – Biblical counselors provide their time and energy as a service to God and a labor of love to individuals *(based on I Thessalonians 2:7-8; I Timothy 1:5)*. Therefore, each counselor serves without any charge or fee, or any financial requirement, actual or implied.

4. **TEAM COUNSELING: A BIBLICAL CONCEPT** – Typically, you will find that biblical counselors work in teams; since team counseling has many biblical benefits, both for the counselee(s) and the counselors *(Proverbs 11:14, 15:22, 18:17, 20:18, 24:6; Matthew 18:16)*. Normally, sessions are conducted by a team of counselors, with one responsible for leading the team and one or two others assisting. You, as a counselee, are also a vital member of the team as you seek to overcome the problems in your life. The most important member of the team, however, is the Lord Himself, in the Person of the Holy Spirit. It is He who will provide the hope, the enabling, and the wisdom (through God's Word) for you to face and deal with your problems *(John 14:26; Romans 5:3-5, 8:26-27; Ephesians 3:16)*.

5. **DISCIPLESHIP AND MATURITY THROUGH BIBLICAL COUNSELING** – Biblical counselors are committed not only to help you overcome the current problem in your life but also to train you to live all your life in a manner that leads to increasing maturity in the Lord *(Psalm 119:165; Proverbs 2:6-12a; Galatians 6:1-5; I Timothy 4:7-8; I John 5:1-5)*. Thus, in the scriptural sense, biblical counseling is a ministry of discipleship that teaches you to walk in God's way even in the midst of serious problems *(based on Matthew 28:19-20; I Timothy 1:5; II Timothy 2:2)*. During the counseling period, one of the assistant counselors will be available to answer any questions or give further information. This counselor will talk with you on a weekly basis between the counseling sessions. Often, this same counselor will continue to contact you to be of further help and encouragement after counseling has been completed.

6. **CONFIDENTIALITY** – A commitment to trustworthiness is an important quality of biblical counselors *(based on I Corinthians 4:2)*. Thus, although your biblical counselor may talk with others about a particular situation, you may be confident that the discussions will be restricted to whatever is necessary to help you overcome your problems *(based on Proverbs 10:18-21, 15:28, 18:8, 25:11)*.

7. **MEDICAL NEEDS** – Biblical counselors believe in considering your total health needs. Your counselor may recommend that you have a full or specified medical examination. If medical assistance is required, counseling will continue at the same time, whenever possible.

8. **ELEMENTS OF BIBLICAL COUNSELING** – Biblical counselors will use all of their biblical counseling training and skill to help you overcome whatever problem is depriving you of the peace and joy that God has promised in His Word. Your counselors will concentrate on four essential elements from Scripture:

    Understanding your problem – There is the need to apply biblical principles to all of your difficulties, not just "fix your feelings" or change your circumstances. Your counselors, in a spirit of gentleness, will make biblical inquiry into the various levels of your problems and help you gain God's perspective on your difficulties (*based on Proverbs 18:13; Isaiah 55:8-9; Mark 7:20-23; Romans 5:3-5, 8:28-29; Galatians 6:1-4; Hebrews 4:12; James 1:2-4, 19, 22-25; 4:17*).

    Your Hope – In Jesus Christ you have a great High Priest who has been tempted in all things, yet without sin (*Hebrews 4:14-16*). Even though you may currently be going through a difficult test or even though every sin common to man may be tempting you, God has promised that He will not allow any trial in your life that is beyond your endurance. He has promised to provide a way of escape so that you may be able to endure it without sinning (*I Corinthians 10:13*), and He will use trials for your benefit as you respond to them in a biblical manner (*Romans 8:28-29; James 1:2-4*).

    Your Change – In Christ, you can learn how to lay aside the old selfish ways of living and put on the new ways of living in a manner worthy of the Lord (*Romans 6:11-13; Ephesians 4:20-24*). In learning to change biblically, you will begin to please the Lord in all respects, bearing fruit in every good work and increasing in the knowledge of God (*Colossians 1:9-12*).

    Your Practice – You need to prove yourself to be a doer of God's Word and not merely a hearer, thus forgetting what kind of person you are and deluding yourself. Only in becoming an effectual doer of the Word will you be blessed in what you do, and only then will you please the Lord (*Hebrews 13:20-22; James 1:22-25; I John 3:22*).

9. **WAITING PERIOD** – If a counseling team is not immediately available to begin extended counseling with you, you will be counseled as soon as possible on a one-time basis. During this session, your counselors will provide a plan for you to follow while you are waiting for the regularly scheduled sessions. You may be encouraged to attend an ongoing Self-Confrontation course while you are awaiting counseling; in this way, you can work on solutions to overcome problems immediately.

10. **LENGTH OF COUNSELING** – Normally, counseling sessions will last one to one-and-a-half hours each week and will continue for eight to ten weeks. If you respond quickly to biblical counsel, the number of counseling sessions may be shortened. However, if the counselor does not observe definite change in the first few weeks, he will seek to identify the cause of the failure, discuss it with you, and help you to correct it.

11. **COUNSELING APPOINTMENTS** – Because effective counseling requires consistency and faithfulness in your applying God's principles, it is important that you reserve the designated counseling time for the entire counseling period, barring unforeseen circumstances (*based on Luke 14:27-30; I Timothy 4:7*). If you find that you are unable to

come to a particular counseling session, please notify the assistant counselor at least 24 hours before the session.

12. **LOCAL CHURCH INVOLVEMENT** – In order to achieve lasting victory over the problems of life, it is vital that each person become established in a consistent Christian walk. The Lord has provided the local church to help in this process *(Hebrews 3:13, 10:24-25)*. Therefore, it is important that biblical counseling sessions be accompanied by church activities that encourage discipleship and fellowship. If you do not have a church home, you are welcome to join us in our church's fellowship. If you are part of another church family, the assistance of your church's leadership may be requested so that you may more fully receive the benefit of all the spiritual resources given to you by God. One of your pastors, elders, or deacons may even become part of the counseling team to provide the most effectual help for you. It is our commitment to do what will best help you walk in obedience to God's Word and thus experience victory over your problems.

13. **MATERIALS NEEDED AND EXPECTATIONS** – You will need a notebook and your Bible at all sessions, including the first. Be sure to bring them each time. Come with high expectations. You will find hope and encouragement even during your first session. From then on, with your cooperation, we are confident that you will find trustworthy and biblical answers for the difficulty that prompted you to contact us.

BIBLICAL COUNSELING RECORD

Date _____ Case No._____ Session No. _____ Length of Session _____

Counselor's Initials _____ Counselee's Initials _____ Estimated No. of Remaining Sessions _____

Evaluation of Last Week's Homework :

1) Bible Memory:

2) Devotions:

3)

4)

5)

This Week's Homework :

1) Bible Memory:

2) Devotions:

3)

4)

5)

Session Notes:

Proposed Topics for This Session:

Levels of Problems:
(As observed in this session)

Feeling:

Doing:

Heart:

Problems to Address in Future Sessions:

(write on back as needed)

Supplement 12, Page 1
Permission is granted to reproduce this form for personal or ministry use.

EXPLANATION OF THE BIBLICAL COUNSELING RECORD

The Biblical Counseling Record is used in biblical counseling sessions. This page is a training form to help you "think" and explore the case biblically.

Date _____ Case No._____ Session No. _____ Length of Session _____

Counselor's Initials _____ Counselee's Initials _____ Estimated No. of Remaining Sessions _____

Evaluation of Last Week's Homework :
   (James 1:22-25)

1) **Bible Memory:**

2) **Devotions:**

3)   (Extensive and intensive questions on biblical progress or failure, with special
4)   awareness given to *Proverbs 16:2, 25; 18:2, 13, 17; 21:2; 26:12* while assurance can be gained from *Proverbs 16:20, 20:5,*
5)   *25:11-12)*

This Week's Homework : *(Joshua 1:8; Matthew 7:24-25, 28:18-20; James 1:22-25)*

1) **Bible Memory:** *(Psalm 119:11)*

2) **Devotions:** *(Psalm 1:1-3)*

3) **Put-offs/Put-ons** *(Ephesians 4:22-24; Colossians 3:5-17)*

4)

5)

Session Notes:

Proposed Topics for This Session:

a. Laying aside the old self and its practices *(Ephesians 4:22; Colossians 3:5-9)*

b. Renewing the Mind *(Romans 12:2; Ephesians 4:23)*

c. Putting on the new self and its practices *(Ephesians 4:24; Colossians 3:10-16)*

Levels of Problems:
(As observed in this session)

Feeling: *(Genesis 4:7; Psalm 38:3-10, 17-18)*

Doing: *(Ecclesiastes 12:13; Luke 6:46; John 3:21, 14:15; I John 5:3)*

Heart: *(Mark 7:20-23; Luke 6:45; Hebrews 12:15)*

Problems to Address in Future Sessions:

(write on back as needed)

© Biblical Counseling Foundation

Permission is granted to reproduce this form for personal or ministry use.

USE OF THE BIBLICAL COUNSELING RECORD

Date _____ Case No._____ Session No. _____ Length of Session _____

Counselor's Initials _____ Counselee's Initials _____ Estimated No. of Remaining Sessions _____

Evaluation of Last Week's Homework :	**This Week's Homework :**
1) Bible Memory:	1) Bible Memory:
2) Devotions:	2) Devotions:
(After the first session, start subsequent sessions here in this section. Asking good questions in this section will reveal pertinent information for use below)	**(This session's assignments are recorded here. The next session will begin by reviewing these assignments)**

Session Notes:

(As your questions continue, record the counselee's responses here. Biblical violations can be categorized under the "Levels of Problems" section as well as providing information to help you determine proposed topics for future sessions)

Proposed Topics for This Session:

(As these areas are discussed with the counselee, new biblical assignments are to be developed for the next session)

Levels of Problems:
(As observed in this session)

FEELING: **(Possible deep-rooted problems and the commitment level of a counselee may be discovered by listening to what is said)**

DOING:

HEART:

Problems to Address in Future Sessions:

(Topics that need to be covered in the future are noted here)

(write on back as needed)

Supplement 12, Page 3

BIBLICAL COUNSELING SUMMARY AND PLANNING

Date of Session: _____ *Case Number:* ___ *Session Number:* _____ *Length of Session:*

Date of Report: _____ *Counselor's Initials:* _____ *Counselee's Initials:* _____

1. Briefly summarize what happened in the counselee's week prior to this past session. List any health changes, important circumstances, and relationship changes.

2. Describe how well the counselee did in completing the last session's homework.

3. List topics and Scriptures covered in this session. How did the counselee respond when each topic was covered?

4. List homework assigned this session.

5. List topics to be covered in future sessions, along with Scriptures for hope, change, and practice.

6. List any specific future homework assignments you think would be valuable in this counselee's life.

7. List biblical practices this counselee still needs to develop.

MY PRESENT SCHEDULE

	MONDAY	TUESDAY	WEDNESDAY	THURSDAY	FRIDAY	SATURDAY	SUNDAY
6:00 a.m.							
7:00							
8:00							
9:00							
10:00							
11:00							
12:00 Noon							
1:00 p.m.							
2:00							
3:00							
4:00							
5:00							
6:00							
7:00							
8:00							
9:00							
10:00							
11:00							

Record activities and responsibilities that you have done this week (or in a typical week). Review GOD'S STANDARDS FOR YOU (Lesson 22, Pages 4-6) under III. Incorporating God's standards into your life.

Supplement 14

MY PROPOSED BIBLICAL SCHEDULE (*Proverbs 16:9; Ephesians 5:15-16*)

	MONDAY	TUESDAY	WEDNESDAY	THURSDAY	FRIDAY	SATURDAY	SUNDAY
6:00 a.m.							
7:00							
8:00							
9:00							
10:00							
11:00							
12:00 Noon							
1:00 p.m.							
2:00							
3:00							
4:00							
5:00							
6:00							
7:00							
8:00							
9:00							
10:00							
11:00							

Schedule the above week in a biblical manner. Diligently maintain your schedule, remembering that God is sovereignly in control of any unforeseen events that may occur. Review GOD'S STANDARDS FOR YOU (Lesson 22, Pages 4-6) under III. Incorporating God's standards into your life.

Supplement 15

© Biblical Counseling Foundation

Permission is granted to reproduce this form for personal or ministry use

GUIDELINES: FREEDOM FROM ANXIETY
(BIBLICAL ACTION AND PRAYER PLAN)

> There are times in which you will have deep concern over various circumstances in life. It is important that you react biblically during such times in order to be a doer of the Word and receive the peace of God that passes all understanding *(based on Isaiah 26:3; Psalm 119:165; Philippians 4:6-9; James 1:25).*

I. **The problem**

    A. People are sometimes affected physically as a result of experiencing fear and worry. For example, you may have heard statements like:

        1. "My son needs to be more responsible, to get a job, and to support his family. Every time I think about him, my stomach gets upset."

        2. "My daughter needs to get off drugs. My appetite has gone, and I can't sleep at night thinking about it."

        3. "Members of my family need to have a spiritual new birth, but they won't listen to me when I talk to them about it. My blood pressure is sky high."

        4. "My husband brings his friends over; and they look at violent, sexually oriented movies. I'm having one migraine headache after another. I'm so worried about how this is affecting the children that I've developed an ulcer."

    B. When faced with the temptations to fear or worry, you must redirect your attention to God's will instead of focusing on yourself and the problem. One of the first steps to take is to pray *(Philippians 4:6-7; Colossians 4:2; I Thessalonians 5:17).* In order to have an effectual prayer life, you must faithfully examine yourself in a biblical manner and remain diligent to please the Lord in all things *(based on I Corinthians 11:31; II Corinthians 5:9; James 1:5-8, 5:16b; I John 3:22).* As part of this process, you are to place your cares upon the Lord *(I Peter 5:6-7)* while continuing to be a doer of the Word *(James 1:22-25).*

II. **The prayer plan**

    A. Each day, read *Philippians 4:6-9.*

    B. In the first column of Supplement 17 titled **My Concerns**, list the deep concerns that you have.

    C. Considering each listed item in turn, mark through the ones you are powerless to do anything about and write them in the middle column **(The Lord's List)**.

    D. In the third column titled **My List**, write down biblical responsibilities that you are to do regardless of any prayer concerns you might have. Also list your responsibilities that are related to your prayer concerns (for example: if you are prayerfully concerned for a believer who is caught in sin, list the first steps you will take to help restore your fallen brother).

1. To review biblical responsibilities for any believer, study the following (a sample list):

    Matthew chapters 5, 6, and 7
    Matthew 18:15-17
    Matthew 22:35-37
    Romans chapters 12, 13, and 14
    Romans 14:3, 4, 10, 13, 17-19
    Romans 15:1-7, 13-14
    I Corinthians 13:4-8a
    Galatians 6:1-2
    Ephesians 4:15, 29-32; 6:1-19
    Philippians 2:3-8, 14-16
    Colossians 3:12-17, 23-25; 4:1-6
    I Thessalonians 5:16-18
    James 1:19-20, 2:14-17, 5:9
    I Peter 3:1-4, 7, 8-12, 13-17
    I John 3:16-18

2. Add to the column titled **My List** as the Holy Spirit continues to reveal what you should do in your everyday activities and responsibilities.

E. Commit (turn over) to the Lord what you have written under **The Lord's List** *(based on I Peter 5:7).* Trust the Lord to do what only He can do *(based on Psalm 40:4-5, 56:3-4; Isaiah 55:8-11).*

F. In prayer, ask the Lord to help you do heartily as unto Him the things you should do and make a commitment to the Lord to do what you have written under **My List** *(based on Colossians 1:9-12, 3:23-24).*

G. Make plans to do those things written under **My List**. *If necessary, use a VICTORY OVER FAILURES WORKSHEET (Supplement 8) or MY PROPOSED BIBLICAL SCHEDULE (Supplement 15).*

H. Review your lists each day and pray about each item. Add to **The Lord's List** and **My List** as necessary and respond accordingly.

I. The **FREEDOM FROM ANXIETY (BIBLICAL ACTION AND PRAYER PLAN)** (Supplement 17) can be used along with any of the other forms in this manual, such as the **BIBLE STUDY AND APPLICATION FORMAT** (Supplement 3), **VICTORY OVER FAILURES WORKSHEET** (Supplement 8), the **"THINK AND DO" LIST** (Supplement 10), and **MY PROPOSED BIBLICAL SCHEDULE** (Supplement 15).

J. You may find it beneficial to reproduce this prayer plan in a notebook that, with your Bible, will become part of your daily devotions.

FREEDOM FROM ANXIETY
(Biblical Action and Prayer Plan) – based on Philippians 4:6-9

My Concerns (All the things about which I am tempted to worry)	The Lord's List (Those things about which I can do nothing)	My List (My responsibilities to fulfill in faithful obedience to the Lord)

Supplement 17